PRAISE FOR THIS BOC

The word *practical* in the title is well-deserved. This text provides a clear explanation of the research process for novice students, yet still provides comprehensive coverage of the foundational ideas involved in the process.

—Wendy J. Brame, Briar Cliff University

This is an excellent textbook for an introductory research course. It deals with the issue of data preparation and sample description in an excellent manner.

—Rhucha P. Samudra, Augusta University

This book offers the beginning student the fundamentals of research in an easy-to-understand, example-rich format.

—Dennis F. Kinsey, Syracuse University

This accessible text covers the basics of research methods, emphasizing quantitative methods and integrating a review of statistics into the discussions of research methods.

—Warren Fincher, Saginaw Valley State University

This is an approachable book for research students. It is written clearly and offers a variety of examples and illustrations to help students learn the concepts.

—Audrey Wagstaff, Wilmington College

This book is a good introduction to beginning student researchers in social sciences, and in particular its discussion of how to do a literature review will help students understand the structure of a scholarly paper.

—Koji Fuse, University of North Texas

This detailed textbook teaches students the basics of research methods using helpful figures and real-world applied examples.

—Nizia Alam, University of Georgia

A Practical Introduction to Real-World Research

A Practical Introduction to Real-World Research

Getting the Job Done

Loreen Wolfer
University of Scranton

Los Angeles | London | New Delhi
Singapore | Washington DC | Melbourne

FOR INFORMATION:

SAGE Publications, Inc.
2455 Teller Road
Thousand Oaks, California 91320
E-mail: order@sagepub.com

SAGE Publications Ltd.
1 Oliver's Yard
55 City Road
London, EC1Y 1SP
United Kingdom

SAGE Publications India Pvt. Ltd.
B 1/I 1 Mohan Cooperative Industrial Area
Mathura Road, New Delhi 110 044
India

SAGE Publications Asia-Pacific Pte. Ltd.
18 Cross Street #10-10/11/12
China Square Central
Singapore 048423

Printed in the United States of America

ISBN: 978-1-5443-7829-9

This book is printed on acid-free paper.

MIX
Paper from responsible sources
FSC
www.fsc.org
FSC® C008955

Acquisitions Editor: Helen Salmon
Editorial Assistant: Natalie Elliott
Production Editor: Astha Jaiswal
Copy Editor: diacritech
Typesetter: diacritech
Proofreader: Lawrence W. Baker
Indexer: diacritech
Cover Designer: Karine Hovsepian
Marketing Manager: Victoria Velasquez

21 22 23 24 25 10 9 8 7 6 5 4 3 2 1

BRIEF CONTENTS

Preface   xv

Digital Resources   xix

Acknowledgments   xxi

About the Author   xxiii

PART I • ESTABLISHING THE ISSUE

Chapter 1 • Overview of the Research Process   2

Chapter 2 • Research Topics, Literature Reviews,
              and Hypotheses   25

PART II • SETTING THE FOUNDATION FOR OBSERVATION

Chapter 3 • Ethics in Research   56

Chapter 4 • Measurement, Validity, and Reliability   75

Chapter 5 • Sampling   98

PART III • METHODS OF GATHERING INFORMATION

Chapter 6 • Experiments   128

Chapter 7 • Survey Research   157

Chapter 8 • Qualitative Approaches and Mixed Methods   184

Chapter 9 • Evaluation Research   213

PART IV • MAKING SENSE AND PRESENTING THE INFORMATION

Chapter 10 • Preparing Quantitative Data   240

Chapter 11 • Descriptive Statistics   271

Chapter 12 • Confidence Intervals and One-Sample Hypothesis Testing   300

Chapter 13 • Hypothesis Testing With Two or More Samples   325

Chapter 14 • Finding the Degree of Association and Prediction   362

Chapter 15 • Presentation of Data   398

Chapter 16 • Qualitative Data Analysis   427

Appendix A: Directions for Statistical Tests in SPSS   447

Appendix B: Directions for Statistical Tests in R and the
Corresponding Output   460

Appendix C: Table of *Z*-scores   482

Appendix D: Answers to End-of-Chapter Problems   487

Glossary   489

References   499

Index   509

DETAILED CONTENTS

Preface   xv

Digital Resources   xix

Acknowledgments   xxi

About the Author   xxiii

PART I • ESTABLISHING THE ISSUE

Chapter 1 • Overview of the Research Process   2

Sources of knowledge   3

Classifying research   9

   Basic versus applied   9

   Qualitative versus Quantitative   10

   Four main research goals   13

A brief discussion of research and theory   17

Steps in the research process   18

Making decisions   21

Challenges   22

Key terms   23

Answers to learning check questions   23

End-of-chapter problems   24

Chapter 2 • Research Topics, Literature Reviews, and Hypotheses   25

Topic formation and research questions   26

   Types of research questions   26

   Characteristics of strong research questions   28

   Steps for creating research questions   29

Literature reviews   29

   The purpose of a literature review   29

   Searching for material   30

   Critically evaluating material   34

   Organizing a literature review   39

Hypotheses   44

   Alternative and null hypotheses   44

   Establishing causality   46

Making decisions   50

Challenges   50

Key terms   53

Answers to learning check questions   53

End-of-chapter problems   54

PART II • SETTING THE FOUNDATION FOR OBSERVATION

Chapter 3 • Ethics in Research   **56**

Brief general history of ethics in research   58
   Respect for persons   60
   Principle of beneficence   62
   Principle of justice   64
   Additional ethical considerations   64
      Anonymity/Confidentiality   64
      Data access and ownership   66
      Participant privacy   66
      Responsibility to society   67
Ethical governance   68
   Institutional review boards   68
   Professional codes of ethics   69
Making decisions   69
Challenges   71
Key terms   73
Answers to learning check questions   73
End-of-chapter problems   73

Chapter 4 • Measurement, Validity, and Reliability   **75**

Moving from concepts to measures   76
Levels of measurement   79
Measurement quality   83
   Validity   83
      Face validity   84
      Criterion validity   84
      Construct validity   85
      Content validity   86
   Reliability   87
   To increase validity and reliability   89
   Measurement error   89
Measure consideration: time dimensions   90
Making decisions   93
   How to choose your measures   93
   Time considerations   95
Challenges   95
Key terms   96
Answers to learning check questions   96
End-of-chapter problems   97

Chapter 5 • Sampling   **98**

Units of observation vs. units of analysis   100
   Unit of observation and analysis risks   102
Sampling terms   103
Probability sampling   105

Types of probability samples **109**

    Simple random sampling 109

    Systematic random sampling 112

    Stratified random sampling 113

    Cluster sample 116

Nonprobability sampling 118

Sample size 120

Making decisions 121

Challenges 122

Key terms 124

Answers to learning check questions 124

End-of-chapter problems 125

PART III • METHODS OF GATHERING INFORMATION

Chapter 6 • Experiments **128**

True experiments 129

  Characteristics **129**

  Types **132**

    Classic experiment 132

    Posttest-only control group design 133

True experiments and study validity 135

  Internal validity **135**

    Selection bias 135

    Instrumentation 136

    Maturation 137

    Testing 138

    Attrition 138

    Reactivity 139

    Contamination 139

  History **140**

    Summary relationship to true experiments 140

  Statistical conclusion validity **141**

  External validity **142**

Quasi-experiments 143

  Characteristics **143**

  Types **144**

    Ex post facto control group design 144

    Before-and-after design 145

    Nonequivalent control group design 145

    Interrupted time series design 146

Factorial design 148

Interpreting experimental output 149

Making decisions 151

Challenges 153

Key terms 154

Answers to learning check questions 154

End-of-chapter problems 155

Chapter 7 • Survey Research — **157**

Question construction: To write or not to write — 159

Survey presentation — 168

Pretesting questionnaires — 171

Common survey types — 172

    Self-reported mailed surveys — **172**

    Telephone surveys — **173**

    Web surveys — **175**

    Interviews — **176**

Validity and reliability — 177

    Validity — **177**

    Reliability — **177**

Making decisions — 178

Challenges — 179

Key terms — 182

Answers to learning check questions — 182

End-of-chapter problems — 183

Chapter 8 • Qualitative Approaches and Mixed Methods — **184**

Face-to-face interviews — 185

    Process — **187**

        Deciding sample size — 187

        Training the interviewer — 187

        Preparing for the interview — 188

        Presentation of self — 188

        Conducting the interview — 189

        Concluding the interview — 190

        Recording the data — 190

Focus groups — 191

Case studies — 193

Field research — 194

    Researcher roles — **195**

        Covert observer — 195

        Overt observer — 196

        Overt participant — 197

        Covert participant — 199

    Selecting a site — **200**

    Developing relationships — **201**

    Identifying subjects — **202**

    Recording information — **202**

    Leaving the field — **204**

Content analysis — 205

Mixed methods research — 205

Making decisions — 207

Challenges — 209

Key terms — 211

Answers to learning check questions   211

End-of-chapter problems   212

Chapter 9 • Evaluation Research   **213**

Basic evaluation components   218

Types of evaluation research   221

   Needs assessment   **221**

   Evaluability assessment   **223**

   Implementation assessment   **225**

   Outcome evaluation   **226**

   Efficiency analysis   **227**

Additional considerations   229

   The role of theory   **229**

   The balance of researcher and program stakeholders   **230**

   How much detail is necessary to report in the findings?   **230**

Quality issues   232

   Validity   **232**

   Reliability   **232**

   Objectivity   **233**

Making decisions   233

Challenges   233

Key terms   236

Answers to learning check questions   236

End-of-chapter problems   237

PART IV • MAKING SENSE AND PRESENTING THE INFORMATION

Chapter 10 • Preparing Quantitative Data   **240**

Coding quantitative data   241

Special coding considerations   244

   Missing information   **244**

   Coding "please specify"   **246**

   Handling "circle all that apply"   **247**

Direct data entry   248

   SPSS: Variable view   **248**

   SPSS: Data view   **251**

Importing existing data   252

Data cleaning   255

Data manipulation   259

   Collapsing categories and creating new variables   **259**

   Creating scales   **262**

      Likert scale   263

      Guttman scale   264

Making decisions   268

Challenges   268

Key terms   269

Answers to learning check questions   269

End-of-chapter problems   269

Chapter 11 • Descriptive Statistics   271

Types of statistical information   272

Deciding and interpreting descriptive statistics   274

Reviewing some basics: Frequencies, proportions, and percent   274

Introducing the statistical teaching approach in this book   276

What am I doing? Summarizing a distribution   277

Measures of central tendency   277

Measures of dispersion   287

Nominal measures: Percent distribution   287

Ordinal measures: Percentage, range and interquartile range   288

Interval/Ratio measures: Variance, standard deviation, and what to do with
skewed distributions   289

SPSS and interpretations   291

What am I doing? Finding a score relative to a distribution   293

Key terms   298

Answers to learning check questions   298

End-of-chapter problems   299

Chapter 12 • Confidence Intervals and One-Sample Hypothesis Testing   300

What am I doing? Estimating a population parameter   302

The logic behind confidence intervals   302

Estimating confidence intervals   303

Increasing our confidence in our estimates   309

What am I doing? Hypothesis testing—One sample   309

The logic behind hypothesis testing   309

One- or two-tailed tests   311

Cautions about hypothesis tests   312

Testing hypotheses: One-sample tests   312

Errors in hypothesis testing   320

Key terms   322

Answers to learning check questions   322

End-of-chapter problems   323

Chapter 13 • Hypothesis Testing With Two or More Samples   325

What am I doing? Hypothesis testing—Two samples   327

Independent vs. dependent samples   327

Two independent samples   328

Two dependent samples   341

What am I doing? Hypothesis testing—Three or more samples   350

Key terms   359

Answers to learning check questions 359

End-of-chapter problems 360

Chapter 14 • Finding the Degree of Association and Prediction 362

What am I doing? Finding the strength of an association
    between variables 363
    Lowest level of measurement: Nominal 364
    Lowest level of measurement: Ordinal 370
    Lowest level of measurement: Interval/Ratio 379

What am I doing? Prediction 383
    Bivariate linear regression 383
    Some additional points 385

Brief introduction to multivariate analysis 386
    Partial correlation 386
    Multiple regression 388

Key terms 394

Answers to learning check questions 394

End-of-chapter problems 395

Chapter 15 • Presentation of Data 398

Univariate data presentation 400
    Tables 400
    Graphs 402
        Bar graph 402
        Pie chart 404
        Line graph 405

Bivariate data presentation 406
    Table 406
    Graphs 409
        Bar graph 409
        Line graph 412

Responsible graphical representation 413
    Y-axis representation 413
    Three-dimensional representation 414

Preparing an oral presentation 417
    Presentation content 417
        Beginning 417
        Middle 418
        End 420
    Presentation delivery 420
        The benefits and pitfalls of visual aids 420
        Presentation of self 421

Challenges of presentations 422

Key terms 424

Answers to learning check questions 424

End-of-chapter problems 425

Chapter 16 • Qualitative Data Analysis   **427**

Preparing qualitative data for analysis   428

    Moving from observations to full recorded data   428

    Creating the infrastructure for analysis   429

    Deciding how to sort through the material?

        Cutting/Pasting or computer?   429

A general approach to analysis   430

    Identifying initial themes   431

    Linking themes   432

        Making connections   432

        Interpreting the themes and connections   433

        Providing evidence of the claims   433

    When to end analysis   434

Specific analytic techniques   434

    Content analysis   435

    Grounded theory analysis   436

        Method 1: Open, axial, and selective coding   437

        Method 2: Attribute, index, and analytic codes   438

    Qualitative network analysis   440

    Discourse analysis   442

Challenges   443

    How can i know whether my analysis is valid and reliable?   443

    How can i increase validity of my interpretations?   443

Key terms   444

Answers to learning check questions   444

End-of-chapter problems   445

Appendix A: Directions for Statistical Tests in SPSS   **447**

Appendix B: Directions for Statistical Tests in R and the Corresponding Output   **460**

Appendix C: Table of *Z*-Scores   **482**

Appendix D: Answers to End-of-Chapter Problems   **487**

Glossary   **489**

References   **499**

Index   **509**

PREFACE

If you are reading this preface, that means you are taking a research and statistics class ... and are probably completely freaking out! If you are anything like my students, you may even be dreading this class. You might be unsure of whether you will "really need" any of this stuff and/or whether you can even make sense of it. A lot of my students, for example, tell me ahead of time that they are scared because they "can't do" or "don't like" math.

I get it. I really do. I have been teaching and researching in the community using the techniques addressed in this book for over 20 years. I have probably seen and heard much of it. In fact, another "hat" I wear is a program evaluator for local social and criminal justice agencies. In that role, I often encounter people who *have* had research methods and/or statistics courses, but they frequently tell me that they don't remember much of them or that what they covered didn't really fit what they see in their agencies.

So I see both sides. I see the college student who is afraid of all of this because methods and statistics require a different way of thinking, and it can be a challenge figuring out how to approach a problem with systematic observation (methods) and analysis (statistics). I also see the professional who just wants to "help people" but finds that they also have to suddenly support their experiences (which are seen as anecdotal) empirically (with numbers and statistics). Even if they do not have to do research specifically, many people "in the field" now need to know how to read the research of others and how to evaluate that information in order to make choices that will fit their available resources.

This book is designed to try and help those two worlds meet in the middle. Traditional methods and statistics books are frequently written with the idea that students will go on to graduate school. If that is the case for you, this book will still give you the basic foundation in methods and statistics, but I am forewarning you that you will go into more detail about both topics once you are in graduate school—maybe even now, depending on the interests of your professor. For those of you who plan on working after college—perhaps in a social service agency, a criminal justice capacity, or some other form of social work—this book will help you "get the job done" for most basic evaluations from start to finish. Because I want students who plan to enter the field immediately or soon after graduation to have a research resource *and* I want to still provide a foundation for those going on to graduate school, there are some characteristics that make this book unique compared to other methods and statistics books on the market.

First, let's discuss the differences regarding learning research methods. There is a difference between research that is done in a laboratory where the researcher has a lot of control over the context of the research and real-world research where the researcher has much less control.

Therefore, this book is a practical approach to learning how to design research especially in real-world contexts where resources may not be able to be 100% controlled by the people involved. As such, this book does not claim to present *all* the aspects of research (or statistics). Methodologically this book does not claim to discuss the nature of every type of validity or reliability concern, every professional code of ethics, every technical term regarding measurement, or every form of data gathering. It will, however, highlight common methodologies that span a variety of social service arenas such as social work, criminal justice, and mental health, as well as general sociology. Those in the field who do remember their research training are frequently frustrated because they soon realize that much of what they learn in an academic research methods class does not translate to their jobs, where randomized samples, service provider control, and/or expensive statistical programs (to name some common complaints I hear) are just not feasible. Furthermore, they commonly lack confidence in how to handle common challenges that arise in applied research. Therefore, to help the academic world meet the applied world, each chapter relating to methodology, where relevant, will have either a summary feature that will aid in decision making and/or a section on common methodological challenges coupled with some suggestions for how to address these challenges in the real world. Because decisions made in individual aspects of methods, such as hypothesis testing, may affect decisions made in other aspects, such as measurement or statistics, I also frequently refer to other chapters in the explanation so students know where to look if they are rusty on a concept or need a refresher as to what various terms or processes mean. This way, students can more easily link material throughout the book and quickly find information that they have forgotten.

The second unique component of this book is its incorporation of statistics for hypothesis testing and association tests right in the same source. Some research methods textbooks do provide limited statistical information, but this usually focuses on descriptive statistics, not inferential ones. I do this for a number of reasons. First, there is some indication that programs are moving to combine research methods and statistics into a one-semester experience. When this is done, it is still important to have a resource that will help students be able to design and analyze basic research, especially if that course is the only exposure to methods and statistics they receive. Second, and somewhat related to the first, many of the community members I work with took undergraduate research methods or statistics courses; however, there was "so much" information (according to them) or they claim that the information was presented in a way that was "just a bunch of techniques" that they either didn't retain or they couldn't link to their current jobs. Although some community members I work with know what some common statistics are, they almost universally (unless they have had some graduate training) do not know *how* to make statistical choices. In other words, they may recognize the term "chi-square" or "*t*-test," but they do not know how to move from their research question expressed in English and the data on their Excel sheet to what statistical test to use. Therefore, this book focuses more on how to make statistical decisions than on how to calculate the decided statistic by hand. *This* leads us to the third difference.

As I just said, unlike traditional statistic textbooks, for the most part, we do not focus on calculating the statistic by hand. There is some use to learning these calculations by hand, perhaps if you are going on to a graduate program; but, in the field, that is less likely to be the case. In recognition of the merit, in some instances, of hand calculations, I do present the formulas for the simpler, more common undergraduate statistics. I just do not walk you through the calculations. We focus on the statistical *decisions* and how to run the decided statistic in SPSS (Appendix A) and R (in Appendix B). I will discuss these approaches more when we reach those chapters, but for now, let me just say that this focus allows us to cover some statistics that are useful in the real world but that are not frequently included in traditional textbooks because the formulas are cumbersome to calculate by hand. This textbook also gives templates for interpretation of these statistics in APA format, as well as interpretation examples based on that template within the body of the text.

However, perhaps one of the most unique aspects of this book, aside from including statistical tests that are more than descriptive, is *how* we approach learning the statistical tests. Traditional statistical textbooks frequently have a section for each statistical test that starts with the test, explains the assumptions, illustrates the calculation, and then discusses how to decide whether or not the null hypothesis is rejected. However, this is not really the *thought* process behind statistics for the real world. Researchers don't usually start with the statistic and then proceed through a checklist of assumptions before they find a test that "fits," and workers in the field with even less exposure to statistics certainly don't either—which may be some of the reasons why the people I have encountered remain mystified by statistics even after having a class. This book always begins with a situation or example and then breaks down the example into a repetitive thought process that I call a "decision tree." Answers to various questions in the decision tree, which are frequently based on the assumptions associated with various statistical tests, lead the student to a possible statistical decision. Therefore, instead of seeing whether a statistic fits a situation, we start with a situation and work through a repetitive decision process until we reach an appropriate possible statistic. This is also why we cover some statistics that are not commonly presented in undergraduate texts. As we are not focused on hand calculations, we can give students the tools to analyze a greater variety of statistics based on the nature of the data, which in the real world is not likely to nicely conform to the basic statistical assumptions for the tests most undergraduate statistics books are limited to.

Therefore, although this textbook will not cover every quantitative or qualitative method of observation or every statistic that fits every data condition, it will still cover many issues—especially ones that are relevant to "getting the job done" in the real world. This book *will* teach what each component of research is; it will address common undergraduate methods; and it will cover a variety of statistics (and the critical thinking skills to reach those decisions) that apply to real-world data even without an advanced degree. It will also discuss how to present these findings to others, including those who do not have a statistical background. In short, it will teach someone the basic tools that will provide them with quality real-world information under real-world constraints. Therefore, it is a practical guide for understanding and making the best research and statistical decisions under a variety of different resource capabilities from the formation of a research topic all the way to sharing statistical findings with a nonacademic audience in a way that will "get the job done."

DIGITAL RESOURCES

A website at **https://edge.sagepub.com/wolfer** contains resources for instructors and students to use with this textbook:

For instructors: Editable PowerPoint slides, a test bank in Microsoft Word and in LMS-ready formats, all tables and figures from the book, and datasets for use in SPSS and R.

For students: e-Flashcards of glossary key terms, and datasets for use in SPSS and R.

ACKNOWLEDGMENTS

I would like to express sincere thanks to Jason Graham for his assistance with the R programming sections of this book. Without his generous donation of time and his patience, the inclusion of that programming option would not have been possible. I would also like to thank Jeff Lasser for his initial interest in this book and the rest of the amazing editorial staff at SAGE for their valuable assistance in bringing this book to fruition. Last, I would like to thank my family—especially my husband, daughters, and parents—for their support during the writing and editing process, as well as for endlessly listening to me as I bounced ideas to them and talked through the book as it took shape.

I am also grateful for feedback from the following reviewers:

- Nizia Alam, *University of Georgia*
- Wendy J. Brame, *Briar Cliff University*
- Lisa L. Bell Holleran, *St. Edward's University*
- Marika Dawkins, *University of Texas Rio Grande Valley*
- Warren Fincher, *Saginaw Valley State University*
- Koji Fuse, *University of North Texas*
- Youngjo Im, *Chicago State University*
- Ajlina Karamehic-Muratovic, *St. Louis University*
- Dennis F. Kinsey, *Syracuse University*
- Samantha Kwan, *University of Houston*
- Kristina Patterson, *Georgia Southern University*
- Rhucha P. Samudra, *Augusta University*
- Victor Thompson, *Rider University*
- Audrey Wagstaff, *Wilmington College (Ohio)*

ABOUT THE AUTHOR

L oreen Wolfer received her PhD from Cornell University and is a Professor of Sociology in the Sociology/Criminal Justice department at the University of Scranton. She is also the Chief Evaluator for the University of Scranton's Center for the Analysis and Prevention of Crime. As such, she has evaluated programs for the Federal Office of Probation, the Office of Youth and Family Services, and various county-level court-sponsored programs. Her other research interests include family and media studies.

ESTABLISHING THE ISSUE

OVERVIEW OF THE RESEARCH PROCESS

In 2018, a gunman using an automatic rifle killed 17 students and staff as well as injured 17 others at Marjorie Stoneman Douglas High School in Parkland, Florida. To the public, this seemed like the most recent incident in an increasing trend of mass school violence that started almost 20 years prior, in 1999, with the mass shootings at Columbine High School in Columbine, Colorado. These visible acts of mass violence in our schools have led parents, community members, educators, and politicians to ask "What can we do?"

If you are reading this textbook, you are most likely majoring in sociology, social work, criminal justice, or some other discipline where you plan on "helping" people and/or you want to find answers to sociological issues like school shootings. But how do you know what works to help people? Or how do you know what are social issues rather than isolated private troubles?

You are most likely learning about the issues, theories, and challenges of your discipline in your other classes; but, how do your professors know what to teach? And if your career goal is to "help people," how will *you* know if your interventions work effectively for as many people as possible? Because you are reading this textbook, you may already suspect part of the answer to these questions: research and statistics. What we know about our social world and how to influence it comes from various types of theory and research. Understanding how to read and to do research is important because making decisions that influence human behavior without evidence can lead to a waste of money at best or additional harm to those we want to help at worst.

SOURCES OF KNOWLEDGE

Take the tragic instances of mass school shootings like Columbine in 1999, Sandy Hook in 2012, and Stoneman Douglas in 2018, just to name some high-profile cases. These occurrences have made the public more sensitive to school bullying and to what feeling like an outsider might lead people to do. But how can we sift through different types of knowledge to answer the question "What can we do?" There are many forms of knowledge people use to answer questions. Four common sources are tradition, experience, common sense, and **authority**. Let's take a look at each in more detail regarding our issue of school violence.

Tradition is the idea that "that is the way it's always been." For example, it is a tradition that when you have a cold, you eat chicken soup. We probably all have memories of mom or someone we love giving us chicken soup when we were sick and we commonly associate that soup with comfort. It's probably a good bet that none of us have scientifically tested whether or not this association is true, but the link between chicken soup, sickness, and comfort is so entrenched in our traditions that the phrase beginning "chicken soup for_____" has become the basis of folk sayings, book titles, and memes, and is just…well…*known*. In fact, it wasn't until fairly recently that scientific study supported this traditional knowledge (Rennard, Ertl, Gossman, Robbins, & Rennard, 2000). To link traditional knowledge to what we can do about school violence, we might realize that Americans have a tradition of confronting problems head-on in a direct manner. Popular slogans such as "Get tough on crime," "War on Drugs," and "War on Terrorism" reflect our tradition of approaching a problem directly by actions such as tightening enforcement to decrease a threat. Therefore, tradition might suggest that in the instance of school shootings, we should implement actions like zero tolerance for various school offenses or by tightening security.

But there are some problems to basing knowledge, especially knowledge to address a problem, on tradition. First, tradition can be distorted. When we think of the past, we tend to pick the pieces that we *want* to remember. For example, Americans tend to have a nostalgic view of the 1940s and the 1950s, which are exemplified by the folk art of Norman Rockwell. We think of the 1950s as a simpler time where neighbors knew each other, people were civically engaged, women stayed home to raise children, and men worked hard to economically support their families. However, what we neglect to remember is that these times were often rife with racial

PHOTO 1.1 Schools have recently implemented many new strategies to reduce school violence. But do they work?

segregation, social isolation of women, the economic dependence of women, and a quiet tolerance of interpersonal violence.

Obviously, our world has changed since then; but that leads to the second problem with traditional knowledge. What was accurate or accepted in the past may not be now. Even a popular comic when I was young had a main character routinely tormenting another by pulling a football away from him every time he was about to kick it and calling him names…and it was considered funny. But this is less likely to be the case today. In fact, the traditional view might also actually be more tolerant of behavior like bullying and fighting. Familiar sayings like "boys will be boys" and "sticks and stones may break my bones but words can never hurt me" hark back to a time when kids were "tougher," so maybe the problem isn't with the violence per se, it's that children today can't handle adversity and, therefore, are not likely to know how to appropriately deal with it. Therefore, traditional knowledge doesn't always account for cultural, social, or statistical change, so maybe we need to continue to look elsewhere for an answer to our school violence problem.

Another source of knowledge is **experience**[1], the old "seeing is believing" adage. If we experienced it, then it must be true. In the case of the Columbine shootings, the two shooters, Eric Harris and Dylan Klebold, came from wealthy families with employed mothers. At the time of the shootings, working middle-class mothers, who embodied a shift in traditional gender roles, were a common scapegoat to many changes being observed in children's behaviors. Presumably, if mothers worked, they were not home by the time their children got out of school; and this lack of supervision was directly responsible for all sorts of adolescent deviance.

---

[1]All bolded terms in the chapters are defined in the Glossary in the back of the book.

The link between these boys' backgrounds and the shootings gave "evidence" to the "seeing is believing" arguments of social and political conservatives. But this form of knowledge is limiting as well. First, it assumes that our personal experiences represent the experiences of *everyone*. Of course, that isn't true. The experiences of an economically disadvantaged female who identifies as a racial minority are not likely to be the same as that of an economically advantaged white male. Secondly, using experience as the basis of knowledge assumes that what worked in one situation will work in another; but again it ignores that the two situations may not be similar. Furthermore, like tradition, experience runs the risk of selective observation. Blaming the actions at Columbine on adolescents having working mothers ignored the millions of other children whose mothers were employed but who did *not* participate in mass school shootings. Lastly, people have a vested means in perceiving their experiences in ways that benefit them. If a student does poorly on an exam, they are likely to blame the professor (the exam was too hard, the professor doesn't like me), which enables the student to feel less bad. The professor, on the other hand, is likely to put the responsibility on the student (the student didn't study hard enough, didn't ask questions in class, and didn't come to office hours for help) to also feel less responsible. The situation is the same (poor test grade), but different interpretations of cause depend on the perspective. Professional feedback (experience) is especially vulnerable to this bias as research has found that professionals in the field have an empirically observable tendency to see improvement whether it exists or not and/or to have more confidence in their ability to judge client progress than more objective measures would indicate (Hannan et al., 2005; Lambert et al., 2003; Worthen & Lambert, 2007). Therefore, at least in the world of research, we should always be skeptical of whether we should believe what we see—at least until we have a better understanding of the context in which we are "seeing" human behavior. So let's keep looking at the other sources of information.

We still have two other common sources of knowledge to address. The third, although not an entirely unique form, is **common sense**, which is the knowledge that stems from combining tradition and experience. If we have been told something long enough (like the chicken soup) and we have experienced it ourselves (hot soup is soothing), then the knowledge "makes sense." The knowledge that makes sense is common sense. Because we already covered the flaws in the two forms of knowledge that contributed to common sense, then common sense as a primary source of information would be flawed for the same reasons.

So what about knowledge stemming from "authority"? Surely experts have it right...after all, they are *experts*. Often, they are right, but we still have to be skeptical. For example, many of you probably have learned from some history teacher in your life that Christopher Columbus made his famous sail to find a viable trade route to China and had a hard time obtaining financing for this expedition because the educated elite in Spain thought that the world was flat and that Columbus (and his expensive ships) would fall off the earth. Your history teachers are experts, correct? Although teachers *are* experts in their field, it turns out that even experts can learn incorrect information because Columbus's flat earth story is a myth. Educated people of Columbus's time studied the works of the ancient Greeks who knew that the world was not flat since 500 B.C. (Singham, 2007). So how did this myth become a "fact" that has been taught in classrooms for so many years? It turns out that Washington Irving, the writer

iStockphoto.com/ecliff6

PHOTO 1.2 Contrary to what you may have learned in history class, Christopher Columbus had no interest in "proving" that the earth was flat. The educated people of his time already knew that.

of stories such as *The Legend of Sleepy Hollow* and *Rip Van Winkle*, embellished what he read in archives about Christopher Columbus when he wrote the explorer's biography. I guess we shouldn't be surprised. After all, Irving *was* a storyteller, not a historian!

Skepticism about even expert knowledge is especially relevant today because now we live in a time where we are seemingly inundated with expert knowledge at every turn. If someone has letters, such as M.D., J.D., or Ph.D., after their name, we assume that they know what they are talking about. However, just because someone has an advanced degree in one field does not make that person an expert in another. I have a Ph.D. in sociology. If I made comments about astrophysics and just signed my comments as Loreen Wolfer, Ph.D., I wouldn't *technically* be lying; but, I wouldn't be honest either because my Ph.D. has nothing to do with the expertise of astrophysics. Especially with the proliferation of online "experts," anyone can share "expert" knowledge, even if it is out of their area of training, they were poorly trained, or their training is outdated. So look at the available information, look at the credentials of an expert, and look at whether that expert is current in their knowledge. Don't just trust someone because they have letters after their name or claim to be an expert.

It may seem as if we got away from our example of school violence, but we really did not. Using tradition, experience, common sense, and even authority as the basis of knowledge has led schools to respond to school violence by installing metal detectors, security cameras, on-site police or security officers, shooter drills, and student/staff identification cards (Fisher, Mowen, & Boman, 2018). So the real question is: Do these measures reduce the original concern, which is the risk of various forms of school victimization? After all, the implementation of any of these measures is costly and we need to know if they work for the original purpose of making schools safer.

Although the evidence is mixed, most research, which address scientific knowledge, suggest that the answer is: no. There is some evidence that implementing these measures may make communities feel safer, give citizens a sense of control over their environment, and increase officials' ability to document incidences of violence for identification and/or prosecution, all of which have some merit. But, contrary to tradition and experience, there is also evidence that the *more* security measures a school employs, the *greater* the likelihood of some form of violence occurring in a school (Crawford & Burns, 2016; Fisher et al., 2018; Tanner-Smith, Fisher, Addington, & Gardella, 2017), which is contrary to the original goal of decreasing school violence. So why would scientific evidence provide such seemingly counter-intuitive information; and why should we give science any merit? Well, there are a couple of characteristics of science (research) that tradition and experience, for example, lack. Unlike the other two forms of knowledge, science is empirical and theoretical. It is empirical in that it is based on direct, objective observation of our world and it is theoretical in that theory provides context and explanation to our observations. For example, to study the effectiveness of school security measures on student safety, Fisher et al. (2018) used data from the Educational Longitudinal Study to test various theories of student safety. They tested opportunity theories that argue that increased security would reduce the opportunity for victimization. This would be consistent with the traditional view of "cracking down" on deviance by limiting opportunities for it and it also "makes sense" from a common-sense perspective. Another group of theories however, called critical theoretical perspectives, argue that security measures would actually degrade the school environment by leading adolescents to think of their schools as dangerous. If students think of their school as dangerous, they will have an increased perception of victimization and feel unsafe. Critical theorists also argue that such measures may weaken social bonds by fostering distrust. According to Fisher et al., a third possible explanation says that schools that employ heavy security measures have other provisional characteristics, such as racial composition, that may lead to differential effects of security on victimization. So science doesn't just document, it puts observations into a broader theoretical context of why. *Why* will increased security decrease (or not) school victimization? We will get to the relationship between science and theory in a bit, but let's first spend some more time distinguishing science from the other avenues of knowledge we identified.

Second, science is systematic. Unlike the other forms of knowledge, science is based on generally agreed-upon steps that are organized, publicized, and recognized by other scientists. We will discuss this overview of the systematic process later in this chapter, but this systematic nature is important because it allows for replication. The more studies that show similar findings, the more confident we are, as researchers, that what we observe is accurate. For example, did you notice earlier that when I said that increased school security does not work, I cited *multiple* studies? The point I made was not based on just my experience or one study, but rather it was based on more than one study that followed the scientific process and reached similar conclusions. Another example of the importance of following this scientific process is a now-classic, albeit infamous, study of arrest and domestic violence in Minneapolis by Sherman and Beck (1984), which found preliminary evidence that arresting men suspected of domestic violence reduced the likelihood of them committing future assaults.

Because Sherman and Beck's findings had not yet been replicated by other studies using the same systematic procedure, they urged caution in interpreting their results; but many law enforcement agencies quickly adopted this approach because it was based on research (expert knowledge since it was published) and it made sense (common sense). However, when the US National Institute of Justice funded replication of the study in six other cities, the deterrent effect of arrest on future assaults was not supported. In fact, this more vigorous study found that arrest actually *increased* the likelihood of future assaults (Sherman, 1992). Because the scientific form of knowledge has systematic steps, replication was able to show that the original findings were not only false but that in reality, the problem of abuse worsened using this tactic.

Last, scientific knowledge is probabilistic and provisional. This means that in research we are never 100% sure; we never prove beyond any doubt that something is absolutely true and/or will always happen in all instances. Instead, science means that we can establish with confidence (such as 95%) that something is *likely* to happen (probabilistic), and the more factors we identify (provisional) the more accurate our findings. In fact, going back to our discussion of school violence, one of the findings at the 95% confidence level (probabilistic) from Fisher et al.'s study (2018) supported the third theoretical explanation by finding that race did affect both the type of victimization students experienced and whether security measures were successful in reducing said victimization. Therefore, Fisher et al.'s (2018) study illustrates both the probabilistic side of science (95% likely to be related) and the provisional nature (when considering race as a factor) of scientific observation. For these reasons, science, which involves research and statistics, is a fifth form of knowledge that is the most suitable for providing information about how to address the problem of school violence. However, this is not to say that the other forms of knowledge are not useful; they definitely can be if they are incorporated into a research design and, as we will see, are especially useful in designing applied and evidence-based research, which is the focus of this book.

Therefore, it is important to be clear what the goals of any research project of intervention are and to base decisions on well-designed and implemented scientific knowledge that may be fueled by the other sources of knowledge. If the main goal of school security measures is to reduce victimization, perhaps the money spent on security measures can be more effectively used elsewhere. If the main goals are community relations and sense of well-being among

iStockphoto.com/mactrunk

PHOTO 1.3 Adopting a program or policy based on one study can be misleading, as was learned by replicating the Minneapolis domestic violence study of Sherman and Beck (1984).

parents (regardless of whether that sense is misplaced), then the aforementioned measures fit the goal. In reality, the goals are probably a bit of both, so the suggestion, if one was familiar with the existing applied research regarding school safety, would perhaps be to utilize some basic forms of security that are comparatively affordable for that area and to use the rest of available funds to experiment or to explore other means of reducing victimization. The point is, without research, basing policy or practices solely on tradition, experience, or common sense may lead to a false sense of security and the misuse of funds better invested elsewhere.

LEARNING CHECK 1.1: AREAS OF KNOWLEDGE

1. Why is experience not necessarily the best form of knowledge to serve as the foundation for program design and evaluation?

2. Identify three ways in which science is a more relevant use of knowledge

for social programs than the other forms of knowledge.

Answers to be found at the end of the chapter.

CLASSIFYING RESEARCH

Basic versus Applied

Although there is some overlap, one of the first points we have to make is the difference between applied research and basic or academic research. **Basic research**, sometimes also called academic, foundational, or pure research, is research aimed at expanding general knowledge for knowledge's sake. This type of research is research for the sake of improving our understanding of some type of phenomena, but it does not seek to solve or correct that phenomena. To go back to our earlier example of school violence, examples of basic research questions could be: Are incidents of school violence becoming more frequent over the last 30 years? Who is more likely to be a victim of school violence? Is online bullying a form of school violence? Basic research, therefore, helps to define the phenomena and to describe the underlying process of it.

Applied research, on the other hand, is research designed to solve practical problems or to address some known phenomena that the researcher sees as problematic. Applied research generally wants to find ways to improve the human experience. Research questions that are applied and relate to our initial example could be: Do antibullying school programs reduce the incidence of school violence? Do harsh punishments decrease future bullying behavior? Do metal detectors increase students' sense of safety? These questions are focused on trying to reduce the incidence or perception of school violence; they are not documenting trends or defining the behavior. They recognize a problem (violence) and will systematically observe whether a policy or program successfully reduces it. Fisher et al.'s (2018) research regarding whether increased security measures in schools reduced student victimization is an example of applied research.

In fact, when it comes to applied research, pure academics are frequently criticized for being disconnected from the realities of professionals in the field. Similarly, in the past, professionals were criticized for basing their conclusions on anecdotal evidence or gut feeling that lacked empirical testing, which, as I already discussed, can be biased. In the social sciences, applied research has broadened not just to refer to research that can be used for practical purposes but also to include research that incorporates into its design the practical experience of those in the field. This newer approach, which actually started in the medical field, is frequently called **evidence-based research** and has become part of a movement to blend research and practice in a way in which practitioners are encouraged to employ practices that have been empirically tested and supported, whereas researchers are encouraged to seek input from practitioners, such as with identification of goals and the development of research concepts, into the research design (Sackett, 1997; Urban & Trochim, 2009).

As I previously said, there is an overlap between basic and applied (including evidence-based) research; and, the two broad forms are complementary to each other. Clearly applied research cannot work to address problems without having the more foundational knowledge about the problem that basic research provides, and foundational knowledge without any idea of how it can be used to better the social world seems to be…well…a futile effort. Therefore, the two forms of research just look at the same issue (e.g., school violence) from the different perspectives of "what is it?" and "what can we do about it?" where neither one is "best."

Qualitative versus Quantitative

I have already used the terms *qualitative* and *quantitative* in passing, but let's discuss them in a bit more detail. Racism, for example, is a very complex, multidimensional topic that might have a different meaning today than it did at the start of the Civil Rights movement over 60 years ago. Furthermore, everyday interactions, and not just blatant newsworthy exhibitions, can be racist. In order to study the more routine concepts of racism, Walton, Priest, and Paradies (2013) used cognitive interviews and focus groups to explore the meaning of racism in everyday life. Cognitive interviews and focus groups are methodological designs in which subjects can express their own definitions or views in an unstructured, fluid way that enables them to "talk it out" so to speak. As such, these designs are examples of **qualitative research** because, in both designs, researchers focused on the detailed nuances of individuals' self-expressed subjective contexts of what racism is today. Once the researchers had all the subjects' definitions in their own words, they searched to see if there were any common themes expressed among those definitions. They did not prompt individuals to agree or disagree with preconceived definitions of racism to achieve a count or to conduct statistical tests. For example, Walton et al. (2013) noted that whether people considered a mundane comment or action to be racist depended on the speaker's intention that surrounded it. To illustrate this conclusion they presented the following:

> Racism is intent. Intent to be mean because someone is different from you that's what I think. (…)
>
> (Focus Group 4, female blue-collar)

> So you can understand sometimes it's maybe a term of endearment but it depends on how it's delivered isn't it, whether the comment is meant to be nasty or not.
>
> (Interview 1, female white-collar)
>
> Walton et al. (2013, p. 81)

Quantitative research, however, is less focused on the subjectivity of individual meaning and more concerned with objectively trying to consistently measure concepts so that they can be numerically analyzed. As such, quantitative research focuses on well-defined concepts by the researcher (as opposed to subjective definitions of the respondent) that are designed to have clear and consistent means of measuring that meaning. Priest et al. (2014) conducted a quantitative analysis of racism where they tested for a statistical connection between self-identified experiences of racism and various mental health outcomes among secondary school students. To do this study, they used the Localities Embracing and Accepting Diversity (LEAD) program, which was a community-based intervention to address racial discrimination and promote cultural diversity among 263 primary and secondary students across five primary and secondary schools in Australia. Priest and colleagues selected seven items and their corresponding answer options that *they* defined as racial discrimination that a child personally experienced and three additional items of discrimination that a child witnessed toward other students. The researchers provided the specific definitions and answer options for the questions about racism in order to *reduce* respondents' subjectivity and variability in how to define racism. In this study, the researchers were not concerned with subjects' definitions of what constituted racism but rather whether subjects experienced what the researchers defined as racist acts (based on the information they gathered from others) and the outcome of these. Another difference is that findings of quantitative information are presented as numerical statistical tests to assess the likelihood that observed differences in the sample might also apply to the larger population rather than quoted excerpts. For example, in their quantitative study, Priest and colleagues note that there was a statistically significant and noticeable relationship between experiencing racial discrimination and loneliness. Last, quantitative research tries to do, as the name implies; it *quantifies* differences between groups.

For example, in 2020 the world experienced the COVID-19 pandemic that changed the world as we know it for at least the foreseeable future. In fact, I am still writing parts of this book while quarantined at home and teaching classes remotely due to the pandemic! While we are still learning about the possible social and economic consequences of this pandemic, groups like the PEW Research Center were able to use large, nationally representative samples of the US population to describe people's early COVID-19 experiences and to *quantify* whether there were any noticeable differences in experience based on factors such as income, race, and gender. By surveying about 11,500 US adults between March 19 and March 24, 2020, and almost an additional 5,000 US adults between April 7-12, 2020, PEW researchers were able to provide some of the earliest, quantified evidence that showed that, in many ways, the coronavirus affected Hispanics and Blacks more negatively than it did whites. For example, PEW researchers found that 61% of Hispanic adults and 44% of Black adults said that they or someone in their household experienced a job or wage loss due to the coronavirus outbreak, compared to just 38% of white adults, and that members of these two groups were less likely to have emergency financial reserves to help them weather this challenge. The findings also indicated that Black (48%) and Hispanic (44%) respondents were more likely to claim that they could not pay some bills or could only make partial payments compared to whites (26%) (Lopez, Rainie, & Budiman, 2020). The large, nationally representative sample and the percentages are all characteristic of quantitative data, as the purpose of the PEW study was to describe trends in who is *more likely* to be affected (a quantitative issue) by COVID-19.

Even with this very truncated summary of both studies, we can identify some common (but not universal) differences between qualitative and quantitative research. First, as I said, quantitative research is more focused on the subject's idiosyncratic expression of a concept and it is the job of the researcher to find patterns in these idiosyncratic expressions across people. In quantitative studies, on the contrary, researchers are more likely to direct the respondent to what the *researcher* means by a concept and the subject will react, also in a predefined way, to that definition, as illustrated by the 10 total items that the researchers in the Priest and colleague's study of racism used. In quantitative research, however, researchers may use information learned in more qualitative studies to reach these definitions. Second, qualitative studies frequently have smaller sample sizes than quantitative ones. Walton et al.'s qualitative study had between 35 and 39 participants (the exact number of participants in each focus group is not presented in the original article), whereas Priest and colleagues' quantitative study had more than 200. Although quantitative studies can be done on smaller samples, having samples larger than 50 is common. Table 1.1 summarizes some of the key differences between qualitative and quantitative research, some of which we will discuss in a bit.

TABLE 1.1 ◆ QUALITATIVE VS. QUANTITATIVE INFORMATION	
Quantitative Research	**Qualitative Research**
• Researcher is expert	• Subject is expert
• Research is deductive	• Research is inductive
• Concepts are clearly defined with specific measures prior to data collection	• Concepts are not defined until after data collection
• Systematic steps for research facilitate replication	• Few or no systematic research steps as replication is less of a research goal
• Data are predominantly numerical	• Data are primarily in the form of subject explanations or descriptions, hence quoted or paraphrased conversations
• Analysis involves statistical tests for inferential significance and association	• Analysis is in the form of general trends. Any numerical analysis is descriptive with no detailed statistical tests for significance or association

Four Main Research Goals

But applied or basic, qualitative or quantitative, are not the only ways research is classified. Within both typology sets, research can serve different goals, which, in turn, have different methodological needs and statistical outcomes. For example, research can be explorative, descriptive, explanatory, or evaluative, or some combination thereof. Explorative research is used for topics that we know little about and/or for which we want a broad, unstructured examination of what is going on. For example, when social media first starting becoming popular (I know, to you all, it was *always* popular), people knew little about how it would affect social relationships. Did social media affect the frequency of face-to-face interaction? How do people work to craft online identities? How do people present themselves online knowing that people from different parts of their social lives (e.g., friends, classmates, parents, potential employers) would all see the same presentation of self? Much of the early research regarding social media was exploratory. Researchers doing **exploratory research** are frequently interested in obtaining a preliminary understanding of phenomena, so this research is frequently qualitative in nature, although it doesn't have to be.

A second purpose of research is description. Almost all research has a descriptive component that broadly describes the demographics of the sample (e.g., 62% of the sample was male and 74% was white) and the research situation (e.g., 82% of participants completed the program) to put a study and its participants into context. There are even statistics that facilitate this (Chapter 11). However, some research begins and ends with description, which is just fine. Common government databases such as the US Census, the Uniform Crime Reports, and the Current Population Survey all aim to describe various aspects of the American experience. **Descriptive research** can also be inferential, where research using a sample aims to describe a wider population that was not directly studied. Examples of these questions could be: What percent of the American population is married? What is the average prison sentence for men compared to women convicted of the same crime? How long does it take for people to get off of welfare?

For example, Solé-Auró and Crimmins (2014) used data from the 2006 Survey of Health, Ageing, and Retirement in Europe, the 2006 wave of the English Longitudinal Study of Aging, and the 2006 wave of the USA Health and Retirement Study to estimate the probability of people aged 50 or older in Spain, England, and the United States, respectively, receiving some form of care. They found that receipt of within home care was more common for men than for women in all three countries and that the elderly in Spain were the least likely to receive care from outside the household. In all three countries, when care was provided outside the household, it was most likely to be provided by a child (Solé-Auró and Crimmins, 2014). This study used large data sets from multiple countries, but it still just describes. Therefore, as just illustrated, descriptive studies can be very large, very detailed, and very informative. Descriptive research is not a "weak" research goal. Researchers just have to be mindful of the kinds of conclusions they can draw with these studies. As the name implies, descriptive statistics do not explain a situation, they do not answer "why," and they simply document or compare.

Explanatory research is the form of research mostly focused on answering "why" or "how." It is frequently associated with establishing a causal connection between issues in a way that is linked to theory. Descriptive research might find that the rate of suicide increased among youth over the past 20 years. Explanatory research would try to figure out why. For example, explanatory research would link variables related to a theory of either social integration, peer association, or even the use of technology to test how well those variables and theory explained any observed variation. Litwiller and Brausch (2013) did just that when they used data from a large-scale community mental health screening of adolescents at 27 high schools in 7 county regions of a Midwestern state in the United States to examine whether cyberbullying and physical bullying affected suicidal behavior differently. They related this comparison to the interpersonal theory of suicide arguing that bullying creates an environmental cause of suicide by making adolescents feel that they do not belong to their environment and that they are a burden to those around them, which in turn ultimately leads to their suicidal behavior. They found that cyberbullying especially correlated with low self-esteem, anxiety, and depression, which when taken together created an environment of isolation and perceived burden. This sense of isolation and of being a burden, in turn, correlated to suicidal behavior (Litwiller & Brausch, 2013). By linking theory and research, these researchers helped shed light on the explanation for why social media may be related to suicidal behavior among adolescents. As you can probably see, explanatory research is more complex than exploratory or descriptive research. It strives to establish a cause/effect relationship (Chapter 2); therefore, it would require clear measures (Chapter 4), probabilistic sampling (Chapter 5), and statistical analysis (Chapters 11–14).

The last purpose of research is evaluation, which can take many forms. It can involve systematically and statistically showing a need for some type of intervention. It can involve systematically and statistically examining whether a policy or program is being implemented as designed. Or, it can be the more obvious examination of whether a policy or program works—whether it produces the desired outcomes. Evidence-based research, which we will be discussing soon, is a form of **evaluation research**; and, as you will see, it can be both descriptive and explanatory. What distinguishes the evaluation goal from the other three goals is its applied focus. So we see that these typologies do not need to exist independently. They *can*, but as we will see later in this book, the strongest studies have components of more than one typology and/or more than one method of observation. Fisher et al.'s (2018) study, for example, exhibited characteristics of both evaluation (Does increased security reduce victimization?) and explanation (Is racial context a contributing factor in explaining the different levels of effectiveness?).

iStockphoto.com/Windzepher

PHOTO 1.4 Can you think of a different research question for each of the four types of research that would fit this picture?

So, why do we need to know the different purposes of research? Although there are many theoretical and academic reasons to know the different types of research, from a more practical perspective it comes down to assessing the strengths/weaknesses of particular studies for your needs. I already mentioned that even if you don't get a job where you are going to regularly be conducting research and collecting data, you *are* likely to have to read and determine

---

✔ **LEARNING CHECK 1.2: FOUR MAIN GOALS OF RESEARCH**

Identify research goal implied in each of the following research topics/scenarios. More than one research goal may be applicable.

1. A researcher examines whether there is a gender difference in the preference for dogs compared to cats.

2. In accordance with the Broken Windows Theory, a researcher tests whether fixing up a neighborhood, both in terms of houses and yards, leads to a reduction in drug-related crime in that neighborhood.

3. Does increased Internet use lead to decreased face-to-face interaction?

Answers to be found at the end of the chapter.

the strength/relevance of the research of others for your various professional interests. Professionals in many fields like sociology, criminal justice, social work, and mental health, are increasingly expected to improve skills, implement programs, and make decisions that are based on the research of others. They are expected to adopt evidence-based practices that stem from evidence-based research. However, without an understanding of research and statistics, it is very difficult to do this. Just because something is published in what appears to be an academic source, does not mean that that information is good. Or, at times you will encounter published studies with contradictory findings. How do you know which study to "believe"? Some of the answers lie in understanding the different typologies we just described and the type of information they produce. We can't think of research as a dichotomy of "good/bad" or "useful/not useful," because the value and usefulness of research frequently lie on a continuum. For example, research that is explanatory aims to do more than research that is purely descriptive; therefore, it should be held to a higher methodological and statistical standard. Or a researcher might have complete control over the design of research that is descriptive or explanatory but not evaluative and that is to be expected. Therefore, identifying the research purpose also helps us recognize when methodological limitations and deciding whether those limitations discount a study are within acceptable bounds of quality and relevance.

But before we move on, I want to take some time to briefly discuss this idea of limitations. If you look at any published scholarly research, you should see that toward the end of the study the researcher will discuss the limitations of the research. A researcher's identification of study limitations is not a weakness to the overall research; it is actually a strength. All research is socially constructed and therefore none of it is perfect. When I say that research is socially constructed, it means recognizing that researchers are merely people who decide how to define a problem, how to measure it, how to sample it, how to record it, and how to analyze it; and, different people may make different decisions about any of these steps. These different decisions made by people (social) influence how a phenomenon is studied (constructed); but, this variability does not mean research is useless. Because it is a systematic, more unbiased (when done ethically) form of observation, it is a stronger foundation for decisions than the other sources of knowledge I discussed. Its systematic nature, as I said previously, also means that it can be replicated and problems with findings, like we saw with the Sherman and Berk (1984) study, can be identified. Therefore, research is better than other forms of observations for many reasons; but it is not perfect. Reputable researchers recognize this and will alert the reader to these issues by noting their own study's limitations, hence the importance of including this in any research report.

We also have to remember what I said in our earlier discussion of the characteristics of science, which is that in research we never "prove" anything. We are never 100% sure. Incidentally, this is the same in the traditional sciences as well. For example, it is a well-known scientific finding that smoking tobacco, eating sugary and fatty foods in excess, and drinking too much alcohol can all contribute to an early death. This does not mean though that you can be 100% sure that if you smoke tobacco, have poor eating habits, and/or drink too much alcohol, you *will* (prove) die young. We can all probably think of people we know who do all three of these behaviors and are quite old *or* we know of people who were "health nuts" and who died before

PHOTO 1.5 Smoking and consuming alcohol are scientifically shown to increase the probability of an earlier death, but that association does not prove that one will die young from smoking and drinking. We probably all know people who have defied this relationship.

they were 60. So this is an example of the continuum. These habits increase the *likelihood* of an earlier death, but practicing these behaviors does not *prove* beyond any doubt that someone *will* die young.

A BRIEF DISCUSSION OF RESEARCH AND THEORY

As mentioned a number of times in this chapter, most forms of research do not happen in a theoretical vacuum. Research tells us what is occurring; theory works on the deeper explanation of why we see what we see. Because this is a research methods and statistics book, it is not the place to get into a detailed discussion of theory. However, in the spirit of "getting the job done," I do briefly want to distinguish theory from ideology because this distinction is relevant to research. Ideologies are explanations that are offered with absolute certainty and frequently get tied into moral debates. As such, ideologies are hard to research because the research is less about objective observation and more about showing support for a specific side. Theory, on the other hand, as I said previously, seeks to find the reason why behind the why. For example, according to Miron and colleagues (2019), in 2017 there were 47% more suicides among 15 to 19 year olds than there were in 2000. As I already covered, some researchers have found a link between social media use and adolescent suicide (Litwiller & Brausch, 2013; Luxton, June, & Fairall, 2012; Van Orden et al., 2010). An ideological approach might stop there. Such an approach would claim that the increased use of social media contributes to adolescent suicide and, as such, would encourage parents to restrict social media usage, monitor their children's behavior online, etc. Now, there might be merit to all of these suggestions, but from a *theoretical* viewpoint, this explanation is insufficient. Contrary to an ideology, a theory would try to explain *why* social media may contribute to teen suicide. It would look for the why of the why. In other words, for the problem of adolescent suicide, an ideology would find the link between social media and teen suicide and stop there. A theory, on the other hand, would think more deeply to try to figure out *why* social media is linked to teen suicide. What is it about being online in that type of environment or what is it about adolescents today, who live in a digital age, that contributes to teen suicide? After all, lots of people, especially teenagers, use social media and most do not attempt suicide. Furthermore, teens have always experienced "angst" during this life stage and they have always experienced peer pressure and bullying. So what about social media makes things different now? That why behind the why is what theory would get at. Furthermore, theory, by its design, is meant to be empirically tested and altered based on the findings, like we saw in the earlier research examples about teen suicide (Litwiller & Brausch, 2013) and school shootings (Fisher et al., 2018). So theories lend themselves to empirical observation, whereas ideologies, though also observable, border on a moral or value-driven focus; and, as we will see in Chapter 2, that does not make good research.

A last word about theory and research is the difference between inductive and deductive research. The classic research model (and the one we will take for much of this book) is that of deductive research. **Deductive research** starts with a review of the existing research to find out what people in the field already know about an issue, a tentative application of a theory (pending a study's findings), a test of hypothesis by observation, and conclusions based on what the evidence suggests, all of which are then related back to theory. In **inductive research**, the researcher begins with observation, finds patterns in the observations, and uses these patterns to form a general explanation (theory) to account for the observations. Inductive research is usually qualitative in order to capture the subjectivity and nuances of the human experience and aligns with most exploratory or basic descriptive research. Deductive research, on the other hand, tends to be (but is not always) more quantitative, focusing more on numbers and establishing statistical trends. Therefore, deductive research tends to focus on more complex descriptive, explanatory, or evaluative research. Both approaches have their strengths and the strongest research designs, as we will later see, work to have components of both approaches.

STEPS IN THE RESEARCH PROCESS

Because the focus of this book is on research *and* statistics I will center our discussion on the systematic steps of the deductive research process, as shown in Figure 1.1. Let's discuss some general points about this process. First, as you see in Figure 1.1, it is cyclical, meaning that current research is based on what we have learned from previously published research. Second, notice that the lines between the steps are just that, lines, not arrows. That is because these steps do not occur as a neat checklist where you cover one step and then move on to the next without ever possibly returning to earlier steps. If new evidence, such as a newly published study, comes to light while researchers are refining hypotheses and measures, then

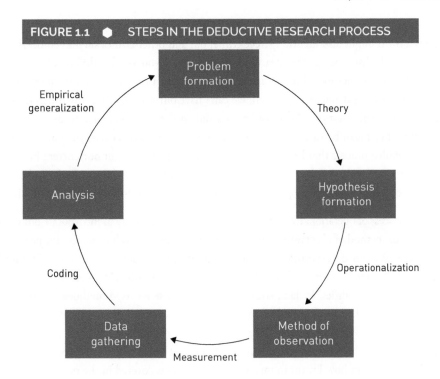

FIGURE 1.1 ⬡ STEPS IN THE DEDUCTIVE RESEARCH PROCESS

researchers will revisit their literature review, possibly add this new information, and perhaps end up altering their hypotheses or measures as a result. Let's walk through this process with an example.

Although the deductive research process is cyclical, we nonetheless have to start somewhere so for us let's start with formulating a research problem, which is essentially what the researcher wants to study. Research topics come from a variety of sources, such as personal interest, bosses, and/or professional needs, but they don't really emerge fully developed on their own. Instead, they are a product of a literature review (Chapter 2) and experience, coupled with theory. I might be interested in studying the relationship between peers and crime; and, after doing a literature review, I might decide that differential association theory is the best fit for the gaps in the research and what I want to study. Based on this, I might refine my research topic to whether age affects the type of criminal behavior children under age 18 exhibit.

Once a researcher has a topic and theory, the researcher might link these steps to hypothesis formation, which is a statement that researchers empirically test. In my example, I might choose to hypothesize that the older the peer group, the more serious the criminal acts they are likely to exhibit. As shown in Figure 1.1, the next steps are to identify and define the concepts relevant to the hypothesis (operationalization, Chapter 4) and to select a method of observation (Chapters 7–10) that will best address these concepts. Let's actually start with what we mean by operationalized concepts. Talk to five of your friends and ask them what crime means. One friend might say that crime is anything that breaks a law. A second friend might provide examples of traditional street crime, such as burglary, assault, and murder, whereas a third might also mention street crime, but add other crimes such as embezzlement and fraud to the list. You get the idea. The point is that if you ask five different friends what crime is, you might get five different answers. This can be a problem when trying to study a phenomenon via the deductive approach; we can't have our subjects thinking different things when we ask them questions. So in order to avoid this, researchers have to be very careful about what they mean by various concepts, the process of which is called operationalization. This is a detailed process that I will explain more in Chapter 4 but for our current brief illustration, I might decide to focus on the specific crimes of petty vandalism, theft, and assault. I might also decide to group my peers into the age categories of 9–12, 13–15, and 16–18.

Once our process of operationalization is complete, then we are ready to incorporate our definitions into our method of observation. There are multiple choices for how to observe people and collect data. We can do experiments or quasi-experiments (Chapter 6), surveys (Chapter 7), interviews (Chapter 7), case studies (Chapter 8), or focus groups (Chapter 8), just to name a few of many possibilities. In fact, strong research will use a mixed-methods approach that incorporates more than one method of observation (which we will discuss later). For now, let's say I decide to conduct a survey of 300 adolescents and to interview a subset of 30 of them. Remember that the lines (rather than arrows) in Figure 1.1 indicate that this process is fluid. So I may have an idea of how I want to measure these terms (as covered in the previous step), but the method of observation I decide to use might lead me to alter these decisions. For example, I might have very specific definitions of crime for the survey to which the respondent answers yes/no regarding whether they ever committed that act; but in the interview, my questions might be open-ended and more ambiguous so I can get a sense of the subjects' definition of their own behaviors. Therefore, in reality, researchers are probably thinking about operational definitions, methods of observation, and measurement simultaneously. However, in order to teach about these processes, we have to treat them as separate steps.

The data-gathering stage is really where we just go out and implement our method of observation. To put it another way: we actually get our data. Once we have our information, we have to somehow make sense of it. We want to find patterns in responses that we can relate to theory and, for us, practical use. For quantitative methods like surveys, for example, much of data analysis involves computers, and computers frequently involve numbers. So our next step is to translate our language responses to numbers that a computer can "read." But even for qualitative methods like interviews, researchers need to clearly articulate and identify themes in responses to organize their data into meaningful patterns. Both of these practices are forms of coding (Chapter 11). In quantitative analysis, computers use this information to summarize the patterns for us via various statistical techniques (Chapters 12–15). In qualitative methods patterns in codes are often identified by the researcher, but computer programs do exist that can help with this sort of analysis as well. In both cases, once research is analyzed it is shared with the academic or professional community and becomes fuel for further research, thereby continuing the cycle.

As I said, this was a very cursory overview of the research process and the general organization of our book. Subsequent chapters will discuss each phase of the deductive process in more detail; and, although research methods and statistics can be very sophisticated, our focus will be on how to "get the job done." Therefore, the material in this book will provide you with the foundation in research and statistics for those of you who plan on going to graduate school, but it will also provide enough basic detail to be useful to those of you who plan on entering your field of choice sooner and need to "get the job done."

✓ **LEARNING CHECK 1.3: STAGES OF RESEARCH**

1. In the deductive research model, where does the researcher learn about what is already known about a research topic?

2. In the deductive research model, where can the researcher get ideas about how to refine his/her researcher interests, to measure concepts and problems that might arise in studying a topic?

3. True/false: Stages of the research process are unique and independent of each other, meaning that once you have completed a stage, you can progress to the next stage without ever needing to go back and reconsider information from a previous stage.

Answers to be found at the end of the chapter.

MAKING DECISIONS

Your overall research goal, whether you decide to do basic or applied research, and quantitative or qualitative research all affect the method of observation that you will select. For example, case studies and focus groups really do not lend themselves to quantitative analysis; likewise, experiments are the best design choice for explanatory studies. To give you an idea of what types of methodologies fit the board research characteristics I discussed in this chapter, Figure 1.2 has a flowchart of one possible way they all relate, along with the chapters for which the different methodologies are covered. Remember, however, that research methods can be very complex. This flowchart is just one possible way of reaching a decision of a method that matches your goals. There are other methodological options that might be viable; and, as I said earlier, the strongest research designs incorporate more than one goal and approach. Therefore, incorporating multiple sections of the flowchart and doing a mixed-methods design is another possibility.

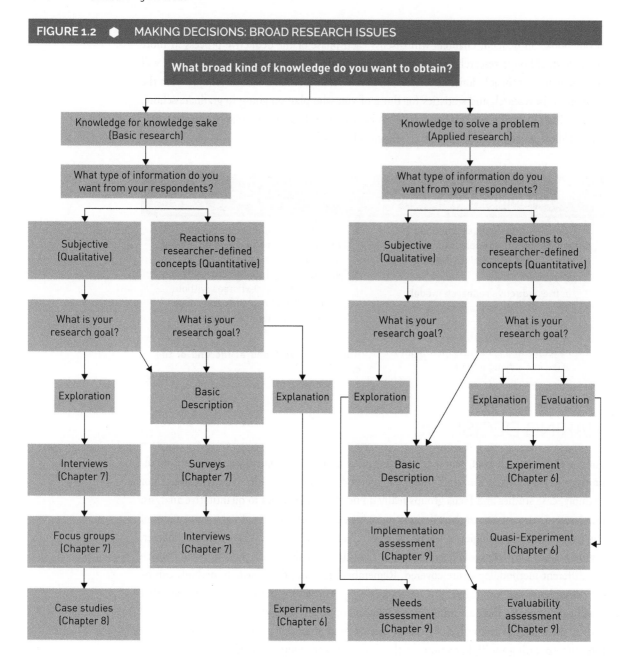

FIGURE 1.2   ●   MAKING DECISIONS: BROAD RESEARCH ISSUES

CHALLENGES

We have not had the opportunity yet to really get into the specifics of research methods or statistics, so we don't have many *methodological* challenges to specifically address here. However, as I cover the individual steps of the research process in more detail in future chapters, I will also identify some common challenges researchers may encounter as well as some possible solutions to those challenges.

Key Terms

Applied research

Authority (knowledge)

Basic research

Common sense (knowledge)

Deductive research

Descriptive research

Evaluation research

Evidence-based research

Experience (knowledge)

Explanatory research

Exploratory research

Inductive research

Qualitative research

Quantitative research

Science

Tradition (knowledge)

Answers to Learning Check Questions

Learning Check 1.1: Areas of Knowledge

1. Some possible reasons are: experience is limited, we have selective perception about our experiences, we tend to interpret experiences in ways that align or benefit us, and experience in one situation does not necessarily translate to other situations

2. Some possible reasons are that science is: (1) empirical (observable); (2) theoretical; (3) systematic (so it can be replicated); (4) probabilistic; and (5) provisional.

Learning Check 1.2: Four Main Goals of Research

1. Descriptive. There is no indication that a causal connection is being made, nor is this testing an intervention.

2. Evaluation: There is an intervention (cleaning up the neighborhood) that is being evaluated to see if it works. If you said explanation, you are

close because in evaluation the intervention is supposed to "cause" a change in the outcome, but because this is an applied cause, even though it is related to theory, it is an evaluation.

3. Explanation: Although there are a lot of factors to be addressed in the research design to make this causal claim, the wording of the question itself implies causality because it implies that internet use is responsible for (or causes) changes in face-to-face interaction.

Learning Check 1.3: Stages of Research

1. Literature review

2. Literature review

3. False. Decisions in the early stages of the process affect the later stages and new information that may come to light at the later stages may cause re-evaluation, and possible changes, to decisions made at the earlier stages.

End-of-Chapter Problems

1. Knowledge that stems from the way we have always done things is knowledge based on
   a. Common sense
   b. Tradition
   c. Experience
   d. Science

2. When we combine traditional knowledge and experience we have what type of knowledge?
   a. Common sense
   b. Science
   c. Expert

3. When we say science is systematic, we mean that
   a. there is a generally agreed-upon order of steps that researchers describe regarding their study that helps other researchers replicate a study.
   b. it is value-free
   c. it is empirically observable
   d. the more criteria (provisions) we can specify, the more likely we will be able to explain our findings.

4. True or False: We use science to prove hypotheses about social behavior.

5. True or False: A study to test the effectiveness of a campus antidrinking campaign would be an example of applied research.

6. True or False: A researcher samples 400 comments to an online article from a reputable news source to study how people react to

disagreeing perspectives online. This would be an example of basic research.

7. A researcher conducted focus groups of 40 children under age 10 to see which toys would be the popular ones coming this holiday season. She is doing what type of research?
   a. Exploratory
   b. Descriptive
   c. Explanation
   d. Evaluation

8. A researcher wants to examine whether an in-prison coaching prisoner on the "soft skills" of interviewing helped them find jobs upon release. What research purpose would this be?
   a. Exploratory
   b. Descriptive
   c. Explanation
   d. Evaluation

9. True/False: A researcher wants to examine the dating experiences of people who identify as gender-fluid, so the researcher conducts interviews with 15 self-identified gender-fluid individuals about their dating practices, transcribes the interviews, finds common themes, and then relates those themes to theory as part of her reporting. This is an example of deductive research.

10. True/False: In deductive research, once a researcher is done with one part of the wheel (process), the researcher moves on to the next, never looking ahead or returning to parts of the process.

RESEARCH TOPICS, LITERATURE REVIEWS, AND HYPOTHESES

What if your research methods/statistics professor walked into the classroom and announced, "Our topic for this semester is gender stratification. You have three and a half months to design a study, collect the data, analyze the results, and write your report." Any idea where to begin? Probably not. "Gender stratification" is not a real research topic; it is too broad. For example, you might choose to focus on examining what percent of women are in upper management positions in a company. Someone else might focus on how husbands and wives separate household responsibilities. A third person might focus on gender differences in the specialties doctors select. Basically, the possibilities for studying gender stratification are as endless as your imagination. This is not necessarily "bad," but for the purpose of identifying a research topic, it is also not very useful.

Sometimes coming up with a research topic or question is really straightforward. Someone may tell you explicitly what they want you to study such as: Did the program reduce delinquency? What percent of high school students experience bullying on school grounds? Which precinct in the county is the most efficient in reducing property crime? Sometimes, however, getting started is hard. Professors or bosses might give you a broad topic, such as gender stratification, but these are not viable *research* topics. These topics need to be refined into something that is meaningful and manageable, and, doing so is the first step of the deductive research process that I discussed in Chapter 1. In reality, the first couple of parts of that deductive research cycle, namely topic formation, literature reviews, and writing hypotheses, are frequently developed simultaneously and establish the foundation for the rest of the research process. Therefore, this chapter focuses on these three initial components to get us started.

TOPIC FORMATION AND RESEARCH QUESTIONS

I have been using the terms *research topic* and *research questions* interchangeably, so what is the difference? In reality, not much. Of all the considerations you will learn in conducting research, getting hung up on what is the difference between a research topic and question is not conducive to "getting the job done." Although I will continue to use them interchangeably, I will probably use the term *research question* a bit more, simply out of habit. However, as I said, they really address the same point: refining what it is your research will address.

Types of Research Questions

Research questions can take many forms, too many to get into an exhaustive list here. To provide a "getting the job done" perspective of research questions, we can borrow from Hedrick et al. (1993), who identified four types of research questions: descriptive, normative, correlative, and impact. **Descriptive research questions** are pretty much what the name implies—they describe something. What percent of prisoners recidivate within 5 years of release? What percent of upper-management positions in medium-sized firms are occupied by women? Not much more needs to be said about these questions because they are directly related to the kind of material I discussed in Chapter 1 regarding the descriptive purpose of research. The second type of research question is **normative questions**, which make a comparison against some types of standard program objectives ("norm") or population comparisons. Normative research questions might be something like if 68% of prisoners nationally recidivate within 3 years of release, how do prisoners in our county compare? Is a peer-tutoring program providing the designed 15 hours of tutoring? Think of these research questions as comparing your interest to some known value or program goal to see how your focus would relate to the norm or standard. The third type of question, **correlative questions**, looks at an association between two variables (X and Y) but does not purport to make any causal claims between them. In other words, correlational research questions might ask things like: What is the relationship between college major and salary 3 years post-college graduation? Is there a relationship between marital status and overall happiness? Correlative research questions might lead to hypothesis testing in order to show that a change in one variable is associated (what we frequently statistically call "correlated") with a change in a second variable, but they do not explicitly aim to test causality. As we will learn later in this chapter, correlation does not automatically mean causation, but it is definitely a component of it. The last type of research question, **impact question**, is more causal. This would be questions like: Does Drug Court participation reduce the risk of re-arrest for drug-related crimes within 3 years of graduation? Does intensive child intervention reduce the need for out-of-home foster care placement for at-risk families? Impact questions imply that some program or policy, for example, creates (causes, impacts) a change in behavior.

iStockphoto.com/Ridofranz

PHOTO 2.1 Can you think of an example of each of the four types of research questions to fit this picture?

✔ LEARNING CHECK 2.1: TYPES OF RESEARCH QUESTIONS

1. What distinguishes normative research questions from descriptive ones?

2. What distinguishes descriptive research questions from correlative questions?

3. Which of the four types of research questions does this question exemplify: What percent of sociology majors have a job or are enrolled in a graduate program 2 years after graduation?

Answers to be found at the end of the chapter.

Characteristics of Strong Research Questions

Regardless of the form, all strong research questions share some common characteristics. First, research questions have to be sufficiently specific. "Gender stratification," the example I gave at the beginning of the chapter, is not specific. Specific questions could be: In dual-earner households, what percent of household activities is done by men and what percent is done by women? Are individuals who identify as racial/ethnic minorities more likely to be in upper-management positions in companies with more than 1,000 employees compared to smaller companies? What percent of the elderly have weekly contact with their children? These examples are not only specific, but they are clear and relatively concise as well.

Research questions also need to be **empirically observable**. This means that the research question has to be about something that can actually be documented. Questions that involve values cannot be documented and are not good research questions. Examples of value questions include: Should the death penalty be federally outlawed? Should men become more involved in childcare at home? Is frequent involvement of grandparents in children's lives important for children's socioemotional development? As we learned in Chapter 1, science can only answer what *is*, what we can *observe*; and "should" questions or questions about importance are opinions and, as such, are unanswerable. Of course, we could make some of these viable questions by shifting the question wording to something like What are people's views regarding a federal outlaw of the death penalty? Do women feel that men should be more involved in childcare at home? What benefits do parents see of having involved grandparents in children's lives? Now, even though we are addressing opinions, we are *documenting* them, and our research goal is a description, not to reach a decision about what we "should" do. In other words, these altered questions are not taking a stand on which opinion we should act on or is more important.

Third, strong research questions or topics should be relevant. In basic research, relevance can be very subjective. What is relevant to a sociologist would not necessarily be relevant to an archeologist. However, relevance can also mean whether research adds to the existing knowledge about a topic in a meaningful way. Identifying relevance is a bit easier in applied research because, in applied research, relevant research is that which will have an impact on real-world experiences or theories. The point is, it is the researcher's responsibility to make the case of relevance for their field.

Fourth, they should also be realistic. What we mean by this is that the question should be able to be studied within the bounds of the available resources, such as the time, money, and skill of the researcher, and it should be sufficiently specific so that what is being studied is clear. There is no point in creating a research question that requires a form of sampling or statistical analysis that is beyond the available economic resources, the available data-gathering skills of the staff, the analytical skills of the researcher, or the availability of the data.

Last, research questions should be able to be studied ethically. We will discuss the types of ethical responsibilities researchers have to their field and subjects in Chapter 3. For now, let it suffice that when it comes to research studies, the end does not justify the means.

LEARNING CHECK 2.2: STRONG RESEARCH QUESTIONS

1. Identify three characteristics of good research questions.

2. Is the following a strong research question? Why or why not?

    How does family structure in high school affect the likelihood an adolescent will enroll in a 2- or 4-year college immediately after high school graduation?

3. Is the following a strong research question? Why or why not?

    Should parents who are unhappy in their marriage stay together for the sake of their children?

Answers to be found at the end of the chapter.

Steps for Creating Research Questions

As I mentioned previously, sometimes research questions or topics are easy to create because someone else—a boss or professor, for example—tells you what to study and what you are told fits the characteristics I just mentioned in the previous section. However, sometimes this is not the case. In those instances, starting with a broad research topic is a viable first step. That topic will just have to be refined and the next step to accomplish this is to read the existing literature, called a **literature review**, which I will discuss in more detail in the next section. For our purposes now, however, I will say that a literature review will help you learn what experts in the field already know about your broad topic so you can eliminate research questions that replicate that knowledge. A literature review will also help you define your problem by giving you ideas of when researchers have found conflicting findings and where there are gaps in existing knowledge. For example, you may find that some research creates more questions than answers and these questions can fuel your focus. Or finding gaps or inconsistencies can help you mold your research question in a way to help resolve the conflict. In a nutshell, your current research should build on the knowledge that already exists and you learn about what is known by studying the published research of others. Third, an honest assessment of your skills and the available resources (such as time and money) can help you further refine your research question. For example, if you have a limited budget, refining your research question in a way that requires a large multiyear study is not useful. On a limited budget, you will need to study a small, specific aspect of an issue. It may take multiple iterations of these steps, especially reviewing the literature and refining your research topic more than once, until you reach a feasible research question and this back and forth further illustrates how stages of the systematic research process covered in Chapter 1 are frequently done simultaneously in the real world.

LITERATURE REVIEWS

The Purpose of a Literature View

As I just discussed, critically reading the research of others and gaining material for a literature review are instrumental in refining research questions. A literature review also helps you place your research question or topic into the broader context of the existing knowledge. It gives you the opportunity to orient the reader to how your research "fits," thereby fulfilling the goal of relevance mentioned in the previous section. The last use of a literature review I will mention in our spirit of "getting the job done" is that it can also give you direction with methodological decisions, thereby alleviating some of the pressure of coming up with all this stuff on your own. Specifically, the methods, findings, and limitations expressed in previous research can give you ideas of how to measure your concepts, what type of sampling techniques are feasible, which methods of observation might be the most appropriate or informative, and potential problems to troubleshoot. It may also give you information on other causes or factors relevant to your topic that you have not previously considered, but which should nonetheless be incorporated into your study. So the literature review, the part of methodology that might, at first glance, not really seem "relevant" to your "real" research, actually serves as the foundation for it.

But first, you have to find the information.

Searching for Material

What to search and where to begin can be daunting. The most logical starting point is your research topic or question. I have already discussed how to select a research question, so the next step is to make note of the keywords in that initial question or topic, keeping in mind that the research question may be refined based on the information you find. For example, if my research question is "Does training police officers to identify people experiencing a mental health crisis reduce arrests in favor of directing perpetrators to mental health treatment?," I might start with the following search terms:

1. Mental health and arrest

2. Crime and mental health

3. Police and mental health and offenders

4. Police and mental health training

The "where" to find information is more detailed. Now, most literature searches occur online via databases called **bibliographic databases**, which you can probably access through your school's library. Common online databases in our fields include ProQuest, JSTOR, ERIC, PsychInfo, SocINDEX, and Sociological Abstracts. Your professor or librarian can probably direct you to what is available at your school. The process of searching these databases is similar to conducting a standard online search in popular search engines like Google or Yahoo; and in some of these databases, you can also refine your search to the type of publication (e.g., if you are just interested in peer-reviewed publications) and the years of interest (such as the last five years). The results will usually contain the title, authors' names, and the abstract, which is a brief (usually 125–200-word) summary of the purpose, methods, and main findings that help the reader identify whether the article is relevant to their interest.

Depending on your school's subscription, you might be able to access the full article right from the database; otherwise, you might have to request it from your library, perhaps for a fee. No one search database is perfect. One database might not have the full text of an article available, but another one might. Likewise, not all journals are covered in all databases; and even if there is overlap, they may not cover the same years. Therefore, it is useful to search more than one database when trying to find material.

Once you have selected a database and have entered keywords, the database will present various studies that might be relevant. These studies might be in peer-reviewed journals, professional journals, dissertations, conference proceedings, books, or newspapers…there are many possibilities. Some researchers claim you should be flexible and search all available materials in any particular order. Others suggest starting with academic journals and then proceeding to professional journals, books, conference papers, and any other potentially relevant sources in that order (Creswell, 2002; Hart, 2001). It is my opinion that for research in general and applied or evidence-based research in particular, academic or professional journals, are a good start, and then proceed to any other possibly relevant forms of material. There are a couple of reasons why I say to start with journals. First, there are generally two types of journals: academic and professional. Academic journals usually contain peer-reviewed articles, whereas professional journals generally do not, but both sources tend to have more vigorous research represented in them than do other forms of sources. Among sources, peer review can be one indicator of quality because it means that two to three identified "experts" in the field critically read the details of a study, provided feedback regarding a variety of issues like contribution, missed available literature, methodology, and statistical analysis, and then made a recommendation

iStockphoto.com/pixelfit

PHOTO 2.2 Much research for literature reviews can now be done online, including obtaining the full text of articles.

regarding publication. Usually, there are four possible recommendations. The most common decision is to deny publication outright, so consequently the research will not even show up in your database search since it is not published. The second possible reviewer's recommendation is to revise the manuscript and resubmit it. This option usually results when a reviewer sees merit to the research but also identifies some substantive issues that he or she feels needs to be addressed before the research is sound enough for publication. In this situation, the reviewers will make specific recommendations as to what the researcher needs to change or address and then the researcher is invited to resubmit the revised work for a new review. The manuscript might still be rejected after the new submission, but this response means that the reviewers are willing to give the manuscript another chance. The third option is a conditional acceptance pending successful changes requested by the reviewers that are generally minor or less methodologically substantial in nature than what would occur with a revise and resubmit decision. The last option is that the reviewers recommend publication of the study as is with no changes. This outcome is the least common among reputable journals, a point that will be especially relevant soon when I discuss predatory journals. Based on these individual recommendations from the two to three people independently reviewing each study submitted, an editor makes a final judgment regarding which of the four outcomes is the official decision. I know I went into more detail about this process than you may have expected, but I did so in order to illustrate the degree of vetting that occurs within peer-review journals. Obviously, this process is more vigorous than what we see in newspapers, news magazines, or online blogs. Although not perfect, as not all journals are equally selective in what they publish, being published in a peer-reviewed journal serves as a preliminary indicator of the quality of a study. Obviously poor studies do not get published, adequate ones do in mid-level peer-reviewed sources, and really good studies get published in the more selective, vigorous journals.

But remember what we learned in Chapter 1. Quality research is not limited to or guaranteed in peer-review research. The research published in professional journals may also be very vigorous; it just may not have been vetted by others. Furthermore, with the push to "publish or perish" in academia, the ease of making websites, and open-access publishing, there has been an increase in what is called **predatory journals**. These are journals that claim to be peer-reviewed, and open access (more in a moment) and promise a fast turn-around between submission and publication if "accepted." Unfortunately, there are some problems with these predatory journals. First, the manuscripts are not adequately peer-reviewed, if at all. Peer-reviewed submissions may take 6–12 months until publication, which may be a little more understandable to you now that you know the detailed process peer-review entails. Predatory journals, however, will accept a manuscript for publication in as little as under a month, indicating that contrary to what they may post on a website, they are not peer-reviewed. Furthermore, remember, it is very rare for a manuscript to be accepted without any suggestion for changes the first time around. Think about it. When was the last time *you* got two to three people to independently come up with the same decision about something basic, like where to eat dinner or what movie to rent? Such a decision is even less likely when two to three people are independently reviewing something as detailed (remember all those stages we saw in Figure 1.1 in Chapter 1?) as a scientific study. This lack of a real peer-review means that the material "published" in predatory journals can contribute to the dissemination of bad information. Second, many predatory journals claim to be open access, which is a way of distributing research studies online free to the reader. Open access is a newer way of sharing scientific information that aims to make this information more available to members of the scientific community who, for whatever reason, cannot afford the costly subscription fees for print journals or online databases. Although there are a variety of ways of funding open access material, a discussion of which is beyond our purposes, predatory journals frequently charge the researcher to make his/her study available to others. Even some reputable journals do this to varying degrees, but predatory journals only use the open access fee to generate their profits with no real benefit to the researcher. Last, in predatory journals, the "publication" could be hard to find and it may disappear over time. Reputable journals, on the other hand, strive to make their material readily available and they archive old volumes.

Fortunately, a simple online search will identify multiple websites that are tracking and listing predatory journals, but no one online source is perfect. Be aware of the reputation of the

BOX 2.1
WHERE TO FIND INFORMATION ON JOURNAL QUALITY

Quality Indicator	What It Is	How to Use the Measure	Possible Sources
Impact factor	The number of citations to a given journal over the previous 2 years divided by the number of research articles and reviews published by that journal	The higher the impact factor, the higher the quality	Social Science Citation Index http://mjl.clarivate.com/cgi-bin/jrnlst/jlresults.cgi?PC=ss Scimago journal and country rank https://www.scimagojr.com/
Eigenfactor	Total number of citations over a 5-year period (does not account for a number of articles published)	The higher the impact factor, the higher the quality	Eigenfactor.org Scimago journal and country rank https://www.scimagojr.com/
h-index	An author-level metric that measures the productivity and scholarly view (based on citations) of a specific author that appears in a journal	The higher the impact factor, the higher the quality	Scimago journal and country rank https://www.scimagojr.com/

journal that houses the manuscripts you are considering for your literature review. If it is on a list of possible predatory journals, ignore the manuscript. If a journal is not on such a list, there is additional information that helps determine a journal's validity and quality. One of these indicators is the journal's **impact factor**, which is a measure of the frequency that the average journal article is cited in a particular year. The higher the impact factor, the more frequently the average article is cited, and the higher quality the journal. Another indicator of quality is the journal's acceptance rate. Many people want to publish in highly respected journals, so more people are likely to submit articles to these journals than the journal has space for publication. For example, one of the most respected journals in sociology is the *American Sociological Review* and according to its editorial report of 2019, the journal had 728 submissions in 2018 and only 6.7% of them were eventually accepted for publication (American Sociological Association, 2019). That means that the rejection rate is close to 93%, which is extremely high and indicates that the reviewers and editors of that journal are highly selective. This selectivity, in turn, increases the likelihood that the studies that *are* published are methodologically strong and relevant to the field. Finally, you can also use the number of citations for a specific published article as an additional measure of the study's usefulness to the field. However, keep in mind that older articles have had more time to accrue citations than newer ones; therefore, the number of citations alone is not a perfect indicator either. As you can probably tell, here, as with many things, it is most useful to use more than one of these criteria in combination, rather than alone, to assess the initial quality of the material you find.

However, a preliminary determination of study quality is just one factor in deciding whether the information that shows up in a database search is worth a deeper look for your purposes. Obviously, a second consideration is the degree to which the study focus and findings relate to your research topic or question, which is also important. Both of these factors (source quality and study relevance) are important places to start deciding what will merit a closer look. I will provide some suggestions to determine study relevancy in the next section, but for now, I am focusing on just how to find possible information. Therefore, although this last suggestion seems like it is out of order (because, as I just said, I will discuss some considerations for determining study relevancy), once you do identify some studies that seem particularly informative to you, one last way of identifying additional studies is to look at the material cited by *these* studies. In other words, if you look at the reference section in these articles you find particularly relevant, you can sometimes find more sources that will also be helpful to your study.

Critically Evaluating Material

Probably one of the hardest parts of a literature review is figuring out how to *critically* evaluate the material you see. You will likely come across many different articles, using different methodologies, different theoretical foundations, and producing different results. How do you know what to believe? There is not an easy answer to this per se. Instead, the answer lies in how you approach and organize the different pieces of information you obtain to facilitate your comparison.

Let's first talk about how to organize the articles you find. Remember, it is very possible that you will have many articles that might be relevant to your topic to consider, and there is no one magic approach to how to deal with them all. Your professor may have some suggestions, but here is an approach I have found that works with my students. First, gather the abstracts and the citations (which will save you time when you want to look up the full text of any articles and when you compile your reference section) of the articles you think might even remotely be relevant to your needs. For example, if we want to study how people on Facebook react to posts that they consider to be inappropriate, I would start by copying and pasting *both* the abstracts and the corresponding full citations into one file that I can read all together. Next, based on a reading of the abstracts, I suggest creating a chart that summarizes the purpose, sample, method of observation, and key findings present in each abstract. I also suggest including a column where you can jot initial links between articles or comments of how particular articles relate to your topic. This chart will serve as the source for an initial weeding of articles because the main points are presented in a way that is easy to compare how the many articles you have collected might fit together. An example of how this chart might look for a study about people's reactions to inappropriate Facebook posts appears in Figure 2.1.

Incidentally, you may not be able to fill in all aspects of the chart based on the abstracts. That is OK for now. Once you have this chart filled in as much as possible, decide right away which articles are not useful to your specific purpose as it is currently defined. I suggest using a color code so you can quickly visualize which articles you have decided not to pursue, but not to delete these articles all together from the chart in case they might be relevant later. The next step is to read the remaining articles, even if you are unsure if they will be useful later, and complete the grid based on the detail presented in the articles.

Once you have these main pieces of information recorded, now you are better able to compare and critically evaluate the articles. We already discussed one issue in evaluating the material, the authority of the source. Remember that not all sources are created equal. Peer-reviewed journals tend to have more authority than newspapers, for example, because, as we said, any published material in peer-reviewed journals has been reviewed by experts in the field before publication. However, as we also learned, not *all* journals claim to be peer-reviewed (look back to our discussion of predatory journals), and, even among those that are truly peer-reviewed, as we also mentioned previously, some journals have more prestige than others.

Even without having a strong methodological background, there are some indicators you can use to start critically sorting the information across studies. One of these indicators is the authority of the author. This really involves the affiliation of the author. In other words,

FIGURE 2.1 ● SUMMARY CHART FOR LITERATURE REVIEW CONSIDERATION

Author	Topic	Sample	Method	Findings	Pros / Cons	Possible Use
Roche et al.	Identify inappropriate posts See reaction to posts	150 college students enrolled in Intro course and who agreed to do study for extra credit points	Created posts and then did survey to see students, reaction to posts (quantitative)	Romantic relationships → inappropriate Passive-aggressive inappropriate Ignore / block / defriend	Con: Not random and no indication if representative of student body Con: Too close to your study interests? Pro: Different topics for some areas of inappropriateness—some replication, some new	Appropriateness comparisons Reaction comparisons Self-disclosure discussion Demographic differences
Glassman	Implications of college students posting drinking pictures on FB	445 college students		Those who post pics were more likely to drink alcohol	Con: 22% response rate questionable—did they compare respondents to population to approximate representation?	An example of negative self-disclosure on Facebook → Can use to create posts
Miller et al.	SNS content appropriateness		Field study	Students aware info post is inappropriate for all		Not sure article focus fits with my study; concerned with some term definitions.
Park & Lee	Why college students use Facebook,t their concern for impression management, and sense of belonging w/ campus life	246 college students	Online survey	Entertainment, relationship maintenance, self-expression, and communication with impression management relate to FB intensity	Pro: Focuses on impression management	See the theme of impression management so this might be useful. I need to read the article to decide further.

Color Key:

Black is info inserted into the chart based on a reading of the initial abstracts obtained.

Gray is articles that are eliminated after the initial abstract reading (1st round).

Light blue is an example of an article that I need to investigate more to decide whether I will actually use it.

Blue is info that was inserted into the grid *after* reading the article.

is the author associated with a known institution, like a university or a government agency? If the authors have an affiliation, it is frequently noted by his/her name on a biography presented at the end of the article. If an affiliation is not noted, you can always search the author online. Having an association with a university of government agency gives some authenticity to the author, rather than having that person be an unknown individual. Another way of identifying the authority of the author is to see whether others have cited that individual or where she/he has published before. Again thanks to the Internet, much of this is available online. A third consideration is the tone of the material. As I mentioned in Chapter 1, science strives to be objective and unbiased. As such, if an author writes emotionally, presents only one side of an argument, and/or does not provide scholarly citations, then that should raise a red flag to the reader. You also want to consider the timeliness of the material. Is the topic currently popular? If so, then you might expect to see rather recent citations. If the topic is novel, however, perhaps the citations will be older; and that will be OK. The point is, you have to have an idea of whether you should expect current citations or not, and then whether a source fulfills those expectations. Furthermore, you want to consider the objectivity of the researcher. For example, has the researcher distinguished between opinions and research findings? Key phrases that show a citation is research based include (but are not limited to):

- Recent data suggest that…

- In laboratory experiments…

- Data from surveys comparing…

- Doe (2012) found that…

- The percentage of men who…

On the contrary, keywords that show a citation is opinion based include (but are not limited to)

- Jones (2014) has argued that…

- These kinds of assumptions…

- Smith has advocated the use of…

Both opinion and research are useful; one just has to make sure they are interpreted correctly. You wouldn't necessarily want to base a $400,000 grant on an opinion as opposed to a research observation.

However, even if the material is written by a well-established expert, has current cites, is objectively presented, and is published in a well-respected journal, that does not mean that you should just blindly accept the material based on face value. You still have a responsibility to methodologically and statistically evaluate what you see. I won't discuss how to evaluate how well researchers have designed their chosen methodology here because most of the considerations are covered later in this book, so you have not learned about them yet. However, here it is worth recognizing that not all methodologies are equal, especially in applied and evidence-based research, so it does merit discussing briefly how different methodologies rank.

At the top of the hierarchy would be **meta-analyses**. Meta-analyses are statistical analysis of the results of many independent studies that are similar enough to be able to have their findings be treated as the data for a new study (Higgins & Green, 2005). Think of this as a statistical analysis of others' statistics, where the findings of other studies are the data for the meta-analysis. When done well, this type of study allows researchers to get more of an overall

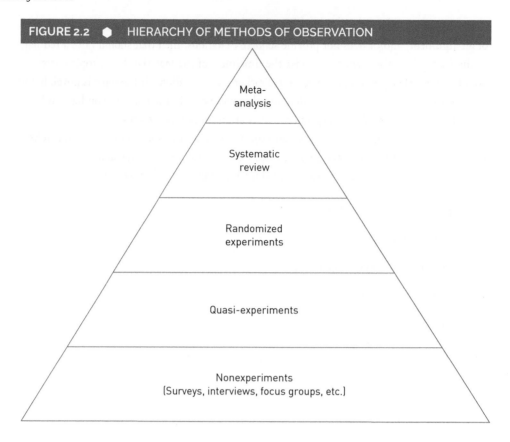

FIGURE 2.2 ◆ HIERARCHY OF METHODS OF OBSERVATION

Meta-analysis

Systematic review

Randomized experiments

Quasi-experiments

Nonexperiments
(Surveys, interviews, focus groups, etc.)

picture of many different studies at once. Of course, the quality of this type of research is only as good as the quality of the studies that serve as this method's data; but, for now, we will assume that when ranking methods, those methods have been carried out as well as can be expected.

Systematic reviews are another tier of research. These are similar in approach to meta-analysis in that they systematically review the findings of multiple studies of similar focus and design; they just produce their results in a narrative form rather than the statistical one, character-istic of meta-analysis. A third tier is **randomized experimental research**, especially ones that are well controlled and involve both random selection (Chapter 5) and random assignment (Chapter 6) because if experiments have these characteristics, researchers are more confident that any change in behavior is due to the independent variable and not some other rival causal factor (Chapter 3). Because experiments are the best methodological means for controlling for factors other than the treatment that might create an observed change in behavior, many researchers consider these types of experiments to be the "gold standard" for establishing a causal connection, especially when evaluating the effectiveness of interventions. Next down in the hierarchy is **quasi-experiments**, which do not involve random assignment but do fre-quently have comparison groups for which statistics (rather than methods) can assess the effects of some rival causal factors. Because this group of methods lacks random selection and assignment, their findings need to be interpreted more cautiously than pure experiments because randomization is the only true way to make sure that groups are equal prior to an intervention. Nonexperimental methods, like surveys, interviews, or focus groups, are toward the bottom end of the hierarchy. However, just because these methodologies are at the bottom of the hierarchy does not mean that they are "bad" choices or do not produce useful information. If we are doing applied research, especially if we are testing a program, these forms of observation are simply less preferred as the *main* way of obtaining evidence than meta-analysis or experiments because they are usually exploratory or descriptive in nature, not explanatory. Remember in the last chapter when we said that the research goal was important because it helped you assess the merit and needs of the research? This is an example of this idea in practice. If your research goal is to describe the need for a particular program, for example, then a nonexperimental method may be all that is necessary to "get the job done" and adequately achieve this goal. However, if your goal is to test program effectiveness (evaluative research), then your goal is more sophisticated and, as such, a more sophisticated method of observation, such as meta-analysis or experiments, is required. Therefore, it is important to know how the different methods rank.

Keeping this ranking in mind, the methodological and statistical considerations you learn as you progress through this book will serve as the foundation for the evaluation of those specific designs when you read the research of others. Furthermore, these points can help you identify which articles in your grid you can discount and omit early on and which ones merit a closer read of the study in its entirety. Once you read all the articles you find relevant, you can fill in the other parts of the grid, including some preliminary notes in the last column that will help you remember linkages, gaps, differences, and/or similarities between articles for when you want to start organizing your literature review. By comparing the findings and methodological detail of different studies, researchers can get a stronger sense of the gaps and contradictions in the existing knowledge that can help them refine their research question to create a testable hypothesis.

Given the systematic and replicable nature of science, the next step is to organize the material in a way that shows others the information flow that led you to your specific focus and that helps to explain how your focus fits into the wider scheme of knowledge.

Organizing a Literature Review

If learning how to critically evaluate material for the literature review is the hardest part of this process, then organizing it has to be a close second. All too often, students treat the literature review like a high school book report where they simply document what each article found and the methods used to obtain those findings. As a result, students often devote one paragraph to each article, where the resulting "literature review" ends up reading like a shopping list instead of a critical analysis of what is known about a topic. However, literature reviews are much more than documentation and no professional (or professor) wants to read a report where paragraph one is about article one, paragraph two is about article two, paragraph three for article three, and so on. Instead, literature reviews are about synthesis, identifying agreement *and* disagreement in what has been found already, identifying gaps in the current knowledge, and wrapping this entire discussion into a critical presentation that will lead the reader to *your* particular focus.

It is not necessary to include every article you read, meaning those that make it past your initial scrutiny of abstracts, in your literature review. Simply put, you will find that some of the articles you read, even after the initial thinning out, will not actually be very useful and therefore have no place in the literature review even after you spent the time reading them. So to help you organize the studies that you did find useful or relevant, think of the entire research project as a story—perhaps not a bestseller, but a story nonetheless. The literature review sets the scene whereby at its conclusion, the reader should have a clear idea of what you will specifically study and why. It is for the other parts of the report—the methods, results, and discussion sections—to continue the story by answering how you did the research, what you found, and the broader social implications of your findings. The articles that are only moderately relevant can be mentioned in passing and/or combined with other studies that have a similar focus or findings, whereas the articles that are highly relevant to the "story" deserve a more detailed discussion such as some summary and evaluation of the studies' methods and main findings.

This is where the grid that you developed in the previous section can be useful. Remember, that grid is a brief summary of the purpose, methods, and main findings of the articles you found. By reading through this, you will start to get an idea of the main issues relevant to your topic, how you might want to refine your topic, and where similarities and differences between the methods and findings of others are. Through the grid, you will also be able to form an idea of how you want to outline your literature review and be able to identify whether there are any gaps in your research that require further exploration and addition to your grid for comparison by you.

In organizing your literature review, you generally want to start by establishing the prevalence of the phenomena. Sometimes this is done in the introduction, but sometimes the introduction and literature review are not distinct subsections, but rather flow into one another. In a sense, the establishment of the phenomena addresses "why we care" about the topic. One quick note about writing introductions: Even though I used the analogy of a story earlier, introductions are not written like a real story with creative writing language or unsubstantiated dramatic claims. Although the material may progress through stages like a story, you are not writing the next bestseller where you have to "grab" the reader's attention to make them want to read more. The people reading research are busy professionals and they really just want to know the bottom line, albeit a well-written bottom line. So as I tell my students when they are writing, "Write what you mean, support what you mean, and move on."

Once the phenomena are established, Creswell (2002) suggests proceeding with a critical discussion of the research that is most relevant to the independent variable(s). Although we will cover independent and dependent variables more in a bit, for now, it is sufficient to say that the independent variable is what will influence the outcome. It is the cause will that make a change in something else, the latter of which is the dependent variable. If the literature review starts with this focus, it is still pretty broad as it is only presenting one part of the researcher's ultimate topic. Creswell argues that the next section of literature should focus on the dependent variable(s), with subsections for each specific dependent variable if there are more than one. In the discussion of the dependent variable, although the writer is not yet linking the material to the independent variable, the reader may be starting to make some of those connections on their

BOX 2.2
LITERATURE REVIEW EXCERPT EXAMPLE

Describing how to present and organize a literature review is one thing; being able to see how it is done is another. So here is a very brief excerpt from a study about intergenerational mobility and drug use done by Dennison (2018) that discusses the role of college graduation in drug use. We can use this excerpt to illustrate some of the point covered in this chapter:

Aside from socioeconomic background, *research also considers the role of one's own achieved SES—or destination status as referred to by mobility scholars (e.g., Sobel, 1981)—on drug use (Boardman et al., 2001; Karriker-Jaffe, 2013; Williams & Latkin, 2007).* Indeed, turning points like socioeconomic achievements are fundamental elements in life-course criminology (Sampson & Laub, 1993), and the way in which achieved SES influences drug use is no exception. **Research shows that college completion is related to lower instances of drug use compared with those with no college education (Martins et al., 2015; White, Labouvie, & Papadaratsakis, 2005). Furthermore, Erickson et al.**

(2016) find that those with a college degree report lower odds of experiencing anxiety, substance use, and other personality disorders, net of sociodemographic and psychological measures. Educational attainment has also been shown to promote self-efficacy (Ross & Mirowsky, 1989) as well as reduce depression (Bjelland et al., 2008).

Prior research notes the importance of employment status on the cessation of drug use (e.g., Faupel, 1988); however, most often considered is the way in which drug use reduces the prospects of stable employment across the life course (see Henkel, 2011). Spans of unemployment are shown to increase drug use (Compton, Gfroerer, Conway, & Finger, 2014; DeSimone, 2002; Hammer, 1992; Henkel, 2011). Moreover, research suggests that unemployment increases psychological distress (Nagelhout et al., 2017), and some find these consequences to be strongest during economic recessions (e.g., Compton et al., 2014).

Source: Dennison (2018, pp. 207–208).

First, notice the synthesis. There are more than 15 citations presented here, yet the excerpt is just two paragraphs long. In other words, there is not a paragraph—or even a sentence—for each study. When multiple studies reach a similar conclusion, Dennison shares that conclusion, cites the studies, and moves on to his next point. For example, look at the italicized sentence. There are three citations about the relationship between socioeconomic status (SES) and drug use and none of those citations are discussed individually; they are *synthesized* into that one point.

Second, notice the bolded text. This section about how college completion relates to a *variety* of factors. The first sentence is about college completion and drug use (with two citations) and the next two are about how college completion relates to other factors that are also related to drug use (with three citations). The bolded italicized paragraph, relates drug use to a new topic, employment, but if you pay attention to what Dennison says, you will realize that although these studies in the bolded italicized text do not directly relate to the points about college graduation, they *do* relate to the points that he mentioned that college graduation can improve. So in other words, Dennison is beginning to frame a

message of how these various factors, even if the parts in one paragraph (e.g., the bolded text) were not directly studied in the next (e.g., the bolded italicized text), all relate.

There is also a clarification or analytical component. If you look at the second sentence in the bolded italicized text section, you will see that Dennison clarifies a broad statement of the importance of employment and the cessation of drug use by *explaining* how studies have approached this relationship and the conditions under which some have found this approach to be strongest. He is not oversimplifying by stating that research has found that drug use and employment are related.

Finally, notice the tone of the writing. Dennison is very direct and factual. He is not "painting pictures," creatively writing to capture a reader's attention or being dramatic. He is not trying to use awkwardly long words to sound smart. He is not stating opinions whether this relationship is justified or important or fair. He does not use quotes from the article to make his point; he is the one writing the synthesis and summary. Furthermore, his sentence structure is varied, but not long-winded. He is not taking 100 words to

(Continued)

BOX 2.2 (*CONTINUED*)

LITERATURE REVIEW EXCERPT EXAMPLE

write what can be expressed in 50. In a nutshell, he is factually summarizing what the research has found, relating studies by identifying when the findings were the same, and comparing them by identifying when approaches added new pieces of information. And he managed to do this, as I said, in about two paragraphs even though he addressed more than 15 studies.

Source: Dennison, C. R. (2018). Intergenerational mobility and changes in drug use across the life course. *Journal of Drug Issues, 48*(2), 205–225. doi:10.1177/0022042617746974

own; therefore, the literature is becoming a bit more directed. Only after the literature for both variables is presented separately, according to Creswell, should the writer then present any literature that links the two. Creswell (2002) argues that this section should be relatively short and limited to studies that are very close to the research questions topically and/or methodologically and where the researcher makes the case for how the current study contributes to this, now specific, knowledge. So essentially the literature review is organized like a funnel where, toward the end of it, the specific direction of the current research and the rationale for the research should be clear to the reader (Figure 2.3)

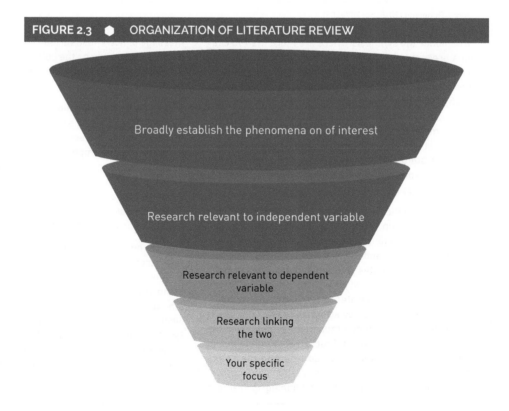

FIGURE 2.3   ●   ORGANIZATION OF LITERATURE REVIEW

Broadly establish the phenomena on of interest

Research relevant to independent variable

Research relevant to dependent variable

Research linking the two

Your specific focus

I just discussed some general guidelines for organizing the material in a literature review, but not actually writing it. Obviously, everyone's style of writing varies, so in the spirit of "getting the job done," I will only highlight three points about actually writing literature reviews. First, as your writing is both summarizing and critiquing, make sure you distinguish between your opinion of the prior research and the conclusions of the authors. Second, if you are noting limitations of prior research, make sure the limitations you focus on are ones that can be avoided, especially in your study. Remember, research is done by people. It may be unfair, for example, to criticize someone for drawing a sample from a localized population rather than the national one because, although a national sample may be ideal, it may also be beyond the accessibility of an individual researcher, including you. Third, in your writing, direct quotations should be used sparingly—if at all (Pyrczak, 2005). Excessive use of quotations of a researcher runs the risk of making the literature review more of an annotated bibliography than a critical analysis. The only time to use direct quotations (and then they need to be cited in the appropriate format) is when something is so incredibly worded that it simply cannot be paraphrased. Let me tell you, that is rare!

BOX 2.3
SUMMARY STEPS FOR LITERATURE REVIEWS

1. Make an initial list of search terms based on your research question.
2. Identify online databases relevant to your topic.
3. Search the databases with these terms.
   a. Keep track of your terms used for each database.
   b. Make decisions about whether to add terms based on the resulting "hits" and, if you decide to add terms, add them to your list to be searched in the multiple databases.
4. Evaluate the resulting material for relevance and quality.
   a. Create a chart listing the various articles that initially seem relevant based on the information in their abstracts like what you see in Figure 2.1.
   b. Make an initial decision about which articles in this chart are not relevant and do not pursue them further.
   c. For the articles that make it past this initial cut, read them in their entirety and fill in any information on the chart that was missing or possibly relevant.
   d. Start to compare articles for similarities, differences, and strength of information (see Figures 2.1 and 2.2).
5. Consider the information you learn for your own study.
   a. Do you need to revise your research question or topic?
   b. Do you have ideas regarding sampling, measurement, method of observation, etc.?
   c. What ethical considerations do you need to consider?
6. Write the literature review.
   a. Consolidate studies with similar points into broad statements with appropriate citations.
   b. Studies that have information that is highly relevant to your focus should be discussed in more detail regarding methodology and relevant findings, while simultaneously incorporating theme with your more general points.

LEARNING CHECK 2.3: LITERATURE REVIEWS

1. Identify two issues to consider when evaluating the strength of a scholarly article.

2. When comparing studies, what type of research (presuming it is done well) is at the top of the methodological hierarchy?

3. When you write literature reviews, which should you start with: a discussion of the independent variable(s) of interest, a discussion of the dependent variable(s), the prevalence, or importance of the phenomena?

Answers to be found at the end of the chapter.

HYPOTHESES

As I mentioned at the end of your literature review, the reader should have a clear sense of your topic, its relevance, what is/is not known regarding it, and your specific focus. If you are doing research for any purpose other than exploration, your literature review might conclude with a testable assertion, called a hypothesis, about how your variables of interest are related. Hypotheses are empirically testable statements that usually have an independent and a dependent variable. There are three issues important in this definition: (1) recognition that hypotheses are statements; (2) the presence of an independent variable; and (3) the presence of a dependent variable. First is the recognition that a hypothesis is a statement. It is not a question of how variables are related; it is a statement, an assertion, that stems from theory and the information learned from the literature review. Students are frequently hesitant to word hypotheses as statements because they are afraid of what will happen if they are wrong. Guess what? *Nothing*. Nothing will happen if you are wrong. You won't fail, your reputation won't be ruined…*nothing* will happen. Sometimes having a hypothesis not be supported is just as informative as when it is, so it is OK to "fail" in this sense. Of course, this all presumes that the methodology and statistics were strong; but we are not ready to evaluate methodology yet.

As I said before, the independent variable is the cause. It is what will create the change. As such, it will come first in time. Common independent variables are demographics like sex, age, and race/ethnicity. As most of these are set at birth, they are likely to be the cause if they are featured in a hypothesis. Similarly, if I am doing evidence-based research and I want to test a program, intervention, or policy, then that program, intervention, or policy is going to be the independent variable because the researcher and/or practitioner sets the parameters of who gets it and it is supposed to create the change. The dependent variable then is the effect. It is the behavior that is being altered because of the independent variable. How we put together hypotheses can vary a few ways, which is what I will cover next.

Alternative and Null Hypotheses

There are two broad types of hypotheses: the null and alternative hypotheses. When students think about hypotheses, they are usually thinking about the alternative hypothesis, also called the research hypothesis, which is the hypothesis of *difference*—it is what we really expect to find based on theory, the research we learned in our literature review, and/or common sense. But believe it or not, this **alternate hypothesis** is not what we really test with statistics. Contrary to what might initially make sense, when I discuss statistics, we are actually testing the null hypothesis, not the alternative hypothesis. The **null hypothesis** is the hypothesis of no difference, where "null" means "nothing." Although I will explain why we statistically test the null in Chapter 12, for now, let's just say that statistics are analogous to a court of law. Think of it this way: In the American criminal justice system, a defendant is assumed to be innocent until proven guilty. In research, the assumption is that there is no relationship between variables (the null hypothesis) until statistics show (remember, we don't "prove") otherwise, meaning that observed differences are real and not likely to be due to chance. So statistically we are focused on rejecting the null of no difference and, therefore, that is what we *statistically* test with our formulas.

BOX 2.4
DIFFERENT HYPOTHESIS TYPES

Hypothesis Type	Example	Relationship	How it is Written
Null	Graduates of Smarty Pants University (μ) earn the same 2 years out of college as other college graduates, which is $43,500	None	$H_0: \mu = 43,500$
Alternate	The income of graduates of Smarty Pants University 2 years out of college (μ) is significantly different than the income other college graduates (average = $43,500) 2 years out of college	Different, no direction specified	$H_u: \mu \neq 43,500$
	The income of graduates of Smarty Pants University 2 years out of college (μ) is significantly higher than the income of other college graduates (average = $43,500) 2 years out of college	Positive (higher)	$H_u: \mu > 43,500$
	The income of graduates of Smarty Pants University 2 years out of college (μ) is significantly less than the income of other college graduates (average = $43,500) 2 years out of college	Negative (less)	$H_u: \mu < 43,500$

The null hypothesis is usually symbolized by "H_0" because "0" means "nothing." The alternate, or research, hypotheses are usually denoted as "H_1," "H_2," etc., where the subscripts are numbers that correspond to the number of hypotheses that researchers have in a study. An alternative hypothesis can take one of the three forms as illustrated in Box 2.4. When I have a hypothesis of a general difference, all I claim is that the two populations are not equal, but I do not take a stance about how they are not equal. On the contrary, I *can* go out on a limb and hypothesize either that my study population is greater than the comparison population *or* that it is less than it. Whether or not I take a stance on how the groups differ should be based on theory, available research (which you learn from doing your literature review), and/or common sense. However, this decision is important because how I word my alternate hypothesis has implications for any statistical analysis that I might do, which I will discuss more in Chapter 12.

Establishing Causality

Not all hypotheses aim to establish causality. If the purpose of your research is descriptive, then your hypothesis may just be a testable statement about who is more or less likely to exhibit a behavior. This would be an **associative hypothesis**. For example, a hypothesis such as "Teenagers from low-income families are more likely to have a child without being married than are teenagers from higher-income families" is an associative hypothesis. It is a testable statement; it has an independent variable (economic background) and a dependent variable (likelihood of having a baby without being married). However, it is not making the claim that income *causes* teens to have a child without being married.

If I wanted this hypothesis to be **causal hypothesis**, to somehow claim that income differences *caused* the differences in unwed birth rates, then I would have to fulfill three criteria. The first criteria of **empirical association** is pretty straightforward. It means that I would have to show that a change in one variable is associated with a change in the other variable. Some call this associative relationship a **correlation**. Association and correlation are essentially the same idea, but "correlation" is really a statistical means of assessing an association; therefore, I will use "association" to mean a relationship and "correlation" as the statistical test of that relationship. If one wants to begin and end with this associative criteria, then one has an associative hypothesis that I mentioned in the previous paragraph. However, there is a common saying in research that correlation does not equal causation. So to move beyond this first criterion (and beyond an associative hypothesis), a researcher has to also fulfill two additional criteria.

The second criteria involves time order and is also pretty straightforward, at least in theory. This means that the independent variable has to come before the dependent variable in time. Because my hypothesis refers to teenagers and I do not expect teens to be economically self-sufficient in our culture, here socioeconomic background would come before deciding to have a baby without being married. Testing whether an intervention changes behavior is another clear example of where the independent variable, the intervention, will come *before* any later change in behavior.

In reality, however, the time–order relationship can be more difficult to establish than it initially appears. For example, take the relationship between mental illness and homelessness. If someone experiences mental illness, it may be difficult for them to maintain a job, which would lead to unemployment and possible homelessness. In this example, the mental illness comes first. However, it is also possible that one could lose their job due to downsizing, have difficulty finding another job, become homeless, and develop mental illness after becoming homeless. In this instance, homelessness is the cause of mental illness, not vise versa. If in my example of SES and unwed parenthood, they were worded slightly differently to read "Having an unwed birth is more common among lower-income individuals," the time–order relationship is less clear. With the wording of this new hypothesis, I do not know which came first—the SES or the unwed birth. The time order might be the same as my original hypothesis, where SES comes first. However, it may be the opposite. A person may be lower-income because of having a child without being married. Single-parent households generally have less income potential than two parents due to only having one possible earner. Consequently, even a slight wording change in hypothesis can lead to very different research possibilities. In applied research, this criteria is usually more easily fulfilled, but the researcher still needs to be sensitive to it.

The last criterion, showing that the association noticed between the variables (criteria one) is nonspurious, is much tougher to fulfill. A **nonspurious relationship** is one in which the association between two variables cannot be explained (is not caused) by a third variable. In my example of premarital birth, not only can we make an association between income, which

iStockphoto.com/bodnarchuk

PHOTO 2.3 Homelessness is a problem for which a casual connection is hard to establish. For example, does having a mental imbalance lead to homelessness or does becoming homeless lead to mental health issues?

I will call "I," and unwed birth ("UB"), I can also argue that teens of higher income ("I") are more likely to go on to college ("C"). Having an infant and attending college is *very* difficult, not impossible, but much more difficult. So I can also argue that those who expect to go to college ("C") are less likely to have an unwed birth ("UB"). All these relationships can be summarized as follows:

1. Income is associated with unwed birth: I → UB

2. Income is associated with likelihood to attend college: I → C

3. Having an unwed birth is associated with the likelihood to attend college: UB → C

If I take these three possible relationships and combine them, I see that income may be directly related to unwed birth, but it may also be related to whether someone plans on going to college, for which an unwed birth is associated with a decreased likelihood of this. I can depict these potential relationships as such:

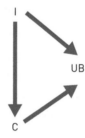

There are other possible causes of unwed birth as well. For example, teens may use pregnancy to "save" a relationship or they may think that having or fathering a baby makes them an "adult." As a result, there are more possible *causes* to unwed birth than just income, so any observed association between income and unwed birth might actually be explained by any of these other rival causal factors, thereby violating the criteria of being a nonspurious relationship. Rival causal factors create spurious relationships that threaten **validity**. I will discuss validity in more depth in Chapter 6, but for now, let's suffice it to say that validity is whether you are observing what you think you are. If I find an association between income and premarital birth but I do not consider these other factors that I mentioned, then I can't really be reasonably confident that any association I see between the two variables is real or valid. The association may be caused by one of these other unmeasured issues. Issues like this, what I call topical rival causal factors, can be identified by the literature review. You may be focusing on income, but some other researchers may have researched the transition to adulthood, and learning about what they found by doing the literature review will give you ideas of how to address this (and other topical issues) in your study. If you want to make a causal connection, you *need* to address other rival causal factors in your study so you can see whether your variable of interest (your independent variable) has any effect on the dependent variable when simultaneously addressing the effects of these other possible causal factors. This is what researchers statistically call *controlling for rival causal factors*. In fact, even though much of the material in this book will focus on bivariate analysis, which means the study of two (bi-) variables (-variate), such as one independent and one dependent variable, to establish a causal connection, unless doing a randomized

LEARNING CHECK 2.4: HYPOTHESES AND CAUSALITY

1. What are the three criteria to establish causality?

2. What does it mean to say "correlation is not causation?"

3. Is the following a null or alternate hypothesis: The more hours of

supplemental training an employee receives, the lower the absentee rate.

Answers to be found at the end of the chapter.

experiment, researchers usually need a multivariate analysis. In a multivariate analysis, you are including not only the main independent and dependent variables of interest (the bivariate relationship) but also the possible rival causal factors that you have identified in your literature review and have therefore incorporated into your method of observation (hence the *multi*variate). For example, with some highly public deaths of African American men at the hands of police and the emergence of the Black Lives Matter movement, there has been a lot of discussion regarding racial injustice in policing. One side of the debate argues that the police are more likely to arrest and use force when encountering minority men, especially Black men, thereby making racial bias a main factor in whether a police-citizen interaction will turn violent. Another view is that race is a correlate (not a cause) to other factors, such as statistics on whether someone is carrying an illegal weapon, age, neighborhood characteristics, and civilian behavior. It is likely that there is merit to both sides, so in order to understand the role of race *while also accounting for* or *controlling for* the other factors, Kramer & Remster (2018) analyzed the conditions around how race and age (their main independent variables) affected the decision to use police force (their dependent variables) using a sample of over two million police stops between 2007 and 2014. The conditions that they accounted for included whether the stop was successful in finding a weapon, other contraband or an arrest (all of which could explain police force), the nature of civilian behavior (whether there were verbal threats, the civilian refused to comply with orders, or whether the civilian was suspected of a violent crime), the length of time the officer observed the civilian prior to the stop, whether the stop occurred at night, local crime rates, and gender, among other factors. The point is that Kramer and Remster tried to statistically determine the effect of race, or racial bias, on the likelihood of a violent encounter with police while *simultaneously* also accounting for these other factors. If racial bias is relevant, then the effect should be statistically significant even if these other factors are also present. Kramer and Remster found that black individuals were more likely to be stopped by police, more likely to be viewed as threatening to officers, and more likely to encounter force by police than whites, even when considering the additional contextual factors noted, thereby indicating that civilian race is, indeed, a factor in police-citizen interaction (2018). As this study illustrates, multivariate statistical modeling can help shed light on very complex social processes.

As if that wasn't confusing enough, rival causal factors can also be methodological or a flaw with the study design. Research design issues that could create spurious relationships threaten what is called internal validity. There are multiple methodological issues that can threaten internal validity and I will discuss those in more detail in Chapter 4.

MAKING DECISIONS

In this chapter, we started learning about some early decisions to make when doing research, namely how to refine your research topic or question, conduct literature reviews, and write hypotheses. However, we are still in the formation part of the research design where we have a lot of freedom in our choices. We are not really at the stage where we are weighing options for design; therefore, although there are decisions to make (such as deciding on the specific research topic or deciding what articles to include in the literature review), they are rather nebulous at this point and depend more on what we find from the work of others rather than what we will specifically design ourselves. Consequently, the flow chart for the making-decisions component of this chapter is really a summary of the considerations I discussed for the stages of topic formation and appears in Figure 2.4.

CHALLENGES

At this early stage in the research process, there are no specific methodological challenges we may need to address; however, there are some common issues arising from searches of the literature and the early stages of considering causality that you might encounter.

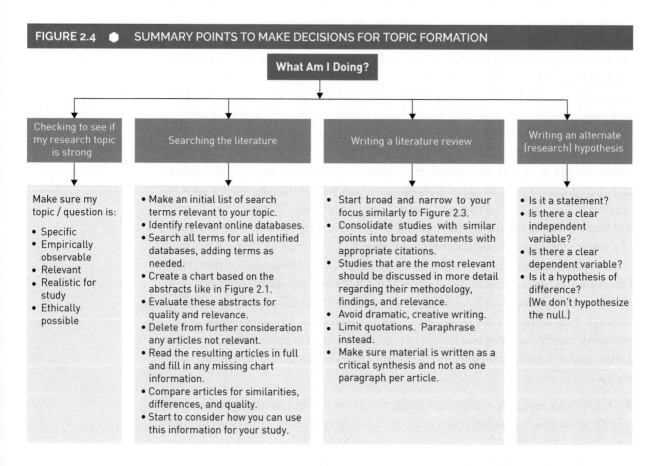

FIGURE 2.4   ●   SUMMARY POINTS TO MAKE DECISIONS FOR TOPIC FORMATION

1. **My review of the literature is not producing anything related to my topic.** I have students come and tell me this *all* the time and the reason is usually two common problems. First, students are looking for literature that is *exactly* on their topic. Allow me to let you in on a little secret: If you have found "enough" research *exactly* on your topic, then your topic has been already studied a great deal and *you* need to find a new approach. In other words, finding a lot of research exactly on your topic is not a good thing! Literature reviews are the review of *related* research…and "related" does not mean an exact replica.

    The second most common reason is that people give up too soon or are too limited in their search. Before you conclude that there really isn't much known about your topic (and therefore that your research may be more exploratory in nature), there are a few points you need to make sure you covered. First, check that you have used multiple databases and multiple search-term combinations within each database. Keep a list of what terms you are using to search and then think of any other combinations of those terms, synonyms, or other ways of getting similar (not necessarily identical) points that you could be using to search instead. Then use all the combinations of these terms for multiple databases. For example, you might not find much information searching for "mental health training for police officers," but you can expand this to searches such as "police and perpetrator mental health," "arrest and perpetrator mental health," "police view of perpetrators in mental crisis," etc. You will find some of the same articles popping up, but you might find new ones as well. Keeping a list is also helpful because you can show that list to someone else who might be able to give you other suggestions of possible search combinations that will help you find material as well.

2. **My search for literature is producing too many possible articles.** When I entered "mental health" and "arrest" into the ProQuest search engine when I wrote this chapter, I received 9,442 "hits." It would take an immense amount of time to scroll (not to mention read the abstracts) through this many hits. If I refine the search by programming ProQuest to only look at peer-reviewed articles, the number drops to 6,776. If I add "full text" as a filter so ProQuest only provides "hits" for articles that I can read in their entirety online, the number drops to 5,651; and if I program it to only include articles published within the past 10 years, the "hits" further drop to 3,099 articles. That is *still* a lot of articles and most of them will not be relevant to my topic. In order to refine the search further, I might need to use multiple terms together, such as "mental health" and "arrest" and "crisis." The point is that basically, you can keep working with the database to further restrict the search parameters and to make your list manageable.

3. **My literature review identified factors other than my main independent variable that are also associated with changes in my dependent variable, but I cannot incorporate all of them into my study so how can I establish causality?** The short answer is that you really cannot; but remember, descriptive research can be very informative. That

earlier phrase I said I give my students about writing what they mean means for them to write succinctly yet cohesively without dramatic flourish, but it also means to simply be clear about what you can and cannot do. Remember, no research is perfect. Discuss these topical rival causal factors (all of them) in the literature review, try to incorporate as many of them that you methodologically and feasibly can, explain why you couldn't incorporate the ones you didn't, and then be honest in your results of about what you can and cannot conclude. Although you cannot conclude causality, the topical rival causal factors you included might speak to the provisional nature of science where the more factors (topical provisions) you can control for (account for), the clearer your descriptive results.

Key Terms

Alternate hypothesis

Associative hypothesis

Bibliographic database

Causal hypothesis

Correlation

Correlative question

Descriptive research question

Empirically observable

Empirical association

Impact factor

Impact question

Literature review

Meta-analysis

Nonspurious relationship

Normative question

Null hypothesis

Predatory journal

Quasi-experiment

Randomized experimental research

Systematic review

Validity

Answers to Learning Check Questions

Learning Check 2.1: Types of Research Questions

1. Normative questions involve comparing the information you will gather to some known standard or norm. Descriptive questions just report a situation without any comparison. One way of identifying a descriptive question is that it will usually involve only one variable or issue at a time.

2. Descriptive questions look at one variable and report what is going on regarding it. Correlative questions look at how the variables relate or correlate.

3. Descriptive. It is only examining behavior two years after graduation, which is one variable.

Learning Check 2.2: Strong Research Questions

1. Any of the following would be valid answers: reasonably specific, empirically observable, relevant, realistic, and ethically able to be studied.

2. Yes. Even though it may need some specification with measurement (e.g., "family structure" will have to be defined), as a research question it fulfills the criteria for being strong.

3. No. Most importantly, it is not empirically observable because it is a value question.

An argument might also be made that it is not sufficiently specific because "sake of the children" is very subjective and hard to define.

Learning Check 2.3: Literature Reviews

1. Possible answers: the authority of the author, the authority of the source, the tone of the material, the objectivity of the researcher, the method of observation

2. Meta-analysis

3. The prevalence or importance of the phenomena

Learning Check 2.4: Hypotheses and Causality

1. The three criteria are (1) association, (2) the independent variable needs to come first in time, and (3) the relationship between the independent and dependent variables cannot be spurious (caused by a third, different, variable).

2. Two variables can be associated (have correlation), but if the relationship does not fulfill the other two criteria, then a researcher should not claim causation.

3. Alternate hypothesis because it shows that the variables do have an effect on each other—whereas one goes up, the other goes down.

End-of-Chapter Problems

1. "How do freshman and seniors differ in their binge drinking behavior?" is an example of what type of research question?
    a. Descriptive
    b. Normative
    c. Correlative
    d. Impact

2. "Does attending a multicultural training seminar improve cultural awareness among employees?" is an example of what type of research question?
    a. Descriptive
    b. Normative
    c. Correlative
    d. Impact

3. Which of the following is a strong research question?
    a. Do treatment courts work?
    b. Should treatment courts be an option for nonviolent drug offenders?
    c. Does attending treatment court reduce the risk of being arrested for a drug-related crime 2 years after completion?
    d. Which offenders are the best candidates for treatment court attendance?

4. What is wrong with the following research topic: Reactions to inappropriate online posts
    a. It is not sufficiently specific.
    b. It is not empirically observable.
    c. It cannot be studied ethically.
    d. Nothing. The topic is fine.

5. True or False: Literature reviews can help researchers refine their research topic.

6. True or False: Newspaper articles are strong sources for material in a literature review.

7. A researcher argues that coming from a high-conflict home where parents fight frequently causes behavior problems, such as disciplinary actions in school and poor academic performance, in children; but, she has failed to account for whether the child exhibited behavioral problems prior to parental conflict, which a review of the literature suggests might be an important factor in child behavior in school. Her causal claim is false because she did not fulfill what criteria of causality?
    a. Association
    b. Time order
    c. Nonspuriousness
    d. Her causal claim is fine; all three components of causality have been met.

8. Which of the following is an example of an alternate hypothesis?
    a. Gender differences in the type of major declared.
    b. Gender has no effect on the type of major declared.
    c. Women are more likely to select majors that lead to helping professions than men.

9. Which of the following is an example of a null hypothesis?
    a. Distance between campus and home is related to the number of times a student goes home.
    b. Distance between campus and home is not related to the number of times a student goes home.
    c. The shorter the distance between campus and home, the less often a student goes home.
    d. The shorter the distance between campus and home, the more often a student goes home.

10. In the following alternate hypothesis, what is the direction of effect: As years of education increases, so does one's income
    a. No direction is specified
    b. Positive
    c. Negative

SETTING THE FOUNDATION FOR OBSERVATION

PART II

3

ETHICS IN RESEARCH

LEARNING GOALS

- Recognize the main historical events leading to the development of current ethical standards
- Identify the three principles of the Belmont Report
- Identify a researcher's ethical responsibilities to subjects
- Understand the role of Institutional Review Boards (IRBs)

Let's pretend you were in a class and the professor said that the class is going to review for an upcoming test by playing a game. When someone gets a question right, they get a point; but if they get it wrong, you, as the person with the highest average in the class, administer an electric shock to this classmate. Every round that a question is answered incorrectly, the electric shock you administer gets stronger. Do you think you would do it? You are probably thinking, "Of course not!" What if that person asking you to administer the shock was a doctor, a police officer, or a military general? Would you be more likely to go along with this? We would like to think that the answer would still be "no," but controversial research by Stanley Milgram in the 1960s suggests that the answer might actually be "yes" more often than we might feel comfortable thinking. Milgram wanted to see whether people would obey those in power, even if doing so was contrary to their personal judgment, or react against those in power if they were abusing their authority. To explore this, Milgram recruited subjects and told them that they would be participating in an experiment that would study the effects of punishment on learning ability and that they would be assigned either to the role of "student" or "teacher." In reality, all the subjects were assigned to be "teachers," whereas confederates, people who are "in" on the experiment, were the "students." The "teachers" were told to administer electric shocks of increasing intensity when the "student" answered questions incorrectly. The shock levels ranged from 15 to 450 V and their intensity was indicated by labels such as "slight shock" or "moderate shock" to "extreme intensity shock" and "Danger: Severe Shock." The highest shock was simply labeled "XXX." In reality, no shocks were administered to the "students"; however, the "teachers" did not know this. "Students" answering incorrectly would start to grunt at 75 V, complain at 120 V, and express increasing levels of discomfort, including loud yelling and complaints of heart pain, as the "volts" continued to intensify. The "student" response would cumulate in silence at the extreme levels. Remember though, all the "student" reactions were fake; but, the "teachers" did not know that. Milgram found that although some "teachers" refused to increase shock levels while they were still comparatively low, even when the researcher tried to encourage them to do so, the majority of the "teachers," even those who were initially reluctant, were willing to administer what they believed to be dangerous levels of shock if the researcher encouraged them to continue. This occurred even if the "teacher" heard the "student's" distress. After the experiment, when asked why they continued to administer possibly lethal shock doses, the most common response from the "teachers" was that the lab assistants told them to and they felt that the lab assistants had scientific authority over them (Milgram, 1974). Thus, Milgram learned that authority means power and that those in authority can get others to do what they want, even if those without authority are initially hesitant. But what was the cost of this information?

iStockphoto.com/Nicola Katie

PHOTO 3.1 Would you administer an electric shock to someone because you agreed to participate in a research study? How high of a shock would you be willing to administer? Are you sure? Milgram's study might lead us to question our answers.

Milgram wasn't alone in this type of experiment. Around the same time, Philip Zimbardo (1972) was conducting his now infamous Stanford Prison Experiment, also about responses to authority, but his study was in a simulated prison rather than in a teaching lab. In his study, Zimbardo used male undergraduates who were randomly assigned to be either prisoners or guards. Guards were given props such as sunglasses and prisoners were assigned prison numbers, rather than names, in order to help the students get into their roles. He then put these "prisoners" and "guards" in a simulated jail-like environment to see how the "guards" and "prisoners" behaved. Zimbardo instructed the "guards" not to use violence, but he found that they quickly developed other forms of aggressive and/or dehumanizing behavior to torment the "prisoners," such as making them do an excessive number of pushups for infractions and waking them by blaring whistles at them. Similarly, although the "prisoners" initially resisted this treatment, they generally became passively hostile to the guards, rather than remind everyone that this was fake and just an experiment. Some prisoners even had emotional breakdowns. In other words, they generally adopted their "prisoner" status even though they complained about it or suffered emotional distress. However, seeing the tapes of the simulated prison, a third party, fearing physical and psychological harm to the prisoners encouraged Zimbardo to end the experiment after just 6 days even though it was supposed to last 2 weeks (Zimbardo, 1972).

Although both of these studies have been criticized recently for design issues, for our purposes, we are more concerned with the ethical issues (Baumrind, 2013; Burger, 2009; Tolich, 2014). Do you think that what Milgram and Zimbardo learned about the influence of authority justified the psychological distress of the subjects? By today's standards that answer is no.

BRIEF GENERAL HISTORY OF ETHICS IN RESEARCH

Studies like Milgram's and Zimbardo's were not actually the first to exhibit questionable ethics. In fact, globally the current focus on ethics in research is in response to unethical medical studies, like those that occurred during World War II in Nazi Germany and the Tuskegee Syphilis Study that took place in the United States. You have probably heard about some of the horrific experiments Nazi doctors performed on their prisoners without the prisoner's consent. But the Nazis are not the only ones who behaved poorly. Between 1932 and 1972 the Department of Health and Human Services in Tuskegee, Alabama, studied 600 Black men, of whom 201 had syphilis, but were not told of their disease, were not told of the risks for not treating this disease, and were *not* provided treatment in order to study the health effects if the disease went untreated. This lack of treatment, even when a successful treatment became available, led to painful deaths for many study participants. When the public learned about this study, the criticism was widespread, especially since there were no consequences to this treatment.

In response to these (and other) unethical biomedical studies, the Nuremberg Code was developed as an early attempt to establish the ethical guidelines of informed consent, voluntary participation, scientific justification for research, and limits for various forms of harm (Dunn & Chadwick, 2004). The Kefauver-Harris Amendment, which focused on studies involving medical drugs, and the Declaration of Helsinki, which involved an external review of research protocols, furthered this early attempt. However, while a start, some of these guidelines were not legally enforceable and others did not address how behavioral or social research differed from medical research. In an effort to develop a broad ethical framework that could be used in various disciplines across the traditional and behavioral sciences, the National Research Act of 1974 was passed when the public learned about the Tuskegee Syphilis Study. This Act created a national commission whose job was to develop guidelines for human subject research and to monitor the administration of these guidelines with clearly expressed consequences for guidelines violation.

One of the most noteworthy outcomes of this law was the generation of the **Belmont Report**, named for Belmont, Maryland, where the committee met to develop their national recommendations for ethical and responsible research. The Belmont Report identifies three universal principles of research: (1) Respect for persons; (2) Beneficence; and (3) Justice. Within each of these principles are additional specific ethical responsibilities, so let's look at each principle in more detail.

PHOTO 3.2 A subject of the Tuskegee Syphillis study being tested by a researcher.

Respect for Persons

One of the most detailed parts of this report is **respect for persons**. Simply put, this means that researchers have to respect the inherent worth of every person and treat them with dignity. There are specific ethical responsibilities that accomplish this. One of these is ensuring **voluntary participation** of subjects. Voluntary participation seems pretty straightforward and means that people choose to let researchers study their lives on their own free will. It also means that subjects are free to *end* study participation any time that they want without fear of negative consequences. However, fulfilling this responsibility is not as simple as it initially appears. After all, the men in the Tuskegee experiment agreed to participate, but as we covered, many were uneducated so they did not really understand what they were agreeing to participate in. The issues of free will and voluntary participation are also important. If you are a prisoner and someone asks to study you, do you *really* have free will to participate? In a prison environment, if a prisoner does not cooperate with authority figures (and a researcher would likely appear as such), prisoners may fear retribution from prison officials. The opposite may also be true. Prisoners may think that if they *do* agree to participate, they appear cooperative, which will lead to favorable reactions from prison officials. Therefore, treating subjects with respect also involves recognizing that some subjects may not be able to truly voluntarily decide whether to participate. These groups are called **vulnerable populations** and include children, who are not of age to give consent, prisoners, and people with impaired cognitive abilities. Under some situations, police or active members of the military might be considered a "special class" of individuals for whom extra care also needs to be made in obtaining voluntary participation because each of these individuals is participating in rigid hierarchical institutions with obedience from lower ranks expected. Therefore, an argument can be made that choosing *not* to participate might have negative consequences for these individuals, as they may fear job loss or disciplinary actions for not following a "suggestion" of a superior. As a result, many IRBs, which I will also cover soon, have different protocols for dealing with these vulnerable populations.

Respect for persons also includes the concept of **informed consent**. Informed consent requires that participants are given any information that might influence their decision to participate in the study. Again, the Tuskegee men were not given full information as many did not realize that they would *not* be given real drugs to treat their syphilis, nor were they even told they had syphilis and that the disease was the focus of the study. So although the Tuskegee subjects consented to the study, they did so without receiving full disclosure about what the study entailed and the corresponding risks associated with it. This leads us to the question of what might affect someone's decision to participate in the study? Many agree that, at the very least, obtaining informed consent involves letting the subject know:

- The purpose of the research

- Any potential risks or harms the participants may experience

- Any benefits the participants may experience

- The procedures used in the research

- Who is funding the research

- Incentives for participation (if any exist)

- That participation is voluntary and the subject can stop participating at any time without penalty

- Whether confidentiality or anonymity is guaranteed

As you can see, that list is longer than just saying, "I am conducting a study about the effectiveness of drug treatment programs. Would you like to participate?" Although some issues are pretty straightforward, others might need clarification. For example, sharing with respondents the purpose of the research does not necessarily mean that you tell them your hypothesis. In order to avoid possible reactivity, where subjects answer in ways that they think will please (or purposely hinder) the research, some deception might be allowable. Zimbardo used deception when he told participants he wanted to study prison life when what he *really* wanted to study was how people adopted and responded to labels of authority. Milgram used deception when he told subjects he was using electric shock to study learning when he was really studying obedience to authority. For all the questionable ethical behavior in these studies, their level of deception was actually OK (Yanow & Schwartz-Shea, 2018). For Zimbardo, the subjects knew they were going to be acting as guards or prisoners and their behavior as such would be recorded. Telling them that the researchers were interested in the effect of labels does not alter what the subjects thought their observed behavior would entail. Likewise, Milgram told people that they would be shocking "learners" who got answers wrong. Regardless of whether "teachers" thought those shocks were to change learning or to examine how people responded to authority, the act of administering (or not) the shock was the same. However, the Tuskegee experiment *did* violate this ethical responsibility because here the researchers' level of deception resulted in direct harm to the participants as the subjects did not know and were never told during the study that they had syphilis (hence they were deceived about a disease), and they did not have the opportunity to seek treatment. Therefore, some deception, to the degree that it is essential to the scientific question and does not foreseeably impact the actions of the subjects in the study, is allowable provided that it is handled carefully where the researcher does an assessment of potential harm *prior* to the study and a debriefing of subjects (letting them know the real purpose of the study, giving them a chance to ask questions, and allowing them to decide whether they want any or all of their data destroyed as a result) *after* the study (Dunn & Chadwick, 2004).

Subjects also need to know whether there is any risk of harm beyond that of everyday life and, if so, what types of harm and what the researcher will do to minimize that risk. The researcher's responsibility to pre-identify and work to minimize the risk of various types of harm really addresses the issue of the second principle, the principle of beneficence, so we will hold off on that discussion until then. For informed consent, the point is that the subject has to be made aware of the risks in order to fully be able to decide whether to voluntarily participate.

Another aspect of informed consent, telling subjects about the procedures involved, means letting them know about your method of observation, such as what you will be asking of them and how long it will take. For example, will they be completing a survey? Approximately how long will the survey take? Are they going to be part of an experiment? If it's an experiment, how will it be decided whether they are in the treatment or control group? What *is* the treatment? Potential participants may not want to become involved with studies that take too long or require a lot of effort on their behalf. In addition to that, some people may be comfortable with an anonymous survey, but not a confidential interview. The point is, it is up to the subject to decide.

Knowledge of the funding agency is also important because it gives subjects a chance to participate or decline based on their own ethical values. For example, a person who is strongly against abortion may not want to participate in a study about sexual behavior that is funded by Planned Parenthood because that person may feel that the findings may be used to fuel a social issue that they do not support. The opposite may also occur; someone might be more willing to participate if they respect the funding agency. Either way, the point is that the subject has the right to decide whether to participate in a study and the funding agency may affect that decision.

If there are any incentives offered to participate, such as a small monetary payment, gift card, or chance to win a larger prize, the potential subject needs to know that as well. Some have argued that offering an incentive may skew voluntary participation because different people may need, and therefore be attracted to, an incentive than others. However, the general consensus is that if using incentives, one should make them small enough *or* run them like a raffle where participation in the study earns someone a *chance* to win a larger prize. Small incentives or a chance to win a prize may encourage people to participate but is not likely to really bias the sample.

One additional point about informed consent is that studies that occur in public spaces, like marches or shopping malls, in which the researcher will have no interaction with the subjects, do not require informed consent. In other words, in public, *anyone* can be observing behavior by the nature of being at the same place at the same time. Therefore, as long as the researcher does not do anything to interfere or inconvenience the individuals observed, anything the researcher sees could also be seen by anyone else. Therefore informed consent is not necessary.

Principle of Beneficence

The second principle of the Belmont Report, the **principle of beneficence**, refers to a balance where the potential benefit from participating in the study should outweigh any possible risks of participation. The goal is, whenever possible, to make sure that risk is "no greater than everyday life." Although minimizing physical risk is obvious, and frankly less common than some other risks in the behavioral or social sciences, there are other forms of risk that also need to be addressed. For example, research should try to not cause psychological harm to participants. If you remember the Zimbardo prison experiment study I mentioned, some suggest that Zimbardo violated the principle of beneficence in three ways. First, Zimbardo's study created both physical harm (as some "prisoners" were physically harassed via the pushups) and psychological harm (as "prisoners" were clearly upset by their experiences). Second, some believe Zimbardo violated the principle of beneficence because he only ended the study early after a third party strongly encouraged him to do so. Last, in order to help "prisoners" get into their role, Zimbardo had them "arrested" at home to start the study. By "arresting" them in public like this, there was a risk of social harm, as neighbors may not know that this was part of an experiment and only saw people they knew getting "arrested" in public. This is how potentially damaging rumors can start. To compound this violation, the "prisoners" did not know that they would be publically "arrested"; therefore, they did not provide informed consent for this.

Legal and financial risks are other risk factors, especially if the research design does not adequately protect the subject's identity (which I will discuss shortly). If a subject's identity becomes known, especially in behavioral or social research, personal issues that otherwise would have remained private may come to public attention, and this attention may produce negative consequences for participants, such as arrest or job loss. For example, if you are studying inner-city gangs and you describe a criminal act of a gang member with enough detail that the police think that they can identify this individual so they put that person under surveillance, and this subject gets arrested, that's legal harm to the participant. Now you may be thinking that if a person commits a crime, then that person deserves to be arrested. This could be a valid argument. However, if it was *your research* that either provided evidence for the police or in some other way led to this individual's arrest, you are now in fuzzy ethical area. Legal harm also does not limit itself to catching individuals in criminal acts. Research may lead to potential harm of participants by the authorities, as Latané and Darley (1970) found when they staged "crimes" in order to study what factors influence bystanders to intervene when they observe something potentially criminal. One of the staged "crimes" was a liquor store hold-up, and one of the witnesses called the police, who arrived with drawn guns.

iStockphoto.com/LightFieldStudios

PHOTO 3.3 What if you agreed to participate in a study about prisoners and guards but did not know that as part of being assigned a "prisoner" role, you would be "arrested" at home in front of your neighbors. Would knowing about this "arrest" influence your decision to participate in the study?

BOX 3.1
POTENTIAL HARMS FOR A SUBJECT

Type of Harm	Effect on:	
	Individual	Wider Society
Physical injury	Physical pain; personal cost of treatment; fear; diminished trust	Cost of treatment (insurance, for example); diminished trust
Psychological injury	Damaged interpersonal relations; personal discomfort	
Legal	Investigation by authorities, arrest	Person or groups are stigmatized regardless of guilt or innocence; cost of criminal justice proceedings
Social	Loss of job; damaged interpersonal relations; stigmatization	Scapegoating, vilifying, or stereotyping of certain groups
Loss of privacy, anonymity, confidentiality	Reduced control over how one presents self to others; public exposure that may lead to other physical, psychological, legal, or social harm	Reduction of general privacy; concern of being continually watched by others

The resulting potential for physical and legal harm to researchers and participants once real police arrived with drawn guns is pretty obvious.

Principle of Justice

The last ethical responsibility stemming from the Belmont Report is probably the most direct. The **principle of justice** means that the risks and benefits of the research are spread across subjects fairly. In other words, one group of subjects should not be at a higher likelihood of becoming the experimental or control group, receiving the benefits of the study, or of receiving the risks. The Tuskegee study clearly violated this by *only* running the study on poor African American men. The designers of the study purposely did not want to expose wealthier whites to the experiences of syphilis so the risks of this study were not distributed justly…in fact, they weren't distributed at all.

Additional Ethical Considerations

Anonymity/Confidentiality

Integral to the fulfillment of many of the ethical responsibilities in the Belmont Report is the protection of a subject's identity. If someone reading the results of the research cannot link responses or experiences to a known individual, then that individual, for example, might be protected from legal or financial harm. Researchers protect a subject's identity through **anonymity** or **confidentiality**, depending on the method of observation. A researcher can provide anonymity when even the researcher cannot match responses to individual subjects. Web or mail surveys that have no identification numbers are examples of methods of observation that frequently provide anonymity to subjects. Sometimes mail or web surveys involve participation incentives; in the case of mail surveys, in order to maintain anonymity, a collaborator may agree to keep an identification sheet that matches the numbers of return envelopes to the person's identity. The collaborator would record who returned the surveys, keep the envelopes with that identification information, and then only give the survey to the researcher, thereby maintaining subject anonymity. In the case of web surveys, many platforms allow researchers to program the survey in a way that keeps one separate file of responding individuals and another separate file with individual survey responses (Chapter 7). Guaranteeing subjects anonymity may be especially useful when studying deviant or private behavior such as drug use, criminal activity, or sex. People may be more willing to report their behavior if they believe that there is no way their responses can be linked to them personally.

However, in most cases, when inexperienced researchers claim that they are providing anonymity, they really mean to say confidentiality. Researchers should promise confidentiality when they *can* match a person's identity to his/her responses, but they promise not to reveal that identity to others. Researchers usually accomplish this by referring to individuals via case numbers or pseudonyms, which are fake names, when the researcher needs to publicize a person's responses. Confidentiality is common in qualitative forms of observation such as interviews or focus groups, but it might also apply to experiments. In the qualitative forms of observation, as we will see in Chapter 8, researchers frequently provide more narrative forms of data presentation, rather than statistical, so it is common that they need to refer to subjects individually. Therefore, the key to maintaining confidentiality in these instances is for the researcher to make sure that she or he does not use too much description or does not mention unique characteristics that would enable those familiar with the research or geographical area to identify the participants. If you remember Walton, Priest, and Paradies's (2013) study about the definition of racism that I discussed in Chapter 1, the researchers presented excerpts quoted from respondents as their data, but they identified respondents as "Focus group 4, female blue-collar" or "Interview 1, female white-collar" where you got a sense of whether the respondent was from a focus group or interview, the respondent's gender, and his/her social class. The researcher knows who the respondents were, but the readers of the research do not.

However, this can be harder to accomplish than you may initially think. For example, in his classic work *Street Corner Society*, William Foote Whyte (1955) studied the social dynamics of young men on the West End of Boston. He provided so much contextual detail on two of his subjects, whom he gave the pseudonyms "Doc" and "Chic," that when another researcher, Herbert Gans, later studied the same area of Boston, he recognized that one of the candidates in an election was one of the people from Whyte's book. He was not alone; members of the community were also able to identify the individual and Gans noted that voters responded to this individual negatively because of what they read in Whyte's book (Gans, 1962). Although researchers like to give subjects context in order to both make their results more readable and to provide some background information on who people are, the risk of violating confidentiality is real even today. I conducted interviews of individuals from the first wave of a local Treatment Court cohort and in trying to reach the balance between describing my subjects while still protecting confidentiality, I could only give gender and drug of choice as individual characteristics. I could not give race because only a few subjects at the time identified as a racial minority and if I presented race as part of the context for respondent quotes, someone reading the report may have been able to identify the clients who were the racial minorities. Therefore, the racial component, which might be key in other research reports, had to remain missing in mine.

Data Access and Ownership

The Internet has undeniably opened up new avenues of research from the ease and affordability of conducting web surveys to the easy storing of data online, to the availability of new social artifacts, like online posts, to study. However, the Internet has created some new ethical considerations as well. For example, would a researcher need to obtain informed consent when studying online posts made in reaction to a news story? What about when researchers want to study comments made in a chatroom? Hudson and Bruckman (2004) studied just this idea: what is considered private online and what is public? If something online is public, then the same ethical issues of informed consent might apply as they would if someone was sitting on a park bench analyzing a political march. As I discussed earlier, in the instance of a public march, if the behavior is not being conducted by vulnerable populations, is occurring in public space where the behavior is visible to all, and the researcher is not influencing subjects' behavior, then obtaining informed consent is probably not necessary. But the same might not apply to chatrooms, even if they are considered public. In fact, Hudson and Bruckman entered 525 chatrooms to see if the participants would "opt-in" to participate in a study and found that of the 766 individuals in these chatrooms, only 4 (yes...*only 4*) chose to "opt-in" to being studied. Hudson and Bruckman suggest that a way around this is to do covert research, a methodological approach that is sometimes warranted but ethically challenging. As Hudson and Bruckman recognize, there are very limited instances in which covert research is viable. It is appropriate only if the research poses no risk beyond everyday life if *not* obtaining informed consent will not hurt the rights or well-being of the subjects if the research cannot be carried out with trying to obtain informed consent, and if appropriate, subjects can be provided with relevant study detail after observation (Hudson & Bruckman, 2004). I will cover covert research more in Chapter 8.

Participant Privacy

Although a respondent has the right to be private by deciding *not* to participate in a study, the right of privacy also extends during the course of the study for those who agree to participate as well. One way this is carried out during a study is the recognition that a respondent has the right to decide to stop participating at any time and would not be penalized in any way for doing so. If a respondent wants to skip questions, end the interview, or leave the focus group,

iStockphoto.com/pondsaksit

PHOTO 3.4 Computers have created an entirely new class of ethical considerations when doing research.

for example, they should be allowed to. It also means that if a respondent decides to "take back" anything he or she shares during the course of a study, the researcher has to respect that and omit the information. Now, a researcher *could* remind the respondent of the importance of the information and the guarantee of confidentiality (which is what is most likely to be relevant in this instance), but a researcher cannot badger a respondent; if a respondent still wants information omitted after a gentle reminder, then the researcher has to comply.

Responsibility to Society

Many social science studies, especially those that involve applied evidence-based research, are likely to occur in a natural setting instead of in a lab like Milgram's (1974) and Zimbardo's (1972) studies did. Because of this, social science researchers have the responsibility to protect not only their subjects from harm but also to protect innocent bystanders who are not directly involved in the study but may be affected by it. Let's face it. In our fields, sometimes subjects behave in undesirable or, quite frankly, illegal ways. For example, if I am doing field research (Chapter 8) among gangs and I learn that the gang I am observing is planning a drive-by shooting in retaliation to a gang member's death, what do I do? Clearly, I have knowledge that my subjects at least might participate in criminal activity that can get any of them, a member of another gang, and even innocent bystanders either seriously injured or killed. In this situation, do I protect the subjects (not cause them legal harm by tipping off the police, for example) or society (make that call and perhaps protect an innocent bystander)? Unfortunately, I cannot provide accurate guidance here. Therefore, all I can say is that in a life-or-death situation, or other similarly serious situations, the researcher's responsibility to society may outweigh any responsibility to subjects. There is no right or wrong answer per se, as what to do is a relative concept, which is called **ethical relativism.**

LEARNING CHECK 3.1: ETHICAL ISSUES

1. What are the three ethical principles of the Belmont Report?

2. If a researcher can match a subject's identity to his/her study information, which should the researcher guarantee: anonymity or confidentiality?

3. Here is a possible research scenario: A researcher wants to see whether playing violent video games leads players to act more aggressively. The researcher measures aggression by the response time to a stimulus where shorter response times are associated with more aggression. To study this, the researcher tells potential subjects only that he is studying their reflexive response time and that he will do this by having subjects watch a violent video and then test how quickly they hit a computer button in response to a visual stimulus. Has the researcher violated informed consent just based on this information? Why/why not?

Answers (to be written upside down at the bottom of the box).

ETHICAL GOVERNANCE

Institutional Review Boards

The National Research Act of 1974 that I mentioned earlier not only created the committee that produced the Belmont Report, it also created ethical oversight committees called **Institutional Review Boards (IRB)** to review potential research projects. These governing agencies are responsible for protecting human subjects and making sure that research protocols avoid ethical violations. Any institution that receives federal funds has an IRB and it frequently consists of a variety of staff members from different areas of expertise (in the case of professional IRBs) or disciplines (in the case of academic IRBs). Although the exact nature of an IRB may vary by the institution, in general, they all review potential research protocols. IRBs frequently have different ethical criteria for different levels of risk/benefits and different degrees of ability to give voluntary informed consent. For example, protocols involving anonymous mailed surveys of the general adult population that pose no risk beyond that of everyday life are likely to entail less ethical scrutiny than is a proposed protocol interviewing elementary school-aged children about their potential use of e-cigarettes, the latter of which involves confidentiality over anonymity (via interviews) for a vulnerable population (children) about a deviant behavior (e-smoking).

IRB applications usually involve a brief overview of the research, which is much shorter than a standard literature review for a published manuscript but which also provides enough information to show the reviewers that the applicant *did* search the literature for relevant information. They also involve a description of the research protocol, with detailed explanations of how individuals will be recruited for the study, whether anonymity or confidentiality will be provided, what any possible harms might be and the researcher's plan to minimize them, and what the benefits are and to whom. Based on this description, it is then the reviewers in the IRB's responsibility to determine whether the research is worth doing and whether the proposed procedures are ethical.

Professional Codes of Ethics

Although the Belmont Report was directed at creating a unifying code of ethics, different disciplines have built off of it to suit their discipline-specific needs. Getting into the specific ethical responsibilities addressed by all the social science disciplines is beyond our scope of "getting the job done," but links for some of the common disciplines appear in Box 3.2.

BOX 3.2
DISCIPLINE SPECIFIC CODE OF ETHICS

Discipline	Location of Ethical Guidelines
Counseling	American Counseling Association https://counseling.northwestern.edu/blog/ACA-Code-of-Ethics/
Criminal Justice	Academy of Criminal Justice Sciences https://www.acjs.org/page/Code_Of_Ethics
Mental Health	American Mental Health Counselors Association https://www.amhca.org/publications/ethics
Psychology	American Psychology Association https://www.verywellmind.com/apa-ethical-code-guidelines-4687465#the-apas-code-of-ethics
Social Work	National Association of Social Work https://www.socialworkers.org/About/Ethics/Code-of-Ethics/Code-of-Ethics-English
Sociology	American Sociological Association https://www.asanet.org/code-ethics

MAKING DECISIONS

I covered multiple ethical issues in this chapter. As we will see when I discuss the different methods of observation, some research designs are more vulnerable to different breaches in ethics than others. Therefore, in this chapter, the "Making Decisions" section for ethics is a table that identifies the individual ethical considerations, reviews what they are, and links them to methods of observation, which I will cover later in the book, that are vulnerable to them. I would like to note, however, that the methods of observation are not the *only* methods for which these issues are relevant. Depending on how you design a study, it is conceivable that any of the issues can be relevant. The material in Box 3.3 just serves as a guide.

BOX 3.3
MAKING DECISIONS INVOLVING ETHICS

Ethical Issue	Questions	Relevant Methods of Observation
Voluntary participation	• Have you told everyone that they can decline participation without penalty? • Have you made sure that if your subjects are vulnerable populations you have built in safeguards for them?	All
Informed consent	• Have you told them the general topic, the reason for the study, the potential harms/benefits (if any of either), guaranteed them anonymity/confidentiality, informed them of their right to privacy (see the following), told them the funding agency? • If you have some deception, have you made sure the deception is absolutely necessary, and have you added a debriefing at the end to explain the real purpose of the research and to give subjects a chance to enact their right to privacy?	All except covert observation
Protection from harm	• Have you considered the possible physical, psychological, legal, social, and economic risks of participation? • If any are present, have you identified steps to minimize the harm?	All, but especially • Experiments • Interviews • Participant observation • Case studies
Principle of justice	• Are your benefits and risks equally distributed across subjects?	All, but especially • Experiments • Participant observation
Anonymity/ Confidentiality	• Have you correctly distinguished whether you are granting the respondent anonymity (meaning you cannot match their identity to their responses) or confidentiality (you can match their identity to responses, but you will protect their identity)?	Anonymity • Surveys Confidentiality • Experiments • Interviews • Participant observation • Case studies
Privacy	• Have you told subjects that they can stop participating at any time? • Have you told subjects that they can skip any questions that they do not want to answer?	All

Ethical Issue	Questions	Relevant Methods of Observation
Data access and ownership	• If studying online behavior, have you considered and made the case for how public the behavior is? • What steps are you taking to ensure the safety of the data while you are actively working with it? • How do you plan on disposing of the data after your analysis?	All
Responsibility to society	• Is the general public at risk as a result of your study's actions? • If you learn of a potential risk to the general population during your study, how will you handle that risk?	All, but especially • Interviews • Participant observation • Case studies

CHALLENGES

Because ethics involves interactions with others, the researcher may not always be in control of the situations. Therefore, there are some gray areas that are worthy of mention.

1. **What if in protecting my subjects, I put society at risk or vice versa?** Unlike clergy or attorneys, researchers have no legal right to confidentiality of subjects. In other words, although we have an *ethical* responsibility to protect subjects' identities, if they do something illegal, we have no *legal* right to maintain that protection. This is why ethical relativism, which I discussed earlier, may be an issue.

2. **What if I cannot avoid some risk?** Sometimes some level of risk is unavoidable. For example, if you are studying the effectiveness of a specific type of counseling intervention for college students who have experienced date violence, it may be unavoidable for subjects to feel psychological distress during the course of your study. How various types of unavoidable risk are handled generally varies based on the topic and the method of observation? Instead of *not* studying this topic, however, presuming that the researcher has a persuasive reason for pursuing this topic, the researcher has the responsibility to bring this risk of harm to the attention of the respondent and perhaps even offer resources to the respondent should they need them. The subject can then decide whether they are willing to take on the risk of participating in the study. For example, in my mention of the potential risk for a study on dating violence, in order to provide informed consent, the researcher should mention the risk and remind the subjects that they can elect to not respond to particular questions and stop participating at any time. The researcher might go as far as identifying a counselor who, prior to the study, agreed to be a resource if someone felt the need to speak to someone to process any uncomfortable feelings that

may have arisen. This way subjects are informed of the possible risks and can decide whether to participate in the study, but if a subject overestimates his or her ability to handle the risks and realizes that they want to stop participation or need some form of help, as a researcher you have presented them with options and have fulfilled your ethical responsibilities to minimize harm.

Key Terms

Anonymity

Belmont Report

Confidentiality

Ethical relativism

Informed consent

Institutional Review Boards

Principle of beneficence

Principle of justice

Respect for persons

Voluntary participation

Vulnerable populations

Answers to Learning Check Questions

Learning Check 3.1: Learning Check Ethical Issues

1. Respect for persons, the principle of beneficence, and the principle of justice.

2. Confidentiality

3. No, because the deception about the purpose of the study is not deception about what is asked of the subject to do. Regardless of whether the purpose is response time or aggression, the subject's actions are the same, namely pushing a computer button.

End-of-Chapter Problems

1. What is the name of the document that established the three main standards for ethical and responsible research?
    a. The Nuremberg code
    b. The Belmont Report
    c. The Institutional Review document
    d. The Tuskegee Report

2. Which of the following indicates voluntary participation?
    a. Subjects can choose to participate in the study or not without fear of negative consequences if they decide not to.
    b. Subjects can stop participating in a study at any time without fear of negative consequences
    c. Neither of the above
    d. Both of the above

3. When a researcher can identify a subject but does not share that identity in any reports, what ethical responsibility is being used?
    a. Principle of justice
    b. Principle of beneficence

    c. Confidentiality
    d. Anonymity

4. Which of the following are types of harm a subject needs to be protected against?
    a. Physical
    b. Psychological
    c. Economic
    d. Legal
    e. All the above

5. True or False: The term *ethical relativism* refers to the recognition that fulfilling one ethical responsibility (such as to subjects) may be contrary to another ethical responsibility (such as to society).

6. Which of the following are a protected class of subjects who might not be able to fully voluntarily be able to decide to participate in a study and/or give informed consent?
    a. Children
    b. Inmates
    c. People with mental challenges
    d. All of the above

7. Which of the following involves the principle of respect for persons?
    a. Voluntary participation and informed consent
    b. Informed consent and protection from harm
    c. Voluntary participation and a balance between benefits and risks of research
    d. Informed consent and protection from harm

8. True or False: A researcher has the responsibility to try and foresee (and prevent) possible social harm to participants.

9. True or False: Like clergy and priests, researchers can withhold information learned in research from authorities in order to protect their subjects over their responsibility to protect society.

10. Who is responsible for reviewing research protocols to make sure that research is ethically sound?
    a. The Nuremberg code
    b. The National Research Act
    c. The writers of the Belmont Report
    d. IRBs

MEASUREMENT, VALIDITY, AND RELIABILITY

How many homeless people do you think live in New York City? A 2019 article in *The New York Times* claims that the number is about 78,000 (Stewart, 2019). However, the Coalition for the Homeless claims that the number is closer to 61,000 (www.coalitionforthe homeless.org). So who is right? Because both numbers are quite large, a difference of 17,000 may not seem like an issue, all things considered unless you are figuring out how to pay for something like the cost of shelter meals for a week or are trying to estimate housing needs.

So the answer to which number is "right" is that they both probably are. The *New York Times* figure refers to an estimate of homeless people who are living in shelters, who sleep on streets, or who sleep in other public spaces like subway stations. The Coalition for the Homeless figure referred to the number of people who sleep each night in the New York City shelter system. The difference in estimates stems from *how* the concept of homelessness is defined and, therefore, what is observed, or measured. How researchers define and measure concepts is important for reaching valid and reliable conclusions—so important, in fact, that these issues deserve their own chapter. Therefore, in this chapter, I am going to complete our coverage of foundational issues by discussing how to move from concepts to measures, the different types of study validity, and the different forms of reliability for which researchers strive.

MOVING FROM CONCEPTS TO MEASURES

Homelessness, gender stratification, academic achievement, recidivism…all of those are **concepts.** They are abstract terms, which give us a mental image of what someone is discussing. If, in conversation, someone mentions "gender stratification," we have an idea that they are not talking about the most recent football statistics, but we are still unclear about *what* they mean by gender stratification specifically. Are they talking about gender stratification in the workplace? In education? In sports? If they mean sports, are they talking about the different marketing power of men's versus women's sports? Are they talking about how women are still having trouble "breaking into" some traditional male sports? What? Concepts can have multiple meanings about which even experts can disagree depending on the theoretical perspective they find relevant, and different meanings can lead to different measures and different conclusions like we saw with the count of homeless people in New York City at the beginning of this chapter. Not only can a concept's definition vary across researchers, but it can also change over time as well. Traditionally gender is a dichotomous social concept that addresses the social roles we attribute to the biological sex of male or female. However, today, the concept of gender is less likely to be defined dichotomously and more likely to be placed on a spectrum between these two extremes. We have even coined a *new* concept, gender fluid, to recognize the move away from a dichotomous classification.

So how do we move from concepts, which are vague, multi-meaning, and temporally sensitive to measures, which are very specific? The process of moving from a concept to a measure is called **conceptualization** and **operationalization** and involves using both theory and prior research to identify what we think is important about the phenomena captured by the concept (Goertz, 2006). Because conceptualization and operationalization are so intertwined, some textbooks use the terms interchangeably and, quite frankly, the distinction is a small one. Here I will really use the term *conceptualization* as a broader overarching idea of refining a research topic into something that can be feasibly observed. To this end, conceptualization involves thinking about what we want to study and how in a broad sense. What is our topic? How would we organize our units of analysis? What method of observation can be most effectively used to study that topic? Clearly, in answering these questions, we have to simultaneously be thinking about the details of what we mean by a concept. At this stage, however we aren't focused on specifying those details just yet but rather on the overarching issues.

iStockphoto.com/FatCamera

PHOTO 4.1 Gender stratification is a concept that can apply to multiple institutions like work, education, the family, and sports.

Operationalization, on the other hand, focuses more on how to specifically define the concepts identified in the conceptualization process. In the deductive research process, researchers have to make sure that their resulting indicators and measures are sufficiently clear for subjects from their population to understand. Sometimes concepts and their indicators are pretty straightforward, such as the concept of age. Most people would agree that a measure asking "What is your age?" means someone's chronological age, not how old they feel. However, other concepts, like the ones I mentioned at the start of this section, are not widely recognized and can take many different forms. Therefore, the operationalization process may involve several steps of increasing specificity until researchers reach indicators. Methodologists have many names for each of these stages or definitions, such as dimensions, conceptual definition, and operational definitions; but for our purpose of "getting the job done," moving from concept to indicator really just means asking ourselves "what do I mean" repeatedly until we have an indicator that is theoretically sound, empirically observable, likely to be understood by the study population, and can be put into a question format to become a measure that is consistent with that definition.

For example, Young (2019) examined whether community resources were more likely to reduce work–family conflict among Canadians with young children compared to other residents. In this instance, there are two broad concepts: community resources and work–family conflict. Both of these concepts give the reader an idea that, for example, the researcher is not examining crime or sports or health care, so "community resources" and "work–family conflict." are abstract terms that serve to orient someone to the focus of study. However, these terms on their own are too broad to be empirically observed. Therefore, Young further defines or answers "what do I mean" to each by specifying, or operationalizing, the terms. For "work–family conflict." Young notes that she means the frequency someone felt that they did not have enough time for family or important people in their life, that they lacked energy to do things with family, that they felt that they could not do a good job at home, and that they could not concentrate on important family and life things each due to the respondent's job.

Each of these four definitions can be empirically observed with a survey question, or indicator, which Young further notes are measured on a five-point scale ranging from "never" to "very often." Young's operationalization process for both "work–family conflict" and "community resources," along with two hypothetical examples of operationalization, appears in **Box 4.1**

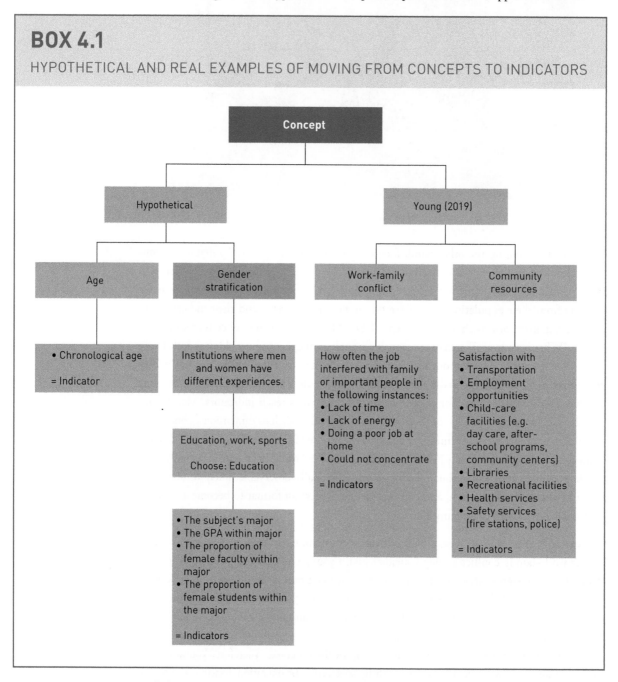

BOX 4.1

HYPOTHETICAL AND REAL EXAMPLES OF MOVING FROM CONCEPTS TO INDICATORS

I will discuss how to move from indicators to measures in the next section, but to summarize, this process involves clearly stating what researchers mean by a concept and making sure that the indicators selected for that concept are clear, empirically observable, and consistent with that definition.

> ✔ **LEARNING CHECK 4.1: CONCEPTS**
>
> 1. How does the operationalization of concepts relate to why different studies might produce different findings about the same topic?
>
> 2. When trying to define concepts, what is the key question to ask yourself and when do you know you may be done asking it?
>
> **Answers to be found at the end of the chapter.**

LEVELS OF MEASUREMENT

The type of indicator you use for a concept will help someone understand what you mean by those vague conceptual terms and the measure you select for that indicator is going to have statistical implications. There are two common ways that people refer to the categories of measures, by type and by level. The first way of categorizing measures is by their general type, which is discrete (also sometimes called categorical) or continuous. **Discrete measures** have a finite set of values that are usually identified by the researcher and do not, in and of themselves, have concrete numerical meaning. For example, gender might have the values (answer choices) of male, female, and other. Or the variable satisfaction with your school might have five values ranging from very dissatisfied to very satisfied. Both examples are discrete measures because the answer choices, what we statistically referred to as **values**, are limited. There are three options for gender and five options for school satisfaction. Furthermore, the numerical codes that I might assign to each value, such as 1 = male, 2 = female, and 3 = other, do not have meaning on their own. If you asked me what Subject 100 answered to gender and I said "2," you would have no idea what "2" means. That "2" just reflects the arbitrary number I assigned to the value of "female" so a computer program would be able to do mathematical calculations on this information (Chapter 10). In other words, the "2" has no real numerical meaning on its own, unlike the answers to continuous variables.

Continuous measures are those for which the values are quantifiable and have meaning on their own. If my measure is "What is your age?" there are many possible values for this measure, too many for a researcher to write every option. Furthermore, if Subject A answers 19 and Subject B answers 23, the values of 19 and 23 have meaning on their own. I do not need an outside source to tell me that 19 refers to 19 years since the person was born. Likewise, the measurement is quantifiable because I can tell how much older or younger subjects are. I know, for example, that Subject A is 4 years younger than Subject B.

The **levels of measurement**, however, refer to a ranking of measures based on the characteristics their values have. Nominal measures are the most basic level of measurement which are discrete measures where the answer choices are mutually exclusive and exhaustive but have no inherent rank order. When I say a measure's values are mutually exclusive it means that, unless otherwise specified by the researcher with a direction such as "circle all that apply," there is *only* one viable answer choice (value) for everyone. Exhaustive, on the other hand, means that

PHOTO 4.2 Race is a complex concept that is measured at the nominal level.

iStockphoto.com/FG Trade

there *is* an answer choice for everyone. Some common nominal levels of measurement are gender, race, religion, and political affiliation.

There are a couple of ways in which these two characteristics of mutually exclusive and/ or exhaustive are frequently violated. For example, if someone decided to measure race as Caucasian, African American, Latino, and Asian, it is clear that this variable is categorical and has no ranking. However, it does not have the characteristics of being mutually exclusive *or* exhaustive. What if someone identifies as biracial? Would that person circle two categories? Ditto for multiracial. Because a respondent could feel that there could be more than one answer choice and there is no evidence that the researcher will specify to circle all that apply, this measure would not be mutually exclusive. However, it also is not exhaustive because what if someone identifies as East Indian? Or Indigenous American? Or Haitian? Therefore, there is also not a choice for everyone.

An argument can be made for not wanting to write every possible race or ethnic identity as an answer choice because doing so would lengthen the survey dramatically. This dilemma is common for measures that are aimed at identification, such as identifying what sports a subject played in college, what types of movies someone likes to watch, and in what types of stores someone usually shops. The possible value options for any of these variables could be very long. The typical solution for this is to include four to five values that the researcher expects to be common responses (Side note: and how do you think the researcher determines this? You probably guessed it—the literature review!) and have the last category read something like "Other (Please specify:_____." Write-in responses that occur frequently can later be coded as additional values once all the data is collected (Chapter 10). I will discuss how to write survey questions in more detail in Chapter 7, but for now, Box 4.2 gives a poor example and corrected examples of how a measure of racial identity might appear on a survey.

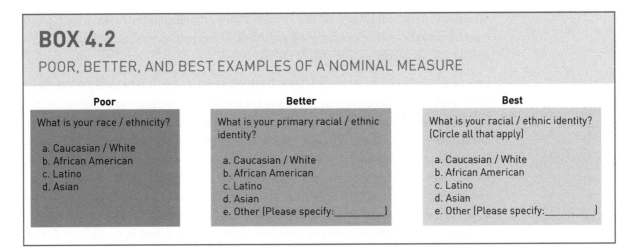

BOX 4.2

POOR, BETTER, AND BEST EXAMPLES OF A NOMINAL MEASURE

Poor	**Better**	**Best**
What is your race / ethnicity?	What is your primary racial / ethnic identity?	What is your racial / ethnic identity? (Circle all that apply)
a. Caucasian / White b. African American c. Latino d. Asian	a. Caucasian / White b. African American c. Latino d. Asian e. Other (Please specify:_____)	a. Caucasian / White b. African American c. Latino d. Asian e. Other (Please specify:_____)

The next level of measurement, ordinal, is also a discreet variable and it builds on the nominal level in that its values are mutually exclusive and exhaustive, but ordinal measures have the additional characteristics that they can be ordered but not in a quantifiable way. A common example of ordinal measures is questions that follow the five- or seven-point Likert scale format. An example of a Likert question would be something like "How excited are you to begin summer vacation?" with the corresponding value options of "Very excited," "Somewhat excited," "No opinion," "Not very excited," and "Not at all excited." These values are mutually exclusive, as it does not really make sense to choose two, and exhaustive since if someone has no opinion that is an option. So, as with all ordinal measures, this question builds on the characteristics of nominal measures. Furthermore, a researcher would know that a subject who responds "Very excited" is more excited than someone who answers "Somewhat excited," so the answer choices are ranked, but the researcher can't say *how much* more excited in numerical terms.

The third level of measurement is interval. As you can probably guess, interval levels of measurement have all of the characteristics of the previous two measures and build on them by having values with meaningful distinctions, but not a true zero point. Therefore, interval measures are a type of continuous measure because their values can directly be unambiguously compared. The Scholastic Aptitude Test, or SAT, is an example of an interval measure because if I compared two scores, such as a score of 700 and a score of 650, I know that the student who scored the 700 scored 50 points higher than the one who scored 650. I can quantify (in other words tell *how much* more or less with a meaningful number) the difference. However, believe it or not, there is no "0" score on the SAT. So, as a measure, there is no true, meaningful zero here.

The last level, also a continuous measure and also building on all the measures that came before, is the ratio level of measurement. You can probably guess that the only remaining difference between the interval level and the ratio one is that now "0" has true meaning, at least in theory. For example, age can be measured at the ratio level. If someone is 18 and another 25, we know the 25 year old is 7 years older than the 18 year old, but we also recognize infants as newborn, 1 day old, 1 week old, etc. Figure 4.1 shows the relationship between the types of measures and the level of measurement and shows an example of how the concept of "social media use" can be measured at each of the four levels.

One comment before I move on: Higher levels of measurement can be collapsed down to lower levels of measurement; however, lower levels cannot be increased to higher levels. If a researcher asks someone "Do you use any social media such as Facebook, Twitter, Snapchat, or Instagram?" and includes only a yes/no response, there is no way that "yes" or "no" can be increased to the number of times a day someone uses social media. However, if you start and includes only a ratio question, you *can* make it nominal by coding all the "0" responses as "no" and any response greater than or equal to "1" as "yes." Because of this, the general consensus is that all else being equal (which I will discuss in Chapter 7), when there is a choice, go with the highest level of measurement possible when deciding what measure to use for an indicator, as you will have more statistical testing options as a result.

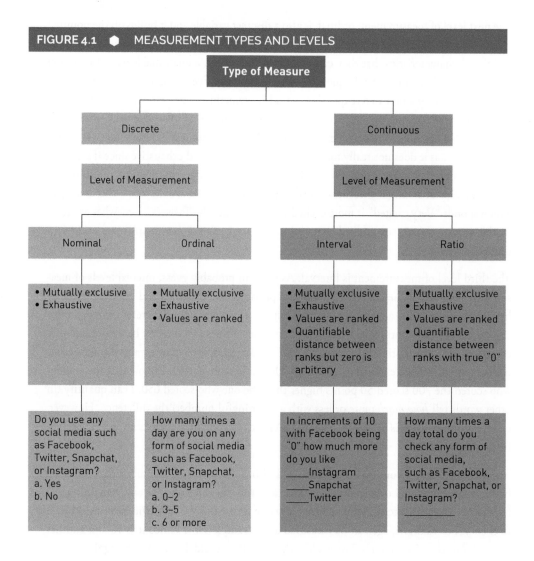

FIGURE 4.1 ● MEASUREMENT TYPES AND LEVELS

LEARNING CHECK 4.2: LEVEL OF MEASUREMENT

1. Which level of measurement has the following characteristics: the values are mutually exclusive, exhaustive, and ranked but without being able to quantify the difference between ranks?

2. Can we make a higher level of measurement from a lower level of measurement? Why/why not?

3. Identify whether the following measure is discrete or continuous and what its level is: How many university clubs do you belong to this semester? _____

Answers to be found at the end of the chapter.

MEASUREMENT QUALITY

How do we know what is a good measure to use? Often the process of operationalizing a concept takes many "drafts" or iterations until the researcher achieves indicators that will produce credible findings. At the risk of sounding repetitive, the literature review (Chapter 2) will come in handy for this and will help streamline some of the process. By reviewing the literature you can get a sense of how other people have operationalized their concepts and the indicators they selected accordingly. However, just because research is published does not 100% guarantee that the measures used in those studies are strong, have been tested for validity, and/or suit your situation. The literature review may give you ideas, but you still need to evaluate that information for your purposes based on your idea of relevance and your understanding of validity and reliability.

Validity

As I said previously, validity refers to whether you are observing what you think you are—in other words, whether your measures, sample, method of observation all produce information that truly reflects what is going on in the population. This is actually much more challenging than may initially appear because, since research is made by fallible people, there are many ways that validity can be threatened. In fact, there are so many forms of validity and threats to these forms that your professor can probably devote a couple of weeks of lecture just to this topic. I will introduce other forms of validity in more detail in Chapter 6 when we discuss experiments, but for now I want to focus on the most basic issue of measurement quality, which is showing the validity of the measure itself, or in other words, identifying whether the measure accurately represents the corresponding concept. If our measures are poor, then the rest of the study will be poor as well. To put it another way, our measures are the foundations for making sure we are studying what we think we are. Quality measures are meaningful, understandable, and are relevant to the research topic, hypothesis, or goals. Measures should also be timely. People are not very good at recalling events, so measures should reflect current or very recent behavior or experiences that contribute to theoretical understanding or, in the case of evidence-based research, something that can currently be used by the agency.

There are many forms of measurement validity that are an important component to overall study validity. I will present four here.

Face Validity

At the very basis of measurement is to make sure our concept has **face validity**, which literally means that the measure makes sense "on the face of it," meaning as a basic logical indicator of a concept. For example, if I want to measure academic performance, a student's GPA at the end of the semester has face validity, because it makes sense as one possible indicator of how well a person did in their classes. However, "number of classes taken in a semester" or "overall view of the professor's teaching skills," while certainly related to academic performance, does not make sense as an indicator of how well someone did in a class. Therefore, these other two measures would not have face validity. Because of its very basic nature, face validity, however, is usually not sufficient as the only form of validity. Just because a measure makes sense does not mean that it is complete or strong. For example, there are some experiences like sexual behavior, income, crime victimization, and some acts of deviance where people might fully understand the measure (it makes sense) but choose to over- or under-report their experiences. Therefore, these measures are not *really* adequately measuring what a researcher hopes to.

You may be thinking that people can over- or under-report for *any* measure. Technically that's true, but the risk is not the same for all measures. Obviously, college students, for example, may be more hesitant to answer a question regarding whether they have ever had unprotected sex than they are to answer a question asking how many classes they are taking this semester. However, if researchers have multiple measures for a concept or if a researcher's measures fulfill some of the other forms of validity, researchers are more likely to detect this kind of bias if it does occur. So let's cover some of these other forms of measurement validity.

Criterion Validity

If we are creating a new measure, we also have to be conscious of **criterion validity**, which is the degree to which people's answers relate in the expected way to other widely accepted measures of a concept. A scale measuring weight would appear invalid if someone who looked skeletal stepped on it and the scale read 200 pounds. We expect people who visibly look extremely thin (what we are measuring with our eyes) to show low weight on a scale (our official measure) and if those indicators contradict, we presume one of the indicators in invalid. Here the outside criterion is what we can see with our own eyes. Establishing this validity presumes (1) that other accepted measures of a concept exist; (2) that those measures themselves were valid; and (3) a researcher has pretested this new measure against the older ones before incorporating it into a full study (de Vaus, 2002). In order to establish this, researchers would run a statistical correlation test and hope to see that the correlation shows at least a moderate association.

PHOTO 4.3 A weight scale can serve as an example of criterion validity. We measure approximate weight with our eyes (heavy, thin, etc.) and expect the scale to give us a number (second measure) that is consistent with our perception. If we saw a super-thin person on a scale that read 250 pounds, we would presume that the scale was invalid (because we trust our eyes more).

iStockphoto.com/golibo

There are two types of criterion validity, both of which have to do with the timing of the relationship between the indicators. If the two measures being compared are occurring at roughly the same time, then we have **concurrent criterion validity**. For example, if a therapist administers a caregiver stress scale to a client who is in her office in response to a crisis and the scale strongly correlates with the other measures of stress the client is experiencing, that is concurrent validity. However, if an indicator is designed to measure a future event, if the measure and the future event (when it occurs) has a high correlation, then we have **predictive criterion validity** because the indicator successfully predicted future behavior. For example, the SAT is designed to predict how well someone will do in college during their freshman year. If SAT scores and student GPA in the first semester are strongly correlated, then the SAT has predictive validity.

Construct Validity

If the correlation between the old and new measure is weak, does that mean that we do not have criterion validity? Possibly. However, the problem may be that the *old* comparison measure is now invalid. Therefore, the researcher might be able to make a theoretical argument that the new measure is related to an underlying factor related to theory and testable with hypotheses. This would be called **construct validity**. Therefore, the new measure would be considered valid pending replication of other studies using the measure and those resulting validity tests. In other words, construct validity is how well a measure tests a theoretical concept that is linked to *why* the measure works the way it does. So it involves validation of the theory underlying a concept. This validity is harder to both understand and to establish than some of the other forms, but Cronbach (1970) suggests that one can establish this validity by

(1) identifying what concepts might account for variation in an indicator; (2) identifing or developing a theory around these concepts; and (3) testing the hypotheses for this relationship empirically. The statistical process of factor analysis can help establish this form of validity. In factor analysis, the researcher inputs a large number of measures (called factors) that are linked by an underlying theory into a computer statistical program and the program runs tests to see which factors measure the same thing (concept) and what the relationship is between factors. In this way, the original large number of potential factors is reduced to a small number that is statistically determined to go together.

Content Validity

Content validity refers to the ability to measure abstract concepts that include multiple dimensions or groups of indicators. It is about how well the measures cover the different meanings of a concept. At the start of our discussion of measurement, I presented the term "gender stratification" and I identified gender stratification in the workplace, education, and sports as just a couple of dimensions of where gender stratification could occur. However, each of these dimensions still needs to be further defined and then in some way related to each other. Tjaden and Thoennes (2000) wanted to study the concept of intimate partner violence, which can have multiple definitions, such as rape, physical assault, sexual assault, psychological abuse, and stalking, to name a few. Interpersonal violence can also occur in a variety of contexts such as dating, cohabitation, or marriage, *and* it could include current or former partners. Therefore to establish content validity, researchers like Tjaden and Thoennes (2000) first need to be very clear about the definitions of their concepts and their corresponding measures because researchers cannot study all forms of such a broad concept simultaneously. For example, Tjaden and Thoennes (2000) defined intimate partner violence to be:

> Rape, physical assault, and stalking perpetrated by current and former dates, spouse, and cohabiting partners, with cohabiting meaning living together at least some of the time as a couple (p. 5).

They also had a clear definition of each type of violence. For example, to define stalking Tjaden and Thoennes borrowed the antistalking code developed by the National Criminal Justice Association (1993), which states that stalking is

> ...a course of conduct directed at a specific person that involves repeated visual or physical proximity, nonconsensual communication, or oral, written, or implied threats, or a combination thereof, that would cause a reasonable person to fear bodily injury or death, with repeated meaning on two or more occasions (National Criminal Justice Association, 1993, as quoted in Tjaden & Thoennes, 2000, p. 430).

Not all measures can address all forms of measurement validity simultaneously; therefore, it is the researcher's responsibility to make the case for which forms of measurement validity relate to his/her study and the steps taken to achieve those forms. A summary of the different types of measurement validity and key questions that identify them appears in Figure 4.2.

FIGURE 4.2 ● MEASUREMENT VALIDITY TYPES

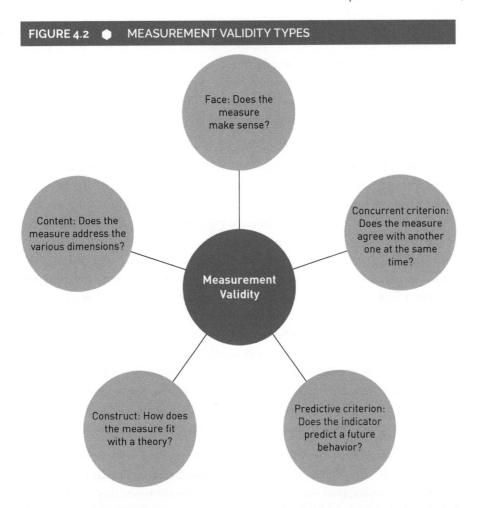

Reliability

Not only should the measure be accurate for a concept, but it also should be reliable. Measurement **reliability** means that the measure will produce consistent results on repeated observations of the same phenomena. For quantitative measures, there are a variety of ways to assess reliability, two of which I will focus on in order to "get the job done," but reliability is also important to qualitative studies. For qualitative data, such as interviews, focus groups, and field research, there are multiple ways of essentially making the same point or observation. In order to analyze this information, researchers have to find patterns in the responses to these questions (measures). Reliability then would be the degree to which different experts read these responses and see the same patterns among them. There is also a statistical test that helps establish this type of reliability, and this will be the third reliability assessment I will discuss.

However, while, as I said, I am going to discuss three ways to assess reliability, it is important to understand that researchers can only estimate reliability; they cannot calculate it exactly (Trochim, Donnelly, & Arora, 2016). A common way to test measurement reliability for quantitative measure is the test-rest method, which is pretty much what the name implies. For this test, the researcher administers the same instrument to the same or similar samples at two time points that are sufficiently close together, but not close enough that the group (if using the same group) remembers what they said to specific questions. For example, if I give a chapter test on Monday to a group of students and give them the same test a few days later, if the questions reliably measure their knowledge of the chapter content, the scores on the tests should not be significantly different. I would assess this difference by doing a correlation test, which I will cover in Chapter 14, but for now, I will just make two points about correlations in this context. The first is that the higher the correlation between the two scores, the more reliable the measure is. The second is that the amount of time between tests can affect the correlation because the more time between tests, the greater the opportunity for change in the factors that can affect the measurement. In other words, if too much time lapses, then the correlation is going to go down regardless of the reliability of the measure.

If researchers are worried that they will not be able to identify a time that is sufficiently close in order to decrease the effect of outside change yet far enough apart so subjects cannot remember their specific answers, then instead of administering the test twice, they could divide the test in half and administer the first half at one point and the second half at another point that is closer in time. This form of reliability test is called a split-half reliability test. For this test, the researcher just has to make sure that there are two sets of items that measure the same concept. The test then is a simple correlation between the total scores between the two tests.

The third form of reliability is more likely to apply to qualitative measures and this is inter-rater, also called inter-judge or inter-observer, reliability. Human observation can be very subjective and inconsistent. For example, what offends me may not offend you or it may offend me now but perhaps it did not in the recent past. In order to reduce this, when looking at qualitative measures, which are known and valued for their subjectivity, researchers have to take steps to increase the likelihood that the interpretations of that subjective content are consistent, and therefore reliable. **Inter-rater reliability** is the technique where two or more raters will need to agree about the meaning of the content as well as whether individual subjects' information reflects that meaning. This agreement can then be tested statistically with a Cohen's Kappa, which looks at the rate of agreement adjusting for random chance. This score varies from 0 to 1, but there is disagreement among researchers as to what intervals are considered slight, moderate, and strong reliability, with most of the cutoffs being determined arbitrarily (Gwet, 2014). In general, however, most researchers consider correlations of at least .7 as sufficiently strong, so we will too.

To Increase Validity and Reliability

There are some steps researchers can take to increase the likelihood of measures and studies being reliable. One of the easiest ways, and a suggestion throughout the later chapters of this book, is to pretest any instrument you plan to use with a representative, but small, sample of the intended subjects. This way you can see whether there are measures, responses, or directions that confuse subjects. In some cases, these pretests can even be accompanied by brief interviews with subjects so researchers can better understand why confusion occurs. When problems are discovered, the researchers should correct the problem and then retest the new instrument on another small, representative sample. Once most of the pretests indicate that there are no questions or confusion, measures are probably ready to be used in the full study.

Measurement Error

However, despite researchers' best efforts, no measure is going to be perfect. Measurement error is unavoidable. Presuming a researcher did everything possible to maximize the validity and reliability of measures, the two remaining possible sources of error are random error and systematic error. **Random error** is just what the name implies. It is an error that cannot be predicted and does not follow any discernible pattern. People can have a bad day or a good day. Some may have gotten enough sleep, others did not. Any of this can affect what people say and do in a study, but it will not affect the overall results in any way because they will essentially balance out. Therefore, random measurement error will add variability in the data (which I will discuss more in Chapter 11), but it will not affect the typical responses in data (also in Chapter 11).

The second form of measurement error is **systemic error** and systemic error differs from random error because, while random error is inconsistent, systemic error is a consistent effect on measurement. For example, if students are taking a test in a room that is very hot, it may affect most of their scores on that test. Systemic error may also occur if there is a pattern among people who choose to skip questions or who choose to participate in the study. Unlike random

---

✔ LEARNING CHECK 4.4: MEASUREMENT QUALITY

1. What part of the research process that we discussed in a previous chapter is a useful way to identify possible valid and reliable measures to use in your study?

2. _____ refers to the consistency in responses to a measure and _____ refers to whether a measure accurately reflects the intended concept.

3. True or False: Due to the subjectivity of qualitative research, researchers cannot establish reliability for their measures.

Answers to be found at the end of the chapter.

error, systematic error can influence the results and bias the study. Therefore, systematic error is something that researchers especially need to be conscious of and I will discuss what to do to reduce this later in this chapter.

MEASURE CONSIDERATION: TIME DIMENSIONS

I opened Chapter 1 with some horrific, fairly recent incidents of school violence that fueled the common belief that school violence is increasingly common and that parents and administrators had to do something to decrease it. But is the rate of school violence really as high as we think? According to data compiled by the National Center for Education Statistics, the total victimization rates for many types of crime on school grounds, including serious violent crime, was lower in 2015–2016 (when these data were collected) than in previous years by both student self-reports and principal reports (U.S. Department of Education, National Center for Education Statistics, 2019). Furthermore, a related report also shows the rate of homicide for students aged 5–18 on school property was lower in 2015–2016 than every year between 2005 and 2010, with the exception of 1 year where they were the same (2008–2009, Digest of Education Statistics, 2018). With the extensive media coverage over some extreme and disturbing acts of school violence, it is easy to see why people have the perception that the frequency of school violence is high and increasing; however, as I just illustrated, the use of longitudinal data analysis suggests that this might not actually be the case. How long researchers measure a concept, what is called the time dimension of the research, is an issue related to measurement that influences the validity and reliability of our findings.

Measuring a concept over multiple years can give you a better idea of trends than can measuring something at one time point. But let's suppose that you were not interested in trends over time and instead you wanted to measure whether peer-reading tutoring helped young children improve their reading skills. To study this you let fourth graders who had an "A" in reading tutor first graders who were having reading trouble. When would you measure the first graders' reading skills to see if your program worked? One month after the program? Two months? How would you know if there was a *change*? Wouldn't you need to measure reading skills *prior* to the tutoring? Determining how many observations to make and the amount of time between them, especially when examining whether a program works or not, is an important issue in measurement.

The most common form of research is **cross-sectional research**, which occurs at only one time point. Lots of studies are cross-sectional. If you receive a marketing survey in the mail, complete it, and don't receive any further surveys from that marketer, that is a cross-sectional survey. Course evaluations are also cross-sectional. I conducted a web survey of faculty, staff, and students at my university to examine whether there were age differences in the types of Facebook posts that people perceived to be inappropriate (Wolfer, 2017, 2018). This too was an example of cross-sectional research. Essentially, cross-sectional surveys provide a snapshot of what people think or do at one point in time and are common for exploratory or descriptive studies (Chapter 1).

However, if you want to see how a measure changes, like in my peer tutoring example, you need to measure the dependent variable before and after exposure to the independent variable. Any time you have two or more time points of data collection you have a **longitudinal research**. In longitudinal studies, researchers can have control over the second criteria of causality, making sure the independent variable comes before the dependent variable (Chapter 2) because researchers can document the dependent variable at various time points and then see if the variable changes *after* they introduce the independent variable. Therefore, longitudinal studies are good for explanation and evaluation, but they can also be useful for description over time, like in our school violence example. There are three types of longitudinal studies that are relevant to us. These are repeated cross-sectional studies, cohort studies, and panel studies (Box 4.3).

Repeated cross-sectional designs, also called trend studies, are the most basic form of longitudinal study and they are frequently used to examine changes in a general population over time. In trend studies, a new sample of the population is drawn at each time point. For example, we have all heard of the challenges of parenting: the "terrible twos," not being able to go to the bathroom or take a shower without someone needing something at that very moment, the sleepless nights with infants or sick children, the constant comparison to cultural expectations, …you get the idea. Being a parent is *tough*. So, how does being a parent affect happiness? Are nonparents happier than parents and has this varied over time? Herbst and Ifcher (2016) studied this very topic using the General Social Survey, which was generally administered yearly between 1972 and 1993 and then biennially afterward. Each administration of the GSS is called a "wave," and

BOX 4.3
DIFFERENT RESEARCH TIME DIMENSIONS

Population	Type of Study	Time 1	Time 2
	Cross-section		
	Longitudinal		
	Repeated cross-section/Trend		
	Panel / Fixed study		
	Cohort study		

each "wave" is a new sample of people. Each of these waves Herbst and Ifcher analyzed included variables identifying parenthood and the question "Taken all together, how would you say things are these days—would you say you are very happy, pretty happy, or not too happy?" This same question has been asked repeatedly in each wave of the GSS, but the people answering the question changed with each wave. As Herbst and Ifcher note, that makes approximately 35 years of information to study the relationship between parenthood and happiness over time. If, on the contrary, the researchers examined the same question but used only one wave of data, say the 1991 wave, they would have been doing a cross-sectional study—at one time point—even though the data set is longitudinal. In fact, we will be doing a cross-sectional analysis of the 2019 wave of the GSS for our discussion of statistics starting in Chapter 11.

If I study the same people at multiple time points, on the contrary, I am doing a panel study, sometimes also called a fixed study because the sample does not change across time and is, therefore, *fixed*. Del Boca, Piazzalunga, and Pronzato (2017) used the Millennium Cohort Study, a longitudinal study in the United Kingdom of 19,000 babies born in the year 2000 to see how early grandparent childcare affected child cognitive outcomes in the United Kingdom. After refining the sample for various characteristics, the researchers had a sample of about 9,000 children, all of whom were studied for four waves (years 2000, 2003, 2006, and 2008), and they found that children with grandparent childcare had a higher vocabulary compared to children who had formal childcare, but at the same time, these children were less ready for school and performed worse on nonverbal reasoning and mathematical concepts. The researchers also found that some of this negative relationship is explained by socioeconomic status, where children from lower-income households benefited in these areas of development more if they attended formal childcare, as opposed to grandparent care. To really examine the impact of grandparent compared to formal childcare, Del Boca et al. (2017) needed to examine the *same* children at each time point, making this a panel study.

iStockphoto.com/monkeybusinessimages

PHOTO 4.4 To see how being a parent affects happiness, do you think that we would get a better picture with a cross-sectional survey or a longitudinal one? Why?

However, if the sample at each time point shares a time-related characteristic, regardless of whether they are the same or different people at each wave, the study is a cohort study, the third type. The common ways people can share a time characteristic are:

- School cohort (freshman, sophomore, junior, senior)

- Birth cohort (Baby-boomers, Millennials)

- Experience cohort (5 years experience, 10 years experience)

The Del Boca et al. (2017) study is actually also an example of cohort study because all of the children in the study share a birth cohort; they were born in the year 2000. Hence cohort studies can be panel studies like the Del Boca et al. study if the same people who share the time dimension are studied over time or it can be a repeated cross-sectional one if new people are selected. If, on the contrary, I replicated the study but drew a new sample of people born in 2000 at each time point, then I would be doing a repeated cross-sectional version of the cohort study.

One of the benefits of panel studies, especially cohort ones, is that studying the same people more than one time helps address some rival causal factors that may make the observed relationship spurious and, therefore, demote a causal goal to a descriptive one. However, these studies can also be expensive, subjects may drop out over time, and subjects may be difficult to contact over time. Therefore, depending on the purpose of the research, a panel study may not be necessary. I will discuss some considerations to help you decide what time dimension to choose later in the chapter in the "Making Decisions" section.

✔ LEARNING CHECK 4.5: TIME DIMENSIONS

1. Which type of time dimension studies people who share a point in time at more than one time point, regardless of whether they are the same people or not?

2. Which type of time dimension is the strongest for assessing change in behavior? Why?

3. A researcher draws a random sample of 75 people who use food stamps to see what types of food they purchase. Based on this information, what time dimension did the researcher use?

Answers to be found at the end of the chapter.

MAKING DECISIONS

How to Choose Your Measures

As the term "level" suggests, there is a hierarchy to the levels of measurement with the nominal level being the lowest and the ratio being the highest. There are some consequences to this ranking. For example, if you know that an indicator is nominal, then you know that any numbers you see in the analysis are arbitrary and there just for the computer program, which might not be able to do the math on language terms. Similarly, knowing the level of measurement gives you an idea of what are meaningful statistics. A computer is not very smart in and of itself and it will do anything you tell it to. If you tell a computer to calculate an average for "gender," which is coded as "1 = male; 2 = female; 3 = other," the computer will dutifully chug out an average of those numbers. However, realizing gender is a nominal measure, you will also recognize that does not make sense to add "genders" and then divide them! Fourth, statistics that involve lower levels of measurement come with fewer statistical assumptions (which we will see in Chapters 12–14) than do statistics with higher levels of measurement, but their resulting ability to generalize to populations from samples is also more limited.

So how do you choose which measure to use? There is no specific easy answer, but there are some considerations. First and foremost is the level of information necessary to address your research goal and what levels and types of measures were used by others who studied this goal. Furthermore, having a sense of the statistical tests you might want to run can also affect your choice of measurement. If you want to run multivariate linear regressions (Chapter 14), for example, then

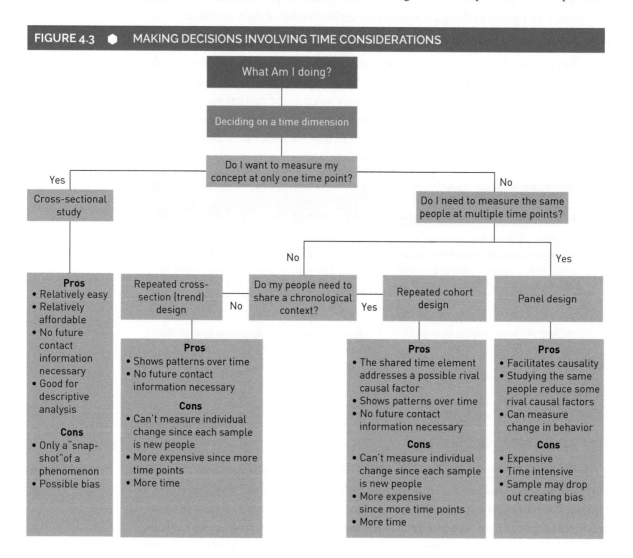

FIGURE 4.3 ● MAKING DECISIONS INVOLVING TIME CONSIDERATIONS

having an interval/ratio-dependent variable, if possible, is preferred. Last, all else being equal or if you truly do not know yet what type of statistics you plan to run, then always go with the highest level of measurement possible. As I discussed earlier, you can always bump a higher level of measurement to a lower one, but you cannot make a lower level of measurement higher.

Time Considerations

There can easily be different time dimensions and sampling considerations for anyone's research question. Therefore, Figure 4.3 presents a flow chart of how various time dimensions fit with some basic research needs along with a summary of some common pros and cons of each option.

CHALLENGES

1. **How can I maximize measurement validity?** There are a couple of ways to maximize measurement validity. One is to use a measure that has already been validated in other studies, which, again, you would learn from a literature review (Chapter 2). Another way is to focus on your indicator presentation. I will discuss this in detail in survey research in Chapter 7, but there are some suggestions that I can mention here that are relevant to any method of observation. One suggestion is to make sure that your questions are clear. This means to make sure that the question wording will have the same meaning to different respondents regardless of their culture, gender, social class, region, or age. To increase this likelihood, a researcher needs to avoid vague wording, slang, or even colloquialisms in question and response wording. Another general comment about question (and indicator) wording is to be simple and direct. Try to avoid long, convoluted questions with many parts embedded within them. With these kinds of questions, subjects can easily get confused, lost, or even just give up. Last, make sure you ask questions that the subjects are qualified to answer. You may not want to ask parents details about the content of the standardized tests given to their children, for example, because in many school districts parents do not get to see these tests and therefore do not know much about specific content.

2. **Because measurement is such a foundational part of any research project, should I make it a focal point of the data collection?**
    Although it is important that measures be administered correctly, it is also important to avoid goal displacement where people perform to the measures at the expense of the overall research goals. This issue is analogous to the common criticisms we heard about the old No Child Left Behind legislation. This legislation intended to reward schools that appear to successfully educate their students to national standards as indicated by standardized test scores and punish those that did not. As such, a common criticism is that education became less about truly reaching students skills, such as how to think, and became more about "teaching to the test," where test scores rather than real comprehension become the goal, cheating on the test to get school resources, narrowing curriculums to focus on test content (Nichols & Berliner, 2007).

Key Terms

Concepts

Conceptualization

Concurrent criterion validity

Construct validity

Content validity

Continuous measures

Criterion validity

Cross-sectional research

Discrete measures

Face validity

Inter-rater reliability

Levels of measurement

Longitudinal research

Operationalization

Predictive criterion validity

Random error

Reliability

Systemic error

Values

Answers to Learning Check Questions

Learning Check 4.1: Concepts

1. Operationalization refers to how concepts are defined and the ensuing indicators that fit those definitions. If researchers use different definitions of the same concept, then they will build measures off of different indicators so different behaviors will be observed.

2. The key question is "What do I mean?" and you are done asking it when you have an answer that is empirically observable and is likely to be understood by your study population (although you should still do a pretest to make sure).

Learning Check 4.2: Level of Measurement

1. Ordinal

2. No. Lower level of measurements lacks specific quantifiable information. Therefore, although we can recode a ratio level to an ordinal or nominal one by combining values and, therefore, reducing specific detail, we cannot create detail from when there was none.

3. It is a continuous measure that is at the ratio level because it is a count for which there is a true "0" value because someone taking the survey might not participate in any university clubs.

Learning Check 4.3: Measurement Validity

1. Construct validity

2. Face validity

3. Content validity

Learning Check 4.4 Measurement Quality

1. The literature review

2. Reliability; validity

3. False. For qualitative methods, we would need more than one researcher to code information and look for consistency in their decisions. This is called inter-rater reliability.

Learning Check 4.5: Time Dimensions

1. Cohort

2. Panel, because it is the sample people studied at multiple time points.

3. Cross-sectional, because the study appears to have been done at only one time point. (There is no evidence that the researcher asked these individuals about their food stamp use multiple times.)

End-of-Chapter Problems

1. Which of the following are characteristics of an ordinal level of measurement?
   a. Mutually exclusive and exhaustive values
   b. Mutually exclusive, exhaustive, and ranked values
   c. Mutually exclusive, exhaustive, ranked quantifiable values that have no true "0"
   d. Mutually exclusive, exhaustive, ranked quantifiable values that have a true "0"

2. Researchers conducting a survey on illegal drug use ask subjects how often they have used illegal drugs in the past week and then re-ask that same question three days later. What reliability test did they do?
   a. Inter-rater reliability
   b. Test-retest reliability
   c. Split-half reliability

3. "Neighborhood integration" is an example of an
   a. Indicator
   b. Measure
   c. Concept
   d. Operational definition

4. True or False: Indicators can have multiple meanings; therefore, it is up to the subject to decide how to interpret them.

5. True or False: Nominal levels of measurement are continuous variables.

6. What level of measurement is the following question: How many colleges did you apply to during your senior year of high school?_____
   a. Nominal
   b. Ordinal
   c. Interval
   d. Ratio

7. A researcher studying weekend partying behavior among college students arrives at a college party, asks some students if they have been drinking alcohol, and then gives them a breathalyzer test to verify if the students are telling the truth. The researcher is establishing what type of measurement validity?
   a. Face
   b. Criterion
   c. Construct
   d. Content

8. In order to study people's attitudes toward gun laws over time, a researcher selects a random sample of 300 people in 2014, a random sample of 280 people in 2016, and a random sample of 300 people in 2018. What is the time dimension of this study?
   a. Cross-sectional
   b. Trend/repeated cross-sectional
   c. Cohort
   d. Panel

9. What type of study examines the same people at multiple time points?
   a. Cross-sectional
   b. Trend/repeated cross-sectional
   c. Cohort
   d. Panel

10. What level of measurement is the following variable and values: "What are your plans after graduation?" 1 = Get a job; 2 = Go to graduate / professional school; 3 = Take a gap year; 4 = Other (please specify:_____).
    a. Nominal
    b. Ordinal
    c. Interval
    d. Ratio

5

SAMPLING

LEARNING GOALS

- Identify the terminology related to sampling
- Distinguish between units of observation and units of analysis
- Understand the relationship between samples, sampling, and study populations using the central limit theorem
- Distinguish between probability and nonprobability sampling techniques
- Be able to select simple random, systematic, stratified, and cluster samples
- Identify the considerations for deciding sample size

After refining a topic and thinking about how to study it, researchers also have to specify who or what to study. Can they study everyone who fits their research interests or do they need to select a subgroup of them? If they select a subgroup, how do they decide who to ask to be in the study? How many people should they study? All of these questions relate to the issue of sampling.

Let's take the first question of whether to study everybody or to select a sub-group instead. The answer largely depends on the research goal. If the research goal is to examine whether a specific program used by relatively few people works for those people, then researchers can probably just study all those people. This is what we call a **population**. A population is all of the people, groups, or artifacts (such as newspaper articles, court reports, etc.) that are relevant to the research question. If the population is small and the research question is specific, like testing a program, then researchers might be able to study the population. If the research goal is a little different and researchers are looking for relational comparisons, such as whether program A works better than program B, then researchers might also be able to study a population instead of a sample (Langbein, 2006). For example, Lum, Hibdon, Cave, Koper, and Merola (2011) wanted to test whether using license plate scanners in crime "hot spots" deterred automotive crime, such as auto theft or the use of stolen plates, better than the "business as usual" approach police traditionally used in those areas. They identified 30 hot spots in a two-jurisdiction area and studied all 30 by randomly assigning 15 to use the license plate technology and 15 to use standard operating procedures. They then looked at all the police logs for a 30-day period to compare effectiveness. Because these researchers compared the use of license plate scanners to their nonuse, they were looking for a relational comparison between these two approaches in just two areas (hot spots). They were not trying to generalize to a larger population, so a sample was not necessary (Langbein, 2006).

However, what if researchers want to study people who live in a specific city or state or who attend a large university? In those instances, the researchers probably can't study all the people who interest them because doing so would require way too much time and money. Sampling is the process of selecting a smaller group of people to observe from a larger population of interest. For example, Niven (2006) wanted to see how negative advertising affected voter turnout in a 2003 mayoral race in West Palm Beach, Florida. At the time of Niven's study, West Palm Beach had more than 80,000 residents, close to 50,000 of whom were registered voters. Niven realized that he could not study everyone in West Palm Beach. It would be too expensive and time-consuming; therefore, Niven selected a subset, called a **sample**, of 1,400 of them. To increase the chance that this subset would accurately represent the population of residents, he had to select them randomly, what researchers call a probability or random sample and which we will learn about soon. Niven then randomly assigned each person to one of seven treatment groups (which varied on the number of negative mailings) or to the control group (who received no negative mailings), and then selected a stratified random subsample of 400 people from his sample of 1,400 (essentially a sample of his sample) to participate in a follow-up survey. By using his selected sampling techniques, and thereby not having to go through the cost and time of studying all 50,000 or so registered voters in West Palm Beach, Niven, was able to learn that the more negative ads a subject received, the more likely that person was to turn out to vote. Thus, samples are a useful and important research tool; and, in this chapter, you will learn the different considerations for selecting samples, why random samples are so important, and how to actually select different types of random (probability) and nonprobability samples.

PHOTO 5.1 Surveying all eligible voters in a city would be way too difficult. Sampling makes it easier.

iStockphoto.com/PeteHendleyPhotography

UNITS OF OBSERVATION VS. UNITS OF ANALYSIS

It is easy to confuse units of observation and units of analysis because in many instances they are actually the same, so now is a good time to introduce that difference. In the most basic sense, **units of observation** is a sampling issue because it is an issue of where the data are collected from, which is what we will be discussing in this chapter. On the contrary, **units of analysis**, refers to what is being compared in data analysis and will be more relevant to our later chapters. Nonetheless, because there is a lot of similarities between how the two are classified, even if not how they are used, it is useful to discuss both now.

If I examined the average Scholastic Aptitude Test (SAT) scores of 25 public universities and 25 private ones, it is not the same as studying 25 students who go to public universities and 25 students who go to private ones. In the first example, I am selecting university-wide scores to compare and in the second I am selecting individual students and comparing them. In this hypothetical example, the units of observation and the units of analysis are the same in each part. However, units of observation and units of analysis can differ and that is where it becomes important to know which is what. For example, Dobbie and Fryer (2014) examined whether attending an exam school, which is a selective public high school that caters to the academically talented, rather than a mainstream public school affected college enrollment and graduation. They wanted to examine whether being in a school embodied only with high-achieving peers influenced college entrance and graduation. They found that, at least in the short term, the type of school attended generally had no effect on these outcomes (Dobbie & Fryer, 2014). Some of their information (such as entrance exam scores) were based on individual information they gathered (units of observation) but were analyzed based on group type (the school), which is a group unit of analysis. This is a good example of how units of observation and units of analysis can differ.

Common units of observation and analysis are individuals, groups, and social artifacts, with individuals probably being the most common of all. Researchers can sample and study individual behaviors, opinions, expectations, performance… you name it. If an individual does it, a researcher can study it. For example, Cole (2016) surveyed over 13,000 recently graduated high school seniors to see whether hours of sleep and the time someone got up for the day affected their SAT scores. Cole observed the sleep hours of individual students, so this is an example of an individual being the unit of analysis. By studying the *individual* reports of hours of sleep and time of waking, he found that students who reported that they woke up after 7 a.m. but got less than 8 hours of sleep, had SAT scores that were significantly higher than all the other groups.

Researchers might also study groups such as families, neighborhoods, schools, work organizations, and civic organizations. Our earlier hypothetical example of the average SAT scores at public versus private universities would be an example of groups as a unit of observation and analysis because I am selecting and comparing schools. Last, social science researchers can also study anything that is created by people and can be systematically observed. These units are called **social artifacts**. Common examples of social artifacts are songs, pictures, legal cases, or speeches, really anything that can be transcribed. For example, continuing with the SAT-themed examples, Kobrin, Deng, and Shaw (2011) analyzed over 6,000 essays that responded to 14 different essay prompts written for the 2006 SAT to examine, among other topics, whether there was a relationship between essay length and SAT essay score. They also examined

PHOTO 5.2 Researchers have to make sure that their conclusions fit their units of observation and analysis. If researchers select school-wide statistics, for example, they cannot make conclusions about the abilities of individual students.

istockphoto.com/Srdjanns74

whether students were rewarded for using the five-paragraph theme (introduction paragraph, three paragraphs of supporting points, one paragraph of conclusion) for writing. The units of observation and analysis were the essays themselves because the researchers examine each essay for its word count and organization and then related those measures to the test score, another social artifact. Never did the researchers have contact with the individual students themselves.

Unit of Observation and Analysis Risks

It is important to be able to understand both the units of observation and the units of analysis in order to determine whether the conclusions of the study are appropriate for the methods and statistics used. When units of observation or analysis are one type, but conclusions are made about another, any research conclusions are inappropriate. To go back to the example at the beginning of this section, what if I sampled the SAT scores of 25 public universities and 25 private ones and found that the average SAT scores between the two types of schools were not statistically significant? Does this mean that students in private schools are no smarter than students in public schools? Not necessarily. Making this conclusion would be inappropriate and an example of the ecological fallacy because researchers cannot make conclusions about small units of analyses (e.g., individual students) when they collect data from larger units of observation (such as private vs. public schools).

The mismatch can move in the opposite direction as well. When researchers study individuals and aggregate them (group them) to make conclusions about groups, they have to be careful not to partake in reductionism. Reductionism takes complex issues and reduces them into simple group differences without considering the individual experiences that might have produced the findings. For example, if a researcher interviewed parents about their level of teen

---

BOX 5.1

THE RELATIONSHIP BETWEEN UNITS OF OBSERVATION AND UNITS OF ANALYSIS

Units of Observation (Data Collected About)	Units of Analysis (Conclusions Are Made About)	
	Individuals	Groups
Individuals	Private high school students tend to have higher standardized test scores than public high school students **Correct Alignment**	Students who attend private schools have higher standardized test scores so private schools create smarter students **Possible Ecological Fallacy**
Groups	The standardized test scores of private high schools are higher than those of public high schools, therefore, the students at private high schools are smarter **Possible Reductionism**	Based on a comparison of average standardized test scores, private high schools have higher standardized test scores on average than public high schools **Correct Alignment**

LEARNING CHECK 5.1: UNITS OF OBSERVATION AND ANALYSIS

1. What is the difference between units of observation and units of analysis?

2. It is appropriate for researchers to use groups as units of observation and make conclusions about individuals (units of analysis)? Why/why not?

3. In an elementary school, administrators want to see whether some classrooms are higher performing than others so they compare the average classroom scores on an elementary standardized test. What are the units of observation?

Answers to be found at the end of the chapter.

monitoring and interviewed teens about their self-reported delinquent behavior and found that the two factors were inversely related (meaning low parental monitoring is associated with higher teen delinquency), the researchers would be committing reductionism if they concluded that in order to reduce teen delinquency, all one needs to do is to improve parental monitoring. In this instance, the researcher *reduced* the complex issue of teen delinquency to parental monitoring and ignored other factors such as the teen's connectedness to school, the job opportunities in the area that would give the teen other means of spending his/her time, and whether the teen was involved in any extracurricular activities (which also reduce the time opportunity for delinquency). Dobbie and Fryer (2014) did not fall vulnerable to reductionism because their goal was to compare school types (groups) to see if the type of *school* attended affected college attendance and graduation. They did not make any conclusions about the capabilities or characteristics of the types of students who attended these schools.

SAMPLING TERMS

There is still one more step to cover before I go into detail about sampling techniques, and that is to address some relevant sampling terminology. Let's do this through a hypothetical example where I want to do a version of Niven's study among the students in my department to see how negative ads affect student attitudes toward presidential candidates. I teach at a private, northeastern university of about 4,000 students. In this instance, I may be tempted to say that my population is college students. However, as I said, given that my university is comparatively small, is on the northeastern coast of the United States, and is private, it is possible that my population of students differs in some ways from a population of students at a large (let's say over 30,000), public university on the west coast. That's why researchers frequently distinguish between a population, which is all possible people who fit a possible criteria, and the **study population**, which is the population from which our samples are drawn. The idea is that study populations are similar to larger populations, but in many instances, we just don't know really how similar they are. Therefore, for our example, all the students in my department constitute my study population.

There are two broad types of samples: those that are selected randomly and those that are not. Those that are selected randomly, as I have already said, are formally called **probability samples**, whereas those that are not selected randomly are called **nonprobability samples**. One of the key factors determining whether a random sample (I will use the terms random and probability sampling interchangeably) is feasible is whether the researcher can obtain an accurate sampling frame. **Sampling frames** are a list of all the elements in a study population; **elements** are the individual units of observation about which a researcher is collecting information, such as individual college students, voters, people in a drug court program, poor mothers, etc. As I said, in many instances, individual elements, or our units of observation, are similar to the units of analysis, although the latter is usually a term for data analysis and the former is a term of sampling (Babbie, 1995). So, in my example, I could obtain a sampling frame of all freshmen to senior students (my elements) in my department.

FIGURE 5.1 ● POPULATIONS, SAMPLES, AND SAMPLING ERROR

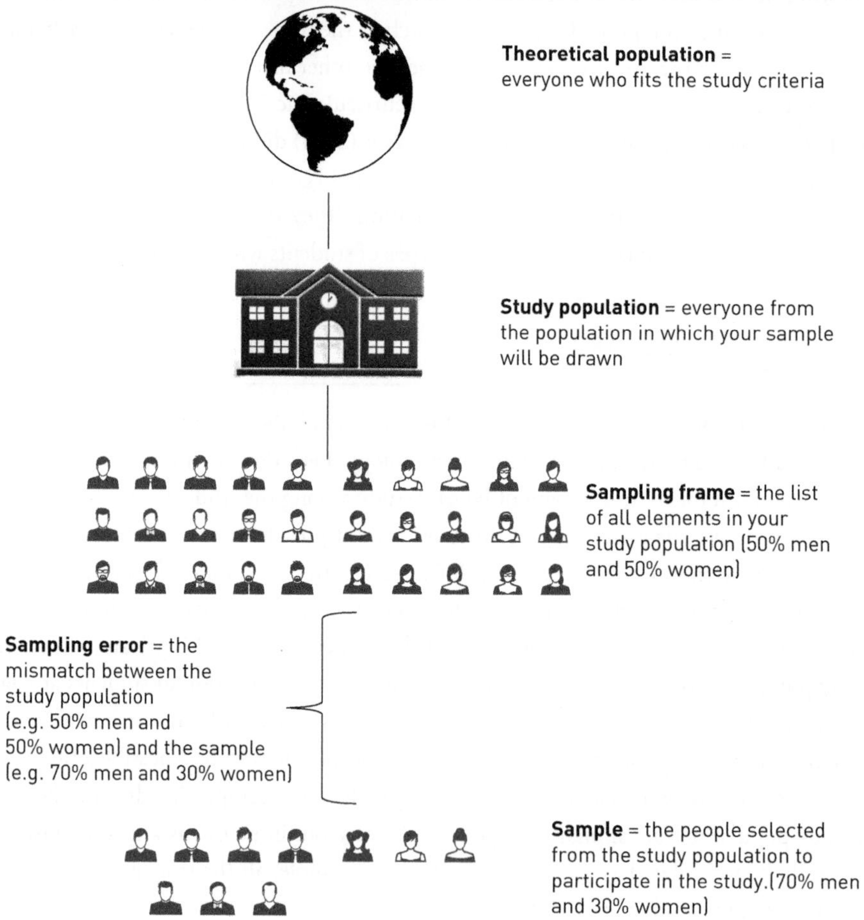

Theoretical population = everyone who fits the study criteria

Study population = everyone from the population in which your sample will be drawn

Sampling frame = the list of all elements in your study population (50% men and 50% women)

Sampling error = the mismatch between the study population (e.g. 50% men and 50% women) and the sample (e.g. 70% men and 30% women)

Sample = the people selected from the study population to participate in the study.(70% men and 30% women)

When researchers sample, no matter how hard they try, they are likely to have some mismatch in representation between the sample they select and the study population it is supposed to represent. For example, 13% of the study population may be African American; but, in a sample, only 5% of it is African American, therefore African Americans would be under-represented in this instance. This mismatch is called **sample error**. If researchers conduct a random sample, they can estimate within a certain level of confidence (such as 95% or 99%) how large the sample error might be. This confidence is called the **confidence level**, and researchers can set it at anything, although 95% is the common minimum usually accepted in the social and behavioral sciences. Figure 5.1 illustrates the relationship between study populations, samples, and sampling error; but to more fully understand this, you need to understand probability theory. So let's get to that next.

PROBABILITY SAMPLING

Of the two broad classes of samples, probability sampling is the type researchers choose when they want to make conclusions about the study population based on the sample; therefore, they need to select a sample that is representative, meaning accurate, of the larger study population. For probability samples, elements are selected randomly in a way that every element has an equal chance (probability) of being selected to be in a study. This sounds straightforward—all a researcher has to do is make sure everyone who qualifies for the study has the same chance of being selected for the study, right? Well, not quite. For example, in my hypothetical study about negative campaign ads and students in my department, if I decided to "randomly" select students who attended some of my colleagues' classes, would every student *really* have an equal chance of being selected? The answer is: no. First, students who skipped that class that day wouldn't have a chance of being selected. Second, a student who I have a particularly good rapport with might have a high chance of being selected to participate because even without thinking about it I might find him/her to be approachable. Third, the opposite also applies: if there is a student in the class who I know does not like me, I may be *less* likely to ask that student to participate because I do not want to make the student or myself uncomfortable. Even if I try to get around this by *purposely* asking that person to participate, this *still* violates the condition of random chance. Do you get the idea? Anything that changes—in any direction— the likelihood of someone being selected for a study means that the people (elements) do not have an equal probability of selection, and, therefore, would not be a probability sample.

Another challenge is that a researcher might not be able to obtain a complete, accurate sampling frame. Although I am less concerned about this with my hypothetical example (because our sampling frame is rather specific and small), what if I wanted to study all 4,000 students at my university? If I went to the department in charge of university housing to get a list of all undergraduates, I would only really be getting a list of undergraduates who live on campus. I would be missing the undergraduates who are commuters or who live in off-campus housing. So, once again, my study is not necessarily representative of *undergraduate* students at my university. Therefore, researchers need to be very careful that the sampling frames they obtain are truly complete lists of the study population they want to use for their research and they need to be clear about any limitations in their sampling process, such as who they are not able to include in a sampling frame.

So why is this idea of random chance so important? Well, because researchers cannot know how a population, even a study population, would *really* respond to study questions unless they study everyone in that population. However, as I mentioned, doing so would require more time and money. Therefore, researchers want to study a subgroup of a population, a sample, to make estimates about what the population, which a researcher cannot observe, would answer. If a sample is randomly selected, researchers can be reasonably sure that the answers to their questions will form a pattern in a predictable manner that helps the researcher get an idea of how the population should respond. In other words, samples provide information that researchers can observe about variables, called statistics, that they can use to make conclusions about the corresponding population values, which we cannot observe. Researchers frequently use different symbols to distinguish between observable statistics and unobservable population parameters (Figure 5.2). For example, when researchers are discussing statistics, the average (for interval/ratio levels of measurement) is commonly indicated by "$\overline{X}$" and in the case of proportions, P_s. For populations, the average is "μ" whereas the proportion (for nominal or ordinal measures) is indicated by P_μ. When researchers want to generalize from samples to populations, doing so frequently requires statistics, and these different symbols help researchers know what information to put where in the formulas.

But I still haven't fully answered the original question "How do we know that our sample can estimate population parameters?" The answer lies in the **central limit theorem**. Let's take a new example, one with a small, manageable population so I can visually illustrate how this theorem works. Let's pretend that I work in a university with only 10 total faculty members. In other words, these 10 faculty are the entire population of faculty at this university. I ask each faculty member to show me the amount of cash they have in their wallet, as illustrated in Figure 5.3.

As I said, because these are the only faculty at this school, they are my entire study population and I can actually calculate the average amount of money in the wallets of this study population. If I add up the amount in each faculty member's wallet (the total equals $180) and divide by the total number of faculty ($n = 10$), I find that the average amount of money faculty members have in their wallet is $18. This $18 is the **population parameter**, or "μ". Remember,

FIGURE 5.2 ●	SYMBOLS FOR STATISTICS AND POPULATIONS		
	Sample		**Population Parameter**
Known?	Yes		No
Relationship?		Sample (known) estimates population parameter (unknown)	
Symbol: Interval / Ratio Variable	$\overline{X}$	estimates	μ
Symbol: Nominal / Ordinal Variable	P_s	estimates	P_μ

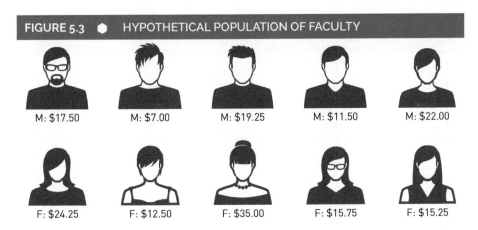

FIGURE 5.3 ● HYPOTHETICAL POPULATION OF FACULTY

M: $17.50 M: $7.00 M: $19.25 M: $11.50 M: $22.00

F: $24.25 F: $12.50 F: $35.00 F: $15.75 F: $15.25

in most instances, researchers do *not* have the population parameter, μ, because the only way to know this is to study the entire population. That is why I wanted to do this example with such as small hypothetical population—so we could see it.

If I decide to sample one faculty member to represent all the faculty, I shut my eyes to randomly pick the faculty member, and I end up with the person who has $7.00 in his wallet; this would be way off from the true population value of $18. This mismatch is the sample error. In reality, I wouldn't know I was far off (remember, I really wouldn't know the population parameter), but if I make conclusions about the study population based on this one member, my conclusions would not be very accurate. Now let's pretend I put this person back into the study population, shut my eyes again, and randomly drew another sample of one person and got the female who has $15.25 in her wallet…closer, but still off.

But what happens if I draw a sample of two people? If I draw a sample of two, I would average those scores, based on what I can observe in the sample. This is the **sample statistic** $\bar{X}$. If I randomly select the female faculty who has $24.25 and the male faculty who has $17.50, their statistics average to $20.88, which is closer to the $18, but still off. If I put these folks back, randomly selected a sample of three people instead of two, and drew the faculty who have $15.75, $22, and $17.5, now my sample mean would be $18.42, which is even closer to my true population mean of $18. As my sample size increases, the likelihood of getting a statistic that is closer to the true population value (parameter) also increases, and Figure 5.4 shows how a plot of sample means would look as the sample size increases.

There are some important things to notice across the graphs. First, you might notice that as the sample size increases, the graphs look more like a curve you have probably seen before called the normal curve. In the normal curve, the peak, the part with the most points, is the true population value. Researchers like the normal curve because it behaves in a predictable manner, and this helps researchers relate the statistics they can see from the sample to the population parameter that they can't see, and I will show you how researchers use the normal curve for statistics in Chapters 12 and 13. The other point you may notice is that the normal curve becomes narrower, or more precise, as the sample size increases. In fact, one way of reducing sampling error (remember, how far off our statistic is from the true population value) is to increase the sample size and to increase my confidence level. Think about it. This makes

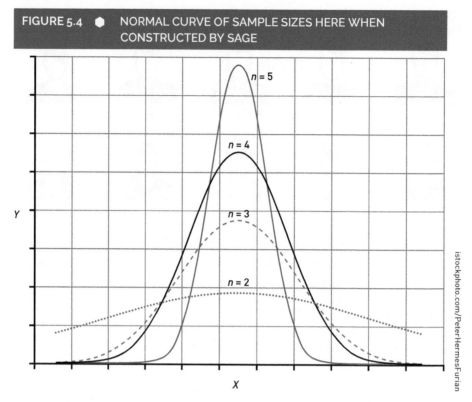

FIGURE 5.4 ● NORMAL CURVE OF SAMPLE SIZES HERE WHEN CONSTRUCTED BY SAGE

sense because if I increase the confidence level from 95% to 99%, I am more sure of my findings (almost 100% sure now). The trade-off (and there are *always* trade-offs) is that my interval is wider because I have now covered almost all (99%) of the normal curve. With a wider interval, my estimate becomes less precise. However, since larger samples create narrower normal curves, the corresponding interval will also be narrow, or more precise. Some researchers have found that this payoff of increased sample size works until samples reach about 2,000, after which the real gains in precision become very modest and may not necessarily justify the higher cost of these studies (Leon-Guerrero & Frankfort-Nachmias, 2018)

Based on this example, probability theory is now more easily understood. **Probability theory** stems from the central limit theorem, which argues that if we take multiple samples of significant sample size (as illustrated by the different graphs of increasing sample size in Figure 5.4), the means of those samples will organize themselves along the normal curve, where the midpoint will approach the true population value. This is true for any variable—whether it is cash in faculty wallets, number of days someone receives cash assistance, the number of online friends a college freshman has…you name it. Because of this predictability, probability theory argues that researchers can actually estimate, through statistical tests, how closely their observed statistic (known) is clustered around the true population value (unknown). In other words, researchers can actually estimate the sampling error. We also know that one sample error in each direction (high and low) of the mean will account for approximately 68% of all the sample means in that distribution, two standard errors in each direction will account for 95% of all the sample means, and three standard errors will account for 99% of all the sample means. Again, I will revisit this in Chapters 12 and 13; but for now, it is enough to understand that if samples are selected randomly, researchers can expect their samples to behave like this.

LEARNING CHECK 5.2: CENTRAL LIMIT THEOREM AND PROBABILITY THEORY

1. What is the relationship between statistics and a population parameter?

2. What is sampling error and how can we estimate it?

3. What happens to the normal curve when the sample size increases?

Answers to be found at the end of the chapter.

Now, researchers don't usually draw 10, 45, or 100 samples of any population. Researchers only draw one. But again, using this information, researchers know that if 68% of their (hypothetical now) multiple samples would be one standard error in each direction, then any *one sample* has a 68% chance of doing the same. We also know that any one sample has a 95% chance of falling between plus/minus *two* standard errors in each direction of the mean, and a 99% chance of falling between plus/minus *three* standard errors of the mean. Again, I will revisit this in more detail in the chapters on statistics, so, for now, let's focus on learning how to draw probability samples.

Types of Probability Samples

Simple Random Sampling

So, now that we know *why* we want to do a probability sample, the next step is learning *how*. The most basic type of probability sample is a simple random sample and it is a good place to start because, as the name implies, it is "simple." The steps for selecting a simple random sample are as follows:

1. Obtain an accurate sampling frame of the study population of interest.

2. Number that sampling frame from 1 to N, where N is the study population size.

3. Select a sample size (more soon).

4. Using a table of random numbers or a computer package with a random number generator, select your sample.

   a. If using a computer package, follow the instructions for your specific package. If you don't have a manual, the Internet can be a great place to find the relevant instructions.

   b. If using a table of random numbers, do the following:

      1. Shut your eyes and pick a random start between 1 and N.

      2. Reading left to right, ignoring spaces (any spaces are simply there to make the numbers easier to read) and line breaks, look at digit increments that correspond to your study population size, selecting however many unique elements (meaning, skip repeat numbers—obviously, you can't study the same person twice!) you need between 1 and N to obtain your sample.

Let's go back to my original hypothetical study of the students in my department. To make sure my sampling frame is as accurate as possible, I need to make sure it is well-defined. So let's clarify that I want to study all the declared sociology majors who are between freshman and senior year. To make this example even more manageable, let's also pretend that my study population only has 60 students in total. Again, in reality, I know that if my study population is so small, I would probably just study the population instead of a sample; but I am going to ask you to suspend disbelief so I can illustrate the process of this theory.

So, for this example, I would obtain a sampling frame of all 60 freshmen to senior sociology majors and number that list from 1 to 60, as shown in Box 5.2. Let's also pretend that we want to sample 20 individuals, so our projected sample size is shown as $n = 20$. (The lower case is to show it is a sample.)

Based on what I described, if using a table of random numbers, I want to pick a random start between 1 and 60 to identify my first element. A subset of a table of random numbers appears both in Box 5.2 and after it.

BOX 5.2
SIMPLE AND SYSTEMATIC SAMPLING

Sampling frame of 60 Sociology/Criminal Justice majors—freshman to senior years

1. Adams, Kim	16. Laker, Roberta	31. Rain, Ross	46. Stein, Mickey
2. Adams, Tony	17. Lee, Sarah	32. Rank, Stephanie	47. Stevens, Janine
3. Aiken, Alexandria	18. Lewis, Edward	33. Rener, Sherry	48. Sullivan, Amanda
4. Baird, Janet	19. Martinez, Jennifer	34. Roth, Wilson	49. Tabor, Joyce
5. Baker, Christa	20. Mara, Chad	35. Rowan, Beverly	50. Takach, Terek
6. Cho, Andrew	21. Mensch, Steven	36. Rowe, Lori	51. Tallin, Ida
7. Clark, Albert	22. Mesola, Wendall	37. Ruane, Ramond	52. Talbot, Liam
8. Feliz, Marvin	23. Nadar, Lashawn	38. Ruddy, Evan	53. Talerico, Thomas
9. Frein, Carl	24. Nelson, Nancy	39. Rudis, Josie	54. Tan, Doris
10. Gaines, Lennie	25. Nevins, Mara	40. Rup, Raven	55. Tanner, Daryl
11. Heinz, Sally	26. Oakland, John	41. Rush, Dave	56. Tanski, Debra
12. Herbert, Danielle	27. Opp, Patrick	42. Sherer, Tim	57. Thomas, John
13. James, Robert	28. Peters, James	43. Schmidt, Kerry	58. Thomas, Pauline
14. Kim, Daniel	29. Peterson, Lanie	44. Shear, John	59. Wendt, Kelly
15. Konda, Herb	30. Polan, Laura	45. Shemaker, Robert	60. Wilkes, Ken

Random numbers:

28374	29560	03827	17327	33827
30283	84**7**72	35736	10264	38265
55600	39911	399⬚0	20890	44923
38622	40383	90081	58223	09231
48274	31001	38579	83885	10472
85739	31319	22957	46259	45285

Simple Random Sample Selected (*n* = 20)		Systematic Random Sample (*n* = 20) *k* = 3	
23. Nadar, Lashawn	39. Rudis, Josie	2. Adams, Tony	32. Rank, Stephanie
57. Thomas, John	02. Adams, Tony	5. Baker, Christa	35. Rowan, Beverly
36. Rowe, Lori	08. Feliz, Marvin	8. Feliz, Marvin	38. Ruddy, Evan
10. Gaines, Lennie	44. Shear, John	11. Heinz, Sally	41. Rush, Dave
26. Oakland, John	33. Rener, Sherry	14. Kim, Daniel	44. Saar, John
43. Schmidt, Kerry	22. Mesola, Wendall	17. Lance, Sarah	47. Stevens, Janine
55. Tanner, Daryl	40. Rup, Raven	20. Lloyd, Chad	50. Takach, Terek
60. Wilkes, Ken	38. Ruddy, Evan	23. Nadar, Lashawn	53. Talerico, Thomas
03. Aiken, Alexandria	58. Thomas, Pauline	26. Oakland, John	56. Tanski, Debra
11. Heinz, Sally	30. Polan, Laura	29. Peterson, Lanie	59. Wendt, Kelly

I shut my eyes, wave my pencil around a few times, and then drop the point. Looking at the section from a table of random numbers, my start (**bolded and italicized**) is the "7" in the "84*7*72" that appears in the second column, second row. I look in two-digit increments from that pencil point because my study population size of 60 has two digits. My first number that would be selected is "77." This is too high, as I only have 60 total people in my sampling frame. Therefore, I ignore this number, continue reading in two-digit increments left to right, and see that my second number is "23." (Remember, the spaces are just for ease of visibility.) This is between 1 and 60, so element #23 is the first element selected to be in my sample. I would continue reading left to right with: 57, 36, 10, 26, 43, 82 (ignored), 65 (ignored) until I have 20 (my sample size) unique (nonrepeat) numbers between 1 and 60. You can see all the elements that would be selected for this sample by looking at the "Simple Random Sample" column in Box 5.2.

As you can probably see, this is a pretty "simple" way of obtaining your sample. However, it is often not a very efficient way. If the study population is large, like it would be if I wanted to study all 4,000 students at my university instead of just those in my department, I would be looking at four-digit increments; and, if I was using a table of random numbers, I am likely to have a lot more numbers in that table *not* apply (e.g., be higher than your sample size) than apply. Think about it. If I am looking for numbers between 1 and 4,000, there would be 5,999 total numbers (numbers 4,001–9,999)—more than my total study population size—that do *not* fit my sampling frame and would have to be ignored. This also does not count the repeat numbers that need to be ignored as well. This relates to the second point. Simple random sampling gets tedious fast if a researcher is drawing a large sample. Furthermore, if the phone rings, my spouse comes home and interrupts me, I leave for the bathroom, whatever, it can be easy to lose my place and then have to start over. Even if I am using a computer program, I might have to input the elements into the program or adapt them somehow to make the program feasible. This too takes time. So, simple random sample is simple, yes; but, it is really only good for a limited type of study population.

Systematic Random Sampling

One approach that tries to address the efficiency issues of simple random sampling is systematic random sampling. In systematic sampling, researchers sample every **kth** element where **k** is a sampling interval that is calculated by taking the study population size and dividing it by the total sample size. If we go back to my original sample of 20 sociology majors from my study population of 60, my interval equals 60/20 or 3. If k was not a whole number, since I can't sample stray arms and legs, I would round this figure to a whole number where anything .5 or higher gets rounded up to the next whole number and .49 or lower gets rounded down. I then use the interval to select elements once I have a random start that is between 1 and k. The steps of systematic sampling are:

1. Obtain an accurate sampling frame of the study population of interest.

2. Number that sampling frame from 1 to N, where N is the study population size.

3. Decide on a sample size. (I will discuss this soon.)

4. Calculate a sampling interval k that is equal to the study population size divided by the sample size.

5. Using a table of random numbers or a computer package with a random number generator, select a random start between 1 and *k*. The first number between 1 and *k* that you select is the first element in your sample.

6. Sample every *k*th element from the starting element in #5 until you reach your full sample size.

Let's explore this process in a bit more detail. Because my interval, *k*, is 3 in my example, I need to find a random start between 1 and 3. So if I shut my eyes, drop a pencil on the 8 (indicated by the boxed number in the set 39980 in Box 5.2), I would just read left to right in the digit increments that correspond to my interval size looking for a number between 1 and *k*. In this instance, that number would be "2." That means that element 2 is the first element to be selected for my sample, followed by 5 (2 + 3), 8 (5 + 3), 11 (8 + 3), 14, 17, etc. I continue with this until I have my desired sample size of 20. The elements that would be selected using this method also appear in Learning Check 5.4 under the "Systematic Sampling" column. You will see, that not all the same elements would be selected depending on what technique I used. That's OK. The point is that regardless of the technique, each element has an equal chance of being selected.

Notice how much faster systematic sampling is over simple random sampling and it still involves random selection because the start is random. In fact, this is so much faster that I could feasibly use this method if I wanted to study all 4,000 students at my university. Say I wanted to sample 200 of the 4,000 students. Using systematic sampling, my sampling unit would be 4,000/200 or 20. Once I pick a random start between 1 and 20 (here looking in 2-digit increments), I simply have to identify every 20th person until I reach 200 people. Still pretty fast.

However, one major caveat with this technique is that one has to make sure there are no patterns in the sampling frame that would lead to bias. For example, if I do a systematic sample of dorm students to explore students' views of dorm life, based on the structure of the dorms, there will be patterns in who is selected. In other words, in a systematic sample, I might end up with a sample of people who all live in the northeast corner of the dorm overlooking garbage bins because of the systematic nature of dorm structure. These students might be less satisfied with dorm life than if I ended up with a sample of students who lived on the southwest side of the building overlooking a pretty campus park. Paying attention to possible patterns in the sampling frame, therefore, is a major consideration for this type of selection.

Stratified Random Sampling

However, as with simple random sampling, there is still a chance that some groups might be under or over-represented in the sample compared to their actual representation in the population. Remember the study population and sample shown in Figure 5.1? In the study population, 50% was male and 50% was female, but in the sample that was randomly selected,

70% was male and 30% was female. I said that this mismatch was the sampling error, and one way to reduce this risk is to do a stratified random sample, where the original study population is separated into groups (called **strata**) that are relevant to the phenomena being studied and then selected randomly (using any other probability sampling techniques) within those groups. For example, Welty et al. (2016) wanted to examine sex and racial/ethnic differences in the prevalence of substance-use disorders among young adulthoods who were delinquent in their youth. In order to obtain a sufficiently diverse sample and to reduce sampling error, Welty and colleagues stratified their sample based on sex, race/ethnicity, age, and legal status. Separating the study population into strata decreases sampling error because now the subgroups are more alike, or homogeneous, based on at least the characteristic that was used to stratify. It is this increased homogeneity on the stratification variable that works to reduce sample error.

There are two types of stratified sampling. The first is proportionate stratified sampling where the proportion of each strata sampled is the same as the proportion of that group in the population. Let's got back to our hypothetical study of students. If I want to do a proportionate stratified sample that increases the likelihood of accurate racial representation, I would first separate my original study population into strata or groups based on race. Figure 5.5 shows that 30% of my study population is white, 20% are Hispanic, 20% are African American, and 10% are Asian American.

I now treat each strata as its own unique study population from which I will sample separately. In other words, I no longer have one study population of 60 students, I have four study populations, one for each separate racial strata. One study population is of the 30 white, non-Hispanic students, another has 12 African American students, a third has 12 Hispanic students, and my fourth has 6 Asian/Pacific Islander students. In a proportionate stratified sample, each group's sample representation reflects that group's proportionate representation in the study population. Therefore, if 50% of my study population is white students, then 50% of my sample of 20 students needs to be white as well. This means I will select 10 white students (20 * .50 = 10) from the white strata. Similarly, I need 20% of our sample to be African American and 20% to be Hispanic, so I would select four students from each of those strata (20 * .20 = 4); and I would select two students who are Asian/Pacific Islander from that strata because they are 10% of the study population (20 * .10 = 2). Keep in mind, the stratification technique just tells the researcher how many from each group needs to be selected; it is not the actual selection of elements. Once the sample size of each group is determined by the proportions representative of the study population, the researcher uses any other probability technique, such as simple random or systematic sampling, to actually separately select the determined number of elements from each strata.

However, sometimes representation is so small that researchers might need to *over-sample* from a group to increase the chances that they will get enough responses for accurate analysis and generalization. In this instance, researchers might want to do a disproportionate stratified sample. Let's continue to work with our sociology department example. Although obviously, all the sample sizes discussed are too low for meaningful analysis (remember, this example is

FIGURE 5.5 ⬡ HYPOTHETICAL STRATIFIED SAMPLE OF STUDENTS

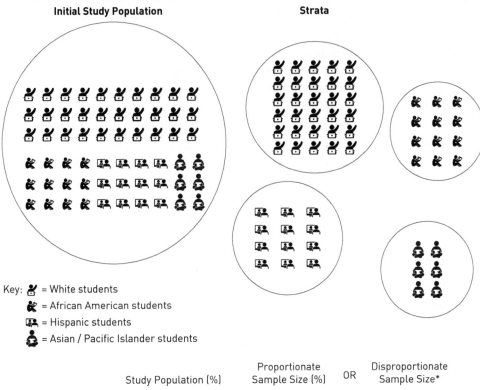

Key: = White students
= African American students
= Hispanic students
= Asian / Pacific Islander students

	Study Population (%)	Proportionate Sample Size (%)	OR	Disproportionate Sample Size*
White	30 (50%)	10 (50%)		5
Hispanic	12 (20%)	4 (20%)		5
African American	12 (20%)	4 (20%)		5
Asian / Pacific Islander	6 (10%)	2 (10%)		5
	N = 60	N = 20		N = 20

* And would need to calculate weights for each strata

hypothetical just to illustrate the process), the sample size of two for Asian/Pacific Islanders is *really* low. In more realistic settings, researchers generally want to make sure that each possible combination of variable values has at least 10 observations in the final sample size. When groups are small, even before researchers distribute them across different variable values, they might want to increase the number from this group in the sample and decrease the number from other, larger groups, like non-Hispanic whites in my example. You may be thinking: "Wait? I can just pick any number I want? Why bother calculating proportions in the first place then?" Well, the answer is not so simple. When you pick strata sample sizes without basing them on their corresponding proportionate representation in the study population, their proportions are no longer representative of that study population. Therefore researchers would have to make up for that fundamentally unscientific strata sample size later by weighting their responses to bring the sample back to study population representation.

In my department example, if I choose to do a disproportionate sample, I might decide to sample five students from each of our four races. I don't need to make the numbers across groups even; in fact, I probably would not. However, as I have such a small hypothetical sample size anyway, I did so here, otherwise there would be little point of any change. In order to return the groups to the proportionate representation in the study population, I would have to instruct the statistical program that I decide to use to take the response of each white, non-Hispanic student (for example) and multiply that response by its corresponding pre-calculated weight. I would have to do this for the three other strata as well and their corresponding weights would generally be different. There are many ways to calculate sample weights, and a full discussion of the nuances of weighting is more appropriate in an advanced research methods class. However, a basic, "get the job done" weight is to take the proportionate sample size (where the sample size did reflect patterns in the study population) and divide that by the disproportionate sample size you selected (which does not). For the White, non-Hispanic subjects, each weight would be 2 (10/5). Therefore, what every white, non-Hispanic student in my sample says would count for what two non-Hispanic white students in the study population would say.

Depending on the size of the study population and sample, researchers can choose to stratify on as many variables as they want. Remember, Welty et al. (2016) stratified on four different variables (sex, race/ethnicity, age, and legal status); but the more variables, the more complicated the sampling process becomes as well. Therefore, most researchers will stratify on only one or two variables. To summarize the steps of stratified sampling:

1. Obtain a sampling frame of the study.

2. Decide on a stratification variable(s).

3. Assign each element in the sampling frame to one strata for each variable or combination of variables.

4. Number the individual strata from 1 to N_s where N_s is the size of that individual strata. Treat each strata now as its own study population with a corresponding sampling frame.

5. Decide on a total sample size.

6. Decide how that total sample size will be split across the strata by deciding to use a proportionate or disproportionate technique.

7. Sample separately within strata, treating each strata as its own unique study population and using one of the other three probability sampling techniques discussed. Therefore, if I have four strata and I decide to do simple random sampling, I would have four unique starts on the table of random numbers and I might be looking at four different number ranges depending on the size of each stratum.

Cluster Sample

All of the probability sample techniques discussed so far imply that the researcher has access to a fairly manageable and accurate sampling frame of elements. Frequently, however, this is not the case. For example, maybe I didn't want to limit the study to students in my department, but instead, I wanted to study all the undergraduate students in my university. Even at my comparatively small university, I really would not want to deal with a list of 4,000 college students! In those instances, researchers sometimes have to break the larger study population into smaller sample units to make the sampling frame more manageable. Researchers then take repeated random samples of sampling units of decreasing size until they obtain a manageable sampling frame of elements. This process is called cluster or multistage sampling. In my example, I might first get a list of all the undergraduate majors offered at my school and include "undeclared" as a major as well (in order to avoid missing freshmen who have not declared a major by my study date). Let's say there are 61 different majors. The majors would be my first sampling unit. I can then randomly select, using any of the previously mentioned techniques, 20 majors (for example) from the 61 listed. Once I select those 20 majors, I can obtain a list of all the students in those 20 majors and the students would be my second sampling unit. Based on that list, I can then randomly select, again using any of the previous techniques, 100 students to actually study. In my example, we used a two-stage cluster process (majors and then students). It is not unusual for studies to involve even more stages. For example, Keyes, Hamilton, and Kandel (2016) used the Monitoring the Future study to examine whether adult drug behavior is shaped by adolescent drug experiences. The Monitoring the Future study is a representative sample of U.S. high school students. Obviously, there are *a lot* of high school students in the United States at any given moment and

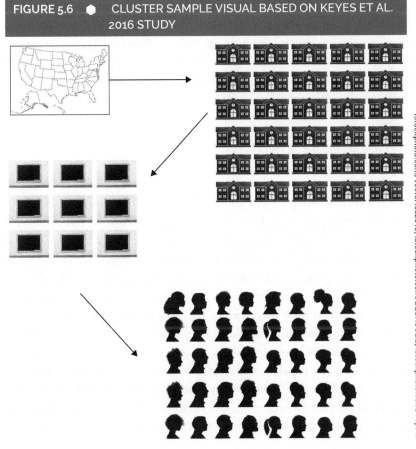

FIGURE 5.6 ◆ CLUSTER SAMPLE VISUAL BASED ON KEYES ET AL. 2016 STUDY

LEARNING CHECK 5.3: PROBABILITY SAMPLING TECHNIQUES

1. Use the sampling frame and information in Box 5.2 to draw a simple random sample of 15 observations from that sampling frame, pretending that your random start is the "2" in the 1st row, 4thcolumn number block of "17327." The 15 elements are listed at the end of this learning check for you to review your answers.

2. Use the sampling frame and information in Box 5.2 to draw a systematic random sample of 15 observations if your starting point is the first "8" in the 5th row, 4th column set of numbers "83885." The 15 elements are listed at the end of this learning check for you to review your answers.

3. If I wanted to do a proportionate stratified sample of students shown in Figure 5.5, but I wanted my sample size to be 30, what would my corresponding sample size be for each group?

Answers to be found at the end of the chapter.

obtaining an accurate sampling frame of them would be impossible. So to make the study population more manageable, those who conduct the Monitoring the Future study first select a random sample of geographical areas (sampling unit 1), then from those areas selected in the first stage, they obtain a random sample of one or more schools in each area (sampling unit 2), then a selection of classes (sampling unit 3) from which up to 350 students may be included (Johnston, O'Malley, Miech, Bachman, & Schulenberg, 2014; Keyes et al., 2016).

Therefore cluster samples are an efficient way of managing large populations for whom obtaining an accurate sampling frame of elements is too difficult. However, again, everything in research comes at a price. The price here is that every time researchers select a sample, they potentially introduce sampling error; but on the positive side, they have a better chance of getting an accurate sampling frame that would not have been feasible otherwise.

NONPROBABILITY SAMPLING

Sometimes random selection simply isn't necessary. For example, if I want to pre-test a survey I wrote before I invest in drawing a larger sample, I might give the survey to a nonrandom sample of my study population to see how well people understand it. In this instance, the main goal of the research is to refine the research instrument, not test a hypothesis or learn specific information about a population. Other times researchers might not be able to do a probability sample because they can't obtain an accurate sampling frame and/or they want to study a population that is hard to identify, like gang members or intravenous drug users. In these instances, researchers either don't need or can't do a random sample; therefore, they would use a nonprobability sampling technique. In nonprobability samples, every element does *not* have an equal probability of selection. As a result, it is harder to know whether your sample is representative of the population of interest, so researchers can't really use statistics to make inferences to a population. Therefore, any conclusions researchers make can only be about their specific sample, but for many of the types of studies I just mentioned, statistics and generalizing to a larger population may not be an overall research goal anyway.

There are many types of nonprobability samples, so I will only highlight some of the ones that are the most common to the behavioral and social sciences. One common technique is a **convenience** sample, sometimes also called an **accidental** or **haphazard** sample. In this instance, the researcher uses a sample that is easily identifiable as relevant to the research purpose but is largely selected based on more technical criteria like ease of accessibility, geographical proximity, and/or availability (Etikan, Musa, & Alkassim, 2015). Comedians like David Letterman and Conan O'Brien, for example, have essentially used this form of sampling when they ask "people on the street" questions to gauge Americans' knowledge (or lack thereof) of various national or world events.

In the second nonprobability technique, convenience samples are very similar to **purposive** samples. Like convenience samples, purposive samples are based on the subjects being easily available and willing to participate, but unlike a convenience sample, which fits a broader criteria of relevance, a purposive sample is *purposely* selected because the researcher believes that these subjects are proficient and/or well informed on the topic of interest based on their own direct experience or knowledge (Etikan et al., 2015). Samples of college students are sometimes purposive samples. Researchers who are interested in the views of college students and who work at colleges or universities may study the behavior of the students in their or their colleagues' classes, not because these students are representative of the college population, but because they are easily accessible to the researcher *and* the researcher knows that, as students of that college, the subjects have the relevant experiences to comment on the topic of interest.

A second type of nonprobability sample is a quota sample. Quota samples are the non-probabilistic equivalent of a stratified sample. Here the researcher aims to select participants from specific groups (e.g., male/females, young/middle age/older) in proportions that mirror the representation in the population; however, these individuals are not selected randomly.

istockphoto.com/Srdjanns74

PHOTO 5.3 Studying homeless people is an example of when a sampling frame is unattainable and a nonprobability sampling technique is necessary.

After leaving the Magic Kingdom at Disney World one day on vacation many years ago, my husband was approached by a Disney cast member to take a survey about his experience in the park that day. My husband is not a social scientist or researcher and he was about to decline the survey. I, seeing a possibility to link this experience to my classwork, was eager to participate in his place. However, when I offered to take the survey, the cast member very politely told me that they already had their "quota of women for the day" and they were looking for male participants. Because Disney cast members have no way of really getting a list of all people who enter the park on any given day, there is no sampling frame. But those doing research still recognize the need for some representation of different groups to obtain a more rounded concept of people's experiences. Hence, this quota sample.

Another common nonprobability technique is the snowball sample. This is essentially the "friend of a friend of a friend" technique and is most useful for hard-to-reach populations. For example, Lanigan and Burleson (2017) used an agency that licenses and trains foster parents as a starting point to identify foster parents with less than 2 years of experience and those with three or more to see how multiple child placements affected that family's ability to transition to the new child. Once initial foster families were identified via this agency, the families recommended other foster families for participation until the researchers had 10 volunteer families participating. Examples of populations for which this technique has been useful are sex trade workers, gang members, survivors of interpersonal violence, and homeless individuals, to name a few (Ding et al., 2005; Schalet, Hunt, & Joe-Laidler, 2003; Simon & Wallace, 2018). Here the researcher identifies a few people who fit the criteria of the population of interest and once these people agree to participate, the researcher asks them for suggestions of other possible participants and how to contact them. When researchers reach these individuals, they repeat the process of recommendations for others to participate. Hence, the sample size "snowballs" by word of mouth.

LEARNING CHECK 5.4: NONPROBABILITY SAMPLING TECHNIQUES

1. How are stratified and quota samples similar and different?

2. How does snowball sampling get its name?

3. What is the main limitation of using a nonprobability technique?

Answers to be found at the end of the chapter.

SAMPLE SIZE

So far I have been talking about how to select samples, but not how many elements to select. That is because deciding sample sizes is not a simple process and depends on many factors. One factor that affects the desired sample size is the purpose of the research. Research that is descriptive and involves relatively few variables allows for smaller sample sizes. However, when research has many variables, even for a descriptive study, or is aimed to test hypotheses, then you need larger samples.

Another consideration is the amount of sampling error one is willing to accept. In my discussion of central limit theorem and probability theory, I already covered that one way to reduce sampling error was to increase sample size; but bigger is only better to an extent. Huge samples are very expensive and, after a certain point, the benefit of going bigger decreases (Leon-Guerrer & Frankfot-Nachias, 2018). Furthermore, the more homogenous the population, the smaller the sample can be. This point relates to the material I covered in stratified sampling. When researchers break the larger study population into specific groups, they make the population homogenous on whatever that group characteristic is…which is why they can draw a smaller sub-sample from that group but still increase the chance of accuracy. Finally, researchers can also decide the sample size based on their desired level of precision. This involves using statistical formulas to decide what final sample size is necessary to achieve results within a selected confidence level (like 95%) and sampling error (like 4%). Being that the purpose of this book, however, is how to "get the job done," a discussion of how to use those formulas is more suited for a more advanced methods class.

You may realize that even with these considerations, I haven't given you a concrete "In instance _____, you need to sample _____ elements." You're right. That's because, as I have shown, that is difficult to do. There is a calculation called a **power analysis** that combines many of these factors into a statistical formula that produces desired sample size, but it is a bit statistically complicated. Therefore, it is beyond our goal of "getting the job done," even though your professor might choose to add this discussion on their own. So the good news is that you have some flexibility as long as you can clearly justify your decisions that led to your chosen sample size. The not-so-good news is that deciding what that sample size should be can still be challenging.

There is one final consideration. Frequently, when researchers discuss choosing a sample size, what they really mean is a *final* sample size. Different methods of observations, as you will learn in the next section of the book, have different response rates. Mailed surveys (Chapter 7), for example, have notoriously poor response rates. If, therefore, I decide I need a final sample of 200 people and I used mailed surveys to gather my information, based on my knowledge of mailed surveys, I know I can expect a response rate of about only 60%, despite my best efforts. Therefore I will need to *over-sample* in order to obtain a final sample of 200. To do this I take my desired final sample size and divide it by the proportion of responses I expect to obtain in order to figure out my *real* sample size for survey distribution. That means that here, I actually need to select about 340 elements to send my survey to (200/0.6 = 333.33 or about 340 to even out the numbers) in order to hope for a return of 200.

MAKING DECISIONS

This chapter presents a lot of considerations for deciding what type of sampling technique to use, and there are even more. However, what we covered here is enough to "get the job done" in most instances. In order to help navigate the main considerations, Figure 5.7 presents a summary flowchart to help you make the main sampling decisions.

FIGURE 5.7 ● SUMMARY FLOWCHART OF POSSIBLE SAMPLING DECISIONS

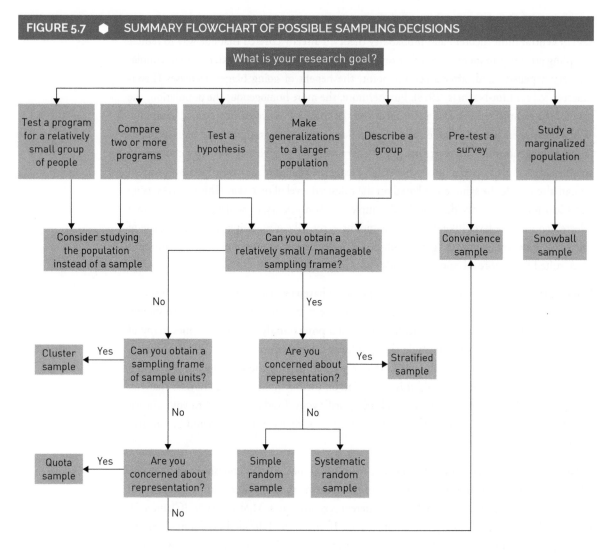

CHALLENGES

Even with our best intentions and planning, sometimes things go wrong when it comes to sampling. Here are some common problems with sampling and some suggestions of what to do if they occur.

1. **I am having a hard time identifying what an accurate study population or sampling frame may be.** Here the literature review that you learned about in Chapter 1 may be of help. You can read similar studies, see how they specified their study populations, and see where they obtained their sampling frames. Remember, one of the key issues is to always be specific about your study population and to try to obtain as accurate a sampling frame from it as possible. If you want to study the reasons behind why people purchase organic food, you might be tempted to sample housewives, presuming that they do the food shopping. However, housewives may be an inaccurate study population because most families today are dual-earners and

husbands may be sharing food shopping duties. Finding similar studies may clue you into this and you can adjust your sampling frame accordingly. For example, instead of sampling housewives, you can consider doing a cluster sample to reach households; once you contact a household, you can ask for whoever does the majority of the food shopping to participate in the study.

2. **I want to generalize to a larger population, but I can't get an accurate sampling frame.** Unfortunately, if you have no sampling frame, you can't do a probability sample, and you can't, with confidence, generalize to the population. The temptation may be to use statistical tests, such as those discussed in Chapter 13, to compare key characteristics of your sample to known values of the same characteristics in the population, hoping to statistically show that your sample is similar to the known population. However, your study will still technically be descriptive and ungeneralizable (Newcomer, Hatry, & Wholey, 2015). It will be in a "gray" area where any description you give is up to the reader to evaluate the relevance to the population.

3. **I do not have the resources to do a large probability sample to test my research question.** One possible direction is to alter your study population by making it more homogenous. Instead of cutting corners with sample size, it may be more appropriate to go back to your research topic and literature review and narrow the focus of your study (and therefore, your study population). For example, instead of learning what kindergarten to 12th-grade parents in a school district feel can be improved about their child's educational experiences, perhaps focus on what parents of high school students feel can be improved. As long as you make sure that your conclusions are *just* about high school parents and not parents of all school-aged children, your study can still be manageable and strong (at least with regard to sample selection). In fact, sometimes focusing on a specific group gives more useful information than focusing on a broad population poorly. Remember, no one study has to do everything.

4. **I conducted a probability sample, but my final sample is not representative of the study population.** Remember, random sampling increases the chance that your resulting sample is an accurate representation of the population; but issues like faulty sampling frames, patterns in nonresponse, general sample error, and/or a combination thereof (and of other factors not mentioned here) can still result in a nonrepresentative sample. If this occurs, you are definitely stuck. There are two common solutions, but neither is perfect. One option is to scrap the sample and start over by selecting a new sample and redoing the study. Obviously, this will be expensive and may not be feasible. Another option is to post-stratify. Here you separate the population into strata *after* you have done the study (and learned the sample is not representative) and correct the imbalance by weighting the observations in the data you already collected to make the sample representative again (kind of like a reverse disproportionate stratified sampling technique). This also isn't ideal because if you have biases in the sample, they will be reproduced—albeit in a weighted version—in the analysis. How to poststratify is beyond the scope of this book, but I did want to let you know that it was an option.

Key Terms

Central limit theorem

Confidence level

Ecological fallacy

Element

Nonprobability sample

Population

Population parameter

Probability sample

Reductionism

Sample

Sample error

Sample statistic

Sampling frame

Social artifact

Study population

Unit of analysis

Unit of observation

Answers to Learning Check Questions

Learning Check 5.1: Units of Observation and Analysis

1. Units of observation is an issue of sampling and refers to whom data are collected from. Units of observation is an issue of analysis and refers to whom conclusions are made.

2. No. Studying groups, but making conclusions about individuals runs the risk of ecological fallacy.

3. Group because what is being selected for comparison is the classroom.

Learning Check 5.2: Central Limit Theorem and Probability Theory

1. Statistics are information about our variables that are based on data, that we can observe, and that are used to estimate the values of our variable in the study population, which we cannot observe.

2. Sampling error is the mismatch between the representation in our sample and the true representation in the study population. If we draw a probability (random) sample, we can use statistics to estimate this.

3. It becomes narrower, or more precise.

Learning Check 5.3: Probability Sampling Techniques

1. 27, 33, 02, 23, 57, 36, 10, 26, 43, 55, 60, 03, 11, 39, 08

2. $K = 60/15 = 4$ so I need a random start between 1 and 4. Based on where I landed on the table of random numbers, that is "3" so my sample is: 3, 7, 11, 15, 19, 23, 27, 31, 35, 39, 43, 47, 51, 55, 59.

3. White: 15, Hispanic: 6, African American: 6, Asian/Pacific Islander: 3.

Learning Check 5.4: Nonprobability Sampling Techniques

1. They are similar in that they both try to separate elements into groups to make sure that different groups are numerically represented in the final sample in proportions that mirror their representation in the study population. They differ in that stratified sampling will select these elements within their groups through a random process, whereas quota sampling will not.

2. Because like a snowball that gets bigger as it rolls, the sample size in this technique gets bigger as elements make recommendations for what additional elements might be.

3. A researcher cannot generalize his/her findings from a sample to the wider study population. He/she can only discuss trends noted among the people he/she directly observed.

End-of-Chapter Problems

1. How do statistics and population parameters relate?
   a. We can observe population parameters so we use them to estimate statistics that we cannot observe.
   b. We can observe statistics so we use them to estimate population parameters that we cannot observe.
   c. We cannot observe either statistics or population parameters and need to estimate both.

2. If we have a sufficiently large random sample, our data are likely to organize itself
   a. Along a straight line
   b. Along the normal curve
   c. In a circular shape
   d. With no observable pattern

3. As our sample size increases, our estimates become
   a. More precise
   b. More random
   c. More variable
   d. More diverse

4. According to probability theory, what percent of my sample means will fall between ±2 sample errors of the true population value?
   a. Approximately 68%
   b. Approximately 95%
   c. Approximately 99%
   d. We cannot estimate this

5. Which probability sampling technique is good for very large study populations?
   a. Cluster random sampling
   b. Stratified random sampling
   c. Systematic random sampling
   d. Simple random sampling

6. Which probability sampling technique is best for making sure subgroups are accurately represented in the sample?
   a. Cluster random sampling
   b. Stratified random sampling
   c. Systematic random sampling
   d. Simple random sampling

7. Which nonprobability technique is similar to a stratified random sample?
   a. Purposive sample

   b. Quota sample
   c. Accidental sample
   d. Snowball sample

8. Which of the following sampling techniques would be the most appropriate for studying prostitutes?
   a. Simple random sample
   b. Stratified sample
   c. Snowball sample
   d. Quota sample

9. In order to conduct a probability sample, what one component of sampling is absolutely necessary?
   a. A paper copy of a table of random numbers
   b. A small study population
   c. An accurate sampling frame
   d. All are necessary

10. Would sampling people in your academic year to represent all students at your college/university be an accurate representation of your college/university students? Why or why not?

11. When a researcher uses individuals as the unit of observation and groups as the units of analysis, the researcher runs the risk of
    a. Reductionism
    b. Cross-sectional design
    c. Violation of the principle of beneficence
    d. Reductionism

12. A researcher samples law firms to compare the proportion of cases won, lost, and settled between the firms. The researcher's unit of observation is
    a. Individuals
    b. Groups
    c. Social artifacts

13. A researcher compares a random sample of 15 rap songs from 2000–2002 to a random sample of 15 rap songs from 2015–2017 to see whether messages about authority figures like police have changed. What is the researcher's unit of observation and analysis?
    a. Individuals
    b. Groups
    c. Social artifacts

METHODS OF GATHERING INFORMATION

PART III

6

EXPERIMENTS

LEARNING GOALS

- Identify the research terms common in experimental designs
- Distinguish between experimental and quasi-experimental designs
- Identify the different forms of study validity and how they relate to experiments
- Identify some examples of both experimental and quasi-experimental designs
- Recognize which topics are appropriate for this type of research
- Understand what to compare in interpreting experimental output

Many of you probably already have a basic understanding of experiments. After all, we "experiment" with lipstick, we "experiment" with recipes, we "experiment" with different types of diets…you name it. If we think we can modify a part of a situation and create a change in behavior as a result, we "experiment." To some degree, this would be correct. For example, if a child reaches for a hot pot, a parent might sternly say "NO!" to distract the child from the danger. However, if the child decides that the pot is just too tempting to go unexplored and reaches for it a second time, now the parent might repeat "NO!" and swat the child's hand away (new behavior). Then the parent waits to see if the child stays away from the hot pot (a change in behavior) or tries to reach for it a third time (the original behavior), so the parent is essentially testing a very basic experiment.

However, the information that we gain from experiments like the ones we do in our everyday lives is not as vigorous as the information we gain from well-designed scientific research. Even if a child stays away from the hot pot after the parent swats the hand away, does that mean the swat *caused* the child to stay away from the pot, or did the child just get tired of the "let's try to touch the thing on the stove" game? So although the logic of our everyday experiments is fundamentally the same as a scientific experiment, the quality of the information learned or the ability to make cause–effect inferences is not.

TRUE EXPERIMENTS

Characteristics

Are you afraid of spiders? Ventis, Higbee, and Murdock (2001) tested two techniques that would help people overcome their fear of spiders on 40 undergraduates who scored highly on a test that measured arachnophobia (fear of spiders) and who expressed an interest in decreasing this fear. Based on these pretest scores, Ventis et al. roughly matched triplets of students and then randomly assigned one student from each matched triplet to one of three groups. One group tried systemic sensitization ($n = 13$), which focused on progressive muscle relaxation in relation to hierarchically organized scenes of a tarantula that were ordered from least to most threatening. The second group experienced humor desensitization techniques ($n = 14$) that involved coming up with different uses for a rubber tarantula and homework assignments regarding humorous word associations with spiders. These students also generally responded to the same tarantula scenes as the systemic group except that two-thirds of the scenes were altered to be humorous and one-third were nonhumorous. Furthermore, the humor desensitizing group was also instructed to provide captions for cartoons involving spiders and coming up with a nickname for the tarantula. The third group was a control group who received neither of these approaches and was just instructed that they would be contacted in a few weeks with a follow-up survey (Ventis et al., 2001). Ventis et al. (2001) found that although students in both the systematic and humorous desensitization groups had a lower fear of spiders at the end of the experiment than the control group, there was no statistically significant difference in posttest fear of spiders between the two experimental groups. In other words, the humorous desensitization approach decreased fear of spiders just as much, no more, than the traditional systemic approach.

Ventis et al.'s study is an example of a **true experiment**. A true experiment has the following characteristics:

1. At least two groups of study

2. Variation in the independent variable (treatment), where one group gets the value of interest and the other does not

iStockphoto.com/JayzCats

PHOTO 6.1 Do you think humor can help someone to get over a fear of spiders? Ventis, Higbee and Murdock (2001) did an experiment to test this idea.

3. Control over the context of the experiment

4. Random assignment to the groups

In Ventis et al.'s (2001) study they had two experimental groups. One group experienced humorous desensitization and the other group experienced systemic desensitization. They also had one control group, for a total of three groups. The **experimental group** is the group that is receiving the treatment and the **control group** is the group that does not. Put another way, the experimental group is the group that experiences the stimulus or situation (the independent variable) and the control group does not. Ventis et al. also had control over the independent variable, which was the type and nature of desensitization that the subjects received. Therefore, the first three criteria for a true experiment are fulfilled. As you will see when I present different types of experiments, not all experiments have control groups; but those that do have a stronger case for causality than those that do not, even though having a control group alone is not sufficient to establish causality.

The criteria of random assignment needs a bit more discussion. Random assignment is different than the random selection I discussed in Chapter 5 but serves the same general purpose. If you recall from Chapter 5, researchers do random selection to increase the likelihood that their samples are accurate representations of the population. If people have an equal probability of selection into a sample, researchers are more confident that the people in a study do not have any systemic bias. But random sampling is about deciding who makes it into a study. Random assignment, on the contrary, is about deciding who gets what treatment once subjects are *already* a part of the study; but, like random sampling, the purpose of random assignment is to increase the likelihood that there is no systematic bias that prevents the experimental and control groups from being similar, which is sometimes called establishing **equivalency**. Essentially, like samples and populations, valid comparisons between treatment and control groups depend on the two groups being fundamentally alike. However, just as some error is likely to remain with random samples, random assignment does not guarantee that the resulting experimental and control groups will have equal numbers of every group represented. The goal is for the groups to be generally alike, where if everyone had an equal probability of being assigned to the experimental or control group, then generally the two groups will be almost identical, even if the number of people in each group is slightly unequal.

The process of random assignment can be as simple or complex as the researcher's skills, resources, and interests. A researcher can write everyone's name on a piece of paper (provided the total sample size is small), put those names in a hat, and the first, say, 15 of 30 names the researcher draws get assigned to the experimental group, whereas the remainder go into the control group. Or I might do a process similar to simple random sampling where I give everyone a number and the first 15 (or how many half is) numbers that appear after a random start (perhaps using a table of random numbers or a computer program) will be in the experimental group and the remainder are in the control group.

Or if I *do* want to make sure that I have the same number of people in each group, I can pair students based on a characteristic and then randomly (through any of the means we just mentioned) assign one member of the pair to each group. This is analogous to stratified sampling (Chapter 5) where researchers separate elements into strata, or groups, prior to sampling and then select elements separately from within each group to be in the study. In theory, this is a great idea. For example, it would increase group homogeneity, which would work to decrease error. However, how do researchers know how many variables are enough to match? And how do researchers know which characteristics are relevant? You might be thinking that researchers can use the literature review for guidance, and they can; but the literature review, although helping researchers identify what is relevant, may not be useful in deciding how many variables to try to match on. Furthermore, in reality, especially in evidence-based research, researchers might not be able to match subjects on many variables and one or two characteristics may be the best they can do. Nonetheless, the general consensus is that some matching, when possible, is preferred to none. Ventis et al. (2001) used both matching and random assignment to better ensure that the groups they wanted to compare were equivalent by grouping subjects into sets of three based on their fear scores (hence matching them on fear) and then randomly assigning one of each of the triplets to either one of the two experimental groups or the control group. Figure 6.1 visually summarizes the ways that researchers can increase equivalency between experimental and control groups.

FIGURE 6.1 ⬡   RANDOM SELECTION, RANDOM ASSIGNMENT, AND MATCHING

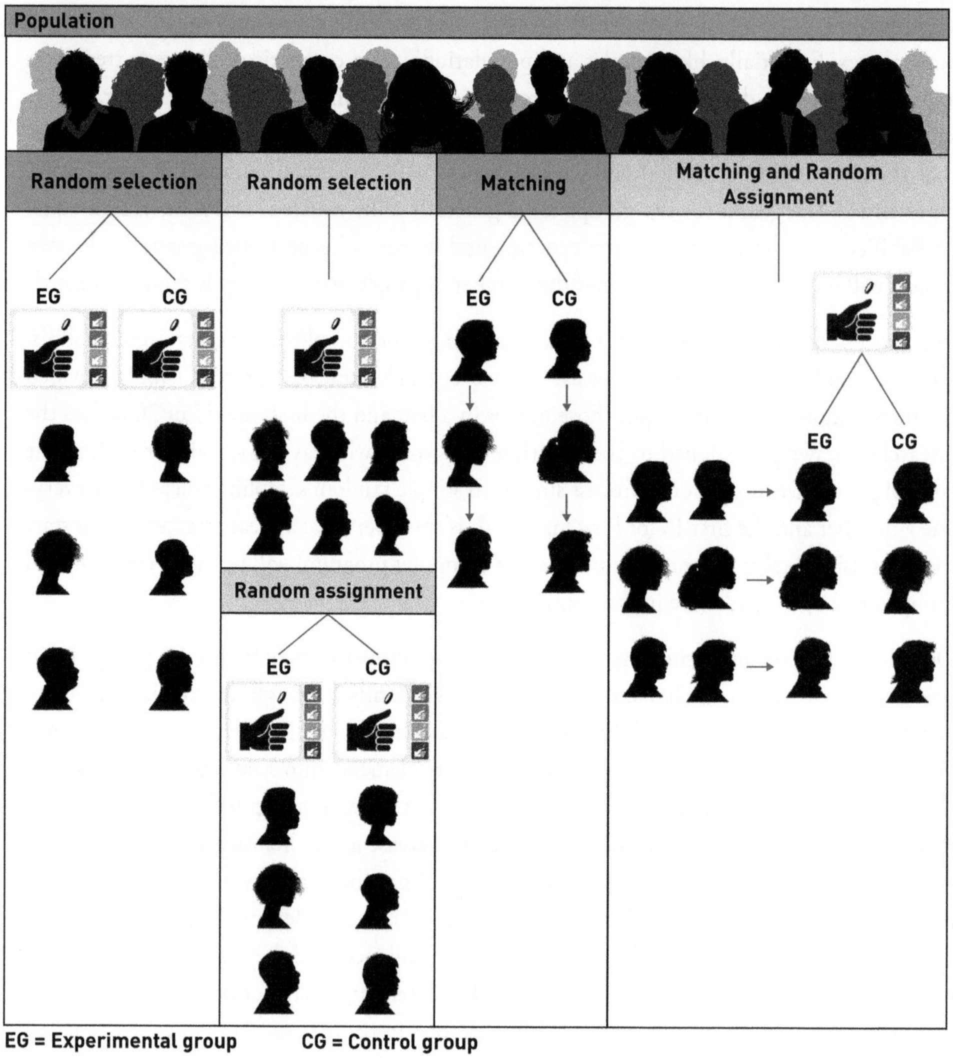

EG = Experimental group   CG = Control group

Types

Classic Experiments

Although some researchers use the term "true experiments" interchangeably with some specific experimental types, like the **classic experiment**, true experiments are really a classification of a group of experiments that fulfill those four criteria I outlined earlier. I don't want us to get hung up on semantics, as doing so is contrary to our goal of "getting the job done," and I only mention it because I want to discuss two common types of true experiments (there are more) in more detail and I don't want to confuse you by naming the first "true experiment" and then trying to explain why the second, which also has all the characteristics of a true experiment, is called something else.

Ventis et al.'s study is an example of the type of true experiment frequently called classic experiment, or sometimes also called a randomized comparative change design or pretest–posttest control group design. Now is a good time to introduce some research notation that will be useful in helping us visually summarize different designs, make preliminary assessments on various methodological risks to validity, and illustrate the ways that experimental findings can be interpreted. A simple notation system to summarize Higbee, Ventis, and Murdock's spider desensitization study, which will also help us compare other experimental designs and quickly make initial conclusions about some common internal validity issues, would look like this:

$$E_1 \quad O \quad X_1 \quad O$$
$$E_2 \quad O \quad X_2 \quad O$$
$$E_3 \quad O \qquad \quad O$$

where the "E" indicates that the groups are equivalent, which is what some researchers call the similarity between the experimental and control group that results from random assignment, the "O" stands for an observation, and "X" stands for the independent variable. When "O" appears before the "X," it is a **pretest**, and when it is after, it is a **posttest**. The subscripts "1" and "2" for the "X" show that there are two different treatments and the group that does not have the "X" is the control group. By this notation, we also see that the second criteria of causality is established where the cause ("X") comes before the final observation (posttest, the second "O" in a line).

I just mentioned that Ventis et al. used a pretest. If you recall, I did not list pretests among the criteria for true experiments, so let's talk about them more a bit. A pretest is a measure of the dependent variable that researchers give prior to any introduction of the stimulus. Pretests are not necessary to test between-group differences because the random assignment to the various study groups presumes that the groups' scores and characteristics are likely to be similar before the experiment; therefore, any difference after the experiment is presumed to be because of the treatment. However, pretests can be useful to determine the magnitude of change, meaning how much the treatment changed behavior within a group at the end of an experiment by making it possible to compare scores before (pretest) and after (posttest) a treatment. In Ventis et al.'s study, their pretest was in the form of the behavioral approach test that they also used to match respondents and to establish the baseline measure of fear, which they would later use to determine the magnitude of any change. It was from the pretest that Ventis et al. learned that although both interventions changed behavior, no intervention worked better than the other because the magnitude of difference in the effect of each treatment was not significantly different from the other.

Posttest-Only Control Group Design

As the name implies, a **posttest-only control group design** is a form of true experiment that does not use a pretest. Chong et al. (2012) used this method to see whether people who play violent video games long term were more likely than short-term users to feel that the storyline expressed in the video game accurately depicted the real world. To study this, they obtained a sample of 135 students who had minimal previous exposure to violent media and

iStockphoto.com/scyther5

PHOTO 6.2 People have always been concerned with whether media affects people's perception of reality. The newest concern is over video games.

the researchers randomly assigned approximately half of the students to play Grand Theft Auto IV, a violent video game, individually for 2 hours twice a week for 6 weeks (for a total of 24 hours) and the other half not to play any video games. In order to track long-term perceptions of reality, all participants (experimental and control) completed a survey halfway through the experiment (at 3 weeks) and at the end (at 6 weeks).

For the study by Chong et al., the schematic would look more like this:

$$E_1 \quad X \quad O_1 \quad O_2$$
$$E_2 \quad\quad O_1 \quad O_2$$

The absence of an "O" prior to the treatment shows that there is no pretest in this design, and the O_1 and O_2 that appear after the "X" show that there are two observations made after the treatment starts (remember, one was at 3 weeks and the other at 6 weeks). This is actually for both groups because even though there is no "X" for the control group, the placement of their "O" directly underneath the "O" for the treatment group shows that posttests are occurring at the same time for both groups.

The researchers found that those who played the game, which involves high-speed car chases resulting in injury or death and rampant drug use, perceived that more people died in car accidents and drug overdoses in reality than did those who did not play the game. Furthermore,

LEARNING CHECK 6.1: TRUE EXPERIMENTS

1. What are the four characteristics of true experiments?

2. How is random assignment different from random selection?

Answers to be found at the end of the chapter.

they found that even though car theft is common in the game, those who played the game were more likely to think that stealing cars was difficult than did those who did not play the game. In this experiment, the researchers elected not to use a pretest in order to not sensitize the subjects to the nature of the study.

There are an infinite number of true (and quasi-) experimental designs that researchers can create. Researchers can have any number of posttests. They can have two pretests or more. They can look at one treatment or multiple ones, although limiting the number of treatments, as I discussed earlier, is a good idea in order to better ensure researcher control over the stimulus. The notation serves as a quick summary of the design that allows others to see how the experiment was organized.

TRUE EXPERIMENTS AND STUDY VALIDITY

We have already encountered the concept of validity in Chapter 4 when I discussed measurement validity; but to recap, validity refers to how accurately a study is measuring what it claims to measure. True experiments are often referred to as the "gold standard of research" because, when done well, they are the best methodological means of addressing many forms of validity and this enables researchers to make causal connections between variables. The main reason for this is their characteristic of random assignment. If subjects are allocated to experimental or control groups at random, then there is no reason to believe that the groups differ in any systematic way prior to the treatment. Therefore, if designed well, any difference in behavior at the end of the study should be because of the treatment and not any rival causal factors (Chapter 2) that might threaten validity.

So now, in order to "get the job done" let's focus on some of the most common types of study validity and the corresponding threats to them as they relate to true experiments.

Internal Validity

Internal validity refers to the types of validity that facilitate causal inferences. If you think back to Chapter 2, I noted that one of the criteria for establishing causality was to make sure that the observed relationship (association) between the independent and dependent variable was nonspurious, or not caused by some factor other than the independent variable. I also said that some of the confounding factors that might get in the way of fulfilling (e.g., hence "confound") these criteria were variables related to the topic that researchers had to make sure they incorporated into the study. But a spurious relationship could also result from methodological problems. In this section, I am going to focus on some of the common methodological issues that might make a relationship between two variables spurious, thereby threatening internal validity.

Selection Bias

One of the common threats to internal validity is selection bias. Selection bias occurs when groups that are being compared are fundamentally different on factors that are not the independent variable. Students frequently confuse this with the idea of the independent variable, so let's look at this another way. If I am comparing two groups, I want those groups to be as similar as possible on all factors (in other words, unbiased) *except* the independent variable. Researchers *want* groups to differ on the independent variable because the differences in the independent variable are what creates the change in the dependent variable. Let's illustrate this with a very simple example. If I want to see whether running a review session before a major exam improves exam scores for an introductory sociology class, and I give the review session to the freshmen and sophomores in my Introduction to Sociology class and compare their test scores to the scores of my juniors and seniors taking the class who did not get the chance to attend a review class, I have a problem of selection bias. If my juniors and seniors do better on the test, I do not really know if my review session was a failure or if upperclassmen, in general, will do better on a test because they are more used to taking college exams than are freshmen and sophomores. If, on the contrary, I grouped my students separately by year (freshman, sophomore, etc.), then randomly selected half of the students in each separate academic year (½ the freshmen, ½ the sophomores, etc.) to attend the review session, whereas the other half did not, and *then* compared their test scores, I am less likely to have selection bias because now the only difference (presuming that there are no other differences than academic year) between the two groups is the value of the independent variable (had the review course/did not have it). Therefore, any difference between scores should be because of the difference in whether someone had the review course. As you can probably guess from this example, one of the main ways to minimize the chance of selection bias is to randomly select subjects (an issue of sampling, Chapter 5) and then to randomly assign subjects to the different treatment options in a true experiment.

Instrumentation

Instrumentation occurs when the measure for a concept changes over the course of a study. Studies of behaviors like crime rates are especially vulnerable to this because what constitutes a crime in one state may not be a crime in another and the very definition of a crime can change. For example, look at the graph in Figure 6.2 of the reported incidents of rape in the last

PHOTO 6.3 If I want to see whether giving a special review class for a test affects test scores, the only variable I want my groups to vary on is whether they get the review class or not. I want the groups to be equal, or close to it, on all other factors in order to reduce selection bias.

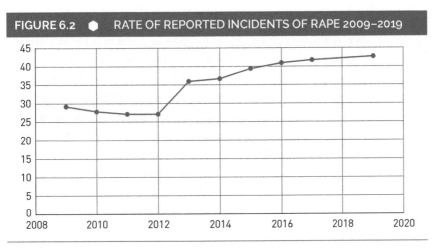

FIGURE 6.2 ● RATE OF REPORTED INCIDENTS OF RAPE 2009–2019

source: Federal Bureau of Investigation https://crime-data-explorer.fr.cloud.gov/explorer/national/united-states/crime. Retrieved on November 15, 2019.

10 years. At first glance, it appears as if the rate of reported rape incidents has increased pretty noticeably since 2012 after which it continued to increase, albeit at a slower rate. Or did it? In 2011 the Federal Bureau of Investigation's Uniform Crime Reporting (UCR) process broadened the definition of rape to include acts of attempted rape that did not involve penetration and acts perpetrated against males as well as females. The change in definition, therefore, will be reflected in statistics starting around 2012, making graphs like this difficult to interpret. For example, how much of any increase in reported rate statistics during this time is because of increased incidence or the broader definition that made more rape behaviors eligible to be labeled a crime? Incidentally, so you do not get a negative view of government statistics, at least based on this example, the UCR *does* track rape under both the old (more restrictive) and new (broader) definition after 2012; but this does not mean that someone else will be carefully watching which set of data to report. In fact, the change under the old definition is not nearly as dramatic, further illustrating the importance of being clear about how concepts are measured (Chapter 4) and whether those measures have changed over time (instrumentation).

Maturation

When studies are long, especially when subjects are very young or approaching old age, changes in the dependent variable may result from the knowledge, experience, or maturity subjects get simply because of time. This is called **maturation**. Think about it. I suspect that you are not the same person you were when you were 10 or 13. You know more, you are likely to be more mature, and you just generally have a different life outlook because you are growing up. This change is going to occur for most young people regardless of whether or not they experience an intervention or experimental stimulus. Again, the study of crime is especially vulnerable to this because it is a well-known fact that younger people commit more crime than do older ones, and many interventions are aimed to decrease crime among younger populations. Therefore, it is hard to determine whether interventions aimed to reduce juvenile delinquency have long-term consequences because of the intervention itself or because the subjects experiencing the intervention are growing up.

Testing

Testing occurs when researchers give a pretest in order to measure behavior change via a posttest at the end of an experiment or treatment. Sometimes the very act of taking a pretest can sensitize subjects to an issue and, consequently, influence their responses at the posttest. Two common tactics to reduce this risk are time and random assignment. The tactic of time is pretty obvious…in theory. It means to ensure that there is enough time between tests, but, in real-time, it can be challenging to establish because there is no clear definition of what an ideal amount of time between observations is. The random assignment inherent in true experiments will help increase the chance that the groups being compared are equal; therefore, if the pretest affects the dependent variable, it will affect it similarly (because the groups are equal at the start) and, therefore, be a constant and not a problem.

Attrition

When studies are longitudinal, even if they are just across two time points, researchers have to be cautious of **attrition**, sometimes also called differential attrition or experimental mortality. Over time it is likely that at least some subjects will drop out of a study; the longer the time span of the study, the more subjects will prematurely leave it. Some dropout is expected, but it becomes a problem if the comparison groups become different because people who share a specific characteristic (e.g., members of a particular racial group, members of the comparison group) drop out disproportionately. When this occurs, bias enters the study and the observed behaviors at the end of the study might reflect this bias instead of the variation in the independent variable. For example, if we wanted to study the effect of housing vouchers on where people decide to live and we used a survey to see where people lived prior to receiving the voucher and after, we need to make sure that the people responding to the survey at each time point are the same. If we see that vouchers improved housing outcomes, but we also see that those who were economically worse off prior to the vouchers were less likely to respond to the survey (they dropped out of the study) at the second time, then we have a threat because of attrition. The people who dropped out disproportionately shared a common characteristic (lower income) and therefore the findings (improved housing) may not be because of the vouchers (the independent variable) but instead because of the higher socioeconomic status of those responding, thereby creating a spurious relationship and a threat to internal validity.

According to Bloom (2008), one way around this is to use an intent-to-treat analysis rather than a pure experiment—control analysis. True experimental research usually only looks at those for whom there is complete information. If someone drops out of the study, it is as if they were never in it and all their early information is ignored. However, in the intent-to-treat approach, the researcher compares all the subjects who started with all the subjects who finished, regardless of whether people dropped out or not. Therefore, with the intent-to-treat approach, the effect of the intervention may actually be underestimated because people will be included in the analysis who did not complete the program. One point in favor of the intent-to-treat approach recognizes that in real life people are allowed to stop treatment or change their minds about being observed. So this approach may be a more accurate assessment of a program in which people can elect to stop participation (Bloom, 2008).

Reactivity

In the 1930s, Roethlisberger and Dixon (1939) designed experiments to either increase or decrease, depending on the specific experimental version, efficiency among workers in the Hawthorne plant of an electric company in Chicago. Roethlisberger and Dixon found, however, that *all* of the experiments increased efficiency, including those designed to actually have the opposite effect. After further investigation, the researchers learned that the workers were not responding to the experimental stimuli; they were actually responding to the researchers themselves. Happy to be part of what they considered an important study, the workers tried to behave in a way that they thought the researchers wanted. This change in behavior resulting from being observed was originally called the Hawthorne effect, but now most people simply refer to it as **reactivity**. Juvenile delinquents who want to appear "cool" to a researcher might act more aggressively than they otherwise would. Bosses who otherwise might be sexist or derogatory toward women might be on "good behavior" for an interview because they know that, regardless of what they feel, others view these behaviors as wrong. Parents who are being visited by caseworkers may resist yelling at their children so they can appear to be nurturing. All of these are examples of how people change their behavior because they are being observed, and doing so will clearly bias and invalidate a study's findings.

You might be asking yourself whether research is ever truly free of reactivity—after all, by voluntarily giving informed consent (Chapter 3), people know they are being studied and, therefore, might present themselves in a way that they hope will give the researcher a favorable opinion of them. In this very rigid view of reactivity, yes all studies are vulnerable to it. However, in reality, researchers can do a few things that minimize the likelihood that it will occur. For example, researchers can choose a method of observation that allows for anonymity (Chapter 3). When subjects think that their responses cannot personally be linked to them, they might feel safer revealing personal information. If a researcher cannot do a study anonymously, such as when conducting interviews, researchers can read subtle clues in body language among respondents that might suggest reactivity and then decide what to do with that subject's information. In field research, researchers can stay in the field long enough where being polite just becomes too hard to maintain. When I was in college, there was a popular show called *The Real World*, whose tag line was that the show was about "what happens when people stop being polite and start being real." It is the same idea in field research. Finally, having sufficiently large sample sizes also can help ensure that those who, despite attempts on behalf of the researcher, are still influenced by the study will be a statistical minority and, therefore, have little real effect on the findings.

Contamination

Contamination, sometimes called diffusion of treatment, is a threat when the comparison group may somehow affect the treatment group or if the comparison group receives some of the treatment of the experimental group. One of the goals of well-designed experimental and treatment conditions is for the experimental and control groups not to have contact with each other. For example, if researchers administer a high school abstinence program to half the

10th-grade class and then compare the sexual behavior of students in the 10th-grade class who receive the program to similar 10th-grade students who do not, what is to prevent the students from talking with each other? If students from both groups can have contact with each other, then we would expect that in normal conversation they might talk about the program. However, if students did discuss it, the study is contaminated because those students not receiving the program are still exposed (through conversation) to some elements of the program.

History

Applied research, more so than basic research, is also vulnerable to **history effects**, which are events outside the study that can affect the dependent variable. For example, if researchers are studying how a new job placement program affects the ability of individuals on public assistance to find jobs and a factory that provided many blue-collar jobs to the target area closed down, that is an event outside of the experiment itself that will undoubtedly affect the subjects' ability to get jobs as available jobs just became more scarce. Another example of a history effect could be an intervention that is being tested at multiple sites. If the delivery of this intervention is not done similarly across sites, say for example one site has providers who are less invested in implementing the program completely as designed, variation in how the program is carried out at different sites can affect the program outcome as well. History issues can threaten causality, but they are beyond the researcher's control. Nonetheless, if a history effect occurs, a researcher needs to identify both it and its possible effect on the study outcome. Consequently, researchers need to pay attention not only to what they are doing but also to what is going on with them and what others are doing.

Summary Relationship to True Experiments

To summarize, with the random assignment that is characteristic of true experiments and the resulting equivalence, anything that affects the behavior in one group is going to have the same type of effect on the second group. Although this may initially sound like a bad thing, it actually is not because this possible risk factor is now the *same* for all of the groups and, therefore, a constant. In other words, if the pretest has an effect on the dependent variable, it will affect *both* the experimental and the control group the *same way* because these groups are equivalent (because of random assignment); therefore, any observed difference between the groups is still because of the treatment, which is the only thing *not* the same for both groups. Could a history effect threaten validity? Not likely because it would still be a constant because of equivalence, making any observed differences between the groups likely to be because of the treatment. Even selection bias, an issue of sampling, would be minimized with random assignment because if there is bias in selection, with random assignment that bias is likely to be distributed equally across the various groups, and, therefore, although there may be problems in representation between the sample and population (a sampling issue), any differences in posttest measurement are still likely to be because of the treatment (an experimental issue). Therefore, random assignment is the key component that makes true experiments the "gold standard" of methodologies by decreasing the effect of many threats to internal validity by reducing them to a constant where the only variability between groups (theoretically) is still from the treatment.

✔ **LEARNING CHECK 6.2: INTERNAL VALIDITY THREATS**

1. Why is it important to avoid selection bias?

2. Although we expect some people to drop out of longitudinal studies, when does this dropout become a threat to internal validity?

3. What are two ways to reduce the risk of reactivity?

Answers to be found at the end of the chapter.

However, true experiments, while the gold standard of methodology for causality, are still vulnerable to some internal validity threats. One of the biggest issues is contamination (Chapter 4), because if the experiment becomes contaminated, the only factor that was supposed to distinguish groups that were presumed equivalent with random assignment is no longer unique to one group. Another risk is local history, which is when an outside event beyond the researcher's control affects only some of the comparison groups, but not all; therefore, even with random assignment, it is not a constant and can now potentially affect the dependent variable. In fact, in reality, it is very difficult for researchers to maintain full control over experimental conditions unless they occur in a laboratory setting, which relates to the next issue.

Statistical Conclusion Validity

As the name implies, **statistical conclusion validity** relates to validity surrounding the statistical tests that determine whether or not there is a relationship between variables. We will encounter this form of validity again in Chapter 12; but for now I just want to highlight some factors in this chapter, especially the three that are relevant to study design, which can threaten this form of validity. The first threat is poor measurement that might lead to over- or underestimating the relationship between variables. We already covered how to create quality measures in Chapter 4, so we don't need to spend more time on that here, but this does illustrate how early research decisions can have an effect on later research conclusions. A second factor is whether there are random environmental effects in the study, such as hot weather, an uncomfortable classroom, or a subject feeling under the weather on observation day that affect subjects' behavior or responses. Random environmental effects are similar to the random error effects we discussed previously; but in true experiments when subjects are randomly assigned to groups, the risk that leads to problems with statistical conclusion validity is relatively small. A third methodologically relevant risk is inconsistency in treatment implementation. This, of course, is a potential problem in *any* experimental design. If those administering the treatment (independent variable) do not do so consistently, then the effects of the treatment may be underestimated, which in turn threatens statistical conclusion validity.

The last two common risks to this form of validity are more statistical in nature so I will only briefly mention them here. The first is when researchers irresponsibly mine data, which means running numerous statistical tests without any theoretical or prior research foundation justifying those tests, until *any* statistically significant findings emerge. In other words, researchers who mine data use a computer program to keep putting in variables in various combinations to see if *anything* suggests a statistical relationship. This is problematic because not only is there no theoretical or research justification for these tests, but if researchers run a sufficient number of tests, especially on larger samples, *some* tests are likely—purely by chance—to produce statistically significant results. That does not, however, mean that those results are meaningful. The second statistical threat involves running statistical tests that are inappropriate for the data and violate the assumptions of that data. These statistical factors can get complex very fast, so as I said, I will postpone this discussion until Chapter 12.

External Validity

The last form of validity that I will cover is **external validity**, which is the ability to generalize the findings in a sample to a wider population. It essentially asks both "How representative are the subjects in the sample to the subjects in the population?" and "How much does the study fit the real world? Therefore, this can be a tricky form of validity to actually claim. In order to truly establish external validity, one would need to replicate the findings of one study with different studies done with different participants in different settings (Robson, 2002). However, obviously, most researchers do not conduct multiple studies of different individuals and settings. Therefore, in most cases, many consider this validity to be fulfilled if the researcher can make the case that the group and settings share characteristics with other groups or settings (Campbell & Stanley, 1963). Second, the factors that make methods of observation like true experiments so strong on internal validity also work to actually weaken external validity. As I mentioned earlier, true experiments are often considered to be the gold standards of research

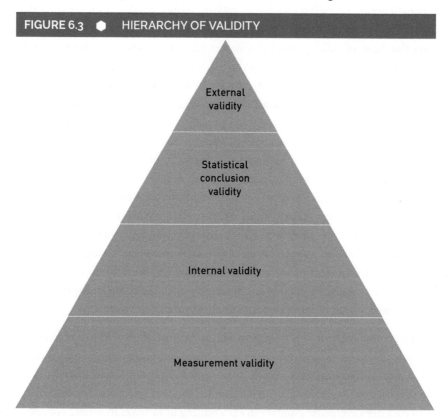

FIGURE 6.3 ● HIERARCHY OF VALIDITY

External validity

Statistical conclusion validity

Internal validity

Measurement validity

LEARNING CHECK 6.3: VALIDITY TYPES AND TRUE EXPERIMENTS

1. Why is random assignment an important part of true experiments?

2. Why are true experiments low on external validity?

3. What threats to internal validity potentially exist for true experiments?

Answers to be found at the end of the chapter.

because researchers control many factors of the study, which increases the ability to make causal conclusions. However, true experiments also frequently involve samples that are smaller than those used in other methods of observation such as **quasi-experiments** (which we will discuss soon) or surveys. The smaller the sample, the harder it is to obtain representativeness in a way that is statistically meaningful, hence the difficulty with establishing external validity. Furthermore, studies, like true experiments, with full researcher control, are somewhat artificial. The findings are, in other words, specific to the controlled condition; but the real world is messy. Therefore, the outcomes from a controlled environment may not apply outside that same controlled environment.

QUASI-EXPERIMENTS

Characteristics

Obtaining participants who can be randomly assigned to a treatment or finding a setting for which the researcher has full control is often very difficult or sometimes even possibly unethical. This is especially true in applied, evidence-based research. The methodological answer to this quandary is quasi-experiments that differ from true experiments in that the subjects are not randomly assigned to the experimental or control group and/or the researcher is less likely to be able to have full control over the implementation of the treatment. In these instances, when researchers want to compare groups, they are most likely to select groups that are comparable in ways relevant to the study topic, such as cities with similar demographics and crime rates or individuals who are eligible for the same services, but the researcher does not randomly decide who gets what. Quasi-experiments are common in evaluation-based research because the researcher is frequently not the person who has control over deciding who will receive a treatment or not. For example, if a local police force wants to test whether their community-oriented policing approach decreases crime, the police force may already be practicing community-oriented policing (the treatment) and the researcher would be responsible for identifying and gathering information on a comparable community that does not utilize this approach, or at least not in the same way. Furthermore, the researcher cannot control officer actions so the researcher cannot control how the community-oriented policing strategies are carried out. The lack of researcher control does not mean that researchers do not study interventions, like community-oriented policing, in the real world. It just means that researchers need to alter the methods of observation and the interpretations of their findings.

I will present four common quasi-experimental designs, but like true experiments, the different number of design types varies only by a researcher's topic, imagination, and resources. These four are just common examples that I picked to illustrate our points.

Types

Ex Post Facto Control Group Design

One common quasi-experimental design is called the **ex post facto control group design** or the posttest-only comparison group design. If you stop to think about the name of these designs and the schematics we discussed earlier, identifying what these designs do is pretty straightforward. For example, in this design there is no mention of random assignment, but there *is* mention of a control group, and the name(s) indicate that only a posttest is used. Therefore, the schematic would look something like this:

$$N \quad X \quad O$$
$$N \qquad\; O$$

where the "N" indicates not random, or not equivalent, and the "X" and "O" have the same meaning as in the true experiments. This design implies that the outcome (dependent variable) will be measured only after the treatment.

So if the experimental group does better on the posttest, does this mean that the treatment worked? Maybe. But maybe not. Because with this design, researchers do not have equivalence *or* a pretest, they have no way of knowing how similar the groups are prior to the treatment. Therefore, although this is a basic design to start with, researchers really have no idea what the posttest means, which leads many to question the utility of this design overall (Gray, 2014).

iStockphoto.com/FatCamera

PHOTO 6.4 What are some ways researchers can experiment to see if programs that try to teach children the risks and protection strategies against sexual abuse work?

Before-and-After Design

Another type of quasi-experimental design is the single-subject design, sometimes also called a one-group pretest–posttest or **before-and-after design**. This is a more basic test to see how an intervention affects one particular group. This would be considered a within-group design because you are only looking for a change in the dependent variable in one group (so "within" the group) from the pretest to the posttest. For example, Brown (2017) studied 1,169 kindergarten students in four school districts in Florida to see whether the *Safe, Smarter Kids* program increased children's knowledge of safety risks and self-protection strategies to prevent sexual abuse. This program focuses on teaching safety rules, distinguishing between a stranger versus a trusted grown-up "buddy," body boundaries, distinguishing between safe and unsafe secrets, and knowing the difference between tattling and reporting (Brown, 2017). Each child was pretested by a trained administrator using 11 close-ended questions prior to the program, and then again 30 days after program completion the child was retested (posttest) to determine what program information the child remembered. The schematic for this experiment would look like:

$$O \; X \; O$$

One of the benefits of this design is that the subjects essentially serve as their own control because this design controls for individual differences by looking at the same people. This design is especially common in applied, evidence-based research because many studies of program intervention are not meant to be generalized to other groups but instead have the main goal of "did it work?" As such, researchers want to see whether a program changes the behavior of those who experience it, much like Brown's (2017) study aimed to do with kindergarteners.

However, even though the goal may not be a comparison between groups, this design is still vulnerable to some of the threats to internal validity that I mentioned previously. The most notable threats are pretest effects, experimental mortality, and instrumentation; and, because of the lack of a comparison group, researchers cannot determine how much change in the dependent variable is because of the treatment or because of one of these possible validity threats without further investigation into the nature of how the experiment was carried out.

Nonequivalent Control Group Design

Probably one of the most common quasi-experimental designs is the **nonequivalent control group design**, which is the nonrandomized equivalent to the classic version of true experiments mentioned previously. This design builds upon the posttest-only control group design by using a pretest and it is an improvement over the before–after test by adding a control group. The basic schematic for this design would look like:

$$N \; O \; X \; O$$
$$N \; O \quad\;\; O$$

Bradford, Steward, Pfister, and Higginbotham (2016) used a nonequivalent control group design to study whether premarital education helped emerging adults form healthy relationships. They recruited individuals using various forms of media, like newspaper and internet advertisements, to voluntarily participate in a Premarital Interpersonal Choices and Knowledge (PICK) program, which is a 6-hour program that utilizes research-based information to help emerging adults recognize the characteristics of a potential partner and learn how to effectively pace an emerging relationship (Bradford et al., 2016). Bradford and colleagues identified 682 individuals who completed the program and who were between the ages of 18 and 25 and compared them to a nonequivalent group of university students recruited from various undergraduate courses from a nearby university. Because the researchers could not control the assignment of individuals to the treatment and control groups, this is a quasi-experimental design. However, Bradford et al. did try to make the groups comparable by limiting the age range of the treatment group, which was actually from a larger population of 2,760 individuals to that which would be comparable to the college students that served as the control.

The researchers administered a pretest that measured subjects' perceived knowledge about relationship skills, relationship warning signs, and partner characteristics to all treatment participants at the start of the program during their Spring 2013 semester. The posttest was administered at the end of the 6-hour PICK program for the treatment groups and 2 weeks after the pretest for the control group. Because these groups were nonequivalent, even though they were roughly matched based on age, Bradford et al. knew that they required to use the pretest to see whether there were noticeable differences in knowledge prior to any PICK participation and they found that there were. The university control group was statistically more likely to be knowledgeable about both relationship skills and partner selection, suggesting that the community treatment group was more at risk for relationship dysfunction. The posttest scores showed that the group experiencing the PICK program improved their posttest scores more than the control group, but that the control did experience a shift in scores as well.

So, what did the researchers learn from this type of study? First, they learned that some members of the community treatment group were more at risk for a dysfunctional relationship than members of the comparison group. They also learned that the nature of taking the pretest may have sensitized subjects, at least in the control group, because their posttest scores increased, but they did not receive the treatment. Researchers then learned that the community group receiving the PICK program did improve their knowledge about functional relationships in some areas. However, researchers do *not* know whether some of this improved knowledge among the treatment groups stems from a possible pretest effect that the change in the control group suggests may have occurred. In reality, the answer might be that both (the program and pretest) had an effect, and the lack in ability to test if and how much change was because of the treatment is one pitfall of many quasi-experimental designs.

Interrupted Time-Series Design

Interrupted time-series designs are longitudinal designs for when programs are started and the data are longitudinally available both before and after the program starts. Sometimes these involve a comparison group, sometimes they do not. For example, I am old enough that I am part of the generation who, when they received their driver's license, there were no driving restrictions or probationary periods as new drivers. But, it also does not take much imagination to realize that some of the most dangerous drivers on the road are young, newly licensed people, simply because they lack the experience to handle many driving situations that no driver's test in the world can anticipate. Today's added distractions of cell phones only make this risk even greater. So many states now have graduated driver's licenses, which grant new drivers more driving privilege as they successfully gain more driving experience; but do they work to reduce motor vehicle crashes and fatalities? Rajaratnam et al. (2015) studied this question using Massachusettss' graduated driver's license program, which was enacted in 2007, and looked at the crash records provided by the Massachusetts Registry of Motor Vehicles for 1 year prior to the enactment of this new legislation and five years afterward. To be included in the study, Rajaratnam et al. defined a crash as an incident that was reported to the police and involved personal injury or property damage in excess of $1,000 or both. As these researchers were most interested in younger drivers, they examined crashes by the age categories of 16–17, 18–19, and 20 years or older. They found that in the year prior to the new legislation, both fatal and nonfatal crashes were highest among the 16–17-year-old drivers and lowest among the drivers aged 20 or older. They also found that after the law went into effect, the greatest decrease in crashes was for the 16–17 year olds followed by the 18–19 year olds, with little change among those aged 20 or older, and that this decrease persisted 5 years after the law was enacted. Therefore Rajaratnam et al. (2015) concluded that the graduated driver's license program contributed to a decrease in crash incidences.

Longitudinal designs are especially useful for evidence-based research because they can help detect a threat to validity that I did not previously cover known as erosion of treatment. Erosion of treatment occurs when the effect of the independent variable wears off over time. Think of it this way. At the start of the semester, are you energized, ready for new beginnings

iStockphoto.com/Aleksandr Zhurilo

PHOTO 6.5 Teen drivers historically have the highest crash records; but now many states have introduced graduated driver's licenses. Interrupted time series designs are one way of evaluating whether they are effective in reducing crashes among new drivers.

LEARNING CHECK 6.4: QUASI-EXPERIMENTS

1. What characteristics of true experiments do quasi-experiments lack?
2. What quasi-experimental design only focuses on within-group change?
3. Interrupted time-series designs are an effective means of identifying what validity threat?

Answers to be found at the end of the chapter.

and new subjects? Well…how do you feel a month into the semester after your first papers and exam start? Less energized? Probably. That decrease in your energetic feelings is analogous to the erosion of treatment. Your initial excitement or "freshness" regarding the start of the new semester *eroded* as the semester wore on. Similar things happen in interventions. When people complete an intervention they are energized and may feel ready for anything that comes their way…and then jobs get hectic, kids get sick or needy, spouses/significant others have needs that require attention…basically, *life* gets in the say. This quasi-experimental design helps identify if a program's effects last a desired amount of time or if they wear off after a while. By tracking crashes for 5 years after legislation introduction, Rajaratnam et al. (2015) were able to show that erosion of treatment was not an issue because the number of crashes 5 years after the program remained lower than the number the year prior to the new legislation.

FACTORIAL DESIGN

So far I have only been discussing experiments with one or two distinct independent variables that are studied, in the case of multivariate designs, separately from each other, like in Ventis et al.'s (2001) study. However, sometimes it is necessary to study two independent variables simultaneously to see how they interact together. This type of experiment would be a factorial design. The simplest form of factorial design is a two-by-two design where the researcher has two variables, each with only two answer choices, for a comparison of four different groups (2 × 2 = 4). Yechezkel and Ayalon (2013) used a 2 × 2 factorial design when they studied 212 Israeli social workers to see if the age of the victim and the nature of the violence influenced whether social workers defined a case as abusive. These workers were randomly assigned to react to one of the four vignettes describing intimate partner violence based on whether the victim was young (aged 37) or old (aged 77) and the type of abuse by her male partner (emotional or physical). Figure 6.4 illustrates the experimental schematic and four possible treatment conditions. The researchers found that social workers were more likely to consider a situation to be abusive in the condition where the event was physical and the victim was younger. On the other hand, when the victim was an older adult, regardless of the nature of the abuse, the social workers were less likely to consider the situation to be abusive. The researchers also found that the response, whether the social worker would suggest a therapeutic or a legal intervention, depended more on the age of the victim than the nature of the abuse. Regardless of the nature of the abuse, social workers were more likely to suggest

FIGURE 6.4 ●	FACTORIAL EXAMPLE FROM YECHEZKEL AND AYALON

Factorial Design

	Victim Age	
Form of Abuse	**Young**	**Old**
Physical	X_1	X_2
Emotional	X_3	X_4

Resulting Experiment

E X_1 0

E X_2 0

E X_3 0

E X_4 0

a therapeutic intervention for the younger victims and a legal one for the older ones. Through a factorial design, these researchers were able to manipulate multiple independent variables to determine if and how a combination of factors influenced perceptions of victims and the corresponding services they received, and the researchers found that independent variables acted in combination, rather than in isolation, to affect social workers' responses.

INTERPRETING EXPERIMENTAL OUTPUT

There are a number of different ways researchers can interpret experimental output. If I illustrate the comparisons with the true experimental design, I have four different types of results that I can start with in order to "get the job done"; but depending on the design, all four comparisons may not be feasible. Let's pretend I have a study where I randomly select 200 teenagers from two area high schools and randomly assign 100 of them to watch two 30-minute documentaries on the effects of vaping and the other 100 to be the control group who does not watch these documentaries. I use a pretest to see how many times all 200 students typically vaped a week before the stimulus and again 1 month after the stimulus. The schematic for this, if you remember, would look like the following, where I have added the letters "A–D" in parentheses to illustrate the different comparisons we can make.

E   O(A)   X   O(B)
E   O(C)   O(D)

The first comparison is between the experimental and control groups' pretest, which is comparison A–C in the above notation. Since this is a true experiment and we rely on random assignment to ensure that the two groups are equal, you should *not* notice any statistically significant difference in the number of times a week the students in these two groups vape. Notice that I say *statistically significant difference*. The number of times a week the two groups vape are not likely to be exact. For example, the experimental group might report vaping an average of 8.6 times a week whereas the control group reports vaping an average of 9.5 times a week. You are not likely to be able to determine whether this 0.9 difference is large enough to suggest that the two groups are fundamentally different (a problem here) or just differences because of normal variation (expected and not a problem) just by looking at the numbers themselves. Depending on the variable measured, you might be able to graph the individual values for subjects and compare the lines or you can do a statistical test to determine whether this difference is real or just by chance, which you will learn about in Chapters 12 and 13. In

PHOTO 6.6 To see if an anti-vaping program is effective, a researcher would look at both between– and within–group comparisons for a true experiment.

my example, since I have a somewhat large sample (100 students in each group) and I gave an average, as opposed to 200 individual data points, I would do a statistical test. So, for now, given my sample size of 200, let's assume that when I say "difference," I mean one that is statistically significant and that some type of statistical analysis has been done to make that claim.

If researchers do find a difference in the pretest scores (comparison A–C), they might have selection bias. Remember, random selection (sampling) and assignment (experiments) minimize the risk of this, but they do not completely guarantee that selection bias will not occur simply by chance. A pretest, however, helps researchers determine whether this validity threat is present in their research.

The second comparison is in the posttest for the experimental and control group (B–D comparison). This is what I referred to earlier as a between-group difference. Between-group differences are what we commonly think of to see if an experiment "works." We compare the group who did get the stimulus to the *other* group, or *between* the experimental and control groups, to see if the stimulus is effective. If the documentaries had an effect on the vaping behavior of the teens in the experimental group, those teens should have posttest scores that are statistically different (and hopefully lower) than those for the control group. However, researchers cannot conclude that the treatment, here the anti-vaping documentaries, successfully led to this difference without first considering two other comparisons.

The third comparison is between the pretest and posttest for the experimental group (comparison A–B), what we have previously called a within-group difference because you are looking at two time points, before and after, for one group. If the posttest did not change from the pretest, the vaping documentary may be ineffective. If the posttest *did* change, then provided that the next comparison does show a difference, the documentaries may have contributed to this change.

The fourth comparison is between the pretest and posttest for the control group (comparison C–D). Because the control group did not experience any stimulus, researchers should *not* see a difference in the pre- and posttest scores among these students. If researchers do see a change in the control group, like we did in Bradford et al.'s (2016) study, there may be a history, maturation, contamination, or testing effect present. Technically, because the groups are equal (and the A–C comparison would confirm or deny this), if any of these validity threats is present, they would affect both groups equally so any C–D changes do not necessarily mean the treatment was ineffective if the B–D change is greater than the C–D change, but it does make the magnitude of effect more difficult to determine.

To summarize, looking only at the posttests for the experimental and control groups (B–D comparison) does not in itself justify whether an experimental treatment influences the dependent variable, and this conclusion is even harder to make with quasi-experimental designs for which there is no random assignment. Other comparisons help identify (and classify as likely or not) potential threats to validity.

MAKING DECISIONS

As I said, even though our common sense approach to establishing causality might not fit many of the validity types you learned about in Chapter 5 when it comes to establishing causality, true experiments are considered the "gold standard" of research because they are the method of observation best suited to addressing the three causality criteria. Therefore, of the four types of methods of observation covered in this book, experiments are especially well suited for explanatory and evaluation research.

The types of hypotheses that are best suited for experiments are those that require some conscious manipulation of the independent variable (the cause). This does not need to be an expensive endeavor. For example, in his classic experiment about peer pressure and conformity, Solomon Asch's study had little to no cost because all he did was get a group of college men into a room to view lines drawn on a board (Asch, 1951). Similarly, Rajaratnam et al.'s (2015) study incurred no cost because they were examining data that were already being collected for other purposes. But if researchers are evaluating an intensive intervention, the costs of the experiment might be much higher.

On the contrary, experiments are ill suited to study topics in which the researcher cannot control or manipulate (or at least identify the introduction of) the independent variable. For example, experiments are not a good design choice for questions such as: Do men do better in research methods courses than women? Does a college degree increase wages? Are girls from abusive homes more likely to be sexually active? Researchers cannot decide or manipulate a person's gender, level of education, or whether a subject experiences an abusive environment.

Another consideration for deciding whether experiments are appropriate is whether the researcher has relatively few variables of interest and the concepts are able to be defined well. For example, the study by Chong et al. (2012) had a very clearly defined independent variable, lengthened exposure to violent video games, which was easy for the researchers to manipulate, as the researchers decided whether a subject played the game or not and for how long.

To summarize, some considerations which will help you "get the job done" in deciding whether experiments are suitable for you are:

1. Is the hypothesis one that involves an independent (treatment) variable that the researcher can manipulate (true experiment) or identify a start date (quasi-experiment)?

2. Is the researcher interested in studying relatively few variables?

3. Can the independent and dependent variables have clearly defined and directly observable indicators?

Deciding which experimental design to choose would involve a different set of considerations, some of which are presented in Figure 6.5. Remember, however, that these are just basic guidelines to "get the job done" and that there are an infinite number of possible experimental approaches.

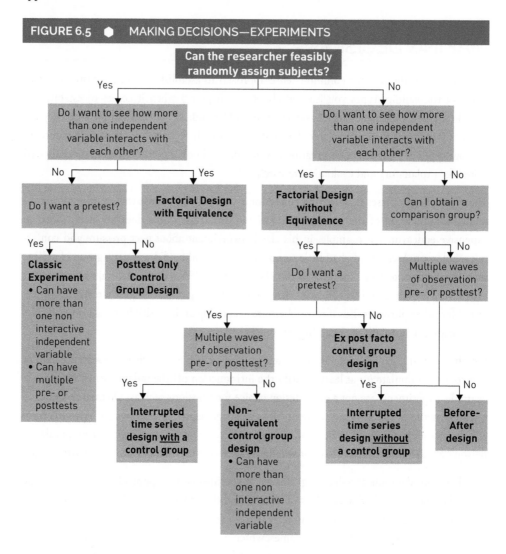

FIGURE 6.5 ● MAKING DECISIONS—EXPERIMENTS

CHALLENGES

1. **How can I ethically deny a control group treatment if I want to do an experiment to test a new intervention?**
   Just because a control group does not get the experimental stimulus does not necessarily mean that it gets *no* stimulus. Especially in applied research, denying the control group *any* treatment might be unethical. For example, if you want to test whether a new form of case management for welfare mothers helps them get off of welfare, you would not necessarily just leave the comparison group with *no* form of casework help and let them flounder on their own! Usually in applied research, while not getting the experimental (new) stimulus, the control group will still get whatever actions were considered "standard operating procedure" and some of the outcome focus is not just on whether the stimulus works, but does it work *better* than what practitioners are already doing (standard operating procedure)?

2. **In order to obtain informed consent do I have to provide full disclosure to the students about the purpose of the study; and if I do, how do I prevent reactivity?**
   As you learned previously in Chapter 3 on ethics, some deception in experiments may be allowed to reduce reactivity as long as what researchers withhold would not affect the participant's ability to give informed consent. For example, Chong et al. (2012) did not tell their subjects that they were studying how video games affected one's perception of reality; but knowing that true purpose or not did not affect the actions of the subjects; therefore, that information did not affect what was being asked of them to participate and would not have been required to be part of informed consent. One of the ways to ethically get around any deception that might be present in an experiment is to debrief the subjects. Debriefing is telling the subjects the true purpose of the experiment after the posttest. Included in the debriefing should be an explanation to subjects that it was not the researchers' goal to deceive them, but in order for the researcher to learn about "XXX," telling them about the real purpose of the research at the time of the study might have unintentionally affected subjects' behavior, and therefore the results.

3. **How can I increase external validity?** Because external validity is an issue of being able to generalize from a study to a population, in order to increase this, a researcher needs to focus on generalizability. One way is to draw a sufficiently large random sample (Chapter 5). However, even if you select a large, random sample, you need to increase the likelihood that people will elect to participate. Depending on your method of observation, how you go about this may differ; but a characteristic that will be the same for all will be how the researcher frames informed consent (Chapter 3). The informed consent wording is one way for you to entice the subject to participate in your study regardless of the method of observation, which can further improve external validity.

Key Terms

Attrition

Before-and-after design

Classic experiment

Contamination

Control group

Equivalency

Experimental group

Ex post facto control group design

External validity

History effect

Instrumentation

Internal validity

Interrupted Time-Series Design

Maturation

Nonequivalent control group design

Pretest

Posttest

Posttest only control group design

Reactivity

Quasi-experiment

Selection bias

Statistical conclusion validity

Testing

True experiment

Answers to Learning Check Questions

Learning Check 6.1: True Experiments

1. True experiments are characterized by (a) at least two groups of study; (b) variation in the independent variable (treatment) where one group gets the value of interest and the other does not; (c) random assignment to the groups; and (d) control over the context of the experiment.

2. Random selection is an issue of sampling where subjects in the population have an equal chance of being selected into the study so that the subjects in the sample accurately illustrate the people in the population. Random assignment, on the other hand, is an issue of experiments where once subjects have been selected (by any means) for study participation, they have an equal chance of being put into either the control or experimental groups.

Learning Check 6.2: Internal Validity Threats

1. Selection bias means that the two groups being compared are unequal on factors *other* than the independent variable (the only factor for which we *do* want them to be unequal); therefore, if selection bias is present, researchers cannot tell if differences at the end of the study are because of the independent variable or the differences between the two groups from the start.

2. Experimental mortality is a problem when people who share a characteristic disproportionately drop out of the study, thereby creating bias.

3. Some possible answers are: choose a method of observation that allows anonymity of

respondents (rather than confidentiality), read respondents' body language to see if they are being honest, spend a lot of time with respondents so they get used to the researcher and begin acting more naturally, and have a sufficiently large sample.

Learning Check 6.3: Validity Types and True Experiments

1. Random assignment is important because it allows the researchers to presume that the groups being compared are not systematically different in any way that would affect the dependent variable prior to the application of the treatment.

2. True experiments are conducted in very specific, controlled environments that allow the researcher to make causal connections; however, in the real world the environment cannot be so controlled, therefore, the findings of a controlled environment may not completely translate to the real, external, world.

3. The main threats to validity are contamination and history if it is localized to only some groups. Pretest effects might also be a factor, but depending on the design selected this may be estimated.

Learning Check 6.4: Quasi-Experiments

1. Random assignment

2. One group before–after design

3. Erosion of treatment (whether the effect of the independent variable wears off over time)

End-of-Chapter Problems

1. When a researcher randomly selects subjects from a population, pairs them on gender and race, and then flips a coin to decide which group gets the experimental treatment and which group acts as the control the research has done
   a. nonrandom assignment
   b. matching without random assignment
   c. matching with random assignment
   d. basic random assignment

2. A researcher wants to test a new teaching technique that incorporates technology in the classroom. The researcher gets permission to gives all the classrooms in Elementary School A the new technology, but Elementary School B elects not to use the new technology so it will serve as a comparison school. The researcher administers a grade-appropriate benchmark of knowledge at the beginning of the school year to both schools and again at the end of the school year. What kind of experiment did the researcher do?
   a. A true experiment
   b. A nonequivalent control group design
   c. A time-series experiment
   d. A within-group before–after design

3. What is the "gold standard" of research?
   a. True experiments
   b. Quasi-experiments
   c. Factorial analysis
   d. Surveys

4. Which quasi-experimental design is good for identifying whether erosion of treatment is a validity threat?
   a. Nonequivalent control group design
   b. Within-group before–after design
   c. Time-series design
   d. Ex post facto control group design

5. Which experimental design allows the researcher to see how two or more independent variables interact to affect the dependent variable?
   a. True experiment
   b. Posttest-only control group design

c. Time-series experiment
d. Factorial design

6. True/False: In order to be a true experiment, random selection is necessary.

7. Which of the following addresses methodological issues that influence whether a researcher can make causal connections?
   a. Measurement validity
   b. Internal validity
   c. External validity
   d. Reliability

8. What threat to internal validity occurs when events outside of the study and researcher's control might affect the dependent variable?
   a. History
   b. Maturation
   c. Selection bias
   d. Reactivity

   For questions 9–12, read the following scenario:

   Hidrobo, Peterman, and Heise (2016) wanted to study whether cash, vouchers, and food transfers targeted to women in Ecuador to reduce poverty also affect intimate partner violence (IPV). The researchers were not able to randomly select individual participants, but they did randomly assign urban centers within two providences to either the treatment or control group. Secondly, within the urban centers assigned to the treatment groups, they further randomly assigned clusters within neighborhoods to one of the three treatments: cash, vouchers, or food. Subjects were surveyed prior to the distribution of the service to establish baseline characteristics and 6 months after intervention. Measures included respondents' household characteristics, labor behavior, women's status in the household, household decision making, and IPV.

9. What type of experiment did Hidrobo et al. (2016) conduct?
    a. A true experiment
    b. A nonequivalent control group design
    c. A time-series experiment
    d. A within-group before–after design

10. What would the notation be for this experiment? (Write-in)

11. Which of the following is unlikely to be a threat to validity based on the study design?
    a. History
    b. Contamination
    c. Selection bias
    d. None of the above is likely to be an issue

12. Which of the following might still be a threat to validity just based on the design alone?
    a. Local history
    b. Contamination
    c. Selection bias
    d. Any of the above is likely to be an issue

7

SURVEY RESEARCH

LEARNING GOALS

- Identify the types of topics suitable for survey research.
- Learn the basic considerations for questionnaire wording and presentation, including when to borrow existing measures and when/how to create unique ones.
- Distinguish between the four broad types of survey research.
- Relate survey research to earlier issues of validity and reliability.
- Recognize different considerations for deciding among the four broad forms of survey research.

Surveys are probably the method of observation that is most familiar to many of you. You may have encountered web surveys, course evaluations (which frequently use a survey format), or even a campus survey through inter-campus mail. Surveys are common when researchers want to obtain the public's view on a variety of social issues and they are a popular form of observation because they are very versatile, are generally affordable, and can reach a large geographically dispersed population. The Pew Research Center, for example, frequently administers surveys to nationally representative samples of US citizens to describe their attitudes regarding many social issues such as the use or views of social media, politics, and race relations, to name

istockphoto.com/ginosphotos

PHOTO 7.1 The United States has yet to elect a female president.

a few topics. One of its recent surveys (as of the writing of this book) is its American Trends Panel, a nationally representative online survey of 4,587 adults that includes questions about people's views of women in leadership positions. According to this survey, 59% of responding adults felt that there were too few women in leadership positions; but women were more likely to feel this way than men (69% compared to 48%, Pew Research Center, 2018). By using a web survey, PeW was able to reach a wide geographical area relatively easily.

So, when are surveys an appropriate method of observation? As I just said, surveys are very versatile and may be appropriate for describing views, like the PeW survey mentioned above does, for describing people's direct experiences, or for recording their self-reported behavior, such as "What forms of social media do you use?," "How many times have you consumed alcohol in the past week?," or "Have you ever had a female boss?" Surveys are not limited to description. They can be explanatory because they can measure multiple concepts via multiple indicators in one instrument. Finally, surveys may also be a useful component of program evaluation by assessing program needs, describing program use, or examining components of program effectiveness (Newcomer & Triplett, 2015). For example, research has long documented that being a foster family can be stressful for all elements of the family: the foster parents, the foster children, and any biological children. One way to help foster parents and their biological children cope with being foster families is to offer respite care or care that gives foster parents a break from their foster duties so they can spend time on their own and/or with biological children. However, this respite care can take many forms and little is known about whether foster parents use this relief, what types they may use, and whether respite care has any measurable effect on family unity. Madden et al. (2016) addressed these gaps using a 42-item survey to explore foster parents' use and perception of the usefulness of different types of respite care on family cohesion and stability, on the ability to care for children, and of foster parent personal well-being. Through these surveys, Madden et al. learned that parents who use a mix of formal and informal respite services reported the most positive experiences, including a reduction in stress and an increase in family stability, than did parents who used either formal or informal forms exclusively. Furthermore, those who exclusively used formal means of respite care fared better than did those who exclusively used informal forms. Therefore, from this survey information, Madden et al. were able to statistically establish a need for providing formal, rather than relying on informal, respite care services to foster families.

There are also some types of information for which surveys are *not* well suited. Surveys are not very good for assessing *past* or recollected behavior. Studies have found that recollected memory is highly variable and therefore potentially problematic for research in general and surveys in particular (Harlow & Donaldson, 2013; Harlow & Yonelinas, 2014). Surveys also are not as strong as experiments or quasi-experiments for assessing whether a program has changed the desired behavior. Because surveys rely on self-report, what one claims to feel or do does not necessarily address what they *really* feel or do. Think about it—have you ever told your parents you were at one place (reported behavior) when you were really at another (actual behavior)? That's the same idea here. Therefore, experimental designs (quasi or true) may be a more objective measure of behavior change.

QUESTION CONSTRUCTION: TO WRITE OR NOT TO WRITE

Depending on the focus of a study and the degree to which others may have examined a topic, researchers might not have to write all of their survey questions, also called **questionnaires**, themselves. Sometimes researchers can borrow the questions developed and used by other researchers, and there are different ways of going about this and some advantages to doing so. One way is to simply borrow some questions created and used by different resources (citing them, of course, to give them credit). Borrowing questions that are used by others is advantageous because doing so can aid external validity (Chapter 4). Because the new study population is not likely to 100% replicate the group or geographical areas of the study from where the new researcher borrowed the questions, if our findings between the two (new and old) studies are similar, researchers have established some level of external validity (Newcomer & Triplett, 2015).

A second way in which researchers do not have to write their own questions is if they use the raw data from someone else's survey for their own analysis. This is called **secondary analysis of primary data**. A variety of surveys and their corresponding data are publically available online. The General Social Survey (GSS), National Longitudinal Studies of Youth (NLSY), and the Panel Study of Income Dynamics (PSID) are three large, publically available data sets based on survey or interview techniques that are extensive and beyond the data gathering means of most individual researchers because the studies are longitudinal with very large samples. Even if researchers do not borrow the raw data itself, they can borrow the questions/answers wording to construct their own particular survey. Last, researchers can incorporate scales, which are frequently constructed from survey question and tested by other researchers for validity and reliability, into their studies. Including scale questions also often helps address concepts that are multidimensional, aiding content validity (Chapter 4). Remember, with proper recognition, copying the questions or using the data of someone else is not cheating; it is replication.

However, there are times when the researcher does need to get creative. Perhaps there are not any measures for a specific program that are applicable, there is a reason for a concept to be measured in a new way, and/or the direction of an analysis is new and there is not any pre-existing measures that fit the situation. When this occurs, the researcher needs to write their own questions. In my experience, students are so used to seeing surveys that they often think that writing survey questions is easy. After all, you have an idea of what you want to ask, you learned how to conceptualize in Chapter 4, so you just take your indicators and put a "?" at the end. Bingo! You have a survey question! Sometimes writing survey questions *is* this easy, especially if you have well-defined indicators, but sometimes—in fact frequently—when we write questions, we also realize that what we thought of as clear is not always clear to others or does not really provide useful information. Let's illustrate this with the hypothetical survey about drug use that appears in Box 7.1.

At first glance, this questionnaire may seem fine to you. However, there is not a single question here that does not have at least one problem. Let's pretend that I am filling out this survey (I will use the terms "survey" and "questionnaire" interchangeably) and I am just getting over an illness that required I take antibiotics. I would have to answer "yes" to the first question because antibiotics are a "drug," but that is probably not the type of drug the researcher

---

BOX 7.1
HYPOTHETICAL SURVEY QUESTIONS ON DRUG USE

1. Have you used any drugs in the past 2 months?
   a. Yes
   b. No

2. How often have you used these drugs?
   a. 1–4 times
   b. 4–7 times
   c. 7–11 times
   d. More than 11 times

3. Did anyone catch you and punish you for using these drugs?
   a. Yes
   b. No

4. How appropriate do you think this punishment was?
   a. Very appropriate
   b. Somewhat appropriate
   c. Not very appropriate

5. What is your race?
   a. White, non-Hispanic
   b. Black/African American
   c. Hispanic/Latino
   d. Asian/Pacific Islander

meant. As a respondent, how am I to know this though? Even something like an over-the-counter medicine to fight headaches is technically a "drug." So if I answer "yes," because I used antibiotics or a headache medicine, but the survey is actually about illegal or recreational drug use, my answer is going to skew the results. Question 1 then is an issue of vague wording and really means that I did not do a good job of selecting indicators when I was operationalizing my concepts. This can happen when the researcher is so focused on what they want to study that they forget that *others* who are not necessarily as familiar with the research topic are the ones actually completing the survey. Questions need to be written very clearly to avoid vague interpretations of what words or the question is really asking.

By the same token, writing survey questions is not the time to show how smart you are by writing long or overly complicated wording or by being indirect (Dillman, 2007). "In your opinion, how well did our customer service staff address the concern that was the purpose of your contact?" is way too long and impersonal and may make the respondent lose interest in the survey. A better approach would be "What is your view of our customer service representative's ability to address your problem?" or even "How would you rate our service representative's ability to solve your problem?" Short, clear, and direct is one of the first guidelines for writing survey questions, always keeping in mind your target audience. Writing a survey to be completed by attorneys would require different wording considerations than writing a survey for someone who did not complete high school.

Incidentally, even though the first question in the example is asking for recollected information, it restricts that past time to a fairly short and recent frame of reference—within the past 2 months. If the question was instead worded "Which drugs have you used in the past?" the respondent may not know whether the researcher means *ever* (If someone tried pot once as a teenager, does that count?) or more recently, such as the last year. Researchers recognize that recollected behavior can be tricky to measure, but sometimes past information is needed. Establishing a short time frame can make this information more accurate. However, the first question still has the problem of vague wording. Does "use" mean the same as "tried once or twice" or does it mean more frequent or consistent use? So that term also needs clarification.

Last, one other point to always keep in mind as you write survey questions (or any other type of research question) that is illustrated in question one: How can I use this information? In this instance, all I may have learned, presuming that the person won't include over-the-counter medication, is whether someone used illegal drugs. I have not, for example, learned *what* kind of drugs, *how many different types* of drugs, or *how often* this person used. Therefore, this question alone is not as informative as it could be, nor is it set up here to be a filter question to additional questions that are relevant (which I will discuss later). In sum, based on the first question alone, we have learned four points about questionnaire wording. Researchers should:

- Write questions to be very specific and a void vague wording that can be subjectively interpreted (e.g., "average," "regularly").

- Write questions using words that are commonly used by your study population.

- If asking for reported behavior, consider bracketing the time span for consideration if including recollected behavior.

- Write questions with a clear idea of how they will use the information provided (that are necessary and useful).

The second question also has a host of problems. First, it asks about "drugs" in the plural. If we ignore the problems of Question 1 and pretend that we understand that "drugs" refers to illegal recreational drug use, Question 2 is still a concern because if I used more than one drug (and the use of the plural "drugs" suggests this possibility), then there might be two different answers for how often. I might have tried Drug A one time, but have used Drug B four times. So how would I respond to this question? That answer is anybody's guess and that vagueness will further contribute to study error. Let's pretend (again—with questions this poor, there will be a lot of "pretending" for the sake of argument) that I did only use one drug and that I used it four times in the past 2 months. Now the issue is which answer choice do I select? Do I circle "a" or "b" because they both have the answer of "4"? You should have been able to identify this problem on your own because the answer choices violate one of the basic rules of measurement that we covered in Chapter 4, namely that answer choices have to be mutually exclusive. To refresh your memory, this means that, unless otherwise specified with something like "circle all that apply," there should be only one answer choice for each person. But there is a third problem with this question as well. What if I did not use any drugs? There is no "0" option, which is also a violation of what we learned in Chapter 4 about measurement because these answer choices are not exhaustive. Even more relevant, however, is that *none* of the questions after Question 1 are relevant to someone who didn't use drugs of any sort. Using the first question to filter respondents who did not use drugs away from the questions not relevant to them would be useful in this instance. Such questions are called **filter questions** and establish **skip patterns** or contingency formats, which directs respondents only to answer questions that are contingent/relevant based on an answer to a previous filter question. I will cover this useful question form later in this chapter when I address how to format various types of surveys. So, for now, we have three additional considerations when constructing survey questions:

- If you are asking for information about something that might occur in the plural (e.g., more than one class, more than one instructor, more than one drug), make sure you can obtain information on individual items as well as the aggregate.

- Make sure answer choices are exhaustive and mutually exclusive unless directed otherwise (e.g., "circle all that apply").

- Use filter questions to avoid asking questions that are not relevant to some participants.

Question 3 illustrates another common problem. It is what researchers call a "double-barreled" question because it essentially asks two questions within a single one. For example, what if someone, such as a teacher, caught me using drugs, but did not punish me? The answer to the first half of the question is "yes" but the answer to the second half is "no"…and, again, that makes it unclear to the respondent how to answer. Fortunately, this problem is easy to identify when the researcher is proofing a draft and it has an easy solution. All the researcher has to do is use their word processing program to search for the word "and" and if it pops up in this manner, make the question into two separate questions.

- Avoid double-barreled questions.

By now you might be noticing some common themes and links to earlier chapters. As I have said throughout the book, methods do not occur in a vacuum. Skills you learned in earlier chapters have relevance to skills you will learn about in later chapters—as we have seen with the importance of answer choice wording. So now you might be able to identify some of the problems with Question 4. First "appropriate" is a very vague term and I might have a different definition of what is/isn't appropriate than you do. So I shouldn't have a question as vague as this. Second, there isn't a neutral category. What if the respondent really doesn't have an opinion on this? If that is the case, there is no answer for this person and either they will just arbitrarily pick one of the three (which can bias results if enough respondents do this) or skip the question altogether (but the researcher will not know why the question was skipped, so they cannot learn anything from its omission). Our new point is, even ignoring the lack of a neutral category, my response choices here are still misleading. Two of the three responses lean toward a favorable view of appropriateness ("very" and "somewhat" appropriate) and only one leans toward a negative view ("not very" appropriate); therefore, these response choices are unbalanced with more options indicating favorable views than negative views, which may bias the results toward the positive. Therefore, it is important to remember that in the social

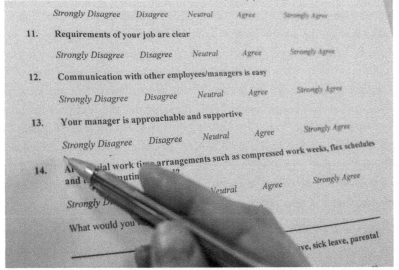

PHOTO 7.2 Can you find the double-barreled question in this survey?

sciences, opinion questions should be evenly expressed among positive and negative perspectives, and, although not universally agreed, many researchers favor a neutral response option, as discussed in Chapter 4.

- Make sure you have the same number of positive and negative answer choices.

- Include a neutral category, preferably situated in the middle of the responses, for opinion-related questions, keeping the answer options an odd number.

The last question is problematic for trickier reasons. Now it is widely recognized that one's race is a matter of personal identity and that people may identify with multiple races simultaneously. Furthermore, obviously, there are more than these four possibilities for racial identification. There are a number of different possible options to correct this. One is the researcher could add "primary identification" to the question if the desired response is one race. Another option is to have multiple questions about racial identification where the questions ask about primary, secondary, and even tertiary identifications for more detailed identification. Regardless, at the very least, the researcher needs to add "Other: Please specify_____" as an answer choice so the respondent can write any clarification they deem relevant. The researcher can then decide how to use that information when coding responses (Chapter 10).

Box 7.2 has one possible way that these survey questions could be asked in better form, but the issues illustrated in this example are only the tip of the iceberg when writing individual questions. Some other considerations include avoiding questions that are leading. "Do you agree that Drug Courts are a good alternative to traditional imprisonment for non-violent drug offenses?" is a leading question for two reasons. First, it is worded as "Do you agree" as opposed to the more balanced "Do you agree or disagree…" or even "What is your opinion…." A second reason this is leading is that the respondent may not feel that Drug Courts are a "good" alternative and the question implies, or leads them, to react as if they are.

Another common issue I frequently see in surveys that are used to evaluate teaching or information sessions is when the question refers to multiple people or issues together so the information cannot be linked to a specific person or issue and, therefore, is not very informative. I have seen this most frequently when surveys are designed to assess people's attitudes toward a training or information session where there may have been more than one presenter. For example, the question may be worded as "How prepared did you find your instructor(s)?" How would someone respond if one instructor was prepared, but the other was not? Furthermore, if multiple respondents answered "Not very" or some other negative response, what has the researcher learned? They may have learned that there was a problem in delivery somewhere, but not where or with whom, so the researcher does not really know what to suggest to change and, therefore, has not learned much from that question.

It is also important to avoid biased wording in surveys. For example, "Do you think responsible parents should vaccinate their children" is a biased question that would put parents who do not believe in vaccinations on the defensive because of the phrase "responsible parents."

BOX 7.2
POSSIBLE IMPROVEMENTS TO SURVEY QUESTIONS

1. In the past 2 months, have you used any non-over-the-counter drugs, such as cocaine, heroin, marijuana, prescription drugs (for nonprescribed purposes or in larger than prescribed doses)?
   a. Yes (Please go to question 2)
   b. No (Please go to question 5)

2. How many times have you used each of the following drugs listed in the past 2 months:
   a. Cocaine _____
   b. Heroin _____
   c. Marijuana _____
   d. Prescription drugs _____
   e. Other (Please specify drug and frequency:_____)

3. Did anyone such as a parent, teacher, or other adult ever catch you using any non-over-the-counter or prescribed drugs?

   a. Yes (please go to question 4)
   b. No (please go to question 5)

4. Did any of these people punish you for your drug use?
   a. Yes
   b. No

5. What is your primary racial identification?
   a. White, non-Hispanic
   b. Black or African American
   c. Hispanic or Latinx
   d. Asian/Pacific Islander
   e. Biracial (Please identify: _____)
   f. Other (Please identify: _____)

Regardless of their view on child vaccination, most parents make the choice that *they* feel is responsible. Another example of a biased wording would be something like "Do you think terrorists on American soil should be prosecuted in America or their country of origin?" "Terrorist" is a very emotional term in our current cultural climate. One group's terrorist is another group's freedom fighter, regardless of the tactics, and "terrorist" creates images of mass destruction.

Another concern, especially relevant to the social sciences, is taking culture into consideration when writing questions. Different terms may have different meanings for people of different cultures. For example, even the seemingly generic term of "family" may have different meanings as to who counts as family depending on that person's culture or location. Some groups focus on the nuclear family unit of spouses and children, other groups include extended family, such as grandparents, aunts/uncles, and cousins, in their common definition of "family," and some even include their pets (Entis, 2016; Knox, 2011; Parker, 2005). As we will see, cultural considerations tend to be even more important to qualitative research (Chapter 8); but, for now, I will just mention this in the context of question-wording.

I am aware that it may seem that this section on how to write survey questions was never going to end. If you remember the beginning of this chapter, however, I did warn that writing questionnaires was more complicated than students frequently think. Thanks to our literature reviews, our expertise, and our boss's mandates, as researchers we may have a very clear sense of what we want to study. As a result, it is easy to forget that our subjects do *not* necessarily have the same firm foundation as we do. Therefore, we really need to use our sociological

istockphoto.com/Morsa Images

istockphoto.com/Rawpixel

istockphoto.com/Nevena1987

istockphoto.com/FatCamera

PHOTO 7.3 Even a concept as "basic" as "family" can have multiple meanings and need to be clarified in a survey

imagination and put ourselves in the place of our respondents, instead of ourselves as researchers, to write questions that will minimize bias and encourage accurate responses to the best of our ability. Respondents who do not understand questions may skip the questions, fill in anything, or—if this happens enough—become frustrated and stop participating altogether. Therefore, to summarize these points and add some others that are more self-explanatory:

- Avoid leading questions that make assumptions about one side of an opinion or that are only worded as "Do you agree" as opposed to the more balanced "Do you agree or disagree" or "What is your opinion?"

- Avoid leading questions that presume that the respondent shares the opinion expressed as a foundation of the survey question.

- Avoid lumping multiple entities (e.g., teachers, session leaders, classes) into the same question if asking the respondent to react to them. If respondents identify a problem, the researcher will not be able to identify where/what to do; therefore, that question will not provide useful information.

- Avoid biased wording that elicits a specific emotional response.

- Keep cultural context in mind when writing questions and try to use terms that have the same meaning in different cultures or specify the meaning of your term in the question to avoid confusion.

- Make sure that the respondent is able to answer the questions asked. Do not presume prior knowledge.

- Consider using both open- and closed-ended questions, but use open-ended sparingly for mail, web, or email surveys as respondents frequently will not answer them in detail (Newcomer, Hatry, & Wholey, 2015).

- Make sure the questions are necessary for the subject matter. Only ask what is needed.

- Make sure there is a logical flow to the survey questions.

- If using a pen/paper survey, make sure questions and/or answer choices all appear on the same page. Do not separate them across pages.

The next section discusses ways to further help reduce bias and nonresponse.

 LEARNING CHECK 7.1: IDENTIFYING PROBLEMATIC SURVEY QUESTIONS

What is wrong with the following survey questions?

1. What is your sex?
   a. Male
   b. Female

2. What is your yearly income?
   a. under $15,000
   b. $15,000–$30,000
   c. $30,000–$40,000
   d. $40,000–$55,000

3. Is the person you are caring for a parent?
   a. Yes
   b. No

4. Do you try and restrain your elderly parent when she/he becomes unruly?
   a. Yes
   b. No

5. What kinds of activities do you provide (with regards to caregiving) for the person you care for (if more than one relative, pick the one you have been providing care for the longest)?
   a. Washing
   b. Cooking
   c. Driving
   d. Administering medication
   e. Paying bills

6. Do you agree that the community provides adequate assistance to family caregivers?
   a. Strongly agree
   b. Agree
   c. Disagree
   d. Strong disagree

Answers to be found at the end of the chapter.

SURVEY PRESENTATION

Question construction is only part of the survey presentation. Would you be interested in completing a survey that had no introduction and/or began with a question such as: "What is your gender?" Probably not. So how surveys are organized and visually presented is important to encouraging subjects' interest and, therefore, possible participation.

Surveys should begin with some type of cover letter or introduction, depending on the survey method you choose. Cover letters (which is the term I will use just for ease) introduce the topic, serve as the first attempt to encourage respondent participation, and establish informed consent. As such, cover letters should be engaging and visually appealing, if possible. As the means of obtaining informed consent, the cover letter should also give the respondent directions on what to expect in the survey and how to complete it, as I already covered in Chapter 3.

Once the respondent begins the survey, the initial questions the researcher asks will set the tone for the survey. Although "What is your gender?" may come off as boring, participants may be equally unwilling to participate in a survey that begins with "How often have you had sex in the past month?" or "Have you ever committed a felony?" Those questions are very personal and might scare off potential respondents. Therefore, just as there is an art to writing questions, there is also an art to survey presentation.

The general rule of thumb is to begin surveys with questions that are related to the survey theme and are interesting but are not threatening. Starting with factual questions that are fairly easy to answer, but not boring, may encourage individuals to participate in your study (De Vaus, 2002 Real; Dillman, 2007; Langbein, 2006). More threatening questions should be placed near the end of a survey because there is a real risk that respondents will stop participating when they encounter these questions. It is also common for questions about the same topic to be placed together with transitions between topics. Contrary to what you might think, ping-ponging between topics is not likely to keep respondents' engaged but instead may frustrate them, and a frustrated respondent is one who is not likely to complete the study.

It is also important to make sure that respondents only answer questions that are relevant to them. Remember the hypothetical survey I began with early in the chapter? What if someone did not use any drugs—over-the-counter, prescription as intended, recreational, or otherwise? Using filter questions is a good way of making sure researchers don't waste respondents' time or frustrate them by asking them things that are not relevant to them. Filter questions direct respondents to only answer those questions that, based on information from a filter question, the respondent knows is relevant. Therefore, as you saw in Box 7.2, the first question is a filter question that directs respondents who answer "no" to skip the questions that pertain to drug use and resume the survey at Question 5.

There are two common ways to present filter questions. The first way is appropriate when the logic path requires more than a couple of follow-ups, called contingency questions. This option is illustrated with question 1 in Box 7.2. In the first question, if a subject answers "no," then questions 2, 3, and 4 are not relevant to that individual, so there is no point in having the subject look at them. Instead, that subject is directed to resume the survey at question 5. On the other hand, if the person answers "yes," then they continue to question 2 and answer all the questions after that.

The second option is more relevant when there are only one or two contingency questions and involves physically drawing the connection to the follow-up question as such:

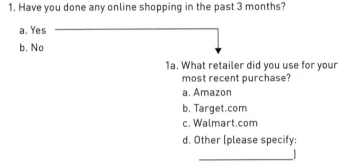

1. Have you done any online shopping in the past 3 months?

    a. Yes

    b. No

            1a. What retailer did you use for your most recent purchase?

               a. Amazon

               b. Target.com

               c. Walmart.com

               d. Other (please specify: _____)

Filter/contingency logic paths can be as simple as the ones I just presented or more complex with logic paths within logic paths. As you will see later in this chapter, some methods of survey design are better at handling complex logic paths than others and, therefore, how complex a path you want needs to be a factor in deciding what type of survey to conduct.

A **matrix format** is another way of presenting survey questions, but this time the goal is to save space and/or identify possible threats to validity for questions with a common theme and similarly worded answer choices. For example, let's say I have four questions about people's attitudes toward the poor, each of which is measured on a 5-point Likert scale ranging from "strongly agree" to "strongly disagree." If I wrote these four questions from top to bottom, as we commonly see, I would take up 27 lines of space (1 line for the question, 5 lines for the responses = 6 lines per question × 4 questions + 3 question spacing lines = 27 lines). Now here are four questions presented in a matrix format:

Please check which response best fits your view of the following issues. The codes for the responses are:

SA = strongly agree   A = agree   DK = don't know   D = disagree   SD = strongly disagree

		SA	A	DK	D	SD
1.	The government should provide low-income families with affordable housing.	[ ]	[ ]	[ ]	[ ]	[ ]
2.	The family one is born into provides the foundation for that person's future economic experiences.	[ ]	[ ]	[ ]	[ ]	[ ]
3.	The poor are lazy.	[ ]	[ ]	[ ]	[ ]	[ ]
4.	The minimum wage provides enough to live on.	[ ]	[ ]	[ ]	[ ]	[ ]

Even with the directions and key to the answer choices, the matrix format is 10 lines. Therefore, when trying to limit survey length, the matrix format is one way researchers can include questions (as long as they are relevant) while still making the survey appear to be comparatively short. However, methodologically, the second reason maybe even more compelling. Notice the third question. This is an example of a **reverse-coded question** where a "strongly disagree" response would show more favorable attitudes toward the poor. When combining reverse-coded questions with a matrix format, it is easy to see whether either someone stopped paying attention to the questions and just checked the same answer all the way down or if they are giving into acquiescence bias by doing the same. For either reason, if someone responds the same way to all the questions, the researcher knows that that survey may be methodologically compromised, at least for that section of questions.

Survey length is also an important consideration for survey design. Asking too many questions will hurt response rate and/or discourage survey completion as respondents get fatigued and stop (Newcomer & Triplett, 2015). How many questions are enough depends on your research topic, purpose, and survey format. Some suggest limiting the length to what a respondent can complete in 10–20 minutes, which may be two to four pages (Langbein, 2006; Newcomer & Triplett, 2015). However, this is a loose guide. I once evaluated a survey aimed at elderly crime victims where the print was so small that I, as a young researcher with good eyesight, had trouble reading it. When I suggested that one way of increasing response was to make the font larger, the person I was speaking to informed me that she learned that surveys for program evaluation were required to be limited to one page. The moral of the story here is that all of these are guidelines to *increase* participation. If something is having the opposite effect, then, by all means, alter the guidelines to your research needs and study population. To summarize the considerations for survey presentation:

- Order questions in a way where the survey starts with an interesting, factual, but nonthreatening question. Save any more personal or threatening questions for the end of the survey.

- Use filter questions to direct respondents away from questions that do not pertain to them.

LEARNING CHECK 7.2: QUESTIONNAIRE FORMAT

1. Where should you place a question about gender: the beginning, middle, or end of a survey? Why?

2. If you want to ask six contingency questions after a filter question, which is better form: separating the questions off to the size of the page and using lines/arrows to direct the respondent after the filter question, or using a logic path that provides directions for the next appropriate question after each answer choice in the filter question?

Answers to be found at the end of the chapter.

- Consider using a matrix format with reverse-coded questions for questions that have a similar theme and answer choices.

- Keep the length of the overall survey in mind. Only ask the number of questions necessary to adequately address all the research goals and concepts expressed in the main purpose.

PRETESTING QUESTIONNAIRES

Even if a survey largely consists of questions that have been borrowed from other researchers or even if researchers carefully constructed each survey question keeping all of these guidelines in mind, researchers still don't know if the questions are clear or accurately interpreted by their study population until they pretest the instrument on a small sample of that population. Pretesting serves multiple purposes. As you learned in Chapter 4 on creating measures, a pretest, sometimes also called a **pilot study**, is a "first-run" where researchers test the administration of the survey instrument on a much smaller scale before they invest the time and money in a larger study (Dillman, Smyth, & Christian, 2014; Gillham, 2007; Willis, 2015). Furthermore, as you learned in Chapter 5, when the research goal is a pretest, researchers do not need a probability sample or a large sample size; therefore, pretests require relatively little effort but can provide big payoffs to survey improvement. There are a variety of reasons why such a trial run can be useful.

In addition to testing whether measures, such as survey questions, are understandable to subjects, pretests can also help identify whether there are any questions that show little variation in responses and/or show a disproportionate amount of non-committal or "don't know" responses (Gillham, 2007). In some cases, especially if only pretesting a few people, researchers might want to couple the pretest with a cognitive interview where researchers interview either the entire pretest sample or a selected number of them to learn about the respondents' thoughts about questions (Willis, 2015). From these interviews, researchers can learn whether respondents are interpreting the questions as designed or if they are providing answers based on different ideas about what the question means. Both pretests alone or in conjunction with cognitive interviews give researchers insights into how people are interpreting questions, whether there are any problems with questions, and if so what might be done to correct those problems.

If problems are identified in the pretest, then the survey can be corrected and tested a second time on a new sample of a few people. This increases the accuracy of the responses in the final, usually larger and more expensive, "real" study for which there are no "do-overs."

COMMON SURVEY TYPES

There are many methods of observation that follow the general questionnaire guidelines, to different extents, that I discussed earlier in this chapter and, therefore, fall under the umbrella of "survey research." Here I will discuss four broad types of those methods in more detail in terms of what they entail, how to do them, and their separate strengths and weaknesses.

Self-Reported Mailed Surveys

Self-reported mailed surveys are one of the most commonly known methods of survey observation. This is the method of observation where a paper/pencil survey is sent to a respondent in the postal mail. This option is best suited for research in which the study population (and therefore, sample) is geographically diverse, respondents need time to reflect upon their answers, respondents are likely to have an interest in the research topic, and/or the topic is one that might benefit from the anonymous response. Think about it. Someone might be more likely to report information about their sex life, their illicit drug use, or their victimization if they were reasonably confident that anyone reading the survey would be unable to link responses directly to them. Therefore, mailed surveys are less vulnerable to the reactivity effect discussed in Chapter 4. They can also be relatively cheap to conduct and they generally contain more closed-, rather than open-ended, questions so they are also relatively easy to code.

To conduct mailed surveys, researchers may create and pretest a pen/paper questionnaire following the guidelines I discussed. Once researchers identify and select a sample, they mail the questionnaire, complete with a cover letter and stamped return envelope, to each selected element. However, the researcher should not consider his/her job to be done. Probably the biggest limitation in mailed survey research is the very low response rate. Have you ever received a survey either at home or in campus mail and just tossed it in the trash? If so, you wouldn't be alone. Response rates as low as 30% are common and, obviously, highly biased simply because of lack of representation (Dillman, 2007; Dillman & Parsons, 2008). I will address some strategies for improving response rates in the "Challenges" section of this chapter because although most apply to mailed surveys, some also apply to other forms of survey design.

Mailed surveys are also vulnerable to response bias because respondents with higher levels of education or a greater sense of social obligation are more likely to respond (Czaja & Blair, 2005; Dillman, Smyth, & Christian, 2014). Likewise, mailed surveys are really a one-shot approach. There is no way for the researcher to clarify or answer any questions respondents might have. Therefore, as mentioned earlier, pretesting a survey instrument is absolutely necessary if this is the method of observation a researcher wants to use.

So some strengths of mailed surveys are that they can reach a wide geographical area and they can be easy to code. However, mailed surveys have additional concerns, such as a low response rate and the inability of the respondent to ask for clarification when needed, that one has to consider before selecting this method of observation, as noted at the end of the chapter.

Telephone Surveys

Telephone surveys are also pretty self-evident; they are surveys done where researchers contact participants over the phone, conduct the survey, and enter the information into a computer program during the course of the survey itself. Like mailed surveys, these surveys are likely to largely consist of close-ended questions, can reach a large geographical population, and are easy to administer. However, unlike mailed surveys, telephone surveys involve interaction with a real person. As a result, they are also sometimes referred to as telephone interviews. This method of observation is faster than mailed surveys and, as just covered, more personal. There are some real benefits to choosing this method of observation. First, telephone surveys frequently can make use of **random digit dialing**, which makes random sampling easier. There are many forms of random digit dialing, but most commonly a machine will call random numbers (whether they are valid phone numbers or not) within a specific exchange, and lists of area code exchange numbers or files of local-based directories can frequently be obtained from commercial sources to make this process even easier. Second, through **computer-assisted telephone interview (CATI)** software, interviewers can directly enter subjects' responses into a computer. This serves a couple of benefits. First, the computer can be programmed to direct the interviewer to specific questions based on the subject's answer to previous ones; therefore,

istockphoto.com/PeopleImages

PHOTO 7.4 Telephone surveys can use computers to handle complex question ordering as well as to input data as respondents provide it.

any skip patterns, which can be potentially confusing to a respondent in a mailed survey or administered incorrectly by a poorly trained or careless interviewer, can be handled with decreased error by the computer. Furthermore, as interviewers enter respondents' answers, they are essentially simultaneously doing data entry, as I will discuss in Chapter 10. Finally, unlike in a mailed survey, here the interviewer can explain or answer questions the respondent may have. This can increase the validity of the information as well as decrease the rate of "don't know" responses.

But no method is perfect so there are still some limitations that need to be considered if choosing this approach. First, the interviewer has to make sure that the person completing the survey is actually the desired respondent. This can easily be addressed, however, if the researcher asks a series of initial questions to make sure that the correct individual is completing the survey. Second, the response rates for phone surveys declined steadily until about 2012, when they stabilized at an all-time low of 9% (Figure 7.1, PEW Research Center, 2017b).

You don't need a research methods class to tell you that a 9% response rate is, quite simply, awful. There are a lot of possible reasons for this drop, some of which include the rise in single-parent homes, the increase in dual-earner households, and the common use of answering machines and/or ID systems that allow people to ignore or screen calls (Tourangeau, 2004).

FIGURE 7.1 ● PEW TELEPHONE GRAPH

Despite overall decrease, response rates have stabilized over past four years

Response rate by year (%)

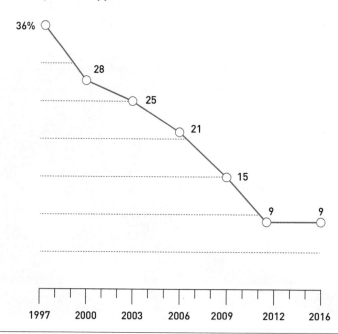

1997   2000   2003   2006   2009   2012   2016

Source: Pew Research Center surveys conducted 1997–2016. "What Low Response Rates Mean for Telephone Surveys."
Note: Response rate is AAPOR RR3. Only landlines sampled 1997–2006. Rates typical for surveys conducted in each year.

Hence multiple callbacks may be necessary before a researcher can obtain a response, which counters some of the efficiency traditionally associated with phone surveys.

Another limitation is that the person completing the survey may get distracted. Children can be crying, dogs can be barking, laundry may be finishing…you get the idea. All of these can conspire to lead to hurried responses, survey drop out, and/or skipped questions.

Web Surveys

Another option is web surveys, also called electronic, online, or Internet surveys, which are surveys done on the Internet. Thanks to the high use of smartphones and the increased availability of free computer use in areas like libraries, now almost three quarters (77%) of Americans go online at least daily and almost a quarter of them (26%) report going online "almost constantly" (Perrin & Jiang, 2018). As a result, web surveys have become an attractive alternative to mail and telephone surveys for some research purposes.

To create a web survey, researchers can draft the survey on pen/paper/computer, and then they need only a minimum of programming skills to upload/create the survey on the web. In fact, many servers are now menu-driven, similar to word processing programs, to make uploading questions even easier. Researchers can then usually contact respondents via an email that contains a link to the server that houses the survey, and there are a lot of free or low-cost servers available to researchers, such as Survey Monkey or Google Forms, which further contribute to the attractiveness of this method of data gathering. The survey itself can then usually be completed on computers, smartphones, or tablets.

Like mail and telephone surveys, web surveys can reach large geographical areas and large samples comparatively cheaply. For example, Döring, Daneback, Shaughnessy, Grov, and Byers (2017) studied online sexual behavior among college students in the United States, Canada, Sweden, and Germany (using one school of higher learning in each country) via an anonymous web survey. According to the researchers, the link to the survey was clicked over 4,000 times and resulted in language 2,270 usable surveys. Each of the surveys was translated into the appropriate and the subjects responded to 24 questions pertaining to involvement in, frequency of, and different types of online sexual activity. The researchers found that, despite any traditional cultural differences between the four countries, there were few differences regarding students' participation in online sexual activities, and when there were differences, they were comparatively small. The researchers suggested that this similarity may be because of the development of a new globalized "net generation" that approaches the Internet in similar ways regardless of their traditional national cultures (Döring et al., 2017). It is through the use of a web survey that the researchers were able to reach a large culturally and geographically diverse sample of people, which would have been very difficult to reach on this scale via other methods of observation.

An additional advantage of this observation method is that subjects can complete web surveys when it is convenient for them, and there is less chance of the survey getting lost. Even if the email is accidentally deleted, unless one's trash file is emptied, the survey can still be easily retrievable. Furthermore, as these surveys are completed electronically, some servers offer basic data analysis, such as frequency distributions and graphs, immediately available to the researcher. For more sophisticated statistical analysis, these servers can also convert the completed data to a form that can easily be imported to other computer programs like Excel, SPSS, or R.

However, complex surveys, such as those with many skip patterns or skip patterns within skip patterns, will still require careful construction and pretesting for survey implementation in order to make sure that the skip pattern organization works correctly when programmed. Furthermore, recent studies have shown that response rates for web surveys are similar to those of mailed surveys (Couper & Miller, 2008). This means the researcher will need to track respondents and conduct follow-up reminders similar to mailed surveys. Last, there is some concern that there is a response bias toward younger people. The same PEW study that showed that about a quarter of Americans report going online "almost constantly" also found that among people between 18 and 39 years old, this percentage was close to 39%, with an additional 49% claiming they go online "multiple times a day." The corresponding percent of those between the ages of 50 and 64 who reported being online "almost constantly" was just 17% (Perrin & Jiang, 2018).

Interviews

Interviews are the most personalized form of survey research and can happen in a variety of ways such as over the phone or face-to-face. Some very common data sets that are called "surveys," such as the GSS, the Current Population Survey, and the National Longitudinal Surveys, are actually interviews that involve the type of questionnaire format discussed in this chapter. These surveys are frequently longitudinal, have large samples of thousands of people, and address a couple of hundred questions (at least) so they are beyond the capabilities of individual researchers to conduct on their own. However, they are also publically available and researchers can access the data collected and use them for their own research purposes. As I mentioned earlier in the chapter, this type of research is often called secondary analysis of primary data because, in the instance I am describing, the researcher who did not gather the data themselves (hence the "secondary") can still analyze the raw data (hence "primary") collected by others. This type of research is nonreactive from the secondary researcher's perspective because the subjects have no interaction with the secondary researcher; therefore, any topics studied or quirks of the researcher's personality will not affect the nature of the data collected.

However, interviews can be a gray area of methodological classification. Some researchers do not think of this method of observation as a type of survey because when an average individual researcher conducts interviews, they are often done face-to-face, are semi-structured, have a limited geographical reach, are more personalized (hence have a high-reactivity risk), and are qualitative with open-ended questions that focus on respondents' subjective meaning of an experience or their detailed explanations of views or events. Because methodologically *conducting* this second form of interview is more common among everyday researchers, I will postpone our discussion of how to conduct face-to-face interviews until the next chapter, Chapter 8, which focuses on qualitative designs.

LEARNING CHECK 7.3: COMMON SURVEY TYPES

1. What are the three possible ways to improve the mail survey response rate?

2. For which of the three survey forms is it possible for the researcher to have responses automatically inputted into a computer program?

3. For which of the three survey forms is random sampling the easiest from a researcher perspective?

Answers to be found at the end of the chapter.

VALIDITY AND RELIABILITY

Validity

As you learned in Chapters 4 and 6, validity is whether the instrument and study design measures what it intends to measure. Of the four methods of observation discussed in this chapter, interviews will most likely have the highest validity followed by telephone surveys because the respondent can ask for clarification from the researcher or express when a question's choices don't really fit with his/her view. Both mailed and web surveys would at be the lower end of validity because, in both instances, these methods predominantly rely on closed-ended questions constructed by the researcher and once the instrument is designed and disseminated, there is no opportunity for clarification or adjustment on behalf of the respondent. This is not to mean, however, that mailed and web surveys do not have validity. Remember, there are different types of validity, and one way of increasing the validity in these methods is to use indicators (survey questions) borrowed and shown to be valid from others.

On the contrary, interviews particularly are also vulnerable to reactivity, which would threaten the validity of the study. Therefore, researchers conducting interviews have to be very conscious of impression management and we will cover this more in Chapter 8.

Reliability

If you remember from Chapter 4, reliability is the consistency of a measure and what is frequently high in validity tends to be a bit lower in reliability. So is the case with survey methodology. The very subjective nature and freedom of expression that make interviews and, to a lesser extent, telephone surveys high in validity also make them a little lower in reliability. Because people can express similar views in a variety of different ways, there is a chance that similar meanings may be missed by different wordings. As a result, codes across expressions may be inconsistent. On the contrary, when answer choices are predominately closed-ended and respondents have a limited number of options from which to choose, they are more likely to select the same answer choice than they are to say the same response or a response that will be interpreted by a researcher the same way when a question is open-ended.

MAKING DECISIONS

So, how do you know which survey form to use? First, there is no one perfect survey form for any given research question. In fact, as I mentioned, I just presented four broad survey options here. There are also multiple variations of these methodologies within each of these categories. Therefore, although the purpose of this book is to "get the job done" and this discussion will do that, your professor may have experience with any of these specific types and supplement what I present herewith greater detail that they feel is relevant. Deciding what survey to use may be a matter of progressing through each of the four points listed in Box 7.3 and determining which group has the greatest number of characteristics that suit your purposes, skill,

BOX 7.3

CHARACTERISTICS OF DIFFERENT SURVEY FORMS

Characteristics	Mailed Surveys	Web Surveys	Telephone Surveys	Face-to-Face Interviews
Money to spend	Not much	Not much	Moderate amount	A lot
Can be implemented quickly	No	Yes	Yes	No
Can be coded/analyzed quickly	Moderate	Yes	Yes	No
What kind of response rate can you anticipate	Low	Moderate	Moderate	High
Researcher control over responses	None	None	Moderate	A lot
Researcher effect on respondents	None	None	Moderate	Possibly a lot
Ability to reach a wide geographical population	Important/ desirable	Important/ desirable	Important/ desirable	Not Important/ desirable
Ability to read body/verbal cues	Not important	Not important	Moderately important	Very important
Need to ask complex questions	Low	Low	Moderate	High
Concern for social desirability bias	Low	Low	Moderate	High
Need facilities/staff	No	No	Some	Yes
A diverse sample is important	Yes	Yes	Yes	No
Respondent needs to be able to read or write	Yes	Yes	No	No

and resources. Nonetheless, there are some considerations that will help you to decide which survey methodology would be the most appropriate for your study.

Incidentally, especially if you are really having trouble deciding one "best" approach, one way to "cover all the bases" is to use a **mixed methods** model that uses more than one form of data gathering, such as mailed surveys and interviews or interviews and experiments. Using more than one method of data collection strengthens research because the weaknesses of one form of data gathering are supplemented by the strengths of another form used.

CHALLENGES

As I said, obviously, there is no one perfect method of survey observation. Here are some common challenges you may encounter if you choose this general method of observation.

1. **I have multiple opinion questions I want to ask, but I am worried that if people feel the same about the first few questions, they will just select the same response for the rest of the questions without reading them.**

   This is definitely a risk when all questions are worded in the same, usually affirmative, direction and it can threaten the validity of the results. If you are concerned about this, one option is to include reverse-coded questions. These are questions in which a negative response actually fits the general hypothesis or confirms previous positive responses. For example, you might fill out course evaluation surveys that ask you to respond, usually on a Likert scale (Chapters 4 and 10), to questions like: "The professor was punctual to class"; "The professor was prepared for class"; or "The professor showed respect for student views." Selecting "strongly agree" or "agree" to these statements gives a positive view of the professor. A reverse-coded question would read something like: "The professor's lectures were dull" or "The professor showed little interest in student concerns." Here "strongly disagree" or "disagree" gives a favorable view of the professor because these are negative statements. Using reverse-coded statements can be a way of checking validity to see if respondents are paying attention to the questions, as opposed to responding as a response set, which is when a respondent reads a few questions and then just select the same response, such as "agree," for all subsequent questions without reading them. Or sometimes respondents select the same answer for all questions because they are exhibiting acquiescence bias where a respondent does not want to appear disagreeable and, therefore, selects "agree" or "strongly agree" to all items (Fowler, 2014). Reverse-coded questions can help identify when subjects are answering as a response set or with acquiescence bias, but not necessarily which one. Regardless though, *either* one is a potential threat to study validity that should be identified even if not distinguished.

   Not all researchers, however, agree that reverse-coded questions are a good idea. Some of the distaste for this approach comes from questions where researchers may mean to write something reverse coded, but instead just confuse the question using double negatives, which pretty much all researchers recognize as a poor question format. Questions using double negatives might read something like "The professor did not write dull lectures." "Not" and "dull" are both negative connotations. To use a different example, a double negative question might read something like: "Do you find it possible or impossible that the majority of poor people never have used welfare." Choosing "possible" as a response, which would seem to be the most positive response, means that you do believe it is *not* possible that the majority of poor people never used welfare. Confused? Yeah...so would a person be who is trying to answer this type of question. So again, avoid double negatives (and just write as clearly and concisely as possible). Reverse wording is not the same as a double negative.

2. **How can I improve the response rate to survey research?**

There are some strategies researchers can use to increase survey response rates, most of which apply to mailed surveys but some can apply to the other survey forms as well. Let's address mailed surveys first. The first suggestion deals with the initial mailing of the survey. In the initial mailing, the researcher needs to make sure to include a well-designed, attractive, and enticing cover letter, include a stamped self-addressed envelope, and, if possible a small monetary incentive. Let's talk about some of these individually. First, I have already discussed cover letters briefly in Chapter 3, as a means of obtaining informed consent, but your cover letter is also a means of enticing the respondent to take the time for your survey. Personalize the cover letter if possible instead of just using a basic "To Whom It May Concern" or "Dear Madam/Sir." Also make it clear that the survey is coming from a credible source that is generally perceived as unbiased (in research), such as a university or government agency. Also, specify whether you are guaranteeing anonymity or confidentiality. Although I discussed in Chapter 4 that it is ethical to let the respondent know if you will know his/her identity (and not disclose it) or if his/her identity will be unknown to you, making sure you include this is not just important for ethics, it may be the difference between whether someone decides to participate or not. Respondents may be more comfortable participating if they realize that no one, including the researcher, will be able to link responses to individual identity. According to Dillman (2000), incentives also indicate a level of trust to the respondent. By giving the respondent a coupon for $2 or $5 to a local store or even as cash shows the respondent that you trust in his/her participation and are therefore already rewarding them for such.

Second, even under the best of circumstances, we can't just rely on one initial mailing to obtain a usable response rate. Respondents may have the best intentions to participate, but sometimes the survey gets misplaced or people's lives get in the way and they forget about it. Therefore, another step to increase the response rate is to send a pleasantly worded reminder postcard. One option is to track how many returned surveys are received starting the day after the mailing. Once the researcher notices that survey return is slowing, they can start the second mailing. Another option is to just automatically do the second mailing 2 weeks after the initial mailing

(Babbie, 1995). Either way, most researchers suggest that the second mailing is just a postcard. This postcard can simultaneously thank respondents who did participate and remind those who did not respond that their participation is important to the research goal.

For maximum response rates, some researchers argue that 2 weeks after the postcard mailing (4 weeks after the initial mailing) the researcher should mail a new cover letter and survey only to nonrespondents (Dillman, 2000; Helgeson, Voss, & Terpening, 2002). This cover letter should more strongly, but still politely, stress the importance of participation. This tactic implies that the researcher has a way of tracking responses, but it does not necessarily mean that to do this one cannot guarantee anonymity. For example, a researcher may have a colleague responsible for assigning and tracking identification numbers on the return envelopes for surveys. The collaborator initially receives the surveys, notes on his/her sheet who has returned the survey but then gives the unopened envelope to the main researcher who has no idea who matches the codes as they open the survey. Dillman (2000) goes so far as to suggest sending a third cover letter and survey via special delivery to the remaining nonresponses after the second mailing. As you can see, the cost of administering mailed surveys can get quite high depending on the number and nature of your follow-up mailings. Therefore, considering the number and nature of follow-up mailings would also be a factor in deciding your target sample size, as discussed in Chapter 5.

The last strategy, which can also apply to web and telephone surveys, deals with the timing of the mailing. How excited are you for the end of the week? I bet you count the minutes until your job or classes end on Friday so you can enjoy the weekend, right? So, if you received a survey, through any means, on a Friday, would you be inclined to complete it? Probably not. People are freshest and most open to participating in studies at the beginning of the week (Wolfer, 2007). So, it is wise for researchers, to the best of their ability, to plan to make contact with subjects at the beginning of the week. Similarly, busy times of life, such as holidays, or when there is a higher than average chance someone will not be home because of vacations, like the summer, may contribute to low response rates, so it behooves researchers to avoid these times to the best of their ability whenever possible (Langbein, 2006; Wolfer, 2007).

Key Terms

Computer-assisted telephone interview

Filter question

Matrix format

Mixed methods

Pilot study

Questionnaire

Random digit dialing

Reverse-coded question

Secondary analysis of primary data

Skip pattern

Answers to Learning Check Questions

Learning Check 7.1: Identifying Problematic Survey Questions

Question 1 should appear toward the end of the survey. Depending on your topic, you might ask about gender rather than sex and have more answer choices along the gender spectrum as a result.

Question 2 should appear toward the end of the survey and its values are not mutually exclusive. Someone earning $30,000, for example, would have to select "b" and "c."

Question 3: what if a person is caring for both parents? This question needs to be reworded.

Question 4 is double-barreled. Someone may try to restrain the parent but not succeed. It is also a poorly worded question, however, because we are not clear what can be learned from a "yes" response.

Question 5 does not address whether someone does multiple tasks, nor does it address whether there are other tasks the individual does that should be recorded under an "other" value.

Question 6 is leading ("do you agree") because the question does not provide both sides of an opinion and there is no neutral "no opinion" category.

All in all, this is a poor survey that is confusing, limiting, and yet also doesn't provide detailed information that is usable or informative.

Learning Check 7.2: Questionnaire Format

1. This would appear toward the end of the survey because, although it is an important demographic, it is not very interesting (so it doesn't go near the beginning) and would disrupt the flow of the survey themes if it appeared in the middle.

2. The second option, the logic path, would be more appropriate here because there are too many contingency questions to easily separate into questions on the side of the main survey.

Learning Check 7.3: Common Survey Types

1. Provide a stamped return envelope, offer an incentive, make the survey attractive, keep it short, plan on receipt for the beginning of a week, and conduct follow-up mailings.

2. Both telephone and web surveys

3. Telephone surveys because of the possible use of random digit dialing.

End-of-Chapter Problems

1. The following survey question: "Was your group leader knowledgeable and prepared?" is an example of a _____ question.
   a. wordy
   b. double-barreled
   c. leading
   d. biased

2. In reverse-coded questions, a positive response such as "strongly agree" indicates
   a. a view that is favorable toward your research topic
   b. a view that is neutral toward your research topic
   c. a view that is negative toward your research topic

3. When asking someone, for example, whether they have children (yes/no) and then directing them to different questions depending on their answer, the question of whether they have children or not is called a
   a. filter question
   b. matrix question
   c. reverse-coded question
   d. biased question

4. One of the biggest challenges of using mail surveys is that
   a. not everyone uses the Internet
   b. people screen calls
   c. they have a very low return rate in general
   d. they are hard to format

5. For which types of surveys can computers be used to help administer contingency paths?
   a. mailed surveys and web surveys
   b. phone surveys and web surveys
   c. interviews and phone surveys
   d. interviews and web surveys

6. Which of the following survey types has the least geographical reach
   a. mail surveys
   b. telephone surveys
   c. web surveys
   d. interviews

7. Which of the following survey types has a fast response rate?
   a. mail surveys and telephone surveys
   b. telephone surveys and web surveys
   c. web surveys and mail surveys
   d. interviews and web surveys

8. Which of the following survey types is generally the most affordable?
   a. mail surveys
   b. telephone surveys
   c. web surveys
   d. interviews

9. Which of the following survey types has the greatest risk of respondent reactivity?
   a. mail surveys
   b. telephone surveys
   c. web surveys
   d. interviews

10. When researchers use the raw data collected by others, such as in large longitudinal surveys/interviews like the GSS or the PSID, they are doing what type of research?
    a. primary analysis of primary data
    b. secondary analysis of primary data
    c. primary analysis of secondary data
    d. secondary analysis of secondary data

11. Write a five-question, closed-ended survey in good form that addresses these variables: a person's academic year, whether they attend campus/college parties, how often they consume alcohol at these parties, if they have ever considered themselves to be drunk, and their major.

12. Go to https://www.surveymonkey.com and program a survey to hypothetically administer the questionnaire you created in #11.

8

QUALITATIVE APPROACHES AND MIXED METHODS

LEARNING GOALS

- Distinguish between face-to-face interviews, focus groups, case studies, field research, and content analysis

- Learn the steps to conducting face-to-face interviews

- Recognize the steps to conducting focus groups

- Identify the main design components of field research

- Distinguish content analysis as a methodology as opposed to the form of data analysis

- Understand what mixed methodology of observation entails

For me, when I was back home, we watch television, see people playing with money… you just feel, you come here, you find money wasting in the street…Yeah, see money in the street! Walking in the street, walking on the street glass [streets made of glass]… Yeah back home, that's the thinking, what we see on television. Yeah, but the first time I enter America, my brother took me to Philadelphia, I saw people begging in the street, I say no, America is different. (Focus Group #4, 08/18/2013, nonrefugee)

…the media had a lot to do with it because when you're back home you have like this, like nice image of America like there is no homeless people. The street is not dirty, there is no…child hunger no like things like that you know. But when you come here it's definitely more prevalent here than anywhere else…Just the street…like trash being on the street, like homeless people on the street…I did not expect to see that (Focus Group #5, 09/01/2013, refugee) (Covington-Ward, 2017, pp. 1021–1022)

These quotes come from a focus group study and suggest that immigrants' preconceived ideas of what America would be like before they arrived turned to surprise when the reality of American life did not meet their expectations. However, the level of description captured in these excerpts is not usually found in more quantitative forms of research like surveys because, by nature, qualitative design is directed at obtaining a deeper understanding of a phenomenon by exploring the complexity and richness of subjects' experiences from the subjects', rather than from the researchers', perspective. In other words, in quantitative research, the researcher asks predetermined questions (e.g. survey questions) and has subjects chosen from predetermined answer options (values) already selected by the researcher. In qualitative data, the researcher asks broad questions, if any, and leaves the subjects to explain their responses in their own words. Qualitative studies also tend to be more organic, evolving, and developing on their own over the course of observation. Therefore, methodologically they are less restrictive.

Depending on your research topic, there are a variety of qualitative methods that might be suitable, but, as the focus of this book is "getting the job done," I will center this discussion on face-to-face interviews, focus groups, case studies, field research, content analysis, and mixed methods.

FACE-TO-FACE INTERVIEWS

In Chapter 7, I introduced interviews as a form of survey research when they use largely quantifiable questionnaires as their main form of design. However, as I also said, many individual researchers are likely to use face-to-face interviews in a more qualitative manner because in this way, researchers can obtain a deeper understanding of sensitive or little-known topics. For example, in general, intimate partner violence against males is a difficult topic to study because it goes against many social concepts of masculinity, so men are unlikely to report its occurrence, making this issue largely invisible. This is especially true for some subcultures, such as Asian/Pacific Islanders or Latinos, who have very strict views of men's roles and of masculinity, making the study of experiences of interpersonal violence among these men particularly difficult (George, 2007; Simon & Wallace, 2018). To address this gap, Simon and Wallace (2018) conducted in-depth face-to-face interviews with eight Chinese male survivors of intimate partner violence to understand their help-seeking behavior or lack thereof. They found that similar to men of other cultures, the issue of "face" in Chinese culture, where men should be able to be competent and responsible for all manners of life, prohibits these men from seeking help because the violation of masculinity inherent in interpersonal violence victimization causes these men to lose "face." Therefore, in order for these men to both define themselves as victims and seek help, they need to perceive social workers as reacting to them professionally, sincerely, and in a way in which it is evident to the victim that the social worker has overcome the shared views of Chinese masculinity. Only in this way can these men maintain "face" (Simon & Wallace, 2018). Understanding the subjective concepts of "face" and social worker reactions to it are levels of meaning that close-ended forms of data gathering, such as mailed or web surveys, are unable to obtain.

Face-to-face interviews are commonly semi-structured where the interviewer has a loose guide of questions to address but may not necessarily use all questions for all respondents or may not use them in the order they are presented (Gray, 2014). This form of interview allows for **probing** by the researcher where, even though the questions are open-ended, the researcher has an idea of the level of information necessary and can, therefore, clarify, reword, or ask to follow up questions that might enable the respondent to give more detailed or specific information. For example, if a researcher is trying to identify the pattern behind young people's drug use, a probe might go like this:

> Interviewer: How old were you when you first tried pot?
> Respondent: I don't know. I was young I guess.
> Interviewer: Would you say you were in high school?
> Respondent: Probably younger?
> Interviewer: Do you think you were in elementary, intermediate, or middle school when you started?
> Respondent: I think it would have been middle school. I know it wasn't elementary and I remember we moved here in middle school and I made a new set of friends, some of whom I still use drugs with today, so probably then.

In this probe, the researcher was able to get the respondent to clarify that the response of "young," which is very subjective and vague, meant "middle school," which is usually between the ages of 11–14 and is, therefore, a more detailed response. Probing can be accomplished in other ways as well. For example, simply staying quiet a few moments may be an effective probe. People are frequently uncomfortable with pauses and are likely to provide information in order to break up the silence (Trochim, Donnelly, & Arora, 2016).

Face-to-face interviews have some additional strengths. They can be useful for testing a hypothesis; for identifying variables to be incorporated into a larger, quantitative study, and for follow-up on special issues of interest when used in conjunction with other forms of surveys (Cohen & Manion, 2011). Face-to-face interviews are also a good choice when the topic of study is complex and might require probing to fully elicit information. However, a common limitation in this design choice is that face-to-face interviews are very time intensive at every stage, from administration to analysis, more so than all the other forms of survey research covered in Chapter 7 as well as many of the qualitative forms of research that I will be discussing in this chapter.

PHOTO 8.1 Interviewers should appear receptive and interested.

Process

1. *Deciding Sample Size*

   Although we already discussed sampling in Chapter 5, a couple of additional points merit mention here. Given the qualitative focus of face-to-face interviews, there is some sample size flexibility. Some researchers argue that one should continue interviewing (and, therefore, selecting individuals) until the point of **saturation** (Glaser & Strauss, 1967). Saturation is the time at which the interviewer is no longer learning anything new from the interviews. Previous work using interviews has shown that, for many purposes, saturation is often reached around 30 interviews, whereas other researchers argue for setting the goal of 60–150 respondents, regardless of saturation (Gerson & Horowitz, 2002; Warren, 2002).

2. *Training the Interviewer*

   A good interview is one that will run almost like a conversation, with the interviewer encouraging information from the respondent in a friendly, open manner. There are a few key elements that facilitate this. First, the interviewer needs to be familiar with the entire study, not just the questions and their format (although, as I will cover, that is important too). This will help the interviewer understand the overall research goals and what level of information is beneficial, which in turn will help the interviewer understand when and how to probe for information. Second, the researcher does need to know the survey instrument inside and out. However, there is disagreement over whether interviewers need to follow the interview script—especially with semi-structured interviews—verbatim. Some suggest that a directed approach is the best goal but at the same time the interviewer should be able to adjust the interview accordingly in a way that works with the conversation (Adams, 2015; Galletta, 2013).

3. *Preparing for the Interview*

Once someone has been identified as a respondent, the researcher needs to contact them to arrange the interview. I won't cover how to obtain contact information here because, presumably, the sampling frame (or population identification) would only include people for whom the researcher has access. Here I will discuss how to arrange the interview once contact is made. The two main issues are choosing the time and location. When possible, as determined by the nature of the research question, the interview should be in a public place that is not very noisy. The research question is important to location because, for example, people may not want to discuss personal issues, like a sexual assault experience, in a restaurant where others can possibly overhear. The preference, when possible, for a public space, is largely for the interviewer's safety, especially if only one person is conducting an interview. If the interviewer is a member of a university or an organization, perhaps there is a conference room that can be privately accessed but is in a building where there are other people if needed. If the interview is to be conducted in the respondent's home, ideally there should be more than one interviewer present. Regardless of location, if more than one interviewer can be present, that is always preferred not just for safety but also because having more than one interviewer can increase the accuracy of the observations, and therefore validity. What one interviewer misses, the other might catch.

The second issue involves the timing of the interview. Unless otherwise requested by the participant, Hagan (1997) suggests that interviews be scheduled between the times of 10:00 am and 8:00 pm so as not to start too early or too late. Within these parameters, the specific time should be primarily determined by what is convenient for the respondent. The interview also cannot be rushed. It is common for the interviewer to arrive 30 min prior to the interview to set up and to stay about an hour afterward to take field notes (Wengraf, 2001).

4. *Presentation of Self*

How interviewers initially present themselves to respondents can go a long way toward establishing the tone of the interview. Because of their highly personal nature, interviews are very vulnerable to the reactivity effects discussed in Chapter 6 so interviewers need to be conscious of their impression management. Those being interviewed may form impressions about the interviewer, which will influence their decision about what to/not to share before the interview even officially starts (Oppenheim, 1992). However, interviewers are in a unique position. On the one hand, interviewers need to present themselves as motivated and knowledgeable, yet humble and interested in the respondent's views or experiences (Leech, 2002; Trochim et al., 2016). On the contrary, they also need to present themselves as objective. They cannot convey surprise or distaste to what the respondent is saying no matter how crazy, appalling, or dull that information is.

One way to self-present is by dress. Interviewers want to keep in mind their population when preparing their dress (Adams, 2015). For example, if I am interviewing trial lawyers, I might want to dress in a suit because to this population. suits symbolize professionalism. On the contrary, if I am interviewing teenagers about their drug use and I arrive in suit, that is likely to set me too far apart from them. That being said, I also probably don't want to show up, as a middle-aged woman, in torn jeans and a sweatshirt—common teenage attire. They would laugh me out of the room (deservedly) as someone who is "posing." In the second instance, I would probably dress in what can be called "dress casual," perhaps some slacks (not too dressy) and a sweater or blouse. The goal of dress is not to pretend you are a member of the group being studied, as you most likely are not, but instead to convey a level of social distance without being unapproachable. For the trial lawyer example, in American culture, the level of the dress above a suit would be cocktail wear; but if I showed up in a cocktail dress, that would just be silly. So there is a level of common sense to this. The point is that how the interviewer dresses requires some thought, as it conveys a message to the participant and can work toward setting the tone of the interview.

Other ways interviewers can make themselves approachable to the respondent are through their language and how they carry themselves. Different cultures have different ways of communicating. What may seem respectful in one culture, such as direct eye contact, may be perceived as challenging in another (Argyle, Henderson, Bond, Iizuka, & Contarello, 1986; McCarthy, Lee, Itakura, & Muir, 2006); therefore, it is important for interviewers to be culturally sensitive to the interaction norms characteristic of their subjects. Similarly, members of subgroups have language, commonly referred to as slang or jargon, that distinguishes them from other subgroups. Knowing cultural norms of interaction and the jargon common to the group ahead of time will help facilitate the interview and establish rapport with the interviewee.

5. *Conducting the Interview*

When conducting the interview, the interviewer needs to focus on being an unbiased, active listener. Active listening does not just mean paying attention to what is being said, but it also means paying attention to *how* things are said. Paying attention and taking notes regarding the interviewee's tone, the emphasis placed on words—or when these change—is an important part of the interview process. Furthermore, respondents should be doing most of the talking. The interviewer should facilitate the respondent's narrative, not dominate it.

Unlike mail or web surveys, interviews also give researchers insight into the respondent's attentiveness, thoughts, and fatigue when the researcher reads the respondent's body language. For example, respondents who start looking at their watch or clock may be getting fatigued and/or are losing interest. This should indicate to the researcher that they either need to wrap up the interview or work to re-engage the respondent. Signs that the respondent is getting distressed may signify to the interviewer that it is time to take a break and revisit that line of questioning later.

Although I said that a good interview may develop a rapport and seem like a conversation, it is *not* a conversation in the conventional sense of a give/take of dialogue. After all, as I also said, being an active listener means the respondent does most of the talking and the interviewer should not interject his/her opinion, even the seemingly innocent agreement with a respondent's statement, for a concern of leading to reactivity. One way to simulate a back/forth conversation without the interviewer really interjecting their views is for the interviewer to repeat back to the interviewee what they said. This has the added benefit of double-checking the accuracy of the interviewer's records and/or getting clarification about any unclear comments.

6. *Concluding the Interview*

Because of the conversational tone of a good interview, ending the interview requires some "wind-down." A good practice for the interviewer is, a few questions from the end, to let the respondent know that the interview is almost over. This mentally prepares the subjects that the interaction will soon be over. Second, the interviewer should ask the respondent if they have any questions/comments. This gives the respondent an opportunity to clarify anything they may feel they did not initially articulate as well as they hoped. A third step is to make sure to thank the subjects for their participation at the end. After all, interviews frequently require more of a time investment on behalf of the respondent than do many other methods of observation; but, thanking a respondent should *always* occur after any study simply to be polite.

7. *Recording the Data*

In most instances, the best approach for capturing interview information is to both take notes (handwritten or typed on some electronic device) and to record the interview itself while conducting it. However, some situations make recording less attractive. Interviews that focus on highly sensitive topics and/or traumatic experiences may make the respondent uncomfortable if recorded, thereby decreasing the quality of the information or even the likelihood of participation in general. If your research focus is one where the respondent might not want to be recorded, it is always important to note the preference for recording in the informed consent letter and the researcher needs to really decide how necessary recording is to data analysis (Adams, 2015).

With or without recording, notes can document nonverbal cues observed or locate key comments the researcher may want to use verbatim. The recorded interview can then be transcribed for later analysis. However, be forewarned. According to Patton (2002), each hour of the live interview takes about 7–10 hr to transcribe.

 LEARNING CHECK 8.1: FACE-TO-FACE INTERVIEWS

1. What types of research questions are interviews most suitable for?

2. What are two main considerations researchers need to keep in mind in preparing for an interview?

3. Identify at least two considerations researchers need to keep in mind for a successful presentation of self in a face-to-face interview.

4. What is it called when researchers ask follow-up questions to vague subject responses in order to elicit a deeper level of information?

Answers to be found at the end of the chapter.

FOCUS GROUPS

The quotes that I opened the chapter with come from Covington-Ward (2017), who conducted five different focus groups of Liberian refugees (*n* = 31) who live in the same Liberian community in Pittsburgh, Pennsylvania. Covington-Ward was interested to see what non-refugee immigration experiences were like and how these immigrant expectations affected these people's ability to adjust to American life.

Focus groups, like Covington-Ward's study, are a qualitative approach aimed at not only gathering information from individual subjects but also seeing whether the expression of views is shaped by the interaction of the subjects. Because people's views can be influenced by the views of those around them, focus group methodology is useful when researchers want to not only study the views but also how those views are formed by the surrounding interactions. It is through the give and take of the discussion that the consensus and themes emerge.

Although the design of focus groups is flexible, most groups share some common characteristics. First, they are usually led by a moderator who guides the discussion with semi-structured questions. The moderator might be the researcher, but it can also be an outside individual. For example, Covington-Ward noted that her focus groups were centered on nine open-ended questions, some of which include what expectations of the United States subjects had before migration, the challenges they faced upon arriving, and their personal transformations since migrating (2017).

Second, focus groups should last between 1 and 2 hr, but there is flexibility in this, and they should be recorded in order to free the moderator to take notes on the interactions instead of trying to record the actual dialogue. Focus groups are also generally small, usually between 6 and 10 people who are similar in social status, the last point of which is important in order to

iStockphoto.com/Juanmonino

PHOTO 8.2 To what degree do you think pre-migration images of the American Dream are unrealistic? Do you think this would affect someone's ability to function well in our society? How could we examine this?

make sure that the participants, who may be strangers, feel comfortable to speak freely (Morgan & Krueger, 1993). Think about it. Would you feel comfortable talking about what could be improved about your department if your professors were sitting in the focus group with you? Of course not. However, the similarity in status does not mean similarity in attitudes or experiences. After all, the similarity in attitudes and experiences would lead to a very boring discussion!

Many of the people in Covington-Ward's study knew each other because they were all part of a rather small Liberian community, so they shared the similar social status of nonrefugee Liberian immigrants. Covington-Ward found that they generally also shared an idealized expectation of American life that made many of them ill-prepared for the racism and lack of knowledge of other cultures Americans exhibit. She also learned that these nonrefugee immigrants experienced many of the same challenges that refugee immigrants experience, but without the social supports that refugees receive in America, all of which can hinder these immigrants' ability to assimilate into the American experience.

Focus groups are best suited for descriptive and exploratory research topics, and they are especially useful in helping to frame basic questions and concepts or to pretest ideas for potential surveys (Krueger, 1988). Focus groups have a number of benefits that can make than a desirable observation choice for certain research questions. One of their biggest strengths is that they are relatively cheap and relatively easy to put together. All a researcher really needs is a meeting space and some recording device, whether audio or video. Furthermore, focus groups provide data the researcher can quickly start to analyze. A researcher might be able to run three or four focus groups in a day, have the dialogue transcribed in a few days, and begin analysis. Analysis of the physical observations can start almost immediately. Last, because the researcher is present and the subjects know of the researcher's role, the researcher can ask for clarification in subjects' responses, probe for more detail when required, and observe nonverbal information like body language (Halcomb, Gholizadeh, DiGiacomo, Phillips, & Davidson, 2007; Stewart, Shamdasani, & Rook, 2007).

There are also some notable limitations to focus group research. For example, sometimes conflicts between group members can arise if topics are especially sensitive. Reactivity is also a risk because subjects might want to make a good impression on each other and, therefore, not respond honestly. Furthermore, if the moderator is not skilled in probing or asking follow-up questions, important information can be missed (Halcomb et al., 2007; Stewart et al., 2007). Last, as with many qualitative methods, researchers have to be careful not to break confidentiality.

✓ LEARNING CHECK 8.2: FOCUS GROUPS

1. Explain two ways in which focus groups and interviews differ.

2. Why should focus groups be homogeneous in terms of the subjects' social characteristics?

Answers to be found at the end of the chapter.

CASE STUDIES

Sometimes the researcher is interested in the experiences of each subject individually in the entirety of a specific context instead of a slice of someone's life as one of many. In these instances, instead of studying hundreds of people or 30 law firms or 20 schools, a case study would look at the entire social context among a few common individuals, such as a couple of families, a community, or a school. In case studies, the nuances of experiences, the sequencing of events, and the context of involvement are examined and described in such detail as to give the reader a sense of place and people studied (Stake, 1995).

For instance, with the publicity of transgender actresses like Laverne Cox and the high-profile gender transformation of Caitlyn Jenner, the topic of transgender identity has become more visible; yet, scientifically we know little about the experiences of these individuals and their families, especially among younger people. Capous-Desyllas and Barron (2017) conducted a case study analysis of four families and their male-to-female transgender children over the course of a year to better understand how those families navigated their child's transition emotionally, institutionally, and socially in our still largely gender binary world. Their goal was to better understand these families' experiences in the education, religious, medical, and mental health areas so that social workers can better promote the health and well-being of these families. As such, Capous-Desyllas and Barron (2017) were not really interested in outlining a strict methodology to follow; instead, they were interested in intensively understanding a specific unit of analysis, here a few units of the family. In this particular study, as in many forms of case study analysis, the researcher actually used multiple qualitative observational techniques, such as interviews of children and their family members, observations of these families in various settings (field research), analysis of email correspondence with the families (qualitative content analysis), and analysis of journals that family members kept (again, qualitative content analysis). Based on this gathered information, the researchers focused on finding commonalities and differences between the cases to ascertain the combination of factors that shape experiences. In doing so, Capous-Desyllas and Barron (2017) were able to learn that all four families had to learn how to navigate unfamiliar gender-variant behavior, they all had to take various steps to prepare their child and themselves for the transition, and they all still expressed concerns for their child's future. Capous-Desyllas and Barron also found that the processes within these commonalities were also frequently similar. For example, they note that all of the families either thought or were told that their child's initial transgender behavior was just a normal phase or something the child would grow out of, so none of the parents labeled their child as transgender from the onset and none realized the gender identity issues that their child was grappling with from a very young age.

Therefore, case study methodology can fit any of the four purposes of research. For exploratory questions, case studies can help define the questions and hypotheses that will serve as the foundation for larger studies. For descriptive topics, case studies can describe an event or group in its context to help describe and understand its functioning. Case studies may be good at explaining causal links because of the nature of depth in which they focus on the unit of analysis, even if they do not have the random assignment or the generalizing capabilities of other methods of observation. Lastly, case studies can help researchers understand the effectiveness (evaluation) of a program or intervention when it is applied to a very small group of individuals (Newcomer, Hatry, & Wholey, 2015; Yin, 2009).

It is important to remember that case studies do not usually involve the generalization of larger populations at all. They are essentially in-depth stories that are able to describe complex processes. As such, case studies are potentially a valuable component to mixed methods designs, where a quantitative method establishes generalizable patterns, and a case study helps to give a deeper understanding of the process that might be behind those generalizable patterns. I will discuss mixed methods later in this chapter.

FIELD RESEARCH

Field research, sometimes also called participant observation or ethnographic research, is a more immersive form of research where the researcher sees the social world of the subjects in that world's totality. It differs from case studies because usually case studies focus on just one or two people in a very specific context, whereas field research focuses on more people in a larger context. However, like case studies and focus groups, field research data are usually in the form of rich subjective dialogue, which, when taken together, are useful in identifying themes. Therefore, participation observation research is a natural study that occurs in the field and, as such, it is especially useful for exploratory or basic descriptive research. For example, Carroll (2018) conducted participant observation of parenting groups for gay fathers in three different locations (California, Texas, and Utah) to investigate stratification in gay fatherhood communities. Specifically, Carroll wanted to explore the community ties and challenges of gay fathers who might be marginalized within the gay community because of being single

iStockphoto.com/SolStock

PHOTO 8.3 Carroll (2018) conducted field research to study the parenting experiences of gay fathers.

parents, a parent of color, or by having their children from heterosexual unions. The author attended monthly meetings for gay fathers in the California setting for approximately 5 years and then performed an additional 20 hr of participant observation in Texas by attending gay parenting events and 10 hr at a gay father's support group in Utah. Both the Texas and Utah sites served as comparisons for the California one. Based on Carroll's observations, she learned that even though existing research suggests that same-sex couples of color are more likely to be raising children than same-sex White couples, gay fathers of color and single gay fathers both saw themselves as socially unique and did not feel that they were visible in the wider society. For example, Carroll's respondent Michael claims:

> "We're all the gay community. But we're again outsiders in that community. And then take another step: We're in the gay community, and the gay community itself is segregated. So we're the Black guys, you know, the Black section of the gay community. And then we're in a smaller—we're in the Black section with children in the gay community. We don't see our image around anywhere." (Black California partnered father via surrogacy, Carroll, 2018, p. 111).

Carroll's approach, overt participant, is one of the four common forms of field research that vary based on the degree and nature of the researcher role.

Researcher Roles

Covert Observer

The most detached form of field research occurs when the researcher observes subject behavior in the natural setting without identifying as a researcher or directly interacting with the subjects. This type of field research is called **covert observer** research and some possible settings for this type of research could be political protests, marches, parties, restaurants/bars, or movie theaters. For example, if I want to study barroom behavior and I sit at a bar observing the conversations and interactions of those around me, but I neither identify as a researcher nor ask fellow bar patrons questions, this would be a form of covert observation (Figure 8.1).

Even based on this limited description, you might be hearing a warning bell in your head right about now regarding informed consent. After all, if you are *covertly* watching people, then they do not know they are being observed and can, therefore, not give informed consent. To some degree, this is certainly true; to avoid covert observation, research is usually done in public spaces where subjects' behavior can be observed by anybody for any reason. If you look back at our discussion of ethics in Chapter 3, I noted that if behavior occurred in a public space, where anyone else could observe the same behavior as the researcher, and the researcher did not interact with the subjects, then informed consent was not necessary because the researcher was just like any other person occupying the same public space. That is the case here.

However, a risk in covert observation is that the researcher might not be interpreting behaviors or situations accurately. Because the researcher never identifies him/herself as such, the researcher cannot ask subjects for clarification or the background context that led to the current behavior by the subjects. For example, a researcher might see two guys get into a physical

FIGURE 8.1   ●   FOUR TYPES OF FIELD RESEARCHER ROLES

fight over a game of pool and conclude that they were drunk or just short-tempered. By not being able to speak with the men, however, the researcher may not realize that the fight started because one of the men was making crude or sexist comments about a woman the other man was secretly interested in. Therefore, it is possible for important meanings or contexts to be masked using this form of observation; therefore, although an option of field research, it is not one of the forms more commonly practiced.

Overt Observer

On the contrary, if I sat at the bar and mentioned to the bartender that I was a researcher and I say the same to anyone who sees me taking notes and asks, then I would be doing overt observation research. Both covert and **overt observer** forms of research are rather passive ways of being in the field, but in overt observation research, once people know I am a researcher, I can obtain informed consent and directly ask them questions about their bar-room experiences. Carroll's (2018) work among gay fathers would be along the lines of overt observation because she was at the events and the participants knew she was a researcher, but her involvement was not directly with the support groups per se. Her involvement was more on the fringe of the group, such as setup and cleanup, which she offered in exchange for being able to make her observations (Carroll, 2018). So a strength of overt observation is that the researcher does not have to hide his or her identity and, therefore, has the ability to ask subjects questions. However, for a more complex understanding of behaviors and the context in which they occur, the researcher would need a higher level of interaction with the subjects. The researcher takes a more active approach with subjects in the next two researcher roles.

Overt Participant

Frequently when we think of participant observation research, we are thinking of the researcher taking a more visible and active role in the research process, and this form, called overt participant, is the most common form of researcher–participant interaction. Because it is so common, sometimes this form also goes by other names, such as participant and observer or participant as observer research, which also recognize the visible and active role of the researcher. In this instance, the researcher fully participates in the activities of the group but also identifies him or herself as a researcher. So if I am at the bar and I am actively seeking out people to speak with, buying people drinks as I talk with them, playing pool and darts, all the time observing their behavior, and letting them know I am a researcher, then I have moved into the realm of **overt participant**. Overt participant can be a useful tool in understanding intergroup dynamics. For example, one researcher, Contreras, moved to California from New York and noticed quiet hostility between Mexican and African Americans, two groups that are frequently associated with hostility with Whites, but not

PHOTO 8.4 Hostility between gangs of different races can make social life unpredictable.

necessarily with each other. So he decided to study the nature of these interactions by asking for introductions from students and colleagues into Los Angeles' Black and Mexican American communities, ultimately focusing his research on Compton and South Central Los Angeles. Contreras notes that he regularly "hung out" at picnics, recreational facilities, parks, and public housing projects, and digitally recorded these conversations (with people's permission) via a recorder unobtrusively stored in his shirt pocket. Contreras's findings reveal that although the crime rates in both areas had seriously dropped the 10 years prior to his field study, distrust between the two groups remained, largely because of the persistent gang presence that got moved to the shadows, rather than removed, with tougher legal reform. The shadowy presence of gangs made it tougher for individuals to judge their risk of victimization. Contreras learned, for example, that any form of driving in these areas, whether it is perceived as too slow or too fast, or even pulling up next to someone at a street light, can quickly escalate into violence if the people nearby associate that behavior with a gang threat, even if the driver is not a gang member. As Contreras reports from a participant he calls "Jayvon":

> "I can't even drive here [Compton] without having to worry about shit," Jayvon explained. "Because let's say there's a car already stopped at a red light and I'm just pulling up to that red light. I gotta be careful with my speed 'cause I don't know if there's [gang] bangers in that car. So if I come up to the light too quick and shit, they might think that I'm trying to roll up on them to do something. But then if I roll up too slow, they might think that I'm creeping up on them to do them bad too. So I gotta always be thinking about my speed when I'm driving the boulevard. I can't be going thirty or forty [miles per hour], but I can't be going ten or fifteen [miles per hour] neither. I can't even pull up to the light and have my car like even with them. 'Cause then they think that I might be planning to do something. I can't even look over 'cause if I make eye contact, they might start something with me. This shit is crazy out here." (Contreras, 2018, p. 270)

Notice the richness of the description given by "Jayvon." This detail is characteristic of overt participant observation that helps the researcher, and those reading the research, get a full sense of the subjects' experiences. However, how would Contreras know that subjects like "Jayvon" are not exaggerating to make their personal experiences seem more interesting? The validity threat of reactivity (Chapter 6) might be setting off the same warning bells as informed consent did with covert observation. Reactivity is definitely a concern in overt participation because now the subject knows they are being observed; however, most field researchers agree that once they are in the field a sufficient amount of time (and what qualifies for this is highly subjective and dependent on the group being studied), their presence does not have as much effect on the subjects. Think about it, as we said when we discussed reactivity in Chapter 6, being on "good behavior" is tiring. If a researcher is around the subjects consistently for enough time, the subjects are likely to come to accept that researcher and stop acting differently because of his/her presence. Because Contreras (2018) conducted his overt participant research on and off over 5 years, from 2011 to 2016, the risk of reactivity in his study is low.

Covert Participant

Probably the least common form of field research is **covert participant** or complete participant research, in which the researcher acts like the group members and does not disclose his/her research role. This form of observation is probably also the most controversial because of the lack of informed consent and the nonpublic venue of most settings. After all, if a researcher pretends or tries to pass as a member of the group being studied in order to make observations, clearly the subjects do not know they are being observed and can't, therefore, give informed consent. Even so, an argument can be made that this is one of the few ways in which to study behavior among marginalized groups or subcultures such as criminals, deviants, or fringe religious groups (Humphrey, 1970; Parker, 1974). For example, Khiat (2010) used his role as a senior prison official to study how prisoners try to influence prison officials in ways that would benefit the prisoners. As Khiat explains, covert observation is important in this context because his role as a prison official is in conflicting interest with his subjects, the prisoners, and with his fellow officers, who he also observed and used as sources of information. Gaining access to a prison in a way that allows a researcher to observe guard–prisoner interaction extensively without reactivity can be almost impossible. Khiat announcing that he will be observing his fellow officers also would definitely limit Khiat's ability to gather this type of information without reactivity. But, due to the nature of his prison role, he is in a unique position to be able to observe the multiple perspectives of the prison system and perhaps use those observations to further the understanding of prison life. As he states in the results, Khiat identified some common forms of manipulation of prisoners to officials. For example, according to Khiat, prisoners frequently used repetition where prisoners individually, and in groups, would continually request previously denied privileges that were not a violation of prison rules from prison officials. By simply not taking "no" for an answer, the prisoners eventually got their way from some of the officials. Khiat also found that prisoners would employ distraction to get fellow prisoners out from situations when they were caught breaking the institutional rules and regulations by prison officials. Other ways prisoners tried to manipulate the prison officials, according to Khiat, were to use excuses for noncompliance, feign ignorance about any issue that might get them or someone else in trouble, and use false compliance, which, according to Khiat, meant that the prisoner complied while the official was watching but then stopped compliance when no longer observed. Khiat was also able to identify three patterns of offical response to these manipulations: (1) idealists, which Khiat identified as those who had no idea they were being manipulated and genuinely believe that the prisoners were there to be rehabilitated; (2) pragmatists, who sometimes acceded to prisoner pressure as long as the influence of the prisoners was discreet, thereby simultaneously allowing the prisoners a morale-boosting "win," but also making officials' lives easier; and (3) authoritarians, who knew they were being manipulated, called the prisoners on this manipulation, and therefore never gave in to the prisoner tactics.

Although potentially informative like Khiat's study, the covert observer form of field research is the least common of the four because it poses numerous risks and issues. I have already covered the ethical violation of informed consent; however, with this form of research, the researcher may be entering the gray area of ethical relativism as well. As an "undercover" observer of the types of populations for which covert observer research is likely to occur, the researcher may witness acts that put others at risk and, therefore, jeopardize the researcher's

iStockphoto.com/Bastiaan Slabbers

PHOTO 8.5 Using one's position as a prison official would provide a unique opportunity to study the dynamics of inmate behavior.

ethical responsibility to society (Chapter 3). Because the researcher's status is not known to subjects, it is harder for the researcher to excuse him or herself from the situation. Another risk results from the deep immersion in the group characteristic of this observation form. By being so deeply immersed in the group, the researcher risks losing their scientific objectivity about the group. This validity threat is known as **going native** and the resulting loss of objectivity may color the researcher's interpretation of the observations, as well as pose a risk of the researcher losing their original identity. Khiat was not undercover as a prison official but rather as a researcher; nonetheless, his identity as a prison official does raise some cautions about his objectivity. Although the potential for bias always remains, the balance in Khati's conclusions is indirect evidence that, although bias can never be completely ruled out, it is less of a concern here than one might normally feel.

Selecting a Site

Once a researcher decides which form of observation to use, they need to select a site that involves not only choosing where you want to do your field research but also gaining access to it. Generally, researchers would select a site that is typical of the topic of interest and one for which they can gain access to. For example, Khiat had easy access to a prison by being a senior prison officer, while Contreras is Dominican, and therefore a member of an ethnic minority, which helped him gain access to the people living in Compton and South Central. In fact, in his work, Contreras notes that even though he was an educated middle-class individual, he was able to relate and gain the trust of those he studied by describing him Bronx upbringing to them (Contreras, 2018).

However, unlike Khiat (2010) and Contreras (2018), Carroll (2018) could not naturally fit into her sites. Therefore, sometimes to gain access to a site, like in Carroll's situation, the researcher needs to get the permission of **gatekeepers** who are people in authority who have the power to permit (or ban) access to the site. Gatekeepers can be formal, like a prison warden, the person who runs a self-help group, or a school principal. However, they can also be informal. Informal gatekeepers can be subjects who have positions of respect or authority among the group the researcher wants to study. As such, these informal gatekeepers can "vouch" for the researcher, which may encourage others to be willing to talk to him or her.

Developing Relationships

It is important for researchers to develop relationships with those they are studying. For example, Khiat already had existing relationships with the other prison officers and inmates, and to get honest information from them and not jeopardize future relationships he had to keep his research secret. However, as I said, most field research is overt, where a researcher is going to identify him or herself to the subjects. Therefore, the researcher has to work to build relationships with the subjects to get them to be willing to share information and act naturally. To this end, there are some suggestions that will help with the development of relations (Rossman & Rallis, 1998; Wolfer, 2007).

A basic suggestion is to be ready to give subjects an honest and believable reason for your study. For field research, deception is not necessary (unless conducting overt participation research, of course) as the researcher will have different levels of interaction with the subjects over an extended period of time. Furthermore, the nature of field research does not involve research questions aimed at testing hypotheses but instead focuses on organically understanding a social process. As such, researchers may need help from subjects to interpret what is being observed so they often need to cultivate the support of key figures, sometimes called **key informants**, in the groups or organizations under study. These key informants can answer questions a researcher has as they arise. Gatekeepers may evolve into key informants; but, these informants may be different individuals and it is good to have between two or three key informants to get a balance of views.

Because field research generally focuses on cultivating some type of relationship with subjects in order to get them to speak freely, it is also important for the researcher to not try to lecture or flaunt his or her knowledge. Researchers are there to learn from the subjects, not show how smart or trained they are. Related to this is the role of observer. Effective fieldwork does not try to direct the subjects' behavior or interrogate the subject regarding the motives behind behavior. It is much better for the researcher to listen, to observe, and to ask questions only if those questions are important or if they clarify an observation. Furthermore, a researcher should not try to be one of the subjects (unless the researcher is doing covert participant research perhaps) because the researcher is likely to come off as fake, which may hurt the relationship with subjects. Last, a researcher should build a rapport with the subjects. This is similar to building friendships in your personal life; however, with subjects, a researcher needs to share personal details sparingly because keeping some of the real "you" to yourself is important to help researchers maintain some objectivity and social distance. Of course, that is easier said than done. The longer a researcher is in the field, the greater the risk that the researcher will create friendships with their subjects, thereby losing their researcher objectivity, and "going native." Furthermore, building rapport should not involve providing monetary assistance or other tangible things in order to form this connection with the subjects. As you can probably guess, building rapport is a balancing act that is more of an art than a science and, therefore, varies based on the individual characteristics of the researcher and research situation.

Identifying Subjects

A common question when learning about participant observation research, especially as an overt observer, is "What counts as a subject?" Are the subjects individuals a researcher comes into frequent contact with? Do people the researcher interacts with tangentially count as subjects? Or do researchers have to explicitly state to *everyone* no matter how much (or little) they interact with them that they are a researcher? The answers to these questions vary. Most field researchers feel that if you are going to have an extended interaction or an in-depth conversation with a person, then that individual would count as a "subject" for whom a researcher needs to obtain informed consent. However, interactions that are superficial or fleeting would not require informed consent, unless the researcher's role as a researcher naturally came up in the interaction, because these instances are less likely to contribute to the overall findings.

Additional questions regarding identifying subjects include: "How do I find subjects?" and "How many subjects are enough?" In the spirit of "getting the job done," I will focus on identifying subjects through snowball sampling and **theoretical sampling**. I have already encountered snowball sampling in Chapter 5 so I will not discuss it again in detail here. I just want to remind you that in this approach the researcher meets additional subjects by word of mouth from current subjects, and, in this way the sample "snowballs," or grows, in size. As to when a researcher has enough subjects from a snowball sample, that's harder to answer. In quantitative research, researchers have general rules of thumb for desired sample sizes, they can use formulas to calculate what they need, or they just make the best with what they have (and realize the resulting possible limitations of the findings). But there is less direction regarding this in field research. When using snowball sampling, researchers generally end the sampling when they reach a predetermined sample size or their time in the field ends.

Theoretical sampling, on the other hand, is a systematic means of identifying subjects based on a researcher's simultaneous processing of the observed information, determining what is relevant, what needs to be checked, and what needs more information. Researchers then select additional subjects based on the new subject's ability to check observations or provide additional information, and sampling stops when no new information is learned (Glaser & Strauss, 1967). For example, in Khiat's (2010) study, he used theoretical sampling and stopped when he had 29 prisoners, 3 senior prison officers, and 9 junior prison officers, which took a little over a year for him to obtain because he felt he had nothing new to learn.

Recording Information

As I have said, good field research will work somewhat like a conversation based on casual, natural interactions. So how would you react if your best friend took the time to record all of your conversations, asking you to slow down so they can write them all down, while also noting your reactions? I suspect you wouldn't like it. You would consider that interaction to be unnatural, and you would likely feel like you are being interviewed or studied…which would be true and would be exactly what researchers do *not* want subjects to feel when doing field research. Anything the researcher does, like asking for clarification or taking notes in front of subjects, that continually reminds subjects that they are being observed, even in their natural setting, increases the chance of reactivity and therefore dilutes the level of internal validity that this form of research prizes. So, asking repeated questions and/or writing information in front of subjects is not a good way of taking field notes. This does not mean that the researcher should not record what they see, however, because they absolutely need to.

In fact, researchers should take copious field notes, which serve as their data, but they have to do so either at the end of the day or at little private moments throughout the day, and not in front of their subjects. Because of the descriptive nature of this method of observation, and the restricted opportunity to record information, it may seem as if the goals and means of producing field notes are at odds with each other. To some extent, they are, but field researchers have figured out some strategies to deal with this seeming contradiction.

Let's first discuss what researchers want to take notes of. Field notes usually consist of direct observations and analytic thoughts. Early in the process, direct observations may be the bulk of the notes as the researcher is still trying to get a feel for the setting and the people. These direct observations should include a description of the settings and the main people the researcher interacted with each observation day. They should also include a chronological recounting of the researcher's experiences and observations of the group for each observation day, especially focusing on any specific events, episodes, or interactions that may have occurred. These observations should be detailed since, as already noted, they are the data. It is in this detail where the nuances of meaning and experiences will be made visible and it is this nuance that should be presented to others in the written analysis. Therefore, unlike more quantitative studies where the evidence is statistical tests of hypotheses, here the evidence is in a detailed recounting of experiences that will show the reader the path that led to the researcher's conclusions. It is also important to record feelings and reactions to what is seen, as well as preliminary analyses of these. The longer the researcher is in the field, the more observations they will have, and the more likely preliminary patterns will become evident. These preliminary connections need to be recorded as they occur because a researcher cannot expect to remember a thought 2 months after it occurs.

But how is a researcher supposed to obtain this detail if they can't write in front of the subjects? There are a number of different strategies for this. First, a researcher might be able to record interactions like Contreras (2018) did by starting and stopping his recorder that he kept unobtrusively hidden once he obtained informed consent. By relying on a recorder for the dialogue, he was free to focus on taking more visual and analytical notes when he had spare private moments rather than trying to record detailed conversations verbatim. However, in doing this, it is important to make sure that the recording material is working and to check it frequently. Otherwise, it is easy to lose an entire day in the field if one is overly reliant on faulty technology.

Another strategy is to make **jottings** of notes periodically. Jottings are short phrases or keywords that will jog the researchers' memory later in the day when they are able to find a lengthier amount of time to record the observations in private. Note the implication in what I just said: field notes should be documented in full the day that they occur. The longer the time span between observation and documentation, the less detailed and poorer quality the data becomes. By being short, jottings can be made in small snippets of time like when going to the bathroom (even if you do not need to—the issue is to excuse yourself to somewhere private), running small errands for the group, or even offering to perform a short task for which you can do alone and have a few minutes to "jot" down some observations.

Leaving the Field

So, how do you know when you have "enough" information and it's time to leave the field? One answer is that your time is up. Sometimes researchers have a finite amount of time to be in the field, so when that time is up, they are done gathering data. Another indicator is the saturation point that I mentioned earlier regarding sampling. Once the researcher feels that there is no new information to be learned relative to the main research focus, then it is time to leave the field. However, *when* to leave the field still does not address *how* to leave the field.

If the researcher did covert participation, leaving the field can be a bit challenging. After all, the reason researchers do this form of field research is they are afraid that they will not obtain informed consent, and those populations who might not give informed consent might also not have a positive reaction to knowing that they were being studied without their knowledge. Even if subjects know they are being studied in the more overt forms of observation, it can still be hard to leave the field. In overt research, the researcher often forms relationships with the subjects on some level, even if the researcher never revealed his or her complete true self. Therefore, subjects might feel betrayed or exploited after the study, especially if the study becomes a publicly well-received book. This sense of betrayal can be exacerbated because once the researcher leaves and re-enters his or her "true" life prior to the research, it is hard to maintain the relationships formed in the field.

Some researchers have tried to give their subjects some input in the write-up of the resulting analysis to make sure that the subjects approve of how the researcher portrayed them (Duneier, 1999). However, this is problematic for a number of reasons. First, a lot of time transpires between leaving the field, transcription of material, data analysis, and report draft. During this time, subjects might mentally review their experiences and alter their perceptions or interpretations of them retrospectively. Second, it is human nature to want to be portrayed in the most positive way possible; so, even if negative portrayals are accurate and important to the understanding of the process, subjects may not want that portrayal to be published. Consequently, giving subjects that level of control over the reporting of the findings can undermine the entire purpose of the research, which is to obtain accurate and, at least to the best of the researchers' ability, unbiased information. As a result, unfortunately, there is no clear answer on how to leave the field, which is highly dependent on the nature of the relationships formed and the subjects' understanding of their role in the entire research process. The only solid advice is to be sensitive to the subjects as you leave the field and to make promises to subjects carefully, sparingly, and only if they can be ethically fulfilled without weakening the validity of the research.

LEARNING CHECK 8.3: FIELD RESEARCH

1. In field research, what is the researcher's role when making his or her identity known and participating with the subjects?

2. What are key informants and why is it important to cultivate more than one?

3. What are some strategies researchers do to avoid taking field notes in front of subjects?

Answers to be found at the end of the chapter.

CONTENT ANALYSIS

Like interviews, content analysis can span a variety of classifications and is somewhat of a gray area methodologically. It can be a method of observation or a method of analysis. It can also be qualitative, quantitative, or both. For example, Schmidt (2016) used content analysis as *both* a methodology and a means of analysis when he wanted to test the hypothesis that the coverage of women's sports in the media has improved, a term he operationalized as an increase in frequency and a change in the depiction of women from supportive to main roles, over the last 30 years. Schmidt's sample focused on sports articles from the *New York Times*, which was purposively selected because it has both male and female readers, and he then used a stratified random sample by week of 1 week per year for the years 1984–2013. In the resulting dates selected, Schmidt then included all of the sports articles that appeared during those selected weeks, eventually obtaining a total of 5,850 articles to analyze (Schmidt, 2016). Schmidt's study design is not an experiment, a survey, or any of the qualitative means covered in this chapter. It is a systematic identification and selection of social artifacts (Chapter 5) to be studied and statistically analyzed. Therefore, as a methodology, content analysis can be exploratory and descriptive (remembering that not all hypothesis tests are aimed at identifying causality) and it can be a nonreactive way of examining opinions or behaviors over time. One con of this approach as a methodology, however, is that it is often atheoretical and as we saw in Chapter 2, linking research to theory is important.

How that information, in Schmidt's case the articles, is analyzed, on the contrary, is a combination of both quantitative and qualitative approaches that are also commonly used in the analysis of the information gathered via the other qualitative methods covered in this chapter. Therefore, as I did with face-to-face interviews, I am going to postpone the discussion of the analytical side of content analysis until Chapter 16, which focuses on ways researchers analyze qualitative information.

MIXED METHODS RESEARCH

As we are nearing the end of the chapters on the different methods of observation, you are hopefully noticing that no method of observation is perfect. Methods that have strong

iStockphoto.com/jemsgems

PHOTO 8.6 Do you think women's sports get the same amount of attention as men's sports? How would you test this theory?

validity, like true experiments, field research, and case studies, tend to have lower reliability. Methods that tend to have higher reliability, like surveys and quasi-experiments, also tend to have lower validity. As a result, you may be asking yourself why people don't just observe social phenomena using *multiple* methods of observation. The traditional answer was that the more methods a researcher uses, the more time, money, and skills a researcher was required to have in order to do these varied methods well. However, now with the strong focus on the role of research in many social science fields, the greater degree of research training in many education programs and jobs, and the use of computers for statistical analysis, a multiple methods research approach is now more feasible.

In recognition of the importance of methodologically balanced information, increasingly researchers *are* using multiple methods to gather data, called mixed-methods research, even though doing so is very complex and the practice is comparatively new. Although mixed-methods research does not mean that the researcher just haphazardly throws two different methods of observation together, there is no clear direction as to what point or how to combine the methods of observation. The most concise definition probably comes from Creswell, Plano Clark, Gutmann, and Hanson (2003), who identify a mixed-methods approach as a study that (1) has both quantitative and qualitative methods, (2) organizes these methods either concurrently or sequentially, and (3) involves the integration of the resulting data. Although there are many different ways in which these objectives can be achieved, the main point is that the researcher needs to make sure that the methods are not just two separate phases of research that are joined together arbitrarily (Creswell et al., 2003; Yin, 2006). The best mixed-methods designs have the information from the different methods feeding each other and answering questions in a comprehensive, rather than separately sequential, manner. Weeks and Schaffert (2019) used a mixed-methods design to study generational differences in the definitions of meaningful work. The first part of their design involved qualitative in-depth interviews of five individuals from four cohorts (Traditionalists, Baby Boomers, Millennials, and Generation X) to see how individuals from different generations defined meaningful work. Their findings revealed that although every generation felt that having a meaningful job is important, each generation also believed that members of the other generations were working for money rather than meaning even though each generation defined meaning differently. For example, although there are differences between each group, Weeks and Schaffert (2019) found that Traditionalists and Baby Boomers were more achievement-oriented (although they differed on how they defined "achievement"), whereas Millennials and Generation X were more about finding balance (although they differed in what and how they sought balance). Weeks and Schaffert (2019) used the information from the qualitative stydy to develop paired answers to the question "My work is meaningful when_____" that were then categorized into four quadrants centered on whether meaning was based on accomplishing for the self or other and whether the item focused more on being (e.g., being in the moment, reflection) or doing (an action). Weeks and Schaffert (2019) used this new measure in a larger quantitative study of meaningful work that they administered to a sample of 298 participants. They found that, for example, in the larger study, Baby Boomers were more likely to choose the "Others" quadrants than were Millennials, as suggested by Study 1, but that the differences noted in Study 1 (the qualitative portion) were not as pronounced in Study 2 (the quantitative one), and they were informative in refining the definition of meaningful work and in supporting, contrary to popular belief, that different generations have meanings more similar than previously thought (Weeks & Schaffert, 2019). As we saw in this research, mixed-methods designs allow researchers generalizability of quantitative studies coupled with the deeper, contextual understanding of qualitative ones (Hanson, Plano Clark, Petska, Crewsell, & Creswell, 2005).

MAKING DECISIONS

There are multiple questions and directions that will get you to a particular qualitative decision, but Figure 8.2 has one path that can be taken. The pros/cons of each decision are listed underneath the particular method. Always remember, if you have the resources, mixing more than one method (mixed-method design) is always a preferable option.

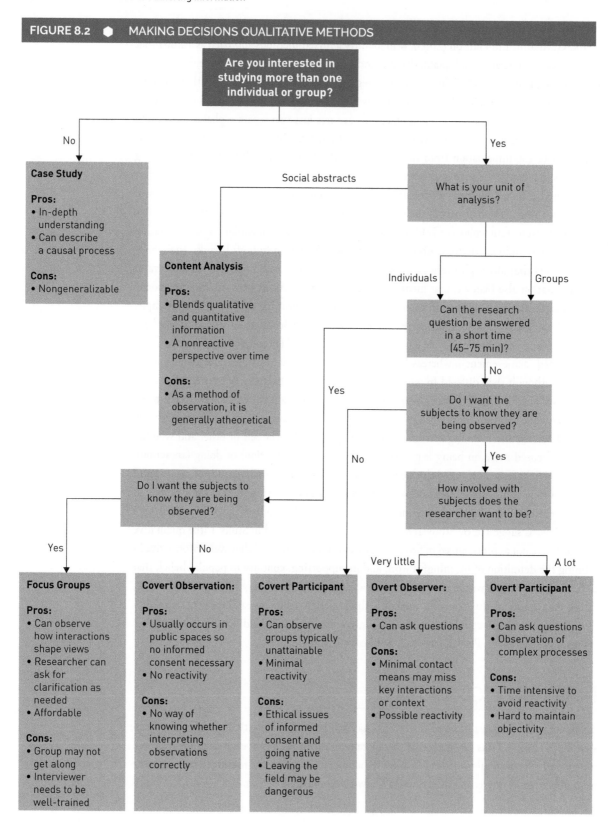

FIGURE 8.2 ⬡   MAKING DECISIONS QUALITATIVE METHODS

CHALLENGES

As I have said numerous times, no observation method is without its challenges, and qualitative methods are no different. Here are some common challenges you may encounter.

1. **How do I know my subjects are being truthful?** The short answer is: You don't. However, in reality, we *never* know if subjects are being truthful. Technically, people can lie on surveys, interviews, and even with their reported behaviors on pre- or posttests for experiments. The only method I have covered for which lying is unlikely is content analysis, because the researcher is studying social artifacts rather than people, so there is no reactivity or covert observation where the subjects do not know they are being studied. However, according to Lincoln and Guba (1985), there are four criteria researchers can use to help determine how trustworthy their information is. These are (1) credibility, (2) transferability, (3) auditability, and (4) confirmability.

   According to Lincoln and Gruba, credibility is the degree to which the researcher's observations accurately reflect the subjects' genuine views or experiences. To increase the likelihood of credible observations, researchers need to minimize subject reactivity, which can be done by staying in the field for a sufficient time, as I discussed in field research, being conscious of how their verbal and nonverbal cues might influence subjects' behavior, minimizing the visibility of any recording devices—basically anything a researcher can think of to make his or her data gathering as unobtrusive as possible, even if subjects know they are being observed. Another way to decrease this risk is to use triangulation, such as using more than one key informant in field research to help interpret observations or more than one coder in content analysis or focus groups to help determine whether the codes have consistent meaning to other people. Both of these work as quality checks to increase the credibility of information.

   Transferability is the degree to which your findings are useful to the field. Although many of the methods discussed in this chapter are not very generalizable because of their subjective focus, findings are transferable when the researcher can identify key aspects of the context of the research and make suggestions for how the findings might manifest in similar contexts. Another way to establish transferability is to make the argument of how participants' characteristics might be comparable to other groups. For example, even though Contreras (2018) studied the experiences of non–gang members in Compton and South Central, he used more than one site and made the case for how the experiences his subjects had might be similar to the experiences of other non–gang members in high-gang areas. Therefore, ways to increase transferability are to make sure that the people, settings, and interactions are fully described. The more detail the better. Likewise, make sure you take the time to try and make the case for how your findings apply to the wider scope of the problem.

   According to Lincoln and Guba (1985) researchers establish auditability when they have clear and detailed documentation of the study procedures so others can follow and evaluate the entire research process. Because many qualitative methods are fluid, meaning that they are not rigid like a mailed survey and can be adapted as information develops, people expect to see methodological changes occur as required. The responsibility of the researcher is just to document these changes and explain their rationale (Davies & Dodd, 2002).

The last of Lincoln and Guba's (1985) criteria is confirmability, which according to them is the ability for others to link the findings of the study to the data. Of all the criteria, this might be the most easily achieved as it usually involves giving illustrations for the various research conclusions. We have seen in our various research examples in this book that the most common way to show the "data" that support findings is to provide quotations or close paraphrases of what subjects say and what the researcher sees. In fact, in many ways, this confirmability is easier for beginning researchers to understand than statistical findings because the resulting narratives are more likely to read like a story than are statistical tests with numbers, odd Greek symbols, and terms like "*p*-values"!

2. **How do I increase the vigor or quality of the information I observe?** The tactics discussed in the previous challenge about how to show your subjects are being truthful contribute to establishing the vigor of qualitative research. There are some more strategies researchers can do as well. For example, in field research, staying in the field for a prolonged time increases the validity of a couple of ways. First, as I already discussed, it decreases the likelihood of reactivity, as being on "good behavior" is not sustainable for most people over an extended period. Second, it allows the researcher time to see patterns, which can then be corroborated with key informants. For case studies or focus groups, vigor can be increased by allowing participant review of transcripts or material. Using multiple coders of transcripts or latent content information can also increase validity and reliability. The bottom line is that with any research, but especially qualitative methods, the researcher needs transparency and detail for all steps.

3. **If I am having extensive involvement with subjects for any length of time, how do I maintain my objectivity?** This is a tough one. The loudest critics claim that qualitative researchers lose their objectivity (e.g., go native) at worst, but even those who do not go native may still struggle with objectivity because researchers who have contact with subjects, for an extended period, cannot help but be influenced by the subjects' perspectives. Hence qualitative researchers are frequently criticized for the subjectivity of their own conclusions. However, the answer to this is that all forms of research have some subjectivity. After all, in quantitative methods, researchers decide topics based on personal, subjective interest. Furthermore, they select indicators and measures that they *think* will produce strong findings, just like qualitative researchers *think* their interpretations are valid as well. In other words, no research is perfectly objective. That being said, again, utilizing the strategies mentioned in the first two challenges will go far in helping the researcher maintain objectivity. Furthermore, breaks from the field, in the case of field research, will also help the researcher "touch base" with his or her specific reality and gain perspective on what is being observed in the field.

Key Terms

Covert observer

Covert participant

Gatekeepers

Going native

Jottings

Key informant

Overt observer

Overt participant

Probing

Saturation

Theoretical sampling

Answers to Learning Check Questions

Learning Check 8.1: Face-To-Face Interviews

1. Research questions that require a more subjective view or explanation, those that are a complementary special focus to the other survey methods, those that want to gather the information that will fuel a later quantitative study.

2. Given the nature of the research question, the most appropriate location is one consideration as is when the interview will be conducted is the second. A third, but less directly relevant consideration, is whether a second researcher can be present for the interview.

3. Answer can be among the following: (a) dressing to maintain some social distance from the population of study while being approachable, (b) conveying a sense of motivated, yet humble, interest in the respondent; (c) being conscious of the cultural norms of interaction among the population being studied; (d) learning the slang or jargon of the studied population.

4. Probing

Learning Check 8.2: Focus Groups

1. Focus groups examine a more specific research question than interviews and in focus groups; the researcher also observes how the interactions between people shape the discussion of the research question.

2. People in focus groups may be strangers; so to feel comfortable expressing their views, the people should be similar in social characteristics.

Learning Check 8.3: Field Research

1. Overt participant

2. Key informants are subjects who the researchers form a more special bond to and who help the researcher understand what the researcher is seeing. It is important to have more than one in order to make sure there is a double check on the interpretations.

3. Some answers may include: making "jottings" instead of full notes, unobtrusively recording information, and finding private time to make quick notes or jottings.

End-of-Chapter Problems

1. If a researcher wants to study people for a topic that can be observed for between 45 and 75 min and for which the researcher's identity is known, the researcher should do
   a. Content analysis
   b. Focus groups
   c. Covert observation
   d. Overt participation

2. Which qualitative method of observation uses social artifacts as the unit of analysis?
   a. Content analysis
   b. Focus groups
   c. Covert observation
   d. Case study

3. Which form of field research would be appropriate for a population for which it is extremely difficult to obtain informed consent to enter?
   a. Covert participation
   b. Focus groups
   c. Covert observation
   d. Case study

4. Which form of observation would be appropriate if the researcher wants to study one unit, such as school, in extreme detail?
   a. Covert participation
   b. Focus groups
   c. Covert observation
   d. Case study

5. When interviewers ask follow-up questions of respondents to try and get respondents to provide a more detailed answer, this is called
   a. Grilling
   b. Contingency questions
   c. Probing
   d. Informed consent

6. True or false: It is important that field researchers take field notes in front of subjects as often as possible in order to make sure they record all observations.

7. In field research, the people who grant the researcher access to a site are called
   a. Helpers
   b. Gatekeepers
   c. Key informants
   d. Research assistants

8. True or false: The most common form of mixed-method research involves a quantitative method combined with a qualitative method.

9. When researchers preliminarily analyze information while they are collecting it in order to determine when they need more information or additional subjects to help clarify observations, they are doing what form of sampling?
   a. Simple random
   b. Quota
   c. Snowball
   d. Theoretical sampling

10. A researcher sits on a bench in plain view of children and parents to study gender dynamics on the playground among preschoolers. What is the researcher's role in this situation?
    a. Overt observer
    b. Overt participant
    c. Covert observer
    d. Covert participant

11. Apply the steps for interviewing to create a hypothetical interview asking people about their ideal type of job, why they like this job, where they see themselves in the next 5 years, and why.

EVALUATION RESEARCH

- Identify how applied research, evaluation research, evidence-based research, and evidence-based practice relate
- Identify the components of a basic systems model of evaluation
- Distinguish between common types of evaluation research
- Identify the considerations specific to evaluation research

To some degree, we have been preparing for this chapter throughout the book. In fact, most of the methods of observation that you learned about in Chapters 6–8 are common components of evaluation research. So you may be wondering: why does evaluation research get its own chapter and why do I need to know about it? Let's tackle the second question first. Unlike basic research or even general applied research, the purpose of evaluation research is to guide practical action, such as deciding whether a program is effective enough to continue as is, if it needs to be altered, or even if it needs to be discontinued. Because it involves *practical* action, it means that this type of research is likely to be used in the real world in the context of people's jobs. Regardless of whether you want to be a child welfare specialist, a police officer, a drug/alcohol counselor, or a mental health advocate ... you name it, as I mentioned early in this book, the courses in your major teach you about skills and tactics that will help you do your selected job. But how do you (or your professors or your boss) know *what* needs to be done or if what you do *works*? As you will learn in this chapter, that's where evaluation research comes in.

So, now back to the first question: Why does this form of research get its own chapter if it entails the *other* forms of research that we have already learned about? Because evaluation research is done in the context of the real world where a researcher does not have full study control, as opposed to a lab where a researcher does have control, there are some methodological considerations and components different from the other forms of applied research that merit mention on their own. Finally, as I have said before, this book is designed to serve as a resource in your future professional life in order to "get the job done." Therefore, a chapter on the ways in which you may encounter these methods and statistics in the "real world" is essential.

Because I have been using the terms *applied research*, *evidence-based research*, and *evaluation research* a lot in this book, let's make sure we know what the differences are when there *are* differences. As you learned in Chapter 1, applied research is aimed at improving the human experience; therefore, it is the foundation for the forms of research in this chapter. However, applied research in and of itself may not be bounded by different stakeholder views and it may not be designed to measure specific outcomes that would help a program operate. An example

BOX 9.1

A SELECTION OF JOBS AND SOME RELEVANT EVALUATION RESEARCH QUESTIONS

Profession	Evaluation Research Questions[1]				Other Examples of Testable Interventions
	Needs	Evaluability	Implementation	Outcome	
Police	Are there any areas in the community that have high incidences of both crime and traffic crashes?	Does the department have the resources to enact and monitor a Data-Driven Approach to Crime and Traffic Safety (DDACTS)?	Are the guidelines of the DDACTS enacted as designed?	By using the DDACTS, were crime and crashes in identified hot spots (needs assessment) reduced?	• Programs to decrease the time for call service • Programs to reduce crime in specific locations • Do neighborhood watch programs reduce crime?

	Evaluation Research Questions[1]				
Profession	**Needs**	**Evaluability**	**Implementation**	**Outcome**	**Other Examples of Testable Interventions**
Social work	Are there any local high schools or groups of students in local high schools who are at a higher risk of dropping out?	Does department or office have the resources to enact and monitor the Reconnecting Youth (RY) program?	Are the guidelines of RY enacted as designed?	Are schools or groups who experience RY more likely to stay in school, decrease disruptive actions, or increase mental well-being?	• Programs aimed at youth who are at risk for foster care • Programs aimed at helping hospital patients connect with natural and community resources • Programs to reduce drug/alcohol dependency • Programs to train first respondents on how to deal with people in mental crisis
Corrections	Are there any groups of prisoners who are at a higher risk for recidivism?	Are the components of the re-entry program observable and trackable? Does the prison have the resources to enact and monitor a re-entry program?	Are the characteristics of the re-entry program being implemented as designed?	Are prisoners who participate in the re-entry program less likely to return to prison within 3 years? If prisoners do recidivate, does it take longer for those who participate in the re-entry program to do so?	• Does providing prisoners with computer courses reduce recidivism? • What system of rewards promotes positive prisoner behavior?

(Continued)

BOX 9.1 *(CONTINUED)*

A SELECTION OF JOBS AND SOME RELEVANT EVALUATION RESEARCH QUESTIONS

| Profession | Evaluation Research Questions[1] | | | | Other Examples of Testable Interventions |
	Needs	Evaluability	Implementation	Outcome	
Therapist	Is there a need to more effectively provide mental health services to college students?	Can digital interventions monitor how often college students download, access, and perform the actions in the digital intervention?	(Presuming the evaluability assessment was positive) How many times was the digital intervention accessed? How often did the student track the requested behaviors?	Did students who use digital intervention report lower levels of anxiety, lower levels of depressive symptoms, or greater overall mental well-being?	• Programs to help survivors of abuse • Programs to help individuals from families that experienced a death by suicide
Public relations					• Programs to improve police–citizen relationships • Programs to reduce the stigmatization of mental health issues • Programs to improve children's views of emergency personnel like firefighters and police

[1]The fifth type of evaluation research, cost-benefit/cost-effective analysis, always asks the question of how the costs and outcomes of the program being tested compared to the current practices; therefore, it is not included in this table.

of general applied research would be a study like the one done by Hyppolite (2017), which statistically examined the degree to which parental mental illness, parental substance abuse, parental incarceration, and poverty independently affected child outcomes such as school failure, criminal behaviors, behavioral difficulties, and drug use. Hyppolite argued that most other studies just focused on parental risk as a broad category (e.g., whether there was parental risk or the degree of parental risk) and not the specific types of risk. Therefore, to examine whether specific types of parental risk affected child outcomes differently, she studied 865 children selected from five US cities. She found that the type of risk did matter and that parental incarceration was the parental risk factor that most negatively associated with the majority of the child outcomes, followed by parental mental illness. She also found that poverty, a commonly used indicator of risk, did not have a significant effect on most of the child outcomes when other risk factors were included in the model (Hyppolite, 2017). As you can see, Hyppolite's research aims to address a problem of human behavior (e.g., negative child outcomes) and has policy implications (e.g., to focus more on understanding the impact of parental incarceration on children rather than the impact of poverty) so it is applied in focus, but it does not assess the need for a specific policy, it does not examine whether a policy is running as designed, and it does not examine whether a specific policy worked; therefore, it is not evaluation research..

A specific branch of applied research is evaluation research, sometimes called evidence-based research, which involves research in an applied setting where different parties involved with a program may want to have a say in the definition of outcomes and the design of the program. In the past, programs were often designed based on personal experience and option rather than research. Now, however, research is increasingly used to establish program need, monitor program implementation, examine program effectiveness, or weigh the costs of the program relative to the benefits. Each of these is a form of evaluation research that you will learn about in this chapter and evidence-based research specifically is generally evaluation research that identifies the best evidence of program merit and is used to design programs, which are then termed **evidence-based practices**. Box 9.2 summarizes some of the distinctions between these various types of evaluation forms and practices.

iStockphoto.com/400tmax

PHOTO 9.1 Applied research is a broad research classification that studies social issues that have policy and program implications, while evaluation research which is a more specific form of applied research that focuses on the need, implementation, outcome, or efficiency of a specific program or policy.

BOX 9.2
SUMMARY OF DIFFERENCES BETWEEN CLASSIFICATIONS OF EVALUATION RESEARCH

Classification	Improve Human Condition	Establish Need	Establish Ability to be Evaluated	Assess Effectiveness	Cost/ Benefit	Direct Program Use
Applied	X					
Evaluation	X	X	X	X	X	
Evidence-Based Research	X			X	X	X
Evidence-Based Practice	X					X

BASIC EVALUATION COMPONENTS

Many social programs are funded, at least in part, by government money, which in turn is funded by taxpayers. Consequently, in order to justify the use of taxpayer funds and to better ensure that these funds are being used for effective programs, the government passed the Government Performance and Results Act of 1993, which required some type of evaluation for all programs receiving government funds (U.S. Office of Management and Budget, 2002). These evaluations usually involve identifying, measuring, and assessing program stakeholders, inputs, processes, outputs, and outcomes with feedback for program improvement. Let's look at each of these components more closely.

Stakeholders are people who have a vested interest in the program and they are a key component of an evaluation that should be part of the process at the very beginning. Stakeholders can include people at every level of program involvement, such as program directors, managers, staff, clients, and even the public. Walker, Hills, and Heere (2017) evaluated whether corporate social responsibility (CSR) programs, which are social programs sponsored by corporations to foster a positive public view of themselves, actually worked to achieve their social reformation goals. To do this, they examined the Socially Responsible Youth Employability Program in the United Kingdom, which was developed by a professional British soccer team and financed by a multinational bank as part of the bank's CSR to bolster employability and life skills through work-related training and motivation for marginalized London youth. The belief was that marginalized youth might not be interested in employability training in general, so soccer was the enticement to spark participant interest. In this context, some of the stakeholders would be the bank, the soccer team, and the marginalized youth themselves.

Each stakeholder may have a different goal, or "stake," they want to see fulfilled by the program. For example, program directors might be concerned with servicing as many clients as

PHOTO 9.2 Companies like to appear socially responsible by sponsoring programs they think will help communities; but, do these programs really work?

possible and at a cost that is more efficient than the cost of the standard operating procedure. Staff might be concerned with whether they have the resources in manpower and skills to carry out the program well, and clients are concerned with obtaining help. Researchers may also be considered a stakeholder because their goal is to produce a vigorous, methodologically sound evaluation. Because of these different goals and perspectives that need to be considered, the main stakeholders all should be able to "come to the table" to discuss what they hope to learn from an evaluation. In Walker et al.'s (2017) study, we can probably say with some confidence that although all the stakeholders had the overarching goal of employment for these youths, the bank was also interested in generating favorable public opinion. The professional soccer team might also have been interested in public opinion but perhaps also in instilling an appreciation for soccer and encouraging youth to develop pro-social employment characteristics, while, the marginalized youth who attended (the clients) probably were hoping to secure some type of job after program completion or just to have a good time. Another important issue with stakeholders is to make sure they are aware of the roles of other stakeholders. Walker et al., for example, stated that a working relationship between the research team, the soccer club foundation, and the bank was negotiated prior to conducting the evaluation.

Stakeholders help identify the **inputs** to a program, which are anything that goes "in" to the program, such as clients, staff, and resources. In the London youth example, the inputs would be the resources necessary to conduct the trainings, such as staff, papers or books, or meeting space. The inputs would also be the youth themselves, as the bank and professional sports team would have decided which applying youths were granted program acceptance.

These inputs shape the program process, which is treatment or service in its entirety and its design. Think of it as the program description: Program X plans to do Y. Walker et al. (2017) give a fairly detailed description of the program process, but to summarize it for our purposes, the program is designed to provide: (1) work-related training, (2) skill and attitude training, (3) leadership in sport training, (4) money skills training, (5) mentoring experience, and (6) other employment opportunities (e.g., volunteering, physical activity, and networking visits) for three 5-hr-a-day sessions during the program week (Walker et al., 2017, p. 57).

However, what is actually done is not always the same as what is designed to be done. Program **output** refers to what is *actually done* and can include indicators such as the number of clients the program served overall, the actual timespan of program involvement, and the detailed nature of what these clients will experience and by whom. Although Walker et al. did not go into much detail about output in their evaluation article, they did mention that the program served 86 youths (the output), who both completed the full program and participated in the pre- and post-program data collection.

The immediate impact of the program on the clients, what most people think of as the "evaluation," is the **outcome**. Outcomes can be "soft," meaning that they are hard to measure and rather subjective, or they can be "hard," meaning that they are more objective and easily observed. According to Walker et al. (2017), the program had two main goals. The first goal was the securing of employment for these youth, which is a "hard" outcome because it is easily and objectively observed. Someone obtains employment or not. Secondary goals focused on fostering self-esteem and marketability, which are "softer" outcomes because they are harder to operationalize and measure objectively (Chapter 4). Recognizing that many soft outcomes are concepts that are multidimensional and vague, Walker et al. adapted scales developed by others to measure self-esteem, self-mastery, perceived marketability, and employability ambition, among other factors, thereby potentially adding both content validity and external validity (Chapter 6) to their study. The point here is that all of these soft concepts can have multiple indicators that are harder to measure than simply determining whether or not someone has a job. Walker et al. (2017) found that the program correlated with improvement in the soft outcomes of self-esteem and marketability, but it did not exhibit much effect on the hard outcome of obtaining employment.

Before we move on, since this *is* a research method and statistics book, I need to take a moment to identify *how* outcomes are identified in a systems model, and that answer is obviously research. Walker et al.'s used a mixed-methods design (Chapter 8) which consisted of pre- and post-questionnaires, an employment tracking postprogram, focus groups, and administrator interviews. In this way, they obtained both qualitative and quantitative information regarding motivations and outcomes. In fact, given the multiple stakeholder goals and components inherent in any program, a mixed-methods design whenever possible is advisable for any evaluation research because the focus on qualitative and quantitative information can be especially informative for the last component of evaluation research, which is the feedback.

The **feedback** component of a systems design is the "where are we going to go now?" or "how can we use this information?" questions. There is no perfect program that is going to work for every single individual, nor is there a program that is likely to be run *exactly* as designed or work *exactly* as designed. In social service arenas, you will often hear about "closing the loop" or "designing the feedback loop," and that is where the feedback becomes relevant. For Walker et al. (2017), their feedback centered on reflections regarding the failure to produce the hard outcome of employment and their suggestions for what the bank and/or soccer team would need to consider moving forward. For example, even though the soft outcomes associated with employability improved, neither the bank nor the soccer team was in a position to offer jobs to the program graduates; therefore, other factors, such as market availability, beyond the control of the two key stakeholder's, overshadowed the effectiveness of the program. People may have the newfound skills for employment, but if jobs are not available, employment is unlikely, regardless of how qualified or willing to work one is. Therefore, the researchers concluded that more thought was necessary when creating these programs regarding what organizations can and cannot control and that stakeholders either need to have some mechanism in place to address these outside factors or they need to alter their goals (Walker et al., 2017).

 LEARNING CHECK 9.1: COMPONENTS OF EVALUATION RESEARCH

1. What part of the evaluation process addresses what the program *is designed* to do?

2. A local agency wants to study a welfare-to-work program directed at men with low levels of education. What would the men, the staff, and the program materials all be considered in evaluation language?

3. What is a key feature that is part of the evaluation process but also distinguishes evaluation research from basic or general applied research?

Answers to be found at the end of the chapter.

TYPES OF EVALUATION RESEARCH

There are many types of evaluation research, but for our purposes of "getting the job done," I will focus on five: needs assessment, evaluability assessment, implementation assessment, outcome evaluation, and efficiency analysis.

Needs Assessment

Workers in the field may feel, based on their daily interactions with clients, that a new program or an adjustment to a program is necessary, but you learned in Chapter 1, personal experience can be biased. Workers, for example, may only see selected types of clients served or they may have their own personal program biases that affect their perceptions of need. A needs assessment, on the contrary, uses systematic methods of observation to more objectively establish "need" based on identified problems or gaps in existing programs. These areas of need might be established by the demographics of a certain population, such as if social

iStockphoto.com/SDI Productions

PHOTO 9.3 Can you think of ways a needs assessment can document the need for a public school district to invest in more computers?

workers are noticing that it is challenging to find foster families for children identifying as a racial minority in a predominantly nonminority county, or there might be gaps in programs that do not effectively address the needs of subgroups of clients. So a prison might be able to record its 3-year recidivism rate to show the need for a reentry program, a welfare agency might show the percent of people in a county whose income falls below the poverty line, or a school might be able to show the percent of students who do not have computer access at home to learn computer skills. All of these are fairly straightforward ways of documenting need.

However, frequently documenting need is not as easy as it may initially appear (and as you are probably learning by now, research rarely is!). For example, which stakeholder's definition of "need" will be used? What do we really mean by "need" anyway? For example, it is unlikely that we will *ever* wipe out recidivism; some people will just be unable to stay out of prison. So what recidivism rate indicates a "need" for intervention? 10%? 20%? This is where the input of stakeholders and multiple indicators would be important. Although there may not be a universal agreement of what recidivism rates are acceptable and what establishes need, there does not necessarily need to be a universal idea. Evaluation research is what is relevant to that agency or organization, so what those *particular* stakeholders agree as the cutoff for need is what is relevant in that situation. In fact, including different indicators that address different stakeholder concerns of need is a way to approach this analysis systematically. As such, need evaluations do not need to be very sophisticated because they are usually only serving as justification for a program and/or as part of a grant application process.

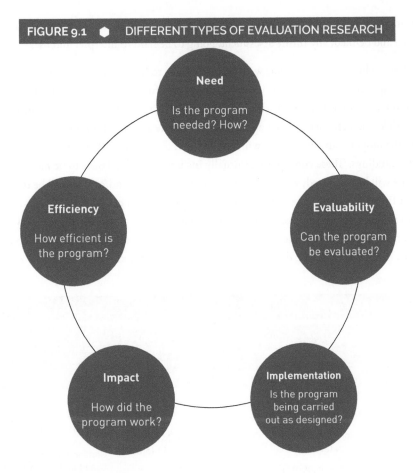

FIGURE 9.1 ◆ DIFFERENT TYPES OF EVALUATION RESEARCH

Need
Is the program needed? How?

Evaluability
Can the program be evaluated?

Implementation
Is the program being carried out as designed?

Impact
How did the program work?

Efficiency
How efficient is the program?

Evaluability Assessment

Just because a need is established and an agency wants to test their program does not mean that that program can actually be evaluated. This is where an evaluability assessment becomes relevant. For a program to be evaluated, a researcher has to make sure of the following:

- Stakeholders can identify each component of the program that they wish to assess, including program eligibility, treatment actions, staff actions, and client experiences.

- There are clear definitions of what indicates success.

- There are ways for the information to be recorded and shared and it is clear who is responsible for recording what.

This stage of the process is usually more qualitative than quantitative in that it involves the analysis of program descriptions and interviews, sometimes in a group setting, with key stakeholders. Frequently through this type of analysis, gaps in knowledge or contradictions may become evident so the feedback would involve reaching an agreement on how to rectify these issues prior to embarking on a full process or evaluation assessment. After all, if the infrastructure is not clearly identified and defined, any future assessment, going to be hard to interpret and use.

When I do evaluability assessments with agencies, I like to first put together what I call a basic **concept map**. This concept map (Figure 9.2) is initially formed after analyzing any program descriptions and eligibility criteria that the agency has documented, coupled with group interviews with key stakeholders. This map allows me to create an understanding of everyone's idea of what the program and evaluation will look like and to identify if there are any obvious gaps in understandings. These concept maps usually include identified issues to be measured, how each issue will be measured, where the indicator can be found, and/or who will be responsible for recording it. Once I make a preliminary concept map, I meet with the key stakeholders again to show them any gaps or contradictions that need to be resolved prior to any evaluation. Common issues I have encountered at this phase include objectives that have no defined outcome, outcomes that have definitions that are not agreed upon by stakeholders, outcomes

---

FIGURE 9.2 ● CONCEPT MAP EXAMPLE

Program Component	Concept	Indicator	Where Measured Note: All are in the pre/post survey adapted from the original program	Notes
Outcomes	1. Creation of a safe haven 2. Child develops a <u>positive view of his/her artistic expression</u>[1] 3. *Improved attitude towards school* 4. *Increased positive peer associations/ sense of belonging* 5. Reduced alienation from others 6. *Improved self esteem*	1. I feel safe being here 2. a. I am creative b. I am talented 3. I enjoy school most of the time[2] 4. a. I get along well with other kids b. I have friends in the program[3] 5. I like being a part of a team 6. a. I can do things as well as most. b. I think there are many good things about me.	1. Pre/Post Q3 2. a. Pre/Post Q4 (old 7) b. Pre/Post Q11 (old 8) 3. Pre/Post Q6 4. a. Pre/Post Q8 (old 14) b. Pre/Post Q12 5. Pre/Post Q14 (old 13) 6. a. Pre/Post Q16 (old 6) b. Pre/Post Q13 (old 9)	Concepts in plain text are from the ARTS Engage program description Concepts <u>underlined</u> are based on the "objectives" listed on the Request for Qualifications form Concepts *italicized* are in both the program description and the Request for Qualifications form NOTE: When there is more than one indicator for a concept, they are not generally spaced together on the pre/post (unless the questions are clearly distinct) to minimize the risk of bias.

---

[1] This was changed from "art skills" because as an immediate goal, "skill" can only be assessed by the instructor and the instructors do not assess individual children. Furthermore, the goal of the program is for the child to feel better through art; therefore, he/she may like art or feel good doing it as a result of the program even if he/she has little talent/skill for the art.

[2] This was changed from "I do well in my subjects in school" because the original question addressed performance (do well) while outcome expressed overall attitude. The goal is to create a favorable view of school, not a favorable view of one's performance in school, which the new question better captures.

[3] The question about friends in the program will be changed in the post test to "I made friends in the program." The goal is to see if peer associations have gone up as a result of program participation.

that have no measures, and a lack of clarity as to who is responsible for obtaining specific pieces of information. An example of a concept map appears in Figure 9.1, and you will see that it presents a means for both the researcher and the stakeholders to keep account of the outcomes that would be tracked in an evaluation, what measures exist, and where to find those measures. The footnotes reflect changes that were made based on continued interviews, and tracking these changes helps all parties remember decisions that were previously made and why.

This concept map can be incorporated into a more sophisticated outline of program processes that is commonly called a **logic model**. Logic models are diagrams that outline each of the components of the evaluation process that I discussed earlier, such as inputs, processes, and outcomes. The concept map would be part of the outcome component where immediate, intermediate, and long-term goals, if applicable, could be specified in detail. The point of the logic model is to clarify at each step of the evaluation process what will be done, by whom, and how it fits with program goals.

As stated earlier, however, not all programs pass the evaluability phase. I will address what challenges researchers might encounter during this phase toward the end of the chapter in the "Challenges" section.

Implementation Assessment

Once the inputs and program processes are identified and clarified, the program is ready for implementation. In reality, programs may already be running prior to the evaluation phase. If this is the case, the program may need to be altered based on any decisions made during the evaluability assessment. This is also illustrated in Figure 9.1, which is an evaluation of an existing program and there are notes in the concept map where measures, as well as program goals, had to be altered. Implementation assessment, sometimes also called a process evaluation, is a systematic way of seeing whether the program is operating as designed. This focuses on examining the nature of service delivery. After all, if the program is not operating as designed, how can stakeholders expect to see the desired results or understand why they observed the effects that they did?

Some program aspects that researchers will want to monitor for an implementation evaluation include decision-making protocols, staff workload, client record keeping, staff training, and worker–client activities. For example, Carter, VanNorman, and Tredwell (2011), in response to evidence that a high number of preschool children exhibited challenging behaviors associated with future negative behaviors, conducted an implementation assessment of the Program-Wide Positive Behavior Support (PWPBS) model that uses a tiered intervention framework to help preschoolers develop socio-emotional skills (Fox, Carta, Strain, Dunlap, & Hemmeter, 2010; Sugai et al., 2000; Tremblay, 2000). Carter et al. (2011) provided detail on the initial training of the program staff and what worked. For example, they learned that giving the staff a lead in the overview of the project created team identity and fostered program willingness. However, they also learned what did not work, such as the staff feeling pressured to agree with the initial design, which might lead to less investment in participation, ultimately reducing effectiveness. Based on these findings they suggested creating a safe haven to let staff provide honest feedback. Publishing implementation assessments are important because they can provide useful information for professionals considering a similar program.

As I mentioned earlier, in reality, programs are rarely carried out *exactly* as designed, which can hurt overall program effectiveness, so implementation assessments are important for identifying areas where the program was not carried out as specified (Patton, 2002). Because programs also usually require some level of political support, findings that show less than desirable effects may lead to program termination. Therefore, it is important to know whether deleterious effects are because the program really did not work or because it was not carried out as designed (so it *might* still work if the program operated as it was supposed to). For example, remember when we discussed survey wording in Chapter 7? If through a well-constructed survey a researcher can identify a specific staff member or a study site (when multiple sites are being used) who is getting negative client feedback and/or is not operating as designed, then that information might be informative to overall program effectiveness by comparing outcomes for those issues separately or removing those issues from part of the analysis to see if the removal produces a different outcome.

Outcome Evaluation

Outcome evaluation, sometimes also called impact analysis, is what most nonresearchers automatically think of when they think of a program evaluation. This type of evaluation addresses "Did the program work?" You already learned in Chapter 6 that randomized experimental designs are the ideal for establishing causality to see if the treatment, or independent variable, created the change in the observed behavior, the dependent variable. Therefore, in order to

iStockphoto.com/artisteer

PHOTO 9.4 Being able to find employment involves more than just a willingness to work and an availability of jobs. What factors do you think are important for job training programs to address?

conclude that the intervention *caused* the change in the desired behavior, a true experiment that uses random assignment would be the best option. For example, it is obvious that there are many potential barriers to finding employment, such as drug addiction, low education, mental health, and market vulnerability. Booshehri, Dugan, Patel, Bloom, and Chilton (2018) evaluated a program that recognizes that exposure to trauma may be an additional barrier to employment. They used a randomized control trial of 103 caregivers of young children who were on Temporary Assistance to Needy Families (TANF) to compare employment outcomes from basic TANF programming (the control group), a 28-week financial education program (a partial intervention), or a 28-week financial education program conducted in conjunction with trauma-informed peer support (a full intervention). They found that although those in the control group were more likely than those in the other two groups to be employed, those in the full program (financial education and trauma-informed peer support) had higher levels of self-efficacy, lower levels of depressive symptoms, and greater earnings overall (hence decreased economic hardship), suggesting that overall the full program was the most effective in improving behavior and economic health (Booshehri et al., 2018).

Obviously, though, also as discussed in Chapter 6, researchers cannot always conduct randomized experiments. Even in my own evaluation experiences, I have encountered situations where I would recommend some form of a randomized experiment only to be told by different stakeholders that random assignment was not possible for political, ethical, and/or resource reasons. In those instances, quasi-experiments, surveys, and qualitative measures might all be viable—and a combination of them in a mixed-methods design would be an optimal alternative to a true experiment—but the results have to be interpreted cautiously and causality cannot really be established.

Aside from the obvious "did it work?" question, more refined outcome evaluation questions might include: (1) Did the program fulfill its desired goals? (2) Did the people who experienced the program benefit more than a comparison group who did not? (3) Were there people within the program who benefited more than others? (4) Do the clients feel that the program benefitted them? and (5) How long does the program effect last? Furthermore, a well-constructed impact assessment can help identify where program problems might also affect these outcomes.

Efficiency Analysis

The last form of evaluation research we will cover is efficiency analysis. I mentioned in our discussion of experiments (Chapter 6) that in applied program studies the comparison is not usually whether a client receives Program A verses no program, but rather whether Program A works better and/or produces more positive outcomes at a lower cost than Program B, which is usually the standard or existing operating procedure. Efficiency analysis, therefore, answers the questions "Do the program's benefits offset its costs?" or "Is this program more efficient than an already existing program?"

There are two common types of efficiency analysis: cost-benefit analysis and cost-effective analysis. **Cost-benefit analysis** focuses on estimating the program costs and the economic benefits of the outcomes. This type of analysis originated in medicine, where the costs of the program (e.g., a new drug) and the outcomes (e.g., lower-cost medical care) are clearer than in the social sciences. For example, what is the economic benefit of a biological mother having her child returned to her? Furthermore, there is a greater variety of stakeholders in social service programs and each may have a different idea of what would be a benefit rather than a cost. Keeping a child out of the criminal justice system may save the economic costs associated with the criminal justice process, but if that child requires intensive social service monitoring, it may increase the cost to social service agencies in terms of staffing.

Because social science outcomes are harder to economically evaluate, researcher efforts generally focus more on a **Cost efficiency analysis**, where the program costs are estimated, but the outcomes are not quantified into economic benefits in and of themselves. Instead, outcomes are evaluated on whether the outcome was achieved or not. Sometimes this can involve financial benefits (such as the money saved from imprisonment, or being on welfare, or needing foster care) or it can be in other types of opportunities (such as family reunification, sense of self-worth, or improved attitudes toward medical care). For example, urban areas are increasingly conscious of trying to promote greenspace in order to protect ecosystems, to create recreational spaces, to foster social connection, and to control urban expansion (Ma & Jin, 2019). However, it is unclear what the overall costs and benefits of creating these spaces are and which greenspace designs (such as greenbelts or greenwedges) would be the most efficient for a city's purposes. Ma and Jin (2019) created economic models to assess different theoretical and structural greenspace models for the city of Beijing, China, which is a rapidly expanding city currently trying to decide how much land to devote to greenspaces and what type. To define effectiveness, Ma and Jin considered such outcomes like how much floor space people will have in apartments, the cost of rent, how many goods residents will be able to buy, whether local markets are likely to be the suppliers of those goods, how traffic and work

iStockphoto.com/cnicbc

PHOTO 9.5 What are some social, as well as economic, outcomes that can be addressed to evaluate how urban green spaces impact a community?

LEARNING CHECK 9.2: TYPES OF EVALUATION RESEARCH

1. What type of evaluation design determines whether an objective evaluation can even be accomplished?

2. Why is conducting an implementation assessment important?

3. Why do social science disciplines such as sociology, social work, and criminal justice focus more on cost-effective analysis rather than cost-benefit analysis for efficiency analysis?

Answers to be found at the end of the chapter.

commutes are likely to be affected, and how such space will affect employment opportunities (which would, in turn, affect the number of people who need public assistance). Some of these outcomes are financial (such as the cost of rent), but others are not (such as how commutes and traffic will be affected). Obviously, these outcomes are hard to define and even harder to predict. Therefore, many cost-benefit or cost-effective analyses require complex forecasting statistical models that are well beyond our focus of "getting the job done" and frankly beyond the capabilities of any undergraduate class. In fact, I really only mention efficiency analysis in general in order to illustrate that it *can* be done, even though *how* to do it is beyond the undergraduate experience.

ADDITIONAL CONSIDERATIONS

What I have covered so far is the decision of what *type* of evaluation study to conduct. As I said earlier, evaluation research gets its own chapter because it poses additional considerations for the research process. In this section, I will discuss some issues researchers have to consider regardless of what type of evaluation they are doing.

The Role of Theory

As you learned in Chapter 1, theory gives the "why" or the context behind empirical findings. However, in applied research, where the purpose of the research is usually to see if something is required, is operating as designed, or has worked, more so than why, an argument can be made that theory is less important (Chen, 1990). On the contrary, many service agencies are moving toward evidence-based practice, which is the integration of evaluation research and theory. If you remember, in evidence-based practice, professionals use research to identify what works and theory to understand why so they can best shape interventions for their own unique populations.

Regardless, knowing how and why something works—or even perhaps, more importantly, does *not* work—is important. If researchers can learn why something does not work, policy makers have an idea of what to change to make another try. Conducting a process evaluation will help to answer these questions and link the observed outcomes to theory.

The Balance of Researcher and Program Stakeholders

In evaluation research, the study topic is not usually selected by the researcher. In other words, researchers do not commonly approach agencies with *their* research interests regarding a program and seek permission to study that program. Instead, when agencies want a program to be evaluated, they approach a researcher to see if the researcher has the interest, skill, and resources to conduct the evaluation. Nonetheless, the researcher arguably *becomes* a stakeholder because like other stakeholders, the researcher has a goal (a well-designed and executed evaluation), and therefore a stake, in the outcome of the final product. I have already discussed how research goals (e.g., randomized studies to establish causality) and agency constraints (e.g., political or economic impediments to such a design) may conflict; so, if that conflict occurs, where lies the balance? There are two views, with an emerging third, on this issue.

One view is the researcher approach, which recognizes that in order for the researcher to remain unbiased to the evidence presented, he or she needs to remain separate from other stakeholders. Based on this information, the researcher identifies the needs of participants and the relevant outcomes with minimal input from other stakeholders (Scriven, 1972). The other option is the stakeholder approach, which recognizes and seeks the input of various stakeholders in the evaluation process, including the researcher as a stakeholder, who now has the stake to make sure that the evaluation accurately represents the concerns of the various parties involved in a program's implementation. As such, this approach recognizes the importance of including different stakeholders in the evaluation design to better ensure that the evaluation results will be used (Patton, 2002); however, because the researcher is seen as an equal among stakeholders, the researcher may either lose objectivity or make compromises that lead to less scientifically sound findings.

An updated version of the stakeholder approach, which is what I have been indirectly favoring in this book, recognizes that at some times the program stakeholders' views might take precedence and at other times the researcher's views might be more visible. This compromise is the integrative approach, which tries to create a project that is responsive to stakeholder concerns while simultaneously trying to obtain objective, scientifically sound results. As such, this approach recognizes that not all stakeholders are likely to view the results the same way, and the answer to whose view "wins," so to speak, is not one that the researcher needs to decide. The researcher will present the evidence and the suggestions (feedback) for how the program can move forward based on that evidence, but ultimately it is the other stakeholders who decide how to use those suggestions.

How Much Detail Is Necessary to Report in the Findings?

Different stakeholders are going to want different levels of information in a report. For example, those who are in administrative positions may just want the bottom line rather than a detailed analysis of each program component. Staff may want to know about the program details so they know what they need to improve upon or keep the same. Funding agencies may have a statistical team who wants to know the statistical justification for each claim. I had an embarrassing lesson in this balance when I wrote my first ever evaluation report for a local drug treatment court many years ago (more than I want to admit!) when evaluation research was much newer as a discipline. At the time I was fresh out of graduate school, and I was contracted to do my first evaluation as a university professor. I wanted to make sure that the presiding judge felt that he was getting his county's money's worth from my evaluation so I put together this detailed report full of graphs, tables, and statistics. I was actually pretty proud of the product ... until he called me, into his chambers to discuss my findings. He kindly sat back in his oversized chair, looked at me and said something to the effect of "This is a really impressive looking document. But I am a busy guy who has no head for numbers. So tell me ... what does it all *mean*?" I was crushed! Even though I had a section on feedback to close the loop, the judge did not understand the evidence I presented to get there. My bruised self-esteem was soothed a little bit, however, when a few days later, I learned that the program coordinator received a call from one of the funding representatives who told her that my report was one of the clearest, most substantiated ones she had ever seen! The moral of this example is that two different stakeholders can have two different views of the very same report.

So how do you give everyone what they want? Well, evaluation research has come a long way in the last 25 years. Now it almost seems to be common sense to those of us who do evaluations to make sure that we organize our reports in this basic template: a table of contents, an executive summary, the main body of the report, and appendices. The table of contents is pretty straightforward and is the same as a table of contents in any other publication, research oriented or not. It tells the reader where various parts of the report begin and end. This way stakeholders who have different interests can easily find the parts of the report that are relevant to them without getting bogged down in reading the sections that are not.

The **executive summary** is also pretty much what the name implies; it gives a brief introduction, a summary of the purpose of the evaluation, the goals of the program, an overview (brief and not very technical) of the methods, the main findings in nonstatistical terms, and the ensuing feedback or suggestions for moving forward. The executive summary basically gives the bottom line and is for anyone who is too busy to read the full report or who does not need all the detail that justifies the feedback and corresponding suggestions. Although I had an executive summary in my first report, I did let some statistical evidence creep into this section, which ended up confusing the judge and rightly so. Statistics were not his area, just like the law is not mine. He was not interested in the statistical evidence; he just wanted my conclusions and suggestions based on them.

The body of the report is where the "meat" of the research is. This would be presented in sections, which are identified in the table of contents, with the more detailed statistical and visual analysis for each component of the report. Those who have a need or interest for the evidence behind what is summarized in the executive summary would use the table of contents to find their relevant section and then read the details in that section. This is the part of the report that interested the funding representative whose job was to oversee the courts' various evaluations. This person had the methodological and statistical background to want to see the numbers and methods. The last section is any appendices forms, … really anything that is supplemental that the researcher feels the sponsoring agency might want to see but is not directly relevant to the analysis presented in the body of the report.

✓ LEARNING CHECK 9.3: OTHER CONSIDERATIONS

1. What does the executive summary entail?

2. When an outcome evaluation is conducted on a comparatively small group in a specific community, which is more important to establish, validity or reliability?

3. Which view of the stakeholder–researcher relationship tries to be sensitive to program stakeholder views while simultaneously recognizing that the researcher is a stakeholder as well?

Answers to be found at the end of the chapter.

QUALITY ISSUES

Validity

Even with the restrictions that are the reality of evaluation research, researchers have to work to create findings that are as objective, valid, and reliable as their resources allow; and they need to be honest about where those quality indicators fall short, perhaps because of those very same resources or, more commonly, lack thereof. I have already addressed that randomized experiments are the best approach to achieve internal validity, and when researchers cannot conduct randomized experiments, they need to spend additional time and resources to address the steps they took to try and achieve this validity (such as what they did to minimize selection bias). Probably one of the most desirous forms of validity claim a researcher wants to make is that of predictive validity (Chapter 4), where the researcher can use the outcomes to predict future behavior accurately. On the contrary, external validity may be less relevant for evaluation research because this form of observation often focuses on a specific site or population, regardless of whether the evaluation focuses on need, implementation, or outcomes. In other words, evaluation research tends to be more specific and, therefore, not about broader generalizations, so external validity is less relevant.

Reliability

Although all studies should strive for reliability, according to Patton (2002), the corresponding importance of reliability and the degree of effort that should be expended to achieve it are somewhat shaped by the nature of the evaluation. For example, if researchers are doing a large-scale outcome evaluation of a national program with multiple sites and a corresponding large budget, then it is fair to expect a more robust attempt to establish reliability. However, if the program being studied, even as an outcome evaluation, is comparatively small and focused on a specific community where the main purpose is just to see if immediate program goals were achieved and whether there were any areas in need of improvement, then reliability is not a major focus.

Objectivity

Objectivity can be difficult to obtain when those doing the evaluation are affiliated with the agency sponsoring the program. In fact, it might even be a conflict of interest. However, again, depending on the resources of an agency (perhaps there are not many funds or, there is no university nearby that has trained and objective people to conduct an outside evaluation), agencies have to make do with what they have. In fact, that is part of the reason for this book and the focus of "getting the job done." This book will give you the basics of how to conduct an entire evaluation on your own if you find you need to, but it will also help you contribute to the stakeholder discussion if you find you do not need to conduct the evaluation, but do need to be a part of it. The key approach to obtaining objectivity, even when subjectivity may be more natural, is to include (and document the inclusion as well as the reasoning) multiple perspectives to give a balanced idea of what is going on. Involving multiple stakeholders from the start is the most expedient way to achieve this.

MAKING DECISIONS

Remember, evaluation research is not a unique method of observation; therefore, the only real decision within the context of the evaluation itself is what type of evaluation to conduct. Figure 9.1, that appears earlier in this chapter, shows how the different evaluation options fit various research questions.

CHALLENGES

1. **Although I have a logic model/concept map created, I still am not sure whether the program can be evaluated. What red flags should I look for that might prevent evaluation of a program?** Patton (2002) identified some warning signs that an objective evaluation might not be possible. One of these is that the stakeholders are not really looking for an honest evaluation, but instead they want the researcher to empirically show that their program is superior to others. For example, under my direction, each year my students learn methods and statistics by designing a basic evaluation for a local agency. Often this is a needs assessment, but sometimes it is a basic quasi-experiment. One year my students worked to create a posttest for an agency, but one of the top stakeholders did not approve it because the answer choices to the close-ended questions were balanced with some negative values. He argued that if we included these negative values, as opposed to just having the lowest value be neutral, there might be negative findings that would hurt the value of his program,

which he "knew" worked well overall. I pulled my students from the project and we did not evaluate his program that semester.

One challenge that would need to be resolved before a program can be evaluated is making sure the staff is on board with the program and their role in recording any data. If the staff is disengaged from the program, disgruntled with the agency they work for, or feel that any data recording is beyond their job description, then they are not likely to carry out the intervention with attention to how it is designed and/or keep substandard records. Either of these situations would obviously affect the program and its corresponding evaluation.

Furthermore, the program of interest needs to be sufficiently different from coexisting programs or the current "standard operating procedure," where the program of interest has unique characteristics that can be clearly identified, defined, and empirically observed. Part of this also means that clients in different programs, such as both a new treatment program or standard operating procedure, should not have any overlap in their program experience, including their service providers. For example, if researchers are trying to test Program A over Program B and part of Program A is a new training for service providers, the same service providers should not be serving both Program A and Program B. Once an individual receives training, that training would be part of the individual's overall work skills, which may affect how that individual treats clients in Program B, a threat to validity that you know is contamination.

2. **What if some stakeholders have unrealistically high expectations of what can be "proven," which I suspect cannot be fulfilled with the available resources?** This can be a challenge for a variety of reasons. Professionals might not have a firm understanding of what can and cannot be empirically shown about the program. Or they have an overwhelming number of outcomes that they want to link to their program, but not the means of measuring (even with help from a researcher) the many competing causes for those outcomes. To minimize this risk, it is important to understand the perspectives of the different stakeholders (administrators, service providers, clients, etc.) and to work together to agree upon the questions and/or outcomes that are the most relevant to the most stakeholders early in the design phase. By limiting the outcomes to ones in which feasible alternative explanations can also be tested will help show (but as we discussed, never prove) whether the observed outcomes are likely to be because of the program.

3. **How can I address the limitations of my available resources?** More so than with basic research, applied research in general and evidence-based research, in particular, have some additional real-world limitations. Not all agencies have the same resources available to them, not all calls for funding require complex evaluation designs, and not all programs can ethically conduct the "gold standard" of randomized experiments (Patton, 2002). Therefore, sometimes "getting the job done" means that the researcher considers what type of evidence and how much will be sufficient

for their purpose and resources. Furthermore, in evidence-based research, more so than basic research, the cultural context of the program and stakeholders, the characteristics of the program itself, and operational issues (like review boards, site-specific obstacles, and the need to rely on others for data gathering) are all challenges that affect the methodological approach, which in turn affect the types of statistics that can be complied and the conclusions that can be made. Therefore it is important to work with stakeholders to explain how to choose appropriate measures (Chapter 4), how to create methods of observation that produce consistent and valid results (Chapters 7–10), and how to analyze that information (Chapters 11–15). This may help them to better understand what their available resources can accomplish or what additional resources they need to obtain.

Incidentally, as I will soon discuss in the next section on statistics, one common resource many agencies lack is access to commercial statistical packages. However, there are some good freeware packages available, one of which is R programming through the use of R Studio. In the chapters involving statistics, I will discuss how to run basic statistical tests in both this program and the commercially available Statistical Package for the Social Sciences (SPSS).

4. **What can I do with the staff's lack of interest in complying with the collection and/or reporting of program data?** This is a tough one as most professionals already feel that they are overworked and underpaid, so gathering data seems like just one more responsibility that you are adding to their already full plate. To minimize the work of professionals, in the design phase, be clear about what kinds of information are already being gathered by the agency and determine whether any of that can be used for evaluation purposes. When additional information is necessary, have the researchers gather data whenever possible, using the service professional as a means of data gathering as a last resort.

Furthermore, making the usefulness of the evaluation clear from the beginning of the process may elicit greater involvement in the data collection process by showing those involved that possible resulting actions are clear. To accomplish this, it is important at every stage of the research process to be clear about what the stakeholder's expectations are for the evaluation. Part of this could involve, during the report, providing a clear list of resulting actions and possible suggestions as to who might be able to carry those actions out. It is also important, in engaging support, to make sure that the reporting documents are targeted to the different audiences. Funding agencies may want more statistical evidence and justification in their reports than do the caseworkers, who will be utilizing the suggestions.

Key Terms

Concept map

Cost-benefit analysis

Cost efficiency analysis

Evidence-based practices

Executive summary

Feedback

Inputs

Logic model

Outcome

Output

Stakeholders

Answers to Learning Check Questions

Learning Check 9.1: Components of Evaluation Research

1. Program process

2. Inputs

3. Feedback

Learning Check 9.2: Types of Evaluation Research

1. Evaluability assessment

2. Implementation assessments examine whether a program is operating as designed. If it is not, then the intended outcomes are unlikely to occur. Even if the program *is* operating as designed, if the intended outcomes still do not occur, then it might be possible to identify if a part of the program, rather than the program in its entirety, contributed to the negative outcomes.

3. Social science disciplines generally focus on cost-effective analysis because many of their outcomes do not have a clear dollar value that can be attributed to them.

Learning Check 9.3: Other Considerations

1. The executive summary is the nonstatistical overview of the material in the following, more detailed, sections of the report. It includes a brief introduction summarizing the purpose of the evaluation, the goals of the program, a brief overview of the methods, the main findings (again, in nonstatistical terms), and the ensuing feedback or suggestions moving forward.

2. Validity, because for specific small programs, the main goal is to gather the best available information to see whether the outcome is achieved.

3. The integrative approach.

End-of-Chapter Problems

1. A local agency runs a veteran's court, which entails veterans attending weekly therapy, weekly posttraumatic stress counseling, biweekly random urine screens, and regular appearances before the veteran's court judge. Which evaluation type would see whether clients are fulfilling these requirements as designed?
   a. Needs assessment
   b. Implementation assessment
   c. Outcome assessment
   d. Cost-benefit analysis

2. For the veteran's court mentioned in Question 1, which evaluation type would see whether the veteran's court is more efficient than traditional court experiences?
   a. Needs assessment
   b. Implementation assessment
   c. Outcome assessment
   d. Cost-benefit analysis

3. The different types of people who have an interest in how a program runs and if it works are called
   a. Stakeholders
   b. Bosses
   c. Clients
   d. Staff

4. The clients, staff, training materials, office space, etc., that go into a program are called
   a. Processes
   b. Stakeholders
   c. Inputs
   d. Outputs

5. True/False: Program output refers to what is accomplished or done in a program rather than what a program is designed to do.

6. True/False: Feedback is a key component of evaluation research that "closes" the loop of an evaluation.

7. The relationship between researchers and stakeholders in which the researcher presents the evidence to the best of his/her ability given the resources and makes suggestions accordingly, but then leaves the other stakeholders to decide which suggestions and goals are the most important to enact is called
   a. Stakeholder approach
   b. Researcher approach
   c. Integrative approach
   d. Evaluative approach

8. Which part of an evaluation report provides the key findings and suggestions, basically the "bottom line," without any statistical discussion?
   a. Executive summary
   b. Table of contents
   c. Report body
   d. Appendices

9. Of the following, what is one of the most desirous forms of validity in evaluation research?
   a. Face validity
   b. Predictive validity
   c. External validity
   d. All the above are equally important

10. Which of the following is a warning sign that a program cannot be evaluated?
    a. Stakeholders are only interested in empirically showing that their program is superior to other programs.
    b. The staff are not supportive of their role in data recording for analysis.
    c. The program is not very unique from the existing program(s).
    d. All the above are warning signs.

MAKING SENSE AND PRESENTING THE INFORMATION

PART IV

PREPARING QUANTITATIVE DATA

LEARNING GOALS

- Be able to prepare information expressed in words to a format understood by a computer

- Learn the coding considerations for different levels of measurement

- Learn how to code a variety of responses such as "other" and "circle all that apply"

- Understand how to prepare data in SPSS and R Studio

- Learn how to clean data

- Learn how to manipulate data like collapsing categories, creating new variables, and creating basic scales

So … now that we have collected our information, what do we do? How do we make sense of all these individual pieces of data? For quantitative information, that answer involves statistical calculations, which are frequently done with a computer program, and many computer programs need numbers for the more complex statistics. This chapter will focus on how to convert non numerical information to numbers that can be read by a computer program in preparation for quantifiable analysis. To accomplish this, I will discuss data coding, possible recoding, data entry, and data cleaning. This chapter will also cover various ways to manipulate data, such as combining categories and creating scales.

CODING QUANTITATIVE DATA

Data coding involves taking the language of the method of observation, whether it is a survey, experiment, agency data, or whatever quantitative method of observation a researcher used, and converting it into a form a computer can recognize. Computers can do complex statistics on thousands of cases involving many variables in a matter of seconds, way before we would even be done writing a formula. However, computers only recognize commands typed into them, they do not have the capabilities of recognizing long, worded questions, which frequently have common words between them. So, for example, computers cannot find a question "what is your gender?" and distinguish it from "If you could pick, what would be the ideal gender of your first child?" Furthermore, some programs cannot recognize the word "male" and compare it to the word "female," but they can compare all cases recognized as a "1" to all those recognized as a "2." But even though the computer can recognize "1" or "2" on their own, these numbers are not likely to have any meaning to people. In quantitative research, coding bridges the gap between our preference for words and the computer's preference for numbers.

For example, take a look at the following hypothetical survey questions:

1. Have you watched any television in the past week?
   a. No (Please go to question 4)
   b. Yes (Please go to question 2)

2. What is your favorite type of television show?
   a. Situation comedy
   b. Drama
   c. Sports
   d. News programs
   e. Other (Please specify:_____)

3. Approximately how many hours of television do you watch a week?_____

4. How accurate do you think television portrayal of real-world violence is?
   a. Very accurate
   b. Somewhat accurate
   c. No opinion
   d. Not very accurate
   e. Not at all accurate

For a computer to recognize this information, I would need to write an abbreviated reference to each question called a **variable name**. These can vary in length, but many programs have eight characters as the default. Of course, with only a few letters to summarize detailed questions, no one would be able to remember what many variable names actually stand for. Fortunately, most computer programs also allow for a **variable label** to be entered, which is frequently a transcription of the question. This is not for the computer, which will search for information based on the variable name, but rather for the researcher, who likely isn't going to remember the meaning of many different variable names.

This information and the following would be tracked in a **codebook**. An example of a possible codebook for the questions I just presented appears in Box 10.1. Notice a couple of points about this codebook before I continue with our coding discussion. The first variables in the codebook do *not* correspond to the first question I presented in the survey. The first variable noted is "Case," which refers to the case number of the particular unit of observation, in this case, the survey. In other words, each individual, group, or artifact, whatever your unit of observation is, needs to have a number so you can identify which information in the computer corresponds to which individual unit. The second item is "coderID" or the "Coder identification." If the main researcher is the only person entering information into the computer, then this variable would not be necessary. However, if there are multiple people entering information, it is important to know who entered what cases in the event that there are systemic problems with data entry that need to be addressed. There are other bookkeeping variables that might be relevant, such as a site ID if the study was done at multiple locations or a wave ID if more than one wave of data is collected. I just gave you the basic variables that might need to be included in addition to the actual survey questions. The third point is the names of the variables themselves. For example "favTVtyp," even if you could decode it to mean "favorite TV type," what does it really mean? Is it your favorite TV show? Favorite television channel? Favorite genre? What? That is also why the variable label, which, as I said, is usually the wording of the question, is important to include in the codebook and the data set. The variable label tells the researcher what specific piece of information or survey question that variable identifies.

The next step in this transformation from the language of words to the language of numbers is to code the values (answer) to each variable (question). Coding of values should be done before data entry and depending on the level of measurement may or may not have meaning. If you recall from Chapter 4, the values of nominal levels of measurement have little numerical meaning and, therefore, neither do their codes. In other words, because these values are just categorical with no ranking, the numerical codes to which they are assigned have no meaning. So, for example, as I said in Chapter 4 for the variable gender, I could assign a code of 1, 111, or 911 to "male," as the number itself makes no difference. For our example, I could code "favTV" as 1 = situational comedy, 2 = drama, 3 = sports, etc., until I reach "Other" simply because that is the order the values appear; but again, the number assigned to each value is immaterial as this variable is a nominal level of measurement. I will discuss what to do with the "Other" category shortly.

BOX 10.1

SAMPLE CODEBOOK

Researcher generated based on survey

Variable Name	Label	Code
Case	Subject ID	
CoderID	Coder identification Sarah Will Sam	 1 2 3
TVwatch	Q1: Have you watched any television in the past week? No YES	 0 1
TVhours	Q2: Approximately how many hours of television do you watch? Note: As answered NA	 99
FavTVtyp	Q3: What is your favorite type of television show? Situation comedy Drama Sports News programs Other NA	 1 2 3 4 5 9
TVreal	Q4: How accurate do you think television portrayal of real-world violence is? Very accurate Somewhat accurate No opinion Not very accurate Not at all accurate NA	 5 4 3 2 1 9

However, with ordinal levels of measurement, the situation changes. Here the values are ranked; therefore, the corresponding codes given to values now have some meaning, where higher codes could mean more or less agreement, depending on the direction of the wording of the question. For example, when I asked, "How accurate do you think the television portrayal of real-world violence is?" the answer choices ranged on a five-point Likert scale from very accurate to very inaccurate, with neutral in the middle. In this instance, "very accurate" is positive toward a perception of accuracy, so this value would get the highest numerical code. On the other hand, if our question was reverse coded, where a negative response actually indicated a high perception of accuracy, the codes would be different. For example, if the question was "In your opinion, how exaggerated do you think the television portrayal of real-world violence is?" with the answer choices on a five-point scale ranging from very exaggerated to very accurate, here a response of "very exaggerated" would imply that the television portrayal is *not* accurate. This is an example of the reversed-coded question I discussed in the chapter on surveys (Chapter 7), so "very exaggerated" would receive a "1" (because it is the furthest away from the concept of "accurate") and the rest of the values would be scored to "5" accordingly.

Interval/ratio levels of measurement are the easiest to code…you *don't*. Remember that one characteristic of these two levels of measurement (Chapter 4) is that the values are quantifiable already. In other words, the answers *are* already numbers—numbers that both you *and* the computer recognize, so no coding is necessary. Hence, in a codebook you might see something like "As answered" (Box 10.1).

You will notice from this section that data sets frequently have more variables than what appears in the actual observation instrument itself. Adding an identification variable for each respondent alone, which is integral to analysis, makes the count of variables in your data set different than your measurement instrument. If you also add variables for coders, data waves, recoded variables, and/or scales, the mismatch between the number of variables in your data set and your original instrument will continue to grow. That is why it is also sometimes useful to add the instrument question number as part of the variable label when the variable is straight from the observation instrument. So for example, my *third* variable in the data set might have a label that reads as "Q1: Have you watched any television in the past week?"

SPECIAL CODING CONSIDERATIONS

Missing Information

Sometimes data is missing for a respondent. Perhaps the question is in a contingency format and based on a subject's answer to the filter question, the subject was directed to skip a subsequent question so that response might be coded something such as "NA" for "not applicable." Sometimes a subject overlooked a question and just forgot to answer it. Or sometimes a subject decided to enact their right to privacy and *chose* not to answer a question. Regardless, the end result is the same: there is no information for the question. In order to distinguish when a respondent didn't answer a question, for whatever reason, rather than when a coder forgot to input information, designating a code for missing information can be useful. There is no single answer for what value should be assigned to missing information and not all computer programs require you to enter such a code. One suggested, but by no means universal, approach is to use "9," for single-digit code values (unless 9 is a viable value), "99" for double-digit, and "999" for three-digit values. In the General Social Survey, which we will be using in the next few chapters, "no answer" is often coded as "9," and "not applicable," which means that the question was not asked of a respondent usually because of a response to previous filter question, is usually coded as "0" (Box 10.2). Again, the point is that including such a code, whatever you decide it to be, helps distinguish between a respondent missing (nothing can be done about it) as opposed to a coder missing (which can be corrected) detail.

BOX 10.2

GSS CODEBOOK EXAMPLE

Codebooks do not all look the same. Below is a segment from the General Social Survey (GSS) codebook:

173.   Taken all together, how would you say things are these days--would you say that you are very happy, pretty happy, or not too happy?

[VAR: HAPPY]

RESPONSE	PUNCH	1972-82	1982B	1983-87	1987B	1988-91	1993-98	2000-04	2006	2008	2010	2012	2014	2016	2018	ALL
Very happy	1	4632	68	2352	64	1918	3131	1715	920	599	538	593	786	806	701	18823
Pretty happy	2	7194	209	4179	216	3368	5907	3125	1676	1100	1184	1094	1403	1601	1307	33563
Not too happy	3	1755	73	903	63	571	1231	643	390	316	317	277	341	452	336	7668
Don't know	8	1	0	1	0	0	4	4	6	2	2	6	6	3	4	39
No answer	9	44	4	107	10	50	61	42	0	6	3	4	2	5	0	338
Not applicable	0	0	0	0	0	0	0	2865	1518	0	0	0	0	0	0	4383

REMARKS: In 1980 and 1987, this question was asked immediately before HAPMAR on Form 3. For Form 1 and 2 this question immediately followed HAPPY. See FORM for the split-ballot forms. See Appendix T, GSS Methodological Report No. 34 and GSS Social Change Report No. 6. See Appendix P. See SATHOBBY- SATHEALT. If planning to perform trend analysis with this variable, please consult GSS Methodological Report No. 56.

IF CURRENTLY MARRIED, ASK HAPMAR

174.   A.   Taking things all together, how would you describe your marriage? Would you say that your marriage is very happy, pretty happy, or not too happy?

[VAR: HAPMAR]

RESPONSE	PUNCH	1972-82	1982B	1983-87	1987B	1988-91	1993-98	2000-04	2006	2008	2010	2012	2014	2016	2018	ALL
Very happy	1	5189	69	2664	55	1974	3163	1576	861	596	544	589	691	726	638	19335
Pretty happy	2	2333	60	1465	49	1087	1796	883	512	343	314	282	425	430	324	10303
Not too happy	3	224	6	131	8	90	139	84	37	30	28	26	39	48	30	920
Don't know	8	16	1	2	0	5	12	7	1	1	2	0	2	1	1	51
No answer	9	34	3	30	3	12	26	15	5	7	4	3	5	8	5	160
Not applicable (Punches 2-5 in MARITAL)	0	5830	215	3250	238	2739	5198	5829	3094	1046	1152	1074	1376	1654	1350	34045

REMARKS: See HAPPY.

The different types of information found in this codebook are as follows (in order):

- GSS question number and wording
- Variable name (VAR)

- Variable values (RESPONSE)
- Numerical code for each variable value (PUNCH)
- The frequency (count) of response for each value for each survey year

Source: NORC. (2019, June). General Social Surveys, 1972–2018: Cumulative Codebook.

Coding "Please Specify"

"Other" as an answer option is really not very informative. All it means is that none of the values the researcher provided fits the respondent's experiences, but it also does not give the researcher any concrete information about what *is* the respondent's experience. On the other hand, surveys would be overbearingly long if researchers listed *every* possible value for some questions even if that were possible, and it probably is not. One way around this is to add the phrase "Please specify:_____" after the "Other" option. This gives subjects a chance to list additional responses relevant to him/her, for example, additional television genres in my earlier example, while still keeping the survey question relatively short. Then the researcher can add values to the data set *after* all the surveys are completed. The easiest way to approach this "other" situation is to look at each survey for which the "other" response was selected, record each new option specified, and tally how many people said something similar. Let's suppose that I distributed my television survey to 200 students and that in addition to the students who selected "a-d" I had the following responses, with their corresponding tallies, written into the "other" category:

Response	Number	Response	Number
Reality TV	26 people	Cooking shows	8 people
Suspense	22 people	Foreign shows	4 people
Talk shows	15 people	DYI shows	3 people
Nature shows	13 people	Other (nothing specified)	12 people
Horror	9 people		

I could take some of these answers and make them *additional* values for the question. There is no magic number for how many subjects should fit a value for that value to be considered unique (e.g. another code in the data set) because different statistical analyses will require different degrees of information. For example, descriptive statistics can deal with fewer observations in each value, whereas linear regressions will require more. As such, even after you make your initial additional codes, you may have to alter them later. So it is best to initially have additional values emerge based on themes that make sense. So for my example, because TV genre is a nominal level of measurement, I could make new categories as such and add them to the previous ones to create the following values:

Response	N
Reality TV	26
Suspense/ Horror	31 (combined suspense and horror)
Talk shows	15
Nature shows	13
Home-related	11 (combined cooking and DYI)
Other	16 (combined other, non specified and foreign)

In the above example, "horror," "cooking shows," and "DYI" had comparatively low tallies for possible statistical analysis. "Horror" can be considered a related theme to suspense, so I combined it with that category; and "cooking" and "DYI" both deal with the home, so that became a new category. There were not enough observations for the "foreign shows" write-in for most statistical analyses and it did not fit in as a theme with any of the other responses; therefore, that write-in had to be grouped with the "other, non specified."

By giving respondents a chance to add genres, I went from a question where I would only know about four specific genres (situational comedy, drama, sports, news), that originally applied to less than half (*n* = 88) of my sample to now having nine genres and one "other" category for the write-in responses that could not be grouped with other responses. Therefore, by simply adding "please specify," I was able to add information for 96 people!

PHOTO 10.1 A seemingly simple question, as "What is your favorite type of television show? such" can have so many possible responses that researchers might be able to create many new values based on the "Other (please specify)" option.

Handling "Circle All That Apply"

In Chapter 4 when I discussed measurement, I said that one of the ways to "release" the criteria of the values needing to be mutually exclusive was to tell the respondent to "circle all that apply." Although this is a pretty easy way to deal with variables where it makes sense that the respondent might have more than one possible response, you may wonder how a researcher codes a question when there is more than one answer choice to select? The answer is that each value would be made into its own yes / no variable. So for example, if I reworded my earlier television question to "Which types of television do you usually watch? (Circle all that apply)," the 10 different options (situational comedy through home-related and the last category of "other") would become their own individual variables, each with a "yes/no" or "circled/not circled" value option. So, in other words, instead of one television question with 10 different possible response values (the five original values and the five new ones), I would have So, for example, I might call these variables (if I keep to eight characters per variable length) fvtvcmdy, fvtvdram, and fvtvsprt, where each variable begins with "fvtv" to indicate that this group of variables is about favorite television show types.

DIRECT DATA ENTRY

When researchers gather data on their own, such as from their survey or their coded experimental information, they have to directly enter that data into a computer. I will illustrate data entry only for the program Statistical Packages for the Social Sciences (SPSS) because it is a fairly intuitive menu-driven program that operates like many word-processing programs you are already probably accustomed to using and using it does not require understanding computer code. Although sometimes people input data into other programs like Excel, R, or a program specific to their field that can then be converted to a statistical package for analysis, I will focus on that process in the next section, "Importing Existing Data."

SPSS: Variable View

To start this process, a researcher would first open the SPSS program that would already be loaded onto a computer. Once the SPSS program is activated, a screen will open up that will list any SPSS files already recognized or allow the researcher to create a new file. To enter data on your own, click "New data" on the top left corner of this screen in the box entitled "New files." This will open a blank screen that looks like this:

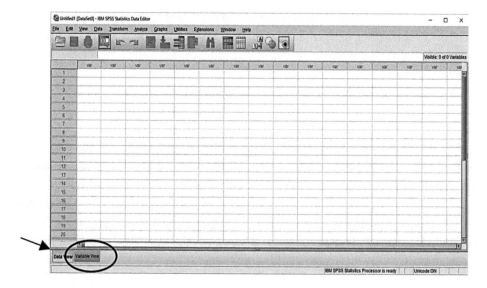

Notice at the bottom left of this screen is two tabs, one labeled "Data View" and the other labeled "Variable View", which is circled in the previous image. The first screen I want to access is "Variable View" because this is where I will program SPSS to recognize the different variables, their corresponding values, and the value codes. There are a lot of features in the "Variable View" tab that SPSS enters in default that are pretty easy to figure out on one's own with a little playing around and are not necessary to discuss in order to "get the job done." So let's focus on the main points.

When you click the "Variable View" tab, the screen changes to look like this:

The first column is labeled "Name" and this is where I would insert the variable name, such as ID, anyTV, favTVtyp, etc. Once I hit "Enter," SPSS will automatically fill in the default settings for a bunch of the other columns to look like this:

For the most part, the "Type" column will be numeric, which is the default that SPSS enters once you put in a variable name. However, sometimes, for example, you might want the variable to be something else, like a date or a string of letters. If I click the "Type" cell for the variable of interest, a new box will open, which will allow me to select some other forms of data. Another column of interest might be the "Decimals" column. The SPSS default is two decimal places to the right of a whole number, but you can change this to any other decimal, such as "0," if your numeric values are all whole numbers. Changing the decimal to "0" would prevent SPSS from showing a code of "1" as "1.00," and although unnecessary from a statistical point of view, it might make the SPSS data view screen (which I will cover shortly) seem less cluttered.

Two other variable options are of particular interest to us. The first is the "Values" column. This is where a researcher tells SPSS what numerical codes go with specific answer choices or values. To continue with my favorite type of television show, the corresponding codes for each answer choice might be:

1 = Situation comedy	6 = Suspense/ Horror
2 = Drama	7 = Talk shows
3 = Sports	8 = Nature shows
4 = News programs	9 = Home-related shows
5 = Reality TV	10 = Other

In order to get SPSS to recognize these codes, I have to label each value individually. To do this, I click the "Value" box for the variable of interest and the following window appears:

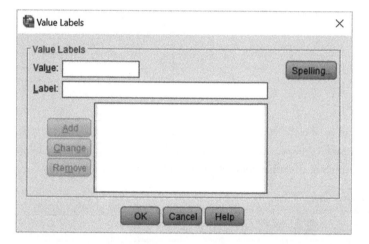

Once I am in this window, I simply type in a value and label in each corresponding box, which will activate the "Add" button. Once I click "Add," I am ready to enter the next value and corresponding label, and so on. Once I have all my values and labels entered, my "Value Labels" window would look like the box below:

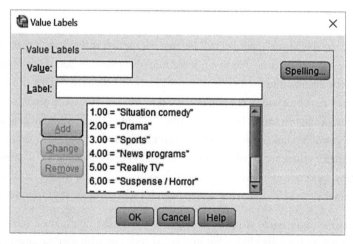

I need to click "OK" to let SPSS know I am done coding this and want the program to now recognize these numbers and their corresponding codes.

The next box is what my "Variable View" in the SPSS data set would look like once I programmed SPSS to recognize the respondent's ID, whether they watched any television, and what their favorite type of television show is.

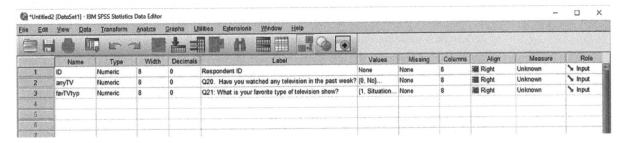

One quick hint: SPSS is capable of copying and pasting, much like a word-processing program. So, for example, if a researcher has a series of questions with the same Likert or yes/no responses, once the researcher enters the coded values, they can highlight the relevant "Values" box, hold "Control C" to copy, move to the empty values box of another variable, highlight/select that new cell, and hold "Control V" to paste, and SPSS will copy the original values into the values for the new variable. You can do the same for variable names. Double click within the "Label" box for a variable label, copy, paste into a new variable label, and then edit any wording to that question. This can be handy, for example, if you have a comparatively long variable label that is measured as a pre- and posttest. You can type in the full variable label for the pretest, add a tag "pre," copy that variable label, paste it into the label field for the posttest variable, and just replace "pre" with "post" by double-clicking into the label box and deleting the "pre." The last point to make is the "Missing" column that is to the right of the "Values" column. This is where you can tell SPSS which of the coded values (if any) that you just entered should be ignored for any statistics. You can select a range of values or one to three individual values.

SPSS: Data View

Once a researcher has all the variables coded, the researcher is ready to actually start entering the data and would now select the "Data View" tab at the bottom of the SPSS screen to change to the data view screen. The screen will now show the variables that the researcher programmed across the top and the researcher will be able to enter the data for each unit of observation (such as the survey for each respondent) as a row.

There are a couple of useful points about "Data view" that I also want to highlight. First, the third button from the right that has the "A" and "1" on it in red allows you to toggle between seeing data entered in English text ("A") or as the numerical code ("1"). This can be useful because it allows coders to enter data via a drag-down menu when in language mode. So, for example, instead of remembering the codes for gender or looking back and forth from a codebook, a coder can put the cursor on a cell under that column, a menu will appear, and the coder can simply select the text of the response and it will be entered. Even if I enter "1" for male when the data view is in "A" mode, I will still see "Male" entered in the corresponding cell. So it allows the coder to enter a value *either* numerically or linguistically but shows the data linguistically. Second, you will also notice that the top row of both the data and variable view pages has the same buttons. That means that you can run statistics from *either* viewing window.

Another useful hint about this window is that for variable names that do not intuitively make sense, all someone needs to do is hover the cursor over a variable name and the coded variable label will become visible along with some basic information about that variable. For example, without reading further, do you have an idea of what the variable "frqtel" measures? Probably not, and if you are entering a lot of variables, especially early in the process before you may have started to memorize some, you are likely to need to be frequently reminded of what it means. Holding the cursor over the variable will open the box you see below that contains information on the variable name and its type. Incidentally, because you can see the values as words, you will also notice that the button we just discussed is depressed, which means that the linguistic values are selected to be visible.

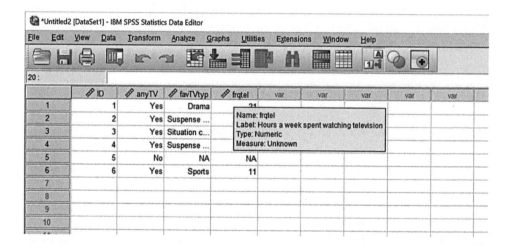

IMPORTING EXISTING DATA

Sometimes, such as with the GSS, data is already coded by people working at the organization collecting the data and is ready to be imported into various statistical programs, like Excel, SPSS, or R. Or agencies might use programs like Microsoft Excel to track client information that will later be statistically analyzed. Although Excel can do some basic statistical tests, it is more limited than SPSS or R. SPSS is a largely menu-driven program and, therefore, is pretty user friendly, but it is also a commercial program, so it can be expensive. R, on the other hand, has the benefit of being free and available to anyone, but it is generally not menu-driven and, therefore, requires some knowledge of computer coding. Because SPSS is more user friendly, I will now discuss how to import data from sources like Excel. (Box 10.3 shows how to import Excel data into R Studio, which is the interface used for R programming.)

BOX 10.3
IMPORTING DATA INTO R STUDIO

If your school or agency does not have access to SPSS, they may have someone who is versed in programming the freeware R, which is usually worked on in the interface of R Studio, which has some menu-driven commands even though the bulk of the data manipulation and statistics require some computer programming, so it is not quite as intuitive or as easily explained as SPSS. Because our purpose is "getting the job done," I cannot teach a complete primer on R programming here. Some excellent sources for R programming are Harris's *Statistics with R: Solving Problems Using Real-World Data* (2020) or Salkind and Shaw's *Statistics for People Who (Think They) Hate Statistics Using R* (2019). There is also a lot of free online help and tutorials with R programming.

As I said in the chapter, I will not focus on coding in R, but because many agencies (1) record information in Microsoft Excel and (2) cannot afford SPSS, in the spirit of helping you "get the job done" in the real world, I will discuss the basics of using R Studio to import data from an Excel file into the R interface.

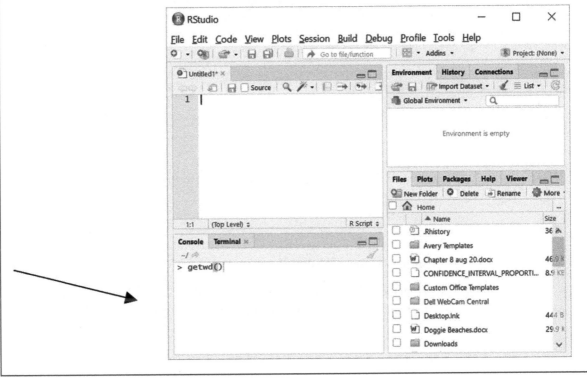

(Continued)

BOX 10.3 (*CONTINUED*)
IMPORTING DATA INTO R STUDIO

The first step is to open R Studio, which you have previously downloaded onto your computer following the online instructions. Any commands you want to type into R Studio will be typed into the command console, indicated by the arrow. One of the first things you want to do in R Studio is to identify the directory R, which is your working directory (where you need to save files for R to find). To do this, the command is:

```
get (wd)
```

R notifies me (not shown) that it will look in my "Documents" directory, so I want to make sure that I save any edited Excel file to my "Documents."

Next, I need to go back to Excel and open the spreadsheet with my relevant data. For our example now, I will work with the data file "GSS2016.xls," which I made when I imported the GSS variables I was interested in from the NORC website (which houses the GSS) to Excel. In Excel, I need to make sure that all the data cells are aligned the same way (e.g., all are left-aligned). This is especially important if data was originally entered into Excel in one computer format (such as an IBM machine) and then is being worked on in another format (such as a tablet).

Select "Save as" from the Excel file menu and when it opens, change "Excel" to "CSV (comma delimited)" as the format and make sure to save this file to the directory that you learned R uses from the "getwd()" command you ran previously.

Now we are ready to read the data into the R programming. The "dstat_df" that you see to the left of the "<-" tells R the name of the data set (dstat) and that it is a data frame (df), and the "read.csv" command tells R to read the data entitled "GSS2016.csv" into this new data frame entitled "dstat_df" in R. When reading in the data files, it is necessary to tell R what values in the data set should be interpreted as missing or unknown and this can be done with the optional argument "na.strings" in the read.csv function. In the GSS data, "NA," "IAP" are frequently identified as missing. For example, the entire command would read:

```
dstat_df <- read.csv("../Data/GSS2016.csv",na.strings = c("NA","IAP","DK"))
```

The steps to do this are fairly straightforward and are as follows:

1. Open SPSS.

2. From the SPSS main screen, click "New data" at the top left corner. This will open up a blank SPSS data file.

3. From the "File" tab, click "Import data" and then "Excel." You will notice that there are other data formats from which you can import data as well. So if, for

example, you are working on a different record-keeping package in an agency, you might be able to import data in the CSV format.

4. This will open up a directory linked to your computer where you can find the Excel file of interest.

5. Once you click the file of interest, a new window entitled "Read Excel File" will open with a lot of default options selected and a preview of your Excel file in SPSS. In the interest of "getting the job done," the most basic and efficient approach is to just click "OK" to this window. It will convert the Excel data to SPSS data, keeping the same variable names and values as they appear in the Excel file. This means that if you have a variable "Race" in the Excel file that has the values "White," "African American," "Hispanic," and "Other," then those values will appear as written words in the SPSS file as well.

When you move data from programs like Excel to another statistical program, you may need to examine how the variables are identified in that second program. I mentioned earlier in that chapter that sometimes data from other sources, such as Excel, may have been inputted in such a way that the values themselves, rather than numeric codes, were entered into the original record/data-keeping program and then carried over as such to the new analysis program. For example, in Excel someone may have inputted the values for gender as "male" or "female" rather than numerical codes, and SPSS and R will likewise read those values as "male" and "female" as a string variable. Although statistical programs like SPSS and R can do basic descriptive statistics like percentages or measures in this form, for a more detailed comparison the program might need numbers. Hence gender would need to be manually converted into numerical form.

Similarly, even if you recode a variable into numbers, SPSS might not recognize it in its appropriate form unless you tell it so. For ordinal variables, for example, not only will the values need to be recoded into numerical values that reflect their ranking, but in "Variable View" you might also need to change the particular value in the "Measure" column to reflect that the variable is nominal, ordinal, or scale (interval/ratio). Recoding language into numerical values is done the same way as if a researcher was entering the information straight into SPSS from a data source like a survey. For interval/ratio variables, the numbers that would be imported in their original form are fine because, by the nature of their level of measurement, they have intrinsic meaning on their own.

DATA CLEANING

Even though I am discussing data cleaning after the initial discussion of getting data into a statistical package, the first step of data cleaning actually occurs before a researcher imports the information into a statistical program. That first step involves looking through your data, whether it is from a survey, experiment, or agency, that is recorded in another program like Excel to make sure that there are no errors. Some errors that you should look for at this stage involve multiple answers for variables for which only one should be selected, incorrectly followed skip formats, and blocks of missing information, such as forgetting to look on back pages of a survey. When these errors are present, the researcher needs to decide whether to omit those subjects from all analyses or to create a variable that identifies different errors (such as skipping entire sections of a survey) and use that variable to track subjects with those errors. The researcher can then compare subjects who did and did not have a particular error to see if there is a resulting bias and then decide whether or not to include those "error" subjects for particular analyses.

The second step in data cleaning is to see whether there are any problems with data entry, such as entering incorrect codes for values. Running a frequency (Chapter 11) is one way of seeing if there are incorrect entries by making sure that all categorical values have a defined label. So in my example of gender, which had five different values assigned to it, I ran a frequency and it produced the following:

What is your gender?	f
Male	56
Female	48
Gender fluid	5
Prefer not to say	12
Other (Please specify:_____)	2
8	1

Clearly, that "8" does not belong and it would be an example of an invalid data entry. I would then find the subject ID for whom the "8" is entered (which is one reason we always add a respondent ID to the data set), look up that subject's survey, see the correct answer, and make that correction. However, there may still be errors in data entry if those errors are valid values. In other words, if a coder makes the mistake of entering the code of male when the subject is a female, running a frequency will not identify that mistake, which is why careful data entry remains an important part of the research process.

In R, the process for checking how the data moved from the first program (such as Excel) to R is a bit different and is summarized in Box 10.4.

BOX 10.4
CHECKING IMPORTED DATA IN R

Once data is read into R, it is a good idea to double-check its format, and there are a few commands we can use to do this. There are many ways to accomplish any task in R, but I will just present one way at any given time (meaning also in the future chapters). If you or your professor are proficient in R programming, you very well might have another approach to the same issue, so feel free to use that approach instead. For now though, here are some common issues and commands in data coding:

For now, I will continue with the data set I read into R in the earlier R programming box entitled "dstat_df." One of the first things we can do is find the number of rows and columns in the data

```
dim(dstat_df)
```

The output we get is

```
[1] 2867 5
```

which tells me that in this data set there are 2,867 rows (which means observations) and five variables.

To see the variable names

```
names(dstat_df)
```

the output we get is

```
[1] "ï..CLASS" "EDUC" "SAVEJOBS" "SEX"
```

```
[5] "TVHOURS"
```

which tells us that the first ([1]) variable is "CLASS" the second is EDUC, up to the fifth, ([5]) which is "TVHOURS."

We can view the first few rows of data with the "heads" command and the last few with the "tails" command, but I will only present the output for the "heads" command.

```
heads(dstat_df)
```

```
tails(dstat_df)
```

The output we get for "heads" is

(Continued)

BOX 10.4 (CONTINUED)

CHECKING IMPORTED DATA IN R

	ï..CLASS	EDUC	SAVEJOBS	SEX	TVHOURS
	<fctr>	<int>	<fctr>	<fctr>	<int>
1	MIDDLE CLASS	16	NEITHER	MALE	1
2	NA	12	NEITHER	MALE	1
3	MIDDLE CLASS	16	NA	MALE	NA
4	MIDDLE CLASS	12	AGAINST	FEMALE	1
5	MIDDLE CLASS	18	NA	FEMALE	NA
6	MIDDLE CLASS	14	IN FAVOR	FEMALE	1

Here we actually learn a lot of information relevant to data cleaning. The first is whether the data has read into R in the right level of information. In R, continuous variables are called "integer" variables and discrete variables are called "factor" variables. So one of the first things we want to do is make sure that the variables are correctly identified as factors for those that are discrete and integers for those that are continuous. We see above that this is all correct. "CLASS," "SAVEJOBS," and "SEX" are all discrete and correctly identified as "fctr" for "factor," whereas "EDUC" and "TVHOURS" are continuous and correctly identified as "int" for "Integer."

Another way to check the structure of the data and make sure that categorical and continuous variables are correctly identified as such in R is to run the string command:

```
str(dstat_df)
```

The output we get is

```
$ ï..CLASS: Factor w/ 4 levels "LOWER CLASS,"..: 2 NA 2 2 2 2 2 4 1 2...
```

```
$ EDUC: int 16 12 16 12 18 14 14 11 12 14...
```

```
$ SAVEJOBS: Factor w/ 5 levels "AGAINST,""IN FAVOR,"..: 3 3 NA 1 NA 2 1 NA 2 NA...
```

```
$ SEX: Factor w/ 2 levels "FEMALE","MALE": 2 2 2 1 1 1 2 1 2 2...
```

```
$ TVHOURS: int 1 1 NA 1 NA 1 2 NA 2 NA..
```

where we can see if each variable is identified as "Factor" or "int."

Sometimes, however, the classification is incorrect. This usually happens when a variable that should be read in as an "Int" is instead read as "Factor" because the continuous variable will have some type of categorical response. For example, if EDUC had values from 1 to 16 and then "more than a college degree" as a 17th option, R will consider EDUC to be a factor variable because in R, characters rank higher than integers. Therefore, as a researcher, if you import data that has any categorical values for an otherwise continuous variable, you need someone to remove those categorical responses. One way is to just change that category to the next highest number and another is to just delete those categorical values. There is no right response, but in order for R to function, the researcher does have to make some decisions in those instances.

Furthermore, data that is ordinal may not be ranked in Excel or, therefore, in R. Therefore, R needs to be programmed to rank the data in order to make the most use out of that level of measurement. In order to see if a variable, such as CLASS, is ordered, we would type

```
is.ordered(dstat_df$CLASS)
```

Given a data frame in R, you can reference individual columns using the "dollar sign notation," which is data_frame_name $ variable name, as we did above.

```
[1] FALSE
```

This output means that CLASS is *not* currently ordered in R. If the variable was ordered, R would return "TRUE" instead. In order to make a factor variable ordered (or ordinal), we have to do two things: (1) Tell R that we intend for the variable to be ordered by setting the "ordered" argument to TRUE and (2) Tell R what order we want the levels of the factor to be in. For example, if we want CLASS ordered from low to high as lower class, working class, middle class, and upper class, we would give the following command:

```
dstat_df$CLASS <- factor(dstat_df$CLASS,ordered=TRUE,levels=c("LOWER CLASS",
"WORKING CLASS","MIDDLE CLASS", "UPPER CLASS"))
```

On the left of the "<-" we tell R that we want this changed for the "CLASS" variable in the "dstat_df" data set, and the commands on the right of the "<-" tell R that we are altering the original "CLASS" variable in that data set. We can now reexamine whether CLASS is ordered by running the same "is.ordered" command and this time we get

```
[1] TRUE
```

This indicates that it is now ordered.

DATA MANIPULATION

Collapsing Categories and Creating New Variables

Sometimes researchers start with a higher level of measurement, like a ratio measure, and need to bump it down to an ordinal level for various statistical reasons. Or sometimes a researcher starts with a five-point ordinal scale only to see that very few subjects responded to one of the categories, thereby also creating some problems with data analysis that requires the values to be recorded. In this instance, a researcher may want to collapse or combine categories. Regardless of what statistical program you use, it is important to make sure to first copy the original variable data into a new variable and then to continue with the changes on the new variable. Making changes to a copy is important because once a researcher begins to recode any information, the original information is lost and cannot be regained without going back to the original data source and re-entering it … for *all* the subjects. Box 10.5 shows an example of both how to recode and how to collapse categories in SPSS. You would have to create a new variable in R Studio as well.

BOX 10.5

COLLAPSING CATEGORIES IN SPSS

Original Variable and Values

How likely or unlikely are
you to vote in the next
presidential election?
VotePres
a. Very likely = 5
b. Somewhat likely = 4
c. Unsure = 3
d. Not very likely = 2
e. Not at all likely = 1

Collapsed Variable and Values

How likely or unlikely are you to vote in
the next presidential election? RECODE
VotePresR
a. Likely = 3 (old values of 5 and 4)
b. Unsure = 2 (old value of 3)
c. Not likely = 1 (old values of 2 and 1)

SPSS

1. Transform → Recode into Different Variable.

2. Move the original variable VotePres from the box on the left to the empty box on the right.

3. Under "Output variable," assign a new variable name and label to the recoded variable. Here the new variable name is VotePresR, where the "R" indicates it is a recode, and the variable label is the same question as the original with "RECODE" in capitals at the end of the question. You can name the new variable anything you like; I just prefer to keep it similar to the original.

4. Click "Change" in the Output Variable box when you have everything renamed.

5. Now to recode. Click "Old and New Values." A box that looks like the one you see below will open. You can enter the old values on the left, give it a new value on the right, and click "OK" *each time* you recode. So for example, I might put in 4 and 5 through the range selection and recode it to 3 (as noted in the first diagram above). I would do this for all values and then click "Continue" when I am done. My finished recoding box should look like the top box on the next page.

6. Click "Continue".

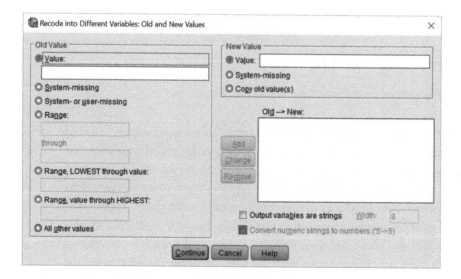

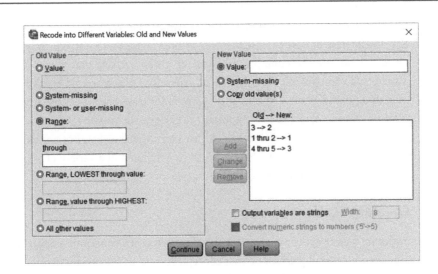

7. Click "OK" at the bottom of the original box and now my recoded variable will be visible as you can see in the last row of data in the figure below, but it will not have any labeled values, which you also see by just the numbers reading down the last column instead of actual text. You will need to tell SPSS what those numbers mean the same way you did when originally inputting the data.

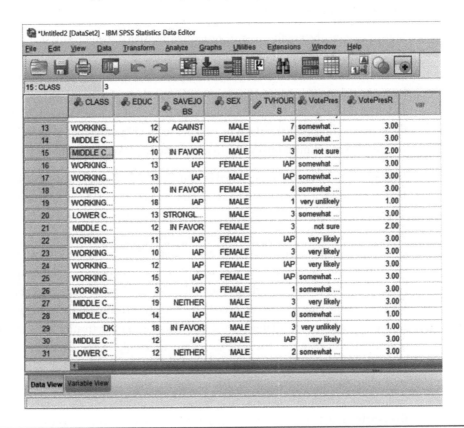

I can also use the same commands to make new variables that only contain select values from an existing variable. For example, if I have a variable for race with seven answer choices, but I am only interested in whether someone is White/Caucasian or not, which is only two answer choices, I can use the same process to make a new variable that makes White/Caucasian a value and combines all the other racial values into a new second category that I can call something to indicate *not* White. It is common for researchers to create new variables based on their existing data and it is important to include the new variable complete with name, label, values, and codes in the codebook that I mentioned earlier. But not only can individual variables be recoded, but variables can also be combined in a variety of ways as well, one of which I will cover in the next section.

Creating Scales

Scales are a means of combining individual measures of a concept to obtain one number that represents an overall position on that concept. A scale, as I defined it here, is, however, different than the Likert response scale I discussed in Chapters 4 and 7. A response scale is what you commonly see when you have collected people's response to *one* measure, where people will frequently say that response is "along a scale" of strongly agree to strongly disagree. The term *scale* as I am using it here, however, refers to a combination of questions, all of which would have the same types of responses.

Scales can either be unidimensional or multidimensional. Unidimensional scales are various measures that are getting at one construct that would theoretically be expressed as low to high. Unidimensional scales are the easiest to interpret and to understand. Multidimensional scales, however, look at two or more dimensions. The Scholastic Aptitude Test is a two-dimensional scale that looks at two dimensions of capability: math and verbal skills. Learning how to develop multidimensional scales is beyond our focus of "getting the job done," but I will cover two common unidimensional scales in a moment: the Likert Scale and the Guttman scale.

Regardless of whether unidimensional or multidimensional, scales serve a variety of purposes. First, they make it easier to understand how numerous individual indicators of a concept relate. It can be hard to interpret findings if you have five different measures of a concept and two suggest one relationship, two suggest another, and one suggests a third. A scale, on the other hand, produces *one* number that *simultaneously* looks at the effects of multiple individual measures. Second, a scale increases the range of responses, which may better capture subjects' variability and, according to some, increase the level of measurement from ordinal to interval or ratio. However, researchers disagree whether treating scales as higher levels of measurement is appropriate (Mangiafico, 2016). Those who favor treating scales as ordinal levels of measurement note that the scale scores are not evenly spaced with inherent quantifiable meaning; those who favor treating them as interval/ratio argue that if scales are sufficiently large, the data may approach a normal or near-normal distribution, thereby allowing for more sophisticated statistical analyses. Regardless, scales do increase the number of categories in the variable and, as you will see in the statistical chapters, researchers use different statistical tests for ordinal measures with comparatively few categories than they do for ordinal measures with many.

Likert Scale

The **Likert Scale** is a common summative scale where the coded response to each included question is added up to a final scaled score. The first step of a Likert scale construction is to identify which items will be included in the scale. Although researchers can decide on the possible items based on their expertise or the information they found in the literature review, they may also find it useful to enlist the help of other experts to identify possible questions for inclusion. One caveat, however, is that all of these items should be measured along the same continuum with the same number of possible values. You cannot combine indicators with three options and five options, for example, on the same scale.

Because not all items will end up in the final scale, it is beneficial to include a multitude of possible items for initial consideration. However, researchers do not agree on the ideal number. Some say you need to start with at least 80 possible items, while others put this number much smaller (Trochim, Donnelly, & Arora, 2016). Nor do researchers agree on the final scale size. Some feel that more is better to get at the greater nuance in possible attitudes, whereas others say that four to eight items are sufficient to avoid long, costly assessments that might result in respondent fatigue (Hinkin, 1998; Nunnally, 1978; Willits, Theodori, & Luloff, 2016). Therefore, the smallest number of final items in the scale seems to be recognized to be around four, but the largest is likely to be determined by your research topic, stamina of your study population, and economic resources.

So how do you decide which items to include in a Likert scale? The most expedient means is to do a factor analysis, which I have discussed previously. This analysis will tell you which items appear to be measured along the same dimension. Others suggest that you can use additional judges to rate each item on a range of 1–5, where 1 is "strongly unfavorable to the concept" and 5 is "strongly favorable to the concept." Notice that the experts are not giving their personal answers *to* the items; they are rating how well they think the item *measures* the desired concept. Therefore, let's say that I have 15 possible items about college satisfaction and three judges. Each judge would rate, on a scale of 1–5, how well an individual item corresponds to their idea of "college satisfaction." These ratings would be added (summed, hence the *summative* scale) to create a new variable (for now a total of 16 variables). To decide which items to include then, you use a statistical package to run a correlation between each of the individual 15 items against the new 16th item, which is the total rating of the scale's appropriateness. Remember, this is not a measure of how people answer the individual questions, it is just a measure of how judges think the items fit the concept. If the individual items have a correlation of about 6 or less (although this is an admittedly arbitrary correlation, it is widely accepted among researchers), they would be omitted from the final scale. Items with a correlation of .61 or higher would be included and then administered to a pretest of subjects who would answer the actual questions (rather than answering how well they think the question fits a concept). The final scale score would then be a summation of these "real" questions.

Likert scales are very common in social and behavioral research. One example that has been used for over 20 years with some revision is the Social Connectedness Scale created by Lee and Robbins (1995). This scale uses eight items to measure the degree of interpersonal

ISTOCKPHOTO.COM/ CREATISTA

PHOTO 10.2 We can use scales to study complex concepts, like social connectedness, which cannot easily be measured by numerous independent indicators.

connectedness someone experiences in his or her social world. Examples of these items are "Even around people I know, I don't feel like I really belong" and "I don't feel related to anyone" and they are coded on a response scale of 1 (strongly agree) to 6 (strongly disagree), where a higher total score indicates greater social connectedness. The scale has achieved high reliability on tests as well as high validity based on factor analysis and correlations with other measures believed related to connectedness (Lee & Robbins, 1998).

Guttman Scale

One of the weaknesses of a Likert scale is that a subject's score does not give the researcher any idea of what the subject said to individual items. The **Guttman scale**, developed by Louis Guttman (1944) during World War II, attempts to address this limitation by organizing the scale along a hierarchy in a way that items are increasingly "difficult" to get an affirmative response from. In this way then, answering in the affirmative to later questions assumes that the subject answered in the affirmative to the previous ones. The Bogardus Social Distance scale is one of the most widely known Guttman scale formats; it measures how closely people are willing to be to members of other groups such as different racial/ethnic groups, people with different types of mental challenges, people who exhibit different forms of deviant behaviors, and other stigmatized groups. For example, Abraham, Bride, and Roman (2013) use a Guttman-based social distance scale to assess public attitudes toward people with alcohol use disorders. To do this, the researchers read subjects a brief vignette that outlined "John's" drinking behavior. The vignette describes John's drinking behavior as increasing over the last month with John being unable to cut back. Consequently, he was increasingly hung over and unreliable and his family now noticed his behavior. Respondents were then asked seven questions that started with how willing they would be to move next door to John. This question was followed by others assessing people's willingness to spend an evening socializing with John, working up to their willingness to serve as John's supervising manager, and culminating in their willingness to have John marry into the family. The way Guttman scales work is that if a subject agrees to have John marry into the family, then the subject should also agree to the previous six indicators because they were less socially close than the last one. Similarly, if a subject was unwilling to move in next door to John, then that subject should also be unwilling to exhibit any "closer" behavior as well. In fact, as soon as a subject identifies an item they are unwilling to do, then that subject should also be unwilling to do *any* future items because they will be organized in degrees of increasing closeness.

The process for creating Guttman scales starts similarly as the Likert scaling process where the researcher should have a clear unidimensional concept, select a large number of possible items to include in the scale (as identified from a literature review or other experts as potentially relevant to a scale), and then have judges rate yes/no as to whether the item is favorable to the concept or not. A researcher then creates a matrix of judge ratings where the judge who agrees with the most items is at the top and the items for which this is in most agreement appear on the left, moving left to right with fewer item agreements. Although this matrix will not show a completely perfect judge rating, the researcher can get the idea of which items have the most and least support and, if there are comparatively few items, make a visual decision on what to include in the scale. If there are many items to be considered, then a scalogram analysis will be necessary, but a discussion of that procedure is beyond our purpose of "getting the job done."

All that is left on the resulting scale is to decide how to respond, how to score the resulting scale, and what a resulting score is likely to mean. Abraham et al. (2013) used a four-point

iStockphoto.com/joshuaraineyphotography

PHOTO 10.3 Guttman scales are frequently used to measure social distance for topics such as race, convicts, drug addicts, and mental health issues. The smallest indicator of social distance, meaning the closest someone is willing to be with the comparison group, is marriage.

response for each question, so their resulting scale ranged from 7 to 28 and had an acceptable reliability score, as indicated by Cronbach's Alpha that I discussed previously. Because each item in their scale had four options of response, their scale score was based on the average of responses. On the contrary, Pharr and Chino (2013) used a hierarchical seven-item scale to examine the association between primary care practice administrators' knowledge of the Americans with Disabilities Act (ADA) and the number of accessibility barriers patients with mobility disabilities experienced that used a simpler yes (coded as 1) and no (coded as 0) format. As a result, their scale ranges from 0 (all responses were "no") to 7 (all responses were "yes"). Pharr and Chino's scale is a simpler example of the Guttman scale because of its yes/no dichotomy and it appears in Box 10.6.

BOX 10.6
PHARR AND CHINO'S GUTTMAN SCALE

Pharr and Chino (2013) used a mixed-methods design to examine primary care practice administrators' knowledge of the Americans with Disabilities Act (ADA) and the number of accessibility barriers patients with mobility disabilities experienced. This design included the creation of a Guttman scale to address administrators' knowledge of the ADA, which appears in Table 3 of their article and is reproduced below:

GUTTMAN SCALE FOR ADMINISTRATORS' KNOWLEDGE OF THE ADA

No. of Responses	V1	V2	V3	V4	V5	V6	V7	Score
6	1	1	1	1	1	1	1	7
5	1	1	1	1	1	1		6
2	1	1	1	1	1	–	+	6
13	1	1	1	1	1			5
1	1	1	1	1	–	+		5
6	1	1	1	1	–		+	5
20	1	1	1	1				4
2	1	1	1					3
2	1	1	–			+		3
1	1	–	1			+		3
3	1	1						2
2	1	–	+					2

V1 = Knew about ADA.

V2 = Knew ADA applied to medical practices.

V3 = Could describe the ADA.

V4 = Could describe the ADA as it applies to medical practices.

V5 = Knew the consequences of not being compliant with the ADA.

V6 = Knew there was a federal tax credit to offset cost of compliance.

V7 = Knew which title of the ADA applied to their medical practice.

+ = Error of inclusion.

– = Error of omission.

CR = 0.94

CS = 0.64.

You will see that there are seven items hierarchically organized in the scale that ranges from the most obvious form of knowledge, which is the existence of the ADA (V1), to the least obvious, which is which title of the ADA applied to their medical practice (V7).

If we accept the hierarchy, subjects earn a score of "7" (row 1) if they were knowledgeable about all seven ADA indicators and, according to the table, there were six respondents who earned this score. Subjects earned a valid score of 6 (row 2) if they knew of the first six indicators (V1 to V6) but not the last one; there were five subjects who fit this pattern (Table 3).

However, there were also two subjects who earned a score of 6, but their pattern was in error (row 3), as they answered yes to the first five indicators, "no" to the sixth (as indicated by the "-" in the V6 column of the 3rd row) and "yes" to the seventh, which, based on the hierarchy of the indicators, should also have been a "no" because the response to the previous indicator was "no." It is because of responses like this that a scale may not achieve a full reliability or scability score of 1.0.

The other response patterns of yes / no that fit the Guttman hierarchy, and are therefore valid, in this instance are the 4th, 7th, 8th, and 11th rows. The "error" patterns, which are response patterns that do not follow the hierarchy, are the 3rd, 5th, 6th, 9th, and 10th rows. The goal of the reproducibility statistic is to see (based on a formula that is beyond our focus of "getting the job done") whether the number of respondents who fit the "correct" hierarchical patterns is sufficiently greater than those whose responses exhibit error (again, based on the established hierarchy of items) patterns. As Pharr and Chino (2013) stated, their scale met the criteria for reproducibility.

Source: Pharr, J., & Chino, M. (2013).

LEARNING CHECK 10.2: SCALES

1. What are two reasons why researchers might want to combine individual indicators into a scale?

2. Which scale is usually based on a five- or seven-point response scale?

3. Which scale, if reliable, allows the researcher to generally know how subjects responded to the multiple scale items based on the scale score?

Answers to be found at the end of the chapter.

MAKING DECISIONS

This chapter essentially serves as the bridge between methods and statistics. For both methods, as you have seen, and statistics, there are many decisions that need to be made. With coding, however, a researcher is generally not making methodological or statistical decisions beyond the numerical code to actually assign to measures. So, as a bridge, this chapter shows how to transition the information gathered via methods into something we can summarize and find meaning in via statistics, rather than what to do in various situations. So there is nothing really relevant to this subsection here.

CHALLENGES

Any challenges in data entry are more likely to stem from a lack of knowledge regarding the statistical program a researcher decides to use rather than in the information already gathered. Challenges in the workings of specific computer programs, whether Excel, SPSS, or R, are beyond our scope of "getting the job done" and are best answered by an outside source versed in the relevant computer program. Therefore, again, as this is a bridge chapter, this subsection is not as relevant here.

Key Terms

Codebook
Guttman scale

Likert scale
Variable label

Variable name

Answers to Learning Check Questions

Learning Check 10.1: Data Coding

1. At the very least you will add an identification number for each subject so you know what instrument to return to if there are coding problems. You might also add variables that correspond to coder identification if more than one person is entering information, a wave if collecting longitudinal data, new variables that might emerge from "circle all that apply," or new variables that might be added to the data set for recoding existing variables or adding scales to the data set.

2. Adding "please specify" gives the researcher the opportunity to keep answer options relatively few in number, and it gives the subject a chance to add additional information if they do not see a value (or more values than what is present) that fits their experiences. The researcher can then look for patterns in response and make additional variable values (answer options) based on what subjects have expressed.

Adding values can help provide more detailed information.

3. For nominal levels, the codes do not matter; any number can be assigned. For ordinal measures, the codes should be ordered where the response that is most affirmative to the research goal gets the highest code; for interval/ratio measures, no codes are necessary because the values are already numeric and have meaning on their own.

Learning Check 10.2: Scales

1. Some possible answers are: scale scores are easier to interpret than multiple responses to individual questions; scale scores offer greater variation, which might lend themselves to more interpretable statistics; they are one measure that can address complex concepts.

2. Likert

3. Guttman

End-of-Chapter Problems

1. What do we call the document, that includes each variable name and its corresponding label as well as each value and its corresponding code?
   a. An executive summary
   b. Literature review
   c. Codebook
   d. Variable list

2. In addition to the research information (e.g., survey information), what else might also appear in a codebook?
   a. Respondent ID
   b. Data wave

   c. Coder ID
   d. All the above

3. True/False: Ideally, the coding order of ordinal measures should follow the pattern of the research goal where the response that is most affirmative to the research goal gets the highest code.

4. On a survey measuring support for the death penalty, a respondent answers "Disagree" on a five-point Likert response to the question

"It is immoral for the state to kill someone as punishment." That response should be coded

a. 5

b. 4

c. 3

d. 2

5. Why add "please specify:_____" to the answer choice "Other"?

a. To save space in listing possible answer options

b. To learn additional detail/answers

c. To increase response rate

d. "a" and "b"

e. "a" and "c"

6. If I have a question that asks juveniles who have gotten into trouble for petty vandalism what specific acts of vandalism they have committed in the past year and I tell them to "circle all that apply," how do I code this variable?

a. Assign each value a number from 1 to the total number of values listed.

b. Make each value its own unique variable with a yes/no response.

c. You can't quantitatively code "circle all that apply responses."

7. True/False: Data cleaning is a step in the data preparation process that can be skipped without risking the quality of the information.

8. Why create scales?

a. They can use one value to simultaneously examine the responses to multiple indicators.

b. They can capture nuances in the differing views of a concept better than a single indicator.

c. They might increase the level of measurement.

d. All the above.

9. True/False: In a Likert scale, if the scale is valid, it is possible to generally figure out how respondents with a particular scale score answered individual questions in the scale.

10. If I administered a Guttman scale that had four items, in this order—I am willing to work in the same office as a known drug addict, I am willing to live next door to a known drug addict, I am OK if a family member dates a known drug addict, I am willing to date a known drug addict—and a person received a score of "2," assuming the scale is valid, what were her responses likely to be?

a. She would want nothing to do with a known drug addict.

b. She would be willing only to work with a known drug addict.

c. She would be willing to work with and live next door to a known drug addict.

d. She would be willing to work with, live next door, and have a family member date a known drug addict.

11

DESCRIPTIVE STATISTICS

LEARNING GOALS

- Distinguish between descriptive, inferential, and associative statistics
- Select, calculate, and interpret appropriate measures of central tendency for the data
- Learn how to identify normally distributed data
- Select, calculate, and interpret appropriate measures of dispersion for the data
- Identify when to use a Z-score and how to calculate it

Now comes the moment we have been building up to, the moment of fun, where we can finally find out what all of our efforts can tell us about the research topic we are interested in. Of course, when I say this is the "fun" part, I realize that from *your* perspective it may also be the part that you might be dreading. In the next few chapters, I want to help you overcome that fear of statistics and numbers in a couple of ways. First, I want to help you decode the statistical process so you see it more as a set of logical decisions than a set of mathematical equations. Second, I want to let you know that after this chapter, we will be doing very little math. You read correctly ... *very little math*! That is because the focus of this book is "getting the job done" and, frankly, in the real world, you are not likely to be doing a lot of the more complex statistics by hand. Depending on the software package you are using, you might not even be doing many basic statistics by hand! However, that being said, I do need to make a plug here that there is definitely merit to learning how to calculate some statistics, especially the basic descriptive ones, by hand because doing so is sometimes faster than plugging information into a computer and it can give the researcher an idea of where the numbers "come from." In fact, your professor might still have you calculate some basic bivariate statistics (Chapters 12–14) by hand, and if you proceed to a higher-level statistics course, you might also encounter hand calculations. However, again, for our purposes of balancing "getting the job done" with learning the decision process of how to select the statistics that best fit your data, after this chapter, there will be very few hand calculations.

Our discussion of statistics is based on the General Social Survey (GSS), which I have mentioned in previous chapters, a survey that addresses a variety of demographics, experiences, and views of social issues of a probability sample of Americans that has been gathered by the National Opinion Research Center (NORC) at the University of Chicago since 1972. I will use the 2016 wave that has 2,867 observations and is available for free by going to the GSS website (http://gss.norc.org/). The data can be downloaded into SPSS, Excel, and R (among other programs), thus making it useful for many of our examples, learning checks, and end of chapter problems. Because I will be using this free data throughout the book, you can download the same variables, practice running the statistics in your professor's preferred statistical program, and double-check your results with my examples.

TYPES OF STATISTICAL INFORMATION

For our purpose of "getting the job done," I will address three levels of statistics: descriptive, inferential, and associative. Without statistics, people generally cannot look at individual pieces of information for a multitude of observations and deduce what is going on. Information on possibly hundreds of variables for possibly hundreds of people is just mind-boggling. Researchers can't even easily see clear relationships between two variables for 50 people by just looking at the raw data. Statistics, therefore, are a way to summarize information and to compare patterns that help researchers put all of those individual pieces of information into a context. In this chapter, I am going to focus on **univariate** descriptive statistics that describe what the sample looks like one variable at a time. Although researchers can describe a sample with **bivariate** comparisons, such as how views of happiness (variable 1) vary by gender (variable 2), I will postpone my discussion of bivariate comparisons, until Chapter 13, so we can ease into the process.

Inferential statistics involve seeing whether information observed in a sample is likely to occur in the population, or whether researchers can "infer" about a population's behavior, which as you learned in Chapter 5 researchers cannot observe, based on what researchers can observe in a sample. Inferential statistics might involve estimating the value of a variable in a population or testing a hypothesis to see if patterns in the sample are likely to also apply to the wider population. Inferential statistics frequently relate to what researchers refer to as **statistical significance**. Associative statistics, on the contrary, sometimes also called **substantive significance** or size effects, tell us how strongly two or more variables are related. To put it another way, **descriptive statistics** tell us what our sample looks like on its own, inferential statistics tell us whether there is a statistically significant difference between variables in the population, and substantive significance, or association statistics, tell us if any difference is big enough to matter.

PHOTO 11.1 In this picture, an example of univariate information would be the gender of the different people in the room. A bivariate example could be how job title (variable 1) varies by gender (variable 2). A multivariate example could be job title by gender, controlling for the effect of years with the company.

I mentioned that statistics can be univariate (focusing on one variable at a time) and bivariate (looking at how two variables relate). They can also be **multivariate**, which, you probably already realize, focuses on the relationship between three or more variables simultaneously. Multivariate statistical techniques are more sophisticated than our basic focus in this book, so I will only discuss basic multivariate analysis briefly in Chapter 14, but I do want to remind you that multivariate analyses are one way to statistically address the topical threats to validity that I discussed in Chapter 2. When researchers conduct multivariate analyses, like Kramer and Remster's (2018) study of police use of force (Chapter 2) did, they are frequently still interested in one or two main independent variables, such as race or age, but they use statistical techniques to see what effect these main independent variables have on the dependent variable(s) while *simultaneously* considering the effect of other variables, such as civilian behavior, neighborhood, and whether a weapon was found present in Kramer and Remster's case. As I also noted in Chapter 2, these additional variables, sometimes called **statistical control variables**, are variables that theory or the literature review suggests might also affect the dependent variable (Chapter 2).

As I said though, I will focus on descriptive statistics in this chapter. I will cover inferential statistics in Chapters 12 and 13 and associative statistics in Chapter 14.

> ### ✔ LEARNING CHECK 11.1: BASIC STATISTICAL TERMS
>
> 1. What is the term used for statistics that look at the relationship between two variables?
>
> 2. What is the relationship between statistical and substantive significance?
>
> 3. How are multivariate analyses helpful in establishing causality?
>
> **Answers to be found at the end of the chapter.**

DECIDING AND INTERPRETING DESCRIPTIVE STATISTICS

Researchers can learn quite a lot by just describing the sample, and I am going to start fairly basic because it might have been a while since many of you have had a math class. All of the statistics I will address in the next few chapters can be calculated for you in various statistical programs, but as I said, the descriptive statistics can also be easily calculated by hand. So in this chapter, I will do hand *and* program calculations; but, before I do that, let's review some basic numerical information.

Reviewing Some Basics: Frequencies, Proportions, and Percent

A **frequency** is pretty much what the same implies. It is how many subjects selected each value for a variable or, to put it another way, how *frequently* each value was selected in a sample, and in statistical formulas it is often represented by f. Remember, the goal of statistics is to summarize information, and the GSS has over 2,800 subjects in the 2016 wave of data. So if I was interested in summarizing some basic descriptive information on whether subjects felt that the government should provide support for declining industries (SAVEJOBS), I would not want to scroll through all 2,800 subjects and hand tally each response. Statistical programs like SPSS and R Studio, which I introduced in Chapter 10, make tasks like this relatively easy and the process/commands for all the tests discussed in this book appear in Appendix A for SPSS and Appendix B for R. However, because the output of SPSS is easier to interpret than that for R, I will always use the SPSS output in the chapter to walk us through the main points while the output for the R commands also appear in Appendix B.

Based on the commands expressed in Appendix A, when I run a frequency I would get the following output:

Statistics

Govt support for declining indust

N	Valid	1,368
	Missing	1,499

Govt support for declining industries

		Frequency	Percent	Valid Percent	Cumulative Percent
Valid	STRONGLY IN FAVOR	252	8.8	18.4	18.4
	IN FAVOR	595	20.8	43.5	61.9
	NEITHER	292	10.2	21.3	83.3
	AGAINST	189	6.6	13.8	97.1
	STRONGLY AGAINST	40	1.4	2.9	100.0
	Total	1,368	47.7	100.0	
Missing	IAP	1,477	51.5		
	DK	13	.5		
	NA	9	.3		
	Total	1,499	52.3		
Total		2,867	100.0		

So what can I learn from this? I see, for example, that 1,368 respondents answered this question. Among the other 1,499 who did not answer this, the majority of *them* ($n = 1,477$) are coded "IAP" for inapplicable, meaning that for some reason this question was not part of their survey so they could not have answered it. I also learn that the most common response was "in favor" with 595 respondents, accounting for 20.8% of the total sample answering this question, as indicated by the "Percent" column. You may have noticed that I said that the 20.8%, appearing in the "Percent" column, was of the *total* sample, which uses the count of 2,867 as the denominator to calculate the percent. This is different from what you see in the "Valid Percent" column, which is 43.5%. The valid percent does not use the total sample size as the denominator but instead uses the total number of respondents who actually answered the question, which in this case was 1,368, as the denominator. As such, the "valid percent" is a more accurate choice to use in reporting statistics.

PHOTO 11.2 Do you think the government should help failing companies?

Descriptive statistics are frequently presented as a percent, whereas the formulas for inferential statistics usually involve proportions. The proportion is just the frequency divided by the desired sample size (either total who participated in the study or total who answered a relevant question). The formula for a proportion is

$$p = f/N$$

where p stands for "proportion," f is the frequency of a response, and N is the sample size. A percent is just a proportion multiplied by 100. So when SPSS gives you the percent as a default, to obtain the proportion, simply move the decimal place reported in either the percent or valid percent (whichever you decide to use) column two places to the left. Therefore, the proportion of the responding sample who are in favor of the government helping industry is .435.

One more column interests us and that is the cumulative percent, which adds ("cumulative") the valid percent as one progresses through the values. The cumulative percent for the first value will always be the same as the "Valid percent" for that value because no values have come before it. The second value will be the sum, again the "cumulative" idea, of the first value and the second. So, in my example, by the time I move to the people who disagree with the statement, I have covered 95.7% of all the valid responses (18.7% + 77.0% = 95.7%). This cumulative percent is more useful when I have interval or ratio variables with many values that I might want to collapse into other categories (Chapter 10). So, for example, if I wanted to collapse an interval or ratio-level variable into three categories, I can look at the cumulative percent to see roughly what values I should include in order to capture 0%–33%, 34%–66%, and 67%–100% of the distribution.

Calculating the frequency and percent is useful for summarizing nominal levels of measurement and ordinal levels that have comparatively few answer choices. However, if one wants to summarize an interval/ratio level of measurement, there may be so many possible answer options that a frequency distribution really is not much of a summary. For example, the GSS may have respondents as young as their early 20s or as old as their 80s, with every age in between! Looking at how many people are each individual, separate age between, say 23 and 81, is still a lot of visual information that is hard to summarize in a meaningful way by just looking at it. One option is to collapse interval/ratio variables down to ordinal levels of measurement for presentation and then to present the frequency information as categories. However, another option is to summarize the data using measures of central tendency and dispersion instead.

Introducing the Statistical Teaching Approach in This Book

Before I discuss more descriptive statistics, I want to take a moment to explain how I will approach the *logic* of statistics, meaning how to make statistical decisions. The approach used to teach statistics in this book is different from that used in many other statistics books. Many books start by identifying the statistic, outlining the necessary mathematical assumptions to accurately use that statistic, the math for the statistic, and then the interpretation. In my 20+ years of teaching, I have found that students find this approach, where the textbook starts with the statistic and then proceeds through the checklist to see if a situation fits the assumptions for the statistic, confusing to apply to real-life situations, where people have to start with the situation instead of the statistic. Therefore, to learn statistics where the situation is the starting point, this book uses what I call a decision tree, or a flow chart, that starts with a problem (rather than the statistical test) and proceeds through a set of decisions, which are often related to the common statistical assumptions, to ultimately lead to a statistical choice. This way, students learn to read the conditions of the data that leads to a statistical decision. The decision tree for descriptive statistics is very simple; however, as the statistical goals become more complex, so does the decision tree. Therefore, although the decision tree may seem unnecessary to you in this chapter, I will still use it in order to get you familiar with the process so that by the time the decisions become more complicated, you are already familiar with the basic approach I am using.

So where do we begin? An overview of our broad statistical decisions for the next few chapters is summarized in Figure 11.1. In the next few sections, however, I will focus on the branch that answers the question of "What am I doing?" with "Summarizing a distribution."

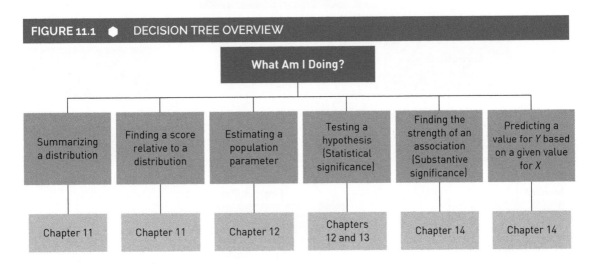

FIGURE 11.1 ●   DECISION TREE OVERVIEW

WHAT AM I DOING? SUMMARIZING A DISTRIBUTION

Most of our earlier chapters on research methods had a section entitled "Making Decisions," which aimed to present some considerations for selecting among different methodological options. The statistical chapters, on the contrary, are almost entirely organized around making decisions based on the initial decision tree question of "What am I doing?." As you saw in Figure 11.1, the first answer is "summarizing a distribution" and the ensuing decisions for that are what I will cover in this section. Each answer to "What am I doing?" leads us down a different path of decisions. Therefore, the decision path that corresponds to "summarizing a distribution" is presented in Figure 11.2 and will serve as our basis for this section of the chapter.

Measures of Central Tendency

Summarizing a distribution involves presenting both the typical response, or **central tendency**, and the distribution of those responses also called **dispersion**. Measures of central tendency and dispersion go together like peanut butter and jelly … they *fit* together. In this section, I will discuss how to decide which measures of central tendency are the most appropriate for your data, how to calculate that **statistic** by hand (as many of you may have encountered these calculations already), how to run them in SPSS (with R programming in a box at the end of most sections), and how to interpret the result.

In general, any measure of central tendency that can be calculated for a lower level of measurement can also be calculated for a higher one, but not vice versa. For example, the mode, or the most frequent response, as you will soon see, is the only appropriate measure of central

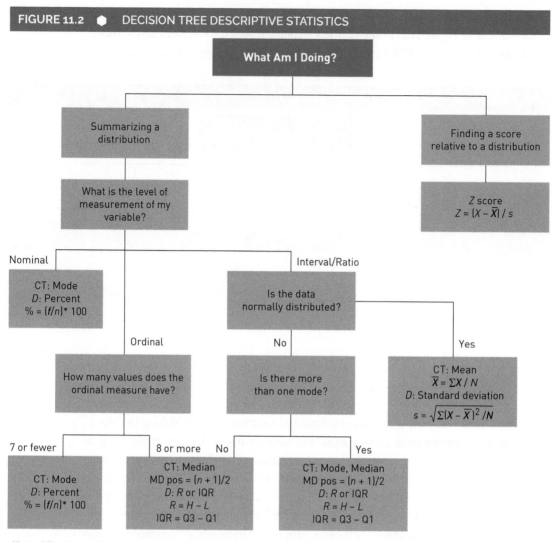

FIGURE 11.2 ⬡   DECISION TREE DESCRIPTIVE STATISTICS

Note: CT = Central Tendency and D = Dispersion

tendency for nominal level of data. Because nominal data is the lowest level of measurement, the mode also has real meaning if calculated for ordinal, interval, or ratio levels of measurement. If you stop and think about this, it makes sense because the characteristics of nominal levels of measurement, which are that the values are mutually exclusive and exhaustive (Chapter 4), are the base characteristics of the higher levels of measurement. Therefore, because each level of measurement builds on the characteristics of the previous one, so do measures of central tendency. So the most frequent response (the mode) for a race variable makes sense, as does the most frequent response for an age variable. However, measures of central tendency that become appropriate at higher levels are *not* appropriate at lower ones. It makes no sense, for example, to calculate the average race because race is a variable whose values have no numerical meaning. It does, however, make sense to discuss the average age, which is measured numerically.

Nonetheless, just because a lower measure of central tendency, such as a mode, *can* be used for a higher level of measurement, like a ratio measure, that does not mean that it is necessarily the most appropriate choice for that higher measure. When deciding a measure of central tendency, a researcher wants to pick a statistic that uses as much information from that data as possible. Simply put, the higher the level of measurement, the more information that is useful to be analyzed. Therefore, a mode will only look at one response (the most common), whereas the mean, or average, equally considers the values of all the responses in the data set. Therefore, if other data considerations are met, the mean would be a better choice for a ratio level of measurement than a mode.

So, let's spend some more time making some statistical decisions about central tendency. There are three common measures of central tendency: the mode, median, and mean. With some exceptions, like how the mean does not apply to nominal data, there are few hard and fast rules as to what to use when; however, in the interest of "getting the job done," I will present a decision tree that will address many possible considerations. Let's pretend that I wanted to look at the hours of TV viewing (TVHOURS) among our GSS sample and I want to be able to describe the sample in terms of not only their TV viewing, but also their gender (SEX), social class (CLASS), and education (EDUC) for context. Incidentally, whenever I use a GSS variable, I will present it in bolded capitalized letters. Whenever I am presenting a variable that I altered (even if from a GSS variable) or created, the variable name will be bolded but lowercase. This will help distinguish between variables I have altered and those that you can directly find in the GSS data set.

Let's take gender first. If I look at the GSS data set, the variable for gender is SEX and if I look in the "value label" box in "Variable View" in SPSS, I see that SEX has two values: male (1) and female (2). Based on these values and what you learned in Chapter 4 on measurement, I know that SEX is a nominal level of measurement. If I follow Figure 11.2, I will see that a variable's level of measurement is a key factor in this part of the decision tree, so if you are rusty on levels of measurement, you might want to take another look at Chapter 4. Based on the information I would follow the decision tree in Figure 11.2 in the following way:

1. **What am I doing?** Describing a sample
   I want to describe, in summary terms, what the gender (SEX) of my sample is

2. **What is the level of measurement of my variable?** Nominal
   I know this by looking in the values section of the "Variable View" frame of SPSS for this variable. There is no ranking to the values "male" and "female"

3. **Decision:** Mode

As I stated earlier, the mode is the most frequent response and it is the only statistic that has any meaning for nominal levels of measurement. This is because, as a statistic, the mode involves no ranking and gives no recognition of the numerical codes that might be assigned to the values since, as we learned in Chapter 10, those codes have no inherent meaning.

There is no real formula for the mode. Researchers just look at a frequency distribution or have a statistical program to identify the value with the most observations (highest frequency).

iStockphoto.com/ m-1975

PHOTO 11.3 Social class is an ordinal measure, but depending on the number of values it has, the statistical choice to summarize it may vary.

I will hold off on how to run measures of central tendency in the statistical programs until I cover all the relevant statistics because I can generally run all (or most) of the measures of central tendency and dispersion (to be addressed in the next section) at the same time. Therefore, for now, I will just focus on making statistical decisions that fit the data.

So if I now want to decide what statistic is relevant for a respondent's self-described social class (CLASS), based on its values, I see that it is an ordinal level of measurement because someone who answers the "working class" is ranked lower than someone who answers "upper class." However, this difference cannot be quantified. I can't say *how much* lower or higher the upper class compared to the working class is. Based on Figure 11.2, my progression through the flow chart would now look like this:

1. **What am I doing?** Describing a sample

2. **What is the level of measurement of my variable?** Ordinal
   → CLASS is ranked based on the values

3. **How many values does the ordinal measure have?**

Here I need to take a break for clarification. This consideration is commonly expressed a bit differently and more along the lines of what the research goal is, such as "Do you want to provide the most common response" or "Do you want to give the middle response?" However, this approach presumes that the researcher first decided on what statistic to use when deciding the measurement part of the research design and then created the variable to suit this statistic. Sometimes the statistics do fuel the methodological choices for measurement; but often, especially in applied research, someone else may have decided what and how to measure behavior or experience, and the person analyzing the data needs to start with that information (the measure) instead of the statistic. No one approach is "right," as we have repeatedly seen, and the statistical decision is likely to be the same either way. But following the decision tree starts with the situation, rather than the statistic, so it favors the second scenario where the researcher has to decide what statistic is appropriate *after* the indicator has been decided and used in data collection.

The traditional measure of central tendency for ordinal measures is the median, which you have probably noticed sounds a bit like "middle" and that's exactly what the median is. The median is the value that divides the distribution exactly in half. Half the cases have scores above the median and half have scores below it. When a researcher's process of operationalization begins with a concept and ends with a measure, then the researcher will need to fit a statistic to that measure. The researcher might not know which summary statistic he or she prefers—to give the most frequent response or the middle; therefore, the next question in the decision tree is the number of values in a measure.

Think about it. A five-point Likert scale ranging from strongly disagree to strongly agree is an ordinal measure but saying that the middle value in a sample is 3.5 does not make a lot of sense, as that would translate that the middle is between, for example, "don't know" and "agree." Again, that does not really make sense. Because ordinal measures commonly have seven values or less (such as in a five- or seven-point Likert scale), researchers are more likely to want to present the most common responses in these cases, as they make the most interpretative sense. Therefore, one possible way to respond to the third decision tree question and reach a decision is:

4. **How many values does the ordinal measure have?** 4

5. **Decision:** Mode

However, what if I created an ordinal scale that combined five Likert questions and ranged from a low score of 5 (most negative) to a high of 25 (most positive). Now my answer to the question about the number of values would lead me to present the median as the descriptive statistic because the median makes sense when a variable has many ranked values. There are not really any ordinal levels of measurement in the GSS that lend themselves to intuitive median calculations, so let's pretend that I gave this scale I created to a sample of 10 people and obtained the following scores:

20 18 24 19 10 8 17 15 21 22

First, 10 is a very small sample size that I am only using to keep the illustration manageable. Second, you will notice that there is no mode in this distribution of scores. No big deal. So now to calculate the median, I do the following:

1. Reorder the scores from low to high.

2. Calculate the median position as $(n+1)/2$ where n, you will remember, is the sample size.

3. Count left to right until you reach the median position you calculated in Step 2. That value is your median.

Sometimes the median position does not come out to a nice even number but instead ends in .5. This is what happens in my example. The median position is calculated by (10+1)/2, which equals 5.5. That just means that the median lies between the fifth and sixth positions. Therefore, if I ordered my responses, my distribution would look like this, with my fifth and sixth position, bolded so you can see where they lie:

8 10 15 17 **18 19** 20 21 22 24

You will notice that my median positions do not fall on the same number. Again, not a problem. All we do is take the average of those two numbers and that is our median. So our median is (18 + 19)/2 = 18.5, or to put it statistically, MD = 18.5. It is OK that the median value is not an actual score in the distribution because the purpose of the median is to identify the point, not necessarily the actual score, where half of the responses are above and half are below. We will encounter the median and SPSS some more in a bit, but one point that is universally clear is that the mean has no real meaning for ordinal levels of measurement.

That brings us to that last statistic, the mean. The mean is the same as the average response and I have two more variables in my example of hours of TV viewing to address: age and TV hours. Looking at the decision tree, I see:

1. **What am I doing?** Describing a sample

2. **What is the level of measurement of my variable?** Interval/ratio
   → **Note:** For statistical purposes, the issue is whether the variable is continuous or not, which you learned in Chapter 4 is either an interval or ratio measure

3. **Is the variable normally distributed?**

Time for another break here. You may remember that I introduced the idea of the normal curve, which is also a distribution, in Chapter 5 on sampling. Just to briefly review, a variable is said to have a **normal distribution** when the mean, median, and mode are relatively equal and form a hump when plotted on a graph. This should make sense to you if you think about it because the mode is the most frequent response, so when graphing responses, the most frequent value should be the highest point on the graph … or the hump. Figure 11.3 shows a normal distribution (Curve A), as well as a positively skewed (Curve B) distribution, a negatively skewed (Curve C) distribution, and a bimodal distribution (Curve D).

The shifts of the "hump" left or right indicate a skewed distribution. If the mode (hump) is toward the left of the curve, the data are positively skewed, where the mode is less than the median, which is less than the mean (Curve B). This may seem a bit counterintuitive to you and you may be asking yourself: If the hump is to the left of the curve, it is lower in value, so how can that be a *positive* skew? The answer is because the skew is actually based on the position of the mean, not the mode. As I just described, in the positive skew the mean is high, hence the "positive" direction. The opposite is the case for a negatively skewed distribution (Curve C) where the mode, and therefore hump, is greater than the median, which is greater than the mean, so it is toward the right. Therefore, a negative skew occurs when

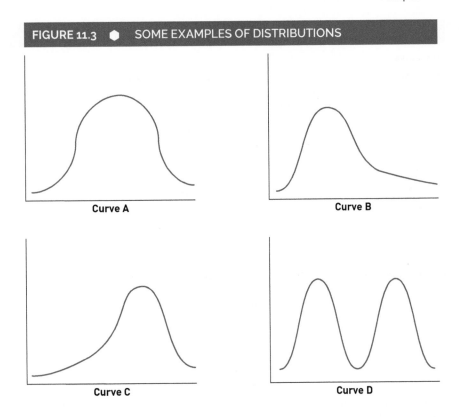

FIGURE 11.3   ●   SOME EXAMPLES OF DISTRIBUTIONS

Curve A

Curve B

Curve C

Curve D

the mean is noticeably less than the median and mode. Finally, Curve D illustrates what a curve would look like when there are two modes (humps). Researchers call this a bimodal distribution; distributions can have even more than two humps if there are more than two modes.

There are a variety of ways to test for a normal distribution, but none of them is perfect and for our purpose of "getting the job done," I will focus on four, most of which are presented in Figure 11.4. All of them can be run in SPSS (Appendix A) and the steps on how to run a histogram, skewness, and kurtosis in R appear in Appendix B. The most common way is to plot the data using a histogram and a normal curve line. As you see with AGE and TVHOURS, rarely in the real world do the data perfectly fit a normal distribution like we saw in Figure 11.3. So the issue is whether the data are *approximately* normally distributed. How can we tell what is close enough? The **histogram** is useful as a first line of defense, so to speak, in identifying normality by making it clear when distributions are definitely *not* normal. For my two variables of interest, education and hours of TV viewing, you see that the distribution for education is closer to a normal distribution than is hours of TV viewing, the latter of which is clearly positively skewed.

Because histograms can be hard to interpret, even with the normal curve superimposed, a second option is the *Q–Q* Plot, which is the **quantile–quantile plot**, which is a little clearer, but ultimately still subjective, determination of whether the distribution is normal. In a *Q–Q* plot,

FIGURE 11.4   ●   TESTS FOR NORMAL DISTRIBUTIONS

Histogram with normal curve

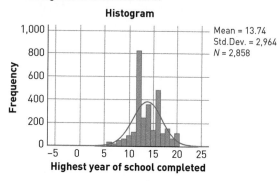

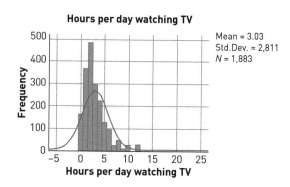

Q-Q **Plot**

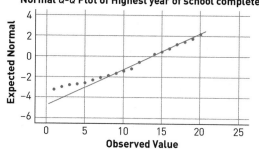

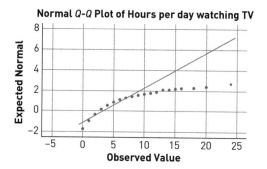

Statistics

		Highest year of school completed	Hours per day watching TV
N	Valid	2,858	1,883
	Missing	9	984
Skewness		−.186	2.811
Std. Error of Skewness		.046	.056
Kurtosis		.824	13.097
Std. Error of Kurtosis		.092	.113

Skewness and Kurtosis

Tests of Normality

	Kolmogorov-Smirnov[a]			Shapiro-Wilk		
	Statistic	*df*	Sig.	Statistic	*df*	Sig.
Hours per day watching TV	.203	1,880	.000	.758	1,880	.000
Highest year of school completed	.149	1,880	.000	.956	1,880	.000

K-S and S-W tests

a. Lilliefors Significance Correction

the black line indicates where your points *should* be if the distribution is normal and the dots are where your observations lie relative to that line. The closer the dots to the line, the closer to a normal distribution your data are. However, the question here, as with the histogram, is how far away from the line is it OK for points to be and for how many of them? If I look at the *Q–Q* plots for the two interval-ratio variables (Figure 11.4), I see that, as the histogram also suggested, the variable TV hours is pretty clearly not a normal distribution, as many of the points deviate from the line. But what about the education variable? Many of the points are very close to the line, but toward the bottom left of the line I see that there is some deviation. Is that deviation too much or are the rest of the points close enough for me to decide that the distribution is *approximately* normal? Tough to tell, but many researchers would probably say that this distribution is close enough. Are there any other options to check?

The answer is, yes. A third test of normality is to look at the statistics regarding the skewness and kurtosis of the curve. I just discussed that the skewness is whether the curve is shifted left or right. Kurtosis is the "tailedness" of the curve, which is influenced by the "squish" or flatness of the curve. For both, a value of "0" indicates a perfect normal distribution, and the further away from "0" the value is, the further away the data are from a normal distribution. As I said, it is unusual for a distribution of real data to have a perfect skewness or kurtosis score of "0"; however, what value of either is acceptable is somewhat arbitrary. Although all agree that the closer to "0" the better, some claim that values, regardless of sign, under 2 are sufficient, whereas others claim that the value needs to be under 1 (George & Mallery, 2010; Tabachnick & Fidell, 2013). If I look at this third piece of information in Figure 11.4, I see that for the TV viewing hours, the skewness and kurtosis are both pretty far from "0," especially the kurtosis, which is over 13. So this is another piece of information that confirms that TV viewing hours are not normally distributed. On the contrary, if I look at the skewness and kurtosis for education, I see that both are pretty close to "0" and under "1." This, coupled with the Q–Q plot, would suggest that education is normally distributed.

The last commonly used tests that I will cover are the Kolmogorov–Smirnov (K–S) test and Shapiro–Wilk (S–W) test both of which are statistical means of trying to minimize the subjectivity of the graphical decisions and the disagreement over appropriate skewness or kurtosis values. The K–S test and S–W test compare your data to what data *would* look like accounting for skewness and kurtosis simultaneously for a normal distribution with the same mean and standard deviation. Although I discuss inferential statistics and these tests more in Chapter 12, for our purposes now, to determine if data are normally distributed, I would want the values in the box labeled (in SPSS) "Sig" to be *greater* than .05. The "Sig" box stands for "significance" based on the probability of error. In the next chapter, I will explain more about what the significance value means and how it relates to the normal curve, but for our purposes now, I will just focus on whether this value is greater than .05 or not. A "Sig" value greater than .05 means that the data are *not* significantly different from the normal distribution, which is what researchers want. Before I get excited, however, that I have a less subjective means of determining a normal distribution, there is a catch here as well. This catch is that the larger the data set, the more likely a researcher is to get a "Sig" value that is *less* than .05 (which is not what researchers want) even if the deviations from normal are slight, and when I say large, I mean 100–200 observations. So, for example, with the GSS data, both tests suggest that the data are *not* normal because the "Sig" value is less than .05 for both tests (Figure 11.4). However, as I also see in Figure 11.4, under the skewness and kurtosis statistics, both of these variables have well over 1,800 observations, so even a slight deviation from a normal distribution, which the histogram and Q–Q plot suggest the education variable has, may produce the results seen in the K–S and S–W tests. Because of this, some researchers argue that when sample sizes are large, there is no need to test for normal distributions beyond a histogram or Q–Q plot (Ghasemi & Zahediasl, 2012; Lumley, Diehr, Emerson, & Chen, 2002). So, given the very large sample size for these two variables, it is not surprising that the slight deviations from normal that we noticed in the other tests were reflected in these statistics.

So, what can I conclude? The first conclusion is that there is no simple test to use in all instances to determine the nature of the data's distribution. Because of this, the decision about whether data is sufficiently normally distributed needs to weigh considerations like sampling technique and sample size against multiple tests for normality, which takes some practice. When data sets are large, such as those found in the GSS, graphs and skewness/kurtosis statistics may be the best option. The second conclusion is that it is easier to tell when data are clearly *not* normally distributed, like the situation with TVHOURS, than when it might be. Therefore, researchers can only do their best to make conclusions about when data *might* be normally distributed, so it is important to be clear what criteria they use for any of their decisions. Taken together and considering the limitations of each test, I would conclude that education is approximately normally distributed, whereas hours of TV viewing are not. So to get back to the decision tree:

3. **Is the variable normally distributed?**
   EDUC: Yes
   TVHOURS: No

4. **Decision**
   EDUC: Mean
   TVHOURS: Median

You all probably know how to calculate the mean because it is probably the best-known measure of central tendency, even though it is more commonly referred to as the average in nonstatistical circles. However, to be consistent with showing formulas and to get used to the common statistical symbols you will see again, the formula to calculate the mean, which is statistically represented by $\bar{X}$ and is read as "X bar," is

$$\bar{X} = \Sigma X / n$$

where

X = individual values of the variable

n = the number of observations; and

Σ = the Greek letter sigma that means "to add"

The mean is a useful measure of central tendency because it considers the value of each individual response in its calculation. If you remember, earlier in the chapter I said that strong statistics consider the contribution or values of more individual points in the distribution. Modes are statistically weak because they only look at one point, the most common. Medians consider the position of every point in order to identify the middle, but they do not consider the *value* of every point. The mean, on the contrary, considers the contribution of the value of each score to the overall distribution and, therefore, uses the most information from the data in its calculation. However, as no statistic is perfect, the mean has a weakness in that it is vulnerable to very high or very low scores that can make the distribution skewed as you saw in Figure 11.4.

Because of this, when a distribution is very skewed, the median is the more appropriate measure of central tendency to use. Technically the mode can also be presented for an interval/ratio level of measurement, but because it only considers one value, while the median considers the relative rank of all scores, the median is generally the preferred statistic. However, if more than one mode exists, sometimes researchers mention the modes in addition to the median.

 LEARNING CHECK 11.2: CENTRAL TENDENCY

1. Which measure of central tendency identifies the score that divides the distribution in half?

2. Which is the strongest measure of central tendency to use for normally distributed interval/ratio data?

3. What does the formula $(n+1)/2$ tell you?

Answers to be found at the end of the chapter.

Measures of Dispersion

I already mentioned that measures of central tendency only give part of the picture. By just giving the typical response, researchers do not know anything about how the responses are organized overall, or the spread of the distribution, most commonly called the dispersion. If 10 is the typical response (regardless of which measure of central tendency is used), a different picture exists depending on the spread of the distribution. A typical response of 10 on a 10-point quiz means something completely different from if the typical score was 10 on a 100-point test. Therefore, knowing the variation among how people answered is important to obtain a complete picture of the information. Although, as with measures of central tendency, there is some discretion in deciding what measure of dispersion to use, commonly the measure of dispersion links with the measure of central tendency. For example, the mean is commonly paired with the standard deviation, not a percent or range. So for our purpose of "getting the job done," I will not treat dispersion as a separate decision process, but instead I will pair dispersion measures with a measure of central tendency based on the variable's level of measurement.

Nominal Measures: Percent Distribution

As a low level of measurement, there are not a lot of statistical options for describing the variability of nominal variables. One option is the Index of Qualitative Variation (IQV); however, unless you are writing more complex statistical reports, it is not often used. In fact, many researchers make do with just presenting the percent distribution of the values using the valid percent that I discussed in frequency distributions. Therefore, for our purposes of "getting the job done," I will do the same.

Ordinal Measures: Percentage, Range, and Interquartile Range

As with measures of central tendency, for ordinal measures, there is some flexibility in the measure of dispersion to report. Although, the range is the traditional measure of dispersion for ordinal measures, when the researcher decides to use the mode as the measure of central tendency, the percent distribution is often given as the corresponding measure of dispersion. After all, it does not make much sense to combine the range with the mode unless one expresses the range in the values or attributes, such as saying "a five-point scale ranging from strongly agree to strongly disagree," instead of the number of viable answer choices.

However, when there are many values, especially ones that are not categorical, for an ordinal level of measurement, researchers frequently pair the median with the range, which is the distance between the minimum and maximum actual response. Sometimes the range is presented as the low and high values (e.g., …on a variable that ranges from 5 to 25) and sometimes the math is done (e.g., …on a variable that ranges across 20 points). The larger the range, the more varied, or dispersed, the answers given to the question.

However, even as a measure of dispersion, the range can be a bit misleading because it is only based on the lowest score and the highest score, which may be outliers, meaning very high or low scores relative to the other responses. In other words, I might give a test to a class where one of the students is a research method whiz kid who earns a perfect score and another student who was out partying the night before got a grade of 30. But what if the next highest score was 93, while the next lowest score was 58? Based on the real scores, the range would be 70 points (100–30); but if I removed these outliers, I would see that the range would be must smaller at 35 points (93–58). The interquartile range is an improvement over the range in that it ignores potential outliers by looking at the range of the middle 50% of the distribution. The formula for the interquartile range (IQR) is:

$$IQR = Q3 - Q1$$

where

Q3 = value at the 75th percent (e.g., *third* quartile), calculated by $n(.75)$

Q1 = value at the 25th percent (e.g., *first* quartile), calculated by $n(.25)$

To figure out where the 25th and 75th percents lie in the distribution, simply take your sample size and multiply it by .25 and .75, respectively. If the position ends in a decimal, again it just means that the value is between two observations. Like when calculating the median, arrange the distribution numerically from low to high and then find the values that correspond to the Q1 and Q3 positions you just calculated. If the values at the two observations are the same, then the value is what is used; if they are different, take the average.

For interpreting the IQR, the researcher would make it clear that they are discussing the middle 50% of the distribution, but then the actual values can be presented as I discussed for the range. For example, one can either state the high and low score, such as "the middle 50% of the scores ranged from 74 to 85) or one can do the math and state something like "the middle 50% of the scores ranged 11 points."

Interval/Ratio Measures: Variance, Standard Deviation, and What to Do With Skewed Distributions

Just like with central tendency, the measure of dispersion used for interval/ratio measures depends on whether the variable is approximately normally distributed or not. If the variable is not normally distributed, like in my instance with hours of TV viewing, and a researcher is presenting the median for central tendency, then the range or interquartile range would most likely be the corresponding measure of dispersion (Figure 11.2).

On the contrary, if the distribution is fairly normal and a researcher decided to use the mean for central tendency, then the variance and standard deviation are accurate measures of dispersion, but the standard deviation is the most commonly paired with the mean for reasons you will see in a moment. Just like the name implies, the variance tells the researcher about the variability of a measure by telling the researcher how close or far from the mean the scores in a distribution generally are. The smaller the variance relative to the mean, the closer the scores are to each other, and the larger the variance, the more spread out the scores are. Although this is pretty easy to grasp—the bigger the number, the greater the spread—the formula for the variance can be confusing because it compares the squared distance of each individual score to the mean:

$$\text{Variance} = s^2 = \Sigma(X - \overline{X})^2/(N)$$

The formula squares this distance to prevent the sum of the individual differences from always being "0," but the problem is that the resulting answer is in squared units, which does not make intuitive sense to us. After all, do you know what a "squared year" is? I sure don't! Therefore, although the variance is an important measure for a quick view of variability, it is most relevant as a factor in the calculations of more advanced statistical tests—which I will cover in the next few chapters—than it is for presenting a descriptive summary to others. That is why the standard deviation, which is just the square root of the variance and, therefore, is not expressed as squared units, is what is most commonly presented with the mean. The formula for the standard deviation (s) is:

$$s = \sqrt{\Sigma(X - \overline{X})^2/(N)}$$

Calculating the standard deviation by hand is time-consuming because the formula has a lot of steps and, therefore, a lot of possibilities for computation mistakes. Nonetheless, it is almost a right of passage in statistics to learn how to calculate the formula, so I present the formula and its steps in Learning Check 11.3, with a sample smaller than researchers would normally use just for the ease of illustration.

BOX 11.1

STANDARD DEVIATION CALCULATION

To illustrate the standard deviation, let's look at the following hypothetical data about the number of disruptions in a day for a classroom of 15 students and compare the number of disruptions of boys versus girls.

Girls			Boys		
Disruptions F	$(X-\bar{X})$	$(X-\bar{X})^2$	Disruptions F	$(X-\bar{X})$	$(X-\bar{X})^2$
0	0–3.43 = –3.43	11.77	3	3–6.25 = –3.25	10.56
1	1–3.43 = –2.43	5.90	4	4–6.25 = –2.25	5.06
2	2–3.43 = –1.43	2.04	5	5–6.25 = –1.25	1.56
2	2–3.43 = –1.43	2.04	5	5–6.25 = –1.25	1.56
4	4–3.43 = .57	.32	6	6–6.25 = –0.25	.06
6	6–3.43 = 2.57	6.60	7	7–6.25 = 0.75	.56
9	9–3.43 = 5.57	31.02	8	8–6.25 = 1.75	3.06
$n = 7$	$\Sigma (X-\bar{X}) \approx 0$	$\Sigma (X-\bar{X})^2 = 59.71$	12	12–6.25 = 5.75	33.06
$\Sigma X = 24$			$n = 8$	$\Sigma (X-\bar{X}) \approx 0$	$\Sigma (X-\bar{X})^2 = 55.48$
$\bar{X} = 24/7 = 3.43$			$\Sigma X = 50$		
			$\bar{X} = 50/8 = 6.25$		
	$s = \sqrt{59.71/7} = \sqrt{8.53} = \mathbf{2.92}$			$s = \sqrt{55.48/8} = \sqrt{6.94} = \mathbf{2.63}$	

In the table above, we see that there are seven girls and eight boys in this class. The formula for the standard deviation is:

$$s = \sqrt{\Sigma (X - \bar{X})^2 / N}$$

In order to calculate this statistic, I need to do the following steps in this order:

1. Calculate the mean, $\bar{X}$, for each group, I have this at the bottom of the first column of each group
2. Compare each individual score to the mean: $(X-\bar{X})$ in the second column
3. Square that answer: $(X-\bar{X})^2$ in the third column
4. Add those values
5. Plug everything into the equation

In this example, we see that the girls exhibited, on average, fewer disruptions ($\bar{X}$ = 3.43) than did the boys ($\bar{X}$ = 6.25), and although the responses were slightly more variable among the girls (s = 2.92), there is not much difference in the variation from the boys (s = 2.63).

✓ LEARNING CHECK 11.3: DISPERSION

1. What measure of dispersion is typically paired with the mode?
2. Why do we use the standard deviation with the mean instead of the variance?
3. If an interval/ratio level of measurement is not normally distributed and has only one mode, what measure of central tendency and dispersion would we most likely report?

Answers to be found at the end of the chapter.

SPSS and Interpretations

As you have probably seen, except with maybe the calculation of the standard deviation, most of the statistical measures of central tendency and dispersion that you learned are pretty easy to calculate by hand. But sometimes a computer can be helpful as well, especially if the sample size is large and/or the researcher wants to calculate the measures for multiple variables simultaneously. In fact, to save time, researchers often do move all their variables of interest to the analysis box or write code to run all the possible statistics—whether the statistic is appropriate for the data or not—at once to save time. If you do this, however, be careful! Statistical programs, regardless of whether they are free or not, do not think; they just compute what you tell them, to regardless of whether the resulting output is garbage or not. So if a researcher uses this shortcut, that researcher needs to make sure to *only* look at the information that is relevant to their statistical decisions.

For example, the output on the next page is the result of telling SPSS (Appendix A) to calculate all the measures of central tendency and dispersion for all the variables we discussed (SEX, CLASS, EDUC, and TVHOURS) at the same time in order to avoid having to individually repeat the set of commands for each specific variable. As I just said, this will produce some "garbage" statistics that are not appropriate or relevant to the data; however, based on the decision tree, I know which statistics *are* relevant for specific variables and they are indicated by the dark-grey-shaded boxes.

For the respondent's gender (SEX) and subjective social class (CLASS), I decided that the appropriate statistics were the mode and percent. The interpretation of the mode is always as the attribute, never the percent or the coded number. Think of interpretations as what you would tell someone who never saw, and has no interest in seeing, the actual data. So if someone asked, "What gender were your respondents?," you would not answer "1" or "55.5%." That would not make sense! Instead, a researcher might respond something like "My sample was almost evenly split between men and women, with a slightly higher percentage of women." Because researchers frequently present many statistics to describe their sample, it is common to present some related variables in the same sentence in order to avoid the choppy writing style of a sentence for each variable. For example, demographics are commonly presented

Statistics

		Subjective class identification	Highest year of school completed	Respondents' sex	Hours per day watching TV
N	Valid	2,843	2,858	2,867	1,883
	Missing	24	9	0	984
Mean		2.36	13.74	1.55	3.03
Median		2.00	13.00	2.00	2.00
Mode		2	12	2	2
Std. Deviation		.699	2.964	.497	2.811
Range		3	20	1	24
Minimum		1	0	1	0
Maximum		4	20	2	24
Percentiles	25	2.00	12.00	1.00	1.00
	50	2.00	13.00	2.00	2.00
	75	3.00	16.00	2.00	4.00

together in a few sentences, so a researcher might report the variable and value, or attribute, like this:

General interpretation: The respondents were generally the <u>value of variable 1</u>

(___%) and <u>value of variable 2</u> (___%).

Example: The respondents were generally male (55.5%) and identified them-

selves as working class (46.8%).

Because hours of TV watching per day were not normally distributed, I decided to use the median and range, and because the range is large (24 hours), I would add the IQR as well. Therefore, my interpretation would be something like this:

General interpretation: The median number of <u>variable 1</u> is <u>(insert median),</u>

which ranges from <u>insert range high and low</u> and the middle 50% of the scores

ranging from <u>insert IQR high and low</u>.

Example: The median number of hours of television watched is 2 with a range

from 0 to 24, and the middle 50% of the scores ranging from 1 to 4.

The interpretation of the mean and standard deviation is a bit different. First, the most meaningful way of interpreting the standard deviation is to compare it to another standard deviation. For example, I could compare the average educational attainment of men and women, and whichever group (men or women) had the lowest standard deviation would have the least variation, or more consistent, responses. A second way of understanding standard deviation is regarding its relationship to the normal curve. Because, as you have learned, the normal curve is symmetrical and predictable, researchers know that one standard deviation in each direction of the mean covers about 68% of the normal curve, two standard deviations in each direction cover about 95% of the normal curve, and three standard deviations cover 99% (**Figure 11.5**).

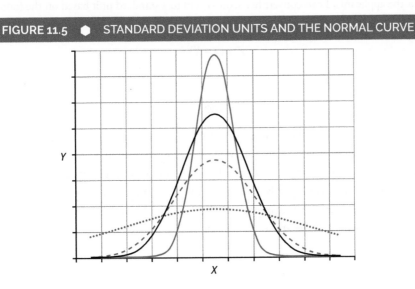

FIGURE 11.5 ● STANDARD DEVIATION UNITS AND THE NORMAL CURVE

However, in reality, researchers rarely relate the standard deviation to the normal curve probabilities. Instead, it is more common to just present the mean and standard deviation and let the reader decide how to use that information.

General interpretation: On average <u>variable 1</u> is <u>(insert mean),</u>

<u>(SD= insert standard deviation)</u>

Example: On average, the highest year of school completed is 12 (SD = 2.96)

WHAT AM I DOING? FINDING A SCORE RELATIVE TO A DISTRIBUTION

I showed in Figure 11.5 that by using the standard deviation and the mean, I can summarize how approximately 68%, 95%, and 99% of a sample responded without looking at the raw data. However, what if I am an employer and I am only interested in interviewing the candidates who score in the top 15% of an aptitude test that I administer. How can I determine what test score that would be? Or, what if I want to know what percent of the released offenders recidivate between 2 and 5 years out of prison but I am not the original researcher so I only have access to the reported mean and standard deviation of the distribution and not the raw data? In both of these situations, I am trying to see how specific scores relate to other scores in a distribution. I can accomplish this is by comparing any score in a distribution to that distribution's average if I convert the normal curve to standardized units, called Z-scores. The Z-score is the number of standard deviations a specific score is above or below the mean.

Let's take my earlier example of an aptitude test. Suppose I have a candidate whose résumé I really liked and who scored 119 on the aptitude test, which among all the candidates had a mean of 110 and a standard deviation of 5.8. In order to see if this candidate scored in the top 15% of the applicants, I can convert her score of 119 to a standard unit based on the following formula:

$$Z = (X - \bar{X}) / s$$

$$= (119 - 110) / 5.8$$

$$Z = 1.55$$

A positive Z-score means that the value of interest lies above the mean and a negative score just means it lies below the mean. In order to make sense of this number, I need to compare it to a table of Z-scores, which appears in Appendix C, but for which a subset appears in Box 11.2 for our reference here. Looking at Box 11.2, you will see that there are three different pieces of information: the Z-score (A), the proportion of the area under the curve between mean and Z (B), and the proportion of the area under the curve beyond Z (C).

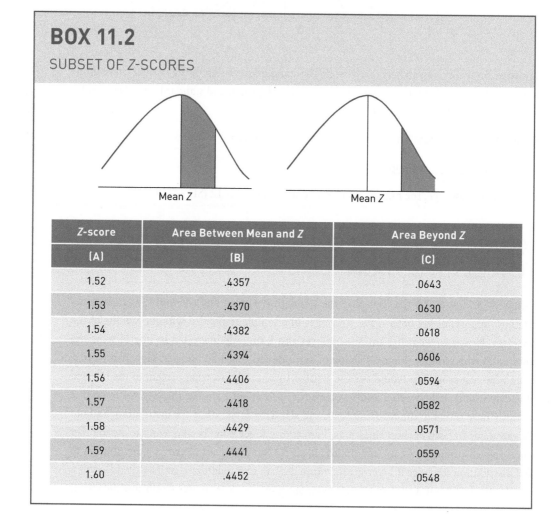

BOX 11.2
SUBSET OF Z-SCORES

Z-score	Area Between Mean and Z	Area Beyond Z
(A)	(B)	(C)
1.52	.4357	.0643
1.53	.4370	.0630
1.54	.4382	.0618
1.55	.4394	.0606
1.56	.4406	.0594
1.57	.4418	.0582
1.58	.4429	.0571
1.59	.4441	.0559
1.60	.4452	.0548

There are a couple of points about the Z-score table. First, you will notice that values are only presented for half the normal curve. That is because the normal curve is symmetrical and the values for columns B and C on the right side of the curve (shown) are the same for the area between mean and Z (column B) and beyond Z (column C) on the left side of the curve. As I said in the Z-score calculation, the only difference is the sign of Z (column A). A positive sign means you are looking at the proportions on the right side of the curve, and a negative sign means you would be looking at the mirror proportions on the left side of the curve. That leads to my second point. Since the values are only presented for half the curve, you will notice that for any particular Z-score (A), the proportion of the area under the normal curve expressed in columns B and C always total 0.5. That is because the entire proportion under the normal curve is 1.0, so half of it is .5.

To get back to my example, I always tell my students to make a quick diagram of the problem so they can visualize what the question is asking. In this instance, my diagram would look like what I have in Figure 11.6.

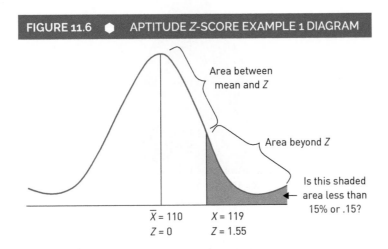

FIGURE 11.6 ⬡ APTITUDE Z-SCORE EXAMPLE 1 DIAGRAM

Area between mean and Z

Area beyond Z

Is this shaded area less than 15% or .15?

$\overline{X} = 110$
$Z = 0$

$X = 119$
$Z = 1.55$

In this figure, the mean of 110 is shown with its corresponding Z-value of "0." Because the Z-score is the standardized units away from the mean, the Z-score for the mean is always a score of "0." I also can draw in my X-value of 119 and its corresponding Z of 1.55. It does not matter whether the diagram is accurate in terms of the spacing of my mean and X-value, as this is just a rough visual to help me see what parts of the Z-score table I am interested in seeing. Since 119 is greater than 110, all that matters is that I locate it to the right of the mean.

I am interested in whether this person's aptitude test was in the top 15%; therefore I am interested in seeing whether the proportion of the curve *higher* than this score is .15 or less. This corresponds to the shaded area of Figure 11.6, and if you compare this shaded area to the figure in Box 11.2, you will see that what I shaded is the "area beyond Z." So to see the proportion of the normal curve that indicates applicants who scored *higher* than this candidate's 119,

I look at Column C for the Z-value of 1.55. I see that my area of interest, the area beyond Z, has a proportion of .0606, which means that 6.06% of the applicants had an aptitude score higher than this candidate's score of 119. Therefore, she is clearly in the top 15%.

I can use the Z-score to find how any scores relate to their distribution. Now let's pretend that I am interested in the percentage of applicants who scored between 100 and 113 on this same test. Figure 11.7 has the diagram that illustrates the parts of the normal curve I am interested in. As I have two scores I want to compare, I will have to convert each score to its own standardized Z-score using the same formula, which produces the following (the subscript for each Z just lets me know which X-value corresponds to which Z-score).

$$Z_{100} = (100 - 110) / 5.8 = -1.72$$

$$Z_{113} = (113 - 110) / 5.8 = .58$$

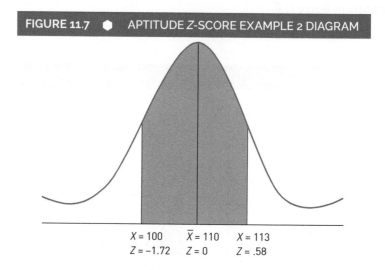

FIGURE 11.7   ●   APTITUDE Z-SCORE EXAMPLE 2 DIAGRAM

| $X = 100$ | $\bar{X} = 110$ | $X = 113$ |
| $Z = -1.72$ | $Z = 0$ | $Z = .58$ |

As you can see in Figure 11.7, now I am interested in the shaded middle area. I need to treat each Z-score independently, so if I look at the Z-values for $X = 100$ first, I see that the first part of the shaded area corresponds to the area between mean and Z for that score. For the second shaded area on the right of the curve, I am also interested in the area between mean and the Z that, in this instance, corresponds to $X = 113$. Therefore, to find the percent of applicants who scored between 100 and 113, I would use the Z-values in Appendix C to find:

$Z_{100} = -1.72$, area between mean and $Z = .4573$

$.4573 + .2190 = .6763$

$Z_{113} = .58$ area between mean and $Z = .2190$

So when I add these sections, I see that 67.63% of the applicants scored between 100 and 113 on the aptitude test even though I never looked at the raw data or a frequency distribution.

Z-scores can be used to find any manner of score combinations. Keep in mind that the Z-score always deals with half of the normal curve. If, for example, I wanted to know what percent of people scored higher than 100, I would only need to calculate the Z-score for 100, which I already noted was –1.72, find the area between mean and Z for the left half of the curve, which I know is .457. The rest of my shaded area would be the entire right side of the normal curve and since the normal curve is symmetrical, that means that half of the scores are higher than the mean. Therefore, in this instance, I do not need to calculate anything for the right side of the curve; I already know that the right side of the mean covers half of the normal curve, so a proportion of .5. To find the percent of applicants who scored higher than 100, I add .4573 and .5 for an answer of .9573, or 95.73%. Don't believe me? Draw it out and work through it.

In this chapter, you learned how researchers summarize variables so they can find patterns in the data and share those findings with others. You also learned how to use the normal curve to find how any response in a distribution of scores relates to other responses based on the mean and standard deviation as opposed to the raw data, which you may not have. In the next few chapters, we will move beyond descriptive analysis and into the realm of inferential statistics, where you will learn how to use sample information to make conclusions about a population.

 LEARNING CHECK 11.4: Z-SCORES

1. Why are only positive Z-scores included in the table of Z-score values?

2. What does the positive or negative Z-score tell you?

Answers to be found at the end of the chapter.

Key Terms

Bivariate	Histogram	Statistic
Central tendency	Inferential statistics	Statistical control variable
Descriptive statistics	Multivariate	Statistical significance
Dispersion	Normal distribution	Substantive significance
Frequency	Quantile–Quarnile, or Q–Q plot	Univariate

Answers to Learning Check Questions

Learning Check 11.1: Basic Statistical Terms

1. Bivariate

2. Statistical significance tells whether a relationship observed in a sample is likely to also occur in the population and substantive significance tells how strongly two variables are related.

3. Multivariate analysis can examine the effects between two variables of interest, while accounting for the statistical effect of topical rival causal factors, which is called statistically controlling, for other factors.

Learning Check 11.2: Central Tendency

1. Median

2. Mean

3. The position of the median or where in the distribution the median value is located. Once the position identified, the actual value in that position is the median response.

Learning Check 11.3: Dispersion

1. The percent

2. The mean is in units like years, pounds, and number of movies, whereas the variance is in squared units (such as squared years, squared pounds, and squared movies), which does not intuitively make sense to us. Therefore, to match the units of dispersion to the units of the central tendency measure, and to make more intuitive sense, we report the squared root of the variance, which is the standard deviation.

3. For central tendency the median, and for dispersion the range and possibly the IQR.

Learning Check 11.6: Learning Check Z-Scores

1. Because they are based on the normal curve, which is symmetrical.

2. The sign of the Z-score tells us which side of the mean the score of interest falls.

End-of-Chapter Problems

1. A researcher is interested in summarizing the region of the country subjects in a nationwide survey are from. The responses are 1 = North, 2 = South, 3 = East, 4 = Midwest, and 5 = West. Which measure of central tendency and dispersion would be appropriate?
   a. Mode and percent
   b. Mode and range
   c. Median and percent
   d. Median and range

2. A survey question asks students how many hours they typically spend studying research methods/statistics in a given week. Which measure of central tendency and dispersion would be appropriate? The responses are:
   7 7 2 10 8 7 4 8 8 7 3 8
   a. Median and percent
   b. Median and range
   c. Mode, median, and range
   d. Mean and standard deviation

3. For a large introductory class, the average test score is 87 with a standard deviation of 3.2. In order to determine what percentage of students earned below a 70, what statistic would I use?
   a. A measure of central tendency
   b. A measure of dispersion
   c. Z-score
   d. A percentage based on looking at all the raw scores

4. On a survey is a question "To what degree do you favor or oppose an armed campus security force?" with answer choices that range from 5 = Strongly favor to 1 = Strongly oppose. Given the following responses, which measure of central tendency and dispersion would be appropriate?
   4 5 5 5 3 4 1 2 5 5 4
   a. Mode and percent
   b. Mode and range
   c. Median and percent
   d. Median and range

5. A survey question asks students how many miles the campus is from home. Which measure of central tendency and dispersion would be appropriate? If you think it is relevant, skewness = .83 and kurtosis = .13. The responses are:
   5 30 24 10 35 60 46 70 44 53 35 90
   a. Median and percent
   b. Median and range
   c. Mode, median, and range
   d. Mean and standard deviation

6. True/False: Statistically, the mean and standard deviation can be used for nominal levels of measurement even though they may not be the best choice.

7. True/False: A Z-score of +1.04 and = 1.04 for the area between mean and Z will be the same.

8. Calculation: In a study of 400 high school seniors, a researcher found that the subjects spent an average of 32 hours a week (s = 2.2) on various electronic devices (cell phones, television, computers, tablets, etc.). What percent of respondents spent less than 35 hr a week on electronic devices? If you think it is relevant (and it may not be to your decisions), the data are normally distributed.

9. Calculation: Fully summarize (central tendency and dispersion) the following responses to the question "How many dates have you gone on in the past 3 months?" If you think it is relevant (and it may not be to your decisions), the data are normally distributed.
   2 6 10 12 15 15 15 18 24 26

10. Calculation: Fully summarize the following responses to the question "How many nights did you go out with friends in the past 3 months?" If you think it is relevant (and it may not be to your decisions), the data is not normally distributed.
    0 6 6 8 9 10 10 12 13 14 20

11. Using the GSS database, summarize the distribution for the following variables: AIDCOL, CHILDS, CCTV, DEGREE, LIFEDTH, and WWWHR.

12

CONFIDENCE INTERVALS AND ONE-SAMPLE HYPOTHESIS TESTING

LEARNING GOALS

- Explain how the normal curve relates to confidence intervals and hypothesis testing

- Recognize when to use confidence intervals and how to interpret their output

- Describe the relationship between confidence levels, alpha levels, and p-values for one- and two-tailed tests

- Identify when to use specific one-sample hypothesis tests and how to interpret the computer output

- Distinguish between Type I and Type II errors when testing the hypothesis

In 2018, the Gallup Poll randomly sampled 1,019 Americans over age 18 to see what crimes worried them the most. According to their findings, cybercrimes topped the list. Gallup found that with a ±4% interval, 71% of Americans are worried about having their personal data hacked and 67% worry about identity theft (Gallup, 2018). But how can Gallup say what millions of Americans are likely to worry about based on a sample of only a little more than a thousand? The Gallup statistic is an example of **inferential statistics** because the researchers at Gallup use statistics based on their sample data of over 1,000 people, which as you learned in Chapter 5, researchers can observe, to *infer* what is going on in the study population, which researchers cannot observe. There is so much that researchers can do with statistics that we can devote multiple semesters to learning the nuances of them; but, as our focus is to "get the job done," I will only cover some of the more common statistics or situations you are likely to encounter if you work in a social service or criminal justice agency.

In this chapter, you will learn the logic behind inferential statistics, estimate population values, and test hypotheses that compare the population from which a sample was drawn to a known population value. In the next chapter, I will discuss hypothesis testing when comparing two or more groups.

Although some of you may have been "OK" with the descriptive statistics I covered in Chapter 11, I suspect that many of you probably consider statistics that relate to hypothesis testing to be a terrifying mix of numbers, magic, and mystery that you are not really sure you are going to "get." Admittedly, learning inferential statistics takes practice. But really, like descriptive statistics, estimating population parameters and hypothesis tests are just a form of logic applied to glorified math word problems. To help you decode those "word problems," I am going to continue using the decision tree process introduced in Chapter 11; but in this chapter, our main answers to "What am I doing?" will be estimating a population parameter or testing a one-sample hypothesis.

There are a few additional points about the next few chapters. First, the body of Chapters 12–14 will primarily focus on how to decode a problem that leads to the particular statistical tests covered in that chapter and the possible ways of interpreting the resulting information in APA format. The actual computer steps to obtain the output continue to be covered in Appendix A for SPSS and Appendix B for R (along with the output for R), and the variable names used in the chapters will be the same as those used in both Appendices for the same test. The purpose of putting the computer steps in Appendices rather than the body of the chapters is to simplify the chapter presentation without getting bogged down in the technical side of how to run two different statistical programs for each statistical test. Second, from now on I will not generally focus on the actual mathematical calculations of these statistics because, as I said in the last chapter, in reality, most of you will not be calculating these statistics by hand in the workplace. However, as I have previously said, there is arguably merit to learning how to calculate these statistics by hand for anyone going on to an upper-level statistics class so your professor may still require you to do some hand calculations. Therefore, the formulas for most of the statistical test decisions, along with the statistical name, appear in the decision tree. Always keep in mind, however, that you can learn the more nuanced and detailed aspects about them in a higher level statistics class or from your professor. Last, I will continue to use the 2016 version of the General Social Survey (GSS) that I introduced in Chapter 11 and to give the variable names in capitalized letters so you can easily identify them and match them to the data set.

Therefore, even without the hand calculations, this chapter will give a solid foundation in what statistical tests to do and how to make sense of the output. In other words, we will essentially "get the job done" for many common applied research situations. But before I get into the statistical decisions, let's learn the basic relationship between population estimates and hypothesis tests.

WHAT AM I DOING? ESTIMATING A POPULATION PARAMETER

The Logic Behind Confidence Intervals

I can't stress enough how important the normal curve is for the discussion of the material in these next few chapters. Most inferential statistics start with two key data assumptions. The first assumption is that the researchers conducted a random sample and the second is that the resulting data are normally distributed. As you learned in Chapter 5, the first assumption of random sampling increases the likelihood of the second assumption, that the data are normally distributed, being fulfilled. If you need a refresher on probability theory, central limit theorem, or the normal curve, go back and read that section in Chapter 5; remember, how to test for a normal distribution is covered in Chapter 11. For our current purposes, a normal distribution is important because it can help explain the underlying concepts behind what population estimates and hypothesis testing do.

I can relate confidence levels, population estimates, and hypothesis testing to the normal curve using the properties of the Z-score that you learned in Chapter 11. If you remember from Chapter 11, Z-scores translate data into standardized proportionate areas under the normal curve. If I want to be 95% confident that I am accurately estimating a population value, I want to cover the entire central 95% of the normal curve, as shown in Figure 12.1A, and the corresponding Z-values of ±1.96 identify this middle interval. The areas outside this middle range of the normal curve, which cover the remaining 5%, 2.5% on each side, are called the **tails of a distribution**, or more simply just the tails, and if the population value actually lies in either of these tails, then this would be the error.

Let's illustrate how researchers use Z-scores to estimate population parameters by walking through a hypothetical study of how much students at my university spent on textbooks this past semester (the population parameter) based on a random sample of 500 of them (the sample). Let's say that in our sample, I found that the average amount these students spent on books this past semester was $625, so $\overline{X}$ = $625, with a standard deviation of $180, or s=$180. Because this is a sample, it is unlikely that my sample average of $625, which is called a **point estimate**, is the exact value in the population. I know there will be a sampling error that will prevent me from identifying the *exact* value in the population. However, based on the central limit theorem (Chapter 5), I also know that if my sample is large enough (and this is), my sample mean is likely to be *close* to the true population mean. To determine how close, I need to decide how sure I want to be of my estimate, meaning I have to decide my confidence level (such as 95%) ahead of time..

Now let's put this information into the context of the normal curve. I can convert my confidence level to a Z-score based on the normal curve and input that information along with my sample information into a statistical formula (which I will come back to soon) to create an interval, that is an estimate within which the true population value is likely to lie. Graphically, this is what I illustrated in Figure 12.1A where, if I chose a confidence level of 95%, I

PHOTO 12.1 How much to do you think students at your school spend a semester on textbooks?

can create an interval where I am 95% sure that the true population parameter lies (the happy emojis), but there is a 5% chance, 2.5% on each side of the curve, that the true population value is outside of this area (the sad emojis). In the textbook study, using the sample information, the Z-score that corresponds to a 95% confidence level, and the statistical formula that fits the data (again, I will get to this soon), I can say that I am 95% confident that students at my university spent between $609.21 and $640.79 on books this past semester. I will come back to this hypothetical study of the textbook cost when we discuss one-sample hypothesis tests, but for now, let's go back to the Gallup data I used at the start of the chapter.

The statistics of 71% and 67%, presented by Gallup, are point estimates because they identify one specific value. They are like the $625 in my textbook study. But the Gallup poll statistics also mention an interval of ±4%. This interval stems from the normal curve and a statistical formula that includes a 95% confidence level, which is the base level of confidence in the behavioral and social sciences. So when we take all of this information together, these statistics mean that the Gallup researchers are 95% confident that between 67% and 75% of the American public is afraid of their personal data being hacked. These numbers are achieved by taking the original 71% and both adding 4% to it (hence 75% on the high end) and subtracting 4% from it (hence the 67% on the low end). Using the same information, I am also 95% confident that 63%–71% of the population is worried about identity theft.

Estimating Confidence Intervals

So, how do we know when our answer to "What am I doing?" is to calculate a confidence interval to estimate a population parameter? Questions such as "What is the value in the population?" or "What percent of Americans feel _____" frequently indicate this statistical

FIGURE 12.1 ⬡ LOGIC OF INFERENTIAL STATS AND THE NORMAL CURVE

(A) Confidence intervals and the normal curve

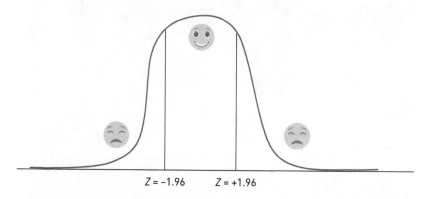

$Z = -1.96$ $\qquad$ $Z = +1.96$

(B) Hypothesis tests and the normal curve

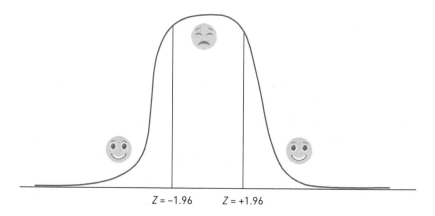

$Z = -1.96$ $\qquad$ $Z = +1.96$

goal. Notice that in both of these questions I am trying to reach a specific number in the wider population. I already covered why I don't want a specific number—a point estimate—so I am going to discuss how to calculate the confidence interval for different data characteristics using the decision tree depicted in Figure 12.2.

Let's suppose that I want to estimate how old people are, on average, when they have their first child (AGEKDBRN). Like in the last chapter, the decision tree in Figure 12.2 is still relatively simple right now, but in order to get used to using it to approach situations (rather than statistics directly), let's still take it step by step starting with the question "What am I doing?"

FIGURE 12.2 ● DECISION TREE FOR A POPULATION PARAMETER AND ONE-SAMPLE HYPOTHESIS TEST

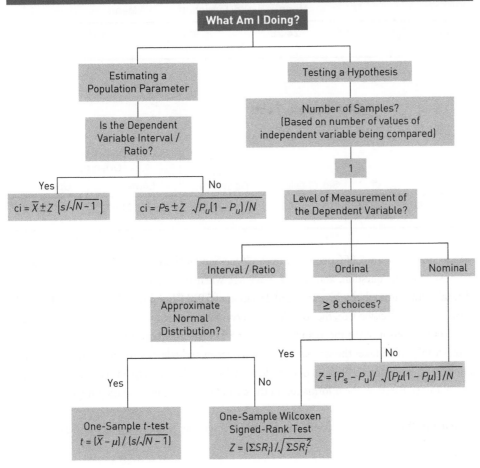

1. **What am I doing?** Estimating a population parameter
   I want an actual number of how old people are when they have their first child.

2. **What is the level of measurement of my dependent variable?** Interval/ratio
   I know this by looking at the values of a variable either in the codebook or data set. (In SPSS this would be in "Variable View.")

3. **Is it normally distributed?** I can assume so based on the large sample size and what we learned in Chapter 11.

4. **Decision:** Confidence interval for continuous variables.
$$ci = \overline{X} \pm Z(s/\sqrt{N-1})$$

What I did above was work through each question of the decision tree until we ran out of questions (considerations) and reached a statistical decision. The computer commands are in Appendices A and B and the SPSS output is below:

One-Sample Statistics

	N	Mean	Std. Deviation	Std. Error Mean
R's age when 1st child born	2,056	24.28	5.918	.131

One-Sample Test

Test Value = 0

	t	df	Sig. (2-tailed)	Mean Difference	95% Confidence Interval of the Difference	
					Lower	Upper
R's age when 1st child born	185.990	2,055	.000	24.276	24.02	24.53

I can see that there are 2,056 people (*N* in the "One-Sample Statistics" table) who have children and answered this question, and their average age when their first child was born was 24.28 ("Mean" in the same table) with a standard deviation of 5.918 ("Std. Deviation"), rounded to 5.92. As we saw in the decision tree, the confidence interval formula used to calculate this statistic looks at the standard error of the mean and we see that SPSS has calculated that as well at .131 ("Std. Error Mean"). SPSS takes the standard error of the mean and relates it to the mean to obtain the confidence interval for a 95% level of confidence, which is what we have in the second table (last two columns). Based on the information in the second table, our interpretation might read:

General: We can be _____ confident that the average [dependent variable] is somewhere between _____ and _____.

Our example: We can be 95% confident that the average age someone has their first child is somewhere between 24.02 and 24.53 years.

Incidentally, I can change the default confidence level from 95% to any percent I want by just clicking on the "Options" box in the one-sample *t*-test and changing the confidence level from the default of 95% to my desired percent (e.g., 99%).

However, what if instead of average age at first birth (a continuous variable) I want to estimate something else, like the percent of people in the population who are confident in our medical institution? In the world of rising health care costs, controversy over vaccinations, and a noticeable number of uninsured individuals, this is an emotional and controversial issue.

Based on the GSS variable CONMEDIC, I see that our answer choices are "a great deal," "only some," and "hardly any." As shown in Figure 12.2, the statistical test and formula for estimating a population parameter for a nominal or ordinal (discrete) variable are different from an interval/ratio (continuous) variable, but the overall logic of the process and the interpretation of the output are the same. Unfortunately, SPSS does not

PHOTO 12.2 How much trust do you think people have in the medical institution?

have a function for calculating confidence intervals for categorical variables unless you download an extension to the program and are willing to keep, or make, your variable dichotomous (such as yes/no). Furthermore, the output produced is not the same as the output for our other statistics in SPSS. For those reasons, *if* your school has this feature downloaded and *if* your variable is dichotomous, you can look at Appendix A for how to use SPSS to calculate this statistic. However, because many of you may not have that extension downloaded *or* your variable is categorical but not dichotomous, we can also use one of the many free online calculators that can do the calculations for us. A couple of examples of these free calculators are:

- http://www.sample-size.net/confidence-interval-proportion/

- http://simulation-math.com/_Statistics/ConfIntervalProportionV2.cshtml

In most of these calculators, you simply have to input the sample size, the frequency of the value of the variable of interest (which you learned how to obtain in Chapter 11), or its proportion, and your preferred confidence level. The calculator will provide you with the resulting interval. For example, if I run a frequency on CONMEDIC (output not shown), I see that there are 1,942 people who answered this question (n), and 694 (f) of them selected "a great deal." Plugging those figures into the calculator for a 95% confidence level, the calculator tells us our population proportion lies between .336 and .379. It is customary to convert the proportion to a percentage when sharing statistical findings with others. Since the general interpretation follows the same pattern as for the last example, here I will just give the example-specific interpretation:

Our example: We can be <u>95%</u> confident that the percent of people <u>who have a</u>

<u>"great deal" of confidence in the medical institution</u> is between <u>33.6%</u> and <u>37.9%.</u>

BOX 12.1
CONFIDENCE INTERVALS AND A CORONAVIRUS VACCINE

In 2020 a global pandemic due to the new COVID-19 infection, commonly called the coronavirus, changed the way of life as we knew it by leading to worldwide closure of businesses, lockdowns in travel, widespread remote education, and individual quarantine, to name a few modifications. As of the writing of this book, much remains uncertain as to how life will move forward and whether a new vaccine will be available. In opinion polls, like the Gallup Poll mentioned at the introduction of this chapter, commonly used large random samples to estimate the population's view on a variety of instances. For example, look at the following graph:

1 in 7 would not get coronavirus vaccine because they distrust vaccines in general

Q: If a vaccine that protected you from the coronavirus was available for free to everyone who wanted it, would you definitely get it, probably get it, probably not get it or definitely not get it? (if probably/definitely not) Is that mainly because you don't trust vaccines in general or you don't think it's necessary in this case?

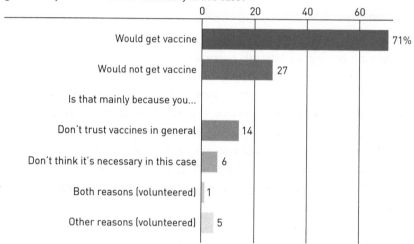

Note: "No opinion" not shown.

Source: May 25–25, 2020, Washington Post-ABC News poll of 1,001 U.S. adults with an error margin of +/- 3.5 percentage points. EMILY GUSKIN/THE WASHINGTON POST

According to this graph, 71% of the population would get a COVID-19 vaccine if one was available. This 71% is an example of a point estimate that makes reporting easier, even though it is unlikely that 71% is actually the true population parameter. Therefore, if you look at the small print, you will see information for the confidence interval, which is where the pollsters statistically think the true population parameter lies. In this instance, the last sentence identified the margin of error as ± 3.5%, which when combined with the point estimate of 71%, becomes the confidence interval. As 95% is the standard confidence level, this information really means that the pollsters are 95% confident that the true proportion of the population (the population parameter) who would get a COVID-19 vaccine is between 67.5% and 74.5%.

Source: Goldstein, A., & Clement, S. (2020, June 2).

Increasing Our Confidence in Our Estimates

I have said multiple times that in statistics researchers want to be at least 95% confident of these estimates, meaning that researchers want to cover 95% of the normal curve with their estimation. If researchers want to be even surer of the findings, they might want to set the confidence level higher, to say 99%. This means that the resulting interval is now wider and will cover almost all of the normal curve. You may think that our findings are not very precise as a result; but, remember as you learned in Chapter 5 on sampling, if researchers have a sufficiently large random sample (and the GSS is both large and random), the curve will be more narrow so that even though the statistic will cover almost all of it at a 99% confidence level, the interval itself will be comparatively small and therefore still precise.

 LEARNING CHECK 12.1: CONFIDENCE INTERVAL DECISIONS

1. If I conduct a random sample of 300 single parents about the hours of TV they allow their children to watch per day and I find a mean of 4.6 (SD=1.06), which statistical formula should I use?

2. At the 97% confidence level which is more precise: a sample of 300 people or a sample of 450 people? Why?

3. Which confidence level, 90% or 96%, covers more area under the normal curve? Why?

Answers to be found at the end of the chapter.

WHAT AM I DOING? HYPOTHESIS TESTING—ONE SAMPLE

The Logic Behind Hypothesis Testing

Hypothesis testing uses the complement of the normal curve logic for estimating a population parameter. In estimating the population parameter, researchers want the observed test statistic to be similar to the population value, so they want it within the bracketed area established by the confidence level and corresponding Z-score (Figure 12.1A). In hypothesis testing, researchers are *comparing* to find some type of *difference*; therefore, they want the value to be *outside* this interval. Inside the interval, where the study population and the population of comparison are the same (similar to our estimate of the population parameter) would be the null region of no difference (hence the "same"). Our *statistical* goal is to reject the null hypothesis of no difference because the assumption is that there is no difference between what is being compared (null hypothesis) unless the statistical information suggests otherwise. Therefore hypothesis testing *wants* to show a difference because researchers would not hypothesize about what is already "assumed" to be true. To keep the graph illustration consistent with the "±" in estimating a population parameter, let's assume that our alternate hypothesis is that the population from which the sample was drawn is just different, or unequal, to the population value of comparison. Therefore, as shown in Figure 12.1B, our "happy place" is what is *not* in the interval, but is outside, in the tails instead.

I can alter our initial textbook example to become a one-sample hypothesis test. Based on data from the College Board's Annual Survey of Colleges (2018), students attending a 4-year college expect to spend $1,240 for books and supplies a year, which would be about $620 for a semester. An example of a hypothesis test would be seeing whether the amount my students spend on textbooks is significantly different from the national average. The null (H_o) and alternative (H_1) hypotheses would be expressed as:

H_o: $\mu = 620$

H_1: $\mu \neq 620$

The "not equal" in the alternate hypothesis just means different; therefore, the population value of my school could be higher (on the right-hand side of the curve) or lower (on the left-hand side). Statistically, this would be called a **two-tailed test** because when I am saying that one population value is higher *or* lower than the other, these high and low ends correspond to areas under the normal curve called tails. Computing the test statistic involves converting the sample information to a standardized equivalent, which results in the mathematical answer that is frequently called the obtained value being compared to a critical value that identifies the cutoff for the null region. The goal is for the obtained test statistic to be greater in magnitude than the critical value, which would put the test statistic in the tail (happy emojis in Figure 12.2B). Researchers frequently establish this cutoff point, which is called the **alpha level**, for what they consider is a sufficiently improbable value (meaning, not likely to be in the null region) in advance and in the social and behavioral sciences; this is typically 95%. The alpha level is a lot like the alpha we discussed with confidence intervals, but the alpha level is technically the proportion of the area under a sampling distribution that has unlikely outcomes (differences) given the assumption that the null is true. The common alpha levels are .05, .01, and .001 and the corresponding critical values for each (depending on the specific distribution of the appropriate test statistic) define the level at which we are sufficiently confident (95%, 99%, and 99.9%, respectively) that our result is improbable enough to risk rejecting the null.

If I calculate the formula by hand, I am not likely to know the exact probability of error, called the *p*-**value**, because with hand calculations we just establish the critical cutoff that corresponds to our alpha. When we do statistics by hand, we want our observed value (the test statistic) to be greater than this critical value and, therefore, somewhere in the tail (the critical region, the smiley emojis, Figure 12.1B) that allows us to reject the null. But when we do statistics on a computer, the computer program tells us exactly where on the normal curve our obtained statistic is by giving us the exact probability of error, or *p*-value. Therefore, we might see *p*= .032, which means the probability of error is 3.2%, or conversely that we are 96.8% sure there is a difference. The smaller the *p*-value, the further into the tail our sample population parameter is from the null region and the higher the confidence we have that the null should be rejected. The larger the *p*-value, the more likely the null is to be true, and therefore we fail to reject it.

So, in a nutshell, statistical tests are formulas that create a standardized observed value for the data that researchers gather and researchers compare this observed value to a corresponding critical value that identifies the cutoff of the null region. Because statistically, researchers are always testing the null (not the alternate hypothesis), researchers assume that the null is true and that what is not in the null region is considered error, even though based on the alternate hypothesis that "error" area is actually the difference researchers are hoping to identify. The complement of that "error" is the confidence level, so researchers then say "we are 95% confident." In many traditional statistics classes (including ones I have taught), students learn these formulas, how to do the math to calculate the obtained value, and then how to compare their obtained value to the critical value that identifies the null region that they look up. If the obtained value is greater than the critical value, then the obtained value is in the "tail" of the distribution and the null is rejected. However, again, in everyday life, people rarely go about calculating statistics by hand.

One- or Two-Tailed Tests

In my textbook example, the alternate hypothesis was that my student study population was not equal to the national population; therefore, as I said previously, the error can be high *or* low. However, if my alternate hypothesis was that my student population spent more (H$_1$: $\mu > 620$) or if it spent less (H$_1$: $\mu < 620$), then in either situation I would have a **one-tailed test** because I am hypothesizing, or taking a stance, that the error is going to be either high (greater than) or low (less than) the null region and, therefore, is only in one tail. As you learned in Chapter 2, whether an alternate hypothesis is a one- or two-tailed test should be based on theory, but such a decision has statistical implications. Statistically, the critical value is lower for one-tailed tests, which, in turn, affects whether researchers reject the null or not. For example, the *Z* critical for an alpha of .05 and a two-tailed test is ±1.96, which corresponds to an error of .025 in each tail, whereas the *Z* critical for a one-tailed test, when the .05 error is *all* either high (>) or *all* low (<), is +1.65 or −1.65 (depending on the side of the curve). Remember, the goal of calculated statistics is to have the magnitude of the observed statistical value (the one calculated) to be greater than the critical value identifying the null region. The sign of the test statistic is important for the alternate hypothesis and to see if our sample statistic is behaving in the same direction, but it is not important per se for determining whether to reject the null because it just illustrates which side of the normal curve your sample falls on. If my observed *Z*-value is 1.83 and I have a two-tailed test, I cannot reject the null because my observed value is less than my two-tailed critical value of 1.96. However, if I have a one-tailed test, my observed value is in the tail because my obtained value of 1.83 is *greater* than my critical value of 1.65, so I would reject the null. Remember, it is irresponsible methodologically to just immediately jump to a one-tailed test because it is easier to reject the null. The decision to use a one-tailed test needs to be justified with theory. Computerized output gives us the exact *p*-value for a two-tailed test, and when researchers have a one-tailed test, the general practice is to take the *p*-value presented in the "Sig." column and divide it by half. As before, the lower the *p*-value, the more confident researchers are of their findings.

Cautions about Hypothesis Tests

It is important to keep in mind that hypothesis tests look for whether any relationships, no matter how strong or weak, that researchers see in our sample are likely to also exist in the study population. With hypothesis testing, researchers can only reject a null or alternate hypothesis. They cannot "prove" a hypothesis in the real world, and it is important to keep that in mind. Furthermore, the ability to reject a null hypothesis or not, as reflected by the *p*-value, is influenced by the sample size. Larger samples produce smaller *p*-values because in larger samples it is easier to detect small differences. By the same idea, the larger you expect the difference to be, the smaller the necessary sample size because this difference, by the nature of its anticipated effect size, will be more easily detected. Hypothesis tests do not provide information regarding whether the degree to which variables co-vary, or change

LEARNING CHECK 12.2: LOGIC OF HYPOTHESIS TESTING

1. If I want to be 99% sure of my findings, how much error am I willing to accept?

2. In hypothesis testing, do I want my observed statistical value (from the formula) to be between the two *Z*-scores or beyond it? Why?

3. Statistically, do we test the null or the alternate hypothesis?

4. If I hypothesize that having a higher level of education leads one to have a higher income, am I doing a one- or two-tailed hypothesis test? Why?

Answers to be found at the end of the chapter.

together, is large enough to argue that there is a *meaningful* relationship, what I identified in Chapter 11 as substantive significance, or effect size, between the variables and which I will cover in more detail in **Chapter 14**.

Testing Hypotheses: One-Sample Tests

So how do you know when your goal is to test a hypothesis rather than estimate a population parameter or find an association? Phrasing that suggests hypothesis testing could be examples such as:

1. Prisoners who attend a county-level re-entry program have lower rates of recidivism 5 years postrelease than do prisoners statewide.

2. Women are more likely than men to support Candidate Jones.

3. People who identify as Asian/Pacific Islanders have smaller families than do people of other races.

PHOTO 12.3 We could hypothesize that children who attend arts programs score higher on tests of self-expression than do children who do not attend such programs. We would be comparing children in these programs to those who are not.

In all of these examples, researchers are *comparing*. You may be comparing a sample to a known population (the first example), you may be comparing two groups (the second example), or you may even be comparing three or more groups (the third example). You may also see language such as "greater than" or "lower than" to imply a direction of effect; but nowhere does the question ask "how strong" is the effect or "how much different." Those latter two questions are more likely to be addressed by the types of statistics that are in Chapter 14 on substantive significance. Nor are we asking for a specific value, such as what percent of prisoners recidivate within 3 years of release, which would be a population estimate instead.

Let's take an example. I can compare the education of women in the GSS with women in the US population, or to put it methodologically, I can test whether the women in the GSS have, on average, different years of education (EDUC) than women in the US population, which is about 13.4 years of schooling (United Nations Development Program, 2018).

Following the decision tree that appears in Figure 12.2:

1. **What am I doing?** Hypothesis test
   I am comparing the population from which my sample was drawn (the GSS data) to a known population value (the national average of 13.4 years of schooling)

2. **Number of samples (based on the independent variable)?** 1
   I have a one-sample hypothesis test when I want to compare the sample population value, which I can only estimate based on my observed sample statistic, such as a mean ($\overline{X}$) to a known population value (μ).

Known population values for comparison are frequently national averages, state averages, averages for an entire school or business, etc. As you can see in the decision tree in Figure 12.2, once I decide I have a one-sample hypothesis test, the next questions relate to the material you learned in the previous chapters:

3. **Is my dependent variable continuous?** Yes, based on the GSS values

4. **Is it normally distributed?** Yes, based on an examination of the histogram, skewness, and kurtosis (not shown)

5. **Decision:** One-sample *t*-test

$$t = (\overline{X} - \mu) / (s/\sqrt{N-1})$$

Notice that point 3 presumes that you can distinguish between the independent and dependent variable, which you learned about in Chapter 2. Furthermore, because of our large sample size (greater than 50), remember you can test for normality focusing on the histogram and *Q–Q* plots learned in Chapter 11.

Here is a good place to note that many statistical tests come with some assumptions, the most basic of which is that the data was selected randomly. Whether additional assumptions are fulfilled or not influences the decision of what statistical test to actually use and are, therefore, usually incorporated into our decision-making process (our decision tree). For example, the one-sample *t*-test assumes that the dependent variable is normally distributed, but if it is not, and you follow the decision tree, you will realize that you would have to use a different test instead. However, to maintain some similarities with more traditional statistics books, I will also state the assumptions for each statistic but note whether that assumption is addressed in the decision tree or elsewhere. The assumptions for the one-sample *t*-test are:

- I have a random sample (fulfilled by the GSS)

- The dependent variable is continuous (addressed in the decision tree).

- The dependent variable is normally distributed (addressed in the decision tree).

Since I have identified that I want to do a one-sample *t*-test and as I am hypothesizing about a general difference (instead of hypothesizing greater or less education), my null and alternate hypothesis would be stated as such:

- H_o: $\mu = 13.4$

- H_1: $\mu \neq 13.4$

Reaching the statistical decision is the hard part. Now what's left is to let the computer do the work and then to interpret the resulting output (Appendices A and B). The SPSS output would be:

One-Sample Statistics

	N	Mean	Std. Deviation	Std. Error Mean
Highest year of school completed	1,585	13.77	2.972	.075

One-Sample Test

	Test Value = 13.4					
					95% Confidence Interval of the Difference	
	t	df	Sig. (2-tailed)	Mean Difference	Lower	Upper
Highest year of school completed	4.952	1,584	.000	.370	.22	.52

The first piece of information I am interested in is the "Sig (2-tailed)" value. That tells me the error level, or p-value, for a two-tailed test. Since the alternate hypothesis is "does not equal," I have a two-tailed test and therefore interpret this number as it is. Remember, in order to reject the null, most situations require us to be at least 95% confident, or to accept a maximum level of 5% error, which is a "Sig. (2-tailed)" value of $p<.05$. My observed value is $p=.000$, which is much less than .05 and, therefore, my decision is that I can reject the null. A general template to present the findings for one-sample t-tests is:

General: A one-sample t-test was conducted to determine if a statistically significant difference existed between [insert variable] from a sample of [insert study population] and the [insert comparison population]. The sample of [variable] reported $M=$_____ (SD=____) is/is not significantly different from the comparison population average of $M=$_____ (t (degrees of freedom)= [_____], $p=$_____).

Our example: A one-sample t-test was conducted to determine if a statistically significant difference existed between the average number of years of education of a sample of women in the GSS and the national average. The GSS sample of women reported an average of $M=13.77$ years of education (SD=2.97), which is significantly different from the national average for women of $M= 13.4$ ($t(1584) = 4.95, p=.00$).

A couple of notes about this output. First, you may have noticed that the formula (on the left side of the equal sign) in the decision tree and the SPSS output are based on the t-distribution. If this was a traditional statistics class where I focused on the hand calculations of formulas, my first hypothesis test discussion would start with the formula for large samples ($N>50$) because that formula involves the **Z-distribution**, which builds on the logic we used for Z-scores and confidence intervals. The Z-distribution is appropriate when using a continuous dependent variable from a random sample that is sufficiently large. However, many computer programs only use the *t*-distribution for this type of analysis because the *t*-distribution addresses *both* large and small samples by accounting for **degrees of freedom**, which are the number of values (or answer choices) that can vary before any constraints are violated.

I know…that doesn't sound like it makes much sense, but it is an important concept so let's briefly take a look at it more closely. Let's pretend I want to pick three numbers that have a mean of 15. If I pick 15 and 20, then the third number I pick has to be 10 in order to get the mean of 15. If I pick 12 and 17, then the next number I have to pick is 16 in order to still get a mean of 15. So in both examples, there are only two scores that are *free to vary* (that you can pick) before you *have* to have a specific third number to average out to your desired mean. Therefore, in both examples, there are two degrees of freedom. Degrees of freedom is a piece of information necessary for determining the critical value in a *t*-distribution and is calculated by $N–1$. As we saw in the example, if I select three observations, two (3–1) are free to vary before the numbers selected become fixed (a specific number to reach the desired statistic). Different statistical tests use different distributions, like the F distribution or the X^2 distribution, that also involve a calculation, degrees of freedom, but by different formulas. Since we are not doing any hand calculations for hypothesis tests, the various formulas for degrees of freedom that correspond to different distributions are less relevant to us. For our current purposes, I just need to know that once the degrees of freedom get sufficiently large, the *t*-distribution becomes indistinguishable from the Z-distribution.

But what would I do if I move through the decision tree (Figure 12.2) and my answer to "Is the dependent variable normally distributed?" is "no"? Many undergraduate statistics texts do

istockphoto.com/Dmytro Aksonov

PHOTO 12.4 The number of hours of television watched per week by the GSS sample is not normally distributed. We need different statistical tests to compare the US population, as indicated by the GSS sample, to another population, such as the number of hours of television viewing by people who live in England or Japan.

not address what to do in this instance because the formulas and calculations can be daunting. However, as we are not making these calculations by hand, we are less restricted by large or complex formula calculations and can, therefore, address some additional statistics that are useful in the real world. Like I discussed in Chapter 11, when I have information that is not normally distributed and cannot, therefore, use the mean accurately, I use the median. A similar logic applies here. When the dependent variable is *not* normally distributed, researchers can use the One-Sample Wilcoxon Signed-Rank test that compares the median of the sample to the median of the population, rather than the two means.

For example, all tests of normality (statistical and graphs) suggest that, contrary to what the large sample size of the GSS would suggest, the real family income of respondents in the 2016 wave of the GSS (REALINC) is *not* normally distributed (data not shown). But what if we wanted to compare the family income of GSS respondents to the family income of US citizens to see if they are statistically different? Since the GSS REALINC variable is not normally distributed, I would need to compare the medians. According to the US Bureau of the Census, the median family income in 2016 was $57,617 (Guzman, 2017). Therefore, following Figure 12.2:

1. **What am I doing?** Hypothesis test
   I am comparing population from which my sample was drawn (the GSS) to a known population value (the median income of US families).

2. **Number of samples (based on the independent variable)?** 1

3. **Is my dependent variable continuous?** Yes, based on the GSS values.

4. **Is it normally distributed?** No

5. **Decision:** One-Sample Wilcoxon Signed-Rank Test (the details of calculating the formula are beyond a basic undergraduate stats class—so let's be grateful for computer programs!)

$$Z = (\Sigma SR_i) / \sqrt{\Sigma S R_i^2}$$

where SR_i stands for the "signed-rank of observation i."

The data assumptions for the One-Sample Wilcoxon Signed-Rank Test are:

- I have a random sample (the GSS is).

- The variable is at least ordinal (covered in my decision tree).

- The variable is interval/ratio; it is not normally distributed (covered in my decision tree).

My null and research hypotheses would be:

H_0: MD = 57,617

H_1: MD ≠ 57,617

I will get the following output in SPSS:

Hypothesis Test Summary

	Null Hypothesis	Test	Sig.	Decision
1	The median of Family income in constant $ equals 57,617.	One-Sample Wilcoxon Signed-Rank Test	.000	Reject the null hypothesis.

Asymptotic significances are displayed. The significance level is .05.

The main focus of the interpretation is the same for this test as it is for the one-sample t-test… and all the other tests, while we are at it. My goal is to see if the significance value is less than .05. Here I see that it is (p=.000), so I would reject the null and interpret the alternate hypothesis by concluding that the family income of the GSS population is significantly different from that of the US population. I could write this as:

General: A Wilcoxon signed-rank test showed that <u>dependent variable </u> for <u>population </u> did/did not significantly differ compared to the <u>population</u>

= ___ , p= _____).

Our example: A Wilcoxon signed-rank test showed that <u>family income</u> for <u>the GSS population </u> did significantly differ compared to the <u>US population</u>

= <u>–32.20, p=.000)</u>.

However, what if my data breaks off the decision tree earlier? What if I wanted to compare the proportion of women in the GSS who had at least a 4-year college degree to the percent of women in the United States with at least a 4-year college degree? In 2016, 33.7% of women in the US population had at least a college degree (US Department of Education, 2018). Given that I saw a significant difference in the median income between the GSS study population and the national average, let's argue that the women in the GSS sample are less likely to have a college degree than the general population.

Remember, your dependent variable determines your level of measurement, so it is important to not fall into the temptation of thinking that your dependent variable here would be "percent with at least a four-year college degree." The *real* dependent variable is whether someone has a college degree or not; as defined, this is a dichotomous yes/no variable. The GSS does not have a variable for college degree per se, but it does have one for highest degree achieved (DEGREE), so for the purpose of our illustration here, I recode DEGREE to "Colldeg," where the values of "bachelors" and "graduate" are combined into "yes" to having a college degree and all other levels were coded as "no." Therefore, the decision tree path would look like this:

1. **What am I doing?** Hypothesis test
   I am comparing population from which my sample was drawn to a known population value

2. **Number of samples (based on the independent variable)?** 1

3. **Is my dependent variable continuous?** No. It is a binomial of yes/no

4. **Decision:** One sample proportion test

$$Z = (P_s - P_u) / \sqrt{\frac{P_u(1 - P_u)}{N}}$$

The data assumptions are:

- I have a random sample (the GSS is).

- I am comparing one sample to a known population value (covered in the decision tree).

- My dependent variable is categorical (covered in the decision tree).

As I am dealing with a proportion here, my null and alternate hypotheses would be:

H$_o$: $P\mu$ =.34 (with rounding)

H$_1$: $P\mu$ <.34

Because the dependent variable is not continuous, I need to run what is called a nonparametric test because these statistical tests do not assume that the data have a normal distribution. The binomial test in SPSS is not very intuitive and there are easy, free calculators that run this statistic available online. Therefore, as our focus is to "get the job done," some online calculators that you can use for this test are:

- Medcalc: https://www.medcalc.org/calc/test_one_proportion.php

- Mathcracker: https://mathcracker.com/z-test-for-one-proportion.php

One of the strengths of these calculators is that your dependent variable does not need to be dichotomous. You can test for one value of any number of nominal or ordinal values, provided you have a comparison population parameter for it. However, because two answer choices in the GSS imply at least a 4-year college degree (the college degree value *and* the graduate degree), I will continue working with the recoded variable of having a college degree or not. Running a frequency in SPSS shows that 479 people out of 1,586 have at least a college degree for a proportion of .30 (data not shown). If I input this information into one of the online calculators, I see that I get an obtained Z-value of 3.63 and a probability of error of .0008.

LEARNING CHECK 12.3: ONE-SAMPLE HYPOTHESIS TESTS

1. Nationally, senior citizens report phone or text contact with their adult children about 3.4 times a month. A sample of 120 Asian/Pacific Islander elderly in the US report an average of 4.1 (s=1.22) phone calls or texts with their adult children a month. Are Asian/Pacific Islander elderly in significantly more frequent contact with their adult children than the national population? What statistical test would you use, and do you have a one- or two-tailed test?

2. A random sample of 460 employers was selected to participate in a study about their attitudes toward ex-offenders. When asked whether they would hire a person who has been to prison, 239 of the respondents said that they would. Nationally, 43% of employers say they would hire some- one who is an ex-offender. Is this sample significantly different than the general population? What statistical test would you use, and do you have a one-or two-tailed test?

3. A researcher is interested in examining the number of hours welfare mothers spend reading to their children who are age 5 or under. She collects a random sample of 80 welfare mothers, found that the hours they spend reading to their children in this age group is not normally distributed, and the median value is 3.8 hr a week. If the median amount of time the national population spends reading to their children under age 5 is 5.5 hours a week, is this difference statistically different?

Answers to be found at the end of the chapter.

When reporting these test results, researchers generally report some descriptive statistics as well. In this case, a frequency will do. Regarding the significance test, I could write something like:

General: A one-sample proportion hypothesis test indicates that

the proportion of [insert population][insert value of interest] of ___ was/ was not

[insert hypothesis direction] than the expected proportion of [insert Pu

value] ($Z=$_____, $p=.$____).

Interpretation: A one-sample proportion hypothesis test indicates that the

proportion of <u>women with at least a college degree</u> of .30 *was lower than the*

expected proportion of .34, (Z=3.63, p =.000).

Errors in Hypothesis Testing

Remember, however, even if researchers conclude that they can reject the null, that does not mean that they have "proven" anything. I will never truly know whether my hypotheses are true or not; I have just established a value (e.g., 95%) that I am comfortable with suggesting it is/is not true. Therefore, even with a 95% confidence level, I recognize that there is a 5% chance I made the wrong decision. In fact, there are two common errors that can occur in hypothesis testing. Box 12.3 illustrates the four possible relationships between our statistical conclusions and what is really happening in the population.

BOX 12.3
TYPE I AND TYPE II ERRORS

	Statistical Decision	
In the Population H_0 is really	**Reject H_0**	**Fail to Reject H_0**
True (should be accepted)	Type I error	Correct decision
False (should not be accepted)	Correct decision	Type II error

As you see, if I fail to reject the null based on my statistic and there really is no difference in the study population (meaning the null is true in the full population), then I have made no errors. Everything aligns. Similarly, if I reject the null and claim there is likely to be a difference based on the study and the difference is true in the population, then I also made the correct decision. However, what if I reject the null based on the statistical tests and tentatively conclude that there is a difference, but in reality, there is not—in other words, the null is actually true in the study population? Remember, since I am never 100% confident, there is a chance (e.g., a 5% chance if I want to be 95% confident) that this can happen. Researchers call this type of error—when we reject the null that, in fact, should *not* have been rejected—a Type I error. If the opposite occurs—we do not reject the null based on our study findings but in reality, there is a difference, so we *should have* rejected the null—when we call this a Type II error.

Since researchers don't know the true population parameter, they never *really* know if they made a Type I or Type II errors. Researchers can reduce the risk of a Type I error by lowering our alpha level because, as you saw earlier, smaller alpha levels correspond to larger intervals (in other words a wider null region) under the normal curve, which decreases our chance of producing a finding outside of the null region. However, you might already have recognized that doing so actually increases our chance of a Type II error. In other words, the two errors are inversely related—reducing the risk of one increases the risk of the other. Therefore, no matter what, once again, researchers have to accept *some* level of error, and *no* research, whether it is in the social or traditional sciences, can ever prove anything. But being 95% confident of something is still better than being 50% sure or not having *any* idea of how confident you can claim findings are!

Key Terms

Alpha level

Degrees of freedom

Inferential statistics

One-tailed test

Point estimate

p-value

Tails of a distribution

t-distribution

Two-tailed test

Z- distribution

Answers to Learning Check Questions

Learning Check 12.1: Confidence Interval Decisions

1. Working through the decision tree: estimating a population parameter → the dependent variable is interval/ratio → Decision ci = $\bar{X} \pm Z(s/\sqrt{N-1})$

2. A sample of 450 people, because larger samples produce smaller intervals at the same confidence level.

3. A 96% sample, because it is 96% of the curve.

Learning Check 12.2: Logic of Hypothesis Testing

1. 1%

2. Beyond it, because hypotheses look for differences (reject the null of *no* difference), and within the bracketed area is the null region.

3. Statistically, we test the null because our research goal is always to *reject* the null by showing our observed statistic is outside of the established null region.

4. One-tailed, because I am arguing that all of the error is in the positive (greater) end of the normal curve.

Learning Check 12.3: One-Sample Hypothesis Tests

1. Working through the decision tree: hypothesis test → one-sample → dependent variable is interval/ratio → it is normally distributed (I know this because means and standard deviations are presented) → Decision: one-sample t-test. The test is one-tailed because it asks for "*more* frequent contact."

2. Working through the decision tree: hypothesis test → one-sample → dependent variable is not interval/ratio → I do not have eight or more answer choices → Decision: one-sample proportion test. This test is two-tailed because it asks for "significantly *different*" and does not take a stance regarding greater or less than (a direction).

3. Working through the decision tree: hypothesis test → one-sample → dependent variable is interval/ratio → it is not normally distributed → Decision: one-sample proportion test Wilcoxon Signed-Rank Test.

End-of-Chapter Problems

For questions 1–7, decide which statistical test should be used for each scenario. Pay attention to the wording of the question. Information such as "average" implies that the mean was calculated as part of the problem, and the mean as a statistic gives information, for example, on the nature of the distribution.

1. A researcher randomly samples 300 senior citizens at a large retirement community about whether they have private health insurance (yes/no). The researchers found that 72% have private health insurance. At the 95% confidence level, what percent of seniors nationwide have some private health insurance?

2. Nationally, women spend an average of 9.2 hr a week on housework. A sample of 115 women in upper management positions reports spending an average of 8.8 hr a week on housework. Do women in upper management positions spend significantly less time on housework? (Note: The use of "average" implies a mean; that statistical choice, in turn, implies some information about the distribution that you learned about in Chapter 12.)

3. A sample of 80 incarcerated individuals attended a re-entry program while in prison. Upon release, 59% were rearrested within 1 year of their release. Is the recidivism rate for these prisoners statistically lower than the national average of 68% who return to prison within a year?

4. A random sample of 400 students at a large university found that the average number of times students go home during the semester is 3.2 ($s=.9$). What is the average number of times college students nationally go home during a semester?

5. In a random sample of 30 women convicted of child abuse, 63%, when asked whether they finished high school (yes/no), replied that they did not. What proportion of women convicted of child abuse in the population did not complete high school?

6. A random sample of 56 sociology/criminal justice freshmen at Grades R Us University had an average math SAT score of 598 ($s=42$). Is this significantly different than the math SAT score of their graduation cohort, which was 527?

7. A random sample of 50 movies released in a 5-year spans show an average of 4.8 instances of intimacy ($s=1.11$). What is the average number of intimate encounters one can expect to see in a movie?

8. Using the GSS data and any computer/web resources available, test whether the population from the GSS works a significantly different number of hours a week (HRS2) than the standard 40 hr.

9. Using the GSS data and any computer/web resources available, estimate what percent of the population has ever read a horoscope or personal astrology report? (ASTROLGY)

10. If people generally consider two children to be the ideal number of children, test, using the GSS data and any computer/web resources available, whether the GSS sample wants significantly more children, on average, than the general population (CHLDIDEL).

11. About a third (32%) of Canadians would either "strongly agree" or "agree" that they would change jobs if they could. Using the GSS data and any computer/web resources available, test whether Americans are more likely to "strongly agree" or "agree" that they would change their jobs if possible (CHNGWRK).

12. Using the GSS data and any computer/web resources available, estimate the average number of children American families have (CHILDS).

13. Using the GSS data and any computer/web resources available, estimate at the 99% confidence level, what proportion of the population use Facebook (FACEBOOK).

14. The Sane Sneaker Co. claims that it has one of the most worker-friendly workplaces in the nation. A survey done by an independent research firm of all employees at the company shows that 43% are "very satisfied" with their work experience. Using the GSS data and any computer/web resources available, see if worker satisfaction at this company is significantly different than satisfaction among the GSS sample (SATJOB).

HYPOTHESIS TESTING WITH TWO OR MORE SAMPLES

LEARNING GOALS

- Distinguish between independent and dependent samples
- Identify when to use two-sample hypothesis tests and the different types
- Distinguish between two-sample tests and tests addressing three or more samples
- Interpret computer output for statistical tests and express the findings in APA format

Sometimes researchers do not compare a sample to a known population value like we did in Chapter 12. Sometimes researchers want to compare two, three, or even four different groups. For example, Maquire, Lowrey, and Johnson (2017) studied whether the nature of police–citizen interaction affects citizens' views of the police. They randomly assigned individuals to watch one of three videos showing different simulated police–citizen interactions during a routine traffic stop. In one set of videos, the officer communicates with the driver in a procedurally just manner; in the second, the officer communicates in a procedurally unjust manner; and in the third, the interaction is in a neutral manner. In this study, Maquire and colleagues did not compare their samples to a known population value; they were comparing three different groups based on different police–citizen interaction experiences. Their findings showed that those who had a positive interaction (procedurally just) with the police were more willing to co-operate with the police and had exhibited greater trust in the police than did those who experienced the other two simulations.

Furthermore, studies of more than one group usually do not mean that the researchers selected these groups separately. Most of the time, like Maquire and colleagues, researchers randomly sample one group of individuals and then randomly assigned those people selected to one of the experimental conditions.

PHOTO 13.1 Does how police interact with the public affect the public's view of them?

In Maquire and colleagues' (2017) study just mentioned, their independent variable was the type of police response witnessed and it had three different values (the three experimental conditions). As a result, this would be a three–sample statistical test—comparing the dependent variable (view of police) based on membership to one of three groups (the different police–citizen encounters). I could also compare multiple groups using other methods of observation. For example, if I conducted a survey and asked someone their main racial identity, I might have a question such as:

What is the primary race for which you identify?

a. White, non-Hispanic

b. African American

c. Latino, non-White

d. Asian Pacific Islander

e. Other (Please specify:_____)

If I want to compare White, non-Hispanics (now just called whites) to African Americans, then I would just look at the responses for people who select "a" or who select "b," so this would be considered a two-sample test. I did not go out and actually *select* two different samples, although I most certainly could have (it just usually isn't as efficient). By a similar argument, if I wanted to compare African Americans, Latinos, and Asian Pacific Islanders,

I would be comparing *three* samples and the statistics in the next section would apply instead. Researchers know how many samples they are comparing based on the number of values of the independent variable they are comparing. If my hypothesis is that white, non-Hispanics have more years of education, on average, than African Americans, my independent variable is race and I am comparing two values of it (white and African American). If, however, my hypothesis is something like Asian/Pacific Islanders have more years of education than whites and African Americans, my independent variable is still race, but now I am comparing three groups (Asian/Pacific Islander, white, and African American).

A lot of statistical options exist for testing two or more samples. In this chapter, I build on Chapter 12 by focusing on hypothesis testing for two or more samples and I will continue to use the decision tree to make our statistical choices. Continuing with the decision tree may seem repetitive, but it is designed to be. The best way to learn statistics is to learn the *thought* process and the critical thinking skills and to make them part of your mental muscle memory. The more frequently you see the types of questions researchers ask themselves when making statistical decisions, the less scary statistics will eventually become.

One last point is that I will also continue to organize our material along the research situation, as opposed to the statistical test, which is why—again—I am going to cover some statistics that are not common in many undergraduate textbooks. Remember, this is possible because of our focus on computer calculations rather than hand ones. As such, I do not need to limit our discussions to formulas that are easier for students to compute by themselves.

WHAT AM I DOING? HYPOTHESIS TESTING— TWO SAMPLES

Independent vs. Dependent Samples

The decision tree for two sample tests appears in Figure 13.1. As you see, there are some new considerations. The first new consideration occurs right after we decide we are comparing two samples, where we need to determine whether or not those samples are independent. **Independent samples** are ones in which being in one group means that you are not in (are *independent of*) the second group. So if you are a freshman in college, for example, that means you also cannot be a senior in college; these two groups are independent. **Dependent samples**, on the contrary, are samples in which whether you are in one group *depends* on being in the other group. This might make a bit more sense using the following examples. Two of the most common ways in which samples are dependent are when researchers do an experiment where participants are measured in a pretest and posttest (Chapter 6). After the experimental treatment, a researcher expects that the experimental group would be fundamentally different from before, so essentially, a *different* group (hence this is considered a two-sample test) even though the subjects are actually the same physical people. So whether a subject takes the posttest *depends* on if that person took the pretest. Another common instance when this occurs is when researchers use experimental matching. A similar logic applies. When researchers match participants, they pair subjects on like characteristics; therefore, whether you are in the study

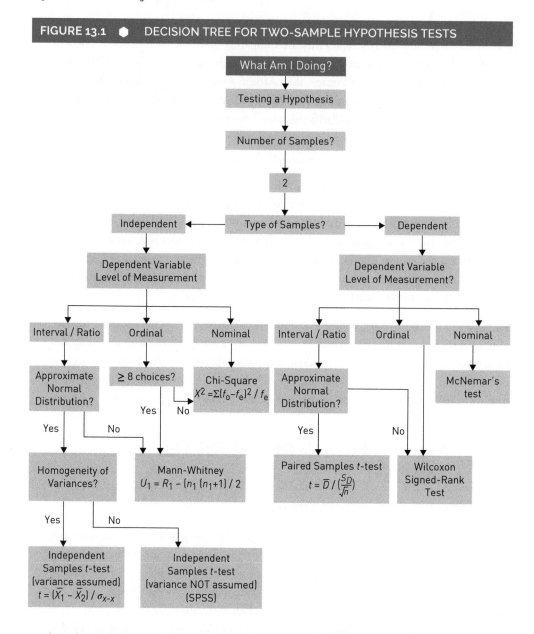

FIGURE 13.1 ● DECISION TREE FOR TWO-SAMPLE HYPOTHESIS TESTS

depends on whether you share the necessary characteristics with another person. Studies on programs or practices in the real world may involve experimentation with matching and/or pre- and posttests, including how to handle these types of samples is a useful statistical tool and, therefore, will be included in our discussion. Let's cover independent samples first.

Two Independent Samples

If researchers have independent samples, following our decision tree in Figure 13.1, we see we next have to determine whether the scores of the dependent variable have **homogeneity of variance**, which is similar variances across the two samples. One way of identifying whether variances are equal is to run a Levene's test for homogeneity in variances. In this test, the null hypothesis is that the groups in the sample have equal variances, which is what researchers want. Therefore, to assume that this is met, researchers actually want a *p*-value that is greater than .05 because that means they *cannot* reject the null. Remember, the null always is that our comparison groups are the same, that there is no difference between them; therefore, this makes sense if we want our variance between the variables to be the same (not different) too. In other words, when the *p*-value is greater than .05 for the Levene's test, the null of equal variances is *true* so the assumption is fulfilled. I will present the SPSS output for this when the test becomes relevant in the decision tree.

 LEARNING CHECK 13.1: GENERAL TWO-SAMPLE CONSIDERATIONS

1. Would the following situation be an independent or dependent two-sample test? Why?

   A researcher wants to see whether a healthy eating program decreases the number of unhealthy snack choices college students make. To study this, she collects a random sample of 30 college students, identifies healthy and unhealthy snack choices, and asks them how many unhealthy snack choices they have made in the past week. These students then experience her program and 2 weeks after its conclusion, she asks them to identify the number of unhealthy snack choices they made in the previous week.

2. Would the following situation be an independent or dependent two-sample test? Why?

   A researcher wants to see whether biology majors attend more campus parties in a semester than sociology majors. She administers a survey to 400 college students and, based on their response to a question identifying their major, she selects biology and sociology majors to compare.

3. A researcher wants to see whether people who have pets score higher on a normally distributed scale about happiness compared to people who do not have pets. As part of his decision information, he runs a Levene's test and obtains a sig value of *p* = .073. (a) Is this an independent or dependent samples test and (b) Does he have equal variances between the groups?

   Answers to be found at the end of the chapter.

We have already discussed all the other considerations in the decision tree, so let's work through the tree with some examples. If I want to examine whether Hispanics (RACECEN1) have more children (CHILDS) on average than African Americans, I can use the GSS data to test this. A respondent's race is the independent variable, and the number of children they have is the dependent variable; therefore, I would proceed through the decision tree as such:

1. **What am I doing?** Comparing—therefore a hypothesis test

2. **Number of samples (based on the independent variable)?** Two
   Hispanics and African Americans

3. **Independent samples?** Yes
   This is not a matched sample or pre-/posttest situation

4. **Dependent variable level of measurement?** Interval/ratio

5. **Approximate normal distribution?** Yes, based on a histogram, Q–Q plot, and skewness and kurtosis (Discussed in Chapter 11, data not shown).

6. **Decision?** Independent sample t-test—but which output is appropriate depends on whether there are equal variances across the populations.

$$t = (\overline{X}_1 - \overline{X}_2) / \sigma_{x-x}$$

$$\sigma_{x-x} = \sqrt{\left(s_1^2 / N_1 - 1 \right) + \left(s_2^2 / N_2 - 1 \right)}$$

The two-sample t-test compares the averages of the two means relative to the variance of the two means. If the between-group difference is sufficiently large, the obtained t-statistic will be greater than the critical value of t that designates the null region. In order to do the t-test, some assumptions need to be met, but many of them are incorporated into our decision tree. These data assumptions are:

- I have a random sample (the GSS is).

- I have independent observations (addressed in the decision tree).

- The dependent variable is normally distributed (addressed in the decision tree).

- I have homogeneity of variances, which means that the variances in our two samples need to be approximately equal (which we determine based on our output—see the last comment in our logic path of the decision tree).

PHOTO 13.2 With some statistical tests, we can compare many groups simultaneously, such as people of different racial identities.

Unlike one-sample tests, where both the null and alternate hypotheses involve only one unknown population parameter, with two-sample tests, *neither* population parameter is known. Therefore, researchers have to represent both groups by the symbol "μ" rather than any real numbers. Because in my example I am taking a stand that one group, Hispanics, has more children and not simply a different number, my alternate hypothesis would entail a one-tailed test. I would, therefore, show the null and research hypotheses as such:

$H_o: \mu_H = \mu_{AA}$

$H_1: \mu_H > \mu_{AA}$

The subscripts of "H" and "AA" are not necessary, but they help us keep track of who is who.

SPSS will produce the following output (with the computer steps in Appendix A and all R programming information and output in Appendix B):

Group Statistics

	What Is R's race 1st mention	N	Mean	Std. Deviation	Std. Error Mean
Number of children	BLACK OR AFRICAN AMERICAN	484	2.04	1.798	.082
	HISPANIC	102	2.22	1.738	.172

Independent Samples Test

		Levene's Test for Equality of Variances		t-test for Equality of Means					95% Confidence Interval of the Difference	
		F	Sig.	t	df	Sig. (2-tailed)	Mean Difference	Std. Error Difference	Lower	Upper
Number of children	Equal variances assumed	.061	.805	-.895	584	.371	-.174	.195	-.557	.208
	Equal variances not assumed			-.915	150.063	.362	-.174	.191	-.551	.202

Before I fully interpret what I see, I need to address that last part of the decision tree, whether I can assume equal variances or not. The Levene's Test for Equality of Variances is automatically calculated by SPSS for the independent sample t-test and the arrow in the above output directs you to that information. All I have to look at is the "Sig." value that is circled above. As I explained earlier in this chapter, I want this value to be greater than .05 and this is $p = .805$, so I can assume equal variances. Therefore, to see if the variables are related, I would look at the top row of data labeled "Equal variances are assumed," that is blocked off by the rectangle. Based on this information, I see that the t-test has a $p = .371$, which is not less than .05 but is also the value for a two-tailed test, which is the default in SPSS. For a one-tailed test, which is suggested by the alternate hypothesis, as I discussed in Chapter 12, I take the significance value and divide it in half, which would give me $p = .186$ (with rounding). This value is still greater than .05, so the decision here would be to not reject the null. A possible general template to present our results is:

General: An independent sample t-test was done to compare [DV] between

[group 1] and [group 2]. There was/was not a significant (not a significant) difference

in the scores for IV level 1 ($M =$ ___, $SD =$ ___) and IV level 2 ($M =$ ___, $SD =$ ___)

conditions; $t(\text{df}) =$ _____, $p =$ _____.

Groups 1 and 2 refer to the two groups I am comparing; M and "SD," as I covered before, stand for mean and standard deviation, respectively, and "df" stands for degrees of freedom, which, as you learned in Chapter 12, refers to the number of observations that are free to vary in a calculation. Therefore, the presentation of results could read something like this:

Our example: An independent sample t-test was done to compare the <u>number of children</u> between <u>African Americans</u> and <u>Hispanics.</u> There was not a significant difference in the average number of children for African Americans (M = <u>2.04</u>, SD = <u>1.80</u>) and <u>Hispanics</u> (M = <u>2.22</u>, SD = <u>1.74</u>); $t($<u>584</u>$)$ = <u>–.90</u>, p = <u>.186</u>.

There are a couple of points to make about this interpretation. First, you will notice that the p-value I presented is *not* p = .371. That is because I have a one-tailed test, and as I said earlier in this chapter, for one-tailed tests we take the reported "Sig," or "p-value," and divide it in half. Therefore, .186 is half of .371. Second, you will notice that the mean for African Americans and the t-obtained value I present here are slightly different from the ones that appear in the SPSS printout. That is because I am reporting two decimal places to the right, which is common but not necessarily universal. As such, I look to the third decimal place in order to see how to round to the second; and, in these instances, I had to round up.

You may be wondering what I would have done if the assumption of equal variances was not fulfilled. In other words, what would I have done if the SPSS output showed that the p-value of the Levene's test *was* less than .05? If that is the case, I simply would have looked at the bottom row of output in the table above where it says "Equal variances *not* assumed" [italics added]. The formula that calculates this bottom row of data is altered from the independent sample's t-test, but the nature of the alterations is beyond our focus of "getting the job done," so I won't delve into that further, especially because the resulting interpretation is the same. I still look at the "Sig." value, just for a different row of information.

Let's take a slightly different problem. According to a Gallup poll, confidence in print and news media went down in 2018 (Saad, 2018). Furthermore, according to the Pew Research Center, about two-thirds of Americans now get their news from social media platforms (Pew Research Center, 2017). Perhaps then, those who are less likely to report faith in the printed press are more likely to spend time surfing the web as an alternative news source. I can use the GSS data to test whether those who do or do not trust the press (CONPRESS) spend different amounts of time on the Internet (WWWHR). To decide what test to run, use the decision tree in Figure 13.1:

1. **What am I doing?:** Hypothesis testing
   Comparing the use of the Internet compared to the view of printed press

2. **Number of samples (based on the independent variable):** Two
   Those who have "a great deal" or "hardly any" confidence in the press

BOX 13.1

INDEPENDENT SAMPLE'S *t*-TEST EXAMPLE IN RESEARCH

How does cognitive and affective empathy or moral disengagement influence young people's bullying roles and does this vary by gender? In order to examine these questions, Haddock and Jimerson (2017) studied 702 6th–8th graders who were recruited as part of a schoolwide bullying prevention program. Among their measures was the How I Feel in Different Situations (HIFDS) questionnaire, which measured cognitive and affecting empathy, and Bandura's Mechanisms of Moral Disengagement Scale (MDS), which measured moral disengagement. Given the nature of the data, different statistical tests were necessary to address the different research questions; but for our example here, we will focus on the independent sample *t*-test that Haddock and Jimerson used to compare these three concepts across male and female adolescents. Here is a subset of their findings:

> An independent sample's *t*-test was performed to assess whether mean moral disengagement, cognitive empathy, and affective empathy scores differed significantly between males and females. The assumption of homogeneity of variance was assessed by the Levene test for each outcome variable and indicated a significant violation of the equal variance assumption for moral disengagement and no significant violation of the equal variance assumption for the empathy variables. Consequently, equal variances were not assumed for moral disengagement when examining differences in mean scores between males and females. The mean moral disengagement score differed significantly between males (M = 48.27, SD = 9.57) and

females (M = 45.19, SD = 8.42), $t(647.143)$ = 4.49, $p < .001$, two-tailed....

The mean cognitive empathy score differed significantly between males (M= 12.7, SD = 3.63) and females (M= 14.18, SD = 3.38), $t(701)$ = -1.49, $p < .001$, two-tailed.

The mean affective empathy score differed significantly between males (M= 12.46, SD= 3.99) and females (M= 16.91, SD= 4.04), $t(701)$ = -4.44, $p < .001$, two-tailed. (Haddock & Jimerson, 2017, p. 7)

Notice a couple of points in the excerpt that relate to our chapter discussion:

- The researchers used the Levene test for the assumption of equal variances and note that it was not fulfilled for moral disengagement but was fulfilled for the empathy variables.

- They note that the mean difference in moral disengagement was statistically significant for gender at the $p<.001$ level and that the score was higher for men (M = 48.27) than women (M = 45.19).

Now, see if you can answer the following questions:

1. Was there a statistically significant difference in the mean cognitive empathy score based on gender? If so, what was the *t*-obtained and the significance value?

2. Was there a statistically significant difference in the mean affective empathy score based on gender? If so, who had the higher score?

Source: Haddock, A. D., & Jimerson, S. R. (2017).

Answers:

1. Yes. The *t*-obtained value was –1.49 and the significance value was $p < .001$ (or a 99.9% confidence level).

2. Yes. Females had the higher score (M = 16.91) relative to males (M = 12.46).

3. **Type of sample:** Independent
    Not a pre/posttest situation or a matched sample

4. **Dependent variable level of measurement?** Interval/ratio

Tests for the normality of distribution of the weekly hours on the internet described in Chapter 11 show that this variable, in fact, is *not* normally distributed (SPSS output not shown). Therefore, to continue the decision tree:

5. **Approximate normal distribution?** No
    A histogram (not shown) suggests a non-normal distribution. Skewness and kurtosis are both over 2

6. **Decision:** Mann–Whitney U

$$U_1 = R_1 - (n_1 \, (n_1+1)) \, / \, 2$$

where "R_1" is the sum of ranks in the first of the two samples and n is the number of elements in that sample. The data assumptions of the Mann–Whitney U test are:

- I have a random sample.

- The dependent variable is ordinal or continuous (addressed in the decision tree by noting an interval/ratio level of measurement).

- The dependent variable is not normally distributed (addressed in the decision tree).

- The independent variable is categorical where there are two values being compared (addressed in the decision tree).

- The two values of the independent variables are independent of each other (addressed in the decision tree).

The Mann–Whitney U test, like the Wilcoxon Signed-Rank Test, covered in Chapter 12, is a nonparametric test that does not require the data to be normally distributed; therefore, the null and research hypothesis for this test are:

H_0: The medians of the two populations are equal

H_1: The medians of the two groups are not equal

The SPSS output for the Mann–Whitney U output and the additional descriptive statistics (in a much-edited form) appear below.

As before, I want to look at the "Asymp. Sig." and since I have a two-tailed hypothesis test, I leave the significance value as it is. Because the value shows $p = .004$, I can reject the null. This output also gives me useful information looking at the ranks because the group with the highest mean rank has the highest value on the dependent variable. Therefore, the output

Ranks

	Confidence in press	N	Mean Rank	Sum of Ranks
Www hours per week	A GREAT DEAL	60	197.27	11,836.00
	HARDLY ANY	432	253.34	109,442.00
	Total	492		

Test Statistics^a

	Www hours per week
Mann-Whitney U	10,006.000
Wilcoxon W	11,836.000
Z	-2.870
Asymp. Sig. (2-tailed)	.004

a. Grouping Variable: Confidence in press

Descriptives

	Confidence in press		Statistic
Www hours per week	A GREAT DEAL	Median	4.50
	ONLY SOME	Median	8.00
	HARDLY ANY	Median	8.00

suggests that those who have "hardly any" confidence in the press spend more time on the Internet. If I want to compare the specific median values of the two groups, I have to look at the third output (the "Descriptives") for this information. Consequently, the interpretation would read something like this:

General: A Mann–Whitney U test indicated that there was (was not) a significant

difference in [dependent variable] between IV level 1 (MD = ___) and IV level 2

(MD = ___),

= ___, p = ___.

Our example: A Mann–Whitney U test indicated that there was a significant difference

in the median hours on the Internet between those who have a great deal of confidence

in the press (MD = 4.50) and those who have hardly any (MD = 8), U = 10,006, p = .000.

Frequently, however, the dependent variable is not continuous. If researchers ask opinion questions like "How likely would you be to vote for a female president?," "How serious a problem do you think global warming is?," or "How willing are you to live within three miles of a halfway house for recovering drug addicts?" then the dependent variable is not measured at the interval or ratio level. As such, even with a random sample, the data will not follow the form of the normal curve and, therefore, researchers need to use a nonparametric test once again. Although there is more than one test that might be appropriate in this instance, a very popular one is the chi-square. For example, some researchers have found that video surveillance can reduce the risk of crime and capture accurate documentation of police–citizen interactions (Bakardjiev, 2015; Blitz, 2013; Heintzelman & Bathon, 2017). However, others argue that

PHOTO 13.3 Do you consider video surveillance a violation of civil liberties or a means of civil protection?

video surveillance is a violation of civil liberties and the Fourth Amendment (Freund, 2015). It may seem reasonable that those who distrust the government might also be less likely to feel that the government has a right to keep its citizens under video surveillance. If I compare those who have a "great deal" and "hardly any" confidence in the federal government (CON-FED), because this is my independent variable and I am looking at two values of it, I have a two-sample test. My dependent-variable view of whether the American government has the right to keep people under video surveillance (CCTV) will determine my level of measurement. I see that for this variable there are four answer choices ranging from "definitely should have the right" to "definitely should not have the right," so it is an ordinal variable. Therefore, following the decision tree:

1. **What am I doing?** Hypothesis testing
   Comparing those with "a great deal" and "hardly any" confidence in the federal government

2. **Number of samples (based on the independent variable):** Two

3. **Type of sample:** Independent
   This is not a before/after or matched design

4. **Dependent variable level of measurement?** Ordinal

5. **Eight or more answer choices?** No. There are four

6. **Decision:** Chi-square
   $X^2 = (f_o\text{-}f_e)^2 / f_e$

The chi-square test is a comparison between the frequencies researchers would expect to see in each cell if the variables being compared were unrelated (called **expected frequencies,** f_e)

and the frequencies researchers actually do see (called **observed frequencies**, f_0) in their data. The goal is for this difference between what researchers see and what they expect to see to be large enough to conclude that one variable is affecting the other. The data assumptions for chi-square are:

- I have a random sample.

- The dependent variable is measured at the nominal or ordinal level (addressed in the decision tree).

- The independent variable is of two or more categorical groups (addressed in the decision tree).

- Few cells have an expected count (f_e) less than 5.

That last assumption about the expected frequencies merits some discussion here. The assumption is that the data cells, which is where a value from each of the variables meets together, have an expected frequency greater than five. For large samples, like the GSS, and/or when comparing variables with comparatively few answer choices, this assumption is usually pretty easy to meet. However, in an applied situation where the sample size might be small or a situation where even one of the variables being compared has many values, this assumption might be violated. To some degree, this can be relaxed as long as less than 25% of the cells have an expected frequency of less than five. In SPSS, identifying what percent of cells have an expected count less than five is pretty easy because SPSS automatically tells us this in a footnote at the bottom of the table, as you will see shortly. However, for other programs, such as R, the researcher does need to obtain this information separately to test this assumption.

Because the chi-square is a nonparametric test, as I said earlier, the alternate hypothesis cannot account for any specified direction of effect, even if the alternate hypothesis conceptually has one. The hypotheses for the chi-square are, in fact, always the same regardless of whether our research hypothesis takes a stand on how the groups differ and are:

H_0: the variables are independent

H_1: the variables are dependent

Saying variables are "independent" is the same as saying they have no effect on each other or are not related. Hence that is the null. Saying variables are dependent means that the value of one variable affects the value of the other one, so that is the alternate hypothesis. Furthermore, as the variables used for chi-square are not interval/ratio, their summary information is not a mean so the comparison is usually shown in a bivariate table, which I will cover in Chapter 15.

Before I go any further, I need to make sure that this chi-square test fulfills that last assumption. If I run the chi-square test on my original variables (Appendices A and B), along with a table showing me the observations for each cell (which are not shown here), I get this output:

Civil liberties - video surveillance * Confid. in exec branch of fed govt Crosstabulation

			A GREAT DEAL	ONLY SOME	HARDLY ANY	DK	Total
				Confid. in exec branch of fed govt			
Civil liberties—video surveillance	Definitely should have the right	Count	19	55	50	2	126
		% within Confid. in exec branch of fed govt	41.3%	28.1%	22.3%	22.2%	26.5%
	Probably should have the right	Count	16	76	92	1	185
		% within Confid. in exec branch of fed govt	34.8%	38.8%	41.1%	11.1%	38.9%
	DK	Count	0	2	4	0	6
		% within Confid. in exec branch of fed govt	0.0%	1.0%	1.8%	0.0%	1.3%
	Probably should not have the right	Count	6	39	44	3	92
		% within Confid. in exec branch of fed govt	13.0%	19.9%	19.6%	33.3%	19.4%
	Definitely should not have the right	Count	5	24	34	3	66
		% within Confid. in exec branch of fed govt	10.9%	12.2%	15.2%	33.3%	13.9%
Total		Count	46	196	224	9	475
		% within Confid. in exec branch of fed govt	100.0%	100.0%	100.0%	100.0%	100.0%

Chi-Square Tests

	Value	df	Asymptotic Significance (2-sided)
Pearson Chi-Square	14.338[a]	12	.280
Likelihood Ratio	14.527	12	.268
Linear-by-Linear Association	6.418	1	.011
N of Valid Cases	475		

a. 8 cells (40.0%) have expected count less than 5. The minimum expected count is .11.

You will notice that the percentage of cells that have an expected count less than five is 40% (the circled part), which is too high. There are a couple of options when this occurs. One option is to do a Fisher exact test, but I am already covering many statistics not included in traditional textbooks, and this test is more complicated than our "getting the job done" focus. There is a second, albeit somewhat less elegant, option available that does not require learning another statistic. With this option, I could either combine values or, in the case of an opinion question, delete the neutral category *if* that category has comparatively few responses. Either of these options will alter both my analysis and, therefore, my expected cell counts. For example, if I have a dependent variable that is a five-point Likert scale ranging from "strongly agree" to "strongly disagree," I might combine "strongly agree" and "agree" into one new category of "agree" and do the same for the two negative responses. If I leave the "no opinion" as the middle choice, I have now gone from five answer choices for the analysis to three. Now I would re-run my chi-square analysis and if collapsing answer choices like this does not correct the problem, I can repeat the process until either: (a) the problem is solved or (b) one has a 2 x 2 table (two values for the independent variable and two for the dependent variable). Once the researcher has a 2 x 2 table, one of two things happens. First, the problem may be fixed and the percent of cells with an expected count less than five is now acceptable. However, if the problem *still* is not fixed, SPSS automatically calculates the adjusted chi-square formula called the Yates chi-square continuity correction for all 2x2 tables and the researcher would just look at the adjusted chi-square value and *p*-value for this statistic instead of for the traditional chi-square.

Or, as I mentioned, if a question is an opinion question and the neutral category has few values, I might choose to code the neutral value as missing, thereby omitting it for the analysis. If you look at the original table for my analysis of view of the federal government and view of video surveillance, we see that relative to the other values, there are very few observations in each of the "don't know" (DK) values. There are only nine people who responded "DK" to view of the federal government and six people who responded the same to the video surveillance question. Therefore in this instance it makes sense to omit the neutral "DK" categories and doing so produces this output:

Civil liberties—video surveillance * Confid. in exec branch of fed govt Crosstabulation

			A GREAT DEAL	ONLY SOME	HARDLY ANY	Total
Civil liberties —video surveillance	Definitely should have the right	Count	19	55	50	124
		% within Confid. in exec branch of fed govt	41.3%	28.4%	22.7%	27.0%
	Probably should have the right	Count	16	76	92	184
		% within Confid. in exec branch of fed govt	34.8%	39.2%	41.8%	40.0%
	Probably should not have the right	Count	6	39	44	89
		% within Confid. in exec branch of fed govt	13.0%	20.1%	20.0%	19.3%
	Definitely should not have the right	Count	5	24	34	63
		% within Confid. in exec branch of fed govt	10.9%	12.4%	15.5%	13.7%
Total		Count	46	194	220	460
		% within Confid. in exec branch of fed govt	100.0%	100.0%	100.0%	100.0%

Table header: Confid. in exec branch of fed govt

Chi-Square Tests

	Value	df	Asymptotic Significance (2-sided)
Pearson Chi-Square	7.705[a]	6	.261
Likelihood Ratio	7.432	6	.283
Linear-by-Linear Association	4.796	1	.029
N of Valid Cases	460		

a. 0 cells (0.0%) have expected count less than 5. The minimum expected count is 6.30.

Now zero cells have an expected count of less than five (this is circled above), so here that assumption is met and I can continue with the interpretation. Incidentally, whenever a researcher changes the nature of the original measure, either by collapsing or by omitting values, the researcher needs to let others know that was done and why, and they also need to make sure that any interpretations of the data are consistent with that change.

But getting back to my problem. As I said, the assumption about expected frequencies is now met so I can proceed by looking at the p-value. As with the other hypothesis tests, I can only reject the null if the p-value is less than .05. Here I have $p = .07$, so I cannot reject the null of independence. As such, the interpretation could read something like this:

General: A chi-square test of independence indicates that there is/is not a statistical relationship between <u>IV</u> and <u>DV</u> (X^2 (<u>df</u>, $N =$ ___) = <u>value</u>, $p =$ _____

a. **When we do reject the null, we might add how the groups compare. For example:** <u>IV Group 1</u> (___%) were more/less likely than <u>Group 2</u> (___%) to <u>value of DV</u>

Our example: A chi-square test of independence indicates that there is no relationship between respondent's <u>confidence in the federal government</u> and their <u>view of whether the government has the right to use surveillance</u> on citizens (X^2 (<u>3</u>, $N =$ <u>266</u>) = <u>7.05</u>, $p =$ <u>.07</u>).

As I do not reject the null, I would not need to compare the percent differences in the dependent variable because any variation I see is presumed to be because of chance. By now you should be seeing a pattern. The *real* issue about statistics is deciding what test is appropriate based on the nature of the data, recognizing the corresponding null/research hypotheses, and looking at the resulting p-value to make the decision about whether to reject the null hypothesis. Once researchers obtain their results, the interpretation of them is pretty standard. You tell people what test you ran, examine the "p-value" to make a decision about the null hypothesis, and give a description of the relevant test output to justify your decision. Because of this, I will now start going into less detail about how we decide to reject the null (or not) and focus on making the decisions, running the tests, and writing a possible interpretation.

Incidentally, if you look at the decision tree in Figure 13.1, you will see that if the dependent variable is measured at the ordinal level and has eight or more answer choices, researchers could use the Mann–Whitney U test that I mentioned earlier in this chapter. The decision to use eight or more answer choices for ordinal levels is a bit arbitrary, meaning there is no strong *statistical* reasoning for this cutoff. However, the reasoning has a *methodological* base. First, many Likert scale questions, which are commonly measured on a five- or seven-point scale, are conducive to easy table presentation and, therefore, chi-square analysis. Related to this is the second point, the larger the table (meaning the more data cells of bivariate relationship) a researcher has, the larger the sample size needs to be to make sure that there is sufficient variation across cells and a sufficient number of observations for analysis in each cell. However, this can be hard to accomplish; researchers are more likely to end up combining answer choices as you learned in Chapter 10 in order to obtain individual cells with enough observation for accurate analysis. However, every time researchers collapse categories, they lose some precision in the measurement because they took specific information and made it more broad or general. Tests like the Mann–Whitney U compare the median response; therefore, collapsing, and the resulting loss of precision, would not be necessary. For all of these reasons, when researchers have ordinal levels of measurement that have more than eight possible answer choices, they might be able to use the same nonparametric tests for nonnormally distributed interval/ratio level measurements because their data will also fit many of the assumptions of those tests.

 LEARNING CHECK 13.2: INDEPENDENT SAMPLES

What statistical test would you use in the following situations?

1. A researcher draws a random sample of 100 college students to see whether ever having a boyfriend/girlfriend (measured as yes/no) affects their view on "friends with benefits" (measured as "OK," "not sure if OK or not," and "not OK").

2. A researcher randomly samples 75 individuals who are married and 75 individuals who are single to see whether their yearly income significantly differs. He finds that income is not normally distributed.

3. You work for a social service agency that claims that membership in your after school program reduces delinquency among troubled youth. You randomly sample 30 youth in your program and find that the average number of delinquent acts they got involved in during the past 6 months was 3.67 ($s = 1.02$). You compare them to a random sample of 45 general youths in a local school and find that their mean delinquent acts in the past 6 months were 4.12 ($s = .89$). Are your youths significantly less delinquent?

Answers to be found at the end of the chapter.

Two Dependent Samples

So far all of my discussions have involved two independent samples. I have not addressed what to use if I have dependent samples as we encountered in Chapter 6 with Ventis, Higbee, and Murdock's (2001) study of humor desensitization to spiders. The GSS data are not appropriate for this section because it is not matched data or a pre/posttest design; therefore, to illustrate dependent samples, let's pretend I did a study where I wanted to test whether participating in a summer library program affects the amount of time adolescents spent watching television after 5 pm. To do this, I asked parents of 15 randomly selected adolescents who signed up for this program to track the number of hours their children spent watching TV after 5 pm for 1 week prior to the program start. I then had the children participate in a summer library program every afternoon for 1 week and had parents track the number of hours their children spent watching TV the week after the program. Based on the decision tree, we would do the following:

1. **What am I doing?** Hypothesis testing
   I am comparing hours watching TV after 5 pm before and after participation in an afternoon community program.

2. **Number of samples (based on the independent variable):** Two
   It seems like one (same kids), but I am arguing that they will be fundamentally different as a result of this program.

3. **Type of sample:** Dependent
   This is a before/after experimental design where whether I measure someone at the later time (posttest) depends on whether that person was measured earlier (pretest).

4. **Level of measurement of dependent variable?** Interval/ratio

5. **Approximate normal distribution?** Yes—based on a histogram, Q—Q plot, skewness, and kurtosis (data not shown).

6. **Decision:** Paired-sample's t-test

$$t = \overline{D} \ / \left(\frac{s_D}{\sqrt{n}} \right)$$

The paired-sample t-test looks at the difference between the two observations on each pair, keeping note of whether the change is positive or negative. So in this formula, the $\overline{D}$ is the mean difference between the pairs and SD is the standard deviation of the differences. The data assumptions for the paired-sample's t-test are:

- I had a random sample.

- The samples are related or dependent (addressed in decision tree).

- The dependent variable is continuous (addressed in decision tree).

- The dependent variable should be approximately normally distributed (tested and therefore addressed in decision tree).

- No outliers in the dependent variable (*not* in the decision tree, but can be tested with the plots as addressed in Chapter 12).

As you see, all but the last assumption is addressed in the decision tree. Once I make it through the tree and decide a paired-sample's t-test would be appropriate, I can just test for that last assumption to make sure.

Because this statistical test focuses on the difference in the pairs, the null and alternate hypotheses will as well. Therefore, in this example, they would be expressed as:

$H_0: \mu_D = 0$

$H_1: \mu_D \neq 0$

where the null is interpreted as the "mean of the true difference is zero" and the alternate hypothesis is that it is not "0." SPSS will produce the output as shown below:

Paired Samples Statistics

		Mean	N	Std. Deviation	Std. Error Mean
Pair 1	Pretest hours TV watching	12.93	15	2.939	.759
	Posttest hours TV watching	11.13	15	2.973	.768

Paired Samples Correlations

		N	Correlation	Sig.
Pair 1	Pretest hours TV watching & Posttest hours TV watching	15	.949	.000

Paired Samples Test

		Paired Differences							
					95% Confidence Interval of the Difference				
		Mean	Std. Deviation	Std. Error Mean	Lower	Upper	t	df	Sig. (2-tailed)
Pair 1	Pretest hours TV watching - Posttest hours TV watching	1.800	.941	.243	1.279	2.321	7.407	14	.000

The first table gives the descriptive statistics for each of the variables (pre- and posttest TV hours), whereas the second gives us the degree of association between the variables, which I will cover in Chapter 14. For now, our main interest is in the third table, which gives us the results of the paired-sample's t-test. This table gives us the mean of the difference between the two variables, the standard deviation of that difference, a 95% confidence interval of that difference, the obtained t-value (and its parameters), and the two-tailed significance value of the test. I am really most interested in the t-value and significance values. As you can see, I would reject the null and, therefore, a possible interpretation is:

General: A paired-sample's t-test was done to compare <u>Variable 1</u> and <u>Variable 2</u>. Findings indicate that there is/is not a statistical difference in Variable 1 ($M =$ ____, SD = ____) and Variable 2 ($M =$ ___, SD = ____; $t(\underline{df}) =$ ___, $p =$ ___)

Our example: A paired-sample's t-test was done to compare hours of TV watched after 5 pm before and after a summer community intervention. Findings indicate that there is a statistical difference between hours of TV watched prior to participation in the program ($M = 12.93$, SD = 2.94) and after ($M = 11.13$, SD = 2.97; $t(14) = 7$, $p(41)=.001$)

But let's go back to the sample of 15 adolescents who attended this library program, and let's pretend that one session of that program involved teaching adolescents how to identify fake news posts online. To test the success of this portion of the program, I showed these students

10 online news feeds, 5 of which were fake, and asked them to identify whether the feed was fake or not. I recorded the number of correct identifications made prior to my seminar and then again after my seminar (using 10 news feeds for the posttest). If I ran a Shapiro-Wilkes test and found that the posttest scores were not normally distributed, I would follow the "No" response to the question "Approximate normal distribution?" When I do not have a normal

---

BOX 13.2

PAIRED-SAMPLE'S *t*-TEST AN EXAMPLE IN RESEARCH

In order to neutralize cultural mistrust of mental health care services, Brooks and Hopkins (2017) used an experimental design to test the effectiveness of a culturally responsive cognitive intervention. Brooks and Hopkins administered the Attitudes Towards Seeking Professional Psychological Help, Shortened Form (ATSPPH-S) to 236 Black students at a historically Black college or university and then administered the Culturally Responsive Cognitive Intervention, which consisted of two informal video presentations. One video exhibited Black doctors at a predominantly Black-staffed medical facility describing their commitment and service philosophy to the community and clients they serve. The second video connected the medical facility and doctors from the first video to the Affordable Care Act (ACA), in order to lead students to think that the centers would be a result of the ACA, thereby activating conscious and unconscious perceptions of trust toward the hypothetical future health care providers. For this group of students, Brooks and Hopkins then readministered the ATSPHH-S to see if the levels of willingness to seek mental health improved after the treatment.

Here is an excerpt from their findings:

> To test this hypothesis, a paired-sample's *t*-test was used to compare the participants' attitudes toward seeking professional psychological help (ATSPPH) responses before and after the intervention. As expected, the analysis revealed that students who received the intervention had significantly higher posttest ATSPPH-S (*M* = 24.66; SD = 13.63) than pretest ATSPPH-S (*M* = 20.78; *SD* = 8.52), *t*(40) = 3.56 *p* = .001, Conditions 3 and 4. (Brooks & Hopkins, 2017, pp. 823–824)

You can see that there were 40 degrees of freedom, the *t*-obtained value is 3.56, and the significance value is *p*<.001.

Now, let's see if you can answer the following questions based on the results presented:

1. Why did Brooks and Hopkins conduct a paired-sample *t*-test?

2. What was the average posttest score?

Source: Brooks, R. T., & Hopkins, R. (2017).

Answers:

1. Because this was a before–after experimental design, being a part of the posttest is dependent on being part of the pretest.

2. The average posttest score was 20.78.

---

distribution in a paired sample, based on the decision tree, I would instead do a Wilcoxon signed-rank test, which is the same choice if I had a paired sample, but an ordinal dependent variable. The process is analogous to comparing the mean difference as we do in the paired-sample's *t*-test, but I am comparing the median difference instead so my hypotheses are:

$$H_0: MD_D = 0$$

$$H_1: MD_D \neq 0$$

The data assumptions of the Wilcoxon signed-rank test are:

- I have a random sample.

- The samples are related or dependent (addressed in decision tree).

- The dependent variable is ordinal or not normally distributed (addressed in the decision tree).

- The distribution of the two groups is symmetrical in shape (*not* addressed in the decision tree, but a histogram, which we learned about in Chapter 11, would help you identify this).

As with the previous test, the last assumption is not covered in the decision tree; therefore, it is a final step that needs to be tested to make sure the choice is appropriate. The most direct way to see if the distribution of the two groups is symmetrical is to run histograms for them (Chapter 11) and visually look for an approximate symmetrical shape. As real-world data are not likely to be *perfectly* symmetrical, some violation of this is tolerated; but if the distribution is clearly skewed, then a data transformation or alternate test, both of which are beyond our scope and are more appropriate for a higher level statistics class, would be necessary. So for us, let's assume that the last assumption is met.

For a two-sample test, in its simplest explanation, the Wilcoxon signed-rank test calculates the absolute difference between the two observations for each case and then ranks from low to high the cases based on this difference. There is more to this explanation than I am presenting here because the process is too complicated for most undergraduate statistics classes, including ones like this that are focused on the computer application rather than the hand calculation. Still, the test itself has quite a lot of utility in the real world, so although we are not going to mention the formula (as it is not one short, easy formula), we will discuss how to run and interpret the test via a computer program. Based on this decision, the SPSS output would look like this:

Descriptive Statistics

							Percentiles	
	N	Mean	Std. Deviation	Minimum	Maximum	25th	50th (Median)	75th
Pretest correctly ID fake news	15	4.47	2.386	0	8	3.00	4.00	7.00
Posttest correctly ID fake news	15	7.20	1.424	5	9	6.00	7.00	8.00

Ranks

		N	Mean Rank	Sum of Ranks
Posttest correctly ID fake news - Pretest correctly ID fake news	Negative Ranks	1[a]	1.50	1.50
	Positive Ranks	13[b]	7.96	103.50
	Ties	1[c]		
	Total	15		

a. Posttest correctly ID fake news < Pretest correctly ID fake news

b. Posttest correctly ID fake news > Pretest correctly ID fake news

c. Posttest correctly ID fake news = Pretest correctly ID fake news

Test Statistics[a]

	Posttest correctly ID fake news – Pretest correctly ID fake news
Z	−3.223[b]
Asymp. Sig. (2-tailed)	.001

a. Wilcoxon Signed-Ranks Test

b. Based on negative ranks.

Because the dependent variable is not a normally distributed continuous (interval or ratio) level of measurement, I would not look at the means. Instead, here I would look at the quartiles and notice that the 50th (the median) and 75th percentile scores are higher in the posttest than in the pretest. An examination of the "Ranks" information supports this. According to the ranks, one person had fewer posttest than pretest news items correctly identified (negative rank); 11 of the 15 adolescents showed an increase pretest to posttest (positive rank); and for 3 of the 15 adolescents, there was no change. If these changes are large enough to conclude that the difference in pre- compared to posttests is not 0, the significance value in the "test statistics" box will be less than .05. Because mine is $p = .004$, it is less than .05 so I can reject the null and conclude that:

PHOTO 13.4 Online news feed

General: A Wilcoxon signed-rank test showed that the [independent variable] did/ did not affect the [dependent variable] (Z = ___, p = ____)/The median changed/did not change from [value of dependent at time 1] to [value of dependent at time 2].

Optional: insert information on 75th quartile if it shows additional change.

Example: A Wilcoxon signed-rank test showed that a seminar on <u>identifying</u>

<u>fake news online</u> did improve adolescents' ability to identify these instances

= –2.89, p = .004). The median number of news sources correctly identified increased

from 4 to 5, with the 75th percentile increasing from 4 to 6.

However, as we see in Figure 13.1, there is one more situation that I need to address and that is what to do when I have a paired sample, but my dependent variable is not continuous. For example, what if I wanted to see whether children feel safe at night (yes/no) after attending a child-centered program on techniques to address childhood fears? I might randomly select 20 children, ask them whether they are afraid of the dark, present this program to them, and then a week later re-ask them whether they are afraid of the dark. As you can see in the decision tree, in this instance I would do the McNemar's test, which is essentially like a paired-sample's t-test but for a variable that has only two answer choices.

1. **What am I doing?** Hypothesis testing
   I am comparing children's fear before and after a program to reduce fear.

2. **Number of samples (based on the independent variable):** Two

3. **Type of sample:** Dependent
   This is a before/after experimental design.

4. **Dependent Variable Level of Measurement?** Nominal

5. **Decision:** McNemar's test

$$X^2 = (b - c)^2 / (b + c)$$

There is one issue with McNemar's test that isn't reflected in the decision tree and that is that the dependent variable has to have only two answer choices. So if you originally have a dependent variable with more than two choices, you need to recode the data to create a new variable that only reflects two choices. As a result, this works on a 2 x 2 table and that directly relates to the formula where "b" and "c" are the observations in what is called the "discordant" cells, or the cells that do not match. Examples of discordant cells are yes/no and no/yes. The assumptions of this test are:

- I have a random sample.

- The independent and dependent variables only have two groups /choices.

- The dependent variable is mutually exclusive, meaning respondents cannot have both values of your dependent variable at any time point.

The null and research hypotheses are:

H_0: The two marginal probabilities of each outcome are the same.

H_1: The two marginal probabilities of each outcome are not the same.

Remember, the GSS is not a paired data set, so, I am illustrating with a hypothetical paired study. In this hypothetical case, I might get output that looks like this:

Test Statistics[a]

	Fear at night—pre and fear at night—post
N	20
Exact Sig. (2-tailed)	.004[b]

a. McNemar Test

b. Binomial distribution used.

Fear at night — pre and fear at night — post

	Fear at night—post	
Fear at night—pre	No	Yes
No	6	0
Yes	9	5

As you can see in the first table, $p = .004$, so I do have a statistically significant difference in fear at night before and after the program. To see how the data changed, I look at the second table, which was generated from the descriptive statistics. We see that there were nine children who were afraid of the dark prior to the program but were not afterward, so the program worked for 9 of the 14 children who were afraid of the dark prior to the programming (the bottom row added is all the children afraid of the dark in the pretest). The interpretation would be something like this:

General: N participants did [insert independent variable]. An exact McNemar's test determined that there was/was not a statistically significant difference in the proportion [dependent variable] pre- and postintervention, $p =$ _____.

Example: 20 children participated in programming to address childhood fears. An exact McNemar's test determined that there was a statistically significant difference in the proportion of children who were afraid of the dark pre- and t-test, $p = .004$.

PHOTO 13.5 Were you afraid of the dark as a child? How can we design and statistically test a program aimed at reducing childhood fears?

LEARNING CHECK 13.3: DEPENDENT SAMPLES

In the following examples, decide whether the sample is dependent or independent. In order to truly distinguish the subtle differences between the two, the basic scenario is the same and only the relevant details vary.

1. A researcher wants to see whether an antivaping program reduces vaping among adolescents. He randomly selects 15 adolescents and asks them how often they have vaped in the past week, gives each of the 15 adolescents the antivaping program, and then asks them to track how often they vaped the week following the program.

2. What if the researcher wanted to study the same program, but instead of the design mentioned in #1, he collected a random sample of 30 adolescents and randomly assigned 15 to the program and 15 as the control group who did not have the program. He asked all 30 how often they vaped the week before and the week after and compared the posttest scores between those who experience the program and those who did not.

3. Same antivaping program as in #1, but in this instance the researcher selected 15 pairs of people who were selected to be the same on gender, race, age (within a year), and frequency of vaping in the prior week. Among those 15 pairs, one individual was assigned to the antivaping program and the other was not. The posttest vaping frequency was then compared between those who experience the program compared to those who did not.

Answers to be found at the end of the chapter.

WHAT AM I DOING? HYPOTHESIS TESTING— THREE OR MORE SAMPLES

I know that I covered a lot of hypothesis tests so far! Believe it or not, we didn't even discuss all the possibilities for two-sample tests (just some of the most common or useful ones in social and behavioral programs). Even so, I still need to address what researchers would do if they want to compare three or more groups. Remember the race variable I presented to introduce two-sample tests? I can use that same variable to compare three (or more) groups as well. Let's pretend I want to compare the ideal number of children (CHLDIDEL) between whites, African Americans, and "Other" races? The decision tree for three or more groups being compared is shown in Figure 13.2.

There are a couple of points that I want to make about looking at three or more samples. First, you may notice that the statistics I will specifically be discussing are all for independent samples. The main reason is that, while possible, dependent samples for three or more groups are less common than they are for two samples. You are most likely to encounter a three- (or more) sample-dependent test when you are comparing three different treatments

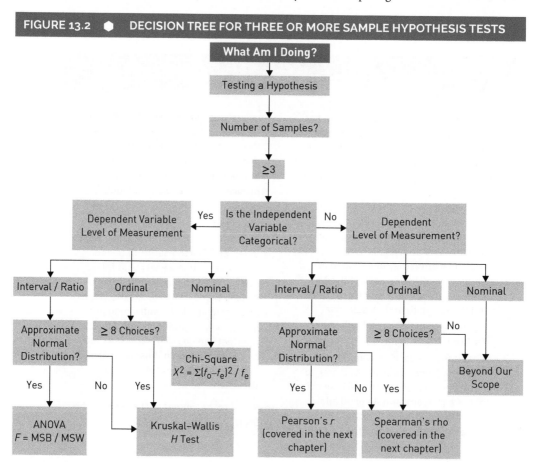

FIGURE 13.2   ●   DECISION TREE FOR THREE OR MORE SAMPLE HYPOTHESIS TESTS

(e.g., standard operating procedure, new treatment option 1, and new treatment option 2) across three matched groups, like Ventis et al. (2001) did. Comparing more than two dependent groups is more statistically complicated to analyze, and, therefore, is more likely to be addressed in advanced methods and statistics classes and is beyond the "getting the job done" approach that I take here. The second observation you may see is that one of our previous tests, the chi-square, can apply here as well. When researchers use the chi-square for three or more groups, the null hypothesis, the alternate hypothesis, the method of running in SPSS (and R), and the interpretation are all the same regardless of the actual number of groups being compared. Therefore, I will not go over this statistic again here. The last point is that there is an entire part of Figure 13.2 that I we will discuss in the next chapter. That is because the statistical tests for those two instances are actually calculated using the association statistic that is obtained from the sample. Therefore, when I discuss the association statistics in the next chapter, I will present them along with the corresponding hypothesis test. That leaves us with two new statistics to address.

Getting back to the earlier example of comparing the number of children across Whites, African Americans, and members of other races, if I follow the decision tree, I would reach the following statistical test:

1. **What am I doing?** Hypothesis testing
   I am comparing people from different races

2. **Number of samples (based on the independent variable)?** Three
   White, African American, and "Other"

3. **Is the independent variable categorical?** Yes

4. **Dependent variable level of measurement?** Interval/ratio

5. **Approximate normal distribution:** Yes—but see the note below

6. **Decision:** One-way analysis of variance (ANOVA)

$$F = \text{MSB} / \text{MSW}$$

Even though the focus of this book is not the formulas per se, the ANOVA merits some discussion. You have learned that scores can vary within a variable because variables are indicators that have more than one answer option—that is the very *definition* of a variable. Statistically, this is called **within-group variation**. When researchers test hypotheses, I stated that they are comparing across values of the independent variable, which addresses **between-group (across) variation**. The one-way analysis of variance (ANOVA) statistic examines whether the differences between groups is large enough relative to the variation within groups to say that there really is a real difference between groups. The ANOVA statistic has a lot of subcalculations, but essentially the statistic will compare whether the mean of the variation between the categories (MSB) is proportionately greater than the mean of the variation with a category (MSW).

There are a few additional assumptions that need to be met before accurately using an ANOVA, all of which can be tested with SPSS or R. As I have before, let's briefly identify the assumptions of this test.

- I have a random sample.

- The dependent variable is an interval/ratio level of measurement.

- The independent variable is categorical with at least three values.

- The populations of the different groups are approximately normally distributed.

- The population variances are equal (homogeneous).

Let me clarify some of these points. First, the assumption of "approximate normal distribution" really means normal distribution *for each category* of the independent variable, but the normality is "approximate" because ANOVA can handle some violation of this. The easiest way to test this is with a histogram of the dependent variable for each group done separately. The second is that the variances in the dependent variable are equal across the groups, much like we discussed in the two-sample *t*-test. I would see if this assumption is met with the Levene's Test of Equality of Variances that we have also covered previously in two-sample tests. If this assumption is met, I would continue with the ANOVA. If it is not, I would just do a Welch ANOVA instead of a one-way ANOVA and a different post hoc test (Games-Howell is common). However, the good news is that when the sample is large, like the GSS, for example, the ANOVA can handle some violation of these assumptions because it is such a robust test (Healy, 2014).

Another hitch in the use of an ANOVA test has to do with what the test itself does. The null hypothesis is that the population means of all the groups are equal, essentially like the independent sample *t*-test for two samples where we said that the average of the *two* groups was the same. Therefore, if we are comparing three groups, we say all three are equal; if we are comparing five groups, all five are equal, etc. In my example, I have three groups, so the null would be that all three are equal. The alternate hypothesis for the ANOVA, however, is that the population mean of at least one group is different. More formally written, the hypotheses are:

$H_0: \mu_1 = \mu_2 = \mu_3$

H_1: At least one is different.

This is the "catch" with ANOVA; it does not give you any information on *which* mean(s) are different, only that one is. In my example, I have the possible group differences:

Whites and African Americans

African Americans and "Other"

Whites and "Other"

Only one of these three sets may be different from each other, or all could be different. The point is that with ANOVA, researchers simply don't know. Therefore, whenever researchers run an ANOVA, they also need to run post hoc, or "after the fact," tests if the test suggests that there is a statistically significant difference between the groups. There are many post hoc tests one can use, but a common one is the Tukey honestly significant difference test, called Tukey HSD or Tukey for short. It is easiest to program SPSS, for example, to run those tests automatically with the ANOVA hypothesis test (Appendix A). If we fail to reject the null, all the group differences will show that they are not statistically significant anyway and would, therefore, be ignored. So here is the SPSS output:

Descriptives

Ideal number of children

	N	Mean	Std. Deviation	Std. Error	95% Confidence Interval for Mean Lower Bound	95% Confidence Interval for Mean Upper Bound	Minimum	Maximum
WHITE	1,335	3.12	1.932	.053	3.01	3.22	0	8
BLACK	305	3.58	1.915	.110	3.36	3.80	0	8
OTHER	181	3.34	1.765	.131	3.08	3.60	1	8
Total	1,821	3.22	1.920	.045	3.13	3.31	0	8

Multiple Comparisons

Dependent Variable: Ideal number of children

Tukey HSD

(I) Race of respondent	(J) Race of respondent	Mean Difference (I-J)	Std. Error	Sig.	95% Confidence Interval Lower Bound	95% Confidence Interval Upper Bound
WHITE	BLACK	−.462*	.121	.000	−.75	−.18
	OTHER	−.219	.152	.319	−.57	.14
BLACK	WHITE	.462*	.121	.000	.18	.75
	OTHER	.243	.179	.365	−.18	.66
OTHER	WHITE	.219	.152	.319	−.14	.57
	BLACK	−.243	.179	.365	−.66	.18

*. The mean difference is significant at the 0.05 level.

Test of Homogeneity of Variances

Ideal number of children

Levene Statistic	df1	df2	Sig.
1.302	2	1,818	.272

ANOVA

Ideal number of children

	Sum of Squares	df	Mean Square	F	Sig.
Between Groups	55.860	2	27.930	7.633	.000
Within Groups	6,652.024	1,818	3.659		
Total	6,707.885	1,820			

That's a lot of output! The first table tells me the mean, standard deviation, and confidence levels (among other points) for each race I am comparing. That may be useful for the write-up of the results if I reject the null. The second table, the "test of homogeneity of variances," tells me if the assumption of equal variances is fulfilled. As we saw with two-sample tests, we want the "Sig." value to be *greater* than .05. Here it is, so my assumption is fulfilled; but, as I said earlier, if it was *not* fulfilled, I would have run a different post hoc test (possibly the Games-Howell),

BOX 13.3

CHI-SQUARE AND ANOVA EXAMPLE IN RESEARCH

DeLuca and Wyman (2012) examined how school engagement related to Latino adolescents' likelihood of disclosing suicidal ideation (SI) to adults. These researchers conducted two studies, but the one relevant here focused on 2,611 students attending schools in Georgia and New York, where at least 10% of the school population was Latino.

The researchers examined whether an adolescent had SI in the previous year (yes/no), whether they told an adult if they did (yes/no), whether they tried to get help (yes/no), and what their level of school engagement was (measured on an interval scale that measured school engagement that was treated as normally distributed). They analyzed the data separately for females and males, and their findings are summarized in the table below:

J Primary Prevent (2012) 33:99–110   105

Table 2 Suicidal ideation, help-seeking behavior, and school engagement for students in Latino-representative schools by race/ethnicity ($N = 2,492$)

Outcome	Female			Male		
	White	African American	Latina	White	African American	Latino
SI in the past year	16 %	11 %	20 %	12 %	8 %	16 %
	122/760	47/349	53/265	65/547	25/304	43/267
Disclosed SI to an adult	27 %	30 %	22 %	26 %	26 %	28 %
	32/118	12/40	11/49	16/61	6/23	12/43
Tried to get help for SI	35 %	28 %	49 %	42 %	22 %	33 %
	41/117	11/39	22/45	26/62	5/23	14/43
School engagement (mean [SD])	2.86 (0.62)	2.76 (0.64)	2.67 (0.67)[a]**	2.75 (0.65)	2.67 (0.69)	2.64 (0.67)

"Latino-Representative Schools" = 8 schools that had at least 10 % or more of student population self-reporting as "Latino/Hispanic." Due to nonresponse from some adolescents regarding disclosure, proportions for female disclosure are different within ethnic/racial groups. A higher mean from these four questions represented a higher level of school engagement ($\alpha = .63$)

SI suicidal ideation, SD standard deviation

[a] Latino versus African American; ** $p < .001$

Three of the dependent variables (SI in the past year, disclosed SI to an adult, and tried to get help for SI) are categorical variables and were therefore tested separately by race within each gender using chi-square analysis (table above). The fourth dependent variable (level of school engagement) is interval/ratio and, therefore was tested using an ANOVA analysis (last row in the table above). The lack of any notation for the six chi-square tests (three for women and three for men) indicates that there was no statistically significant relationship between the variables studied. However, the researcher did find a statistically significant relationship between race and school engagement for females (as indicated by "**").

So now you use the information in the table to answer the following questions:

1. At what probability level was the null rejected for race and school engagement among females?

2. Was there a statistically significant relationship between race and school engagement for males? What evidence do you have for your answer?

3. Among females, which race had the highest level of school engagement?

4. Among females, for what races was there a significant difference in school engagement?

Source: De Luca, S. M., & Wyman, P. A. (2012).

Answers:

1. The $p<.001$ level.

2. No, there was no statistically significant relationship between race and school engagement for males, and we know this because there are no asterisks by the output.

3. Whites, because they have the highest mean of 2.86.

4. The only statistically significant difference was between Latino and African-American females (see footnote "a").

which can be selected from the same pane in SPSS where I selected the Tukey test. The third table is the actual ANOVA results. As with the other tests, I am initially interested in the "Sig." value and, as it is less than .05, I can reject the null and be 95% confident that there is a difference in the population means.

Since I reject the null and ANOVA does not give me information regarding which groups differ, I now look at the post hoc tests. Looking at the p-values ("Sig" column), I notice a few things. First, some of the information is repetitive. The Tukey output compares one value to each of the other values individually—for *each* value, *each* time. Therefore, the first row is "White" compared to "Black," and the information there will be the same as later in the table where the reference value is "Black" compared to "White." Second, the table tells us that the difference in the ideal number of children is significant for Whites compared to Blacks (mean difference = –.462, p = .000) only. None of the other comparisons have p-values that are less than .05; I only report the detail for statistically significant group comparisons. Therefore, one possible interpretation of these findings is:

General: An ANOVA test showed that [dependent variable] did/did not

differ based on [independent variable] (F (dfb, dfw) =___, p = ____).

Note: If the difference is statistically significant add: Post hoc

tests reveal that there is a significant difference between [IV value 1]

= ____, SD = ____) and [IV value 2] (M = ____, SD = ____).

Note: Repeat this, in some form for any significant differences,

adding who is more/less likely to do something based on the means if inclined.

Example: An ANOVA test showed that a respondent's identified ideal number

of children significantly differed by race (F(2, 1818) = 7.63, p = .000), but only

between Whites and African Americans. A Tukey post hoc test reveals that White respondents preferred fewer children (M = <u>3.12</u>, SD = <u>1.93</u>), on average, than did

<u>African American</u> respondents (M = <u>3.58</u>, SD = <u>1.92</u>).

Based on Figure 13.2, you can see that we have one more new statistic to cover: what to do when we are comparing three or more samples, the dependent variable is interval/ratio, but it is *not* normally distributed or if it is ordinal but with too many categories to make a meaningful chi-square test. For example, what if I wanted to test whether people who believed in life after death (POSTLIFE) were more likely to attend religious services frequently (RELAC-TIV). Based on the decision tree:

1. **WAID?** Hypothesis testing
   I am comparing people with different concepts of life after death

2. **Number of samples (based on the independent variable):** Three
   The choices are yes, don't know, and no to the answer of belief in life after death.

3. **Is the independent variable categorical?** Yes

4. **Dependent variable level of measurement?** Ordinal

5. **Are there eight or more answer choices?** Yes—11 different values

6. **Decision:** Kruskal–Wallace H test

This is not a statistic that is covered in many undergraduate statistics textbooks, largely because the formula to calculate this statistic by hand is long. That is why the formula is also not presented in the decision tree.

The data assumptions for this test are:

- I have a random sample.

- The independent variable has three or more categories of comparison (addressed in the decision tree).

- The samples are independent (addressed in the decision tree).

- The dependent variable is ordinal or not normally distributed, if continuous (addressed in the decision tree).

- The distribution of the dependent variable for each group has the same shape or variability (*not* addressed in the decision tree).

As with some other statistics I discussed, this last assumption needs some more explanation. Basically, if the distributions of the dependent variable have the same shape for each value of the independent variable, then researchers can proceed with the Kruskal–Wallace H and compare the medians of the dependent variable. If the distributions are different, however, researchers can still do this test; they just compare the mean ranks, which are a little less intuitive than comparing the actual medians. For our purposes, I will just discuss the more conservative interpretation of the mean rank of values.

This statistic is based on the chi-square distribution that I covered earlier, although the formula for use is different (and not of concern to us because we are not calculating these statistics by hand). The null and research hypotheses are:

H_0: the sample groups are from identical populations

H_1: at least one group is from a different population

To test the assumption of similar distributions, all you have to do is run a histogram for the distribution of the dependent variable for each value of the independent variable, as discussed in Chapter 11.

Ranks

	Belief in life after death	N	Mean Rank
How often does R take part in relig activities	No	495	1,061.11
	Don't know	268	1,157.98
	Yes	2,082	1,543.16
	Total	2,845	

Test Statistics[a,b]

	How often does R take part in relig activities
Chi-Square	186.642
df	2
Asymp. Sig.	.000

a. Kruskal Wallis Test

b. Grouping Variable: Belief in life after death

The data show that I can reject the null (p = .000 here) so the interpretation would be:

General: A Kruskal–Wallis H test shows that there was/was not a statistically significant difference in [underline]dependent variable[/underline] between the different [underline]independent variable[/underline], X^2(df) = ____, p = ____ with a mean rank score of ____ for [underline]condition 1[/underline], ____ for [underline]condition 2[/underline], and ____ for [underline]condition 3, continuing for however many conditions you have[/underline].

Example: A Kruskal–Wallis H test shows that there was a statistically significant difference in how <u>often someone participates in religious activities</u> between the different <u>views of life after death</u>, X^2(2) = <u>186.64</u>, p = <u>.000</u> with a mean rank score of <u>1,061.11</u> for those who <u>do not believe in life after death</u>, a mean rank score of <u>1,157.98</u> for those who do <u>not know if they believe</u>, and a score of <u>1,543.16</u> for those who <u>do believe in life after death</u>.

LEARNING CHECK 13.4: THREE OR MORE SAMPLES

1. A researcher administers a life satisfaction scale (answers range from 15 to 75) to people who are married, separated/divorced, and single to see if satisfaction varies by marital status. She finds that the scale is not normally distributed for all three groups. What test should she use?

2. A researcher is examining average GRE scores for students who went to a public school in either working-class, middle-class, or upper-class public school districts, or a private school to see if the scores vary. She finds that the scores are normally distributed within the three groups. What test should she use?

3. A researcher wants to know if owning a pet (owns/does not own) varies by whether a family has no children, one to two children, or three or more children. What test should she use?

Answers to be found at the end of the chapter.

Because like the other parametric tests, the research hypothesis does not make any stance on *how* the variables are related, I could run nonparametric post hoc tests, similar to what we did with the ANOVA, to see what groups have the difference; but for the purpose of "getting the job done," comparing the mean ranks is sufficient here. The mean ranks may not tell us which groups are statistically significant, but they do tell us how the groups compare. The higher the mean rank, the more likely that condition is to exhibit the dependent variable.

As I mentioned earlier though, all the materials in this chapter and the previous one only give the researcher an idea of whether there are differences between groups; this material does not give any insight as to whether any of the observed differences is meaningful. To assess that, researchers need to measure the degree of variation between variables, what is sometimes called effect size or substantive significance. Therefore, this is what we will focus on in the next chapter.

Key Terms

Between-group variation
Dependent samples
Expected frequency

Homogeneity of variances
Independent samples
Observed frequency

Within-group variation

Answers to Learning Check Questions

Learning Check 13.1: General Two-Sample Considerations

1. Dependent test. The same students are asked about their number of unhealthy choices before the program (sample 1) and after (sample 2). Whether you answer the survey at the end of the program depends on you being in the study and answering the survey at the beginning.

2. Independent test. Students do not need to be a biology major, to be a sociology major, so the two groups are independent.

3. (a) Independent, because you cannot simultaneously have and not have pets, but also because this is not a before/after or matched methods design. (b) Yes, because $p = .073 > p = .05$.

Learning Check 13.2: Independent Samples

1. What am I doing? Testing a hypothesis --> 2 samples --> independent --> dependent variable is ordinal --> has fewer than 8 answer choices. Decision: Chi-square $X^2 = (f_o - f_e)^2 / f_e$

2. What am I doing? Testing a hypothesis --> 2 samples --> independent --> dependent variable is interval/ratio --> not an approximate normal distribution. Decision: Mann–Whitney U: $U_1 = R_1 - (n_1 (n_1+1)2$

3. What am I doing? Testing a hypothesis --> two samples --> independent --> --> dependent

variable is interval/ratio --> it is normally distributed (implied by use of mean and standard deviation). Decision: Independent sample t-test, $t = (\bar{X}_1 - \bar{X}_2)/\sigma_{X-X}$

Learning Check 13.3: Dependent Samples

1. Dependent. This is the sample people tested in a before–after design.

2. Independent. This is not a before–after design or a matched sample.

3. Dependent. This is a sample where pairs of elements are matched (selected to be the same) on gender, race, age, and frequency of vaping.

Learning Check 13.4: Three or More Samples

1. What am I doing? Testing a hypothesis --> 3 samples --> independent --> dependent variable is interval/ratio --> it is not normally distributed (NOTE: the dependent variable can also be taken as an ordinal level of measurement with more than 8 answer options). Decision: Kruskal–Wallace H Test

2. What am I doing? Testing a hypothesis --> four samples --> independent --> dependent variable is interval/ratio --> it is normally distributed. Decision: ANOVA, $F = MSB/MSW$.

3. What am I doing? Testing a hypothesis --> 3 samples --> independent --> dependent variable is nominal. Decision Chi-square.

End-of-Chapter Problems

For questions 1–8, decide which statistical test should be used for each scenario. Pay attention to the wording of the question. Information such as "average" implies that the mean was calculated as part of the problem, and the mean as a statistic gives information, for example, on the nature of the distribution.

1. A researcher randomly samples 280 people to determine whether a region of residence (east, midwest, west) affects their level of support for a border wall (does not support, no opinion, supports).

2. Based on a random sample of 220 college students (100 athletes and 120 nonathletes), is the GPA of college athletes ($M = 3.42$, $S = .78$) and nonathletes ($M = 3.61$, $S = 1.02$) significantly different?

3. As part of a random sample of 134 college students, a researcher examines whether the number of times a student texts his/her parents varies based on their academic year (freshman, sophomore, junior, senior). Using various statistics, he finds that the dependent variable is approximately normally distributed based on the values of the independent variable.

4. A social service agency wants to test whether its parenting program reduces caregiver stress. Its administers a caregiver stress scale that ranges from 4 (no stress) to 20 (extreme stress) to 20 caregivers under age 40 who are at risk of losing their children before the program and 1 week after their program completion. They find that the scores on the scale are not normally distributed at either time point and that the distribution of the scores for the groups is approximately symmetrical.

5. In the same study as mentioned in #4, the researchers want to see whether this program affects the number of positive interactions (as self-reported based on a checklist of behaviors) between the caregiver and child based on the caregiver's age (under 21, 22–30, 31–40). They find that the number of positive interactions is not normally distributed across the age groups.

6. Educators in an online sociology/criminal justice program at DegreesRUs.com want to know whether the earnings of their first-year graduates are significantly different from the earnings of first-year graduates at brick-and-mortar universities. They conduct a random sample of 35 graduates of their program and a random sample of 40 individuals who graduated from a sociology/criminal justice brick-and-mortar program. They find that the average salaries of the two groups are not normally distributed.

7. A researcher randomly sampled 175 individuals to determine whether their preferred social media platform (Facebook, Snapchat, Instagram, Other) varied by age (under 25, 26–40, over 40).

8. A researcher matches 40 inmates based on race, gender, and age category and randomly assigns 20 to an intensive prison-based re-entry program that has among its components a session for helping ex-inmates find employment. She then compares the number of days it takes to find employment that lasts more than a month upon release for the two groups. The dependent variable is normally distributed.

Questions 9–15 are based on GSS data.

9. Using the GSS data and any computer/web resources available, test whether there is a statistically significant relationship between a respondent's view of the number of politicians they think are corrupt (CORRUPT1) and their confidence in the executive branch of the federal government (CONFED).

10. Using the GSS data and any computer/web resources available, test whether a person's level of education (practice the skills learned in Chapter 11 and recode DEGREE into less than high school degree, high school degree, at least some college) affects how many children they feel are ideal to have (CHLDIDEL). Use

the normal $Q–Q$ plot to test for approximate normality.

11. Using the GSS data and any computer/web resources available, test whether people who are currently working for money (WORKNOW) have more years of education (EDUC) than those who are not working.

12. Using the GSS data and any computer/web resources available, test whether the number of children someone has (CHILDS) varies by their view of sex before marriage (PREMARSX)? Use $Q–Q$ plots to test for approximate normality.

13. Using the GSS data and any computer/web resources available, test whether the real income, when expressed as constant dollars

(REALINC), varies by gender (SEX)? Use $Q–Q$ plots to test for approximate normality.

14. Using the GSS data and any computer/web resources available, test whether those who have more confidence in our educational institutions (CONEDUC) feel that the government assists low-income college students (AIDCOL).

15. Using the GSS data and any computer/web resources available, test whether the size of the household (HOMPOP) varies based on one's subjective class identification (CLASS). Use $Q–Q$ plots to test for approximate normality and note that for CLASS, only values 1–4 have real meaning, so you should practice coding that you learned in Chapter 11 to recode this variable to keep values 1–4 and have all other values recoded as "missing."

FINDING THE DEGREE OF ASSOCIATION AND PREDICTION

LEARNING GOALS

- Explain how measures of association complement statistical tests of inference
- Distinguish when to use, how to run, and how to interpret different measures of association
- Conduct and interpret bivariate linear regression
- Explain how partial correlations can provide information about how variables are related
- Explain how to run and interpret multivariate linear regression

What if you have an awful headache and you are at the store deciding which medicine to buy to make it go away. You have narrowed your choices to the two leading brands: Headache Away and Pain Be Gone. Headache Away costs more than Pain Be Gone, but the label claims that it has been clinically proven to work significantly faster than other leading headache medicines. Tempted to buy Headache Away? The company selling it sure hopes you are! But what is Headache Away's claim *really* saying? Just because the medicine may work "significantly" faster only means that the time test subjects report their headache being gone between the two brands is less, but the claim alone does not tell you *how much* less. What if the difference is only a few seconds? Do you *really* think you are going to notice a three-second difference in relief, and would that very short span of time be worth the extra cost of Headache Away? This example illustrates the importance of understanding both significant and substantive statistical differences. As you have spent the last two chapters learning, significant difference is whether we can be reasonably confident that there is a difference between groups, but substantive significance, sometimes also called **effect size** or associative significance, tells us whether that difference is large enough to truly be meaningful. In our headache example, Headache Away's claim is sound; they are not lying because their clinical trials showed a significant difference between the brands. But if the time difference is only 3 sec, then the brands are not meaningfully different and Headache Away is not being completely transparent because doing so would not serve its marketing purposes.

In this chapter, you will first learn about some basic measures of association, followed by basic models of prediction and multivariate analysis.

PHOTO 14.1 If you were selecting between two headache medicines, how much faster is meaningful to you to determine that Drug A is meaningfully faster acting than Drug B?

WHAT AM I DOING? FINDING THE STRENGTH OF AN ASSOCIATION BETWEEN VARIABLES

Once again, the level of measurement of the variables is one of the main factors for deciding what measure of association might be appropriate for the data, but the main question now for our purpose of "getting the job done" is "What is the *lowest* level of measurement?" This needs a bit more explanation before I continue. When the two variables you want to relate are the same level of measurement, the statistical choice, as you will see, is usually pretty straightforward. However, there are a lot of times when researchers want to compare variables that are different levels of measurement. For example, according to Mather, Scommegna, and Kilduff (2019), people aged 65 and over account for about 16% of the population; and, as this age group is working longer, they are also more likely to live alone because of divorce, are less likely to have family near them, and are more likely to need nursing home care as they age. The United States is not alone in this; consequently, the role of the government in providing aid to the elderly is being debated globally, with some evidence showing that women, parents, and those with more liberal political views were more likely to support government intervention in providing for elder care (Caïs & Folguera, 2013; Silverstein & Parrott, 2001). I can examine the views of government involvement in elder care in the GSS sample using the AIDOLD variable, and if I wanted to see how strongly this variable was related to a subject's gender, measured by the variable SEX, I would be comparing an ordinal measure (AIDOLD) to a nominal one (SEX). You already learned that higher levels of measurement contain all the characteristics of measures that are lower in level (Chapter 4) and, therefore, the statistics that fit lower levels of measurement also fit higher ones, but not vice versa (Chapter 11). Therefore, although you will learn about some special statistics such as eta, which can be used when the dependent variable is interval/ratio but the independent variable is a dichotomous nominal measure, for our purposes of "getting the job done," it is a general practice to use the measure of association that corresponds to the lower level of measurement. Therefore, in my example of the government's role in helping the elderly, the statistic I would select for association is what will fit the nominal measure. In the next few subsections, I will discuss what these measures are for each level of measurement, and the decision tree for statistics of association appears in Figure 14.1.

Lowest Level of Measurement: Nominal

In my example of the government's role in elder care, based on the decision tree from Chapter 12, I know that to test for statistical significance, I would use the chi-square statistic. To see the strength of the association, I would follow this chapter's decision tree.

1. **What am I doing?** Finding the strength of an association

2. **What is the lowest level of measurement of the two variables?** Nominal
   AIDOLD is ordinal and SEX is nominal

3. **Do I have a clear independent variable?** Yes
   SEX is always in an independent variable in the social sciences

4. **Do I have a continuous dependent variable?** No

5. **Decision:** Lambda (λ) or Cramer's V (V)1.

$$\lambda = (E1 - E2)/E1$$

$$V = \sqrt{X^2/N(m)}$$

FIGURE 14.1 ● DECISION TREE ASSOCIATION

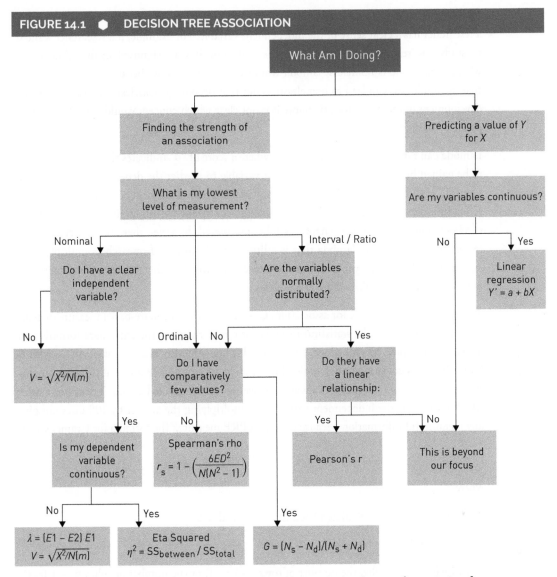

There are a couple of statistics researchers could use to assess the degree of association for nominal levels. A common one to use is lambda, which is a measure that looks at the **proportionate reduction of error (PRE)**, meaning that the statistic looks at the errors a researcher would make in predicting the dependent variable while ignoring the independent variable ($E1$) and compares that to the errors one would make predicting the dependent variable while now considering the contribution of the independent variable for each category of the dependent variable ($E2$). The formula for $E2$ is:

$$E1 = N = \text{Mode of dependent variable}$$

$$E2 = \Sigma(N_k - \text{Mode}_k)$$

where N_k = the sample size of a column

Mode_k = the mode for that column.

However, lambda is an **asymmetrical measure of association**, so it is only appropriate when a researcher has a clear sense of the independent variable. For example, if a researcher wanted to study the relationship between whether someone has a diagnosed mental illness and whether he or she is homeless, lambda would not be appropriate because there is evidence that mental illness can lead to homelessness but that becoming homeless can also lead to the development of mental illness; therefore it is not clear which concept would apply as an independent variable.

Lambda can range in value from .0 to 1.0, where a score of "0" indicates that there is nothing to be gained by looking at the independent variable to predict the dependent variable and a score of "1" indicating that the independent variable predicts the dependent variable without error. Interpreting lambda on the 0–1.0 scale is consistent with how most other measures of association covered in this chapter will be interpreted; however, there is another way that researchers can interpret lambda that is a little more intuitive. If researchers multiply their lambda value by 100, they can look at the "percent improved predictability." I will discuss this more soon when we look at some SPSS output.

The other nominal statistic for association, Cramer's V, is a chi-square-based measure of association, meaning that the statistical formula for Cramer's V has the chi-square formula you learned in Chapter 13 embedded within it. This statistic also ranges from 0 to 1, with 0 indicating no association and 1 indicating a perfect association. Because it is based on chi-*square*, the value of Cramer's V is always positive. However, unlike lambda, it does not matter which measure is the independent variable and multiplying the answer by 100 does not give any meaningful information because it is not a PRE measure. The formula for Cramer's V is

$$V = \sqrt{X^2/N(m)}$$

where

X^2 = chi-square value calculated from that statistical test

N = total sample size

m = whichever is smaller, the number of rows — 1 (r–1) or the number of columns – 1 (c–1)

The SPSS commands to run both of these association statistics can be done from the same command box as the chi-square (Appendix A), whereas the commands to run Cramer's V in R is in Appendix B; as of this writing, there was not an active package to download to run lambda in R.

The resulting SPSS output would look like the figure on the next page.

There are some points worth noting about this output. First, as I said, I can do my statistical and substantive testing at the same time for this type of analysis. Second, I know that no cells have an expected frequency of less than five, so my chi-square fits that assumption and, therefore, based on my p-value of p = .000, I can reject the null. Therefore, there is a statistically significant relationship between gender and view of the government's role in helping the elderly. Third, the lambda value I want to look at is the circled one where "Govts resp: Provide for the elderly Dependent" because that is the test value for when that variable is the dependent

Govts resp: provide for the elderly * Respondents sex Crosstabulation

			Respondents sex MALE	Respondents sex FEMALE	Total
Govts resp: provide for the elderly	DEFIN SHOULD BE	Count	250	422	672
		% within Respondents sex	44.5%	52.4%	49.2%
	PROBAB SHOULD BE	Count	226	309	535
		% within Respondents sex	40.2%	38.4%	39.1%
	PROB SHOULD NOT BE	Count	67	61	128
		% within Respondents sex	11.9%	7.6%	9.4%
	DEFIN SHOULD NOT BE	Count	19	13	32
		% within Respondents sex	3.4%	1.6%	2.3%
Total		Count	562	805	1367
		% within Respondents sex	100.0%	100.0%	100.0%

Chi-Square Tests

	Value	df	Asymptotic Significance (2-sided)
Pearson Chi-Square	15.604[a]	3	.001
Likelihood Ratio	15.433	3	.001
Linear-by-Linear Association	14.887	1	.000
N of Valid Cases	1367		

a. 0 cells (0.0%) have expected count less than 5. The minimum expected count is 13.16.

Symmetric Measures

		Value	Approximate Significance
Nominal by Nominal	Phi	.107	.001
	Cramer's V	.107	.001
N of Valid Cases		1367	

Directional Measures

			Value	Asymptotic Standard Error[a]	Approximate T[b]	Approximate Significance
Nominal by Nominal	Lambda	Symmetric	.010	.010	.949	.343
		Govts resp: provide for the elderly Dependent	.000	.000	.[c]	.[c]
		Respondents sex Dependent	.021	.022	.949	.343
	Goodman and Kruskal tau	Govts resp: provide for the elderly Dependent	.004	.002		.002[d]
		Respondents sex Dependent	.011	.006		.001[d]

a. Not assuming the null hypothesis.

b. Using the asymptotic standard error assuming the null hypothesis.

c. Cannot be computed because the asymptotic standard error equals zero.

d. Based on chi-square approximation

variable. The lambda has a value of .000, indicating that gender contributes nothing to the ability to predict subjects' views of whether the government should provide for the elderly. Fourth, the Cramer's *V* supports lambda's findings by having a value of .107, which is very close to 0. Although a Cramer's *V* value hovering around .1 pretty clearly suggests almost no relationship, because a score of 1, which is a perfect relationship, is basically unheard of in the real world for a simply bivariate association, even if the two variables are strongly associated, it is harder to determine what values suggest a strong relationship. Therefore, researchers try to identify range of values to indicate what could be considered weak, moderate, and strong relationships, but there is no agreement on how to interpret the magnitude of these statistics. Therefore, while not universally agreed upon, a loose guideline to interpret the magnitude of the effect of the various association measures appears in Box 14.1. So, both measures of association show that although there is a statistical relationship between view of the government's responsibility to care for the elderly and gender, the effect size is so weak that there is essentially no substantive relationship.

BOX 14.1

INTERPRETATION OF THE MAGNITUDE OF VARIOUS ASSOCIATION STATISTICS

Statistic	Range of Values	Strength of the Bivariate Association
Cramer's *V*	.00–.10 .11–.25 .26 or higher	Weak Moderate Strong
Eta Squared	.01 .06 .14	Small Medium Large
Gamma and Spearman's rho	.00–.30 .31–.60 .61 or higher	Weak Moderate Strong
Pearson's *r*	0–.09 .10–.19 .20–.34 .35–.49 .50–.69 .79–.99 1.0	No relationship Weak relationship Moderately weak relationship Moderate relationship Moderately strong relationship Strong relationship Perfect relationship

One possible way of interpreting this is:

General: Using the information on the <u>independent variable</u> to predict <u>dependent variable</u>, we reduced our error of prediction by __% and a Cramer's *V* suggests a

_____ relationship.

Our example: Using the information on gender to predict the view of whether the government should provide care for the elderly, we do not reduce our error of prediction at all (lambda = 0), which is supported by a Cramer's V value very close to 0, indicating that these two variables are not substantively related.

In order to get an idea of how an interpretation might read when there is a substantive relationship, let's pretend that my findings produced a lambda of .43 and a Cramer's V of .32. If that were the case, the interpretation would read:

Pretend Interpretation: Using the information on gender to predict the view of whether the government should provide care for the elderly, we reduced our error of prediction by 43% and a Cramer's V suggests a strong relationship (V = .32).

But what if I wanted to see how strongly years of education (EDUC) varied by gender (SEX)? Now, if I look at the decision tree in Figure 14.1, I see that there is another path.

1. **What am I doing?** Finding the strength of an association

2. **What is the lowest level of measurement of the two variables?** Nominal
   SEX is nominal

3. **Do I have a clear independent variable?** Yes

4. **Do I have a continuous dependent variable?** Yes
   CHLDIDEL is continuous

5. **Decision:** Eta Squared

$$\eta^2 = SS_{between}/SS_{total}$$

In this case, I would use eta squared, which is another PRE-based measure, but one that is based on the ANOVA statistic that you learned about in Chapter 13 and is easy to calculate based on the ANOVA output. In SPSS, you will get the following output:

Report

Ideal number of children

Respondents sex	Mean	N	Std. Deviation
MALE	2.99	807	1.721
FEMALE	3.40	1,014	2.047
Total	3.22	1,821	1.920

Measures of Association

	Eta	Eta Squared
Ideal number of children * Respondents sex	.107	.011

ANOVA Table

			Sum of Squares	df	Mean Square	F	Sig.
Ideal number of children * Respondents sex	Between Groups	(Combined)	76.569	1	76.569	21.003	.000
	Within Groups		6,631.316	1,819	3.646		
	Total		6,707.885	1,820			

As the above output shows, I can reject the null because my p-value is less than .01 (p = .000), my mean number of ideal children is somewhat different for men and women ($\overline{X}$ = 2.99 for men) and ($\overline{X}$ = 3.40 for women), but my eta-squared value is very small (η^2 = .01). As a PRE measure, I would take this value and multiply it by 100 to get the explained variance, so in this instance, my interpretation could be something like:

General: <u>Variable 1</u> and <u>Variable 2</u> are/are not statistically related and considering <u>Independent variable</u> when predicting <u>Dependent variable</u> does/does not improve predictability by ___% (F(<u>dfb</u>,<u>dfw</u>) = <u>F observed</u>, p = ._____, η^2 = _____).

Our example: Gender and the number of children someone feels is ideal are statistically related and considering gender when predicting the number of children someone feels is ideal improves predictability by only 1% (F(76.57, 6,631.32) = 21.00, p = .000, η^2 = .01).

Even so, it is unlikely to get really large values for eta-squared. Therefore, a common rule of thumb proposed by both Cohen (1988) and Miles and Shevlin (2001) is that an eta-squared value of around .01 would be considered a small effect, a value around .06 a medium effect, and a value around .14 or higher a large effect (see Box 14.1).

There are a couple of additional notes about eta squared as well. First, each categorical effect has its own eta squared. So when there are multiple variables, partial eta squared is the more accurate measure to use because it looks at how much of the unexplained variance in the dependent variable is based on a particular independent variable (X) of interest when there are multiple independent variables considered. So when there is only one variable, which is all I am discussing here because of our focus on "getting the job done," partial eta squared and eta squared are the same.

Lowest Level of Measurement: Ordinal

Because ordinal up to ratio measures are ranked, now measures of association can address the direction of the relationship as well as the magnitude. Researchers can say that two variables have a positive or a negative relationship. A **positive relationship** means that the two variables are moving in the same direction—if one increases, so does the other, and if one variable decreases, so does the second. A **negative relationship**, on the other hand, means that the two variables are moving in opposite directions, whereas when one variable increases, the value of the other variable decreases and vice versa. There are a multitude of possible measures of association for two ordinal levels of measurement but in the spirit of "getting the job done," I will focus on two: gamma and Spearman's rho.

BOX 14.2

ETA-SQUARED EXAMPLE IN RESEARCH

Are your parents involved in your college life? Do they help you select your courses or advocate on your behalf with professors? Or is this social perception of the increased involvement of parents in their young adult children's lives overstated? Pizzolato and Hicklen (2011) note that despite the claims of increased parental involvement in their college-aged children's lives, there is little empirical evidence on the degree or effects of this involvement. Therefore, they studied 747 undergraduates at a public Midwestern university to determine if these students involved their parents in decision making and, if so, how. The main finding was that the majority of students did not actually involve their parents in decisions, including the important decisions students described (Pizzolato & Hicklen, 2011). The researchers then examined whether there were demographic differences in parental involvement in decision making. They found there was an interactive effect between gender and class year so they split the file and analyzed this statistically significant relationship more closely. Here is an excerpt of their findings:

> The file was split by sex in order to examine the effect of class year on parent involvement separately for females and males. A one-way ANOVA showed that there were statistically significant differences at the $p < .05$ level in parent involvement for females by class year, $F(5, 617) = 4.87$, $p = .001$. Despite reaching statistical significance, the actual difference in mean scores between groups was small; eta squared was .04.
>
> ... Significance in the frequency of parent involvement by student class year was also evident in males as determined by a one-way ANOVA, $F(5, 282) = 4.63$, $p = .001$, and this significance was found to be practically significant as well, with an eta squared of .08. (Pizzolato & Hicklen, 2011, p. 677)

Based on the ANOVA test, we see that for females there were statistically significant differences for parental involvement by class year at the $p < .05$ level; in fact, the p-value was less than .001 based on the statistical evidence, but according to the researchers, the substantive effect was small because the eta-squared was only .04. So considering this presentation of results, see if you can answer the following:

1. Was there a statistically significant effect of parental involvement by class year for either males? What is your evidence?

2. For whom was the relationship between parental involvement and class year stronger? Males or females? What is your evidence?

Source: Pizzolato, J. E., & Hicklen, S. (2011).

Answers:

1. Yes. According to the results, $p<.001$ for the males as well.

2. It was stronger for the males because their eta-squared value of .08 is larger than the value of .04 for the females.

LEARNING CHECK 14.1: NOMINAL ASSOCIATION MEASURES

1. Which is a PRE measure, Cramer's V or lambda?

2. A researcher wants to know whether children who do not live with both biological parents (yes/no) are more likely to have disciplinary problems at school (yes/no). What tests should be used for statistical significance and substantive significance?

3. A researcher studying the relationship between major and whether someone decides to go to law school found a lambda of .28. What does this mean (e.g., How would it be interpreted)?

Answers to be found at the end of the chapter.

If I continue with my earlier example of people's view of the government's role in providing care for the elderly and I wanted to relate that to the subject's social class, the decision tree would proceed as such:

1. **What am I doing?** Finding the strength of an association

2. **What is the lowest level of measurement of the two variables?** Ordinal **AIDOLD** is ordinal and **CLASS** is ordinal

3. **Do I have comparatively few answer categories?** Yes, both are under 5

4. **Decision:** Gamma

$$G = (N_s - N_d)/(N_s + N_d)$$

You may have noticed in the SPSS Crosstabs box used to calculate Lambda and Cramer's V that the box on the right has options for calculating some measures of ordinal association, one of which is Gamma. Gamma is a PRE measure that compares the number of pairs that are ranked the same on both variables, called same-ordered pairs, or N_s, to the rank of pairs which are different, otherwise known as inverse-ordered pairs, or N_d. Same-ordered pairs are cells in which the pair of variables are ranked the same way relative to a comparison cell. For example, if you look at Figure 14.2A, if I start with the dark-blue-shaded cell, which I will call the reference cell, this cell is low on the independent variable (column) and the dependent variable (row). All the cells for which the values for *both* the independent and the dependent (a pair of values) are higher than this reference cell are shaded as light blue. For example, if I look at the cell marked "A," both the independent and dependent variable values went from low to medium, so they are *both* higher on the variables than the reference cell. The cell marked "B" went from low (reference cell) to high on the independent variable (column) and from low on the reference cell value of the dependent variable (row) to medium, also an increase even though one that is not as big as low to high. I would do this for every cell individually until I reach the end of the table.

FIGURE 14.2 ●   THE LOGIC OF SAME- AND INVERSE-ORDERED PAIRS

(A)

Dependent variable	Independent Variable		
	Low	Medium	High
Low	Reference cell		
Medium		A	B
High			

(B)

Dependent variable	Independent variable		
	Low	Medium	High
Low			Reference cell
Medium	B	A	
High			

PHOTO 14.2 What factors do you think might affect someone's view of whether the government should give aid to the elderly?

The process is similar, but in the reverse, for the inverse-ordered pairs, where the value of one variable will go up relative to the reference cell (dark blue, Figure 14.2B), whereas the other goes down. Figure 14.2 illustrates what some inverse-ordered pairs would be if I start with the cell, in dark blue, which is highest on the independent variable (column) but lowest (hence in an opposite, or inverse, direction) on the dependent variable. Now, the light-blue-shaded cells are also moving in opposite directions to the reference cell. For example, the light-blue-shaded cell "A" moved *down* from high to medium on the independent variable (column) relative to the reference cell and *up* from low to medium on the dependent variable (row). Therefore, the ranked values of the light-blue-shaded pair are moving in a different direction from the reference pair. This process of inverse and same-ordered pairs is done for each cell in the table and there is a formula that calculates how these pairs relate. However, because in our spirit of "getting the job done" I am not focusing on hand calculations, we do not need to cover these formulas here, although your professor may choose to. I am simply using these tables to illustrate the *concept* of the same and inverse-ordered pairs. Because of this, I am not getting into the hand calculation of Gamma here, as now we are going to primarily be using SPSS or R for the computations; however, even so, there is a caveat that we need to discuss before moving forward.

Because the coding of ordinal variables is somewhat arbitrary and does not always reflect the actual rank of the values, the researcher needs to be aware of the coding scheme if intending to use the Gamma statistic. If the researcher is coding all variables on his or her own and following the advice for coding ordinal measures that I discussed in Chapter 10, where values that are consistent with the researcher's research goals are coded higher, then the caveat is already addressed. However, when using data coded by someone else, such as with the GSS, the practice of coding responses of higher rank a higher numerical code value may not be followed. For example, where the response is that the government "definitely should be responsible" for providing care for the elderly, the variable AIDOLD is coded as "1" (because it appears first in the answer options) and, thus would appear first on a bivariate table, and the value "definitely should not" is coded as "4." This presentation of rank, where the most positive response is actually coded as the lowest rank, would alter the sign of the Gamma statistic and could lead to a confusing interpretation of results. As such, it is easy to use the recoding skills learned in Chapter 10 to simply reorganize these codes, and I will now call this new recoded variable aidoldrc, where the "rc" indicates that the variable has been recoded. Once I recode this data and run a Gamma, again, using the same process as I did for Lambda and Cramer's *V*, but now selecting "Gamma" instead, I get the following output:

Government should provide aid for the elderly - recode * Subjective class identification Crosstabulation

			Subjective class identification				
			LOWER CLASS	WORKING CLASS	MIDDLE CLASS	UPPER CLASS	Total
Government should provide aid for the elderly - recode	Definitely should not be	Count	4	12	13	3	32
		% within Subjective class identification	3.1%	2.0%	2.3%	6.5%	2.4%
	Probably should not be	Count	3	53	70	2	128
		% within Subjective class identification	2.3%	8.7%	12.4%	4.3%	9.5%
	Probably should be	Count	34	225	255	16	530
		% within Subjective class identification	26.0%	36.8%	45.2%	34.8%	39.2%
	Definitely should be	Count	90	322	226	25	663
		% within Subjective class identification	68.7%	52.6%	40.1%	54.3%	49.0%
Total		Count	131	612	564	46	1,353
		% within Subjective class identification	100.0%	100.0%	100.0%	100.0%	100.0%

Symmetric Measures

		Value	Asymptotic Standard Error[a]	Approximate T^b	Approximate Significance
Ordinal by Ordinal	Gamma	-.232	.040	-5.747	.000
N of Valid Cases		1,353			

a. Not assuming the null hypothesis.

b. Using the asymptotic standard error assuming the null hypothesis.

Chi-Square Tests

	Value	df	Asymptotic Significance (2-sided)
Pearson Chi-Square	51.733[a]	9	.000
Likelihood Ratio	53.638	9	.000
Linear-by-Linear Association	25.342	1	.000
N of Valid Cases	1353		

a. Three cells (18.8%) have expected count less than 5. The minimum expected count is 1.09.

To illustrate my earlier discussion of same-ordered and inverse-ordered pairs with this example, one pair of values would be "Lower class and Definitely should not be." Both values are the lowest possible value for the independent and dependent variables. To have a *pair* of values that is ranked both higher (I can't have any pairs where both variables in the pair are ranked lower because the values of this pair are the lowest), one option would be the pair "Working class" and "probably should not be." In this instance, the working class is ranked higher than the lower class and "probably should not be" is ranked higher than "definitely should not be." Therefore, both values in the second pair are ranked higher than the first pair. On the contrary, if I start with the most extreme inverse rank of the upper class, which is the highest value of the independent variable, and definitely should not be allowed to conduct video surveillance, which is the *lowest* on the dependent variable, now I have an inverse-ordered pair. A comparison inverse-ordered pair would be middle class, a move down in rank for the independent variable, and "probably should not be," a move up in rank for the dependent variable. Therefore, these values are moving in the opposite, or inverse, direction of that first pair. There are additional same-ordered and inverse-ordered pairs in this example that factor into the calculation of Gamma. I am just illustrating the concept with these individual examples.

Gamma, like other measures of association, ranges in magnitude from 0 (no relationship) to 1 (perfect relationship), with the sign showing the direction of the relationship score rankings. Gamma can be interpreted in two ways. As a PRE measure, Gamma, which my output shows here has a value of –.23, can be multiplied by 100 to represent the percentage of improvement in predicting the dependent variable by taking into account the independent variable, and as such would follow the same template of interpretation as Lambda.

> **Our example:** Using the information on social class to predict the view of whether
>
> the government should provide care for the elderly, we reduced our error of prediction by
>
> only 23%.

Gamma can also be interpreted more like the next two measures of association I will cover, which is Spearman's rho and Pearson's *r*, by discussing the relative strength of the relationship between the variables, where closer to 0 indicates a weaker relationship and closer to 1 is a stronger relationship. However, as with Cramer's *V*, interpreting any value in between 0 and 1, such as a score of .23 or .40 on its own is more difficult because, in reality, a bivariate relationship of real data is very unlikely to produce high values close to 1. Although no researcher is likely to question whether a value of .75 is strong or not, as it is fairly clear that it would be, one might consider a value of .35 to be weak, whereas another might consider it to be moderate. Nonetheless, Box 14.1 presents as an admittedly somewhat arbitrary, but commonly accepted, guideline interpretation of strengths for Gamma that would lead to this possible interpretation, coupled with the interpretation for statistical significance:

> **Our example:** Statistical tests reveal that social class and view of whether the
>
> government should provide care for the elderly have a statistically significant but weak
>
> inverse relationship where the higher the social class, the less likely one is to feel that the
>
> government should care for the elderly ($X^2(9) = 51.73$, $p < .01$, $G = -.23$).

In the same SPSS box where I could select Gamma, there are some other ordinal measures of association mentioned that I want to recognize briefly, even though I will not go into detail about them for our purpose of "getting the job done." These are Somer's *d*, Kendall's Tau-b, and Kendall's Tau-c. All four of the ordinal measures (including Gamma in that count) that appear in this SPSS box look at the rank pairs and all have their relative strength interpreted similarly to that which I presented for Gamma in Box 14.1; however, Gamma is the only PRE measure and, therefore, is the only one of the four in which if a researcher multiplies the value by 100, the researcher can determine the percent of improved predictability. There are some additional differences between Gamma and the other three measures. First Gamma is a **symmetrical measure** of association, which means that its value is the same regardless of which variable is your independent variable. Somer's *d*, however, is asymmetrical and is calculated by a formula that considers not only the same-ordered (N_s) and inverse-ordered (N_d) pairs but also pairs that are tied (in the same column) on the independent variable. Hence, when researchers have a strong sense of the independent variable and want to include that additional information, they might choose to use Somer's *d*. Kendall's Tau-b includes consideration of pairs tied not only on the independent variable but on the dependent variable as well, so it includes the most information in the data and, like Gamma, it does not matter which variable is the independent one. However, tau-b is most appropriate for tables that are square, meaning that the two variables have the same number of answer choices (e.g., a 2 × 2 or 3 × 3 table). When the variables do not produce a square table, Kendall's tau-c would be the appropriate choice. Again, however, Gamma works in all of these situations and that is why it is the statistic I focused on. I mention the others because they all build off the basic calculations involved in Gamma, are run from the same command in SPSS, have similar interpretations for relative strength, and your professor may want you to learn them. The differences are summarized in Box 14.3.

BOX 14.3

HOW CATEGORICAL ORDINAL MEASURES OF ASSOCIATION RELATE

Measure of association	PRE measure	Requires identification of independent variable	Requires a square table
Gamma	Y	N	N
Somer's *d*	N	Y	N
Kendall's tau-b	N	N	Y
Kendall's tau-c	N	N	N

However, what if I wanted to determine the strength of the association between two ordinal levels of measurement that were created as scales, ordinal measures that had too many answer choices to make a meaningful summary bivariate table, or between an ordinal measure with a lot of values and an interval/ratio measure? For example, various opinion polls and academic sources have documented the decline in frequency of formal religious attendance and religious membership. A case in point is that in 1938, 73% of Americans responded to a Gallup poll that they belong to a church, synagogue, or mosque, but in 2018, this figure had dropped to only 50% (Jones, 2019). What if I wanted to see whether age and the frequency of church attendance were related, where older people were more likely to attend church regularly than younger people? In the GSS sample, I would use the variable ATTEND for the frequency of church attendance, which has eight values ranging from never to more than one time a week and age (AGE), which is a ratio measure. Following the decision tree, I would see:

1. **What am I doing?** Finding the strength of an association

2. **What is the lowest level of measurement of the two variables?** Ordinal
   ATTEND is ordinal

PHOTO 14.3 Thinking of people you know, do you think age and frequency of attending religious services are related?

3. **Do I have comparatively few answer categories?**
   No. ATTEND has many options, as does AGE, which is a ratio measure.

4. **Decision:**

   Spearman's rho $r_s = 1 - \left(\dfrac{6ED^2}{N(N^2 - 1)} \right)$

   where "D" is the difference of the relative rankings of cases (D).

You may remember that in Chapter 13's decision tree (Figure 13.2), I mentioned that in hypothesis testing sometimes researchers encounter a situation in which the number of groups they want to compare, based on their independent variable, is not categorical and their dependent variable is interval/ratio. In this instance, a researcher has too many groups, based on the independent variable, to compare. I also mentioned that if the dependent variable was not normally distributed, I would calculate a Spearman's rho (Figure 13.2) but that I would discuss this statistic in Chapter 14 instead of in Chapter 13. That is because, while a measure of association, I can relate the resulting Spearman's rho statistic to the t-distribution for hypothesis testing using the following formula:

$$ t = r_s \sqrt{(N - 2)/\left(1 - r_s^2\right)} $$

$$ \mathrm{df} = N - 2 $$

When I run the SPSS, the output (appears in the next page), which includes a p-value for a hypothesis test based on this formula, is produced appears on the next page.

What you see here is called a **correlation matrix**, and you will notice that it is symmetrical. This means that the values of "1" form a diagonal where the correlation values under the line of that diagonal are the same as the correlation values above it. That is because correlation

Correlations

Spearman's rho			Age of respondent	How often R attends religious services
Spearman's rho	Age of respondent	Correlation Coefficient	1.000	.146[**]
		Sig. (2-tailed)	.	.000
		N	2,857	2,840
	How often R attends religious services	Correlation Coefficient	.146[**]	1.000
		Sig. (2-tailed)	.000	.
		N	2,840	2,850

**. Correlation is significant at the 0.01 level (2-tailed).

statistics are calculated for all pairs of variables, regardless of the order the variables are in. Therefore, a computer program will run the statistic for age by religious attendance *and* religious attendance by age. The variables are the same, only the order the computer reads them in is different; therefore, their correlation value is the same as well. In fact, when presenting correlation matrixes in written reports, it is common to only present information on half the diagonal.

As with the other measures of association, a value of 0 means that there is no association between the variables, whereas a score of 1 means that there were no disagreements in the ranks of the variables and, therefore, that the two variables are a perfect fit. The sign indicates the direction of the relationship where, as before, a positive sign means that the two variables are moving in the same direction and a negative sign means that they are moving in opposite directions. Again, however, any bivariate relationship is not likely to have a value of 1 in the real world, so the interpretation of the relative association between two variables via a Spearman's rho are along the same lines as it is for other ordinal tests that I presented earlier and that is summarized in Box 14.1. Therefore, in this instance, my interpretation would read something like:

Our example: Statistical tests reveal that respondent age is weakly and positively associated with the frequency of attendance at religious services ($r_s = .15$, $p < .01$).

✓ LEARNING CHECK 14.2: ORDINAL ASSOCIATION MEASURES

1. A researcher is interested in studying the strength of the relationship between support for gun control (support/unsure/do not support) and political views (liberal/moderate/conservative). What measure of association would be appropriate?

2. A researcher examining the relationship between college students, score on a social attachment scale that is not normally distributed, and their reported number of Facebook friends finds the following information: $r_s = -.43$, $p < .05$. What would a possible interpretation of these findings be?

Answers to be found at the end of the chapter.

Lowest Level of Measurement: Interval/Ratio

What if a researcher wanted to see whether there was a relationship between education (EDUC) and the age someone had his or her first child (AGEKDBRN)? Both are continuous variables, so if I follow the decision tree, we see:

1. **What am I doing?** Finding the strength of an association

2. **What is the lowest level of measurement of the two variables?** Interval/ratio

3. **Are the variables normally distributed?** Yes based on a histogram, skewness, and kurtosis (not shown)

4. **Do the two variables have a linear relationship?**

Before we continue, I need to discuss some of these considerations a bit more. First, notice that statistically, researchers are more concerned with whether a variable is continuous, and thereby an interval *or* ratio level of measurement, rather than whether the variable is specifically an interval or a ratio measure. This is because the only real difference between the two variables if you recall from Chapter 4 is whether "0" is arbitrary or not. If the answer to the normal distribution question is "no," a researcher would conduct a Spearman's rho, which I just discussed, because that measure of association does not make any assumptions about the data other than that the measures are ordinal. Second, researchers need to establish whether the two variables have a linear relationship. The easiest way to estimate this is to conduct a scatterplot to see if the relationship between the two variables is linear or not. Four scatterplots appear in Figure 14.3, which is illustrated in the next page.

As you can see in Figure 14.3 on the next page, the points in scatterplots A and B are somewhat cigar-shaped, which indicates a linear relationship. If I run a scatterplot, based on SPSS graphing commands learned in Chapter 11 for education (EDUC) and the age when a subject had his or her first child (AGEKDBRN), the result would look like this:

The super-imposed shape shows that the dots tend to cluster in a cigar shape (although not a perfect one), suggesting a linear relationship. The second piece of information that I see is that points are angled upward and to the right a bit, indicating a positive relationship. Because the angle is not very steep, I suspect that the relationship, or effect size, will be somewhat weak. So, to continue with the decision tree:

5. **Do the two variables have a linear relationship?**
   Yes

6. **Decision:** Pearson's *r*

Pearson's *r*, officially called Pearson's Correlation Coefficient, is a measure of linear association that can also identify the direction of the relationship as positive or negative (as indicated by no sign or a "-" sign) and the magnitude of the relationship on a range of 0 to 1. In SPSS, I would use the same command path to calculate Pearson's *r* that I would use for Spearman's rho because the choice of Pearson's *r* is in the same SPSS box (Appendix A), which produces the following output shown after Figure 14.3:

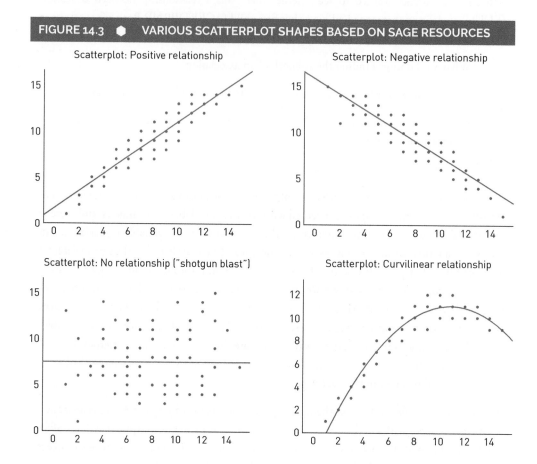

FIGURE 14.3 ● VARIOUS SCATTERPLOT SHAPES BASED ON SAGE RESOURCES

A= POSITIVE LINEAR, B=NEGATIVE LINEAR, C=SHOTGUN NO RELATIONSHIP AND D=A CURVILINEAR

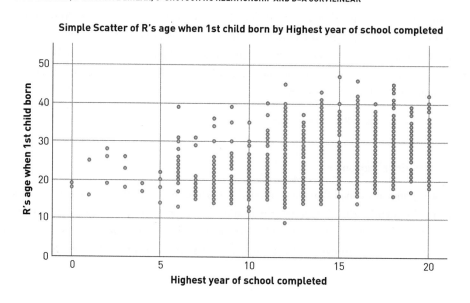

Simple Scatter of R's age when 1st child born by Highest year of school completed

Correlations

		R's age when 1st child born	Highest year of school completed
R's age when 1st child born	Pearson Correlation	1	.413**
	Sig. (2-tailed)		.000
	N	2,056	2,050
Highest year of school completed	Pearson Correlation	.413**	1
	Sig. (2-tailed)	.000	
	N	2,050	2,858

**. Correlation is significant at the 0.01 level (2-tailed).

Because Pearson's r applies to levels of measurement that are quantifiable, the interpretive meaning for different values, even though they are still somewhat arbitrarily defined, is more nuanced and appears in Box 14.1 with the interpretation of the other association statistics. Furthermore, like Spearman's rho, the Pearson's r statistic can be related to the t-distribution in order to test for statistical significance, as mentioned back in Chapter 13. In fact, the formula and degrees of freedom are the same as those when using Spearman's rho, with the substitution of Pearson's r for rho into the formula.

$$t = r\sqrt{(N-2)/\left(1-r^2\right)}$$

$$df = N-2$$

Consequently, the interpretation of this output would follow a similar template as that for Spearman's rho and the other measures of association with the exception that I would say:

Our example: Statistical tests reveal that education has a moderate positive statistically significant relationship with how old someone is when they have their first child ($r = .41$, $p < .01$).

Last, Pearson's r, when squared also acts as a PRE measure, the coefficient of determination, that can be interpreted as the other PRE-based measures were. In this instance, the R^2 value is .17, indicating that 17% of the variation in the age when someone has their first child is explained by their highest level of education.

BOX 14.4

PEARSON'S *R* IN RESEARCH EXAMPLE

Undeniably social media has become an integral way for many to stay connected with their social networks, to learn about new products, and to keep abreast of current events. Advertising online is a delicate balance between addressing people's fear of missing out (FOMO) on new products or trends while making sure that the consumers are not inundated with so much content that they experience "social media fatigue" and withdraw from the product.

To study how FOMO and social media fatigue relate to consumptive patterns, Bright and Logan (2018) analyzed 518 surveys from a representative sample of the US social media users. According to these researchers, when consumers "opt in" to receive branded content by liking specific social media pages, the receipt of the special offers or deals that result may reduce these people's FOMO by making them feel privy to the most current benefits. However, overuse of this practice by advertisers may have the unintended consequence of increasing these same consumer's social media fatigue. Bright and Logan (2018) conducted Pearson's *r* analyses to see how factors such as FOMO, attitudes toward brands, and attitudes toward advertisers relate to social media fatigue. A subset of their findings appears below:

	1	2	3	4	5	6	7
1. Social media fatigue	1.00						
2. Social media privacy	0.43**	1.00					
3. Fear of missing out (FOMO)	0.48**	0.18**	1.00				
4. Attitude toward brands	0.35**	0.30**	0.50**	1.00			
5. Attitude toward social media	0.15**	0.23**	0.43**	0.49**	1.00		
6. Attitude toward social media advertising	0.16**	0.10*	0.33**	0.48**	0.32**	1.00	
7. Social media advertising intrusiveness	0.13**	0.11*	−0.07	−0.22**	−0.17**	−0.50**	1.00

Table II.
Pearson correlation coefficients among key variables

Notes: $n = 518$. $*p < 0.05$; $**p < 0.01$

To read this matrix, all the instances where the correlation coefficient is 1.0 are where the variable is correlated against itself. Furthermore, only one half of the correlation matrix is presented because the information above the imaginary diagonal line (the line indicated by all the 1.0 values) is repetitive of what is below it and, therefore, omitted. What is left is to read the unique correlation coefficients. For example, the correlation coefficient of .43 that you see in the first column, the second row, is the strength of the relationship between social media fatigue (indicated by the "1") and social media privacy (indicated by the "2"). Similarly, the coefficient of .18 that you see in column 2, row 3, is the strength of the relationship between social media privacy (#2) and FOMO (#3). By matching the numbers on the top row with the column numbers, you can see which two variables a coefficient represents.

To practice interpreting this output, consider each of the following:

1. What is the variable that has the weakest relationship with social media fatigue?

2. What is the variable that has the strongest relationship with social media fatigue?

3. What is the correlation between attitudes toward brands and attitudes toward social media advertising? Is it positive or negative? What does that mean?

Source: Bright, L. F., & Logan, K. (2018).

Answers:

1. Social media advertising intrusiveness, because it has the smallest correlation coefficient of .13.

2. FOMO, because it has the highest correlation coefficient of .48.

3. .48 (Column 4, Row 6). It is positive, which means that as attitudes toward the brand increases, FOMO also increases.

LEARNING CHECK 14.3: INTERVAL/RATIO ASSOCIATION MEASURES

1. What shape should a scatterplot have to indicate an approximate linear relationship between two variables?

2. A researcher found that the correlation between immediate family size and socioeconomic status was −.57. What does this mean?

3. Based on the information in #2, how much of the variance in this sample's socioeconomic status would be explained by family size?

Answers to be found at the end of the chapter.

WHAT AM I DOING? PREDICTION

Bivariate linear regression

Measures of association can give you an idea of how strongly variables are related, but what if you wanted to see how much each year of education affected the age one first becomes a parent? In other words, can researchers examine how each additional year of education one obtains affects the age when they first become a parent? If we follow the decision tree, you see:

1. **WAID?** Finding how much a unit change in the independent variable affects the dependent variable

2. **Were the observations selected randomly?**
   Yes

3. **Are both variables measured at the interval/ratio level?**
   Yes.

4. **Is there a linear relationship between the variables?**
   As we saw from the earlier scatterplot, yes.

5. **Decision:** Linear regression

$$Y' = a + bX$$

where: $b = \dfrac{\Sigma(X - \bar{X})(Y - \bar{Y})}{\Sigma(X - \bar{X})^2}$

$a = \bar{Y} + b\bar{X}$

If the formula looks familiar to you, it is because it is the basic equation for a line where:

Y' = the value of the dependent variable

a = the Y-intercept, which is the predicted value of Y when $X = 0$

b = the slope that represents the effect of a unit change in X on the dependent variable (Y)

c = a given value of the independent variable

However, this is not the equation of any old line. I mean, I could draw multiple lines through a scatterplot, but that does not mean that it would be the line I want to use. This is the formula for a **linear regression line**, sometimes also just called a regression analysis, which uses an estimation technique called **least squares analysis** to find the straight line that best fits the data points by touching as many points as possible while simultaneously minimizing the distance between all the X and Y relationships exhibited in the data, hence the Y' in the formula as opposed to just Y. That's why the regression line is statistically described as being drawn to touch each conditional mean of Y. The graph below is the same scatterplot that we looked at earlier, but now it has a regression line drawn through the points. When we run a linear regression in SPSS, it produces the following output:

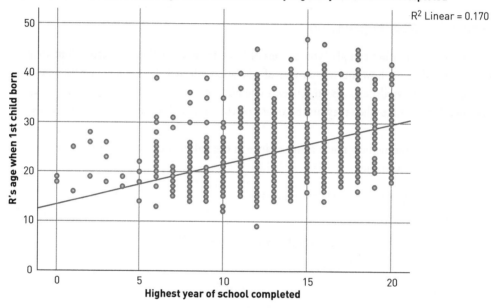

Simple Scatter with Fit Line of R's age when 1st child born by Highest year of school completed

Model Summary

Model	R	R^2	Adjusted R^2	Std. Error of the Estimate
1	.413[a]	.170	.170	5.396

a. Predictors: (Constant), Highest year of school completed

Coefficients[a]

Model		Unstandardized Coefficients B	Std. Error	Standardized Coefficients Beta	t	Sig.
1	(Constant)	13.438	.542		24.772	.000
	Highest year of school completed	.806	.039	.413	20.494	.000

a. Dependent Variable: R's age when 1st child born

In this output, I learn quite a few points. First, I see that Pearson's r is .413, which, as I already discussed in the previous section, indicates a moderately positive association between the two variables. Second, I see the R^2 value of .17, which I also discussed above. Third, the slope or "b" is .81 (with rounding), which tells us that for each year of education, the age someone is when they have their first child increases .81 years. The sign of the slope should be the same sign as the Pearson's r because characteristics of the slope are part of the Pearson's r calculation and both are positive, so they are in fact the same. Fourth, education has a statistically significant effect on the age of first birth because the "Sig" value is less than .05 (in fact, it is less than .01). Fifth, I see that "a" for the resulting linear equation is the "Constant" and is 13.44 (with rounding).

Therefore, based on all of this information, the linear regression line would read:

$$Y' = 13.44 + .81\,X$$

I can use this regression line equation to predict one's age at first birth for different levels of education. For example, if I wanted to see at what age people with a high school degree generally have their first child, would substitute 12 in for X and get

$$Y' = 13.44 + .81\,(12) = 23.16$$

I see that people with a high school degree generally have their first child around age 23. However, as we know, any statistical test is not going to exactly fit all people all the time; therefore, researchers also do not expect that *every* person who only has a high school degree will become a parent for the first time at age 23.16 years. The regression line gives us the tool to make the best guess based on the variation seen in the data.

Some Additional Points

There are some points that are important to note about linear regressions. The first is that sometimes if a scatterplot reveals a curvilinear relationship, the relationship can be "linearized" by transforming the data, such as by taking the log of the X variable. This type of data transformation is beyond both our focus of "getting the job done" and most undergraduate statistics textbooks. Therefore, I am just mentioning it here to make you aware of the possibility.

Another point is that sometimes researchers want to predict a dependent variable that is *not* continuous. That type of prediction can be done, but it involves nonlinear statistical methods that are not as easily interpretable as linear methods and, therefore, once again beyond our goal of "getting the job done." However, if you take an upper-level undergraduate statistics class or a graduate-level statistics class, you are likely to learn these nonlinear techniques.

 LEARNING CHECK 14.4: BIVARIATE REGRESSION

1. In order to see an approximate linear regression, a scatterplot should have what shape?

2. The sign of the slope should be the same sign as for what other statistic?

3. Using the regression line calculated in the chapter, predict the age a sub-ject is likely to become a parent if they have a four-year college degree (in other words, education = 16 years).

Answers to be found at the end of the chapter.

BRIEF INTRODUCTION TO MULTIVARIATE ANALYSIS

I have been discussing statistical and substantive significance, even prediction, from a bivariate perspective for the past three chapters; however, in reality, clearly, it is unlikely that *one* independent variable is going to be the sole, or have even a noticeably strong, effect on any dependent variable. As I have been periodically saying throughout this book—the real world is complicated and messy. Plus, as you learned in Chapter 2, the literature review is likely to suggest that numerous factors other than the independent variable of interest affect the dependent variable, and sometimes even each other. Therefore, although a detailed discussion of how to conduct multivariate analysis is beyond our goal of "getting the job done," there are some basic points I can make about multivariate analysis here and some points I want to make about multivariate contingency tables for categorical analysis in Chapter 15.

Partial Correlation

In the previous section, we examined the effect that education has on the age someone has their first child; however, other variables like religion, race, political views, attitudes toward children, and/or marital status could all also affect how old someone is when they first become a parent. **Partial correlation** is a statistic researchers use to see how an original bivariate relationship changes when they add the effects of a third variable, which you have already learned is frequently called a **control variable**. If you recall from earlier, I found that the original bivariate correlation between someone's years of education (EDUC) and the age they first became a parent (AGEKDBRN) is .41. This original bivariate relationship is called the **zero-order correlation** because it is controlling for zero additional factors. Once I add a control variable, such as the father's level of education (PAEDUC) as a measure of the socioeconomic status of someone's childhood, then I have a **first-order correlation** because I have added the first control variable to the original bivariate relationship. If a researcher adds a second control variable, then the partial correlation is a second-order correlation and so on.

Partial correlations lead to three possible outcomes. One possibility is that the bivariate and partial correlation produce similar values, such as if the partial correlation between age and year someone becomes a parent controlling for father's education produced a partial correlation coefficient of .40. This is not much different from my bivariate correlation of .41 and this outcome suggests a **direct relationship** between education and age of parenthood where the third variable, father's education, has no effect on this original bivariate relationship.

A second possibility occurs when the partial correlation is much weaker, for example, a value of .30, than the bivariate correlation, and this outcome would indicate either a **spurious** or **intervening relationship**. We have already encountered the concept of a spurious relationship in Chapter 2, which is when an observed relationship between two variables is actually caused by a third, sometimes topical or sometimes methodological, influence that is what is really affecting the dependent variable. So in a spurious relationship, the third variable Z

FIGURE 14.4 ● POSSIBLE CONTROL VARIABLE RELATIONSHIPS

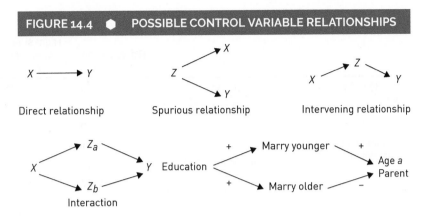

has an effect on both X and Y (Figure 14.4). An example would be how the socioeconomic background one grew up in (as indicated by father's educational attainment, Z) affects one's educational attainment (X) and also affects when someone has their first child (Y). The other reason for a lower partial correlation would be when the third variable, Z, has an intervening effect where the real relationship is not really between X and Y but is instead through the third variable Z, where X affects Z and then Z, in turn, is what affects Y. So, for example, imagine that our third variable Z was the age at first marriage. An intervening relationship would be where education (X) affects the age of first marriage (Z) and the age someone marries, in turn, affects the age in which they become a parent (Y). Statistically, spurious and intervening effects are the same, and the partial correlation (statistic) is noticeably lower. Therefore, deciding which is the reason, a spurious or intervening relationship for the observed effect has to be decided on other factors, such as theory, information from other studies, and/or the time order.

The last relationship I will cover is an **interaction**, which occurs when the X–Y relationship is different for different values of Z. For example, if the age of first marriage, Z, exhibits an interaction effect with education, I might see that people who have higher levels of education but marry younger (perhaps while in school or very soon after obtaining a degree) will also become parents sooner relative to people who also have higher levels of education but pushed off marriage to later (so they had children later). In this instance, both variables, education *and* age at first marriage, exert their own effect on the age when a person first becomes a parent. Interaction effects cannot be tested by partial correlations, but they are important considerations, so researchers need to explore their data to see if this might be relevant.

The output for the partial correlation (appears in the next page) between education (EDUC) and the age someone had their first child (AGEKDBRN) while controlling for the father's level of education (PAEDUC) (Steps to run the statistic are in Appendices A and B):

As you see, the partial correlation of .34 is noticeably less than the zero-order correlation of .41; therefore, I would conclude that father's education (Z) creates either a spurious or intervening relationship. Because father's education comes first in time, this relationship is likely to be intervening.

Correlations

Control Variables				R's age when 1st child born	Highest year of school completed
Highest year school completed, father	R's age when 1st child born	Correlation		1.000	.341
		Significance (2-tailed)		.	.000
		df		0	1477
	Highest year of school completed	Correlation		.341	1.000
		Significance (2-tailed)		.000	.
		df		1,477	0

Multiple Regression

Another useful tool for analysis is multiple regression, which I will illustrate with three independent variables, though if the sample size is large enough, it can accommodate many more. The general formula for a multivariate linear regression is:

$$\hat{Y} = a + b_1 X_1 + b_2 X_2$$

where

$\hat{Y}$ = the predicted score on the dependent variable

X_1 = the score on the independent variable X_1

X_2 = the score on the independent variable X_2

a = the score on the Y-intercept when both X_1 and $X_2 = 0$

b_1 = the partial slope of Y and X_1, meaning the unit change in Y for X_1 when X_2 is held constant (controlled)

b_2 = the partial slope of Y and X_2, meaning the unit change in Y for X_2 when X_1 is held constant (controlled)

If, for example, I wanted to see how a person's education (EDUC), his/her father's education (PAEDUC), and SEX influence the age that a person had his/her first child (AGEKDBRN), I have a multivariate analysis. However, notice that although all the variables that I have been discussing up to this point have been an interval/ratio level of measurement, now I added the variable SEX, which is nominal. Obviously, some very important factors, such as race, gender, and marital status, cannot be measured at a continuous level so researchers need to have a way to include these into the linear regression formula. The answer is to recode categorical variables into **dummy variables**, where each categorical *value* becomes a 0 to 1 *variable* with a code of 1 if that particular value was selected and the code of 0 if it was not. So, for example, the GSS codes SEX as 1 = male and 2 = female. I would make this a dummy variable by making a new variable, which I will call male (remember, the lower case means this is not a GSS variable) that I will code as 1 if a person is male and 0 if a person is female. Therefore, in a regression, the Y-intercept will be the dependent value for a person who is female and the the Y-intercept *and* the coefficient for **male** will be the dependent value for someone who is male. The number of dummy variables to make from an existing variable is determined by k-1, where k is the number of values in the original variable. So, for example, if a researcher has a variable for race with four categories—White, Black/African American, Hispanic/Latino, and Other—the researcher might have the following three (4–1 = 3) dummy variables:

White = 1 if White, 0 otherwise

Black/African American = 1, 0 otherwise

Hispanic/Latino = 1, 0 otherwise

I do not need a fourth category for Other because if White = 0, Black/African American = 0, and Hispanic/Latino = 0, then the respondent must be "Other." The value of the original variable that is not included in the regression is called the **reference category** or reference group and the variables that do appear in the model are always interpreted compared to the reference group. So for our gender example, the resulting information would be interpreted something like "being male as opposed to female" and our race example might be something like "being White as opposed to some other race" or "being Hispanic/Latino as opposed to being some other race." If the coefficient is positive for the dummy variable, then the dependent variable is higher for that group than the reference group, and if it is negative, then the dependent variable would be lower. If the regression coefficient is statistically significant, then the difference between the dummy group and the reference group is also statistically significant.

I want to make one more point before I move on with an illustration. In SPSS, independent variables can be entered into the regression equation a variety of ways, but I will just mention two of the most common: **enter**, sometimes also called forced entry, and stepwise methods. The "Enter" method is used when there is a theoretical justification, frequently based on a literature review, for putting all desired independent variables, regardless of whether any particular variable ends up being statistically related to the dependent variable or not, into the regression model. In a **stepwise regression method**, SPSS will include or remove one independent variable at each step starting with the independent variable that has the strongest statistical significant effect on the dependent variable, followed by the independent variable that has the next statistically significant and strongest effect (in magnitude) on the dependent variable and so on until there are no more independent variables significantly contributing to the overall model.

Let's illustrate some of these points using the **entry regression method** to analyze the hypothesis that the higher one's education level (EDUC), controlling for father's education (PAEDUC) and sex (**male** as the dummy variable, female as the omitted reference variable), the older one is when they first became a parent (AGEKDBRN). For our purposes of "getting the job done" and just illustrating how to run and interpret this type of analysis, we will assume that we have tested and verified that all the assumptions for linear regression are met.

Model Summary

Model	R	R^2	Adjusted R^2	Std. Error of the Estimate
1	.443[a]	.196	.194	5.268

a. Predictors: (Constant), male, Highest year of school completed, Highest year school completed, father

ANOVA[a]

Model		Sum of Squares	df	Mean Square	F	Sig.
1	Regression	9,973.737	3	3,324.579	119.801	.000[b]
	Residual	40,960.260	1,476	27.751		
	Total	50,933.997	1,479			

a. Dependent Variable: R's age when 1st child born

b. Predictors: (Constant), male, Highest year of school completed, Highest year school completed, father

Coefficients[a]

Model		Unstandardized Coefficients		Standardized Coefficients		
		B	Std. Error	Beta	t	Sig.
1	(Constant)	12.792	.669		19.113	.000
	Highest year of school completed	.726	.051	.370	14.337	.000
	Highest year school completed, father	.090	.037	.063	2.452	.014
	male	2.234	.277	.188	8.054	.000

a. Dependent Variable: R's age when 1st child born

As with a bivariate regression, the unstandardized Beta column gives us the slope, here called the **partial slope**, for each variable's contribution to the regression. Our regression line would read:

$$\hat{Y} = 12.792 + .726(EDUC) + .090(PAEDUC) + 2.234(male)$$

The equation tells us that the age the subject has his/her first child increases .726 years with each year of education when holding constant father's education and being male; it increases .090 years for each year of father's education while holding constant the other two variables, and being male will add 2.234 years to when someone has their first child when holding constant the other two variables in that instance. To put this another way, the equation tells us that if we have two people who have the same number of years of education and whose fathers have the same number of years of education, but one person is male and the other is female, then the

Chapter 14 ■ Finding the Degree of Association and Prediction

male will likely have his first child about 2.234 years later than the other person with the same characteristics but is female. We also know by looking at the "Sig. value" in the "Coefficients" table that all three variables have a statistically significant effect on the age one has his or her first child.

However, the units of measurement in a multivariate analysis are likely to be different. In our example, three of our four variables have years as the units of measurement (*years* of education, *years* of father's education, age *in years* when someone has their first child) and one does not (gender has individuals as the unit of measurement). In fact, frequently many of the variables are likely to involve different units of measurement, some may be in years, others in dollars, and others in individuals, for example. So how do researchers know which variable has the greatest effect? The coefficient in the equation that I just discussed gives us unit change, but that is not directly comparable across different levels of measurement and the significance value just gives researchers the statistical change. The standardized slope coefficient, frequently called the beta and symbolized by β, converts the values of the variables into a standardized measure analogous to what the Z-score does that you learned about in Chapter 11. The larger the beta value, regardless of whether it is positive or negative, the stronger the effect of that variable on the dependent variable. In our case, I see that being male has the strongest effect, when simultaneously considering the effect of the other independent variables, on the age someone becomes a parent because it has the highest beta value of .277. (Remember, the constant is not a variable, it is the Y-intercept, so its beta value is not relevant here).

Two final pieces of information. As some of our earlier statistics showed, researchers can use the information in the multivariate regression to calculate the PRE of all the variables together for explaining the variance of the dependent variable. This measure is called R^2. We see in our example that we have an R^2 value .196, which means that the subject's education, father's education, and gender explain 19.6% of the variation in the age someone has their first child. If I take the square root of R^2, I have Pearson's multiple correlation coefficient, which measures the linear relationship between the dependent variable and all the combined independent variables. In our example, the square root of .196 is .442, which suggests that our variables combined have a moderate relationship on the age a subject becomes a parent.

BOX 14.5
MULTIVARIATE REGRESSION RESEARCH EXAMPLE

Specialty courts, like drug treatment courts, mental health courts, and veterans courts, are courts that are designed to address the needs of specific populations. Veterans courts were developed to address the needs of veterans with mental illnesses who were appearing in drug and mental health courts by allowing veterans with eligible offenses (and this varies by the individual programs) to be diverted from incarceration in favor of a more specialized form of treatment that usually involves regular court appearances, some form of community-based treatment, and veteran-specific interventions. The intensive nature of these programs means that not all veterans who enter will successfully complete them. In order to study what influences premature program termination, Johnson and colleagues (2016) conducted phone surveys with

(*Continued*)

BOX 14.5 (*CONTINUED*)

MULTIVARIATE REGRESSION RESEARCH EXAMPLE

ASSOCIATION COURT VARIABLES PREDICTING THE PERCENTAGE OF SUBJECTS TERMINATED FROM VC PROGRAMS USING STEPWISE LINEAR REGRESSION

Steps	R^2	Adjusted R^2	Degrees of Freedom	F	p-Value
11	.723	.442	11.65	6.474	<.001 *
Final model			Beta (SE)	Standardized beta	p-value
Constant			.538 (.462)		
Behavioral contracts[a]			−.194 (.066)	−.271	.005*
Allow reserve/guard[a]			−.428 (.096)	−.414	<.001*
Accept veterans outside jurisdiction[a]			.146 (.064)	.219	.027 •
Later phases permit less stringent testing[a]			−.310 (.098)	−.300	.002*
Phase progression based on measurable goals[a]			352 (.156)	.322	.001*
Post-plea veteran defendants[1]			.257 (.093)	.249	.008*
Works in close partnership with Va health care network[a]			−.679 (.259)	−.232	.011*
Conducts frequent drug and alcohol testing[a]			.660 (.275)	.225	.019 *
Brief incarceration[a]			−.409 (.153)	−.239	.009*
Court classification[b]: veterans* court			.190 (.071)	.262	.009*
Sanctions arc more severe for failure in immediate goals[a]			.168 (.067)	.231	.015*

*p-value <.05
a Coded as 0 = court did not use this criterion/strategy, 1 = yes, court did use this criterion/strategy
b Coded as 0 = no, 1 = yes, for whether a veteran's treatment

302 Veterans Justice Outreach representatives of veterans courts to examine what was most predictive of a court's percentage of clients terminated from the program.

Using a stepwise linear regression model produced the output that you saw on the previous page.

This output shows that it took 11 iterations, or steps, to achieve the final model and that the variables in this model predict an adjusted 44.2% (Adjusted R^2 = .442) of the total variance in the percentage of clients terminated. Furthermore, this total variance prediction is significant at the $p < .001$ level. We also see that the strongest factor influencing the rate of termination is whether the program allows reserve/national guard veterans (Standardized Beta = −.414) and that this factor is related to lower rates of termination, as indicated by the negative sign. We can learn some other things from looking at this table as well, but it's time for you to try by answering the following questions:

1. What is the Y-intercept in the regression line?

2. What factor had the weakest effect on the percentage of clients terminated? Does this factor increase or decrease the rate of termination? How did you know this?

3. What factor had the second strongest effect on the percentage of clients terminated and what can we say about this effect?

Source: Johnson, R. S., Stolar, A. G., McGuire, J. F., Clark, S., Coonan, L. A., Hausknecht, P., . . . Graham, D. P. (2016).

Answers:

1. The Y-intercept is the "Constant" in the output and it is .538 in this instance.

2. The weakest variable was whether the court accepted veterans outside of the jurisdiction (standardized beta = .219), but it increases the percentage of termination as indicated by the lack of a sign (so the assumption is positive).

3. The second strongest predictor is whether phase progression is based on measurable goals, as indicated by a standardized beta of .322. We can say that this variable has a statistically significant, as indicated by $p<.001$, positive effect on percentage of clients terminated, which means that the programs with measurable goals for phase progression have a higher percentage of clients terminated from the program.

 LEARNING CHECK 14.5: MULTIVARIATE ANALYSIS

1. When a first-order correlation (partial correlation) is not much different from the zero-order correlation, what is the relationship between X, Y, and Z?

2. If I have a variable that addresses the type of college someone attends, which is coded as 1 = community college, 2 = public 4-year university, 3 = private 4-year university, 4 = private 4-year college, and 5 = other, ignoring any possible issues with sample sizes, how many dummy variables would I create based on this?

3. In #2, if I decided to omit "2-year junior college or community college" from the analysis, this dummy variable would be called what?

Answers to be found at the end of the chapter.

Key Terms

Asymmetrical measure of
    association
Control variable
Correlation matrix
Direct relationship
Dummy variable
Effect size
Entry regression method

First-order correlation
Interaction (relationship)
Intervening relationship
Least squares analysis
Linear regression line
Negative relationship
Partial correlation
Partial slope

Positive relationship
Proportionate reduction of error
Reference category
Spurious relationship
Stepwise regression method
Symmetrical measure
Zero-order correlation

Answers to Learning Check Questions

Learning Check 14.1: Nominal Association Measures

1. Lambda

2. Statistical Significance: chi-square; Substantive Significance: Cramer's V and/or lambda

3. Interpretation: Considering major when trying to predict whether someone attends law school improves predictability by 28%.

Learning Check 14.2: Ordinal Association Measures

1. Based on the text, we would use gamma; however, as shown in Figure 14.1 tau-b would also be appropriate because this is a square table.

2. Interpretation: There is a statistically significant, moderate inverse relationship between the number of Facebook friends and scores on a social attachment scale ($r_s = -.43$, $p < .05$).

Learning Check 14.3: Interval/Ratio Association Measures

1. A cigar shape.

2. A value of $r = -.57$ means that there is a moderately strong inverse relationship between family size and socioeconomic status, which

means as family size increases, socioeconomic status decreases.

3. The explained variance, a PRE measure, is determined by squaring the Pearson's r value. So $.57^2 = .3249$, so 32.49% of the variance in this sample's socioeconomic status is explained by their family size.

Learning Check 14.4: Bivariate Regression

1. Cigar

2. Pearson's r

3. $Y' = 13.44 + .81 (16) = 26.4$

Learning Check 14.5: Multivariate Analysis

1. A direct one, which means that the control variable Z has no effect on the original bivariate relationship between X and Y.

2. I would create k-1 values so 5–1 = 4 dummy variables.

3. The reference group or reference category where each of the remaining variables (based on the remaining categories) would be interpreted as "attending a _____ compared to a community college."

End-of-Chapter Problems

1. Which of the following is a PRE-based measure of association?
   a. Cramer's V
   b. Lambda
   c. Gamma
   d. a and b
   e. b and c
   f. a and c

2. A researcher examines the strength of the relationship between marital status and happiness and finds a lambda of .24. What does this mean?
   a. That there is a weak relationship between marital status and happiness (no direction).
   b. That there is a weak positive relationship between marital status and happiness.
   c. The marital status explains about 24% of the variation in happiness.
   d. b and c.

3. In a regression line equation, the slope can tell you
   a. the direction of effect/relationship between the independent and dependent variables
   b. which variables are statistically significant
   c. the magnitude of effect/relationship between the independent and dependent variables
   d. where the line crosses the Y-axis

4. The bivariate correlation between family size (X) and the hours husbands contribute to the household (Y) is .38. When adding a measure of political liberalism (as indicated by a normally distributed index value) as a control variable (Z), the partial correlation is .39. What is the nature of this relationship?
   a. A direct relationship
   b. A spurious relationship
   c. An intervening relationship
   d. An interaction

   For questions 5–13, decide which tests of statistical *and* substantive significance would be appropriate for each scenario.

5. A researcher is interested in whether neighborhoods with an active crime watch program (yes/no) have fewer police reports for property crime in a 12-month span (which is normally distributed).

6. A researcher is interested in seeing how education level (less than a high school degree, high school degree, at least some college) affects concern for the environment (little, moderate, high).

7. A researcher is interested in seeing how the percent of urbanization and homicide rate are related. Both variables are normally distributed and appear to have a linear relationship.

8. A researcher is interested in seeing how race (White, Black, Hispanic, Asian/Pacific Islander, Other) is related to first-year college attrition (returned for sophomore year, did not return).

9. Are hours of television viewing in a week related to introversion (the latter of which is based on a non normally distributed scale)?

10. Does gender role ideology (traditional/nontraditional) affect one's view of whether mothers of young children should have a full-time job if not economically necessary (yes/unsure/no).

11. How strongly is the view of abortion (positive, neutral, negative) and social class (upper-middle class, middle class, working class) related?

12. How strongly are gender and favorite type of pet (measured as dog, cat, reptile, fish, other) related?

13. A researcher is interested in seeing whether being a social science major (measured as yes/no) affects hours of volunteering in a given semester (the latter of which is normally distributed).

Questions 14–17 are based on GSS data.

14. Using the GSS data and any computer/web resources available, test the statistical and substantive relationship between a respondent's view of the number of politicians they think are corrupt (CORRUPT1) and their confidence in the executive branch of the federal government (CONFED).

15. Using the GSS data and any computer/web resources available, test the statistical and substantive relationship between education (EDUC) and the number of children one has (CHILDS).

16. Using the GSS data and any computer/web resources available, test the statistical and substantive relationship between how often a person feels that they have extra time (BORED) and number of children one has (CHILDS).

17. Using the GSS data and any computer/web resources available, test the statistical and substantive relationship between education (EDUC) and hours spent on the Internet (WWWHR).

Questions 18–23 are based on the following SPSS output:

Model Summary

Model	R	R^2	Adjusted R^2	Std. Error of the Estimate
1	.429[a]	.184	.183	1.506

a. Predictors: (Constant), Age of respondent, Highest year of school completed, Gender

ANOVA[a]

Model		Sum of Squares	df	Mean Square	F	Sig.
1	Regression	1,451.932	3	483.977	213.518	.000[b]
	Residual	6,435.120	2,839	2.267		
	Total	7,887.052	2,842			

a. Dependent Variable: Number of children

b. Predictors: (Constant), Age of respondent, Highest year of school completed, Gender

Coefficients[a]

Model		Unstandardized Coefficients B	Std. Error	Standardized Coefficients Beta	t	Sig.
1	(Constant)	1.958	.160		12.224	.000
	Highest year of school completed	-.123	.010	-.219	-12.908	.000
	Gender	-.162	.057	-.048	-2.849	.004
	Age of respondent	.034	.002	.357	21.051	.000

a. Dependent Variable: Number of children

18. How much of the variance in the number of children someone has is explained by their highest education, being male (gender), and their age?
   a. 43%
   b. 18%
   c. 1.5%
   d. 2%

19. Of the three independent variables, which one(s) has(have) a statistically significant effect when simultaneously controlling for the others on the number of children someone has?
   a. Education
   b. Being male (gender)
   c. Age
   d. They all do

20. Which of the following is an appropriate best-fit regression line formula based on this information?

a. $Y' = 1.96 + -.12(\text{education}) + -.16 \text{ male} + .03 (\text{age})$

b. $Y' = .16 + -.01(\text{education}) + -.06 \text{ male} + .00 (\text{age})$

c. $Y' = 12.22 + -12.91(\text{education}) + -2.85 \text{ male} + 21.06 (\text{age})$

21. How many children is a male, college graduate who is 40 years old likely to have (with rounding)?

a. 0

b. 1

c. 2

d. 3

22. Which variable has the strongest effect on the number of children someone has?

a. Education

b. Being male (gender)

c. Age

d. We can't tell

23. True/false: Education and the number of children have a positive relationship.

PRESENTATION OF DATA

Just like there is a lot of information researchers can learn by describing a sample, testing their hypotheses, and examining the strength of associations, there are a lot of different ways researchers can convey that resulting information to others. For example, look at information about online dating sites and apps at the top of the next page and ask yourself: What age group experienced the greatest change in the use of online dating sites or mobile apps?

In which presentation, the graph or the table, was it easier for you to find the answer? You probably answered the graph because the bars allow you to quickly see who has the biggest gap (change) quickly. On the contrary, if I first asked you what age group was the most likely to use online dating or apps in 2015, you might have said the table because it is faster to hone in on the year by looking at the column. Or it may be that no matter the question, you just prefer looking at a graph because it is "prettier" or more interesting looking than a table. Don't cringe if that is what you were thinking; many feel the same way! After all, we all know the saying "a picture is worth a thousand words." The point is, depending on what you are trying

% in each age group who have ever used an online dating site and/or mobile dating app

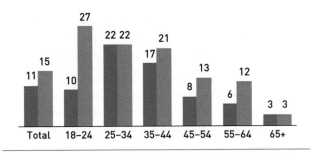

Source: Survey conducted June 10 to July 12, 2015. PEW RESEARCH CENTER

Use of online dating sites or mobile apps by young adults has nearly tripled since 2013		
	Year	
	2013	2015
Age group		
Total	11	15
18–24	10	27
25–34	22	22
35–44	17	21
45–54	8	13
55–64	6	12
65+	3	3

to show, different forms of presentation may share your message more effectively, and, contrary to the saying, pictures do not always make things clearer. It is also important to learn different options for presenting data because researchers do not usually directly distribute their statistical computer output to share our findings. As you saw in the previous four chapters, statistical output frequently produces more information than those reading our results need or want to see. Therefore, an effective and efficient presentation of information is one that removes unnecessary information and instead presents information in a way that facilitates a quick summary or comparison. Therefore, in this chapter, I am going to discuss how to most accurately present these various forms of data summary and comparisons.

UNIVARIATE DATA PRESENTATION

Tables

The most common way of presenting quantitative information for multiple categorical variables is a **frequency table**, which is a tabular display of how often each value for different variables was selected by a subject. As you saw in Chapter 11, computer output might provide *too* much information when running a frequency; therefore, it is the researcher's job to determine the most relevant information and present it to others. Although there are many ways researchers can present a frequency distribution, it is probably easiest to understand some of the most common elements using an example, such as what I present in Box 15.1.

BOX 15.1
FREQUENCY DISTRIBUTION

TABLE 15.1 ⬡   DESCRIPTIVE STATISTICS FOR SELECT VARIABLES FROM THE GSS

Who Should Provide for School	% (*n*)
Government	79.4 (1,071)
Private companies/for profit organizations	5.6 (76)
Non profit organizations/charities	4.7 (63)
Religious organizations	0.6 (8)
Family, relatives or friends	9.7 (131)
Total	1,349
Women are not suited for politics	
Agree	18.7 (353)
Unsure	4.3 (81)
Disagree	77.0 (1,454)
Total	1,888
Respondent age	
18–32	22.2% (634)
33–47	24.9% (711)
48–62	28,6% (818)
63–77	17.5% (500)
78 and older	6.8% (194)

General Social Survey, 2016 wave.

For example, you will notice that any table should have a table number and title for easy reference. In Box 15.1, Table 15.1, for example, shows that it is the first table in Chapter 15, and the title tells us that the material within the table focuses on descriptive statistics. Second, each variable should have a short heading, such as "Who should provide for school?" that provides a general idea of what is being categorized, along with labels for each value, or response, that are somehow set off from the main variable to show that they are values and not a different variable. This can be done, for example, using a few spaces or an indent to distinguish the values from the variable. The corresponding descriptive statistic is also presented and labeled. For example, for categorical variables, the researcher would probably include the percentage and frequency of occurrence for each value. Sometimes each of these will be in a separate column; however, if they are in the same column, as in Box 15.1, it is customary to have the percent be the main piece of information and the frequency be presented in parentheses. The point is that *both* the percent and the frequency should be presented as they give context to each other.

I mentioned that the frequency tables are really only useful for categorical variables measured at the nominal or ordinal level. To understand why, look at a subset of the frequency table for the GSS variable "AGE" that is produced by SPSS. The number of rows only represents one-third (look at the bottom of cumulative percent column) of the possible values and the table is already pretty long.

tatistics Viewer

rm   Insert   Format   Analyze   Graphs   Utilities   Extensions   Window   Help

Age of respondent

		Frequency	Percent	Valid Percent	Cumulative Percent
Valid	18	7	.2	.2	.2
	19	33	1.2	1.2	1.4
	20	26	.9	.9	2.3
	21	33	1.2	1.2	3.5
	22	44	1.5	1.5	5.0
	23	49	1.7	1.7	6.7
	24	35	1.2	1.2	7.9
	25	56	2.0	2.0	9.9
	26	42	1.5	1.5	11.4
	27	58	2.0	2.0	13.4
	28	42	1.5	1.5	14.9
	29	56	2.0	2.0	16.8
	30	54	1.9	1.9	18.7
	31	57	2.0	2.0	20.7
	32	42	1.5	1.5	22.2
	33	54	1.9	1.9	24.1
	34	49	1.7	1.7	25.8
	35	56	2.0	2.0	27.8
	36	52	1.8	1.8	29.6
	37	58	2.0	2.0	31.6
	38	44	1.5	1.5	33.1
	39	42	1.5	1.5	34.6

This is no summary! Someone looking at this table would not be able to get a quick understanding of any patterns in the data, other than that there are a lot of possible values. If a variable was continuous and had comparatively few values, then a frequency distribution might still be meaningful, but even then there are probably other ways of more clearly visualizing the information.

One way around this issue for continuous variables is to collapse or combine values. There are a variety of approaches to this. One common approach is to decide how many categories, which are also called intervals, a researcher is interested in. For example, I might decide I want to use five categories to summarize age. I can then use the computer to identify the range of responses for the variable AGE, which in this instance ranges from 18 to "89 or older." I will discuss what to do with this "89 or older" category in a moment, but for now, let's just treat the data as having a high value of "89." Therefore, based on these values, the range is 71. To find the approximate interval size, I would take the range and divide it by the number of intervals I decided to use. In this instance, the intervals will all cover approximately 14.2 years, which is awkward, so I will round it to 15. There are a couple of guidelines about interval creation. First, I need to make sure that my intervals are mutually exclusive, which means that each value is represented in only one interval. The second is that the intervals also have to be exhaustive, meaning that there *is* an interval for each possible value in the data set. So this means that my lowest interval needs to contain my lowest observed value and my highest interval needs to contain the highest score. If you remember from Chapter 4, these two criteria are the basic criteria for all levels of measurement. The third is the general rule of thumb where the intervals should be the same size, which in this instance is 15. However, I say that this is a "general" rule of thumb because sometimes there are outliers that, if a researcher wanted to keep the intervals of the same size, might mean adding some intervals where there would be no observations until the researcher reached the highest and that interval might have too few observations to be statistically viable. Therefore, sometimes these collapsed frequency distributions might be open-ended at the extremes, such as "under 20," or we see in our case "89 or older." Putting all of this together, I get the intervals for age that appear in Box 15.1.

Graphs

The same information that can be presented in a frequency table can also be presented as a graph. Sometimes, as we saw at the start of the chapter, the visual of bars, lines, or wedges can get a researcher's point across more efficiently than a list of numbers. There are a variety of graph types and, like with tables, some are better suited for certain types of variables than others. I will cover three common graphs here.

Bar Graph

When values are discrete, such as nominal or ordinal measures with few values, a **bar graph**, like the one I presented at the beginning of this chapter, is a useful way of presenting the information. For example, I can represent information for the variable FEPOL, one of the variables I used in the frequency table, as a bar graph that would look like the information on the next page from SPSS (as always, the steps for SPSS and R are in Appendices A and B, respectively).

Graph 1: View of Whether Women Are NOT Suited for Politics

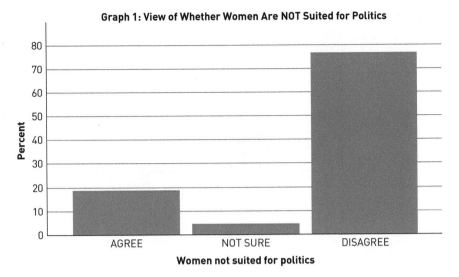

There are some points to notice about this bar graph. First, the graph has a title and there are labels for the *X*-axis, *Y*-axis, and categories. If there are multiple graphs, there may also be a graph number. These labels help readers find specific charts quickly for their interests. Second, it is not in three dimensional (3-D). Three-dimensional bar charts may look impressive at first glance; however, they are not the preferred form of data presentation among researchers and we will revisit this later in the chapter. Last, notice that there are lines, called **axis lines**, that run the entire length of the chart corresponding to the ticks on the *Y*-axis. This is because once you move away from the *Y*-axis, it becomes harder to visualize what values the top of the bars represent on the far right. Although this is not really a problem when the variable has only three values, like with my view of women in politics example, this becomes more of an issue when the variable has many values. For example, compare the following two graphs:

Graph 2: Simple Bar Percent of Main Source of Information about Science and Technology

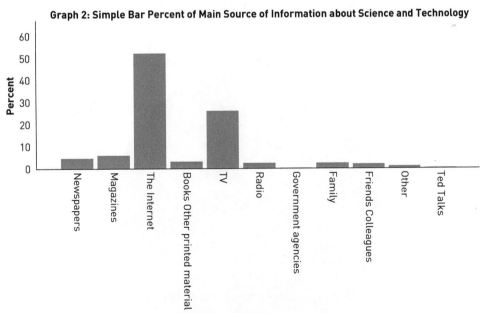

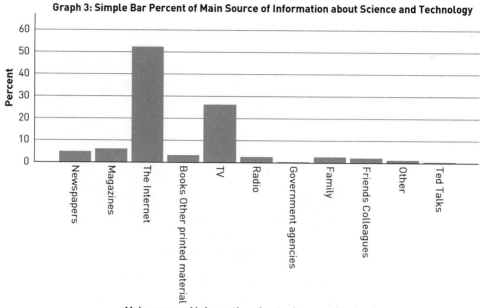

Graph 3: Simple Bar Percent of Main Source of Information about Science and Technology

It is really hard to get a sense of what percent of people get their news from family or even from the radio, aside from the conclusion of "very little," based on the graph on the top (Graph 2). However, by looking at the graph on the bottom (Graph 3) and using the *Y*-axis lines, I can see that the percent is less than 5% (half of the space) and probably somewhere around 3%.

Pie Chart

Researchers could also use a **pie chart** to show the relationship between values of nominal or ordinal measures, like FEPOL, where instead of bars, each value is represented by a wedge of a circle, otherwise known as a *pie*.

Graph 4: GSS Respondents´ Views of Whether Women are NOT Suited for Politics

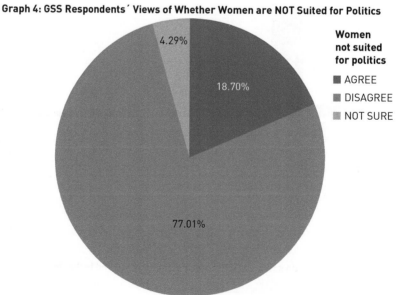

There are a few characteristics of good pie charts. Like bar graphs, pie charts should have a number and title. They should also have some means of distinguishing the wedges from each other. This can be done by different colors, as we see above, or it can be different using different types of fill, like dots or lines. The third characteristic of good pie charts is to make sure that each wedge is labeled both by its variable value and by its proportion of the circle (p. 416). For example, if you look ahead to graph A in Box 15.4, can you really identify what portion of the pie is indicated by the blue and black sections? I would be surprised if you could. It's obvious that they are close, but how close and what real proportion of the pie? The percentage labels are often necessary to make a distinction clear. Last, notice that the pie chart of FEPOL is two dimensional (2-D). It may not look as fancy and as impressive as some pie charts that you might see in magazines and newspapers that are 3-D, but among researchers it is more accurate. We will revisit the issue of 3-D representation later in the chapter, so for now we will just say that pie charts in good form are 2-D.

Line Graph

Sometimes, especially in longitudinal and evaluation research, researchers want to show change across time. For example, what if I wanted to see how people's view of women in politics has changed over time? I could do this by tracking the percent of GSS respondents who agreed that women are not suited for politics since the beginning of GSS data collection. The commands in SPSS would also appear in the same graphing window as the bar graph and pie chart, but now a researcher would just drag a **line graph** to the editing window instead of one of the other formats. This will produce a graph that looks like this:

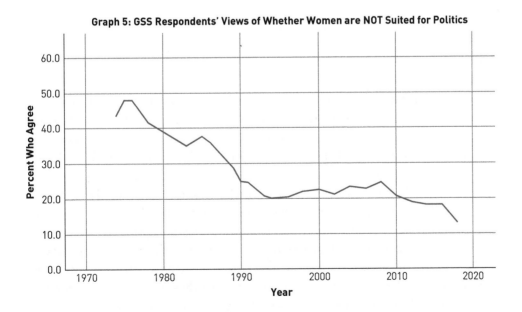

Graph 5: GSS Respondents' Views of Whether Women are NOT Suited for Politics

Line graphs such as this are especially useful in evaluation research with time series designs. In Chapter 9 on evaluation research, I mentioned the importance of extending posttest information for a few years, if possible, in order to see if the effects of the intervention wore off, that is, if there is an erosion of treatment effect. A line graph can also be used to show whether the independent variable is responsible for a change in behavior or whether the dependent variable was already changing, due to other factors, regardless of the intervention.

Although univariate presentation helps summarize characteristics of the sample, these presentations do not compare how two or more variables relate, nor do they express statistical or substantive association tests. For those goals, a researcher needs a means of sharing bivariate (or multivariate) information with others.

LEARNING CHECK 15.1: UNIVARIATE DATA PRESENTATION

1. For categorical variables, how are percentages and raw numbers typically presented?

2. How are continuous variables presented in a frequency table?

3. Should univariate graphs or pie charts be presented in 3-D? Why/why not?

4. On a graph, what is the purpose of grid lines?

Answers to be found at the end of the chapter.

BIVARIATE DATA PRESENTATION

Table

Frequently researchers use tables to show bivariate relationships and to report statistical tests. As you have probably realized by now, there is no one way to do *anything* in methods or statistics, but that does not mean that there are no commonly accepted ways or even easier ways of accomplishing the same goal. Therefore, in our effort to "get the job done," I will discuss one of the easier ways, from an interpretive perspective, to present bivariate tables. Let's use the chi-square information that I presented in Chapter 13 when I tested how the confidence someone had in the federal government affected their view of video surveillance. As we have seen, sometimes statistical packages provide too much output or output that is relevant to a researcher's decision making and interpretation, but that is not necessarily when presenting the "bottom line" to someone else, such as in a written report or presentation. So what I want to focus on here is how to take that information from our chi-square output and put it in a form that I could present to others and that might look something like this:

Table 15.2: Whether the Government Should Be Able to Conduct Video Surveillance by Confidence in the Federal Government				
Whether the government should have the right to conduct video surveillance	**Confidence in the Federal Government**			
	Hardly any	**Only some**	**A great deal**	**Total**
Definitely should not have the right	15.5%	12.4%	10.9%	**63**
	[34]	[24]	[5]	
Probably should not have the right	20%	20.1%	13%	**89**
	[44]	[39]	[6]	
Probably should have the right	41.8%	39.2%	34.8%	**184**
	[92]	[76]	[16]	
Definitely should have the right	22.7%	28.4%	41.2%	**124**
	[50]	[55]	[19]	
Total	**220**	**194**	**46**	460

$X^2 = 7.71$, $df = 6$, $p > .05$

There's actually a lot going on in Table 15.2, so let's break it down. As with all the univariate presentation forms I discussed earlier, bivariate tables should be numbered and have a title. It is customary for bivariate table titles to be presented as the dependent variable (e.g., view of video surveillance) by the independent variable (confidence in the federal government). Second, the independent variable should read down the columns (top of the table) with a column heading identifying the variable and a label for each of the corresponding values. I will explain the reasoning behind this in a moment. The dependent variable, therefore, appears along the rows and is also indicated by corresponding row and value labels.

Bivariate tables also should have row and column **marginals**, values in bold, which are the univariate totals for each value of the variables. They are bold in the table so you can find them. *Cell* is the term for the areas of the table where the two variables intersect, here shaded in the medium color. For example, there are 34 people who have hardly any confidence in the government (variable 1) *and* who feel that the government definitely should not have the right to conduct video surveillance. Each cell is likely to have a percentage (more in a moment) with its corresponding frequency of observations, the latter which is usually in "()."

A few more points about bivariate table construction are that the total sample size should appear in the bottom right corner. Here that number is 460. The data source should also appear under the table if it is not a primary data set used for the analysis of the entire report. Last, any statistical tests might also appear at the bottom of the table, although if more than one bivariate analysis appears in the same table, usually only statistically significant *p*-values are indicated and the statistical evidence appears in the text as opposed to the table. However, there is a lot of variability in this.

Now that I listed the basics, let's discuss some of these in more detail. The practices of placing the independent variable down the column and then percentages with respect to the column marginal facilitate the presentation of information to others in a few ways. First, when people have bivariate tables, they usually want to make comparisons, and the most common comparison they want to make is between groups. So for example, researchers frequently will want to compare the views *between* those who have hardly any confidence in the federal government and those who have a great deal of confidence more so than they want to compare how views vary among, or *within*, just those who have hardly any confidence in the federal government. Within-group comparisons are perfectly valid and can provide some useful information, but these comparisons are not usually the *main* interest of researchers.

This relates to the second point: researchers are comparing between groups, then the natural comparison will be something like "_____% of people who have hardly any confidence in the federal government feel that the government definitely should have the right to use video surveillance compared to _____% of the people who have a great deal of confidence in the government." When calculating a percent, whatever marginal is at the end of the phrase "of _____," such as "of those who have hardly any confidence," would be the denominator. Therefore, in this instance, to calculate the percent for the cell, which remember is any part of the table that has information for two variable values simultaneously, a researcher would take the frequency of the cell and divide it by the column marginal for which that cell lies. So let's break it down for the example I started:

Cell = square where "hardly any" and "definitely should have the right" meet.

Frequency = 50

Column marginal = 220

Percent that should go into the cell: 50/220 = 22.7%

I can learn quite a lot from this table. First, I see by looking at the marginals that the majority of the respondents feel that the government probably should have the right to conduct video surveillance (column marginal, $n = 184$). I also see that the majority of respondents also have hardly any confidence in the government (row marginal, $n = 220$). Both of these statistics, you will recall from Chapter 11, are the mode. Presenting the table and calculating the percentages this way allow me to also easily see that those who have hardly any confidence in the federal government are less likely to feel that the government definitely should have the right to use video surveillance (22.7%) compared to those who have a great deal of confidence in the government (41.2%). I also see, by the chi-square value presented at the bottom of the table, that these variables are *not* statistically related at the $p < .05$ level. When the researcher presents multiple bivariate comparisons within one table, the researcher is not likely to identify the individual statistical test detail in the table but will give this detail in the text of the Result section. Instead, the researcher is just likely to identify which comparisons are statistically significant usually using some sort of symbols, such as "*" for a significance value less than .05, "**" for a significance value less than .01, and "***" for a value less than .001.

BOX 15.2
HOW TO INTERPRET A BIVARIATE TABLE WHERE *N* IS THE DENOMINATOR

Table 15.3: Whether the Government Should Be Able to Conduct Video Surveillance by Confidence in the Federal Government

Whether the government should have the right to conduct video surveillance	Confidence in the Federal Government			
	Hardly any	Only some	A great deal	Total
Definitely should not have the right	15.5%	12.4%	10.9%	63
	(34)	(24)	(5)	
Probably should not have the right	20%	20.1%	13%	89
	(44)	(39)	(6)	
Probably should have the right	41.8%	39.2%	34.8%	184
	(92)	(76)	(16)	
Definitely should have the right	22.7%	28.4%	41.2%	124
	(50)	(55)	(19)	
Total	220	194	46	460

As you see in Table 15.3, the marginal and cell counts are the same as in the table presented in the chapter. Only the percentages, and therefore, the interpretation of them, change. So, for example, our between-group comparison might now read something like this:

> The majority of the sample has hardly any confidence in the federal government and feels that it should probably not have the right to conduct video surveillance (20.0%) compared to 16.5% of the sample who has only some confidence in the federal government and feel that it probably should not have the right to conduct video surveillance and 3.5% of the sample who feels a great deal about the federal government but also shares similar beliefs about video surveillance.

The above interpretation is not statistically wrong; it is just more wordy and makes the between-group comparison harder to see how changes in the independent variable correspond to changes in the dependent variable.

Graphs

Bar Graph

Bar graphs are a useful way to quickly show the relationships between categorical variables, and I will discuss two common ways to present bivariate bar graphs. When using bivariate bar graphs, the bars represent the number or percent of cases by category for the dependent variable, the *X*-axis is the categories for the independent variable, and the *Y*-axis is the count or percent of the observed values on the dependent variable. Let's continue with the example of GSS respondents' views of video surveillance that I introduced in Chapter 13 in our discussion of chi-square so you can see the continuity between the statistics we ran in earlier chapters and the visual presentation I am discussing in this one. To see if the view of whether the government should be allowed to use video surveillance (CCTV) varied by respondents' confidence in the federal government (CONFED), the values of the independent variable (CONFED) will be represented by the actual bars in the bar graph and the values of the dependent variable (CCTV) will be on the *X*-axis with their count or percent. Because the sample sizes for each value of CONFED are so varied, I will use the percentage that will appear on the *Y*-axis.

Bivariate bar graphs are commonly presented in one of two ways. The bars can appear next to each other as they do on the graph on the top, or they can be stacked like the graph on the bottom. Stacked bar graphs are particularly helpful when there are a lot of categories on the grouping (bar) variable. Presenting all the groups horizontally can make the chart cluttered, but presenting them vertically frees space on the *X*-axis.

I can compare the percentages in the top bar graph for each *X* value to the percentages that appear in the earlier bivariate table and see that they are the same. For the stacked graph, you

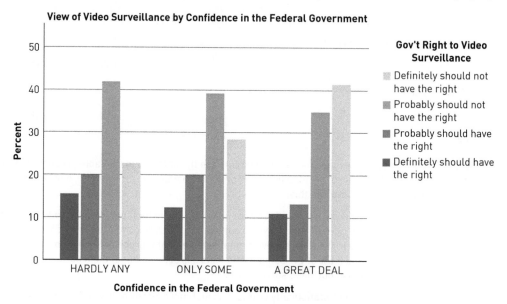

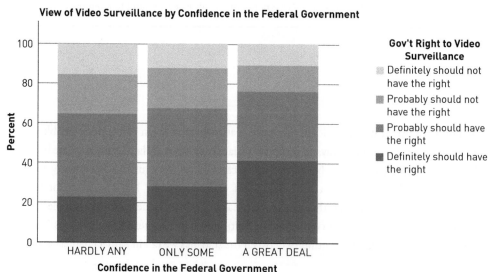

will see that each category of *X* tallies to 100%, once again reinforcing that the column totals (see the earlier bivariate table) should total 100%.

Incidentally, these graphs have the bars going vertically, but sometimes if the value labels are long, a vertical representation can be challenging because the value labels on the *X*-axis can get cluttered and hard to read. Presenting the bar graphs horizontally may help this problem because there may be more room along the vertical axis to present longer labels. Box 15.3 shows an example of a stacked horizontal bar graph that examines the interest in COVID-19 news for different variables.

BOX 15.3
HORIZONTAL STACKED BIVARIATE BAR GRAPH IN RESEARCH

In the spring of 2020, the world experienced a new pandemic stemming from the coronavirus, also known as COVID-19. Many people were quarantined to their homes, and some became avid consumers of the news in an attempt to learn more about this novel, and life-altering, virus. The PeW Research Center surveyed 8,914 US adults who are members of the Center's American Trends Panel about how much they followed the news about COVID-19.

Here is an excerpt of their findings:

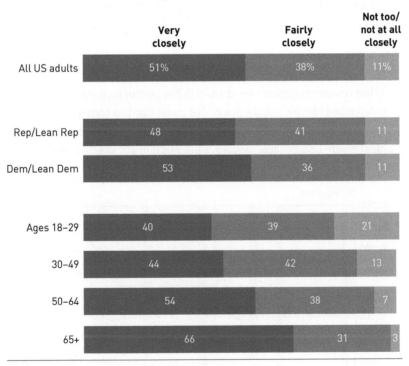

High interest in COVID-19 news cuts across party, age
% of US adults following news about the COVID-19 outbreak …

	Very closely	Fairly closely	Not too/ not at all closely
All US adults	51%	38%	11%
Rep/Lean Rep	48	41	11
Dem/Lean Dem	53	36	11
Ages 18–29	40	39	21
30–49	44	42	13
50–64	54	38	7
65+	66	31	3

Note: Respondents who did not give an answer not shown.

Source: Survey of U.S. adults conducted March 10–16, 2020.

"Americans Immersed in COVID-19 News; Most Think Media Are Doing Fairly Well Covering lt"

PEW RESEARCH CENTER

(Continued)

BOX 15.3 (*CONTINUED*)

HORIZONTAL STACKED BIVARIATE BAR GRAPH IN RESEARCH

This chart from the PEW Research Center actually has three graphs embedded within it. The top graph is a univariate bar graph that looks at all US adults and finds that about half (51%) followed the news "very closely." The second two graphs are both bivariate. The middle graph is for political orientation and the bottom graph represents age. The middle graph shows that there is only a slight difference where Democrats or those leaning toward that orientation were slightly more likely (53%) to watch COVID-19 news very closely than were Republicans/those leaning toward that orientation (48%).

Now you try using the bottom graph examining the relationship between age and news watching to answer the following questions:

1. What age group was most likely to watch COVID-19 news "very closely"?

2. What age group was most likely to report watching COVID-19 news "not too/not at all closely"?

Source: Mitchell, A., & Oliphant, B. (2020, June). Majorities think the news media have done a good job overall covering COVID-19 but have exaggerated the risks. Pew Research Center (March 18, 2020). Retrieved from https://www.journalism.org/2020/03/18/majorities-think-the-news-media-have-done-a-good-job-overall-covering-covid-19-but-have-exaggerated-the-risks/

Answers:

1. The 65+ age group (66%)

2. The 18–29 age group (21%)

Therefore, as I said, there are many ways to present bivariate information; I just presented two basic ones in the spirit of "getting the job done." Your professor might show you additional versions.

Line Graph

When researchers present two variables in line graphs, each separate line represents a value of the independent variable and the points that create that line correspond to the values of the variable over time. For example, if I wanted to look at income (dependent variable) over time for different racial groups (independent variable), a line graph might look like this:

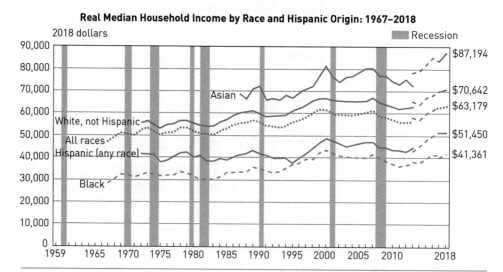

Real Median Household Income by Race and Hispanic Origin: 1967–2018

Source: US Census Bureau, Current Population Survey, 1968–2019 Annual Social and Economic Supplements.

LEARNING CHECK 15.2: BIVARIATE DATA PRESENTATION

1. Which appears first in a bivariate table or graph title, the independent or dependent variable?

2. Which variable, the independent or dependent, typically reads down the column, and why?

3. What is the difference between marginals and cells in a bivariate table?

4. In a bivariate bar graph, should the bars be presented vertically, horizontally, on top of each other, or does it not matter?

Answers to be found at the end of the chapter.

RESPONSIBLE GRAPHICAL REPRESENTATION

Y-axis Representation

Undeniably one of the most controversial issues in contemporary American society is race, and one of the areas in which people expect to experience racial tolerance is in education. But what if a teacher was obviously racist? Should that individual be allowed to teach? It is not for us to get into a debate about having a racist teacher; however, it *is* relevant to see how the GSS sample responds to this issue and to use that information to illustrate responsible graphical representation. Here is a graph of how the GSS respondents feel about whether a racist teacher should be allowed to teach.

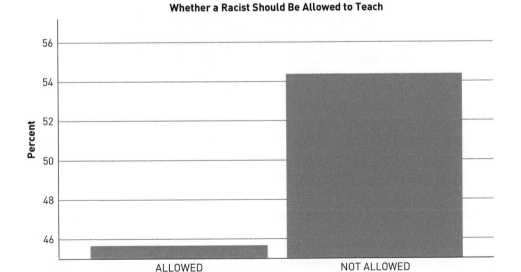

A look at this graph suggests that the GSS sample overwhelmingly feels that a racist teacher should not be allowed to teach…or does it?

This graph is actually distorted on two counts. First, the scores on the *Y*-axis do not begin at 0. The *Y*-axis actually begins at 44 with the first axis line at 46. This gives the impression that very few people agree (indicated by the very low bar) that a racist teacher should be allowed to teach. Understandably, due to space limitations in some forms of publication, sometimes starting the *Y*-axis at 0 is not always practical. In those instances, the responsible reporting action is to have the graph start at "0" and then show a break in the *Y*-axis with a "≈" to indicate a break in numbering, where the next number after the "0" is a higher level. This draws the attention of the reader to the fact that the *Y*-axis is truncated.

Second, notice the size of the intervals. The intervals are measured every 2 percentage points. If we look at this more closely, we see that the percent who feel a racist teacher should be allowed to teach is a bit over 45% (45.7%), whereas those who feel that a racist should not teach is 54.3% … two percentages that are a lot closer numerically than this graph would suggest. In fact, if I scale the graph more accurately, we see that the same information should really look like this:

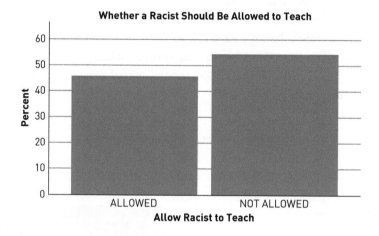

The use of small intervals, like 2%, for the *Y*-axis can artificially inflate small differences. So a comparatively small difference of about 10% can be made to look very large. Not starting at "0" and playing with *Y*-axis intervals run the risk of distorting the graph and both are examples of irresponsible graphical presentation.

Three-Dimensional Representation

Remember, the purpose of graphs is to give readers a quick visual of how data are organized. Graphs that are shown in 3-D undeniably look "cooler" or "prettier" than those presented in 2-D, but is coolness or prettiness the purpose of graphs? The answer is: no.

Three-dimensional graphs are often misleading because the angles and shading can make proportions look different depending on how the graph is rotated. Box 15.4 contains a 2-D pie chart created by the Pew Research Center regarding people's view of the effects

BOX 15.4
2-D VERSES 3-D GRAPHICAL REPRESENTATION

In 2018 the PeW Research Center compared how people get their news sources. Here is their presentation:

Now look at four ways that you might see the same information presented in 3-D form:

Half of Americans say online dating has had neither a positive or negative effect on dating, relationships

% of US adults who say...

Online dating sites and apps have had a ___ effect on dating and relationships

Compared to relationships that begin in person, relationships where people first meet through a dating site or app are...

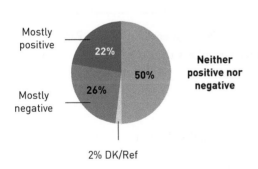

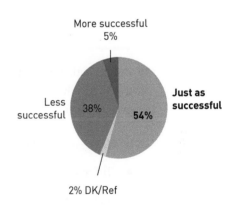

Source: Survey of U.S. adults conducted Oct. 16–28, 2019.

"The Virtues and Downsides of Online Dating"

PEW RESEARCH CENTER

Source: Anderson, M., Vogels, E. A., & Turner, E. (2020, June). The virtues and downsides of online dating. Pew Research Center (February 6, 2020). Retrieved from https://www.pewresearch.org/internet/2020/02/06/the-virtues-and-downsides-of-online-dating/

BOX 15.4 (*CONTINUED*)
2-D VERSES 3-D GRAPHICAL REPRESENTATION

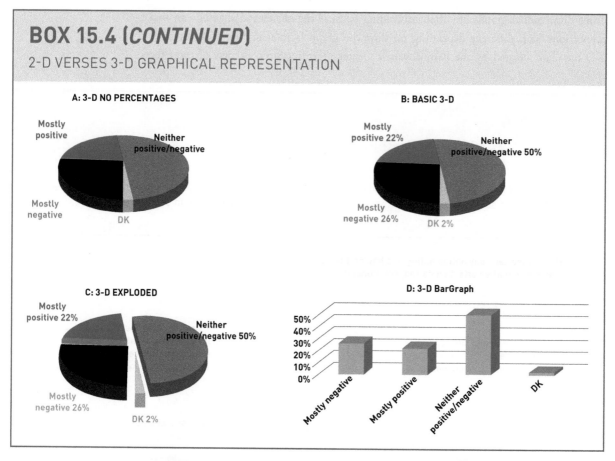

of online dating apps and sites on people's relationships. What PeW presents is the methodologically preferred format that exemplifies the points that we will discuss in this chapter, namely:

- The graph is 2-D

- The wedges are different colors to distinguish the values

- The wedges are labeled as to what they represent

- The wedges have their actual percentage noted as well

Now look at the other graphs, all of which are some ways that the same information could be and have been presented for different topics. We have already discussed Graph A. In addition to the problems of being 3-D, as I said, it does not have any wedge percentages represented. This makes it difficult to discern between "mostly positive" and "mostly negative." Graphs B and C are two common ways of presenting 3-D pie chart information. Again, they may look prettier than the original 2-D version, but the 3-D throws off the perspective. If you compare the black and blue areas, the 3-D portion of the black makes that wedge seem larger, as if it is a greater proportion of the pie, than it really is. In fact, the percentages show that there is little difference between the blue and black wedges, so the 3-D presentation makes the graph misleading. Graphs B and C differ in that Graph C is an example of an **exploded pie chart**, which means that the segments are separated. This can be done in either 2-D or 3-D, but it is common in 3-D because it is visually appealing. Again, however, the 3-D exaggerates small differences in wedge size. The last graph, D, is an example of a 3-D bar graph. This too is misleading for a number of reasons, but mostly because at a quick glance, which remember is one of the goals of visuals like graphs, it can be unclear whether someone should read the front part of the rectangle or the back. Therefore, although computer programs make it pretty easy to create visually stunning graphs and charts, if those graphs confuse the data rather than clarify it, those graphical presentations are basically worthless.

PREPARING AN ORAL PRESENTATION

Professional and academic journals have different formats for how they want their research articles and reports to be written, but they generally follow a similar format as that presented in Chapter 9 on evaluation research, with the notable exception that the executive summary discussed in evaluation reports is replaced by both an **abstract**, which is usually a 100–200 word summary of the purpose, methods and main findings, and a more detailed introduction/literature review (Chapter 2). Therefore, I will not cover the written presentation in this chapter.

Sometimes, however, researchers not only write their finding but they also present them to others, and oral presentations do not quite follow the same pattern as do written ones. For example, in written reports, researchers spend a lot of time summarizing and evaluating the existing research. Furthermore, written reports are more impersonal, where researchers do not really concern themselves with connecting with their audience. In other words, written academic or professional research reports do not start with some witty line or "hook" to engage readers. Readers of these reports are frequently concerned with the bottom line and are reading the report to learn either the methodology, the findings, the challenges, or some combination thereof. The researcher–audience relationship, however, is different for oral presentations. The audience of a presentation may have similar goals as the audience reading a report, but it is often difficult for those hearing material to grasp it to the same degree as those reading it. After all, unlike with a written report, a person listening to a presentation cannot go back and reread sections until the material "sinks in." Therefore, in this section, I am going to present some key components, and some suggestions, for presenting a successful presentation.

Fundamentally there are two important components of any presentation: the content and the delivery. I will examine both in more detail in the next two sections.

Presentation Content

Beginning

Any presentation, written or oral, has a concrete beginning, middle, and end. A key difference though is that in a written research report, the beginning essentially is a review of the literature. In a presentation, the audience is rarely ever interested in the preexisting literature except in the most superficial sense. They want to know who you are, what you have to say, and what it all means. Therefore the beginning of the presentation serves to connect with the audience. Some common ways to connect with the audience include presenting a personal story, a related "aha" moment in your life, or an anecdotal story about the topic. For example, a personal story can be about how you got involved in the presentation topic. This could be something related to your personal life or some inconsistency or observation you made that piqued your interest in the topic. Even if this is something you researched because your boss told you to, you can still begin with a story of how you got interested in the field that led you to that job and that particular boss! Or if you truly are doing research because it is part of your job description rather than something that your own experience or curiosity drove you to, you still might be able to bridge to the main content with a de-identified anecdotal story of one of your study participants.

The beginning can also serve to let the audience know the basic structure of what is to come, such as how long you will be speaking and when questions from the audience will be welcome (e.g., at the end). If you have any handouts, the beginning would also be the time to distribute them.

However, the beginning should also serve to entice the audience to *want* to listen to what you have to say. A common pitfall of presentations is that the presenter is so focused on what he or she wants to say to the audience that the audience's interest in the presentation is forgotten. Therefore, it is important to know your audience ahead of time in terms of what they hope to learn from your talk and their level of familiarity with the general topic. You can then weave this information into the content of your beginning.

Notice a common theme in this section: personalize the beginning to engage the audience's interest and inform them of what is to come but be brief. No one will want to listen to a presentation, no matter how important the content, if a presenter jumps right into the known literature on the topic and the methods of observation employed.

Last, as a presenter, you need to portray enthusiasm for your presentation. If you are dull and monotone, it will be easy for your audience to tune you out and drift into their own thoughts of other, probably unrelated, topics. On the contrary, you are not an infomercial trying to "grab" their attention to sell your product. The balance is to show that you are excited about the topic, that the topic is worthy of *their* interest, and to do so in a way that does not move your presentation into buffoonery, the latter of which will hurt your credibility.

Middle

The middle is the heart of the presentation where you make your case to the audience. There are a variety of ways to structure this. One option is to present your evidence in a way that will lead the audience point by point to your ultimate conclusion. This is frequently what professors will do in a lecture. We frequently have a topic for the day, we make points about that topic, and then ultimately we lead the class to some kind of conclusion based on those points by the end of the period. Although this approach may work in the classroom, it may be less successful in professional presentations if the audience is not the sort who wants to be taught per se. So, if you decide upon this approach, it needs to be carried out carefully to avoid sounding condescending to fellow professionals. However, if the purpose of your presentation is to establish the need for something, such as a new intervention, then this approach may be the most appropriate because the presentation *is* essential to teach about a situation in order to establish why the intervention is needed.

A second approach takes the opposite direction by starting with the conclusion and then presenting the points supporting the path to that conclusion. This may be easier for the audience to understand because they essentially have the "punch line" at the start of the presentation and then, as they listen to the facts in support of that conclusion, they can assess their reaction to those facts in light of the conclusion.

A final approach that I will cover here (although, clearly there are more) is appropriate when the topic of the presentation is more controversial and/or has multiple perspectives or "sides." In this instance, if the main goal of the presentation is to convince the audience of your particular perspective, then one way to organize the middle is to present both sides of the situation, focusing on the evidence refuting one side and favoring the other.

When presenting the crux of the material, it is important for the presenter to remember to avoid using abstract or conceptual language or too much jargon. Presentations need to be clear and comparatively concise. Information overload is a very common risk in presentations. You may have a ton to say, but by knowing your audience, you can cull that large amount of information down to what is most relevant *at that point*. Sometimes, however, you are unavoidably in a situation where what you need to present is very complex. One approach in this instance is to introduce a visual diagram of the entire process early in the content portion of the presentation as a reference, basically the punch line, and then during the presentation, use smaller visuals that will eventually build to that original diagram once again at the end. In other words, present the whole first so the audience gets a sense of where you are going in the presentation, but then progress through that diagram piece by piece in a cumulative manner as the main content of your presentation, with explanation, so that by the presentation's end, the audience can see how that whole was built.

Last, for the middle part of the presentation, it is also more important to cover the "what" rather than the "how." For us in this book, that means that we would not spend much time on the details of the method of observation or the specific statistical tests run. Instead, we would focus more on the findings and their use or relevance. Of course, we should always *know* that other information in case it comes up in audience questions, but it should generally not be included in core presentation content.

End

The presentation end is your last chance to drive home your main message, as supported by a very brief recap of a few points. It can be useful to also let the audience know that the presentation is approaching the end by using verbal cues such as "In summary," "Putting this all together," or even a couple of words linking back to the story you started with in the beginning.

Presentation Delivery

The Benefits and Pitfalls of Visual Aids

It is almost unheard of today to have a presentation that is *not* accompanied by visual aids, and many of you are probably already familiar with the mechanics of using tools like whiteboards, posters, or PowerPoint. However, just because you know the mechanics of how to use them does not mean that you know how to use them *effectively*. But what do I mean by "effectively"? Well, for example, strong visual aids are:

- Simple

- Focus on illustrating complex processes or summarizing a few key points

- Keep the audience visually engaged

These sound pretty simple, yet they are frequently violated. For example, here are some mistakes that are commonly made with presentations:

- The font is too small for the audience to see.

- The font and background color do not have enough contrast to facilitate viewing.

- The slides have too much information, such as many bullets or long sentences of description.

- The animation effects are excessive, distracting, and/or do not contribute to the message of the slide.

- The presence of visual aids inadvertently causes the presenter to read the slides rather than look at and engage the audience.

Many of these issues are interrelated. For example, when presenters have too much text on the screen, the visual aid is acting more as a notecard for the presenter than a tool for the audience, so the presenter falls into the trap of reading the presentation, which disengages him or her from the audience. In fact, presenters should barely read *any* notecards during a presentation. Reading breaks the story and the connection between the presenter and the audience so it should be minimized, if not avoided altogether, whenever possible … and it is *always* possible with enough preparation.

Similarly, very short video clips (less than 15 sec or so) can be useful to engage the audience, but if you have multiple videos and sounds in your presentation, it can get distracting very quickly. Basically, keeping the visuals simple, making sure their inclusion facilitates the overall message, and using them as a supplement to what you are saying are key to their successful inclusion in a presentation.

Presentation of Self

Personal delivery style is another important part of the successful presentation equation as well. I suspect that you all know the basics of presenting: be well-groomed, dress appropriately for the audience, and make sure your clothes are clean. But delivery also involves your body language and the use of your voice as well. For example, as alluded to earlier, speaking in a monotone that is flat and dull is going to disengage your audience. If you do not appear to find this material interesting or exciting, why should they? On the contrary, you also need to be conscious of not speaking too quickly or sounding hyper-excited. Again, presentations are not infomercials! You can speed (within reason) or slow your voice down depending on whether you are trying to get the audience incited about something or you want them to stop and think. How you pitch your voice can also key listeners into important themes or points that you want them to notice.

PHOTO 15.1 Giving a presentation is a lot more than just reading a pre-written speech.

Using your body language can also help you get and keep the attention of your audience. Periodically moving around the presentation area, rather than hiding behind a table or podium for the duration of the presentation, will help keep the audience's attention as the human eye generally tracks movement. Standing, rather than sitting, projects confidence and authority. Standing also makes it easier for you to make eye contact with various audience members, creating the impression that you are talking "to them."

Handling questions also involves the presentation of self and it might be the most nerve-racking part of any presentation because it cannot fully be prepared or practiced ahead of time. However, most audience questions stem from them missing a point you made, seeking clarification, or misunderstanding something. In these instances, the presenter can repeat the question, both to make sure the presenter heard it correctly and to give others the opportunity to hear it if they did not, make eye-contact with the questioner, and then pose the answer to the entire audience with periodic references back to the original questioner.

LEARNING CHECK 15.3: ORAL PRESENTATIONS

1. How can presenters connect with an audience?

2. What are three possible approaches to presenting the main content (middle) of a presentation?

3. Identify two common problems to avoid when using visual aids in a presentation.

Answers to be found at the end of the chapter.

CHALLENGES OF PRESENTATIONS

1. **Someone asked a question that I do not know the answer to.**
   This definitely might happen, and it can definitely throw you off track when it does. But you can recover. At the very least, acknowledge that you do not know the answer and thank the person for their perception. You can then perhaps say that it is an area that you will explore at the next opportunity. When you do not know the answer to someone's question, you might also take the opportunity to open the question to the rest of the audience and start a debate. If the issue is that you did not understand the question, then politely let the individual know that and ask them to clarify. Whatever you do, do **not** just come up with an answer off the top of your head. Someone in the audience is likely to recognize that off-the-cuff and ill-thought response for what it is and they may call you on it, which would cause more embarrassment than simply admitting that you do not know.

2. **What if I get a heckler in the audience who simply refuses to be receptive to my research and message?**
   Although most people who attend presentations based on research are receptive to at least being open to what the presenter has to say, on the rare occasion you might find

yourself dealing with an individual who is very confrontational to your message. One of the first points to keep in mind is that you are unlikely to convince this person to change his/her view during the presentation itself. Therefore, the response that is most likely to aid *your* credibility is for you to remain calm and polite. You can thank the heckler for their view and perhaps briefly restate (more for others' benefit than this individual's) the reason for yours and, if you are so inclined, tell the person you would be interested in debating the issue more at a future opportunity. Again, above all else, however, remain calm and polite because that will translate into others perceiving you as confident and unfazed.

Key Terms

Abstract

Axis lines

Bar graph

Exploded pie chart

Frequency table

Line graph

Marginal

Pie chart

X-axis

Y-axis

Answers to Learning Check Questions

Learning Check 15.1: Univariate Data Presentation

1. The percentage is the main piece of information with the raw number in parentheses.

2. They are collapsed into categories (e.g., bumped down to an ordinal presentation).

3. No, because 3-D presentations can make it harder to actually interpret what the bars or pie slices represent, which is contrary to the purpose of a graph.

4. Gridlines help the reader determine the values of *Y* as the graph moves away from the *Y*-axis along the *X*-axis.

Learning Check 15.2: Bivariate Data Presentation

1. Second. The order is dependent variable by independent variable.

2. The independent variable typically reads down the column because the percentages are typically calculated with respect to the independent variable to make between-group comparisons easier.

3. Marginals are the frequency of an individual, univariate value, whereas a cell is the frequency of how often a combination of two values occurs, hence they are bivariate.

Learning Check 15.3: Oral Presentations

1. Presenters can connect by personalizing the topic to the audience, such as through a personal story of how one got involved in the field or an anecdote.

2. One approach is to present the material in a way that will lead to the conclusion at the end. A middle approach is to present the conclusion first and then the points that led to it. A third approach is to present multiple sides or perspectives and then the evidence supporting your side and refuting the others.

3. Any of the following would apply: Font that is too small; not enough contrast between the font and background color to facilitate viewing; slides have too much information; animation effects are excessive, distracting, and/or do not contribute to the message of the slide; and when the presence of visual aids inadvertently causes the presenter to read the slides rather than look at and engage the audience.

End-of-Chapter Problems

1. For the variable "How difficult do you think research methods is?" take the following data and make a frequency distribution. The variable is coded from 1 (not at all difficult) to 5 (very difficult).

   3 4 2 5 5 4 2 1 1 2 3 4 5 4 3 4 4 4 5 3 2

2. True/False: Bar graphs should be presented in 3-D to increase clarity.

3. In a bar graph, what is the purpose of axis lines?
   a. To let the reader know what the bars represent.
   b. To let the reader know what the X-axis represents.
   c. To let the reader know what the Y-axis represents.
   d. To help the reader match bar tops to Y-axis values across the graph (the length of the X-axis).

4. True/False: In a pie chart, the wedges should be kept together to create an intact circle.

5. Not concerning oneself with statistical tests, identify three things (there are more than three but at least identify three) that are wrong with Table 15.4:

Table 15.4: Gender by View of Whether Job Is Interesting		
	Gender	
Job is Interesting	Male	Female
Strongly agree	17.6%	17.3%
Agree	22.3%	21.7%
Neither	5.5%	6.3%
Disagree	3.4%	3.4%
Strongly disagree	1.6%	1.0%

8. What is a common way bar graphs can be distorted?
   a. The colors used for the bars, wedges, or lines do not have a clear relationship to each other.
   b. The Y-axis does not begin at "0" and there is no indication of a break in counting for space.
   c. The Y-axis increments are very small so that small differences appear large.
   d. Both "b" and "c."
   e. Both "a" and "b."

9. In presentations, what are some ways to engage with the audience?
   a. A short story of how you got involved in the field
   b. An "aha" moment related to the topic
   c. A brief anecdotal story that can personalize the topic
   d. Any of the above

10. Which approach to organizing the middle content of an oral presentation is typically the easiest for people to follow?

a. Assemble the story piece by piece, building to the conclusion at the end.

b. Start with the conclusion and then identify the steps that led to that conclusion.

c. Present all sides to the story and then your points to support your side or message.

11. Which of the following is not good in a presentation visual aid?

a. Simple messages or slides

b. High contrast between the background color and font color

c. Many points or a lot of text on each slide

d. A font size that is large enough for the audience to see

12. Which of the following are ways to keep the audience engaged in your presentation

a. Periodically move around the staging area

b. Speaking in a monotone

c. Pitch your voice differently to either incite the audience or get them to think

d. "a" and "b"

e. "a" and "c"

16

QUALITATIVE DATA ANALYSIS

LEARNING GOALS

- Identify the basic steps in preparing qualitative data.

- Explain the general approach to qualitative data analysis (QDA).

- Distinguish between the four analytic strategies of content analysis, grounded theory analysis, social network analysis, and discourse analysis.

- Identify some common ways of presenting qualitative analysis.

I think because she knows that my desire level is a lot higher than hers, typically, that she would be upset. She would think something is wrong … she would think something weird was going on if I said no I don't want to. (Hudson, p. 136)

It's keeping up appearances for my wife at least. Because to some extent I think she buys into the stereotype that men are more sexually active or have more sexual desire. So if I'm not doing that, I think she feels sexually inadequate? So sometimes I'll feign sexual desire even if I'm not into it just so she feels good about herself. (Justin, age 30, p. 137)

(Murray, 2018)

The two quotes above suggest that women might not be the only gender to experience stereo-types regarding sexual expectations. These quotes are men's responses to how well their actual sexual desire matches the male sexual script that expects men to continually have a high sex drive. In order to explore how men's actual desires match with their perceived pressure to act a certain way, Murray (2018) conducted semi-structured interviews with 30 heterosexual men between the ages of 30 and 65 who were in relationships at the time of the study. Through these interviews, she learned that men feel pressure to conform to the social script of mas-culinity that presumes a high and relentless sex drive even when their personal interest is momentarily low. These descriptions at the start of the chapter and in Murray's research also indicate that men feel that they have to adhere to this script not just for wider social accep-tance but also in order to save the feelings of someone else, thereby suggesting that the women in these men's lives also subscribe to this masculine sexual script.

In this chapter, I will focus on the tools researchers use to analyze the subjectively rich data like Murray (2018), Covington-Ward (2017), and Carroll (2018) gathered into something that can be patterned to explain or describe human behavior. As always, there are many approaches to analyze qualitative data, and entire books have been written on this topic alone. Our pur-pose is to "get the job done," so I will focus on a couple of approaches common to the social sciences.

PREPARING QUALITATIVE DATA FOR ANALYSIS

Moving from Observations to Full Recorded Data

Although quantitative data preparation largely involves the fairly structured coding process dis-cussed in Chapter 10, preparing data for qualitative analysis is more variable. However, in the spirit of "getting the job done," I will nonetheless present some common steps, albeit not rules, to accomplish qualitative data coding. One of the first steps is for a researcher to transcribe the data, ideally starting as soon as possible (Baptist, 2001). For example, the quick observational jottings that were noted in Chapter 8 should be transcribed the same day that they are recorded in order to avoid forgetting what the jottings mean. Similarly, transcriptions of early interviews should start before too many have been conducted. Not only does early transcription minimize the risk of the researcher forgetting details, but it also enables the researcher to start to see pat-terns in the data simply by continually exposing themselves to the information.

Related to frequent and early transcriptions is to periodically take the time to read through these notes while still in the field or conducting interviews. In fact, preparing and analyz-ing qualitative data means being prepared to read and re-read the data many times. What I am describing here is just the initial read-throughs for researchers to familiarize themselves with the data in order to identify gaps and questions while still in a position to gather more information. At this stage of data preparation, researchers should read to question the data, and while they are reading, they should ask themselves what additional information from the subjects or what type of observations do they need in order to complete the picture.

Creating the Infrastructure for Analysis

Once a researcher is satisfied with the data obtained, whether it is field observations, focus group notes, interviews, or social artifacts collected, it is time to organize that data for a more in-depth analysis. The first, and perhaps most important, step in this process is to make a master data copy of all the data gathered in its original form and store it somewhere other than the copy from which you will work. That means a full, unedited copy of all field notes, all interview transcripts, all documents gathered … you name it. If you took written notes that are not computerized, that means perhaps photocopying everything. If your data are transcribed into a computer file, then the process is simpler and just involves making an extra copy. If the data are audio-collected or videoed, make a copy of those too. Keep this copy in an alternate, safe location. The point is, even though this may sound tedious, in qualitative research a researcher may have invested tens of hours or days of data gathering … and all it takes is one computer crash, one lost briefcase, or one program error to lose *all* that hard-earned data. Having a backup in an alternate location can very feasibly present the loss of the entire project.

According to Warren and Karner (2005), if researchers have multiple types of data, such as field notes and interview responses, they should organize the data first by type and then by chronological order within type. If researchers only have one form of data, they can go right to the chronological ordering. Part of this process is to make new files for this reorganized data because this new data form is where the researcher will start analysis. Another step in the data organization stage is for the researcher to keep a log of the main information relevant to their study, such as the name of all subjects, IRB forms, meeting locations or observation settings, dates, and any additional documents.

Deciding How to Sort Through the Material? Cutting/Pasting or Computer?

As with anything, there are pros and cons to deciding whether or not to use a computer program. The "old school" way of sorting through the information to identify themes involves the cutting and pasting of printed transcripts or field notes. In a common version of this approach, the researcher prints at least one copy of the transcript of the data, reads through it to identify quotes that seem particularly relevant to the research question, cuts out each of those quotes (keeping some of the original context or at least noting it somewhere), and pastes the quote onto an index card. On the back of the index card, the researcher would write who said the quote and the context in which it was said. The researcher might also note where the quotation appeared in the transcript (e.g., page number). Once all the relevant quotes are on index cards, the researcher sorts these quotes into similar piles, which will serve as the basis for the themes.

One benefit of this approach is that it is easy to gather frequencies to determine the most common themes by simply counting the cards and the researcher can see whether there are any patterns based on the individual or the context by reading the back. In fact, by keeping this information on the back (name and context), it also helps protect against some bias as the researcher is unlikely to remember who said what quote while sorting quotes into themes.

A limitation of this approach, however, is that it uses a lot of paper and it can be time consuming to continually read and work to sort quotes into themes. Therefore, the scissors and paper approach may be useful for analytical approaches where initial themes are already identified and then it is a matter of matching quotes to those themes and then examining the remaining, unassigned quotes, to see if new themes emerge.

Another option is to use qualitative data analysis (QDA software to identify themes and how often they occur). There are a number of QDA software programs on the market that serve different purposes. For example, Word or Excel can be useful for tracking simple coding and analysis-like counts. Other software such as NVivo or MaxQDA can help identify patterns in the text, create network diagrams, and identify codes.

Some strengths of QDA programs are that they may save time from the traditional cutting, pasting, and manual sorting of the previous methods and they may also help decrease human bias or error. However, programs like these also run the risk of creating too many analytic codes that end up muddying the overall story rather than clarifying it. Therefore, there are both electronic (computer programs) and nonelectronic (a team of coders) approaches to increase reliability. Which approach is the best fit for you depends on your research goals (e.g., computer programs might help you see social networks more efficiently), cost (programs are more expensive), time (a team of coders takes more time), and level of data (comparatively short transcripts can sometimes be done more easily without a computer)? As always, there is no perfect fit.

 LEARNING CHECK 16.1: PREPARING QUALITATIVE DATA

1. When should researchers transcribe their notes—at the beginning, during, or end of research?

2. When creating the infrastructure for analysis, what is the first thing a researcher should do?

3. Identify one strength and one weakness of using computer software to sort through qualitative data.

Answers to be found at the end of the chapter.

A GENERAL APPROACH TO ANALYSIS

Once the data are organized, then the researcher needs to read and re-read the data some more to get a sense of the main themes and any subthemes underneath them. By transcribing the data and doing some of the preliminary reading and organization discussed in the previous section, the researcher may already have a sense of where to begin this process. Some qualitative researchers even suggest creating *new* folders that correspond to each theme and subtheme in order to better be able to read through these sections in the future.

There are many tactics to use when reading through material and looking for themes. Therefore, in this section, I will just discuss the broad, more general approach to analyzing qualitative information that spans a variety of observational techniques, such as focus groups, field research, and interviews. Then in the next section, I will discuss more specialized approaches to analysis that are better suited to some qualitative methods of observation relative to others.

Identifying Initial Themes

Once all the data are collected, now is the time for a more focused reading of the material where keywords or phrases should somehow be identified, such as by underlining, highlighting, or making notes in the margin. Sometimes this is called **first-level coding** as it is the first stage where a researcher might actually note specific codes for various passages in the transcript, via assigning labels or tags to the text. These notes serve as a first attempt to find patterns and to give meaning to the observations. During this reading, it is also recommended to make notes, usually in the margins, of questions, reminders, or other general points a researcher wants to keep in mind as they continue to work through the material. For example, Dhillon and Smith (2019) conducted over 100 interviews to study how they felt about cyberstalking and how it could be managed. Their ultimate goal with this information was to try and identify actionable objectives to combat cyberstalking and their first level of coding identified approximately 200 value responses, which addressed respondents' views of the norms of cyber distribution and appropriateness, which ultimately led them to identify possible objectives that could be useful to organizations to prevent cyberstalking (Dhillon & Smith, 2019).

Some observations a researcher might be looking for during this initial coding might be the identification of important experiences or ideas present in the data. These identifications might be words or sentences that a researcher highlights but not necessarily assigns meaning to as of now. The identifications just form the initial means of trying to sort the data. A researcher also might start taking notes about preliminary links between these ideas. A common way to accomplish this is the **constant comparative method,** where classification is identified as similar or different to each other and where the units that are identified as similar then become part of the same category. It is important for a researcher to take notes on *why* the researcher considers meaning units to be similar because doing so will "solidify" the rules for defining codes later on. This continues until all meaning codes have been classified into some type of theme and the number will grow every time meaning units are considered to be meaningfully different. Although there is no set number of themes researchers need, there is a balance between giving enough meaning to content but also keeping the number of themes within a manageable limit. More complex topics will require more categories than simpler ones. The main issue is to make sure that the categories are clear and distinct enough to simplify the data while also being reflective of the data. For example, Dhillon and Smith (2019) eventually clustered those initial 200 value responses into 75 subobjectives, which were further classified into 5 fundamental objectives, which the researchers defined as fundamental to deciding whether a behavior is normatively appropriate or normative for distribution, and 15 means objectives, which are whether a behavior exists more as a means of obtaining a fundamental objective.

Once a researcher thinks they have a preliminary list of themes with corresponding definitions and examples, the researcher reads through the material again to make sure these factors accurately reflect what the subjects said. Remember, researchers are still just recording here, not analyzing per se, and it is natural for themes to change over time as researchers refine their definitions where some may become obsolete, divided into new categories, or emerge as new categories.

Linking Themes

Identifying themes in the data is just the preliminary part of data analysis. Now a researcher has to actually make sense of those themes by somehow linking them together into a meaningful pattern or message. Again, there are many general approaches to this, but in the spirit of "getting the job done," I will focus on a more basic approach for beginners that involves three steps identified by Warren and Karner (2005). These steps are:

1. Making connections between themes
2. Interpreting the themes and connections
3. Providing evidence of claims

Making Connections

Making connections involves deciding how the themes and subthemes a researcher has identified relate to each other. According to Warren and Karner (2005), one way to accomplish this is through outlines, much like you might draft for a college paper or a literature review (Chapter 2) that order information either randomly, temporally, or analytically (meaning logically). However, qualitative researchers also frequently use diagrams as a means of illustrating the connections between themes. For example, a researcher might make a **cluster diagram** in which the categories are drawn in relation to each other. This can be done where the size of the circle will represent the importance of the category to the overall research goal with larger circles indicating categories of greater importance, or if all categories are presented as the same size, a cluster diagram might show how categories relate to each other via linkages. Furthermore, a researcher might see if categories overlap. Some might stand alone.

Another option is to make a **flowchart**. For example, the 15 means objectives (subthemes) that Dhillon and Smith (2019) ultimately linked to the five larger fundamental objectives (main theme) for cyberstalking prevention can affect each other as well as more than one fundamental objective. Therefore, the linkage between these objectives can be complicated. In order to elucidate the process, Dhillon and Smith presented the cluster diagram reproduced in Figure 16.1.

FIGURE 16.1 ● CLUSTER DIAGRAM

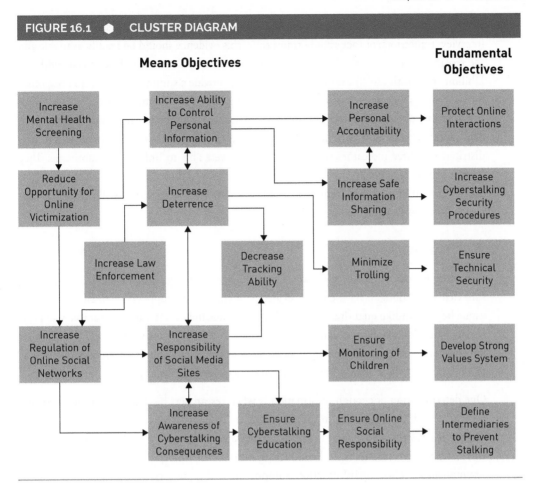

Source: Dhillon and Smith (2019, p. 153).

Interpreting the Themes and Connections

Warren and Karner (2005) identify two different means of relating the linkages in the previous section to answered questions (Emerson, 2001). The first is **emic meaning,** which is understandings of the situation from the subjects' perspective, as expressed by the subject, and **etic meanings,** which are the researcher's understandings of the situation or themes. Etic understandings are actually often based on the subject's emic interpretations, but here the researcher will also link the material to the questions, concepts, and theories relevant to their discipline. So in this sense, not only is the material linked to each other (the first step), but now they are also linked to the discipline relevant to the study.

Providing Evidence of the Claims

According to Warren and Karner, in qualitative research, data get meaning from the researcher-organized framework; therefore, the specific data itself are essential to providing the evidence for what the researcher frames. Because, as I described in the earlier steps, researchers often create separate files for each theme and subtheme with corresponding transcribed field notes, interview transcripts, or focus study transcripts, this evidence should be readily available and the researcher can select the best quotes to give context to the theme. To continue with the Dhillon and Smith (2019) example, the researchers provide a summary of common responses for each means objective as well as a corresponding quote. For example, for the means objective "increase ability to control personal information," Dhillon and Smith note that respondents wanted to be able to control how their personal information is shared, stored, and distributed—three indicators that the researchers were able to link to this subtheme. They further provide a quote as "I want as many options on social media as possible to prevent as much personal information from being publically available" to specifically illustrate this subtheme (Dhillon & Smith, 2019, p. 151).

When to End Analysis

According to Baptist (2001), the issue is not necessarily having *enough* codes as it is making sure that your codes all have enough evidence in the data to support them. But this is still vague because unlike quantitative research where a researcher sets a desired sample size prior to data collection, qualitative data collection is dynamic and the answer to "Do I have enough information?" or "Do I have enough codes?" might contribute to the researcher's decision as to when to leave the field and/or stop interviewing or running focus groups.

One determination of enough information is when researchers have addressed the preidentified themes with enough data to support them and they have identified and supported new themes in a way that contributes to an overall message of the findings without any gaps. This is why continually transcribing and conducting initial read-throughs of those transcripts while simultaneously collecting information is important to this approach.

Another possible determination is the approach of saturation, which for analysis has a meaning similar to that addressed in Chapter 8 about sampling. In analysis, saturation is the point in which themes or subthemes are at the point where meaning is becoming repetitive.

LEARNING CHECK 16.2: GENERAL APPROACH TO ANALYSIS

1. Identify two things researchers might look for during the initial coding of data.

2. True/False: Researchers should aim to identify between 10 and 25 themes in their data.

3. What is the difference between emic and etic meaning in data?

Answers to be found at the end of the chapter.

SPECIFIC ANALYTIC TECHNIQUES

There are many techniques for analyzing qualitative information, but as the focus of the book is "getting the job done," I will present four that are common to the social sciences.

Content Analysis

In Chapter 8, I mentioned that content analysis was one of those odd beasts that could be both a method of qualitative observation (e.g., when the units of observation was a random sample of social artifacts) and a means of qualitative analysis. Because in applied research, which is our subtle focus of "getting the job done," it is more likely to be relevant as a means of qualitative analysis, in Chapter 8 I also said that we would discuss the steps for how to conduct content analysis here.

From an analytic view, content analysis generally involves separating the data into both its manifest content and its latent content. The **manifest content** is the content that is more direct and easily observed, such as a count or identification of clearly, unambiguously defined occurrences. For example, in Schmidt's (2016) research on the depiction of women in sports news articles (Chapter 8), the manifest content was the format of the article, the type of article, the topic, the length, and the sources. All of these characteristics, once identified, are easy for other researchers to observe. For example, if Schmidt counted the number of times "female" showed up in an article, I understand "female" and if I had a copy of the articles he used, and counted the number of times that word appeared, I should be pretty close to his, if not exact. Consequently, manifest content tends to be high on reliability. However, counts do not really give the context or the meaning behind the information. What if an article that had a high count for the number of times "female" was mentioned was about how females should *not* be allowed to play certain sports? That would have a different meaning than if the article was promoting female sports. So a count alone is not sufficient. That is why researchers also look at the latent content of the material.

The **latent content** is the codes researchers give for the meaning of what they see in the social artifacts, which is why this method is included in the qualitative chapter even though it involves quantitative analysis. Schmidt borrowed themes from other researchers to give meaning to the latent content which were whether the articles (1) were respective of women, (2) sexualized women, (3) were about fights, assaults, or scandals involving women, or (4) were about women in domestic or supportive roles along gender lines (Schmidt, 2016). He had similar codes for articles about men where the gender perspective was just switched as appropriate. Therefore, for example, the fourth code would be whether the articles featuring men involved men in *their* supportive roles as father, husband, boyfriend, etc. Because latent content aims to put the words into context, it is higher on validity than manifest content; however, because that meaning is a bit more subjective (what I consider to be a sexualized story you might not), it is lower on reliability. Because of this, the lead researcher will often enlist the help of others to also independently code material and then compare the consistency in the codes to establish reliability. For example, in Schmidt's case, he used two other coders to code 400 overlapping articles and found that these three coders had an agreement rate of about 92%, which is considered acceptable (Schmidt, 2016).

Even though content analysis is a technique for analyzing qualitative information, as you probably guessed, it has some quantitative elements—after all, manifest content is obviously quantitative. Schmidt's research addressed both. Since the purpose of this chapter is not statistics, in nonstatistical terms, Schmidt found that there was only a little increase in the mention of female sports over the last 30 years and that any observed increase happened in spurts. Furthermore, when there were articles about women in sports, they had a lower word count than the articles about men's sports, which is also a quantitative measure. Qualitatively, Schmidt also found that the thematic portrayal of men and women changed even less over time, with females most likely to be mentioned as the wives, girlfriends, or mothers of male athletes. According to Schmidt, this persistent imbalance may be because the vast majority of the articles for whom the writer's name was mentioned were written by men, and female writers were more visible only in the articles from more recent years (Schmidt, 2016).

Grounded Theory Analysis

Another approach, one that is frequently used in evaluation research, is grounded theory, which involves the simultaneous collection and analysis of data where concepts form from the data only (Charmaz, 2006). In other words, concepts don't start with preidentified categories but instead form from the *ground up* in the data (Charmaz, 2014; Glaser & Strauss, 1967) and end, rather than start, with theory formation. For example, in the study about male sexual scripts that I used in the opening of this chapter, Murray (2018) states that during the study, she met with a larger research team to discuss the categories that were emerging in the codes and when the group could not answer the questions about those categories, additional questions were added to the interviews to be asked of future respondents. For example, Murray notes that early in the interviews, the researcher noticed that the majority of men reported never saying "no" to sex; but the researchers were unsure whether this was because of these men's sex drive (confirming the script) or if the men felt pressure to say "yes" (refuting the script). Furthermore, if the men felt pressure to conform to the script, why did they feel this pressure and from whom? As a result of these early findings and new research questions, Murray added questions to the original interview script to try and find answers.

iStockphoto.com/tommaso79

PHOTO 16.1 Can you think of any reasons why a man, rather than a woman, might feel pressure to have sex?

Many variations of grounded theory have emerged since Glaser and Strauss's initial work, but I will focus on two.

Method 1: Open, Axial, and Selective Coding

According to Strauss (1987), the first stage, **open coding**, involves four main steps. The first is to have a specific and consistent set of questions to continually apply to the data, such as "What is this about?" This allows the researcher to see whether the data fit the original research goals. The second step is to code as many categories with corresponding examples as possible in order to capture the many nuances in the data. Third, the researcher should continually work to link the data to theory. In other words, researchers do not wait to apply theory at the end of data analysis, but instead periodically throughout data collection and analysis try to link the data to theory to see where theoretical perspectives may fit. Last, Strauss (1987) suggests that researchers do not concern themselves with looking for patterns among traditional variables like demographics (age, race, gender, etc.) unless these variables emerge independently in the data. In other words, in quantitative analysis, these variables are almost always included as statistical control variables, with the researcher assuming that they will have some effect on the research question and, therefore, need to be addressed statistically. According to Strauss, this is not the case in open coding.

Although open coding helps identify themes in the data, the second stage of **axial coding** helps to see how they link. According to Strauss and Corbin (1998), axial coding focuses on issues like the context around which themes arise, the conditions that led to certain observations, and the actions or consequences of these conditions or actions that may link categories together. In this sense, axial coding moves beyond description to analysis by relating themes to each other in a combination of inductive and deductive reasoning. Murray (2018), for example, states that during her stage of axial coding, the previously coded categories of "pressure to initiate" and "pressure to say yes to sex" were combined into the category "social pressure to appear to have a high desire." She then defined this theme as "An episode in which men indicate they may have otherwise wanted to say no to sex but felt it would not bring about a favorable response from their female partner" (p. 136).

Axial codes can take various forms. For example, they might address causal conditions that are the events or variables that actively lead to the occurrence or development of the phenomenon. Or axial codes might be context codes that identify the background or the context that influences the active causal codes previously noted. Action codes, another type, are purposeful activities that subjects do in response to circumstances or conditions, whereas the consequences of these strategies—whether intended or not—would be consequence codes.

In order to put the information into a coherent story, the last stage of **selective coding**, sometimes also called theoretical coding, occurs, which is the process of picking one category (e.g., "selecting" it) to be the reference category around which the other themes will be organized and which will serve as the central explanation linking the other categories (Daly, 2007).

For example, Murray's (2018) original research question was to explore how men's actual sexual behavior reflected society's prescribed male sexual scripts. Her core category that emerged and that she used as her central theme was that men are pressured to exhibit a high interest in sex, which they do not always feel (2018). Much of her discussion focused around themes of context and the reasons (causal codes) men feel such pressure and what they do as a result (action codes).

Method 2: Attribute, Index, and Analytic Codes

The second approach to grounded theory is to identify attributes, index, and analytic codes. In this method, the most basic codes are the **attribute codes,** which are factors such as demographics (age, race, gender, occupational status, etc.) or contextual variables (e.g., neighborhood, school, different research sites) that may affect subjects' behaviors. These are the more obvious or easily identifiable codes independent of any input on behalf of the researcher or subjects' actions. The second level, **index codes,** are codes related to broad topics in the data. For example, in interviews, index codes might correspond to the topics covered in specific interview questions. McDaniel, Gazso, Mitchell, and Wu (2014) were interested in how low-income people's support relationships, both instrumental (such as through economic aid) and emotional, came to be defined as family. To accomplish this, they interviewed 70 individuals representing 20 aging families by choice, meaning people who identify as a family without the traditional biological connection. The initial contact person had to be low income and had to have at least one child (to address the aging process) and, for the purpose of this research piece, were in midlife or later. McDaniel and colleagues' (2014) description of their methodology noted that after transcribing and translating each transcript they used QSR International's NVivo software to help identify passages that had common elements that could be grouped into themes. McDaniel and colleagues state that they assigned initial index codes, such as "meanings of family" and "supports given" based on their interview questions. The answers to questions can be considered a sublevel of index codes. For example, in McDaniel's study, three women named Lin, Yusheng, and Jun, two of whom were biologically related and one who was not, identified as a family of choice. Lin, a low-income 48-year-old mother of two, said this of her friend Yusheng (age 83): "Feel like family, yes … She's 83 years old … when I arrived to Canada I did some business, yeah. She is helping me to build restaurant" (p. 405). Similarly, Yusheng identified close ties with other Chinese immigrants, of whom Lin was one, that she considered family because they helped her when her husband died and she helped them because they too were immigrants. Lin's mother Jun (age 73), the third member in this family of choice, comments about Yusheng: "I have a very close friend … All the way we help each other" (p. 405). McDaniel and colleagues took answers like this and coded them into the subtheme of "shared experiences are what count" (p. 405) because the respondents identified their shared immigration experiences as an integral component of why they created their family of choice (McDaniel et al., 2014).

PHOTO 16.2 Who do you consider to be family? Do you have any nonbiological people you consider to be family? Why?

Aside from creating index codes from any questions posed to the subjects, researchers will also get a sense of what is important as they transcribe (if they are the ones doing the transcribing) and/or read through the data. By asking yourself the question "So what?" that I mentioned earlier, researchers are likely to see what is interesting and/or relevant to the overall research question. These answers then can also become index codes.

The creation of index codes facilitates the formation of **analytic codes,** which are codes that address what the content of the index codes mean, and they may even link the index codes to theory. For example, another index code that McDaniel and colleagues created was the "meaning of support," further subdivided into "if you got it, don't question it" and "good enough support" (2014). To them, these codes reflected that among low-income elderly, the perception of support was more important than the effectiveness of that support. In other words, how practically useful support was or was not was less relevant to these family members of choice than was a member's *feeling* of being satisfied with the offer of support. Understanding the context, in other words, analyzing *why* people felt happy with the support that was "good enough," were the analytical codes (McDaniel, et al., 2014). The analytic coding can also link concepts in the data to theory and to the literature, further illustrating that the process of creating and linking analytic codes is ongoing.

Regardless of the method used to code data, thematic analysis, or grounded theory, the end result is an account of the data that has theoretical utility and validity. Ideally, researchers want this theoretical model to fit the empirical data but also to be general enough to fit related situations outside of the data as well. Achieving this frequently requires both finding patterns among the codes that can be used to explain occurrences and addressing alternative explanations and cases that do not fit the pattern and thereby examining how those cases fit with the formulated theory.

Qualitative Network Analysis

Qualitative network analysis builds off the fundamentals of social network analysis but is adapted to combine visual network maps with qualitative interviews, observation, and/or analysis of documents (Ahrens, 2018; Herz, Peters, & Truschkat, 2015). Although this is a fairly complex and varied approach to QDA, for our purpose of "getting the job done," I will just highlight some of the main components of it. Regardless of the complexity, most approaches involve a version of using the data to first make a social network map that shows the connections between subjects and uses the interview data to give cultural and social context to those connections (Herz, Peters, & Truschkat, 2015).

For example, on the network side of the analysis, researchers might answer structural, positional, and actor-specific questions such as:

- Are there clusters of networks within the larger one? (structural)

- Is there any overlap between clusters? (structural)

- How do the clusters differ? (structural)

- Are there some actors who occupy similar positions in different networks? (positional)

- Which actors have multiple connections? (actor-specific)

- Which actors serve as the only connection to other actors? (actor-specific)

- Are there any actors who connect multiple networks that would otherwise be isolated? (actor-specific).

Interviews or field observation then give context to or elaborate on the nature of these relationships in order to provide a deeper measure of the context.

For example, behavioral health has been moving to an integrated approach to dealing with mental health issues, and one emerging component of that approach is peer providers. However, there is a lot of variation on the specific role of peer providers in these teams. Therefore, Siantz, Rice, Henwood, and Palinkas (2018) studied 24 programs affiliated with the Los Angeles County Department of Mental Health's Innovations that had a peer component. They sent the peer providers in these programs a web-based social network survey tailored to their program, and they conducted semi-structured interviews with each peer provider. Although the researchers used a variety of complex analytic tools, in the spirit of "getting the job done," the basic gist is that they used a computer program to create a visualization of the social network of these peer providers and conducted a qualitative analysis, rooted in grounded theory, to give context to those networks.

According to the researchers:

> Social network analysis revealed that peer providers…were in network subgroups that ranged from high to medium to low status …. Qualitative data suggested that this positional variation was related to the peer provider's responsibilities (e.g., outreach vs. ongoing engagement or case management), population served (e.g., formerly homeless individuals vs. underserved ethnic communities), and background (e.g., in recovery from mental illness vs. cultural and linguistic broker for clients). **Source:** (Siantz, Rice, Henwood, & Palinkas, 2018, p. 543)

The researchers also included network maps, code examples, and other examples of linkages, which appear in Box 16.1. For example, in Box 16.1 you can see in the first two types of network maps, which are identified as having a peer with high centrality (Type), that the gray box

BOX 16.1
QUALITATIVE NETWORK ANALYSIS IN RESEARCH

Table 5 Care coordination network subtypes. (Color table online)

Network type	Network visualization	Illustrative quote
Type 1: Peer has high centrality, and felt central to team		"The psychiatrist might know how to give the guy meds, or the doctor knows how to prescribe the meds, and this is how it's supposed to happen, but then we have us who… who know the client."—Network A, IMHT
Type 2: Peer has high centrality, but felt periphery to team		"They just turn up their nose to me and everything that I do. 'Cause the client community is…you know, is my strength, you know what I'm saying? As a peer advocate I don't go to the staff meetings. They just let me do my thing, you know what I'm saying? They let me do my thing."—Network B, IMHT
Type 3: Peer has low centrality, but felt central to team		"My team is very supportive… everyone has, a good positive vibe. We all work as a team. We all make sure that we get our things done on time. If I have a question and I go to a therapist or go to (names boss) or I go to (other name) and ask them, they are very helpful with me."—Network M, ICM

Source: Siantz, E., Rice, E., Henwood, B., & Palinkas, L. (2018).

representing the peer is closer to the other black boxes, whereas the other two types, which are identified as peers with low centrality, have the gray peer box set more apart from the boxes. This is network analysis. But aside from where the peer was actually located (network analysis) was how the peer felt as a member of the team (qualitative analysis). The quotes on the right-hand side of the box illustrate reasoning for the second half of the typology, which is whether the peer *felt* central or peripheral to the team.

The network analysis showed how peers were related and the qualitative information provided the answers to why the classifications were made.

Discourse Analysis

As the name implies, discourse analysis examines the meaning and social context of language, especially how it relates to social power. After all, communication is not just about what is said but also about *how* it is said. For example, a teenager who responds to a parent with a calm "that's fine" as they grab the car keys and walk out the door when the parent tells them to be home before midnight has a different meaning than a teenager who sighs in exasperation, says "that's fine," grabs the car keys, and slams the door on the way out. In both instances, the actual language is "that's fine." However, the first instance suggests that the teenager is actually OK with the restriction, so the request really is fine; but in the second, the response suggests that the teenager is *not* OK with the reaction and the language perhaps suggests they are fed up or are being sarcastic. These are two very different meanings to the same language. The meaning of language and how it is used can also change over time. Language to describe groups that were acceptable in the 1920s or 1930s is probably not acceptable today. For example, nobody refers to women today as "gals." Therefore, discourse analysis might focus on

- how the language relates to current social, political, or economic contexts
- how the language expression reflects current cultural norms of communication
- how body language or tone gives context to verbal expressions
- how language is used to express a person's values or beliefs
- how the presence of others affects verbal and physical language
- how language is used to achieve specific reactions or behaviors from others
- the context of the language—is it spoken dialogue? A speech? A rally?

Although there are a variety of ways to approach discourse analysis, just as there is for any form of analysis, I will focus on the approach proposed by Fairclough. According to Fairclough (2001), there are three levels of discourse analysis: description, interpretation, and explanation. The first level, description, focuses on the linguistic features of a text such as the vocabulary (words used, euphemistic expression, and style), grammar, and textual form. The second level, interpretation, focuses on how a speaker produces the text and the interpretations of that production. According to Fairclough, the last step, explanation, involves looking at how language provides cues that reflect power on three different levels: societal, institutional, and situational (2001). The key to discourse analysis is that it recognizes that language is not just words but also a reflection of social interaction, culture, and power.

LEARNING CHECK 16.3: SPECIFIC ANALYTIC TECHNIQUES

1. In content analysis, _____ content is high on validity and low on reliability.

2. In grounded theory analysis, what are some examples of axial codes?

3. How do the two methods of grounded theory presented differ?

4. Which of the four specific techniques covered focus on mapping the connections between people and the meaning given those connections?

5. What are Fairclough's three levels of discourse analysis?

Answers to be found at the end of the chapter.

CHALLENGES

How Can I Know Whether My Analysis Is Valid and Reliable?

Reliably identifying codes and the data that capture this information is one of the biggest challenges of qualitative research. Team coding is one way to increase reliability. Having a group of researchers read the transcripts, discuss the codes, and reach a consensus can help reliability. It is, however, also very time consuming. Another option is to use the QDA software mentioned earlier to identify themes, networks, or and how often they occur. Using a computer program minimizes the risk of personal bias or error.

How Can I Increase the Validity of My Interpretations?

One strength of qualitative research is its subjective nature, but this can also be an issue because the researcher needs to make it clear why the researcher's subjective interpretation of that information should be believed. One step in this direction is to clearly document every decision and the thought process behind it. This may not appear in every report, but a researcher should document decisions while fresh in case they are needed. A second step is to be consistent in the interviewing skills and analysis so that another researcher can replicate the steps and interpretation of the observations.

Triangulation is a third technique to increase validity. Frequently this means using other sources of information, such as documents or the perspective of another observer, to verify the information. When different sources of information reach the same interpretations, that reinforces validity. Also, a researcher can make note of his/her own biases and the steps the researcher took to check the data and ensure that the conclusions are reflective of the data and not these biases. Therefore, even though qualitative information aims to capture the differences in subjective meaning, there are steps researchers can take to increase the validity of their interpretations of that information.

Key Terms

Analytic code

Attribute code

Axial coding

Cluster diagram

Constant comparative methods

Emic meaning

Etic meaning

First-level coding

Flowchart

Index code

Latent content

Manifest content

Open coding

Selective coding

Answers to Learning Check Questions

Learning Check 16.1: Preparing Qualitative Data

1. During

2. The first thing is to make a master data copy and secure it somewhere other than where the main data are being edited or analyzed.

3. Strengths include saving time and a possible decrease in human bias in interpreting information. Weaknesses include a risk of creating too many analytic codes to be useful for pattern identification.

Learning Check 16.2: General Approach to Analysis

1. Things researchers might initially look for in the data include important experiences, important ideas, preliminary links between ideas, and why ideas may be preliminarily linked.

2. False. There are no set goals for the number of themes to identify. More complex topics will likely lead to the identification of more themes than simpler topics.

3. Emic meaning is the meaning that subjects give (and express in the data) to their own experiences, whereas etic meaning is the meaning that the researcher gives to the data

based on both the subjects' emic meanings and the researcher's discipline.

Learning Check 16.3: Specific Analytic Techniques

1. Latent content.

2. Some types of axial codes include causal codes, context codes, action codes, and consequences.

3. The first method (open, axial, and selective coding) focuses on continually identifying basic codes through asking the data "what is this about" (open codes), linking those codes via new codes (axial codes), and then selecting a few main codes (selective codes) to serve as the central storyline of the presentation. The second method is less concerned about an overall storyline and instead starts with basic demographic or contextual observations in the data that are correspondingly coded (attribute codes), put into context via specific questions—such as interview or researcher questions(index codes)—and then analyzed (analytic codes). Remember, both form from the ground up (inductively) and have some overlap.

4. Qualitative network analysis.

5. Description, interpretation, and analysis.

End-of-Chapter Problems

1. Which of the following are parts of the early steps in preparing qualitative data?
   a. Transcribe any observational or recorded information
   b. Create a master data copy
   c. Develop axial codes
   d. "a" and "b"
   e. "b" and "c"

2. When reseachers have multiple forms of qualitative data (e.g., field notes and interviews), to organize data, one approach is to organize by
   a. Date only, regardless of types
   b. Type first and then date within type
   c. Type only regardless of date
   d. Organizing data is not important

3. Which of the following is a benefit of the cut-and-paste technique for organizing data?
   a. It saves paper
   b. It helps protect against bias as the researcher is unlikely to remember people or contexts tied to specific quotes
   c. It is efficient
   d. It creates many analytic codes that help clarify the meaning

4. When identifying initial themes, what are some things researchers might record?
   a. Initial theme impressions
   b. Questions raised by the data
   c. Reminders of points a researcher might want to follow up on
   d. All the above

5. True/False: In qualitative analysis, it is sufficient just to identify themes in the data without any furthers analysis.

6. According to Warren and Karner (2005), what are the three steps to linking themes?
   a. Identifying themes, connecting themes to each other, connecting themes to theory

   b. Linking the themes to questions, linking the questions to theory, providing evidence of the theoretical link
   c. Connecting themes, interpreting the themes, providing evidence for the interpretations
   d. Connecting themes, connecting theory, questioning theory

7. What are some ways in which researchers can show how qualitative themes are linked?
   a. Cluster diagrams
   b. Flowchart
   c. Bivariate table
   d. "a" and "b"
   e. All the above

8. A researcher is studying the grieving process among people who have lost someone close to them by suicide. In analyzing the data, the researcher notices a theme of blame toward the individual based on comments respondents have made such as: "He was always a moody person" and "She wanted a lot of my time" as well as themes of self-blame: "Maybe if I just called him more" or "I wanted to spend more time with her, but my job prevented it." In these examples where the respondent is giving meaning to both the individual who committed suicide and their own reaction to it would be an example of:
   a. Emic meaning
   b. Etic meaning
   c. Normative meaning
   d. Theoretical meaning

9. Dr. Jones is studying political speeches from the most recent presidential election. As part of his analysis, he counts how often the Democratic and Republican candidates use the terms *environment, greenhouse, emissions,* and *sustainability*. The count of these terms is the
   a. Unit of analysis
   b. Latent content
   c. Manifest content
   d. Reliability test

10. In one method of grounded theory, we have the stages of open, axial, and selective coding. Which of these stages involves picking a reference category around which the other themes will be organized?
    a. Open coding
    b. Axial coding
    c. Selective coding
    d. All the above

11. Which are some forms that axial codes might take?
    a. Causal conditions
    b. Context codes
    c. Action codes
    d. All the above

12. One method of grounded theory coding involves attribute, index, and analytic codes. Which code addresses demographic and/or contextual variables?
    a. Attribute codes
    b. Index codes
    c. Analytic codes
    d. All the above

13. Which specific analytic technique might examine how a subject's word choice reflects power differentials?
    a. Content analysis
    b. Grounded theory analysis
    c. Qualitative network analysis
    d. Discourse analysis

14. Which specific analytic technique might examine how a subject's peer associations work to influence self-esteem based on those subjects' descriptions about how they feel around certain groups of friends?
    a. Content analysis
    b. Grounded theory analysis
    c. Qualitative network analysis
    d. Discourse analysis

15. Which specific analytic technique might examine how textbooks treat the issue of male victimization in interpersonal violence?
    a. Content analysis
    b. Grounded theory analysis
    c. Qualitative network analysis
    d. Discourse analysis

APPENDIX A: DIRECTIONS FOR STATISTICAL TESTS IN SPSS

The directions to run the statistical tests covered in Chapters 11–14 in SPSS all appear in this Appendix and are organized by chapter; therefore, the variable names that appear in these directions correspond to the GSS variables used for the statistical examples in the relevant chapter. The tests can all be run from the top command menu in either the "Variable View" or the "Data View" tabs.

CHAPTER 11

Frequency Distribution

1. Analyze → Descriptive Statistics → Frequencies

2. Once in this box, move the variable of interest (SAVEJOBS) from the box on the left to the box on the right. Click OK.

In the analysis field, SPSS presents variables in alphabetical order by variable name, not by label. To get a sense of where your particular variable is, hold the cursor over a variable name to see what its corresponding variable label is and repeat until you get to your variable of interest. You can also move more than one variable into the box on the right to do the statistics on multiple variables at once.

Normality Plots

1. Analyze → Descriptive Statistics → Explore

2. Move the variables of interest from the box on the left to the box on the right.

3. Click the "Plots" option on the right.

4. Select "Normality tests with plots."

Central Tendency and Dispersion

1. Follow the steps to calculate the "frequency distribution" but do *not* click "OK" yet.

2. Select the "Statistics" box. The window that appears at the top of the next page will open

3. Select the statistics of choice; click "Continue."

4. You will be back to the command box for "Frequencies" so click "OK."

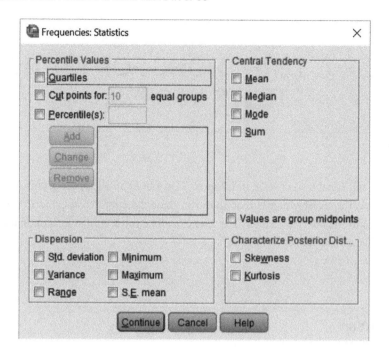

CHAPTER 12

Confidence Intervals

Interval/Ratio measures

1. Analyze → Compare means → One-sample *t*-test

2. Move the variable of interest (AGEKDBRN) from the box on the left to "Test variable" on the right.

3. Click "OK."

You might notice that if you search SPSS you will not find anything that specifically states "confidence intervals" in the "Analyze" menu. That is because, in SPSS, a one-sample hypothesis test (which we will see again shortly) produces the confidence interval information as part of its output, so SPSS (and us) uses that instead.

Nominal/Ordinal Measures

The steps to calculate a confidence interval for proportions in SPSS are easy if you have (1) a dichotomous (two-answer choice) variable and (2) the SPSS extension, but the output is not in the same format as the output for our other tests. The SPSS commands are:

1. Utilities → Confidence Interval Proportion

This will open the following screen:

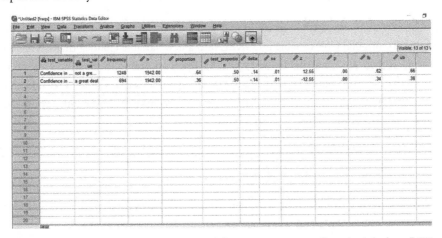

You want to put the variable of interest in the top row (I had to recode the variable to be dichotomous, hence the lower case "r" at the end of the variable name) and pick your confidence level. You are limited to 95% or 99%.

The resulting output will actually be a new data set:

There is actually a lot more on this data set than we need for our purposes to "get the job done." We are interested in the second row, which is "a great deal" (identified in the second column of the second row), and the last two columns of that row. "lb" stands for "lower bound" for the lower part of the confidence interval and "ub" stands for "upper bound," for the upper part. Therefore, basically, the data set is telling us that we are 95% confident that between 34% (lb) and 38% (ub) of people have "a great deal" of confidence in the medical institutions.

Hypothesis Tests: One Sample

One-Sample t-Test

1. Analyze → Compare means → One-sample *t*-test

2. Move variable of interest from left box to right. Here our variable is "EDUC."

3. For the "test value," enter the population mean of comparison. Here it is "13.4" (see Chapter 12).

4. Select "OK."

One-Sample Wilcoxon Signed-Ranks Test

1. Analyze → Nonparametric Tests → One sample

2. In the box that opens, click the tab at the top entitled "fields."

3. Move all the variables from "test fields" (the left box") to "fields" (the right box).

4. Now move *just* REALINC from "fields" (the left box") to "test fields" (the right box). (Yes, you are moving it *back* to the box on the right, but it is easier to move just the one variable over than trying to find it in the list on the right and then move the variables around it to the left).

5. Click the "settings" tab at the top.

6. Select "Customize tests" and select "Compare median to hypothesized (Wilcoxon Signed Rank Test)."

7. Enter the hypothesized median as "57617."

Binomial Hypothesis Test (with Output)

If I am using the SPSS binomial test, there is an additional assumption that my dependent variable is a dichotomous 0/1 variable. (I recoded the original GSS variable DEGREE into a new variable Colldeg that is yes/no to having a college degree). Furthermore, there are a few slightly odd ways this test works in SPSS. First, the test proportion we enter applies to the category that's first encountered in the data. So the hypothesis that's tested depends on the order of the cases. So if we want to test college, we either need college to appear first (have the lower code) or use the proportion for *noncollege* as our reference proportion.

To run this test in SPSS, we do the following:

1. Analyze → Nonparametric tests → Legacy Dialogs → Binomial

2. Move the variable of interest (colldeg) that I created from the variables listed in the box on the left to the box on the right.

3. Put the population parameter of comparison in the "test proportion" box. The proportion .50 is the default, but we will change it to .66 since it can only take two decimal places to the right. We use the computed value of .66 because noncollege educated is listed first (it has a code of 0) and if 34% of the population *has* a college degree, then 100%–34% = 66% who do *not* have a college degree. The 66% as a proportion is .66.

4. Click "Options" and select "descriptive."

This will produce the following output:

Descriptive Statistics

	N	Mean	Std. Deviation	Minimum	Maximum
Whether the respondent has a college degree	1,586	.3020	.45928	.00	1.00

Binomial Test

		Category	N	Observed Prop.	Test Prop.	Exact Sig. (1-tailed)
Whether the respondent has a college degree	Group 1	No	1,107	.70	.34	.000
	Group 2	Yes	479	.30		
	Total		1,586	1.00		

CHAPTER 13

Independent Samples *t*-Test

1. Analyze → Compare Means → Independent samples *t*-test

2. When the new box opens, move the dependent variable "CHILDS" to the "Test variable" box and the independent variable "RACECEN1" to the "Grouping variable box."

3. Select which two values of RACECEN1 you want to compare. Looking at the variable in "Variable view," we see that African American has a code of "2" and Hispanic a code of "16." Click the grouping variable, and under "define groups" enter "2" for group 1 and "16" for group 2.

4. Click "OK."

Mann–Whitney *U* Test

1. Analyze → Nonparametric Tests → Legacy Dialogs → two Independent Samples

2. Move the dependent variable WWWHR into the "Test Variables List."

3. Move CONPRESS into the "Grouping Variable" box.

4. Select "Define groups" and enter "1" (a great deal) for group 1 and "3" (not a lot) for group 2.

5. Click "Continue."

6. Click "OK."
   Since the dependent variable is not normally distributed, as I stated, I would need to compare the medians instead of the means. There are a couple of ways to do this. One way is to do the following:

7. Analyze → Descriptive Statistics → explore

8. Move the dependent variable WWWHR into the "Dependent list" and the independent variable CONPRESS into the "Factor List."

9. Select "Statistics" and when the box opens up, select "Descriptives" and then "OK."

10. Select "OK" in the main analysis box.

Chi-square Test

1. Analyze → Descriptive Statistics → Crosstabs

2. Move the independent variable (CONFED) to the "Column(s)" box and the dependent variable (CCTV) to the "Row(s)" box.

3. Click "Cells" on the right of the box and click "column" in the "Percentages" box.

4. Click "Continue."

5. Click "Statistics" on the right side of the box and click "chi-square" at the top.

6. Click "Continue."

7. Click "OK."

Paired Sample *t*-Test

1. Analyze → Compare Means → Paired Samples *t*-test

2. Enter the first paired variable (here tvpre) into "Variable 1" and the second (tvpost) into "Variable 2." (Note: The variables are not capitalized since this is hypothetical data and not from the GSS.)

3. Click "OK."

Wilcoxon Signed-Ranks Test

1. Analyze → Nonparametric Tests → Legacy Dialogues → two related samples

2. Enter the first paired variable (here prefake) into "Variable 1" and the second (postfake) into "Variable 2."

3. Make sure "Wilcoxon" is checked for "Test type" (it is the default).

4. Click the "Options" box on the right and select "Descriptives" and "Quartiles" and click "Continue."

5. Click "OK."

McNemar's Test

The SPSS commands are actually the same as noted above for the Wilcoxon Ranked Test, but (1) insert the new variables and (2) in step 3 instead of clicking "Wilcoxon," click "McNemar" a couple options down. Therefore:

1. Analyze → Nonparametric Tests → Legacy Dialogues → two related samples

2. Enter the first paired variable (here prefake) into "Variable 1" and the second (postfake) into "Variable 2."

3. Make sure "McNemar" is checked for "Test type."

4. Click the "Options" box on the right and select "Descriptives" and "Quartiles" and click "Continue."

5. Click "OK."

Analysis of Variance (ANOVA)

1. Analyze → Compare Means → One-way ANOVA

2. Move your dependent variable (CHLDIDEL) to the "Dependent List" and your independent variable (RACE) to the "Factor list."

3. Click the box "Post Hoc" and select "Tukey" then "Continue." (Note: if you don't assume equal variances and run the Welch ANOVA instead of the one-way ANOVA, you could select the Games–Howell post hoc test. The interpretation is the same, just the formula used for calculation differs.)

4. Click "Options" on the right and select "Descriptives" and "Homogeneity of variance" test in order to test that assumption.

Kruskal–Wallace H

1. Analyze → Nonparametric Tests → Legacy → K Independent samples

2. Move the dependent variable (RELACTIV) to the "test variable" box and the independent variable (POSTLIFE) to the "grouping variable" box.

3. Set the values of the independent variable. Note: They need to be expressed as a range; you cannot skip values.

4. Make sure "Kruskal–Wallace" is selected.

5. Click "OK."

CHAPTER 14

Lambda and Cramer's *V*

1. Analyze → Descriptive Statistics → Crosstab

2. Put the independent variable (SEX) in the column box and the dependent variable (AIDOLD) in the row box.

3. Select "Cells" on the right and program to percentage down the columns.

4. Click "Statistics" on the right and within that, select the following boxes:

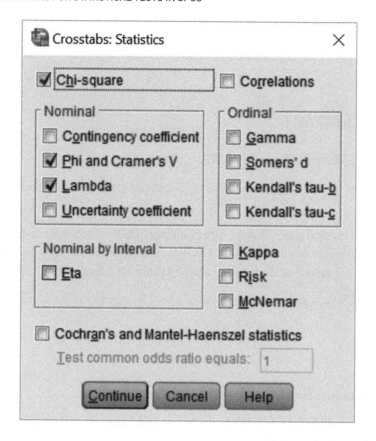

5. Click "OK."

Eta-squared

There are a couple of ways to run this test in SPSS, but I will use the following method, which is one of the more direct ways to run the statistic when there is only one independent variable.

1. Analyze → Compare Means → Means

2. Move the dependent variable (CHLDIDEL) to "Dependent variable" and the independent variable (SEX) to the "Layer 1 of 1" box.

3. Under "Options" click "ANOVA table and eta" under "Statistics for first layer."

4. Click "Continue."

5. Click "OK."

Gamma and Somer's *d*

Follow the same directions as for Lambda and Cramer's *V* but instead of selecting those two statistics, choose either Gamma or Somer's *d*.

Spearman's rho

1. Analyze → Correlate → Bivariate

2. Move the two variables of interest (AGE and ATTEND) from the box on the left to the box on the right.

3. Select "Spearman" under "Correlation Coefficient."

4. Select "two-tailed" for significance.

5. Select OK.

Pearson's *r*

The commands are the same for Spearman's rho but select Pearson's *r* instead.

Linear Regression

1. Analyze → Regression → Linear

2. Move the dependent variable (AGEKDBRN) to the "dependent" box and the independent variable (EDUC) to the "independent(s)" box.

3. Select the "Statistics" box and make sure "estimates" and "model fit" are selected.

4. Click "OK."

Partial Correlation

1. Analyze → Correlate → Partial

2. Move the *X* (EDUC) and *Y* (AGEKDBRN) to the "Variables" box.

3. Move *Z* (PAEDUC) to the "Controlling for" box.

4. Click "OK."

Multiple Linear Regression

1. Analyze → Regression → Linear

2. Move the dependent variable (AGEKDBRN) to the "dependent" box and all independent and control variables of interest (male, EDUC, PAEDUC) to the "independent(s)" box.

3. Choose either "stepwise" or "entry" method.

4. Select the "Statistics" box and make sure "estimates" and "model fit" are selected.

5. Click "OK."

CHAPTER 15

Univariate Presentation

Bar Graph

1. Go to Graphs → Chart Builder.
   - A box might show up asking you to double-check that your variables are the appropriate measurement level of your graph. For example, you probably do not want to do a pie chart on an interval/ratio level of measurement.

2. Click OK if the level of measurement in the "Measure" column in the variable view field in SPSS accurately reflects the level of measurement of your variable. For a bar graph, SPSS should recognize the variable's level of measurement to be nominal or ordinal.
   - If SPSS has the level of measurement misidentified (e.g., if FEPOL is listed as a "scale" variable, which is what SPSS calls interval/ratio measures), then double-check the measure and make sure it actually is nominal or ordinal; if it is, then change the SPSS classification accordingly.
   - If SPSS is correct, and you mistakenly thought the variable was a different level of measurement, then select a different means of data presentation.

3. Once the variable is correctly identified and appropriate for a bar graph, when you click "OK," SPSS will open a window that looks like this:

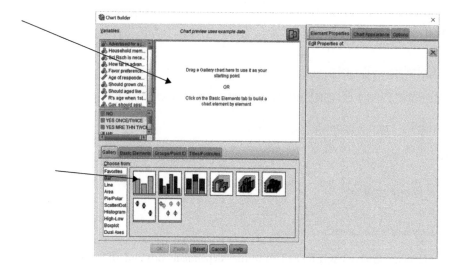

   - You will see that researchers can choose the form of their graph in the lower left part of the window.

4. Select the first set of bar graphs (where the second arrow (smaller arrow) is) and drag that to the white window near the top (where the first arrow (larger arrow) is). This window will now look like this:

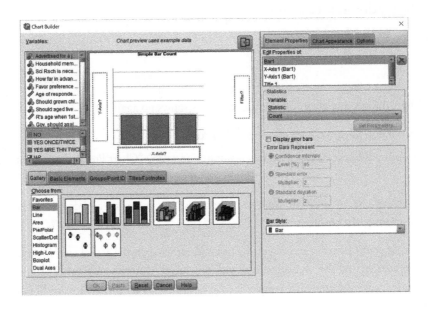

5. Now you drag the variable of interest (FEPOL) to the *X*-axis box at the bottom of the chart you see. The categories of the variable will automatically appear along the *X*-axis as will the observation count on the *Y*-axis.

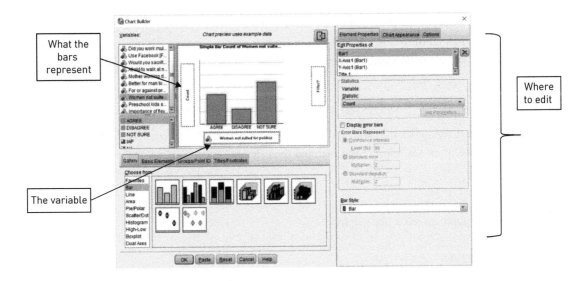

6. Edit the chart as needed by playing with the right side of the window (the black bracket). For example, you can:

    • Change the color of the bars (under "Chart appearance").

    • Change the *Y*-axis to percent (under the "Statistics" window).

- Change axis labels (by clicking on the relevant component under "Edit properties").
- Change the title (also under "Edit properties of," but make sure you click the title in the "Chart Preview" window for any changes to be accepted).

7. Click "OK."

Pie Chart

1. Graphs → Chart Builder and click "OK" if the value box shows up again

2. In the Gallery window at the bottom left, select "Pie/Polar."
   - Only one option is likely to appear, so move that option to the "Chart Preview" screen at the top of the window.

3. Select the variable of interest (FEPOL) from the "Variables" box at the top and drag it to the "Slice by?" box that is at the bottom of the pie chart.

4. To make sure that your pie wedges represent the percent, rather than the actual count, under "Element Properties" on the right and the "Statistics" box within it, select "Percentage()" for the statistic. (The percent is preferred because it addresses the total sample size. 10 out of 10 is very different from 10 out of 100!).

5. Click "OK."

This will produce a color-coded pie chart where the colored wedges represent the value percentages with a legend telling you what wedge represents what value. However, what this will not automatically do is let you know what percent each wedge represents. Many researchers would consider this an important omission because most people can only visually distinguish the relationship between values when they are very pronounced. However, when values are closely represented, it can be hard to distinguish which value is just a little more or less common. Therefore, adding the percentage of each wedge is important and to do this, one needs to continue editing the pie chart *after* SPSS initially creates it. Therefore:

- In the SPSS Output file where the pie chart is present, double click the pie chart to activate the editor.

Once the editor is activated, right-click the pie chart and select "Show data labels." Alternately, double click the pie chart that was produced in the Output file, select "Elements" and then "Show Data Label."

Line Graph

Follow the steps for bar graph but select line graph.

Bivariate Presentation

Table

1. Analyze → Descriptive Statistics → Crosstabs

2. Move the independent variable (CONFED) to the "Column(s)" box and the dependent variable (CCTV) to the "Row(s)" box.

3. Click "Cells" on the right of the box and click "column" in the "Percentages" box.

4. Click "Continue."

5. Click "OK."

Bar Graph

1. Graphs → Chart Builder and click "OK" if the value box shows up again.

2. Select either side by side or stacked for your format.

3. Move the independent variable (CONFED) into the "X-axis" bar.

4. Move the dependent variable (CCTV) into the "Cluster on X" box at the top of the graph viewing window.

5. In "Element Properties," select "Bar 1."

6. In "Element Properties," select "Statistics" and "Percentage ()."

7. "Set Parameter" select "Total for Each X-Axis Category" in order for the bars to represent the percentages down the columns like would appear in a table.

Line Graph

Follow the steps for bar graph but select line graph.

APPENDIX B: DIRECTIONS FOR STATISTICAL TESTS IN R AND THE CORRESPONDING OUTPUT

The directions to run the statistical tests covered in Chapters 11–14 in R all appear in this Appendix and are organized by chapter; therefore, the variable names that appear in these directions correspond to the GSS variables used for the statistical examples in the relevant chapter. Command boxes are distinguished by the shaded boxes and output boxes are distinguished by the clear outlined boxes.

CHAPTER 11

Frequency Distributions

In order to run a frequency in R, I will work with the data set I introduced in Chapter 10 that is named "dstat_lw_df" using the table command to create a new table and then to run it. So to run measures of central tendency and some dispersion measures, our command would be:

```
Jobtable<-table(dstat_lw_df$JOBSAT)
Jobtable
```

STRONGLY AGAINST	AGAINST	NEITHER
40	189	292
IN FAVOR STRONGLY IN FAVOR		
595	252	

Notice, however, that this is just the frequency of responses. In order to get the frequency, cumulative frequency, and proportions (which could be converted to percentages by just moving the decimal two places to the right), I could run the following commands:

```
cbind(Freq=table(dstat_lw_df$SAVEJOBS),
Cumul=cumsum(table(dstat_lw_df$SAVEJOBS)),
relative=prop.table(table(dstat_lw_df$SAVEJOBS)))
```

	Freq	Cumul	relative
STRONGLY AGAINST	40	40	0.02923977
AGAINST	189	229	0.13815789
NEITHER	292	521	0.21345029
IN FAVOR	595	1116	0.43494152
STRONGLY IN FAVOR	252	1368	0.18421053

Central Tendency, Dispersion, and Normality Plots

A basic way to calculate measures of central tendency and dispersion in RStudio is to use the "Summary" command. To illustrate this, I will continue to work with the data set I introduced in Chapter 10 that is named "dstat_lw_df."

Remember, the name I gave this data set does not have to be the same name you give your conversion from the GSS. Mine is named this way just so I can keep track and remember that this is the data set with the descriptive variables— "dstat"—and that it is mine—"lw." The "df" tag is helpful for me to know the file is a data file.

So to run measures of central tendency and some dispersion measures the command would be:

```
summary(dstat_lw_df)
```

```
        CLASS                    EDUC
LOWER CLASS  : 286        Min.  : 0.00
WORKING CLASS:1330        1st Qu.:12.00
MIDDLE CLASS :1146        Median :13.00
UPPER CLASS  :  81        Mean  :13.74
NA's         :  24        3rd Qu.:16.00
                          Max.  :20.00
                          NA's  :9


             SAVEJOBS             SEX
STRONGLY AGAINST  : 40      FEMALE:1591
AGAINST           : 189      MALE :1276
NEITHER           : 292
IN FAVOR          : 595
STRONGLY IN FAVOR : 252
NA's              :1499
      TVHOURS
Min.      : 0.000
1st Qu.   : 1.000
Median    : 2.000
Mean      : 3.031
3rd Qu.   : 4.000
Max.      :24.000
NA's      :984
```

The above is the output. I know what is relevant because of the decisions I made in the decision tree. I can find the central tendency and dispersion for SEX, CLASS, and SAVEJOBS in this output because all three of those variables are categorical, what R calls factors. However, EDUC and TVHOURS, on the other hand, are continuous and I do not know what the data look like yet so I do not know whether I want the median and range/IQR or the mean and standard deviation. So, for now, focusing on SEX, CLASS, and SAVEJOBS, I can identify or calculate the following based on the output above:

```
SEX: The mode is "female" (n=1,591)
    Valid percent: 1,591/2,867 = 55.49%
    Total percent: Same since no "NA" responses

CLASS: Mode = "Working class" (n=1,330)
  Valid percent (I have to calculate)
        = 1,330/2,843 = 46.78%
   Total percent (again, I calculate)
        = 1,330/2,867 = 46.39%

SAVJOBS: Mode = "in favor" (n=595)
    Valid percent: 595/1,386 = 43.49%
    Total percent: 595/2,867 = 20.75%
```

Now let's figure out whether to look at the median or the mean for EDUC and TVHOURS by running a histogram, skewness, and kurtosis. To start with the histogram, I would use the "hist" command for "histogram," identify the data set, and the variable of interest using "$," which is R's way of identifying a specific variable. To get the information for EDUC, the command would read:

```
hist(dstat_lw_df$EDUC)
```

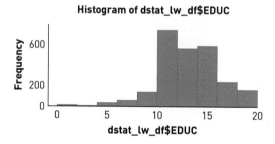

Histogram of dstat_lw_df$EDUC

The above output shows a slight shift to the right, but the responses themselves are pretty normally distributed around a central hump, just like I saw in our discussion of SPSS.

Now let's try for TVHOURS:

```
hist(dstat_lw_df$TVHOURS)
```

Here I see that the data are definitely skewed. But let's check the skewness and kurtosis before deciding. In order to test skewness and kurtosis, the "moments" package needs to be installed (first line) and then run (second line). First, do this:

```
install.packages("moments")
library(moments)
```

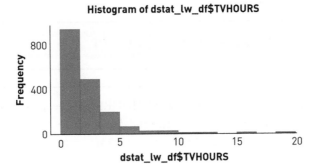

Q–Q Plot with Reference Line

I included the command that will put the reference line in a different color (here blue).

```
qqnorm(infer_lw_df$EDUC,pch=1,frame=FALSE)
qqline(infer_lw_df$EDUC,col='blue", lwd=2)
```

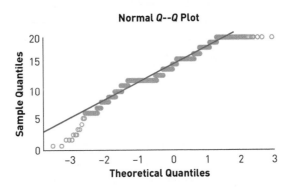

I also want to illustrate how to run skewness and kurtosis so we have a nongraphical method of testing normality in R as well; however, I am only going to show how to calculate this for TVHOURS for illustration. Each statistic is run with its own separate command, but I have to make sure that R knows not to include the missing ("NA") in the calculation because if I do not, and I try to run either skewness or kurtosis, I would get "NA" as the output because, as covered in Chapter 10, lettered responses outrank numerical ones in R. So to tell R not to use the "NA" in the calculation, I have to set the "na.rm" command, which stands for "NA remove" to "TRUE."

```
skewness(dstat_lw_df$TVHOURS,na.rm=TRUE)
```

```
[1] 2.809179
```

```
kurtosis(dstat_lw_df$TVHOURS,na.rm=TRUE)
```

```
[1] 16.05903
```

Skewness and kurtosis statistics reinforce the decision that TVHOURS is skewed; therefore, I would look at the information from the "summary" command and the decision tree and decide to use:

```
EDUC: Mean = 13.74
TVHOURS: Median = 2
```

I can complete the dispersion information for TV hours using the "summary" output because the information to calculate the range and the IQR is both part of that information.

```
TVHOURS: Range = 1 - 24 (based on "Min" and "Max.")
        IQR = 4 - 1 (based on "3rd Qu." and "1st Qu.")
```

Now I just need the standard deviation for EDUC and this is a fairly simple R command, but as I did for skewness and kurtosis, I need to tell R to ignore the missing values using the same na.rm=TRUE command.

```
sd(dstat_lw_df$EDUC,na.rm = TRUE)
```

```
[1] 2.963886
```

I see that the standard deviation for EDUC with rounding = 2.96.

CHAPTER 12

As always, I need to use the commands learned in Chapter 11 to first load my data into R. For my own bookkeeping clarification, I made separate data sets for the different variables used in each statistical chapter. The smaller subsets of variables enable me to better visually check the data every time I load it. Therefore, the data set I am using in this chapter is entitled "GSS_inferential2_csv.csv," which I am renaming in R to "infer_lw_df."

```
infer_lw_df <- read.csv("../Data/GSS_inferential2_csv.csv",na.strings =
c("NA","IAP","DK","AS MANY AS WANT","DK,NA","SEVEN+","EIGHT OR MORE","DK NA","89 OR
OLDER"))
```

Always check that your data read correctly. You can use the following commands "dim," "str," "head," and "tail" that you learned in Chapter 10. If you need to check the order and possibly re-order any factor (discrete) variables, remember you can do so with the commands you also learned in Chapter 10. Here I will just focus on the statistics covered in this chapter.

Confidence Intervals

Interval/Ratio Measures

In order to calculate the confidence interval, I need to first find the mean, standard deviation, and sample size of the variable of interest in order to program them into R. I also need to set the parameters of the interval, recognizing that because the interval needs to cover both the high and low ends of the normal curve, I need to divide the total error (such as 5%) over two tails (2.5% in each tail). Let's first find the mean (a in R), standard deviation (s), and sample size (n) of the variable AGEKDBRN with the following commands you learned in Chapter 12.

```
summary(infer_lw_df$AGEKDBRN)
```

```
Min. 1st Qu.   Median   Mean  3rd Qu.  Max.   NA's
9.00      20.00    23.00   24.28  28.00    47.00  811
```

```
sd(infer_lw_df$AGEKDBRN,na.rm = TRUE)
```

```
[1] 5.918386
```

Then to calculate the confidence interval to estimate the population parameter:

```
a<-24.28
n<-2056
error<-qt(0.975,df=n-1)*s/sqrt(n)
left<-a-error
right<-a+error
left
```

```
[1] 24.02396
```

...and the other side:

```
Right
```

```
[1] 24.53604
```

Putting all of this together, I am 95% confident that 24.02 is the lower end of the confidence interval and 24.54 is the upper end.

Confidence Intervals

Nominal/Ordinal Measures

To find the confidence interval for proportions, I need to find the point estimate, which I cannot do until I filter out the missing values with the "na.omit" function and save that variable as a new data set, which I will call "medic_confidence_df"

```
medic_confidence_df=na.omit(infer_lw_df$CONMEDIC)
n=length(medic_confidence_df)
```

Now I can find the number of respondents who answered "a great deal" by comparing the new data set "medi_confidence_df" with the factor "A GREAT DEAL" and compute the sum. Dividing that sum by *n* gives the proportion who felt they had "A GREAT DEAL" of confidence in medicine.

```
k=sum(medic_confidence_df=="A GREAT DEAL")
pbar=k/n;pbar
```

```
[1] 0.3573635
```

I see that the proportion who answered this value, or the point estimate, was .3574 or 35.74%. Now I can estimate the standard error:

```
se=sqrt(pbar*(1-pbar)/n);se
```

```
[1] 0.0108746
```

As there are two tails in the normal distribution, the 95% confidence level would mean the interval would be at the 97.5th percentile of the normal distribution at the upper tail, which is given by qnorm (.975), which I multiply, based on the formula to the standard error to compute the margin of error.

```
e=qnorm(.975)*se;e
```

```
[1] 0.02131382
```

```
pbar+c(-e,e)
```

```
[1] 0.3360497 0.3786774
```

With rounding, I see that we are 95% confident that the proportion who have a great deal of confidence in medicine is .34 to .38, or 34% to 38%.

Hypothesis Tests: One Sample

One-Sample t-Test

As before, I have to define the values of the sample mean (xbar), the population mean (mu), the standard deviation (*s*), sample size (*n*), the formula, and then tell R to calculate the formula. Because, based on the chapter information, I only want this information for women, I need to first make a new data set that separates this information just for women, which I will call "female.educ" (top line), and then run the *t*-test command (second line).

```
female_educ <- infer_lw_df[infer_lw_df$SEX == "FEMALE" , ]$EDUC
t.test(female_educ,mu=13.4,alternative="greater")
```

This will produce the following output:

```
One Sample t-test


data: female_educ
t = 4.9523, df = 1584, p-value = 4.059e-07
alternative hypothesis: true mean is greater than 13.4
 95 percent confidence interval:
13.64685 Inf
sample estimates:
mean of x
 13.76972
```

If I wanted to make this a one-tailed test that is less than, I would just change the "alternative" comment to "=less," and if the alternative hypothesis is "not equal," then the same command would read "=two.sided."

One-Sample Proportion Test

To do a one-sample proportions test, comparing the percent with a college degree or more I need to define the number of successes (x), in other words, the frequency of the value of interest, which I can find with the summary function discussed earlier, the total sample size (*n*), and the probability to test against (*p*), which is determined the same way as discussed in the chapter. The phrase "correct =" is a logic R uses to indicate whether the Yates's continuity correction is needed (which is really important if the expected frequencies are <5). Discussing Yates is beyond our scope, but since the sample size is much greater than 5, I will set this to "FALSE."

Based on the information I learned from the summary command (not shown):

```
prop.test(x=479,n=1,591,p=.34,correct=FALSE)
```

```
   1-sample proportions test without continuity
   correction

data: 479 out of 1591, null probability 0.34
X-squared = 10.746, df = 1, p-value = 0.001045
alternative hypothesis: true p is not equal to 0.34
95 percent confidence interval:
 0.2790293 0.3240661
sample estimates:
       p
 0.3010685
```

This output includes the Pearson's chi-square statistic because this bases the outcome on a Goodness of Fit test, which is a chi-square-based measure; the probability value ($p<.001$); the 95% confidence interval (.28–.32); and a Ps, which is the probability of having a college degree.

If I want to make this a one-tailed test, just as I did with the one-sample *t*-test, I would just add "alternative="less" if the direction is less than or "alternative="greater" if the direction is greater than. The greater than example would read:

```
prop.test(x=479,n=1591,p=.34,correct=FALSE, alternative="greater")
```

```
   1-sample proportions test without continuity
   correction

data: 479 out of 1591, null probability 0.34
X-squared = 10.746, df = 1, p-value = 0.9995
alternative hypothesis: true p is greater than 0.34
95 percent confidence interval:
0.2825027 1.0000000
sample estimates:
      p
 0.3010685
```

Wilcoxon Signed Rank

```
wilcox.test(infer_lw_df$REALINC, mu = 57617, alternative = "two.sided")
```

```
   Wilcoxon signed-rank test with continuity
   correction

data: infer_lw_df$REALINC
V = 456340, p-value < 2.2e-16
alternative hypothesis: true location is not equal to 57617
```

In R's calculation of the Wilcoxon Signed-Rank Test, I only interpret the p-value; I do not give a corresponding test statistic.

CHAPTER 13

I am going to continue working with the "infer_lw_df" data set I created from the GSS data in Chapter 12, so let's presume that these data are already read into R.

Independent Sample t-Test

Based on the decision tree in Figure 13.1, I need to see if I have homogeneity of variances and, for us, this involves running the Levene's test. In order to run this test, I need to install and run the package "cars" into R.

```
install.packages("car")
library(car)
```

The command for the Levene's test is "LeveneTest"; then I need to tell R the dependent variable, the independent variable, and the data set, which houses those variables. Note: I had to create a new variable called "HISPBL" that had two categories of "Hispanic" and "Black."

```
Levene.test(CHILDS~HISPBL,infer_lw_df)
```

This gives me the following output:

```
Levene's Test for Homogeneity of Variance (center = median)
      Df F value Pr(>F)
group 1 0.1351 0.7133
    577
```

From this, I see that the p-value is > .05 (it is .7133) so I can assume equal variances. Therefore, I would run the independent samples t-test doing the following:

```
t.test(infer_lw_df$CHILD~infer_lw_df$HISPBL)
```

```
        Welch Two Sample t-test
data: infer_lw_df$CHILD by infer_lw_df$HISPBL
t = -1.0599, df = 147.24, p-value = 0.2909
alternative hypothesis: true difference in means is not equal to 0
95 percent confidence interval:
 -0.5496789 0.1659016
sample estimates:
mean in group BLACK mean in group HISPANIC
     1.966527         2.158416
```

As always, the numbers are a bit different in R than in SPSS because R automatically produces the Welch test. Although the assumption of equal variances is the default, I can add the var.equal = FALSE option to specify unequal variances and a pooled variance estimate. As we learned in Chapter 12, I can also use the alternative="less" or alternative="greater" option to specify a one-tailed test.

Mann–Whitney U Test

In order to run the Mann–Whitney U test for those who had "hardly any" and "a great deal" of confidence in the press, I first have to tell R to ignore the middle response of "only some." To do this, (1) I saved a new data set "NEWCON-PRESS" with the same old values as CONPRESS to avoid accidentally changing the original data variable (top line); (2) I created a new data set that is based on this newly recoded variable, which I will call "NEWCONP," that will be programmed to ignore (drop) the level "only some" (second line); and then (3) double-checked the new variable with the "summary command"

```
NEWCONPRESS,_infer_lw_df$CONPRESS
NEWCONP<-droplevels(NEWCONPRESS,c("ONLY SOME"))
Summary(NEWCONP)
```

```
HARDLY ANY      A GREAT DEAL      <NA>      NA's
963              159              930       815
```

Now I am ready for the Mann–Whitney U test:

```
wilcox.test(WWWHR ~ NEWCONP,data=infer_lw_df
```

```
data: WWWHR by NEWCONP
W = 15914, p-value = 0.004108
alternative hypothesis: true location shift is not equal to 0
```

I see that my p-value of .004108 is less than .05, so I reject the null and the alternate hypothesis is presumed true.

Chi-Square Test

The test for chi-square is most easily done in two steps. The first involves making the bivariate table where the first variable presented would be the row, or dependent variable, and the second would be the column or independent variable. This is the top line. The second line is necessary to have the table be presented in proportions, which I can later convert to percentages. The "2" in the command tells R to use the second variable (the column variable) as the denominator for the proportions.

```
mytable<-table(infer_lw_df$CCTV, infer_lw_df$CONFED)
prop.table(mytable,2)
```

	HARDLY ANY	ONLY SOME
Definitely should not have the right	0.1545455	0.1237113
Probably should not have the right	0.2000000	0.2010309
Probably should have the right	0.4181818	0.3917526
Definitely should have the right	0.2272727	0.2835052
	A GREAT DEAL	
Definitely should not have the right	0.1086957	
Probably should not have the right	0.1304348	
Probably should have the right	0.3478261	
Definitely should have the right	0.4130435	

Now I can run the chi-square statistic

```
(chisq.test(mytable))
```

```
Pearson's Chi-squared test

data: mytable
X-squared = 7.7046, df = 6, p-value = 0.2606
```

I see that my *p*-value of .2606 is not less than .05 so I cannot reject the null.

Two Dependent Samples Tests

In order to run these tests in R, I had to create a data set for my hypothetical summer camp study. A screenshot of this data set in Excel appears below. Copying these data into Excel and importing it into R in order to practice these commands is also a good way of practicing the importing skills learned in Chapter 10.

I named the resulting data set "paireddata_csv" and all the following examples are based on that.

Paired *t*-Test

To determine if the paired *t*-test is appropriate, I ran the tests for normality that we have already learned and those commands and output are not shown here. You can check Chapter 11 for the commands to run those tests. To run the paired *t*-test, the command is "t.test" and then I need to specify the data set and variables I want to test as well as set the paired command to "TRUE":

```
t.test(paireddata_csv$prehrstv, paireddata_csv$posthrstv, paired=TRUE)
```

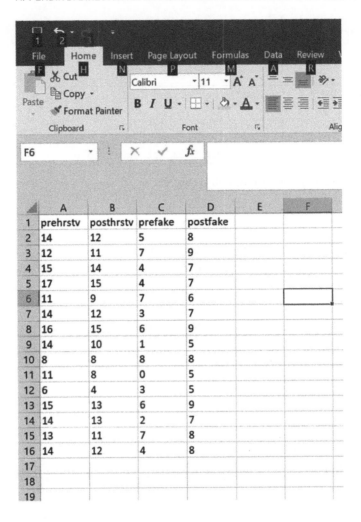

The output looks like this:

```
Paired t-test

data: paireddata_csv$prehrstv and paireddata_csv$posthrstv
t = 7.4075, df = 14, p-value = 3.314e-06
alternative hypothesis: true difference in means is not equal to 0
95 percent confidence interval:
 1.278823 2.321177
sample estimates:
mean of the differences
          1.8
```

The information I am most interested in is the *t* obtained value of 7.41 (with rounding), the degrees of freedom (14), and the *p*-value, which is .0000003314, which is essentially a *p*=.000.

Wilcoxon Signed-Rank Test

The commands for the Wilcoxon signed-rank test is the same as I described in Chapter 12 for one-sample tests with the exception that instead of comparing the ranks to mu, the ranks of the two variables are compared.

```
wilcox.test (paireddata_csv$prefake, paireddata_csv$postfake, alternative="two-sided")
```

The output looks like this:

```
Wilcoxon rank-sum test with continuity correction

data: paireddata_csv$prefake and paireddata_csv$postfake
W = 32.5, p-value = 0.0008431
alternative hypothesis: true location shift is not equal to 0
```

The *p*-value of .0008431 rounds to $p=.001$, so the null is rejected.

McNemar's Test

In order to produce the table that we saw in SPSS, I need to first program R to run the table using the same table commands covered in Chapter 12. I named the table "feartable" and remember that what appears first is the row variable and what appears second is the column variable. This will help me visualize the relationship between the pre- and post-test scores.

```
feartable<-table(paireddata_csv$prefear, paireddata_csv$postfear)
feartable
```

The output looks like this:

```
      No Yes
No   6   0
Yes  9   5
```

```
mcnemar.test(paireddata_csv$prefear, paireddata_csv$postfear), correct=TRUE
```

The output looks like this:

```
McNemar's Chi-squared test with continuity correction

data: paireddata_csv$prefear and paireddata_csv$postfear
McNemar's chi-squared = 7.1111, df = 1, p-value = 0.007661
```

Even though the *p*-value is slightly different from the one produced by SPSS, the overall message of both methods (SPSS and R) is that the null will be rejected.

Analysis of Variance (ANOVA)

Now that I am discussing independent samples again, I am returning to my R data set "infer_lw_df" for this section; but, again, to not risk changing the original data set, I am renaming it to "idealchild_df" (top line) and working from there. To program R to run an ANOVA and to see which groups have significant differences, the process involves more steps than it does with SPSS. The programming text would start with:

```
idealchild_df = infer_lw_df
idealchild_df$RACE=factor(idealchild_df$RACE,labels=c("BLACK","WHITE","OTHER"))
idealchild_df$RACE=as.factor(idealchild_df$RACE)
idealchild.mod1 = lm(CHLDIDEL ~ RACE, data = idealchild_df)
summary(idealchild.mod1)
```

This will return the following, which creates the residuals and information for R to later read with the ANOVA command:

```
Call:
lm(formula = CHLDIDEL ~ RACE, data = idealchild_df)

Residuals:
  Min 1Q Median 3Q Max
-2.9436 -0.4626 -0.4626 0.5374 3.5374

Coefficients:
        Estimate Std. Error t-value Pr(>|t|)
(Intercept) 2.94361 0.05191 56.704 <2e-16 ***
RACEOTHER -0.10312 0.08422 -1.224 .221
RACEWHITE -.48102 .05748 -8.368 <2e-16 ***
---
Signif. codes: 0 '***' .001 '**' .01 '*' .05 '.' .1 ' ' 1

Residual standard error: .8467 on 1,602 degrees of freedom
(1,262 observations deleted due to missingness)
Multiple R-squared: .05157, Adjusted R-squared: .05039
F-statistic: 43.55 on 2 and 1,602 DF, p-value: < 2.2e-16
```

The ANOVA is then run:

```
anova(idealchild.mod1)
```

```
Analysis of Variance Table

Response: CHLDIDEL
       Df Sum Sq Mean Sq F-value Pr(>F)
RACE 2 62.44 31.2203 43.553 < 2.2e-16 ***
Residuals 1,602 1,148.36 .7168
---
Signif. codes:
0 '***' .001 '**' .01 '*' .05 '.' .1 ' ' 1
```

The overall Pr(>F) value shows that the *p*-value is <.001, so the null would be rejected. In order to see where the biggest differences are, in R we would look at the confidence intervals.

```
confint(idealchild.mod1)
```

```
    2.5 %    97.5 %
(Intercept) 2.8417866 3.04543144
RACEOTHER -.2683061    .06206968
RACEWHITE -.5937755   -.36827248
```

The intercept is the confidence interval for the value of "BLACK," which was the omitted category based on how R ran the statistics.

Kruskal–Wallace *H* Test

In order to run the Kruskal–Wallace test, the command needs to read the dependent variable by the independent variable.

```
kruskal.test(POSTLIFE ~ RELACTIV, data=infer_lw_df)
```

The output looks like this:

```
Kruskal–Wallis rank-sum test

data: POSTLIFE by RELACTIV
Kruskal–Wallis chi-squared = 187.34, df = 8, p-value < 2.2e-16
```

As always, we are interested in the p-value and this is $p<.001$.

CHAPTER 14

As with the previous two chapters, I will continue to use the "infer_lw_df" data for these commands.

Cramer's V

Because, as we saw from the formula, Cramer's V is based on the chi-square statistic, I need to first calculate the chi-square as I did in Chapter 13.

```
tbl=table(infer_lw_df$AIDOLD,infer_lw_df$SEX)
tbl
chisq.test(tbl)
```

```
                  female male
defin should be      422  250
defin should not be   13   19
prob should be       309  226
prob should not be    61   67
```

To run the Cramer's V afterward, I need to first install the "lsr" package (top line) and run it (second line):

```
install.packages("lsr")
library(lsr)
```

Remember, the data set I created for chi-square in was entitled "tbl":

```
(lsr::cramersV(tbl))
```

```
[1] 0.106839
```

Eta Squared

In order to run eta squared, I need to first install and open a package that will recognize the statistic. I chose to use the package "sjstats" and the first two lines of the command install (line 1) and load (line 2) this package. I then can run the ANOVA statistic (line 3) and get the resulting output (line 4):

```
install.packages(sjstats)
library(sjstats)
anova1<-aov(infer_lw_df$CHLDIDEL ~ infer_lw_df$EX)
summary (anova1)
```

```
               Df Sum Sq   Mean Sq   F-value    Pr(>F)
infer_lw_df$SEX  1  4.5      4.541    6.034     0.0141 *
Residuals      1603 1206.3   0.753
---
Signif. codes: 0 '***' 0.001 '**' 0.01 '*' 0.05 '.' 0.1 ' ' 1
1,262 observations deleted due to missingness
```

Now I am ready for the eta squared on the output file created above:

```
eta_sq(anova1)
```

```
          term etasq
1 infer_lw_df$SEX 0.004
```

Remember, the value will be different from that produced by SPSS due to the different handling of missing information; however, even so, this result shows that there is no real improvement in predictability.

Gamma

```
with(infer_lw_df,DescTools::GoodmanKruskalGamma(AIDOLD,CLASS))
```

```
[1] -0.0404526
```

Spearman's Rho

For our data, because the GSS gave labels to ordinal measures that have many values, R reads those as factors and therefore I cannot do a test like Spearman's rho on them until I first tell R to read them as numeric. The order per line of the following commands is: (1) tell R to read "AGE" from the data frame "infer_lw_df" as the X value; (2) read the variable "ATTEND" from the data frame "infer_lw_df as both Y and as numeric; (3) run a Spearman's rho on the data:

```
x<-infer_lw_df$AGE
y<-as.numeric(infer_lw_df$ATTEND)
cor(x, y, method = "spearman", use = "complete.obs")
```

```
[1] -0.1170546
```

Pearson's r

In order to conduct a Pearson's r, I need to use a scatterplot to see if the two variables have a linear relationship. To do a scatterplot in R, I need to tell R which variables (and the data set they come from) are my X and Y variables. The first two lines do this, whereas the third line programs the scatterplot, and the fourth line tells R to draw a best-fit regression line through it.

```
x<-infer_lw_df$EDUC
y<-infer_lw_df$AGEKDBRN
plot(x,y,main="EDUC BY AGEKDBRN",xlab="EDUCATION",ylab="NUMBER OF
CHILDREN",pch=19,frame=FALSE)
abline(lm(y~x,data=infer_lw_df),col="blue")
```

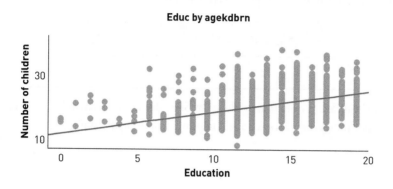

The command for Pearson's *r* is the following, where the *X* variable is presented first (and the dataset in which it is found) and the *Y* variable (with its dataset) second:

```
cor(infer_lw_df$AGEKDBRN,infer_lw_df$AGE, method = "pearson", use = "complete.obs")
```

Bivariate and Multivariate Regression

When running a linear regression in R, I create a new output (here called "reg"), which is the result of the linear model ("lm") for which the dependent variable is listed first followed by all the independent variables to include in the analysis. If I am doing a simple bivariate analysis, there is only one additional variable, the independent variable. If I am doing a multivariate analysis, I would just include all the additional variables. In order to avoid repletion, I will just illustrate the process from a multivariate perspective. So, this command appears on the first line. The second and third lines recognize the linear model output ("reg") and then tell R to summarize this linear output.

```
reg <- lm(AGEKDBRN~EDUC + PAEDUC + MALE, data=,infer_lw_df)
reg
summary(reg)
```

```
Call:
lm(formula = AGEKDBRN ~ EDUC + PAEDUC + MALE, data = infer_lw_df)

Coefficients:
(Intercept) EDUC PAEDUC MALEMALE
  12.79235 0.72644 0.09025 2.23441

Call:
lm(formula = AGEKDBRN ~ EDUC + PAEDUC + MALE, data = infer_lw_df)

Residuals:
Min 1Q Median 3Q Max
  -13.5926 -3.7327 -0.8656 3.1730 19.3439

Coefficients:
Estimate Std. Error t-value Pr(>|t|)
(Intercept) 12.79235 .66930 19.113 < 2e-16 ***
EDUC .72644 0.05067 14.337 < 2e-16 ***
PAEDUC 0.09025 .03681 2.452 .0143 *
MALEMALE 2.23441 .27744 8.054 1.64e-15 ***
---

Signif. codes:
0 '***' 0.001 '**' 0.01 '*' 0.05 '.' 0.1 ' ' 1

Residual standard error: 5.268 on 1476 degrees of freedom
  (1,387 observations deleted due to missingness)
Multiple R-squared: .1958, Adjusted R-squared: 0.1942
F-statistic: 119.8 on 3 and 1476 DF, p-value: < 2.2e-16
```

The "Coefficients" output is what I am particularly interested in for writing the resulting best fit multivariate linear regression line because it gives me the estimates as well as which variables statistically significantly contribute to the overall model. Based on this, our regression line would read (with rounding):

$$Y' = 12.79 + (.73)EDUC + .09(PAEDUC) + 2.23(male)$$

I also see that PAEDUC has the weakest statistical relationship (one star for a p-value of $p<05$), whereas the other two variables have a $p<.001$ error. It also gives me the adjusted R^2 as well, which is .1942 here, meaning that 19.42% of the variance in the age at which someone becomes a parent is explained by their years of education, their father's years of education, and by their gender.

R does not give you the standardized beta weights to see which variables have the strongest effect, while simultaneously considering the effects of the other variables, on the dependent variable; but it can be calculated using the rest of the information in this output if so desired (but those calculations are beyond our scope of "getting the job done").

Partial Correlation

Partial correlation in R is very sensitive to missing values; if I keep my initial data set of "infer_lw_df" as it is, it will delete cases for the variables I am interested in even if the missing values are for variables I am *not* interested in. Therefore, the first line tells R to make a new dataset, one that I just call "working_df," so I know that it is just the one I am currently working that will only contain the variables I am interested in running the partial correlation for (EDUC, AGEKDBRN, PAEDUC). The second line now creates a second data set that will omit all the missing values just for those three variables. The third line is the line that runs the partial correlation on this new data set that is just based on the three variables of interest for the cases for which there is all information.

```
>working_df<-read.csv("../Data/working.csv",na.strings=c("NA","IAP","DK"))
> infer_lw_df2 <- na.omit(working_df)
> pcor.test(infer_lw_df2$EDUC,infer_lw_df2$AGEKDBRN,infer_lw_df2$PAEDUC)
```

The resulting output is this:

```
  estimate p.value statistic n gp Method
1 0.341372 1.103161e-41 13.95801 1480 1 pearson
```

CHAPTER 15

I can use R to run all the graphs mentioned in this chapter except for pie charts, and I will continue to work with the data set "infer_lw_df" that was used in the previous three chapters.

Univariate Data Presentation

Bar Graph

The top line saves the frequency information into a new data set "counts," which will be referenced in the "barplots" command (second line). The "main=" command sets the title of the graph and "xlab" tells R what to label the *X*-axis:

```
counts <- table(infer_lw_df$FEPOL)
barplot(counts, main="Whether a female should NOT be a politician",
xlab="Number of Respondents")
```

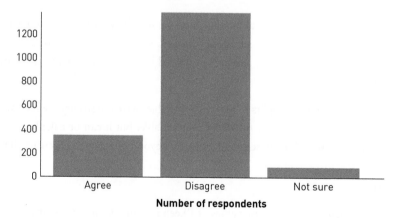

Line Graph

For the line graph, I had to create a new data set that looked at the view of women in politics over time. I called this data set "GSS_line," so I knew that it was the separate data for the line graph. In the command, I need to define the *X*- and *Y*-axes for R and what values of the *X* variable I wanted to plot (group =1). The "geom_point()" adds the data points on the line.

```
ggplot(data=GSS_line, aes(x=Year, y=Agree, group=1)) +
geom_line()+
geom_point()
```

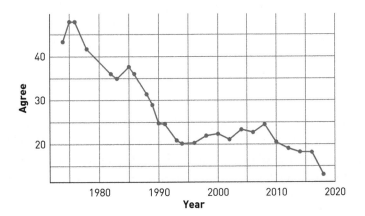

Bivariate Presentation

Table

R bivariate output for tables is a good example of why we need to learn how to present tables for others. As before, we need to define the table where the variable that is mentioned first is what will read across the rows (so the dependent variable if a hypothesis test) and the second variable is read down the columns (so the independent variable). This is what the command in the first line does. In the second line, the command tells R to calculate proportions (which we would convert to percentages for presentation) and to use, in this instance, the second variable (column variable) for the denominator.

```
mytable<-table(infer_lw_df$CCTV,infer_lw_df$CONFED)
prop.table(mytable,2)
```

```
                                    HARDLY ANY
Definitely should not have the right     0.1545455
Probably should not have the right       0.2000000
Probably should have the right           0.4181818
Definitely should have the right         0.2272727


                                    ONLY SOME
Definitely should not have the right     0.1237113
Probably should not have the right       0.2010309
Probably should have the right           0.3917526
Definitely should have the right         0.2835052


                                    A GREAT DEAL
Definitely should not have the right     0.1086957
Probably should not have the right       0.1304348
Probably should have the right           0.3478261
Definitely should have the right         0.4130435
```

Bar Graph with the "NA" Missing

Running a bivariate bar graph in R is a bit more complicated than running just a single variable. First, there are three packages that need to be loaded (or first installed if they are not installed using the "install.package()" command. Then there are separate commands to ignore missing values (fourth line), identify how variables will be grouped (fifth line), summarize the bivariate relationship (sixth line), calculate the percentages, and run the bar graph with labels that can be read.

```
library(dplyr)
library(ggplot2)

library(scales)

infer_lw_df3 <- na.omit(select(infer_lw_df,CCTV,CONFED))

grouped_df <- group_by(infer_lw_df3,CONFED,CCTV)

result_df <- summarise(grouped_df,cctv_confed_num=n())

result_df <- mutate(result_df,percentage = cctv_confed_num/sum(cctv_confed_num)*100)

ggplot(result_df,aes(x=CONFED,y=percentage,fill=CCTV)) +

geom_bar(stat="identity",position = position_dodge(preserve = "single")) +

scale_x_discrete(labels = wrap_format(10)) +

xlab("Confidence in the Gederal Gov't") +

labs(fill = "Gov't Right to Video Surveillance")
```

The output will look like this:

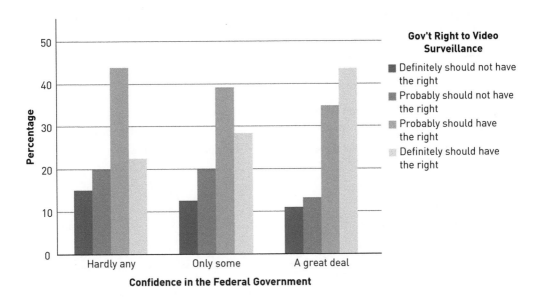

Bar Graph Stacked

```
mytable<-table(infer_lw_df$CCTV,infer_lw_df$CONFED)
prop.table(mytable,2)
barplot(prop.table(table(infer_lw_df$CCTV,infer_lw_df$CONFED),2),xlab = "Confidence in
the Federal Government", main = "Views of Video Surveillance by Federal Government")
```

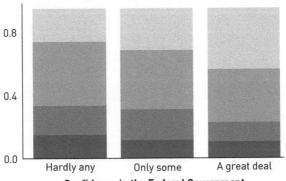

APPENDIX C: TABLE OF Z-SCORES

The values in column A are Z-scores. Column B lists the proportion of area between the mean and a given Z. Column C lists the proportion of area beyond a given Z. Only positive Z-scores are listed. Because the normal curve is symmetrical, the areas for negative Z-scores will be exactly the same as the areas for positive Z-scores.

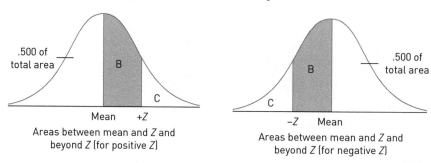

Areas between mean and Z and beyond Z (for positive Z)

Areas between mean and Z and beyond Z (for negative Z)

THE STANDARD NORMAL TABLE

A	B	C	A	B	C	A	B	C
Z	Area Between Mean and Z	Area Beyond Z	Z	Area Between Mean and Z	Area Beyond Z	Z	Area Between Mean and Z	Area Beyond Z
.00	.0000	.5000	.14	.0557	.4443	.28	.1103	.3897
.01	.0040	.4960	.15	.0596	.4404	.29	.1141	.3859
.02	.0080	.4920	.16	.0636	.4364	.30	.1179	.3821
.03	.0120	.4880	.17	.0675	.4325	.31	.1217	.3783
.04	.0160	.4840	.18	.0714	.4286	.32	.1255	.3745
.05	.0199	.4801	.19	.0753	.4247	.33	.1293	.3707
.06	.0239	.4761	.20	.0793	.4207	.34	.1331	.3669
.07	.0279	.4721	.21	.0832	.4168	.35	.1368	.3632
.08	.0319	.4681	.22	.0871	.4129	.36	.1406	.3594
.09	.0359	.4641	.23	.0910	.4090	.37	.1443	.3557
.10	.0398	.4602	.24	.0948	.4052	.38	.1480	.3520
.11	.0438	.4562	.25	.0987	.4013	.39	.1517	.3483
.12	.0478	.4522	.26	.1026	.3974	.40	.1554	.3446
.13	.0517	.4483	.27	.1064	.3936	.41	.1591	.3409

A	B	C	A	B	C	A	B	C
Z	Area Between Mean and Z	Area Beyond Z	Z	Area Between Mean and Z	Area Beyond Z	Z	Area Between Mean and Z	Area Beyond Z
.42	.1628	.3372	.72	.2642	.2358	1.02	.3461	.1539
.43	.1664	.3336	.73	.2673	.2327	1.03	.3485	.1515
.44	.1700	.3300	.74	.2703	.2297	1.04	.3508	.1492
.45	.1736	.3264	.75	.2734	.2266	1.05	.3531	.1469
.46	.1772	.3228	.76	.2764	.2236	1.06	.3554	.1446
.47	.1808	.3192	.77	.2794	.2206	1.07	.3577	.1423
.48	.1844	.3156	.78	.2823	.2177	1.08	.3599	.1401
.49	.1879	.3121	.79	.2852	.2148	1.09	.3621	.1379
.50	.1915	.3085	.80	.2881	.2119	1.10	.3643	.1357
.51	.1950	.3050	.81	.2910	.2090	1.11	.3665	.1335
.52	.1985	.3015	.82	.2939	.2061	1.12	.3686	.1314
.53	.2019	.2981	.83	.2967	.2033	1.13	.3708	.1292
.54	.2054	.2946	.84	.2995	.2005	1.14	.3729	.1271
.55	.2088	.2912	.85	.3023	.1977	1.15	.3749	.1251
.56	.2123	.2877	.86	.3051	.1949	1.16	.3770	.1230
.57	.2157	.2843	.87	.3078	.1992	1.17	.3790	.1210
.58	.2190	.2810	.88	.3106	.1894	1.18	.3810	.1190
.59	.2224	.2776	.89	.3133	.1867	1.19	.3830	.1170
.60	.2257	.2743	.90	.3159	.1841	1.20	.3849	.1151
.61	.2291	.2709	.91	.3186	.1814	1.21	.3869	.1131
.62	.2324	.2676	.92	.3212	.1788	1.22	.3888	.1112
.63	.2357	.2643	.93	.3238	.1762	1.23	.3907	.1093
.64	.2389	.2611	.94	.3264	.1736	1.24	.3925	.1075
.65	.2422	.2578	.95	.3289	.1711	1.25	.3944	.1056
.66	.2454	.2546	.96	.3315	.1685	1.26	.3962	.1038
.67	.2486	.2514	.97	.3340	.1660	1.27	.3980	.1020
.68	.2517	.2483	.98	.3365	.1635	1.28	.3997	.1003
.69	.2549	.2451	.99	.3389	.1611	1.29	.4015	.0985
.70	.2580	.2420	1.00	.3413	.1587	1.30	.4032	.0968
.71	.2611	.2389	1.01	.3438	.1562	1.31	.4049	.0951

A	B	C	A	B	C	A	B	C
Z	Area Between Mean and Z	Area Beyond Z	Z	Area Between Mean and Z	Area Beyond Z	Z	Area Between Mean and Z	Area Beyond Z
1.32	.4066	.0934	1.62	.4474	.0526	1.92	.4726	.0274
1.33	.4082	.0918	1.63	.4484	.0516	1.93	.4732	.0268
1.34	.4099	.0901	1.64	.4495	.0505	1.94	.4738	.0262
1.35	.4115	.0885	1.65	.4505	.0495	1.95	.4744	.0256
1.36	.4131	.0869	1.66	.4515	.0485	1.96	.4750	.0250
1.37	.4147	.0853	1.67	.4525	.0475	1.97	.4756	.0244
1.38	.4612	.0838	1.68	.4535	.0465	1.98	.4761	.0239
1.39	.4177	.0823	1.69	.4545	.0455	1.99	.4767	.0233
1.40	.4192	.0808	1.70	.4554	.0466	2.00	.4772	.0228
1.41	.4207	.0793	1.71	.4564	.0436	2.01	.4778	.0222
1.42	.4222	.0778	1.72	.4573	.0427	2.02	.4783	.0217
1.43	.4236	.0764	1.73	.4582	.0418	2.03	.4788	.0212
1.44	.4251	.0749	1.74	.4591	.0409	2.04	.4793	.0207
1.45	.4265	.0735	1.75	.4599	.0401	2.05	.4798	.0202
1.46	.4279	.0721	1.76	.4608	.0392	2.06	.4803	.0197
1.47	.4292	.0708	1.77	.4616	.0384	2.07	.4808	.0192
1.48	.4306	.0694	1.78	.4625	.0375	2.08	.4812	.0188
1.49	.4319	.0681	1.79	.4633	.0367	2.09	.4817	.0183
1.50	.4332	.0668	1.80	.4641	.0359	2.10	.4821	.0179
1.51	.4345	.0655	1.81	.4649	.0351	2.11	.4826	.0174
1.52	.4357	.0643	1.82	.4656	.0344	2.12	.4830	.0170
1.53	.4370	.0630	1.83	.4664	.0336	2.13	.4834	.0166
1.54	.4382	.0618	1.84	.4671	.0329	2.14	.4838	.0162
1.55	.4394	.0606	1.85	.4678	.0322	2.15	.4842	.0158
1.56	.4406	.0594	1.86	.4686	.0314	2.16	.4846	.0154
1.57	.4418	.0582	1.87	.4693	.0307	2.17	.4850	.0150
1.58	.4429	.0571	1.88	.4699	.0301	2.18	.4854	.0146
1.59	.4441	.0559	1.89	.4706	.0294	2.19	.4857	.0143
1.60	.4452	.0548	1.90	.4713	.0287	2.20	.4861	.0139
1.61	.4463	.0537	1.91	.4719	.0281	2.21	.4864	.0136

Z	Area Between Mean and Z	Area Beyond Z	Z	Area Between Mean and Z	Area Beyond Z	Z	Area Between Mean and Z	Area Beyond Z
2.22	.4868	.0132	2.52	.4941	.0059	2.82	.4976	.0024
2.23	.4871	.0129	2.53	.4943	.0057	2.83	.4977	.0023
2.24	.4875	.0125	2.54	.4945	.0055	2.84	.4977	.0023
2.25	.4878	.0122	2.55	.4946	.0054	2.85	.4978	.0022
2.26	.4881	.0119	2.56	.4948	.0052	2.86	.4979	.0021
2.27	.4884	.0116	2.57	.4949	.0051	2.87	.4979	.0021
2.28	.4887	.0113	2.58	.4951	.0049	2.88	.4980	.0020
2.29	.4890	.0110	2.59	.4952	.0048	2.89	.4981	.0019
2.30	.4893	.0107	2.60	.4953	.0047	2.90	.4981	.0019
2.31	.4896	.0104	2.61	.4955	.0045	2.91	.4982	.0018
2.32	.4898	.0102	2.62	.4956	.0044	2.92	.4982	.0018
2.33	.4901	.0099	2.63	.4957	.0043	2.93	.4983	.0017
2.34	.4904	.0096	2.64	.4959	.0041	2.94	.4984	.0016
2.35	.4906	.0094	2.65	.4960	.0040	2.95	.4984	.0016
2.36	.4909	.0091	2.66	.4961	.0039	2.96	.4985	.0015
2.37	.4911	.0089	2.67	.4962	.0038	2.97	.4985	.0015
2.38	.4913	.0087	2.68	.4963	.0037	2.98	.4986	.0014
2.39	.4916	.0084	2.69	.4964	.0036	2.99	.4986	.0014
2.40	.4918	.0082	2.70	.4965	.0035	3.00	.4986	.0014
2.41	.4920	.0080	2.71	.4966	.0034	3.01	.4987	.0013
2.42	.4922	.0078	2.72	.4967	.0033	3.02	.4987	.0013
2.43	.4925	.0075	2.73	.4968	.0032	3.03	.4988	.0012
2.44	.4927	.0073	2.74	.4969	.0031	3.04	.4988	.0012
2.45	.4929	.0071	2.75	.4970	.0030	3.05	.4989	.0011
2.46	.4931	.0069	2.76	.4971	.0029	3.06	.4989	.0011
2.47	.4932	.0068	2.77	.4972	.0028	3.07	.4989	.0011
2.48	.4934	.0066	2.78	.4973	.0027	3.08	.4990	.0010
2.49	.4936	.0064	2.79	.4974	.0026	3.09	.4990	.0010
2.50	.4938	.0062	2.80	.4974	.0026	3.10	.4990	.0010
2.51	.4940	.0060	2.81	.4975	.0025	3.11	.4991	.0009

A	B	C	A	B	C	A	B	C
Z	Area Between Mean and Z	Area Beyond Z	Z	Area Between Mean and Z	Area Beyond Z	Z	Area Between Mean and Z	Area Beyond Z
3.12	.4991	.0009	3.27	.4995	.0005	3.42	.4997	.0003
3.13	.4991	.0009	3.28	.4995	.0005	3.43	.4997	.0003
3.14	.4992	.0008	3.29	.4995	.0005	3.44	.4997	.0003
3.15	.4992	.0008	3.30	.4995	.0005	3.45	.4997	.0003
3.16	.4992	.0008	3.31	.4995	.0005	3.46	.4997	.0003
3.17	.4992	.0008	3.32	.4995	.0005	3.47	.4997	.0003
3.18	.4993	.0007	3.33	.4996	.0004	3.48	.4997	.0003
3.19	.4993	.0007	3.34	.4996	.0004	3.49	.4998	.0002
3.20	.4993	.0007	3.35	.4996	.0004	3.50	.4998	.0002
3.21	.4993	.0007	3.36	.4996	.0004	3.60	.4998	.0002
3.22	.4994	.0006	3.37	.4996	.0004	3.70	.4999	.0001
3.23	.4994	.0006	3.38	.4996	.0004	3.80	.4999	.0001
3.24	.4994	.0006	3.39	.4997	.0003	3.90	.4999	<.0001
3.25	.4994	.0006	3.40	.4997	.0003	4.00	.4999	<.0001
3.26	.4994	.0006	3.41	.4997	.0003			

APPENDIX D: ANSWERS TO END-OF-CHAPTER PROBLEMS[1]

CHAPTER 1

(1) b; (2) a; (3) a; (4) False; (5) True; (6) True; (7) Exploratory; (8) Evaluation; (9) False; (10) False

CHAPTER 2

(1) a; (2) d; (3) c; (4) a; (5) True; (6) False; (7) c; (8) c; (9) b; (10) b

CHAPTER 3

(1) b; (2) d; (3) c; (4) e; (5) True; (6) d; (7) a; (8) True; (9) False; (10) d

CHAPTER 4

(1) b; (2) b; (3) c; (4) False; (5) False; (6) d; (7) b; (8) b; (9) d; (10) a

CHAPTER 5

(1) b; (2) b; (3) a; (4) b; (5) a; (6) b; (7) b; (8) c; (9) c; (10) No. Each year of education exposes students to more information so, for example, freshmen and seniors are not likely to have similar views/experiences; (11) a; (12) b; (13) c

CHAPTER 6

(1) c; (2) b; (3) a; (4) c; (5) d; (6) False; (7) b; (8) a; (9) b; (11) d; (12) a

CHAPTER 7

(1) b; (2) c; (3) a; (4) c; (5) b; (6) d; (7) b; (8) c; (9) d; (10) b

CHAPTER 8

(1) b; (2) a; (3) a; (4) d; (5) c; (6) False; (7) b; (8) True; (9) d; (10) a

CHAPTER 9

(1) b; (2) c; (3) a; (4) c; (5) True; (6) True; (7) c; (8) a; (9) b; (10) d

CHAPTER 10

(1) c; (2) d; (3) True; (4) b; (5) d; (6) b; (7) False; (8) d; (9) False; (10) c

---

[1] The answers are for objective chapter questions or for statistical formula identification questions only.

CHAPTER 11

(1) a; (2) c; (3) c; (4) c; (5) d; (6) False; (7) True; (8) $Z=1.36$ so the area between mean and $Z =.4131$ and to determine the proportion less than 35 we also need to include the entire left half of the normal curve. Therefore, $.4131 +.5000 =.9131$. So the percentage of respondents who spent less than 35 hours a week on electronics is 91.31%; (9) The average number of dates respondents went on in the last 3 months was 14.3 with a standard deviation of 7.00; (10) The median number of nights someone went out with friends in the past 3 months was 10 with a range of 21 nights and the middle 50% of the distribution ranging between 6 and 13 (12.5) nights.

CHAPTER 12

(1) confidence interval: proportion; (2) one-sample t-test; (3) one-sample proportion hypothesis test; (4) confidence interval: means; (5) confidence interval: proportion; (6) one-sample t-test; (7) confidence interval: means

CHAPTER 13

(1) chi-square; (2) independent samples t-test; (3) ANOVA; (4) Wilxcoxon Signed-Rank test; (5) Kruskall–Wallace; (6) Mann–Whitney U; (7) chi-square; (8) paired-sample t-test

CHAPTER 14

(1) d; (2) c; (3) a; (4) a; (5) Independent-samples t-test, eta-squared; (6) chi-square, Gamma; (7) Pearson's r t-test, Pearson's r; (8) chi-square, Cramer's V or lambda; (9) Spearman's rho t-test, Spearman's rho; (10) chi-square, lambda; (11) chi-square, Gamma; (12) chi-square, lambda; (13) Independent-samples t-test, eta-squared; (18) b; (19) d; (20) a; (21) b; (22) c; (23) False

CHAPTER 15

(2) False; (3) d; (4) True; (5)–(7) Title should be dependent variable by independent variable; there are no row marginals, there are no column marginals, the total sample size is not given, the percentages are not calculated with respect to the independent variable (e.g., the column percentages do not equal to 100%), there are no raw number observations presented in the cells; (8) d; (9) d; (10) b; (11) c; (12) e

CHAPTER 16

(1) d; (2)b; (3) b; (4) d; (5) False; (6) c; (7)d; (8) a; (9) b; (10) c; (11) d; (12) a; (13) d; (14) c; (15) a

GLOSSARY

Abstract: A 100–200-word summary of the purpose, methods, and main findings of a study.

Acceptance rate: The proportion of scholarly manuscripts that are published in a given year relative to the number of manuscripts submitted for the same time period. The lower the acceptance rate, the higher the quality of the journal.

Alpha level: In hypothesis testing, this cutoff point for which a researcher considers is a sufficiently improbable value that is outside of the null region.

Alternate hypothesis: A testable assertion of difference.

Analytic code: In the method of grounded theory analysis that involves attribute, index, and analytic codes, this is the last stage of coding, which addresses the content of the index codes and links the codes to theory.

Anonymity: When a researcher cannot detect a subject's identity, thereby protecting that identity from being revealed in any study reports.

Applied research: Research aimed to address phenomena that a researcher sees as problematic or to solve practical problems in a way to improve the human experience.

Associative hypothesis: A testable statement with an independent and dependent variable but which does not attempt to establish a causal connection.

Asymmetrical measure of association: An association measure for which it is important for the researcher to have a clear sense of which variables are independent and dependent, respectively.

Attribute code: In the method of grounded theory analysis that involves attribute, index, and analytic codes, this is the first level of coding, which refers to demographic factors that might affect subjects' behaviors.

Attrition: A threat to internal validity that occurs when too many subjects stop participating in a study over time and/or when subjects who share a specific characteristic disproportionately drop out from either the experimental or control group, making the groups no longer comparable.

Authority: A form of knowledge that stems from "experts."

Axial coding: In the method of grounded theory analysis that involves open, axial, and selective coding, this is the middle stage of coding that links data themes.

Axis lines: Lines that run in the background of a graph that helps a reader follow the Y-axis values across the X-axis.

Bar chart: A graph that represents the values of categorical data with rectangular bars where the high represents the count of proportion for each value.

Basic research: Research aimed at obtaining knowledge for the sake of knowledge.

Before-and-after-design: A type of quasi-experimental design that has only an experimental group but has both a pre- and posttest.

Belmont report: The document that identifies the three universal principles of ethical and responsible research, which are respect for persons, beneficence, and justice.

Bibliographic database: An online collection of references to published information such as scholarly journals, conference proceedings, newspapers, government publications, and books.

Bivariate: Statistical comparisons that examine how two variables relate to each other.

Causal hypothesis: A testable statement where the independent variable is believed to create (cause) the change in the dependent variable.

Central tendency: Statistical test that summarizes the typical sample response to a variable.

Classic experiment: A form of true experiment that has at least two groups, a pretest and a posttest.

Cluster diagram: A means of linking qualitative themes where the themes are linked to each other with circles with, perhaps, different circle sizes representing the various degrees of importance of a theme to the overall research goal.

Cluster sample: A probability sampling technique where researchers take repeated random samples of sampling units of decreasing size until they obtain a manageable sampling frame of elements.

Codebook: This contains information about the structure of the data, such as variable names, labels, and values with their corresponding codes.

Cohort study: A form of longitudinal research in which different subjects participate at each time point, but all subjects share a reference point in time (e.g., graduated same year of college, are of same birth cohort, have worked at a company for the same amount of time).

Common sense: A form of knowledge that stems from a combination of experience and tradition.

Computer-assisted telephone interview: A computer program used in telephone interviewing that can digitally tell interviewers what questions to ask and in what order as well as allow the interviewer to immediately record the answers in the computer, thereby saving the step of data entry.

Concept map: In evaluation research, this can be an outline of program goals, inputs, measures, and who will be responsible for gathering/tracking information.

Concepts: Abstract terms that give people a mental image of a behavior or phenomena.

Conceptualization: The process of refining a research topic into something that can be feasibly studied.

Concurrent criterion validity: A form of criterion validity that assesses the agreement between two or more measures of the same concept that are being measured at the same time.

Confidence level: In sampling, this is the percentage of all the possible samples in a sampling distribution that is statistically expected to contain the true population parameter of a variable. In statistics, it is how sure a researcher is that the statistical output reflects the true population value of the phenomena being tested.

Confidentiality: When the researcher knows a subject's identity, but protects that identity by not revealing it in any reports of the study. Subjects might be referred to as numbers, letters, or pseudonyms instead, for example.

Constant comparative method: A general form of qualitative coding where themes are identified as similar or different to each other and where the units that are identified as similar then become part of the same category.

Construct validity: A form of measurement validity that bases the validity of a measure by its relationship to theory and testable hypotheses, which is considered valid pending replication by other studies' use of the same theory and measure.

Contamination: A threat to internal validity that occurs when the comparison group may somehow affect the treatment group or if the comparison group receives some of the treatment of the experimental group.

Content validity: A form of measurement validity that addresses a measure's ability to cover the multiple meanings of abstract concepts.

Continuous measure: A measure whose values can be quantified. Interval and ratio measures are continuous measures.

Control group: In experiments, this is the group of comparison that does not receive the experimental treatment.

Control variable: Variables other than the main independent variable that might influence the dependent variable and are, therefore, included in the statistical analysis.

Convenience sample: A nonprobability sampling technique in which the subjects are broad members of the target population but are mostly selected because of their availability, geographical proximity, and/or willingness to participate.

Correlation matrix: A table showing the correlation coefficients between variables.

Correlation: A statistical test establishing an association between variables.

Correlative question: A type of research question that looks at an association between variables but does not purport to make any causal claims.

Cost-benefit analysis: A form of evaluation research that focuses on estimating the program costs and the economic benefits of the outcomes

Cost efficiency analysis: A form of evaluation research that focuses on estimating the program costs compared to whether the outcome was achieved or not (and not the economic benefits of the outcome).

Covert observer: A form of field research where the researcher hides their identity as a researcher and does not directly interact with subjects but observes and records subjects' behavior.

Covert participant: A form of field research where the researcher hides their identity as a researcher even though they interact with subjects as they observe subjects' behavior.

Criterion validity: A form of measurement validity that examines the degree to which responses for a specific measure behave similarly to responses to other widely accepted measures of the same concept.

Cross-sectional research: Research for which data are gathered at only one point in time.

Cumulative percent: This adds the percentages of a value from the first to the last, where at the last value 100% of the responses have been accounted for.

Deductive research: An approach to research that starts with a review of existing research, formation of a hypothesis that tests a theory, creation of a fixed method of observation, analysis, and conclusion.

Degrees of freedom: The number of observations of data that are free to vary before constraints are violated when estimating statistical parameters.

Dependent samples: Samples in which being in one sample or having specific sample characteristics is necessary (dependent) for being part of the second sample, such as in before/after experimental designs and matched samples.

Descriptive research: Research whose main purpose is to describe or document a phenomenon.

Descriptive research questions: Research questions that intend to document an experience or phenomena.

Descriptive statistics: Statistics that summarize or compare patterns in sample data without trying to relate those patterns to the wider population.

Direct relationship: When a partial correlation indicates that the third, control, variable does not seem to have an effect on the original bivariate relationship.

Discrete measures: Measures whose values are categorical and have no inherent quantifiable meaning on their own. Nominal and ordinal measures are discrete.

Dispersion: Statistical tests that summarize the spread of a distribution of sample responses to a variable.

Dummy variable: A means of converting categorical variables into numerical ones in order to be able to run regression analyses.

Ecological fallacy: A research problem that occurs when researchers make conclusions about small units of analysis when their units of observation are larger. For example, researchers cannot gather data based on groups and make analytical conclusions about individuals.

Effect size: See substantive significance element individual units of observation about which a researcher is collecting information.

Emic meaning: In qualitative data analysis, this is the meaning that subjects give to their experiences.

Empirical association: Being able to show that a change in one variable is associated with a change in another variable.

Empirically observable: This means that a phenomenon can be directly observed and documented.

Enter regression method: A regression method where all the variables a researcher is interested in analyzing are put into the equation regardless of whether the variable has a statistically significant effect on the dependent variable or not.

Equivalency: A term used in experimental design to indicate that the subjects have been randomly assigned to either the experimental or control group and, therefore, should be similar on factors other than the treatment.

Ethical relativism: A situation in which adhering to an ethical responsibility to subjects might jeopardize the ethical responsibility to society or vice versa.

Etic meaning: In qualitative data analysis, this is the meaning that researchers give to the data based on the subject's own interpretations (emic meaning) as well as the perspective of the researcher's discipline.

Evaluative research: Research that has an applied focus such as assessing whether a program or policy is operating as designed or if it is creating the desired effect.

Evidence-based practices: Programs designed based on the findings of research.

Evidence-based research: A form of applied research that started in the medical field but has expanded to the social and behavioral sciences that blends the knowledge and experiences of those in practice with the best available research in the field.

Executive summary: In evaluation reports, this is the bottom-line summary that briefly summarizes the purpose of the evaluation, the goals of the program, a brief nontechnical overview of the research methods, the main findings in non statistical terms, and the ensuing feedback or suggestions for moving forward.

Exhaustive values: This is a characteristic of measurement that requires that there be a value for all possible responses for a measure.

Expected frequency: In the chi-square statistical formula, this is the approximate number of observations we would expect to see in each cell if the two variables were independent, meaning unrelated.

Experience: A source of knowledge that comes from our first-hand observation of facts or events.

Experiment: A form of research where the researcher controls the manipulation of the independent variable (treatment) to observe the effect of it on the dependent variable. See randomized experiment and quasi-experiment.

Experimental group: In an experiment, this is the group that received the treatment that the researcher intends to study.

Explanatory research: Research that tries to answer "why" a phenomenon occurs, often via testing of a theory.

Exploded pie chart: A pie chart in which the segments of the pie are separated.

Explorative research: Research involving topics for which little is known and therefore it focuses on a broad, comparatively unstructured examination of a phenomenon.

Ex post factor control group design: A type of quasi-experimental design that has an experimental and control group, a post test but no pretest.

External validity: Forms of validity that refer to the generalizability of sample findings to the outside population.

Face validity: The most basic form of measurement validity that assesses whether the measure is a logical indicator of a concept.

Feedback: In evaluation research, this "closes the loop" by suggesting or raising questions about what to do next and/or how to use the information learned.

Filter question: A question whose answer will determine which set of subsequent questions a subject will answer.

First-level coding: Initial codes researchers make in qualitative data analysis.

First-order correlation: A partial correlation that adds the first (one) control variable to a bivariate comparison.

Flowchart: In qualitative data analysis, this is a visual means of linking themes in the data.

Frequency: A statistical term used to describe how many sample subjects responded to each value of a variable.

Frequency table: A tabular display of how often each value for different variables was selected by a subject.

Gatekeepers: In field research, these are people in authority who have the power to permit or ban access to a research site.

Going native: A risk of field research in which the researcher starts to identify with the subjects they are studying, thereby threatening the researchers' scientific objectivity and possibly affecting the researcher's interpretation of the observations.

Guttman scale: A measure that consists of the summation of responses to hierarchically related individual questions and from which, if the scale is accurate, original question responses can be deduced.

Histogram: A graphical representation of the distribution of data that is commonly used to determine whether a distribution is normally distributed or not.

History: A threat to internal validity that refers to when events outside of the study can affect the dependent variable.

Homogeneity of variances: When two or more samples have similar variances across the samples.

Impact factor: A measure of the frequency that the average journal articled is cited in a particular year. This serves as an indicator of journal quality; the higher the impact factor, the more frequently the average article is cited and the higher the journal quality.

Impact question: A research question that tries to establish a causal connection between variables.

Independent samples: When being in one sample means that you are not in the second sample.

Index code: In the method of grounded theory analysis that involves attribute, index, and analytic codes, this is the middle level of coding that relates to broad topics in the data.

Inductive research: An approach to research that starts with observation based on a looser design of observation, identification of patterns in the data, and then the formation of a general explanation (theory) to account for those patterns.

Inferential statistic: Statistical tests that relate observed sample data to unobserved population characteristics.

Informed consent: An ethical obligation for a researcher to tell potential subjects any information about the study that might influence their decision to voluntarily participate in that study.

Inputs: In evaluation research, this is anything that goes into a program, including clients, staff, and resources, that will need to be tracked in a study.

Institutional review boards: Ethical oversight committees responsible for protecting human subjects and making sure that research protocols avoid ethical violations.

Instrumentation: A threat to internal validity in which an observed association between two variables is at least partially causing a change in how the variables are measured over time.

Interaction (relationship): A type of spurious relationship in which the original bivariate relationship of X and Y is different for different values of a third variable, Z.

Internal validity: Types of validity that are part of study design and that help facilitate causal inferences.

Inter-rater reliability: A technique to establish reliability where two or more individuals agree to the ratings or meaning of subjective information.

Interrupted time series design: A type of quasi-experimental design that is longitudinal. It might have both a control group and/or a pretest.

Interval level of measurement: A level of measurement where the measure's values are ordered, can be quantified, have meaning, but for which the value of "0" is arbitrarily set.

Intervening relationship: A type of spurious relationship where the main independent variable X affects a third variable Z, which in turn is what produces the change in Y.

Jottings: In qualitative research, these are short phrases or keywords that will jog the researcher's memory later in the day when they are able to find a lengthier amount of time to record the more detailed observations in private.

Key informant: In field research, this is a member of a key figure in the sample who helps the researcher interpret observations and who answers researcher questions about events.

Kurtosis: A measure of the "tailedness" of a distribution. Higher/shaper peaks in the curve produce longer tails while lower/flatter peaks produce shorter tails.

Latent content: In qualitative analysis, these are codes used to give meaning to observed content, and it is common in content analysis.

Least-squares analysis: The mathematical analysis used to determine the best-fit regression line for observed data.

Likert scale: A summative measure where the coded response of individual questions all measuring the same dimension of a concept and which are usually individually asked in a five- to seven-point Likert format are added to produce a total value, which is the scale score.

Linear regression line: A straight line that is the best fit for the observed relationship between two normally distributed interval/ratio measures.

Line graph: A graph that is commonly used to show trends over time.

Literature review: A survey of the existing scholarly work on a topic that summarizes, compares, and evaluates the existing research to identify contradictions and gaps in knowledge or theory.

Logic model: Diagrams that outline the individual components of an evaluation process.

Longitudinal research: Research for which data are gathered at more than one time point.

Manifest content: A form of qualitative analysis that focuses on elements that are easily identified and counted, such as specific words, phrases, or themes. This is common in content analysis.

Marginal: The univariate information at the end of rows or columns in a bivariate table.

Matrix format: A condensed way of presented similarly responded questions where the questions read down the column and the same options read across rows.

Maturation: A threat to internal validity in which an observed association between two variables is at least partially caused by the subjects aging over time.

Mean: A measure of central tendency used for normally distributed interval/ratio data that indicate the average response.

Median: A measure of central tendency for ordinal levels of measurement and higher that indicates the midpoint of a distribution where 50% of the sample responses are above and 50% are below.

Meta-analysis: A quantitative form of research that studies the findings of similar independent studies to reach conclusions about a body of research.

Mixed methods study: A form of research that combines qualitative and quantitative methods that complement each other's strengths and weaknesses to obtain a more valid observation of a phenomenon.

Mode: A measure of central tendency that identifies the most frequent value in a distribution.

Moderator: In focus groups, moderators guide the discussion with semi-structured questions.

Multivariate: Comparisons that involve three or more variables.

Mutually exhaustive values: This is a characteristic of measurement that requires that there be only one value for each indicator (measure) that a subject can select, unless the indicator specifically states to "circle all that apply" or some equivalent direction.

Negative distribution: In a distribution, this occurs when most of the scores in a distribution (mode) are clustered on the right (higher) side of the tail.

Negative relationship: When measuring association, this means that the variables are moving in opposite directions. As one variable increases in value, the other decreases.

Nominal level of measurement: A level of measurement where the measure's values are mutually exclusive and exhaustive but have no inherent order.

Nonequivalent control group design: A type of quasi-experimental design that has both a control and experimental group as well as both a pre- and posttest. It is the quasi-experimental version of the true classic experiment.

Nonprobability sample: A collection of sampling techniques in which each element in the study population does not have an equal chance (probability) of being selected for the sample.

Nonspurious relationship: In causality, this refers to ways to show that any observed relationship between independent and dependent variables is not created by some outside factor.

Normal distribution: Also known as the bell curve, this is a distribution where the mode, median, and mean are essentially equal.

Normative research question: A type of question that makes a comparison against some type of standard or population.

Null hypothesis: A testable assertion of no difference with the statistical assumption.

Observed frequency: In the chi-square statistical formula, this is the number of sample observations that are in each cell of comparison.

Obtained value: In hypothesis testing, this is the answer to a statistical formula that is compared to a critical value of the same distribution to determine whether the null hypothesis should be rejected.

One-tailed test: In hypothesis testing, this refers to when the critical area to reject the null is either in the right or left tail of the distribution, but not both.

Open coding: In the method of grounded theory analysis that involves open, axial, and selective coding, this is the first stage of thematic coding that tries to identify the main themes in the data.

Operationalization: The process of defining abstract concepts into something that can be empirically observed.

Ordinal level of measurement: A level of measurement where the measure's values are ranked but the distance between ranks cannot be quantified/have no numerical meaning.

Outcome: In evaluation research, this is the immediate impact of the program.

Output: In evaluation research, this is what is actually done in the program.

Overt observer: A form of field research where the researcher makes their identity as a researcher known to subjects but does not meaningfully interact with subjects.

Overt participant: A form of field research where the researcher makes their identity as a researcher known as they directly interact with and observe subjects.

Panel study: A form of longitudinal research in which the same subjects are studied at each time point.

Partial correlation: This measures the degree of association between two variables while addressing the effects of additional variables simultaneously.

Partial slope: In a multiple regression equation, it is the relationship between a predictor variable and a dependent variable that is independent of other predictor variables.

Pie chart: A circular graph that is divided into sectors where each sector represents a proportion of a variable's value as part of a whole.

Pilot study: A pretest of a methodological design, such as a survey, on a small set of subjects in order to determine whether subjects have any problems with question wording or format.

Point estimate: The singular value in a probability sample that is obtained to approximate the population parameter.

Population: All of the people, groups, or artifacts that are relevant to a research question.

Population parameter: A characteristic of the study population that is usually unknown so is estimated with a sample statistic computed from a probability sample.

Positive relationship: When measuring association, this means that the variables are moving in the same direction. As one variable increases in value so does the other and vice versa.

Positive skew: In a distribution, this occurs when most of the scores in a distribution (mode) are clustered on the left (lower) side of the tail.

Posttest: An observation that occurs after a treatment.

Posttest only control group design: A type of true experiment that has at least two groups and a posttest, but no pretest.

Predatory journal: Journals that appear as scholarly journals but that often are not peer reviewed, do not follow the accepted academic standards for publishing, and offer fast publication, often for a fee. These journals undermine the ability to screen the quality of research that is shared among academics and professionals.

Predictive criterion validity: A form of criterion validity that assesses the degree to which one measure will predict the future behavior on a second, related, measure of the same concept.

Pretest: An observation that occurs prior to a treatment.

Principle of beneficence: An ethical requirement established by the Belmont Report requiring that potential benefit to a subject for participating in a study should outweigh any possible risks from study participation.

Principle of justice: An ethical requirement established by the Belmont Report requiring that any potential risks and benefits of any study are spread across subjects fairly.

Probability sample: A collection of sampling techniques in which each element in the study population has an equal chance (probability) of being selected for the sample.

Probing: A methodological tactic common in qualitative research where the researcher asks subjects follow-up questions to vague or confusing answers in order to obtain a more in-depth level of response.

Proportionate reduction of error: Statistical tests of effect size that compare the errors a researcher would make in predicting the dependent variable while ignoring the independent variable relative to the errors one would make predicting the dependent variable while now considering the contribution of the independent variable for each category of the dependent variable.

Purposive sample: A nonprobability sampling technique where subjects are selected based on their proficiency, knowledge, and/or direct experience with the phenomena of interest as well as their accessibility, geographical proximity, availability, and/or willingness to participate.

P-value: Short for probability of error value; this is the likelihood that your null hypothesis is true. Lower p-values suggest that your data are unlikely if the null is true.

Qualitative research: Research in which the data are not in numbers but instead are in the contextual language of the subjects. Qualitative research frequently focuses on in-depth understanding of information for which little is known.

Quantile-Quantile, or Q–Q plot: A linear graphical representation of where data should be if the distribution is normal compared to what data actually look like.

Quantitative research: Research for which the data are expressed in numbers via statistical analysis. Quantitative research often focuses on testing hypotheses and theories.

Quasi-experiment: A form of experimental research where the subjects are not randomly assigned to the experimental (treatment) or control (nontreatment, comparison) group.

Questionnaire: A set of questions, often with corresponding answer choices, that researchers use to learn about a phenomenon.

Quota sample: A nonprobability sampling technique that aims to select participants from specific groups in proportions that mirror the representation in the population; however, these individuals are not selected randomly.

Random digit dialing: A form of sampling used with telephone interviews in which subjects are selected randomly by a computer based on their telephone number.

Random error: Measurement error due to unpredictable events or nondiscernable patterns. Because the error follows no pattern, it is unlikely to affect a study.

Random experiment: A form of experimental research where the subjects are randomly assigned to the experimental (treatment) or control (nontreatment, comparison) group.

Ratio level of measurement: A level of measurement where the measure's values are ordered and can be quantified (have numerical meaning), including the value of "0."

Reactivity: A threat to internal validity in which subjects behave atypically because they are being observed.

Reductionism: A research problem that occurs when researchers make conclusions about complex issues based on simple group differences without accounting for individual issues that might produce those group differences.

Reference category: When using dummy variables, this is the 0–1 dummy variable created from a categorical variable that is omitted from the analysis in order to serve as a comparison.

Reliability: A study of measure's ability to produce consistent results on repeated observations of the same phenomena.

Repeated cross-sectional design: Longitudinal studies in which new subjects are selected for each time point.

Reverse-coded question: A question where a negative response is actually supportive of the main research question or goal.

Sample: A smaller group of people, groups, or artifacts elected from a larger population of interest to study.

Sample error: The mismatch between the characteristics of a sample selected and the study population from which that sample was drawn.

Sample statistic: A characteristic of a sample that was selected randomly and that can be observed and, therefore, used to estimate a population parameter.

Sampling frame: A list of all elements in a study population from which a sample is drawn.

Saturation: In qualitative research, saturation is the point in which researchers no longer substantively learn new information from subjects, thereby suggesting that sampling is complete and no new subjects need to be added to the study.

Scale: A means of measuring complex concepts by combining multiple-related individual measures into one new conglomerate measure.

Scientific knowledge: Testable information obtained from systematic definition, observation, and analysis.

Secondary analysis of primary data: A form of research in which a researcher analyzes raw data in a new way that was gathered by someone else.

Selection bias: A threat to internal validity that occurs when researchers are comparing groups that are different on factors other than the treatment or independent variable.

Selective coding: In the method of grounded theory analysis that involves open, axial, and selective coding, this is the last stage of coding in which one theme is picked to be the reference category around which the other themes will be organized and which will serve as the central explanation linking the other categories.

Simple random sample: The most basic probability sampling technique in which each element in the study population has an equal chance of being selected into the sample.

Skewness: The degree to which a statistical distribution shifts left or right relative to a normal distribution.

Skip pattern: A series of questions that are answered based on a conditional response to a filter question.

Snowball sample: A nonprobability sample technique where the researcher obtains subjects based on word-of-mouth recommendations of current subjects.

Social artifact: A unit of observation or analysis that refers to material produced by people and that can be systematically observed, such as songs, books, speeches, and movies.

Split-half reliability test: A test of reliability where a researcher makes sure that there are multiple measures of the same concepts, splits those measures across two similar groups, and then statistically correlates the scores across the group to see if there is high agreement.

Spurious relationship: When an observed bivariate relationship is actually caused by a third variable outside of the original two.

Stakeholders: From a research perspective, these are people who have vested interest in a program and who, therefore, should have a voice in the design of research related to that program.

Statistic: A way to summarize and to compare patterns in information observed in data.

Statistical conclusion validity: A form of validity surrounding the statistical tests that determine whether or not there is a relationship between variables.

Statistical control variable: In multivariate analyses, these are variables other than the main independent variable(s) of interest that might affect the dependent variable and threaten validity if not included in the model.

Statistical significance: A threshold, usually a minimum of 95%, that helps determine whether an observed result is likely because of chance (hence the null hypothesis cannot be rejected) or a phenomenon of interest.

Stepwise entry method: A form of regression analysis where the computer builds a best-fit regression model by including variables based on the strength of association, where variables that have no effect are omitted from the model.

Stratified random sample: A probability sampling technique where elements in the study population are first separated into similar groups (strata) and then randomly selected from within those groups.

Study population: The population from which a sample is actually selected.

Substantive significance: A determination of effect size that indicates whether any observed difference between variables is large enough to be meaningful.

Symmetrical measure: These are statistical tests of association for which it does not matter which variable is the independent or dependent variable.

Systematic reviews: A form of research that, like a meta-analysis, systematically reviews the findings of multiple studies of similar focus and design, but that presents its findings in a narrative (rather than statistical) form.

Systematic sampling: A probability sampling technique where every kth element in the study population is selected to be in the sample after a random start between 1 and k.

Systemic error: A source of measurement error that is caused by some consistent or predictable influence that can affect the outcome of a study.

Tails of a distribution: The part of distribution that is furthest from the mean.

t-distribution: A probability distribution used to estimate population parameters when the sample size is small and/or the population variance is unknown. As sample size increases, the t-distributions resemble the Z-distribution.

Testing: A threat to internal validity in which an observed association between two variables is at least partially caused by the subjects taking a pretest.

Test–retest reliability: A test of reliability where a researcher tests either the same group at two different time periods or across two similar groups, and then statistically correlates the scores across the group to see if there is high agreement.

Theoretical sampling: In qualitative research, this is a systematic means of identifying subjects based on a researcher's simultaneous processing of the observed information, determining what is relevant, what needs to be checked, and what needs more information. Additional subjects are selected based on the new subject's ability to check observations or provide additional information.

Time dimension: The amount of time in which a study is conducted.

Traditional knowledge: A source of knowledge that stems from "how things have always" been done.

Two-tailed test: In hypothesis testing, this refers to when the critical area to reject the null can be in the right or left tail of the distribution.

Unit of analysis: An issue of data analysis that refers to what is being compared.

Unit of observation: An issue of sampling that refers to the nature of what is being selected to study.

Univariate: Summarizing or examining one variable without relating it to other variables.

Validity: Whether research findings truly represent the topic being studied.

Valid percent: The percentage of respondents who select a value, which is calculated by dividing the frequency of the value response by the total number of subjects who actually answered the question rather than the total sample size.

Values: A term used to refer to the answer options to questions or measures.

Variable label: In a codebook, this is usually the full-working question that corresponds to a piece of data, such as a full-survey question.

Variable name: This is usually a shortened name given to a piece of information, such as a survey question, that is used for computer identification of specific pieces of data.

Vulnerable population: People, such as children, prisoners, and individuals with impaired cognitive abilities, who might not be able to adequately make decisions about voluntary participation in a research study.

X-axis: On a graph, this is the horizontal axis that corresponds to the independent variable.

Y-axis: On a graph, this is the vertical axis that corresponds to the dependent variable.

Z-distribution: Otherwise known as the normal distribution, this distribution helps find probabilities and percentiles of large, continuous, randomly selected data.

Zero-order correlation: Also known as a bivariate correlation where there are no additional (control) variables being examined.

Z-scores: A statistical process that translates data into standardized proportionate areas under the normal curve that allows for the comparison of specific scores to the curve regardless of the units in which those scores are measured.

REFERENCES

Abraham, A. J., Bride, B. E., & Roman, P. M. (2013). Public attitudes toward persons with alcohol use disorders (AUDs): The role of social contact and treatment-seeking behavior. *Sociological Focus, 46*(4), 267–280.

Adams, W. C. (2015). Conducting semi-structured interviews. In K. E. Newcomer, H. P. Hatry, & J. S. Wholey (Eds.), *Handbook of practical program evaluation* (pp. 492–505), Hoboken, NJ: John Wiley & Sons, Incorporated.

Ahrens, P. (2018). Qualitative network analysis: A useful tool for investigating policy networks in transnational settings? *Methodological Innovations.*

Anderson, M., Vogels, E. A., & Turner, E. (2020, June). *The virtues and downsides of online dating. Pew Research Center.* Retrieved from https://www.pewresearch.org/internet/2020/02/06/the-virtues-and-downsides-of-online-dating/

Argyle, M., Henderson, M., Bond, M., Iizuka, Y., & Contarello, A. (1986). Cross-cultural variations in relationship rules. *International Journal of Psychology, 21,* 287–315.

Asch, S. E. (1951). Effects of group pressure upon the modification and distortion of judgment. In H. Guetzkow (Ed.), *Groups, leadership and men: Research in human relations* (pp. 177–190). Pittsburgh, PA: Carnegie Press.

Babbie, E. (1995). *The practice of social research* (7th ed.). Albany, NY: Wadsworth.

Bakardjiev, D. K. (2015). Officer body-worn cameras-capturing objective evidence with quality technology and focused policies. *Jurimetrics, 56*(1), 79–112.

Baptiste, I. (2001). Qualitative data analysis: Common phases, strategic differences. *Forum Qualitative Sozialforschung/Forum: Qualitative Social Research [Online Journal], 2*(3). Retrieved from www.qualitative-research.net/fqs-texte/3-01/3-01baptiste-e.htm

Baumrind, D. (2013). Is Milgram's deceptive research ethically acceptable? *Theoretical & Applied Ethics, 2*(2), 1–18. University of Nebraska Press.

Bjelland, I., Krokstad, S., Mykletun, A., Dahl, A. A., Tell, G., & Tambs, K. (2008). Does higher education protect against anxiety and depression? The HUNT study. *Social Science & Medicine, 66,* 1334–1345.

Blitz, J. M. (2013). The fourth amendment future of public surveillance: Remote recording and other searches in public space. *American University of Law Review, 63*(1), 21–86.

Bloom, H. (2008). The core analytics of randomized experiments for social research. In P. Alasuutari, L. Bickman, & J. Brannen (Eds.), *The SAGE handbook of social research methods* (pp. 115–133). Thousand Oaks, CA: SAGE.

Boardman, J. D., Finch, B. K., Ellison, C. G., Williams, D. R., & Jackson, J. S. (2001). Neighborhood disadvantage, stress, and drug use among adults. *Journal of Health and Social Behavior, 42,* 151–165.

Boca, D. B., Piazzalunga, D., & Pronzato, C. (2018). The role of grandparenting in early childcare and child outcomes. *Review of Economics of the Household, 16*(2), 477–512.

Booshehri, L. G., Dugan, J., Patel, F., Bloom, S., & Chilton, M. (2018). Trauma-informed temporary assistance for needy families (TANF): A randomized controlled trial with a two-generation impact. *Journal of Child and Family Studies, 27*(5), 1594–1604.

Bradford, K., Stewart, J. W., Pfister, R., & Higginbotham, B. J. (2016). Avoid falling for a jerk(ette): Effectiveness of the premarital interpersonal choices and knowledge program among emerging adults. *Journal of Marital and Family Therapy, 42*(4), 630–644.

Bright, L. F., & Logan, K. (2018). Is my fear of missing out (FOMO) causing fatigue? Advertising, social media fatigue, and the implications for consumers and brands. *Internet Research, 28*(5), 1213–1227.

Brooks, R. T., & Hopkins, R. (2017). Cultural mistrust and health care utilization: The effects of a culturally responsive cognitive intervention. *Journal of Black Studies, 48*(8), 816–834.

Brown, D. M. (2017). Evaluation of safer, smarter kids: Child sexual abuse prevention curriculum for kindergartners. C&A. *Child & Adolescent Social Work Journal, 34*(3), 213–222.

Burger, J. M. (2009). Replicating Milgram: Would people still obey today? *American Psychologist, 64*(1), 1–11.

Caïs, J., & Folguera, L. (2013). Redefining the dynamics of intergenerational family solidarity in Spain. *European Societies, 15*(4), 557–576.

Campbell, D. T., & Stanley, J. C. (1963). *Experimental and quasi-experimental designs for research.* Chicago, IL: Rand McNally.

Capous-Desyllas, M., & Barron, C. (2017). Identifying and navigating social and institutional challenges of transgender children and families. *Child & Adolescent Social Work Journal, 34*(6), 527–542.

Carroll, M. (2018). Gay fathers on the margins: Race, class, marital status, and pathway to parenthood. *Family Relations, 67*(1), 104–117.

Carter, D. R., Van Norman, R. K., & Tredwell, C. (2011). Program-wide positive behavior support in preschool: Lessons for getting started. *Early Childhood Education Journal, 38*(5), 349–355.

Charmaz, K. (2006). *Constructing grounded theory: A practical guide through qualitative analysis.* Los Angeles, CA: Sage Publications.

Charmaz, K. (2014). *Constructing grounded theory* (2nd ed.). Thousand Oaks, CA: Sage.

Chen, H. (1990). *Theory-driven evaluations.* Newbury Park, CA: Sage.

Chong, G., Mun, Y., Teng, S., Zin, K., Siew, A., Cheng, S., ... Skoric, M. M. (2012). Cultivation effects of video games: A longer-term experimental test of first and second-order effects. *Journal of Social and Clinical Psychology, 31*(9), 952–971.

Coalition for the Homeless. (2019, July). *Basic facts about homelessness: New York City.* Retrieved from https://www.coalitionforthehomeless.org/basic-facts-about-homelessness-new-york-city/

Cohen, J. (1988). *Statistical power analysis for the behavioral sciences* (2nd ed.). Hillsdale, NJ: Erlbaum.

Cohen, L., & Manion, L. (2011). *Research methods in education* (7th ed.). London: Routledge.

Cole, J. S. (2016). Do later wake times and increased sleep duration of 12th graders result in more studying, higher grades, and improved SAT/ACT test scores? *Sleep and Breathing, 20*(3), 1053–1057.

College Board. (2019, March). Enrollment data. *Annual Survey of Colleges; NCES, IPEDS Fall 2016 Enrollment data.* Retrieved from https://trends.collegeboard.org/college-pricing/figures-tables/average-estimated-undergraduate-budgets-2018-19

Compton, W. M., Gfroerer, J., Conway, K. P., & Finger, M. S. (2014). Unemployment and substance outcomes in the United States 2002–2010. *Drug and Alcohol Dependence, 142,* 350–353.

Contreras, R. (2018). From nowhere: Space, race, and time in how young minority men understand encounters with gangs. *Qualitative Sociology, 41*(2), 263–280.

Couper, M. P., & Miller, P. V. (2008). Web survey methods introduction. *Public Opinion Quarterly, 72*(5), 831–835.

Covington-Ward, Y. (2017). "Back home, people say America is heaven": Pre-migration expectations and post-migration adjustment for Liberians in Pittsburgh. *Journal of International Migration and Integration, 18*(4), 1013–1032.

Crawford, C., & Burns, R. (2016). Reducing school violence: Considering school characteristics and the impacts of law enforcement, school security, and environmental factors. *Policing: An International Journal of Police Strategies & Management, 39,* 455–477.

Creswell, J. C. (2002). *Educational research: Planning, conducting, and evaluating quantitative and qualitative research.* Upper Saddle River, NJ: Merrill Prentice Hall.

Creswell, J. W., Clark, Plano., V, Gutmann., M, & Hanson, W. (2003). Advances in mixed methods design. In A. Tashakkori & C. Teddlie (Eds.), *Handbook of mixed methods in the social and behavioral sciences.* Thousand Oaks, CA: Sage.

Cronbach, L. J. (1970). *Essentials of psychological testing.* New York, NY: Harper & Row.

Czaja, R., & Blair, J. (2005). *Designing surveys: A guide to decisions and procedures.* Thousand Oaks, CA: Sage.

Daly, K. J. (2007). *Qualitative methods for family studies and human development.* Thousand Oaks, CA: Sage Publications.

Davies, D., & Dodd, J. (2002). Qualitative researcher and the question of rigor. *Qualitative Health Research, 12,* 279–289.

De Luca, S. M., & Wyman, P. A. (2012). Association between school engagement and disclosure of suicidal ideation to adults among Latino adolescents. *Journal of Primary Prevention, 33*(2–3), 99–110.

Dennison, C. R. (2018). Intergenerational mobility and changes in drug use across the life course. *Journal of Drug Issues, 48*(2), 205–225.

DeSimone, J. (2002). Illegal drug use and employment. *Journal of Labor Economics, 20*, 952–977.

De Vaus, D. A. (2002). *Surveys in social research* (5th ed.). London, UK: George Allen & Unwin.

Dhillon, G., & Smith, K. J. (2019). Defining objectives for preventing cyberstalking. *Journal of Business Ethics, 157*(1), 137–158.

Digest of Education Statistics. (2018). *Table 228.10. School-associated violent deaths of all persons, homicides and suicides of youth ages 5–18 at school, and total homicides and suicides of youth ages 5–18, by type of violent death: 1992–93 through 2015–16.* Retrieved from https://nces.ed.gov/programs/digest/d18/tables/dt18_228.10.asp on July 19, 2019

Dillman, D. A. (2007). *Mail and internet surveys: The tailored design method* (2nd ed.). Chichester, UK: John Wiley.

Dillman, D. A., & Parsons, N. L. (2008). *Self-administered paper questionnaire.* London, UK: Sage.

Dillman, D. A., Smyth, J. D., & Christian, L. M. (2014). *Internet, phone, mail, and mixed-mode surveys: The tailored design method* (4th ed.). Hoboken, NJ: Wiley.

Ding, Y., Detels, R., Zhao, Z., Zhu, Y., Zhu, G., & Zhang, B. (2005). HIV infection and sexually transmitted diseases in female commercial sex workers in China. *Journal of Acquired Immune Deficiency Syndrome, 38*, 314–319.

Dobbie, W., & Fryer, R. G., Jr. (2014). The impact of attending a school with high-achieving peers: Evidence from the New York city exam schools. *American Economic Journal: Applied Economics, 6*(3), 58–75.

Döring, N., Daneback, K., Shaughnessy, K., Grov, C., & Byers, E. S. (2017). Online sexual activity experiences among college students: A four-country comparison. *Archives of Sexual Behavior, 46*(6), 1641–1652.

Duneier, M. (1999). *Sidewalk.* New York, NY: Farrar, Straus, and Giroux.

Dunn, C. M., & Chadwick, G. L. (2004). *Protecting study volunteers in research.* Boston, MA: Thomson.

Emerson, R. M. (2001). The face of contemporary field research. In *Contemporary field research* (2nd ed., pp. 27–53). Prospect Heights, IL: Waveland Press.

Entis, L. (2016). Pets are basically people. *Fortune.* Retrieved from http://fortune.com/2016/09/07/pets-are-basically-people/

Erickson, J., El-Gabalawy, R., Palitsky, D., Petten, S., Mackenzie, C. S., Stein, M. B., & Sareen, J. (2016). Educational attainment as a protective factor for psychiatric disorders: Findings from a nationally representative longitudinal study. *Depression and Anxiety, 33*, 1013–1022.

Etikan, I., Musa, S. B., & Alkassim, R. S. (2015). Comparison of convenience sampling and purposive sampling. *American Journal of Theoretical and Applied Statistics, 5*(1), 1–4. doi:10.11648/j.ajtas.20160501.11

Fairclough, N. (2001). *Language and power.* London, UK: Pearson Educational Limited.

Faupel, C. E. (1988). Heroin use, crime and employment status. *Journal of Drug Issues, 18*, 467–479.

Fisher, B. W., Mowen, T. J., & Boman, J. H. IV. (2018). School security measures and longitudinal trends in adolescents' experiences of victimization. *Journal of Youth and Adolescence, 47*(6), 1221–1237.

Fowler, F. J., Jr. (2014). *Survey research methods.* Thousand Oaks, CA: Sage.

Fox, L., Carta, J., Strain, P. S., Dunlap, G., & Hemmeter, M. L. (2010). Response to intervention and the pyramid model. *Infants & Young Children, 23*(1), 3–13.

Freund, K. (2015). When cameras are rolling: Privacy implications of body-mounted cameras on police. *Columbia School of Law and Social Problems, 49*, 91–133.

Galletta, A. M. (2013). *Mastering the semi-structured interview and beyond.* New York, NY: NYU Press.

Gallup. (2018). Cybercrimes remain the most worrisome to Americans. *Gallup.* Retrieved from https://news.gallup.com/poll/244676/cybercrimes-remain-worrisome-americans.aspx?g_source=link_NEWSV9&g_medium=TOPIC&g_campaign=item_&g_content=Cybercrimes%2520Remain%2520Most%2520Worrisome%2520to%2520Americans

Gans, H. (1962). *The urban villagers.* New York, NY: Free Press.

George, D., & Mallery, M. (2010). *SPSS for Windows step by step: A simple guide and reference, 17.0 update* (10th ed.). Boston, MA: Pearson.

George, M. J. (2007). The 'Great Taboo' and the role of patriarchy in husband and wife abuse. *International Journal of Men's Health, 6*(1), 7–21.

Gerson, K., & Horowitz, R. (2002). Observation and interviewing: Options and choices. In T. May (Ed.), *Qualitative research in action* (pp. 200–225). Thousand Oaks, CA: Sage.

Ghasemi, A., & Zahediasl, S. (2012). Normality tests for statistical analysis: A guide for non-statisticians. *International Journal of Endocrinology and Metabolism, 10*(2), 486–489. doi:10.5812/ijem.3505

Gillham, B. (2007). *Developing a questionnaire* (2nd ed.). London, UK: Continuum.

Glaser, B. G., & Strauss, A. S. (1967). *The discovery of grounded theory: Strategies for qualitative research.* New Brunswick, NJ: Aldine Transaction.

Glassman, T. (2012). Implications for college students posting pictures of themselves drinking alcohol on Facebook. *Journal of Alcohol and Drug Education, 56*(1), 38–58.

Goertz, G. (2006). *Social science concepts: A user's guide.* Princeton, NJ: Princeton University Press.

Goldstein, A., & Clement, S. (2020, June). 7 in 10 Americans would be likely to get a coronavirus vaccine, Post-ABC poll finds. *The Washington Post.* Retrieved from https://www.washingtonpost.com/health/7-in-10-americans-would-be-likely-to-get-a-coronavirus-vaccine-a-post-abc-poll-finds/2020/06/01/4d1f8f68-a429-11ea-bb20-ebf0921f3bbd_story.html

Gray, D. E. (2014). *Doing research in the real world.* Washington, DC: Sage.

Guttman, L. (1944). A basis for scaling qualitative data. *American Sociological Review, 9,* 139–150.

Guzman, G. (2017). *Household Income: 2016.* U.S. Census Bureau, 2016 American Community Survey. Retrieved from https://www.census.gov/content/dam/Census/library/publications/2017/acs/acsbr16-02.pdf

Gwent, K. L. (2014). *Handbook of inter-rater reliability: The definitive guide to measuring the extent of agreement among raters* (4th ed.). United States: Advanced Analytics, LLC.

Haddock, A. D., & Jimerson, S. R. (2017). An examination of differences in moral disengagement and empathy among bullying participant groups. *Journal of Relationships Research, 8,* 15.

Hagan, F. (1997). *Research methods in criminal justice and criminology* (4th ed.). Boston, MA: Allyn and Bacon.

Halcomb, E. J., Gholizadeh, L., DiGiacomo, M., Phillips, J., & Davidson, P. M. (2007). Literature review: Considerations in undertaking focus group research with culturally and linguistically diverse groups. *Journal of Clinical Nursing, 16*(6), 1000–1011.

Hammer, T. (1992). Unemployment and use of drug and alcohol among young people: A longitudinal study in the general population. *British Journal of Addiction, 87,* 1571–1581.

Hannan, C., Lambert, M. J., Harmon, C., Nielsen, S. L., Smart, D. W., & Shimokawa, K. (2005). A lab test and algorithms for identifying clients at risk for treatment failure. *Journal of Clinical Psychology: In Session, 61,* 155–163.

Harlow, I. M., & Donaldson, D. I. (2013). Source accuracy data reveal the thresholded nature of human episodic memory. *Psychonomic Bulletin & Review, 20,* 318–325.

Harlow, I. M., & Yonelinas, A. P. (2014). Distinguishing between the success and precision of recollection. *Memory (Hove, England), 24*(1), 114–127.

Hart, C. (2001). *Doing a literature search.* London, UK: Sage.

Healey, J. F. (2014). *Statistics: A tool for social research* (10th ed.). New York, NY: Thompson.

Heintzelman, S. C., & Bathon, J. M. (2017). Caught on camera. *International Journal of Education Policy and Leadership, 12*(6), 1–16.

Helgeson, J. G., Voss, K. E., & Terpening, W. D. (2002). Determinants of mail survey response: Survey design factors and respondent factors. *Psychology and Marketing, 19*(3), 303–328.

Henkel, D. (2011). Unemployment and substance use: A review of the literature (1990–2010). *Current Drug Abuse Reviews, 4,* 4–27.

Herbst, C. M., & Ifcher, J. (2016). The increasing happiness of US parents. *Review of Economics of the Household, 14*(3), 529–551.

Herz, A., Peters, L., & Truschkat, I. (2015). How to do qualitative structural analysis: The qualitative interpretations of network maps and narrative interviews. *Forum: Qualitative Social Research, 16*(1), 1–24. Article 9.

Hidrobo, M., Peterman, A., & Heise, L. (2016). The effect of cash, vouchers, and food transfers on intimate partner violence: Evidence from a randomized experiment in northern Ecuador. *American Economic Journal Applied Economics, 8*(3), 284–303.

Higgins, J. P. T., & Green, S. (2005). *Cochrane handbook for systematic reviews of interventions*. On-line book: URL. Retrieved from http://www.cochrane.org/resources/handbook/hbook.htm

Hinkin, T. (1998). A brief tutorial on the development of measures for use in survey questionnaires. *Organizational Research Methods, 1*(1), 104–121.

Hudson, J. M., & Bruckman, A. (2004). "Go away": Participant objections to being studied and the ethics of chatroom research. *The Information Society, 20*, 127–139.

Humphreys, L. (1970). *Tearoom trade*. London, UK: Duckworth.

Hyppolite, M. L. (2017). Understanding child outcomes within a multiple risk model: Examining parental incarceration. *Social Sciences, 6*(3), 82–103.

Johnson, R. S., Stolar, A. G., Mcguire, J. F., Clark, S., Coonan, L. A., Hausknecht, P., ...Graham, D. P. (2016). US Veterans' Court programs: An inventory and analysis of national survey data. *Community Mental Health Journal, 52*(2), 180–186.

Johnston, L. D., O'Malley, P. M., Miech, R. A., Bachman, J. G., & Schulenberg, J. E. (2014). *Monitoring the future national survey results on drug use, 1975–2013*. Ann Arbor: University of Michigan Institute for Social Research.

Jones, J. M. (2019). *U.S. church membership down sharply in past two decades*. Retrieved from https://news.gallup.com/poll/248837/church-membership-down-sharply-past-two-decades.aspx

Karriker-Jaffe, K. (2013). Neighborhood socioeconomic status and substance use by U.S. adults. *Drug and Alcohol Dependence, 133*, 212–221.

Keyes, K. M., Hamilton, A., & Kandel, D. B. (2016). Birth cohorts analysis of adolescent cigarette smoking & subsequent marijuana and cocaine use. *American Journal of Public Health, 106*(6), 1143–1149.

Khiat, H. (2010). Secondary adjustment in prisons: Prisoners' strategies of influence. *Qualitative Sociology Review, 6*(2), 146–159.

Knox, D. (2011). *Marriage & family*. Belmont, CA: Wadsworth, Cengage.

Kobrin, J. L., Deng, H., & Shaw, E. J. (2011). The association between SAT prompt characteristics, response features, and essay scores. *Assessing Writing, 16*(3), 154–169.

Kramer, R., & Remster, B. (2018). Stop, frisk, and assault? Racial disparities in police use of force during investigatory stops. *Law & Society Review, 54*(4), 960–993.

Krueger, R. A. (1988). *Developing questions for focus groups*. London, UK: Sage.

Lambert, M. J., Whipple, J. L., Hawkins, E. J., Vermeersch, D. A., Nielsen, S. L., & Smart, D. W. (2003). Is it time for clinicians to routinely track patient outcome? A meta-analysis. *Clinical Psychology Scientific Practice, 10*, 288–301.

Langbein, L. (2006). *Public program evaluation: A statistical guide*.

Lanigan, J. D., & Burleson, E. (2017). Foster parent's perspectives regarding the transition of a new placement into their home: An exploratory study. *Journal of Child and Family Studies, 26*(3), 905–915.

Latané, B., & Darley, J. M. (1970). *The unresponsive bystander: Why doesn't he help?* Englewood Cliffs, NJ: Prentice-Hall.

Lee, R. M., & Robbins, S. B. (1995). Measuring belongingness: The social connectedness and social assurance scales. *Journal of Counseling Psychology, 42*, 232–241.

Lee, R. M., & Robbins, S. B. (1998). The relationship between social connectedness and anxiety, self-esteem, and social identity. *Journal of Counseling Psychology, 45*, 338–345.

Leech, B. L. (2002). Asking questions: Techniques for semi-structured interviews. *PS: Political Science & Politics, 35*, 665–668.

Leon-Guerrero, A., & Frankfort-Nachmias, C. (2018). *Essentials of social statistics for a diverse society* (3rd ed.). Washington, DC: Sage.

Lincoln, Y. S., & Guba, E. G. (1985). Paradigmatic controversies, contradictions, and emerging confluences. In N. K. Denzin & Y. S. Lincoln (Eds.), *Handbook of qualitative research* (2nd ed., pp. 163–188). Thousand Oaks, CA: Sage.

Litwiller, B. J., & Brausch, A. M. (2013). Cyber bullying and physical bullying in adolescent suicide: The role of violent behavior and substance use. *Journal of Youth and Adolescence, 42*(5), 675–684.

Lopez, M. H., Rainie, L., & Budiman, A. (2020). Financial and health impacts of COVID-19 vary. *PEW Research Center*. Retrieved from https://www.pewresearch.org/fact-tank/2020/05/05/financial-and-health-impacts-of-covid-19-vary-widely-by-race-and-ethnicity/

Lum, C., Hibdon, J., Cave, B., Koper, C. S., & Merola, L. (2011). License plate reader (LPR) police patrols in crime hot spots: An experimental evaluation in two adjacent jurisdictions. *Journal of Experimental Criminology, 7*(4), 321–345.

Lumley, T., Diehr, P., Emerson, S., & Chen, L. (2002). The importance of the normality assumption in large public health data sets. *Annual Review of Public Health, 23*, 151–169.

Luxton, D. D., June, J. D., & Fairall, J. M. (2012). Social media and suicide: A public health perspective. *American Journal of Public Health, 102*(Suppl 2), S195–S200. doi:10.2105/AJPH.2011.300608

Ma, M., & Jin, Y. (2019). Economic impacts of alternative greenspace configurations in fast growing cities: The case of greater Beijing. *Urban Studies, 56*(8), 1498–1515.

Madden, E. E., Chanmugam, A., McRoy, R. G., Kaufman, L., Ayers-Lopez, S., Boo, M., …Ledesma, K. J. (2016). The impact of formal and informal respite care on foster, adoptive, and kinship parents caring for children involved in the child welfare system. *Child & Adolescent Social Work Journal, 33*(6), 523–534.

Maguire, E. R., Lowrey, B. V., & Johnson, D. (2017). Evaluating the relative impact of positive and negative encounters with police: A randomized experiment. *Journal of Experimental Criminology, 13*(3), 367–391.

Mangiafico, S. (2016). *Summary and analysis of extension program evaluation in R, v. 1.2.1*. New Brunswick, NJ: Rutgers Cooperative Extension. Retrieved from http://rcompanion.org/documents/RHandbookProgramEvaluation.pdf

Martins, S. S., Kim, J. H., Chen, L., Levin, D., Keyes, K. M., Cerda, M., & Storr, C. L. (2015). Nonmedical prescription drug use among US young adults by educational attainment. *Social Psychiatry and Psychiatric Epidemiology, 50*, 713–724.

Mather, M., Scommegna, P., & Kilduff, L. (2019, October). *Population Reference Bureau*. Retrieved from https://www.prb.org/aging-unitedstates-fact-sheet/

McCarthy, A., Lee, K., Itakura, S., & Muir, D. W. (2006). Cultural display rules drive eye gaze during thinking. *Journal of Cross-Cultural Psychology, 37*, 717–722.

McDaniel, S., Gazso, A., Mitchell, B., & Wu, Z. (2014). Liminality and low-income aging families by choice: Meanings of family and support. *Canadian Journal on Aging, 33*(4), 400–412.

Miles, J., & Shevlin, M. (2001). *Applying regression and correlation: A guide for students and researchers*. London, UK: Sage.

Milgram, S. (1974). *Obedience to authority: An experimental view*. New York, NY: Harper.

Miller, R., Parsons, K., & Lifer, D. (2010). Students and social networking sites: the posting paradox. *Behaviour & Information Technology, 29*(4), 377–382.

Miron, O., Yu, K.-H., Wilf-Miron, R., & Kohane, I. S. (2019). Suicide rates among adolescents and young adults in the United States, 2000–2017. *JAMA, 321*(23), 2362–2364. Retrieved from http://dx.doi.org/10.1001/jama.2019.5054

Mitchell, A., & Oliphant, B. (2020, March). Majorities think the news media have done a good job overall covering COVID-19 but have exaggerated the risks. *Pew Research Center*. Retrieved from https://www.journalism.org/2020/03/18/majorities-think-the-news-media-have-done-a-good-job-overall-covering-covid-19-but-have-exaggerated-the-risks/

Morgan, D. L., & Krueger, R. A. (1993). When to use focus groups and why. In D. L. Morgan (Ed.), *Successful focus groups*. London, UK: Sage.

Murray, S. H. (2018). Heterosexual men's sexual desire: Supported by, or deviating from, traditional masculinity norms and sexual scripts? *Sex Roles, 78*(1–2), 130–141.

Nagelhout, G. E., Hummel, K., DeGoeij, M., M. C., DeVries, De H., Kaner, D., & Lemmens, P. (2017). How economic recessions and unemployment affect illegal drug use: A systematic realist literature review. *The International Journal of Drug Policy, 44*, 69–83.

National Criminal Justice Association. (1993). *Project to develop a model anti-stalking code for states (NCJ 144477)*. Washington, DC: U.S. Department of Justice, National Institute of Justice.

Newcomer, K. E., Hatry, H. P., & Wholey, J. S. (2015). *Handbook of practical program evaluation*, Hoboken, NJ:John Wiley & Sons, Incorporated.

Newcomer, K. E., & Triplett, T. (2015). Using surveys. In K. E. Newcomer, H. P. Hatry, & J. S. Wholey (Eds.), *Handbook of practical program evaluation* (pp. 344–382). Hoboken, NJ:John Wiley & Sons, Incorporated.

Nichols, S. L., & Berliner, D. C. (2007). *Collateral damage: How high-stakes testing corrupts America's schools*. Harvard Education Press.

Niven, D. (2006). A field experiment on the effects of negative campaign mail on voter turnout in a municipal election. *Political Research Quarterly*, *59*(2), 203–210.

NORC. (2019, June). *General Social Surveys, 1972–2018: Cumulative Codebook*. (p. 391 on document and 400 on pdf) Retrieved from http://gss.norc.org/documents/codebook/gss_codebook.pdf (p. 391 on document and 400 on pdf)

Oppenheim, A.N. (1992). *Questionnaire design, interviews, and the attitude measurement* (2nd ed.). London, UK: Pinter.

Parker, J. (1974). *View from the boys: A sociology of down-town adolescents*. Newton Abbot, UK: David & Charles.

Parker, L. (2005, March 15). When pets die at the vet, owners call lawyers. *USA Today*.

Park, N., & Lee, S. (2014, March 15). College students' motivations for Facebook use and psychological outcomes. *Journal of Broadcasting & Electronic Media*, *58*(4), 601–620.

Patton, M. Q. (2002). *Qualitative research and evaluation methods* (3rd ed.). Newbury Park, CA: Sage.

Perrin, A., & Jiang, J. (2018, February). About a quarter of U.S. adults say they are "almost constantly" online. *Pew Research Center*. Retrieved from http://pewrsr.ch/2FH8dCJ

Pew Research Center. (2016, October). 15% of American adults have used online dating sites or mobile dating apps. *Pew Center Research*. Retrieved from https://www.pewinternet.org/2016/02/11/15-percent-of-american-adults-have-used-online-dating-sites-or-mobile-dating-apps/

Pew Research Center. (2017a, March). *News Use Across Social Media Platforms 2017*. Retrieved from file:///C:/Users/R92578987/Downloads/PJ_17.08.23_socialMediaUpdate_FINAL.pdf

Pew Research Center. (2017b, January). *What Low Response Rates Mean for Telephone Surveys*. Retrieved from https://www.pewresearch.org/methods/2017/05/15/what-low-response-rates-mean-for-telephone-surveys/

Pew Research Center. (2018, January). Women and Leadership 2018. *Pew Center Research*. Retrieved from http://www.pewsocialtrends.org/2018/09/20/2-views-on-leadership-traits-and-competencies-and-how-they-intersect-with-gender/

Pharr, J., & Chino, M. (2013). Predicting barriers to primary care for patients with disabilities: A mixed methods study of practice administrators. *Disability and Health Journal*, *6*(2), 116–123.

Pizzolato, J. E., & Hicklen, S. (2011). Parent involvement: Investigating the parent-child relationship in millennial college students. *Journal of College Student Development*, *52*(6), 671–686.

Pyrczak, F. (2005). *Evaluating research in academic journals: A practical guide to realistic evaluation* (3rd ed.). Glendale, CA: Pyrczak.

Rajaratnam, S. M. W., Landrigan, C. P., Wang, W., Kaprielian, R., Moore, R. T., & Czeisler, C. A. (2015). Teen crashes declined after Massachusetts raised penalties for graduated licensing law restricting night driving. *Health Affairs*, *34*(6), 963-1-970.3.

Rennard, B. O., Ertl, R. F., Gossman, G. L., Robbins, R. A., & Rennard, S. (2000). Chicken soup inhibits neutrophil chemotaxis. *In Vitro*, *118*, 1150–1157.

Robson, C. (2002). *Real world research* (2nd ed.). Oxford, UK: Blackwell.

Roche, T. M., Jenkins, D. D., Aguerrevere, L. E., Kietlinski, R. L., & Prichard, E. A. (2015). College students' perceptions of inappropriate and appropriate Facebook disclosures. *Psi Chi Journal of Psychological Research*, *20*(2), 86–96.

Roethlisberger, F. J., & Dixon, W. J. (1939). *Management and the worker*. Cambridge, MA: Harvard University Press.

Ross, C. E., & Mirowsky, J. (1989). Explaining the social patterns of depression: Control and problem solving—or support and talking? *Journal of Health and Social Behavior*, *30*, 206–219.

Rossman, G. B., & Rallis, S. F. (1998). *Learning in the field: An introduction to qualitative research*. Thousand Oaks, CA: Sage.

Saad, L. (2018, June). *Military, Small Business, Police Still Stir Most Confidence*. Gallup. Retrieved from https://news.gallup.com/poll/236243/military-small-business-police-stir-confidence.aspx

Sackett, D. L. (1997). Evidence-based medicine. *Seminars in Perinatology, 21*, 3–5.

Sampson, R. J., & Laub, J. H. (1997). A life-course theory of cumulative disadvantage and the stability of delinquency. In T. P. Thornberry (Ed.), *Developmental theories of crime and delinquency* (pp. 133–161). New Brunswick, NJ: Transaction Publishers.

Schalet, A., Hung, G., & Joe-Laidler, K. (2003). Respectability and autonomy: The articulation and meaning of sexuality among girls in the gang. *Journal of Contemporary Ethnography, 32*(1), 108–143.

Schmidt, H. C. (2016). Women's sports coverage remains largely marginalized. *Newspaper Research Journal, 37*(3), 275–298.

Scriven, M. (1972). Pros and cons about goal-free evaluation. *Evaluation Comment, 3*, 1–7.

Sherman, L. W. (1992). *Policing domestic violence: Experiments and dilemmas*. New York, NY: Free Press.

Sherman, L. W., & Berk, R. (1984). *The Minneapolis domestic violence experiment*. Washington, DC: The Police Foundation.

Siantz, E., Rice, E., Henwood, B., & Palinkas, L. (2018). Where do peer providers fit into newly integrated mental health and primary care teams? A mixed method study. *Administration and Policy in Mental Health and Mental Health Services Research, 45*(4), 538–549.

Silverstein, M., & Parrott, T. M. (2001). Attitudes toward government policies that assist informal caregivers: The link between personal troubles and public issues. *Research on Aging, 23*(3), 349–374.

Simon, C. T. M., & Wallace, T. W. H. (2018). Disclosure of victimization experiences of Chinese male survivors of intimate partner abuse. *Qualitative Social Work, 17*(6), 744–761.

Sobel, M. E. (1981). Diagonal mobility models: A substantively motivated class of designs for the analysis of mobility effects. *American Sociological Review, 46*(6), 893–906.

Solé-Auró, A., & Crimmins, E. M. (2014). Who cares? A comparison of informal and formal care provision in Spain, England and the USA. *Aging & Society, 34*(3), 495–517.

Stake, R. E. (1995). *The art of case study research*. Thousand Oaks, CA: Sage.

Stewart, D. W., Shamdasani, P. N., & Rook, D. W. (2007). *Focus groups: Theory and practice* (2nd ed.). Thousand Oaks, CA: Sage.

Stewart, N. (2019, May 30). New York's Toughest Homeless Problem. *The New York Times*.

Strauss, A. L. (1987). *Qualitative analysis for social scientist*. New York, NY: Cambridge University Press.

Strauss, A. L., & Corbin, J. (1998). *Basics of qualitative research* (2nd ed.). Thousand Oaks, CA: Sage.

Sugai, G., Horner, R. H., Dunlap, G., Hieneman, M., Lewis, T. J., & Nelson, C. M. (2000). Applying positive behavior support and functional behavioral assessment in schools. *Journal of Positive Behavior Interventions, 2*, 131–143.

Tabachnick, B. G., & Fidell, L. S. (2013). *Using multivariate statistics* (6th ed.). New York, NY: Pearson.

Tanner-Smith, E. E., Fisher, B. W., Addington, L. A., & Gardella, J. H. (2017). Adding security, but subtracting safety? Exploring schools' use of multiple visible security measures. *American Journal of Criminal Justice, 43*, 102–119.

Tjaden, P., & Thoennes, N. (2000). The role of stalking in domestic violence crime reports generated by the Colorado Springs Police Department. *Violence and Victims, 15*(4), 427–441.

Tolich, M. (2014). What can Milgram and Zimbardo teach ethics committees and qualitative researchers about minimizing harm? *Research Ethics, 10*(2), 86–96.

Tourangeau, R. (2004). Survey research and societal change. *Annual Review of Psychology, 55*, 775–801.

Tremblay, R. E. (2000). The development of aggressive behavior during childhood: What have we learned in the past century? *International Journal of Behavioral Development, 24*, 129–141.

Trochim, W. M., Donnelly, J. P., & Arora, K. (2016). *Research methods: The essential knowledge base* (2nd ed.). Stamford, CT: Cengage.

United Nations Development Report. (2018, March). *Human Development Indices and Indicators: 2018 Statistical Update Briefing note for countries on the 2018 Statistical Update United States*. Retrieved from http://hdr.undp.org/sites/all/themes/hdr_theme/country-notes/USA.pdf

Urban, J. B., & Trochim, W. (2009). The role of evaluation in research-practice integration working toward the "Golden Spike." *American Journal of Evaluation*, *30*, 538–553.

U.S. Census Bureau.(2019, October). *Current Population Survey, 1968 to 2019 Annual Social and Economic Supplements*. Retrieved from https://www.census.gov/library/visualizations/2019/demo/p60-266.html#

U.S. Department of Education, National Center for Education Statistics. (2018, March). *The Condition of Education 2018 (NCES 2018-144), Educational Attainment of Young Adults*. Retrieved from https://nces.ed.gov/fastfacts/display.asp?id=27

U.S. Department of Education, National Center for Education Statistics. (2019). *Indicators of School Crime and Safety: 2018 (NCES 2019-047)*. Retrieved from https://nces.ed.gov/fastfacts/display.asp?id=49

U.S. Office of Management and Budget. (2002). *Government and Performance Results Act of 1993*. Washington, DC: U.S. Office of Management and Budget, Executive Office of the President.

Van, Orden., A, K., Witte, T. K., Cukrowicz, K. C., Braithwaite, S. R., Selby, E. A., & Joiner, T. E. (2010). The interpersonal theory of suicide. *Psychological Review*, *117*(2), 575–600.

Ventis, W. L., Higbee, G., & Murdock, S. A. (2001). Using humor in systematic desensitization to reduce fear. *The Journal of General Psychology*, *128*(2), 241–253.

Walker, M., Hills, S., & Heere, B. (2017). Evaluating a socially responsible employment program: Beneficiary impacts and stakeholder perceptions. *Journal of Business Ethics*, *143*(1), 53–70.

Walton, J., Priest, N.C., & Paradies, Y. (2013). "It depends how you're saying it": The complexities of everyday racism. *International Journal of Conflict and Violence*, *7*(1), 74–90.

Warren, C. A. B. (2002). Qualitative interviewing. In J. F. Gubrium & J. A. Holstein (Eds.), *Handbook of interview research: Context and method* (pp. (pp. 83–102)). Thousand Oaks, CA: Sage.

Warren, C. A. B., & Karner, T. X. (2005). *Discovering qualitative methods: Field research, interviews, and analysis*. Los Angeles, CA: Roxbury Publishing.

Weeks, K. P., & Schaffert, C. (2019). Generational differences in definitions of meaningful work: A mixed methods study. *Journal of Business Ethics*, *156*(4), 1045–1061.

Welty, L. J., Harrison, A. J., Abram, K. M., Olson, N. D., Aaby, D. A., McCoy, K. P., & Teplin, L. A. (2016). Health disparities in drug- and alcohol-use disorders: A 12-year longitudinal study of youths after detention. *American Journal of Public Health*, *106*(5), 872–880.

Wengraf, T. (2001). *Qualitative research interviewing: Biographic narrative and semi-structured methods*. London, UK: Sage.

White, H. R., Labouvie, E. W., & Papadaratsakis, V. (2005). Changes in substance use during the transition to adulthood: A comparison of college students and their noncollege age peers. *Journal of Drug Issues*, *35*, 281–306.

Whyte, W. F. (1955). *Street Corner Society*. Chicago, IL: University of Chicago Press.

Williams, C. T., & Latkin, C. A. (2007). Neighborhood socioeconomic status, personal network attributes, and use of heroin and cocaine. *American Journal of Preventive Medicine*, *32*, S203–S210.

Willis, G. B. (2015). *Analysis of the cognitive interview in questionnaire design*. Oxford, UK: Oxford University Press.

Willits, F. K., Theodori, G. L., & Luloff, A. E. (2016). Another look at Likert scales. *Journal of Rural Social Sciences*, *31*(3), 126–139.

Wolfer, L. (2007). *Real research: Conducting and evaluating research in the social sciences*. New York, NY: Pearson Education, Inc.

Wolfer, L. (2018). Disapproving but invisible: College student and adult views, reasons, and responses to on-line posts about alcohol. *Online Journal of Communication and Media Technologies*, *8*(2), 55–80.

Worthen, V. E., & Lambert, M. J. (2007). Outcome oriented supervision: Advantages of adding systematic client tracking to supportive consultations. *Counseling and Psychotherapy Research*, *7*, 48–53.

Yanow, D., & Schwartz-Shea, P. (2018). Framing "deception" and "covertness" in research: Do Milgram, Humphreys, and Zimbardo justify regulating social science research ethics? *Forum: Qualitative Social Research*, *19*(3), 1-31.

Yechezkel, R., & Ayalon, L. (2013). Social workers' attitudes towards intimate partner abuse in younger vs. older women. *Journal of Family Violence*, *28*(4), 381–391.

Yin, R. K. (2006). Mixed methods research: Are the methods genuinely integrated or merely parallel? *Research in the Schools, 13*(1), 41–47.

Yin, R. K. (2009). *Case study research: Design and methods* (4th ed.). Thousand Oaks, CA: Sage.

Young, M. (2019). Does work-family conflict vary according to community resources? *Family Relations, 68*(2), 197–212.

Zimbardo, P. (1972). The psychology of imprisonment. *Society, 9(6)*, 4–8.

INDEX

abstract 30, 35–36
academic journals 31
academic research 9
acceptance rate 34
accidental sample 119
acquiescence bias 180
active listening 189
aidoldrc 374
alpha level 310
alternative hypothesis 44–46
analysis of variance (ANOVA) 350–355
analysis risks 102–103
analytic codes 439
anonymity 64–66
appendices 230
applied research 9–10, 28, 31, 216,
        228, 233
association 46
    chi-square-based measure of 366
    decision tree 365
    interval / ratio measures of 365,
        377–383
    nominal statistic for 364–370
    ordinal measures of 370–376
    symmetrical measure 375
associative hypothesis 46
associative significance 362
associative statistics 272
asymmetrical measure of
        association 366
attribute codes 438
attrition 138
auditability 209
authority (knowledge) 5, 7
average 106, 286
biased wording 164
axial coding 437
axis lines 403

bar graphs 402, 405, 409
basic research 9–10, 28
before-after design 145
behavioral/social research 59, 62–63
Belmont Report 59, 64, 69
    ethical responsibilities in 64
beneficence, principle of 61–64

between-group difference 150
between-group (across) variation 351
bibliographic databases 30
binomial test in SPSS 319
bivariate comparisons 272
bivariate correlation 386
bivariate data presentation
    bar graph 409
    graphs 409–413
    line graph 412
    table 406–408
bivariate regression 365, 383–385
bivariate relationship 48
body of report 231
Bogardus Social Distance scale 264

case studies 193–194
categorical variables 79, 401, 409
causal hypothesis 46
causality
    establishing 46–49, 135
    gold standard of methodology 141
cell 407–408
central limit theorem 106,
        108–109, 302
central tendency 277, 287
    measures of 277–287
chi-square test 328, 335–340, 350
classic experiments 132–133
classic research model 18
closed-ended questions 167, 177
cluster diagram 432
cluster sample 116–118
codebook 242–245
coder identification (coderID) 242
coding
    considerations 244–247
    data 241, 248
    handling "circle all that apply" 247
    "please specify" 246–247
    quantitative data 241–244
    of values 242
coefficient of determination 381
cognitive abilities 60
cognitive interviews 11, 171
Cohen's Kappa 88

cohort study 93
common sense (knowledge) 5, 8
community-based intervention 11
community resources 77
complete participant research 199
complex surveys 176
computer-assisted telephone interview (CATI)
      software 173
concept map 224, 232
concepts 79
   definition 76
   to measures 76–78
conceptualization 76, 77
concurrent criterion validity 85
confidence intervals
   for categorical variables 307
   for continuous variables 305
   decisions 309
   estimation 303–307
   interval/ratio measures 465
   logic behind 302–303
   nominal/ordinal measures 465–466
confidence level 105, 107
confidentiality 64–66
confirmability 210
confounding factors 135
constant comparison method 431
construct validity 85–86
contamination 139–140
content analysis 205, 209, 435–436
content validity 86, 160, 219
contingency formats 162
contingency questions 169
continuous measures 79, 81
continuous variables 402
   confidence intervals for 305
control groups 129–131, 133, 139,
     149, 150
   pretest and posttest for 151
control variable 386
controversial research 56
convenience samples 119
correlation 46
correlation matrix 377
correlative research questions 26
cost-benefit analysis 227
cost-effective analysis 228
cover letters 168
covert observation 195–196
covert participant 199–200
Cramer's V 364, 366–369
   formula for 366
credibility 209
criterion validity 84–85
cross-sectional research 90
cumulative percent 276

data
   access 66
   cleaning 256
   direct entry 248–253
   importing existing 253–255
   manipulation 259–266
   coding 241, 248
data-gathering stage 20
data presentation
   bivariate 406–413
   challenges of 422–427
   responsible graphical representation
     413–417
   univariate 400–406
data source 407
deception 61, 201
decision making 21–22
   ethics in research 69–71
   evaluation research 231
   experiments 151–152
   measurement 93–95
   qualitative approaches/method 207–208
   quantitative data 268
   sampling 121
   survey questions 179
   time dimensions 95
Declaration of Helsinki 59
deductive research process 18, 77
   steps in 19
degrees of freedom 316
dependent samples 327–328, 349
dependent variables 40, 46, 48, 51
description level 442
descriptive analysis 297
descriptive research 13–14, 51, 192, 194
descriptive research questions 26
descriptive statistics 255, 301, 320, 334, 401
   deciding and interpreting 274–277
   decision tree for 276–278
   frequencies 274–276
   information types 272–273
   percent 274–276
   proportions 274–276
   statistical teaching approach 276–277
   summarizing distribution 277–293
   interval/ratio measures 289
   measures of central tendency 277–287
   measures of dispersion 287–293
   nominal measures 287–288
   ordinal measures 288–289
   SPSS and interpretations 291–293
differential attrition 138
diffusion of treatment 139
direct data entry 248–253
direct observations 203
direct relationship 386

discordant cells 347
discourse analysis 442–443
    levels of 442
discrete measures 79
dispersion 277, 291
    measures 287
disproportionate stratified sample 114
distribution 283
    score relative to 293–299
double-barreled 162–163
double negatives 180
drugs 162
dummy variables 388

ecological fallacy 102
effect size 312, 358, 362
efficiency analysis 226–227
electronic surveys 175
elements 104, 116, 131
emic meaning 433
empirical and theoretical 7
empirical association 46
empirically observable 28
enter regression method 389
equality of variances 331
equivalency 130–131, 140
erosion of treatment effect 147, 406
errors 256
    in hypothesis testing 320–324
    type I and II 321
establishing equivalency 131
eta 364
eta squared 369–371
ethical and responsible research 59
ethical behavior 61
ethical issues
    anonymity 64–66
    confidentiality 64–66
    data access 66
    of informed consent 66
    ownership 66
    principle of justice 64
    responsibility to society 67
    voluntary participation 60
ethical relativism 67, 199
ethical responsibilities
    in Belmont Report 64
ethics in research 56–58 *See also* ethical issues
    anonymity/confidentiality 64–66
    challenges 71–74
    data access 66
    decision making 69–71
    general history of 58–67
    informed consent 60–62, 66
    ownership 66

participant privacy 66–67
    principle of beneficence 62–64
    principle of justice 64
    respect for persons 60–62
    responsibility to society 67
ethnographic research 194
etic meanings 433
evaluability assessment 222–223
evaluation process 223
evaluation research 14, 213–216
    additional considerations 227–230
    challenges 232–237
    classifications of 217
    components 217–220, 220
    decision making 231
    quality issues 230–231
    types of 220–227
evidence-based practices 216, 228
evidence-based research 8, 10, 14–15, 31, 44, 67, 131,
        143, 147, 216, 233
executive summary 231
exhaustive 79, 80
expected frequencies 336
experience (knowledge) 4
    nuances of 193
experimental designs 159
experimental groups 129–131, 133, 135, 139, 144,
        149–150, 327
    pretest and posttest for 150
experimental mortality 138
experiments 128–129
    challenges 153–156
    decision making 151–152
    factorial design 148–149
    humorous desensitization 130
    interpreting experimental output 149–151
    quasi-experiments 143–148
expert knowledge 6
explanation level 442
explanatory research 14
exploded pie chart 415
explorative research 13
exploratory research 192
ex-post facto control group design 144
external validity 142–143, 153, 159, 219, 231

face-to-face interviews 176, 185–190
    process 187–190
face validity 84
factorial design 148–149
factors 86
field research 194–205
    researcher roles 195–200
filter questions 162, 168–169
financial harm 63, 65

first-level coding 431
first-order correlation 386
fixed study 92
focus groups 11, 191–192
follow-up question 169
forced entry method 389
foundational research 9
four scatterplots 379
frequency 274–276
frequency distributions 400
frequency table 400
funding agencies 229

Games-Howell 352
gamma 370, 372–376
gatekeepers 201
General Social Survey (GSS) 91, 159, 272,
    279, 301
going native 199, 201
gold standard
    of methodology 141
    of randomized experiments 233
    of research 135, 151
good pie charts 405
Government Performance and Results Act of 1993 217
graphical representation 413–417
    oral presentation 417–422
    three-dimensional representation
        414–417
    Y-axis representation 413–414
graphs 401–406, 409–413
    bar graph 401–404, 409–412
    line graphs 405–406, 412
    pie charts 404–405
grounded theory analysis 436–440
    attribute codes 438
    axial coding 437
    index codes 438–439
    open coding 437
    selective coding 437
GSS. *See* General Social Survey
Guttman scale 262, 264

haphazard sample 119
Hawthorne effect 139
histograms 283, 314
history effects 140–141
homogeneity of variance 328
hypotheses/hypothesis
    alternative and null hypotheses 44–46
    establishing causality 46–49
    statistical tests of 203
    types 33

hypothesis testing
    cautions about 312
    chi-square test 335–341
    errors in 320–324
    logic behind 309–312
    logic of 312
    Mann–Whitney *U* test 333–335, 340
    one- or two-tailed tests 311
    one-sample proportions test 467–468
    one-sample tests. *See* one-sample hypothesis test
        paired *t*-test 470–471
    three or more samples 350–359
    two dependent samples tests 341–349
    two samples 327–348

independent
identifying subjects 202
impact analysis 224
impact factor 34
impact research questions 26
implementation assessment 223–224
incentives 62
independent samples 327–341
    t-test 329–333
independent variables 40, 44, 46, 48, 51
index codes 438, 439
Index of Qualitative Variation (IQV) 288
inductive research 18
inferential statistics 272, 300–301
informal gatekeepers 201
informed consent 60–62, 168, 190,
    197, 204
    ethical issues of 66
inputs 218, 221
Institutional Review Boards
    (IRB) 68–69
instrumentation 136–137
integrative approach 229
interaction 387
inter-judge reliability 88
internal validity 231
    attrition 138
    contamination 139–140
    instrumentation 136–137
    maturation 137
    reactivity 139
    selection bias 135–136
    testing 138
    threats 141
Internet 66
internet surveys 175
inter-observer reliability 88
interpersonal theory 14
interpersonal violence 86, 185

interpretation level 442
interpretations 291–293
interpreting experimental output 149–151
interpreting questions 171
interquartile range (IQR) 288
inter-rater reliability 88
interrupted time-series design 146–148
interval/ratio levels of measurement 81, 244, 289, 379–385, 402
intervening relationship 386, 387
interviewers 174
  and respondent 187
  training 187
interviews 176–177
  concluding 190
  conducting 189
  face-to-face 185–190
  preparing 188
inverse-ordered pairs 372, 374

jottings 203

Kendall's Tau-b 375
Kendall's Tau-c 375
key informants 201
knowledge
  areas of 9
  of funding agency 62
  sources 3–9
Kolmogorov-Smirnov test (K-S) 285
Kruskal-Wallis H test 357
kurtosis 285, 334

lambda 365–366
latent content 435
least squares analysis 384
legal harm 63
level of measurement 79–83, 242, 363
  continuous 81
  decision making 93–95
  interval 81
  interval/ratio 244
  lowest 364–370
  nominal 79
  ordinal 81
Levene's test 328
  for equality of variances 331
Likert scale 262–263
linear regression line 384–385
line graphs 405, 412
linking theory 14

literature reviews 29–44, 83
  challenges of 50–54
  critically evaluating material 34–39
  definition 29
  excerpt example 41–42
  organization of 39–43
  purpose of 29–30
  searching for material 30–34
  steps for 43
  summary chart for 36
local history 141
logic behind confidence intervals 302–303
logic models 223
longitudinal designs 147
longitudinal studies 91

mailed surveys 121, 172–173, 176
manifest content 435
Mann-Whitney *U* test 333–335, 340
marginalized groups 199
marginals 407
marketability 219
master data copy 429
matrix format 169–170
maturation 137
McNemar test 347
mean 278–279, 282, 286, 292, 344, 358
  standard error of 306
measurement
  challenges 95–97
  concepts to 76–78
  decision making 93–95
  levels of 79–82
  quality. *See* quality measurement
  time dimensions 90–93
  types and levels 82
  validity 86–87, 95
measurement error 89–90
measures of central tendency 277–287
  for ordinal measures 281, 288
medians 281–282, 286, 344
menu-driven program 253
meta-analyses 37–38
methods of survey observation 172
mixed-methods
  approach 20–21
  designs 194, 219, 225
  model 179
  research 205–207
moderator 191–192
modes 277, 279, 286–287
multidimensional scales 262
multiple graphs 402
multiple regression 388–397

multistage sampling 117
multivariate analysis 273, 386–397
multivariate linear regression 388, 391
mutually exclusive 79–80

National Research Act of 1974 59, 68
needs assessment 220–221
negative relationship 370
network maps 441
nominal levels of measurement 79, 81, 242, 287, 364–371, 402
nonequivalent control group design 145–146
nonexperimental methods 38
nonparametric test 319, 334, 337, 341
nonprobability sampling 104, 118–120
nonspurious relationship 47
normal curve 107–108, 295, 302, 304
    and statistical formula 303
normal distribution 282, 285, 302, 334
    tests for 284
normative research questions 26
null and research hypotheses 317, 330, 348, 352, 357
null hypotheses 44–46
number of citations 34
numerical codes 242
Nuremberg Code 59

objectivity 231
observation method 20, 62, 65, 69, 142, 158, 172, 176, 205–206, 241
    hierarchy of 38
observed frequencies in chi-square 337
obtained value 310
one-group pretest-posttest 145
one-sample hypothesis test 305, 309–324
    one-sample proportion hypothesis test 318–319
    one-sample t-test 312–316
    One-Sample Wilcoxon signed rank test 317–318
one-tailed test 311
one-way Analysis of Variance (ANOVA) statistic 350–355
online databases 30, 33
    online dating sites 398
    online surveys 175
open access 32
open coding 437
open-ended questions 167, 191
operationalization process 20, 76–78
oral presentation 417–422
    content 418–420
    delivery 420–422
    self 421
ordinal levels of measurement 81, 244, 288, 370–378, 402
outcomes 219

outcomes evaluation 224–225
outliers 288
overt observation research 196–197
overt participant 197–198

paired sample t-test 342–344, 347
panel study 92–93
Panel Study of Income Dynamics (PSID) 160
paper/pencil survey 172
partial correlation 386–387
partial slope 390
participant and observer 197
participant observation research 194, 197, 202
participant privacy 66–67
participation observation research 194
Pearson's correlation coefficient (r) 379, 382, 384
peer-reviewed journal 31, 35
percent 274–276
percentage 288
percent distribution 287
personal identity 164
physical harm 62, 64
pie charts 405
pilot study 171
"please specify" 246–247
point estimates 302–303, 308
population 99, 103–104, 106
population parameter 106–107, 277, 301–311
    and one-sample hypothesis test 304, 309–311
    and confidence intervals 301–308
positive relationship 370
post hoc test 353
posttest 133, 150
    experimental and control groups 151
posttest only control group design 133–135, 144
potential harm 63–64
power analysis 121
PRE. See proportionate reduction of error
predatory journals 32–33
predictive criterion validity 85
predictive validity 231
preliminary assessments 133
pretest 89, 133, 150, 171
pretest-posttest control group design 133
principle of beneficence 62–64
principle of justice 64
probabilistic and provisional 8
probability sample 99, 104–118
    techniques 118
    types of 109–118
probability theory 108–109, 302
probing 186
process evaluation 223

professional codes of ethics 69
professional journals 31
program evaluation 224
program involvement 217
program stakeholders 230
Program-Wide Positive Behavior Support (PWPBS)
      model 224
proportionate reduction of error (PRE) 365
proportionate stratified sampling 114
proportions 274–276
   formula for 275
ProQuest search engine 51
psychological harm 62
pure research 9
purpose of the research 61
purposive samples 119
p-value 310, 340

qualitative approaches/method 20
   case studies 193–194
   challenges 209–213
   content analysis 205
   face-to-face interviews 185–190
   focus groups 191–192
   making decisions 207–208
   quantitative and 205
qualitative data analysis (QDA)
   challenges 443–446
   general approach to 430–434, 434
   identifying initial themes 431–432
   linking themes 432–434
   preparing 428–430
   software programs 430
   specific analytic techniques 434–443
qualitative network analysis 440–442
qualitative research
   strength 443
   vs. quantitative research 10–12, 13
quality issues 230–231
   objectivity 231
   reliability 231
   validity 230–231
quality measurement 83–90
   to increase validity and reliability 89
   measurement error 89–90
   reliability 87–89
   validity 83–86
quantile-quantile (Q-Q) plot 284
quantitative data
   coding 241–244
   data cleaning 256
   decision making 268
   direct data entry 248–253
   importing existing data 253–255

quantitative measure 436
quantitative research, qualitative research vs. 10–13
quasi-experimental research 38, 142
   characteristics 143–144
   types 144–148
questionnaires 159, 160–161, 185
   format 171
   pre- and post 219
   pretesting 171–172
quota samples 119

random assignment 130, 132–133, 138, 140–141, 224–225
   process 131
random digit dialing 173
random environmental effects 141
random error 89–90, 141
randomized comparative change design 133
randomized experimental research 38, 225, 231
   See True Experiments
random sample 99, 104
   See Probabilty Sample
range 288
ranking of measures 79
ratio level of measurement 81
reactivity 139, 192, 198
recoding language 255
recording information 202–204
reductionism 102
reference category 389
reference group 389
reliability 87–89, 177–178, 231
repeated cross-sectional designs 91
reputable journals 32
research
   basic *vs.* applied 9–10
   classifying 9–17
   decision making 21–22
   deductive 18
   description 13–14
   evaluation 14
   explanatory 14
   explorative 13
   goals 13–17
   inductive 18
   linking theory and 14
   mixed methods 205–207
   overview of 2–3
   qualitative *vs.* quantitative 10–13
   sources of knowledge 3–9
   stages of 21
   steps in 18–21
   and theory 17–18
   time dimensions 91
   universal principles of 59

researcher approach 228
researcher-audience relationship 417
researcher-participant interaction 197
researcher roles
  covert observer 195–196
  covert participant 199–200
  developing relationships 201–202
  identifying subjects 202
  overt observer 196–197
  overt participant 197–198
  recording information 202–204
  selecting a site 200–201
research hypothesis 44
research method 219
research questions
  correlative 26
  creating, steps for 29
  decision making 49
  descriptive 26
  eliminate 29
  impact 26
  making decisions 49
  normative 26
  strong, characteristics of 28
  types of 9, 26–27
respect for persons 60–62
respondents 166, 189
  interviewer and 187
response scale 262
response set 179
responsibility to society 67
responsible graphical representation
  three-dimensional representation 414–417
  Y-axis representation 413–414
reverse-coded questions 170, 179, 180, 244
risk of harm 61
rival causal factors 48, 51, 93
role of theory 229

same-ordered pairs 372, 374
sample error 105
samples 99, 104
  probability 109–118
  size 120–121
  types of 104
sample statistic 107
sample units 117
sampling 98–99
  analysis risks 102–103
  challenges 122–127
  cluster 116–118
  decision making 121
  error 104, 107–108, 114, 302
  frames 104, 105, 110, 119
  nonprobability techniques 104, 118–129
  probability techniques 104–118
  terms 103–105

units of analysis 100–103
  units of observation 100
saturation 187, 433
saturation point 204
scales
  Bogardus Social Distance 264
  Guttman 262, 264
  Likert 262, 263
scatterplots 379–380, 384–385
science 7
  and theory 7
scientific knowledge 7, 8
secondary analysis of primary data 159
selection bias 135–136, 140, 150
selective coding 437
self-esteem 219, 229
self-explanatory 166
self presentation 188, 421
self-reported mailed surveys 172–173
Shapiro-Wilk (S-W) tests 284–285, 343
significant difference 362
simple random sampling 131, 109–113
single-subject design 145
size effects 273
skewed distribution 282
skewness 285, 334
skip patterns 162
snowball sampling 120, 202
social artifacts 101
Social Connectedness Scale 263
social harm 63
Socially Responsible Youth Employability
      Program 217
social media 13, 17, 82
social network analysis 427, 440, 441
social science researchers 101
social sciences 165
social service 301
socio-emotional skills 224
sophisticated statistical analysis 176
Spearman's rho 350, 365, 368, 370,
      375–379, 381
split-half reliability test 88
spurious relationship 386
stacked bar graphs 410–412
stakeholder approach 228
stakeholders 217–218, 223
  program 228–229
standard deviation
  calculation 290
  formula 289
  mean and 292
  units and normal curve 293
standard errors 108–109
  of mean 306
standardized slope coefficient 391
Stanford Prison Experiment 58
statistical conclusion validity 141–142

statistical control variables 273
Statistical Packages for the Social Sciences
      (SPSS) 234, 248, 274, 291–293
  binomial test in 319
  collapsing categories in 260–261
  commands 366
  data view 251–253
  linear regression, 384
  variable view 248–251
statistical significance 149, 272
stepwise regression methods 389
stratified random sampling 113–116
strong research questions 28–29
study groups 101
study populations 103
substantive significance 273, 312, 358,
      363, 386
survey length 170
Survey Monkey 175
survey questions
  challenges 179–183
  construction 159–168
  decision making 179
  on drug use 160
  forms characteristics 178
  identifying problematic 167
  possible improvements to 165
  presentation 168–171
  pretesting questionnaires 171–172
  reliability 177–178
  types 172–177
  validity 177
survey research, writing 161
symmetrical measure 375
systematic error 89–90
systematic process 8
systematic random sampling 110–113
systematic reviews 38
systemic desensitization 130
systemic group 129
systems design, feedback component of 219

table of contents 229
tables 400–402, 406–408
tails 302
  of distribution 302
t-distribution 315–316
telephone interviews 173
telephone surveys 173–175
testing 138
test-rest method 88
theoretical coding 437
theoretical sampling 202
theory 7
  research and 17–18
threatening questions 168
three-dimensional representation 414–417

three or more samples hypothesis
      testing 350–359
time dimensions 90–93
  decision making 95
time-order relationship 47
traditional knowledge 3–4
transcribe the data 428
transferability 209
trend studies 91
triangulation 443
true experiments
  and study validity 135–143
  characteristics 129–131
  definition 129
  external validity 142–143
  history 140–141
  internal validity 135–140
  random assignment inherent in 138
  statistical conclusion validity 141–142
  summary relationship to 140–141
  types 132–135
Tukey honestly significant difference (Tukey HSD)
      test 353–356
two samples hypothesis testing 327–348
  decision tree for 328
  dependent samples 327–328, 341–348
  independent samples 327–341
two-tailed test 310–311, 314

unidimensional scales 262
units of analysis 100–103
units of observation 100
  and analysis risks 102–103
univariate data presentation 400–406
  graphs 402–406
  tables 400–402
universal principles of research 59

vague wording 161
validity 48
  and reliability 160
  construct 85–86
  content 86
  criterion 84–85
  external 142–143
  face 84
  hierarchy of 142
  internal 135–140
  interpretations 443–446
  measurement 86, 87, 95
  predictive 230
  statistical conclusion 141–142
  study 135–143
  types 143
valid percent 275, 287
values 79

variability 289
variables 363–385
   label 241
   names 242
variances 289, 352
voluntary participation 60
vulnerable populations 60

web-based social network 440
web surveys 175–176, 189
weighting 115
Welch ANOVA 352
Wilcoxon signed-rank test 318, 334, 344–346
within-group design 145
within-group difference 150

within-group variation 351
writing survey questions 161
written report 417

x-axis 403

Yates chi-square continuity
      correction 338
y-axis 403

Z-distribution 315
zero-order correlation 386
Z-scores 293–297, 302